Blockchain and AI Amalgamation for IoT Applications Beyond 5G

RIVER PUBLISHERS SERIES IN DIGITAL SECURITY AND FORENSICS

Series Editors:

The "River Publishers Series in Security and Digital Forensics" is a series of comprehensive academic and professional books which focus on the theory and applications of Cyber Security, includingData Security, Mobile and Network Security, Cryptography and Digital Forensics. Topics in Prevention and Threat Management are also included in the scope of the book series, as are general business Standards in this domain.

Books published in the series include research monographs, edited volumes, handbooks and textbooks. The books provide professionals, researchers, educators, and advanced students in the field with an invaluable insight into the latest research and developments.

Topics covered in the series include:-

- Blockchain for secure transactions
- Cryptography
- Cyber Security
- Data and App Security
- Digital Forensics
- Hardware Security
- IoT Security
- Mobile Security
- Network Security
- Privacy
- Software Security
- Standardization
- Threat Management

For a list of other books in this series, visit www.riverpublishers.com

Blockchain and AI Amalgamation for IoT Applications Beyond 5G

Editors

Sudeep Tanwar

Department of Computer Engineering, Marwadi University, Rajkot, Gujarat, India

Maniklal Das

Dhirubhai Ambani Institute of Information and Communication Technology (DA-IICT), Gandhinagar, India

Abderrahim Benslimane

Avignon University, Avignon, France

Rajesh Gupta

Department of Computer Engineering, Marwadi University, Rajkot, Gujarat, India

River Publishers

Routledge
Taylor & Francis Group
NEW YORK AND LONDON

Published 2026 by River Publishers
River Publishers
Broagervej 10, 9260 Gistrup, Denmark
www.riverpublishers.com

Distributed exclusively by Routledge
605 Third Avenue, New York, NY 10017, USA
4 Park Square, Milton Park, Abingdon, Oxon OX14 4RN

Blockchain and AI Amalgamation for IoT Applications Beyond 5G / by Sudeep Tanwar, Maniklal Das, Abderrahim Benslimane, Rajesh Gupta.

Routledge is an imprint of the Taylor & Francis Group, an informa business

ISBN 978-87-4380-904-3 (hardback)
ISBN 978-87-4380-909-8 (paperback)
ISBN 978-87-4380-906-7 (online)
ISBN 978-87-4380-905-0 (master ebook)
ISBN 978-87-4380-908-1 (ePub)
DOI: 10.1201/9788743809050

Contents

Preface

Nowadays, the majority of IoT-based systems are built using centralized client-server, cloud servers, strong database, and the internet. Two major limitations of the IoT centralized infrastructure have been observed: (1) the single point failure, which can potentially topple the entire system, and (2) the lack of trust between the entities involved in the system. To overcome the aforementioned limitations, decentralized architectures can be used for peer-to-peer (P2P) communications among the nodes. However, these systems have several privacy and security concerns, which can open the doors for intruders to launch various attacks. A large number of applications are using IoT devices for the betterment of the service, like smart home, smart factory, smart city, secure vehicular AdHoc network, etc. The future is that 5G drives IoT deployment, and to maintain security, IoT devices will utilize Blockchain. To secure an IoT network, a lot of blockchain solutions are available, and few operate on fast, trusted networks, while others work faster on unreliable networks. For the situation where a new blockchain operates efficiently and rapidly over unreliable networks, then 5G-enabled IoT devices can utilize the same in real time. Security may not be the only task for the utilization of blockchain can also take part for data distribution, as it works in a faster mode. However, as per the knowledge of the editor, an independent mathematical proof for the fast solutions is still unavailable. After the availability of the mathematical proof, a perfect environment is possible where fast and trusted nodes have been connected in the network and can take advantage of 5G by using specific cloud or fog layers.

So, a blockchain-based decentralized system is one of the solutions, which has the ability to store information in an immutable manner and requires no centralized database. In addition to this, it also provides a way to track and execute transactions among various participants in a trusted environment. With the usage of strong encryption with public–private key pairs, blockchain also provides high levels of security to its participants. Some decentralized applications (DApps) are available in the market that have been developed using IoT and blockchain. Using IoT infrastructure, the "information sharing" of devices can be done with the use of embedded sensors and sufficient network connectivity. The omnipresent network connectivity, which is very difficult to achieve in the modern era, can be achieved with 5G. These technologies decrease the latency by 100 times as compared to 4G. Moreover, integrating blockchain with IoT enables to maintain an immutable ledger of transactions of information exchange. By achieving this in a decentralized P2P manner, the "middle-man-attack" can be eliminated, which allows the users to share without relying on a trusted third party.

Motivated by the aforementioned discussion, in this edited book, we aim to provide an overview of the integration of blockchain with 5G-enabled IoT for industrial automation. Then, we discuss some open issues and challenges that may hinder the growth of blockchain technology.

Section 1: Laying foundation: Blockchain and AI amalgamation in 5G-IoT

The chapter "Introduction of Blockchain and 5G-enabled IoT Devices" explores how the fusion of blockchain and 5G-enabled IoT devices is transforming smart systems with enhanced speed, security, and decentralization. 5G offers ultra-fast, low-latency connectivity for large-scale IoT networks, while blockchain ensures secure, transparent, and tamper-proof data exchange. This integration addresses key challenges like data privacy, trust, and scalability by enabling peer-to-peer communication and automated processes through smart contracts. It eliminates reliance on centralized systems, reducing vulnerabilities and improving network resilience. Together, blockchain and 5G empower real-time, intelligent IoT ecosystems across industries, paving the way for secure and efficient digital infrastructure in the era of hyper-connectivity.

The chapter "A Review on Blockchain-enabled Decentralized Architecture in 5G-IoT Network" explores the convergence of blockchain and IoT, emphasizing how their integration enhances security, transparency, and automation in decentralized systems. It highlights blockchain's role in addressing IoT challenges such as data integrity, privacy, and trust through its tamper-proof and decentralized architecture. The chapter reviews key technologies, including smart contracts, consensus mechanisms, and edge computing, and presents real-world applications across smart cities, healthcare, energy, and manufacturing. Despite immense potential, challenges like scalability, interoperability, and resource constraints remain. The chapter concludes with insights into emerging solutions and future research directions for secure and efficient blockchain-enabled IoT environments in the 5G era.

The chapter "Integrating Blockchain and IoT: Opportunities, Challenges, and Applications" focuses on a comprehensive review of blockchain-enabled decentralized architectures in 5G-IoT networks, emphasizing enhanced security, transparency, and automation. It explores how blockchain's immutable, distributed ledger, combined with 5G's ultra-low latency and high bandwidth, transforms IoT ecosystems. The chapter discusses the integration benefits, including improved data integrity, trustless device interactions, and efficient resource sharing through smart contracts. It also addresses key challenges such as scalability, interoperability, energy consumption, and privacy concerns. Through real-world applications in supply chain, healthcare, smart cities, and automotive sectors, the review demonstrates how this fusion drives innovation and creates secure, resilient, and intelligent networks.

This chapter, "Case Studies and Prototypes for Blockchain and Artificial Intelligence (AI) Integration in 5G-enabled Internet of Things (IoT) Systems: Toward Secure, Intelligent, and Efficient Paradigms," presents a comprehensive exploration of integrating blockchain, AI, and 5G in IoT ecosystems. It highlights how blockchain enhances security, transparency, and trust, while AI supports intelligent decision-making and data analytics, and 5G enables ultra-fast, low-latency communication. The chapter outlines technical frameworks, layered architectures, and smart applications in healthcare, cities, agriculture, and manufacturing. Case studies and prototypes illustrate real-world implementations, addressing issues like data privacy, authentication, and system scalability. The synergy of these technologies offers transformative potential for secure, intelligent, and efficient IoT networks, paving the way for resilient infrastructures and next-generation digital services.

Section 2: Security and privacy enhancement in 5G-IoT using blockchain and AI

The chapter "Enhancing Data Security and Privacy in 5G-IoT Using Blockchain Technology" presents a secure and scalable framework that integrates blockchain technology with homomorphic encryption to address data privacy and security concerns in 5G-IoT networks. It highlights the vulnerabilities of centralized architectures and proposes a decentralized model using blockchain's immutable ledger and distributed structure. Homomorphic encryption ensures secure computations on encrypted data, preserving confidentiality during processing. The chapter also explores applications in healthcare, smart cities, and finance, illustrating how this model supports secure data sharing, real-time access, and improved trust. Simulation results and comparative analysis confirm the enhanced accuracy, reliability, and efficiency of the proposed approach over existing methods.

The chapter, "Interconnected Integrity: Securing IoT Networks with Blockchain Technology," explores how blockchain technology can be leveraged to enhance the security of IoT networks. It details the inherent vulnerabilities of centralized IoT architectures and demonstrates how blockchain's decentralized, immutable ledger mitigates risks such as data tampering, unauthorized access, and single points of failure. Key components like consensus algorithms, cryptographic techniques, and smart contracts are discussed as crucial elements in establishing trust and secure data transmission. The chapter also highlights real-world applications and case studies, illustrating blockchain's role in ensuring robust authentication, transparent audit trails, and privacy preservation, ultimately paving the way for resilient and secure IoT ecosystems in various domains.

The chapter, "An Adaptive Approach for Cloud Security Using Cloud Service Tool, Blockchain, Protocols, and Algorithms," explores an adaptive approach to cloud security, integrating cloud service tools, blockchain technology, security protocols, and algorithms. It discusses how cloud service tools can enhance security by monitoring and managing cloud resources, while blockchain provides decentralized, transparent mechanisms for secure data storage and transaction verification. The chapter highlights the role of security protocols in safeguarding cloud communications and the application of advanced algorithms for threat detection and mitigation. By combining these technologies, the approach offers dynamic, scalable solutions to address evolving security challenges in cloud environments.

The Chapter, "Blockchain-enabled VPN Security," presents how blockchain technology enhances the VPN (virtual private network) security. It examines how blockchain's decentralized, immutable ledger can be leveraged to improve VPN authentication, data integrity, and privacy. By integrating blockchain with VPN protocols, the chapter discusses how it can eliminate reliance on central authorities, thus reducing the risks of man-in-the-middle attacks and data breaches. The use of blockchain for secure key exchange, decentralized logging, and real-time monitoring is explored as a means to bolster VPN security and provide a more resilient, transparent, and tamper-proof network infrastructure.

Section 3: Intelligent traffic modeling in vehicular ad hoc networks

The chapter, "Smarter Security: Blockchain and AI-driven Identity Management for Next-generation IoT," presents the integration of blockchain and artificial intelligence (AI) for advanced identity management in next-generation IoT systems. It highlights how blockchain's decentralized, immutable ledger enhances security by providing tamper-proof authentication and access control, ensuring secure device interactions. AI-driven algorithms are employed to analyze user behavior and predict potential security threats, enabling adaptive, real-time responses. The chapter also discusses how this combination improves scalability, efficiency, and privacy for IoT networks, offering a smarter and more robust identity management framework. This approach addresses the growing complexity and security challenges in the rapidly evolving IoT landscape.

The chapter, "Enabling Automated Network Services Using Zero Touch Technology for Intelligent 5G-IoT Communication," discusses the use of Zero Touch technology to enable automated network services in the context of intelligent 5G-IoT communication. It explores how Zero Touch technology can automate network configuration, provisioning, and management, reducing manual intervention and enhancing network efficiency. The chapter focuses on the integration of 5G and IoT, emphasizing the need for scalable, flexible, and intelligent network services that can dynamically adapt to varying demands. By leveraging machine learning and AI, Zero Touch technology ensures seamless communication, faster deployment, and improved service quality, making it a key enabler for the next-generation 5G-IoT ecosystem.

The chapter, "Blockchain and AI Integration for Enhanced Security and Intelligence in 5G-IoT," explores the integration of blockchain and AI to enhance security and intelligence in 5G-IoT ecosystems. It highlights how blockchain ensures data integrity, decentralized trust, and secure device authentication, while AI provides real-time analytics, threat detection, and intelligent decision-making. The synergy between these technologies addresses critical challenges such as data breaches, unauthorized access, and network vulnerabilities in 5G-enabled IoT environments. The chapter also examines use cases and architectures demonstrating how blockchain-AI fusion can support autonomous, secure, and efficient IoT operations, making it a powerful approach for building resilient and intelligent next-generation communication networks.

The chapter, "Enhancing Environmental Monitoring and Sustainability through 5G-IoT Integration with AI and Blockchain," presents how the integration of 5G-IoT with AI and blockchain can revolutionize environmental monitoring and promote sustainability. It explores the role of 5G in enabling real-time, high-speed data transmission from distributed IoT sensors, while AI processes this data for predictive analysis and informed decision-making.

Blockchain adds a layer of security, transparency, and immutability to environmental data, ensuring trust and accountability. The chapter highlights applications such as pollution tracking, resource management, and disaster detection, demonstrating how this integrated approach can drive smarter, data-driven environmental solutions for a more sustainable future.

Section 4: Applications of blockchain and AI in 5G-IoT

The chapter, "Exploration of Conditional Privacy Preserving and Authentication Protocols for Internet of Vehicles," delves into conditional privacy-preserving and authentication protocols tailored for the Internet of Vehicles (IoV). It addresses the need for secure communication and user privacy in vehicular networks, where vast amounts of sensitive data are exchanged in real-time. The chapter explores advanced cryptographic techniques and authentication mechanisms that ensure data integrity, prevent unauthorized access, and support conditional anonymity – allowing identity revelation only under specific legal conditions. By analyzing existing protocols and proposing improved models, the chapter highlights how conditional privacy and robust authentication enhance trust, security, and efficiency in connected vehicle environments, contributing to safer and smarter transportation systems.

The chapter, "Solutions of Blockchain and Artificial Intelligence for 5G-Internet of Things in Agriculture," explores innovative solutions combining blockchain and AI for enhancing 5G-enabled IoT applications in agriculture. It highlights how 5G ensures high-speed, low-latency connectivity for real-time data collection from IoT devices such as sensors and drones. AI is used to analyze this data for crop health monitoring, predictive analytics, and resource optimization. Blockchain adds a secure, transparent layer for data sharing, traceability, and trust among stakeholders. The chapter presents use cases demonstrating how this integrated approach boosts productivity, sustainability, and decision-making in smart farming, ultimately transforming the agricultural sector through technological convergence.

The chapter, "Smart Travelling Bag: Leveraging Blockchain for Enhanced Travel Security and Efficiency with 5G Technology," introduces the concept of a smart travelling bag powered by 5G technology and secured through blockchain integration. It explores how 5G enables real-time tracking, seamless connectivity, and fast data transmission for location updates and status monitoring. Blockchain ensures secure data storage, tamper-proof ownership records, and transparent access control, enhancing both security and trust during travel. Features such as digital locking, lost-bag alerts, and automated check-in are discussed. The chapter demonstrates how combining these technologies improves travel efficiency, prevents luggage mishandling, and offers a smarter, more secure travel experience in today's fast-paced, connected world.

Prof. (Dr.) Sudeep Tanwar

Prof. (Dr.) Maniklal Das

Prof. (Dr.) Abderrahim Benslimane

Dr. Rajesh Gupta

List of Figures

List of Tables

List of Contributors

Aziz, Khalid, *School of Computer Applications, Lovely Professional University, India*

Bagga, Neha, *School of Computer Science and Engineering, Lovely Professional University, India*

Bangar, Nidhi, *Department of Computer Science and Engineering, Institute of Technology, Nirma University, India*

Bhavsar, Madhuri, *Department of Computer Science & Engineering, Nirma University, India*

Bhinde, Priyal, *Department of Computer Science and Technology, Nirma University, India*

Boi, Favour Oluchi, *Department of Computer Engineering, Elizade University, Ilara-mokin, Nigeria*

Chaturvedi, Vijit, *Amity Business School, Amity University, India*

Dedkawala, Neel, *Department of Computer Science and Technology, Nirma University, India*

Dixit, Sheetal Kumar, *Department of Computer Science & Engineering, Nirma University, India*

Dua, Sakshi, *School of Computer Applications, Lovely Professional University, India*

Elesemoyo, Isaac Oluwafemi, *Department of Computer Engineering, Elizade University, Ilara-mokin, Nigeria*

Gohil, Keyaba, *San José State University, San Jose, California, United States*

Grewal, Vinit, *Department of Computer Science and Engineering, Lovely Professional University, India*

Gupta, Prabal, *Department of ECE, SCSE, Lovely Professional University, India*

Gupta, Rajesh, *Department of Computer Engineering, Marwadi University, Rajkot, Gujarat*

Heli, Detroja, *Department of Computer Science and Engineering, Institute of Technology, Nirma University, India*

Jain, Rahul, *Department of Computer Engineering, Marwadi University, India*

Jindal, Kiran, *Mehr Chand Mahajan DAV College for Women, India*

Kalra, Sheetal, *Department of Computer Science and Engineering, Lovely Professional University, India*

Karthikeyan, N, *Computer Science and Engineering, Vellore Institute of Technology, India*

Kathiria, Preeti, *Department of Computer Science & Engineering, Nirma University, India*

Kaur, Jaskeerat, *Department of Computer Science and Engineering, Institute of Technology, Nirma University, India*

Kaur, Sandeep, *Department of Computer Science, GN Girls College, India*

Khanna, Heena, *School of Computer Applications, Lovely Professional University, India*

Koshti, Yash, *Department of Information Technology, UVPCE, Ganpat University, India*

Kovilpillai J, Judeson Antony, *School of Advanced Computing, Alliance University, India*

Kumar, Rishi, *Department of Computing, Universiti Teknologi Petronas, Malaysia*

Kumari, Aparna, *Department of Computer Science and Engineering, Institute of Technology, Nirma University, India*

Malik, Rohit, *SCA, Lovely Professional University, India*

Mansi, Thakkar, *Department of Computer Science and Engineering, Institute of Technology, Nirma University, India*

Mehra, Manik, *School of Computer Applications, Lovely Professional University, India*

Mehta, Deepak Kumar, *Department of Computer Science & Applications, Mandsaur University, India*

Mishra, Sejal, *Department of Computer Science Engineering, NIET, India*

Mohanraj, A, *Department of Computer Science and Engineering, Sri Eshwar College of Engineering, India*

Nachiappan, Balusamy, *Department of Information Technology, Prologis, United States*

Ogunniyi, Julius Olasunmibo, *Department of Computer Engineering, Elizade University, Ilara-mokin, Nigeria*

Olowu, Adekemi Joanne, *Department of Computer Engineering, Elizade University, Ilara-mokin, Nigeria*

Oyewole, Oyeyemi Temitayo, *Department of Computer Engineering, Elizade University, Ilara-mokin, Nigeria*

Rajkumar, N, *School of Advanced Computing, Alliance University, India*

Rana, Roshni Pankaj Kumar, *Department of Computer Science and Engineering, Institute of Technology, Nirma University, India*

Rathore, Nitin, *Department of Computer Science and Engineering, Institute of Technology, Nirma University, India*

Sahnan, Akshay, *Technical Specialist, Apple, Inc.*

Shah, Ayushi, *Department of Computer Science and Engineering, Institute of Technology, Nirma University, India*

Sharma, Sheetal, *Nilkamal School of Mathematics, Applied Statistics & Analytics, NMIMS University, India*

Shilpa, *School of Computer Applications, Lovely Professional University, India*

Shoran, Preety, *School of Sciences, Christ University, India*

Singh, Sartaj, *School of Computer Applications, Lovely Professional University, India; School of Computer Applications, Guru Nanak Dev University, Regional Campus, India*

Singhi, Rushina, *Nilkamal School of Mathematics, Applied Statistics & Analytics, NMIMS University, India*

Tanwar, Sudeep, *Department of Computer Engineering, Marwadi University, Rajkot, Gujarat*

Trividei, Keshini R, *Department of Computer Science and Engineering, Nirma University, Ahmedabad, 382481, India*

Varshney, Nitin, *Department of Computer Engineering, Marwadi University, India*

Venkatesh, R, *Department of Physics, PSNA College of Engineering and Technology (Autonomous), India*

Viji, C, *School of Advanced Computing, Alliance University, India*

List of Abbreviations

ABC	Always better control
AES	Advanced encryption standard
AH	Authentication header
AI	Artificial intelligence
AML	Anti-money laundering
AR	Augmented reality
AUC	Area under the curve
AVISPA	Automatic validation of internet security protocols and apps
BCM	Blockchain manager
BFT	Byzantine fault tolerance
BGP	Border gateway protocol
BH	Bunch-head
BT	Blockchain technology
CDR	Call detail record
CE	Customer edge
CEA	Controlled environment agriculture
CHAP	Challenge-handshake authentication protocol
CK	Common key
CNN	Convolutional neural network
CTF	Counter terrorism funding
DDoS	Dispensed denial-of-carrier
DeFi	Decentralized finance
DES	Data encryption standard
DKMS	Decentralized key management systems
DLT	Distributed ledger technology
DoS	Denial-of-service
DPoS	Delegated proof of stake
DSS	Decision support systems
E2E	End-to-end

EA	Evolutionary algorithm
EAP	Extensible authentication protocol
ECC	Elliptic curve cryptography
EHR	Electronic health record
eMBB	Enhanced mobile broadband
EOQ	Economic order quantity
ESP	Encapsulating security payload
ETSI	European Telecommunications Standards Institute
EVM	Ethereum virtual machine
FIFO	First-in-first-out
GAN	Generative adversarial network
GDPR	General data protection regulation
GIS	Geographic information system
GPS	Global positioning system
GPU	Graphics processing unit
HIPPA	Health Insurance Portability and Accountability Act
IaaS	Infrastructure as a service
IAM	Identity and access management
IDM	Identity management
IDS	Intrusion detection system
IoT	Internet of Things
IoV	Internet of Vehicles
ITS	Intelligent transportation systems
IVO	Initial coin offering
JIT	Just-in-time
KGC	Key generation center
KNN	K-nearest neighbor
KYC	Know your customer
LER	Label edge router
LTE	Long-term evolution
M2M	Machine-to-machine
MAC	Media access control
MAC	Message authentication code
MDM	Mobile device management
MEC	Mobile edge computing
MIMO	Multiple input multiple output
MitM	Man-in-the-middle

ML	Machine learning
mMTC	Mass machine-type communications
MNO	Mobile network operator
NFT	Non-fungible token
NFV	Network function virtualization
NIC	Network interface card
NIST	National Institute of Standards and Technology
NLP	Natural language processing
OBU	Onboard units
OCF	Open Connectivity Foundation
OFDM	Orthogonal frequency-division multiplexing
ONF	Open Network Foundation
OOP	Object-oriented programming
P2P	Peer-to-peer
PA	Precision agriculture
PaaS	Platform as a service
PAP	Password authentication protocol
PBNM	Policy-based network management
PCA	Principal component analysis
PFMI	Principles for financial market infrastructure
PHR	Personal identification record
PK	Public key
PoS	Proof of stake
PoW	Proof of work
PPP	Point-to-point protocol
PQC	Post-quantum cryptography
QKD	Quantum key distribution
QoE	Quality of experience
QoS	Quality of service
RAN	Radio access network
RBAC	Role-based access control
RFID	Radio frequency identification
RL	Reinforcement learning
RNN	Recurrent neural networks
ROC	Receiver operating characteristic
RPA	Robotic manner process automation
RSA	Rivest–Shamir–Adleman
RSU	Road side unit
SaaS	Software as a service

SASE	Secure access service edge
SCM	Supply chain management
SDN	Software-defined networking
SIEM	Security information and event management
SK	Secret key
SON	Self-organizing network
SOS	Sensor Observation Service
SQL	Structured Query Language
SSCM	Site specific crop management
SSL	Secure socket layer
STB	Smart traveling bag
SVM	Support vector machine
TA	Trusted authority
TBA	Traceback authority
TCB	Trusted computing base
TCP	Trusted computing platform
TLS	Transport layer security
TPD	Tamper proof device
TPM	Trusted platform module
TPS	Transactions per second
TSS	Trusted platform support service
TTP	Trusted third party
TWN	Total worker node
UAV	Unmanned aerial vehicle
UDP	User datagram protocol
UE	User equipment
URLLC	Ultra-reliable low latency communication
VK	Verification key
VPN	Virtual private network
VR	Virtual reality
WSN	Wireless sensor network
ZKP	Zero knowledge proof
ZTN	Zero-Touch Network

Section 1

Laying the Foundation: Blockchain and AI Amalgamation in 5G-IoT

1

Introduction of Blockchain and 5G-enabled IoT Devices

R. Venkatesh

Department of Physics, PSNA College of Engineering and Technology (Autonomous), India
Email: sukatesh@gmail.com

Abstract

The convergence of blockchain technology and 5G networks within the Internet of Things (IoT) creates a paradigm shift in digital connectivity. This chapter is an introduction to the confluence of blockchain and 5G functionalities and the scope they create when integrated with IoT ecosystems, beginning with a general overview of the evolutionary road of IoT on its impactful journey within various sectors. Then it continues to explain blockchain technology, which demonstrates that owing to its decentralized and immutable nature, immense attention has drawn in various fields much beyond the confines of cryptocurrencies like Bitcoin. Then it proceeds to outline the full potential of 5G networks and how they represent an unprecedented promise of speed, ultra-low latency, and enormous connectivity and discusses how 5G creates a hyper-connected world, where data can be transmitted in real time and applications follow high bandwidth end.

Further, it would explore the integration of the process between blockchain and 5G on how these combined elements provide significant benefits to transform the IoT ecosystem. The innovation of new routes for effective and efficient working will unfold by combining aspects of security, transparency, and decentralization through blockchain with the increasing speed and scalability functionalities of 5G. Further, the next chapters are going to represent the practical application and use cases in the integration of blockchain and 5G in IoT ecosystems of various sectors of industries. It

DOI: 10.1201/9788743809050-2

then digs into the challenges and concerns brought about by this merger and the future direction and societal implications of blockchain and 5G-enabled IoT devices. Through all this, it aims to infuse insights into the transformative impact of this combination on industries and society at large, paving the way for a smarter, more interconnected future.

Keywords: Blockchain, 5G networks, Internet of Things, IoT, digital connectivity, scalability, hyper-connected world, security.

1.1 Understanding the Convergence of Blockchain and 5G in IoT

1.1.1 Evolution of IoT:A brief overview

The Internet of Things (IoT) technology evolution has been an outstanding technological journey, significantly changing how we interact with our surroundings and make use of data. As we trace back the convergence of the late 20th-century radio frequency identification (RFID) technology and early sensor networks, we would find that the concept of IoT was a way to connect physical objects so that they could communicate data over networks [1]. The widespread implantation of internet devices became critical for developments that made it possible to establish the very broad IoT ecosystems that we experience today in the early 2000s (Figure 1.1). Additionally, developments in wireless communication protocols, including Wi-Fi, Bluetooth, and cellular networks, have also further expanded IoT adoption due to their capability in allowing easy and seamless connection among devices and systems and allowing them to exchange data freely. In addition to this, the discovery of cloud computing greatly paved the way by providing the capability of scalable storage and processing, key requirements that were necessary for handling tremendous volumes of data originating from these devices [2]. Of course, it also saw the emergence of edge computing that decentralizes data processing and analysis to the edge of the network and finds solutions to latency problems, as well as raises capabilities in real-time decision-making capabilities. Standardization efforts and the development of interoperable frameworks have been pivotal in ensuring that not only are IoT devices across different industries and platforms compatible but also secure [3].

Moreover, with the augmentation of machine learning and artificial intelligence algorithms, IoT systems have learned and understood the data better, leading to predictive maintenance, personalization in the user experience, and effective resource management in healthcare, manufacturing, agriculture,

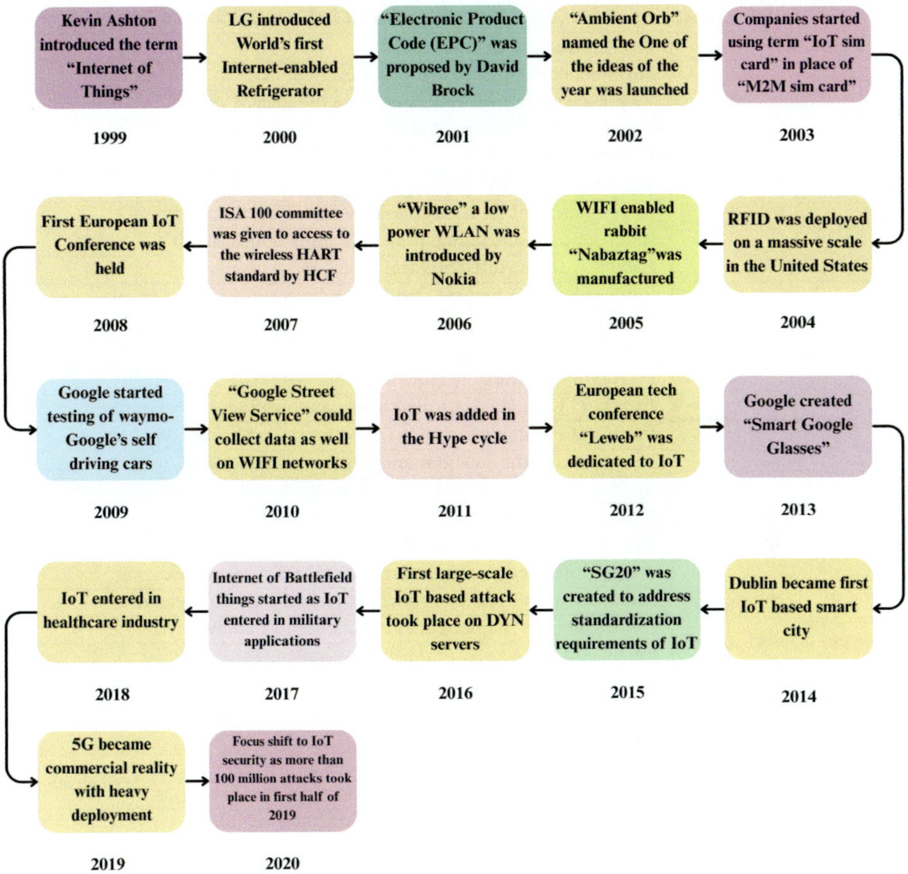

Figure 1.1 The evolution of IoT technologies from 1999 to 2020. Image adopted from [26].

transportation, and smart cities. With such modern developments in the IoT sector, trends like the rollouts of the 5G network, advancements in quantum computing, and even exploration into other types of distributed ledger technology known as blockchain promise further expansion of its capabilities and applications [4]. Challenges such as cybersecurity vulnerabilities and data privacy concerns and the need for frameworks of regulation continue to arise with the integration of IoT into our daily lives and global industries, not only changing the way we relate to technology but also the physical world. Table 1.1 gives a systematic view of the evolution of IoT, showcasing some of the most important events and technologies that have influenced the development of IoT from its discovery to its widespread application across the spheres.

Table 1.1 Historical context and pivotal events in IoT's development lifecycle.

Time period	Key events and developments
1980s	Early conceptualization of connecting devices to the internet.
	Visionaries and researchers explore the idea of "smart" objects.
	First experiments in remote device control over the internet.
	Example: Simple home automation systems.
1990s	The term "Internet of Things" was coined by Kevin Ashton.
	Development of RFID technology for object identification.
	Initial discussions on the potential applications of IoT.
	Example: Smart refrigerators.
Early 2000s	Expansion of embedded systems and sensor technologies.
	Advancements in wireless communication standards (Wi-Fi, Bluetooth).
	Prototyping of early IoT devices and systems.
	Example: Remote-controlled home appliances.
2010s	Proliferation of consumer IoT devices (smart homes, wearables).
	Rise of Industrial IoT in manufacturing and logistics.
	Introduction of smart city initiatives using IoT technologies.
	Cloud computing enables scalable IoT deployments.
	Example: Platforms like AWS IoT.
Current trends (2020s)	Integration of edge computing for real-time data processing.
	Advancements in AI and machine learning for IoT analytics.
	Deployment of 5G networks enhancing IoT connectivity.
	Focus on IoT security and privacy challenges.
	Example: Initiatives like the IoT Cybersecurity Improvement Act.
Future directions	Expansion of IoT into healthcare, agriculture, and environmental monitoring.
	Standards development for interoperability and integration.
	Continued innovation in IoT applications and use cases.
	Example: Like smart grids and connected vehicles.

Rise of internet-connected devices: That marked a huge change, especially during the early 2000s, with the proliferation of internet-connected devices and the onset of consumer-level smart technology. This brought in the whole era of smartphones to smart appliances and a whole lot of wearable devices, which helped individuals check their devices via network connectivity and gain remote monitoring and control over them. It was during this period that the proliferation of IoT ecosystems became critically helped by wireless communication protocols like Wi-Fi and Bluetooth, which made it simple to share data between devices.

Technological advancements: Advances in cloud computing played an important role in scaling and functionalities provided by IoT. Such large-scale cloud-based systems make possible the huge data storage, management, and processing, enabling real-time analytics and insights from the terabytes of generated data through IoT devices. On the other hand, there is edge computing, which reduces latency by decentralized data processing and analysis at the network's edge, hence reducing the data flow across the network and decreasing bandwidth utilization. This improves responsiveness in applications that require rapid decision-making capabilities.

Standardization and interoperability: Once the ecosystems started expanding, their growing complexity became pressing enough to be standardized and interoperable. There are industry efforts and standards organizations involved in establishing protocols and frameworks that ensure compatibility and security across different forms of IoT devices and platforms. In order to foster collaboration, innovation, and robustness in such a complex ecosystem that can easily be integrated with existing infrastructure and technologies, such standards have been very important.

Integration of AI and machine learning: Integration of AI and ML capabilities into the IoT has transformed its capabilities to empower devices to analyze data, learn patterns, and make autonomous decisions. AI-powered analytics have opened up new possibilities in predictive maintenance, personalized experiences, and adaptive automation across various industries. Edge-deployed machine learning algorithms enhance real-time processing capabilities, empowering IoT devices to intelligently respond to changing conditions without relying on centralized cloud resources.

Sector-specific applications and future trends: IoT applications have spread across sectors, affecting and transforming healthcare, manufacturing, agriculture, transportation, and smart cities. In the healthcare area, it has enabled remote patient monitoring and easy generation of a personal treatment plan. In manufacturing, it enhances operations through predictive maintenance and processes in supply chain management. Critical future trends of IoT include the extensive roll-out of 5G networks, promising superior connectivity, and greater numbers of connected devices with less latency and bandwidth. Trends in quantum computing and blockchain technologies also promise to improve the security and scalability of IoT, as well as make the data more integral to itself.

Challenges and considerations: The growth and widespread use of IoT have been impressively tremendous, but in all that development, it poses several significant problems to the user community, especially in relation to cybersecurity vulnerabilities, data privacy, and the complexity of regulations. So, collaboration with current industry stakeholders, policymakers, and technology developers is paramount for setting up such great security measures, privacy guardians, and well-structured regulatory frameworks, keeping in view the safe protection of individual user data as well as responsible use of these technologies. These factors will critically shape IoT's future trajectory to maximize its potential in driving innovation, efficiency, and sustainability across global economies and societies as it continues unfolding.

1.1.2 Understanding blockchain technology

Blockchain is a new technology in the space of digital record-keeping that offers a decentralized approach to storing and handling data (Figure 1.2). Put in simple terms, blockchain refers to a distributed ledger system that uses a linear, chronological chain to put together transactions and add them to blocks. This system leads to the decentralization aspect of this nature, in which, instead of relying on a central authority, the ledger is maintained by a network of computers based on various nodes around the world [5]. The whole blockchain is copied by each node, and hence, manipulation or changes in a chain cannot exist without it coming to the attention of other nodes as well. To understand blockchain, one needs to appreciate its basic principles and operational workings. In short, it is a decentralized digital ledger distributed over a network of computers called nodes. Transactions, or rather blocks of transactions, are secured by cryptography and arranged successively to form an immutable chain. Agreement mechanisms like proof of work (PoW)[1] or proof of stake (PoS)[2] ensure nodes agree that a given set of transactions is valid; therefore, adding an extra layer of security and trust to the network. It removes all intermediaries completely, allowing peer-to-peer transactions to go through without transparency or traceability. This functionality extends further to even smart contracts that can provide full automation and enforcement of agreements without intermediaries [6].

Application in blockchain beyond what is described merely as cryptocurrencies, blockchain goes on to change many industries with improved efficiency and transparency in supply chains, strong identity management, and decentralized applications promising change across the globe in different

---

[1]Proof of work is a mechanism that allows for miners to solve complicated mathematical problems or riddles in order to verify transactions and validate the blockchain while earning a reward in the process.

[2]Proof of stake, where a consensus mechanism relies on validators producing new blocks and accepting transactions based on the number of coins that they hold and are willing to "stake" as collateral.

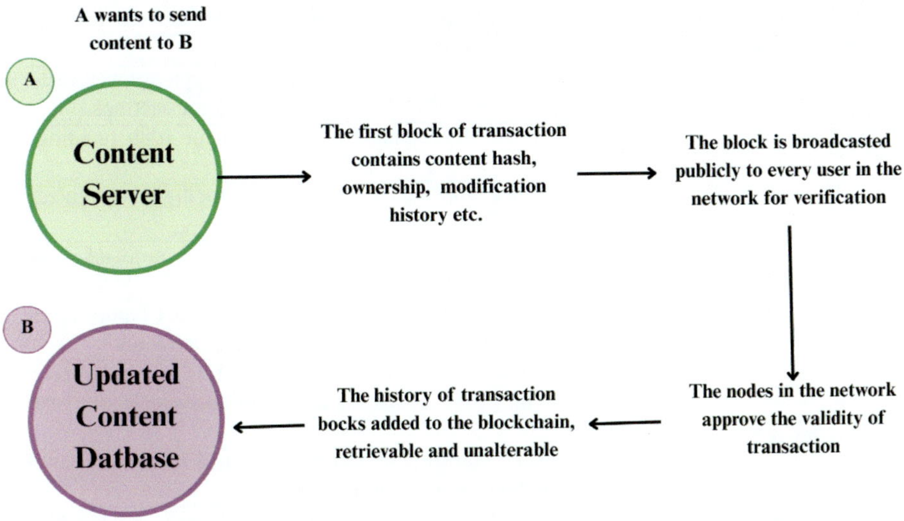

Figure 1.2 Fundamental concepts of blockchain technology.Image adopted from [27].

sectors [7]. Table 1.2 provides a structured overview of the historical background and key developments in blockchain technology, highlighting its evolution from the conceptual stage to its current and future applications across various industries and domains.

Decentralized and distributed ledger: At its core, blockchain operates as a decentralized and distributed ledger. Unlike traditional centralized systems where data is stored and managed by a single entity (like a bank or a government), blockchain distributes data across a network of computers (nodes). Each node maintains a copy of the entire blockchain, ensuring transparency and resilience. Transactions are grouped into blocks, which are linked together in a chronological chain, hence the name "blockchain."

Cryptographic security: Blockchain relies heavily on cryptographic techniques to secure transactions and ensure the integrity of the data stored on the ledger. Each block is included in a cryptographic hash of the previous block, creating a chain that proves to be virtually impossible to alter previous records without changes occurring on subsequent blocks. Moreover, transactions in the blockchain are secured via public-key cryptography so that each participant has a public key or address and a private key. The private key is used to sign the transaction, thus proving ownership, and only that owner can spend the funds.

Table 1.2 Historical context and pivotal events in the development of blockchain technology.

Time period	**Key events and developments**
1980s	*Cryptographic foundations*: Concepts of cryptographic techniques laid the groundwork for secure digital transactions.
	Hash functions: Development of cryptographic hash functions for data integrity.
	Digital currency proposals: Early proposals for digital currencies and electronic cash.
1990s	*Hashcash*: Adam Back introduces Hashcash[3], a proof-of-work system to limit email spam.
	DigiCash: Introduction of DigiCash[4] by David Chaum as an electronic cash company using cryptographic protocols.
Early 2000s	*Bitcoin whitepaper*: Satoshi Nakamoto published the Bitcoin whitepaper in 2008, describing a peer-to-peer electronic cash system.
	Genesis Block: The Bitcoin network launched in January 2009 with the creation of the Genesis Block[5].
	Proof-of-work: Bitcoin implements proof-of-work as a consensus mechanism.
	Blockchain concept: The term "blockchain" is coined to describe the distributed ledger technology behind Bitcoin.
Mid to Late 2000s	*Altcoins*: Development of alternative cryptocurrencies (altcoins) using blockchain technology.
	Ethereum: Vitalik Buterin proposes Ethereum in late 2013, introducing smart contracts and a programmable blockchain.
	Enterprise adoption: Businesses start exploring blockchain for applications beyond cryptocurrencies.
2010s	*Blockchain 2.0*: Rise of blockchain platforms supporting smart contracts and decentralized applications (dApps).
	Hyperledger project: Launch of Hyperledger project by Linux Foundation to support blockchain-based distributed ledgers.
	ICO boom: Initial coin offerings (ICOs) gain popularity as a fundraising method for blockchain projects.
	Regulatory challenges: Governments and regulators begin addressing legal and regulatory frameworks for blockchain and cryptocurrencies.

[3]Hashcash is the proof-of-work system, and it has been used to limit spam e-mail and denial-of-service attacks, forcing senders to perform computational work.

[4]DigiCash was an early form of digital currency that enabled anonymous transactions using cryptographic methods.

[5]The Genesis Block is the first block that gets created in a blockchain; it defines from where the history of the ledger began.

Table 1.2 *Continued.*

Time period	Key events and developments
Current trends (2020s)	*DeFi (decentralized finance)*: Emergence of DeFi platforms leveraging blockchain for financial services.
	NFTs (non-fungible tokens): NFTs gain popularity for digital art and collectibles on blockchain.
	Blockchain interoperability: Efforts toward interoperability between different blockchain networks.
	Sustainability: Focus on improving blockchain's energy efficiency and environmental impact.
Future directions	*Scalability solutions*: Development of scaling solutions like Layer 2 protocols and sharding[6].
	Privacy enhancements: Integration of privacy-preserving technologies into blockchain networks.
	Integration with IoT and AI: Exploration of blockchain applications in the Internet of Things (IoT) and artificial intelligence (AI).
	Regulatory clarity: Continued development of regulatory frameworks to support blockchain innovation.

Consensus mechanisms: Consensus mechanisms are protocols that guarantee nodes that are operating in the network will agree on the validity of the transactions submitted to the blockchain. Different blockchain networks have various forms of consensus mechanisms – proof of work and proof of stake, and the list is endless. Such mechanisms do not allow an attacker to interfere with the blockchain in any way, making the network secure and working fully.

Immutable and transparent transactions: Once the transactions are put on the blockchain, they become virtually undeletable or unerasable, thanks again to the cryptographic hashing and the consensus mechanisms described above. It is like an open ledger of all transactions, available for all network participants, yet with pseudonymous addresses, so that the identity of the concerned persons is not surrendered by this process.

Smart contracts and programmability: The smart contract concept on blockchain technology refers to self-executing contracts the very terms of which are written directly into lines of code. Smart contracts allow self-enforcing arrangements automatically, no matter how complex, once predefined conditions are satisfied, thereby eliminating the need for intermediaries and reducing transactional costs. With smart contracts, programmability on the blockchain is appended and applied to a wider scope of applications

[6] Sharding refers to the method of partitioning a huge dataset into smaller, multiple data pieces, called shards, to improve database performance and scalability.

outside of even simple monetary transactions, like supply chain management, decentralized finance (DeFi), voting systems, and more.

Applications and use cases: This technology is applied in many different aspects, including finance, because it has enabled faster and less expensive cross-border payments, such as remittances, and issued and managed digital assets known as cryptocurrencies. In supply chain management, blockchain can track and ensure the provenance of goods, providing clarity in their origin and authenticity. Its applications are multiplied further in healthcare by ensuring secure, interoperable health records; and by way of governments exploring the potential of transparent voting systems and more efficient public service delivery.

Challenges and future developments: Despite its potential, blockchain faces challenges such as scalability, energy consumption (particularly in PoW systems), regulatory uncertainty, and interoperability between different blockchain networks. Ongoing research and development are focused on addressing these challenges and improving blockchain's efficiency, scalability, and usability. Future developments include the integration of blockchain with emerging technologies like AI and IoT, as well as advancements in privacy-preserving techniques such as zero-knowledge proofs and homomorphic encryption.

1.1.3 Unraveling the potential of 5G networks

An enormous amount of promise is coming with the combination of 5G technology and blockchain; it promises to improve data security efficiency in various fields. This high-speed, low-latency platform that 5G offers makes possible real-time communication of data. The blockchain provides a safe and decentralized ledger for transactions. This synergy can be beneficial for ensuring applications like smart cities where devices communicate seamlessly and securely and ensure data integrity in everything – from traffic management and supply chain logistics – while being safe for use. Together, they can make up a much more integrated, reliable, and transparent digital ecosystem.

Unraveling the potential of 5G networks unveils a profound shift in wireless technology that transcends previous generations like 4G long-term evolution (LTE), heralding a new era of connectivity with unparalleled capabilities (Figure 1.3). At its core, 5G promises to deliver ultra-fast data speeds, significantly surpassing those of 4G, with theoretical peak speeds potentially reaching 10 Gbps or higher [8].

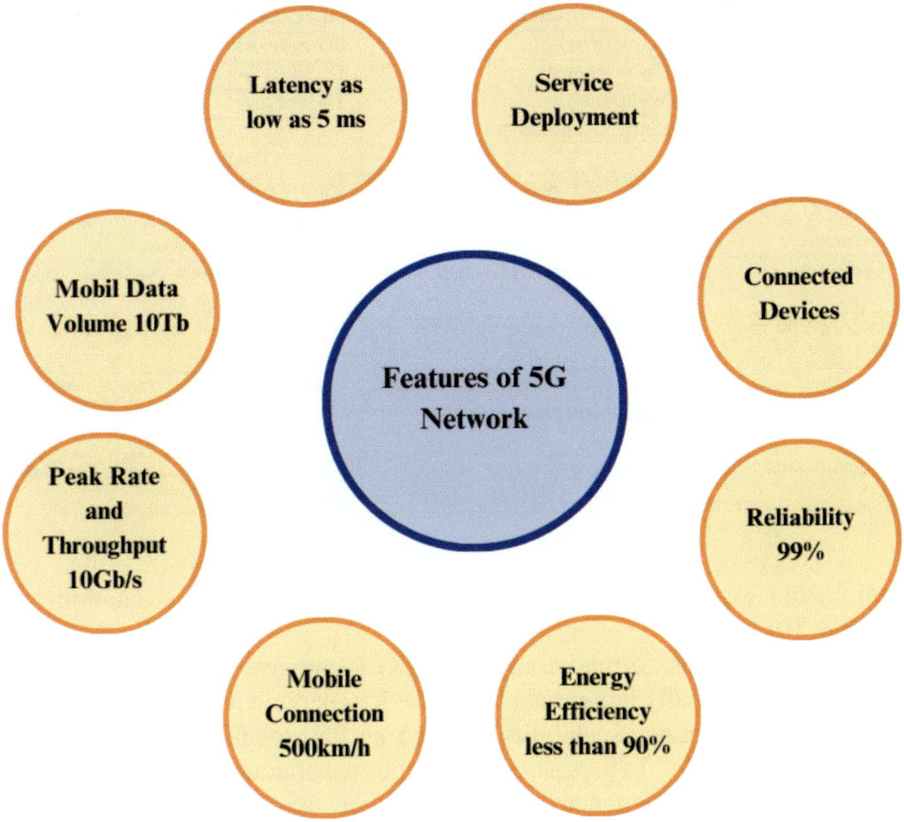

Figure 1.3 Standout feature of 5G networks.Image adopted from [28].

This exponential increase in speed transforms the way data is transmitted and accessed, enabling quicker downloads of large files, seamless streaming of high-definition content, and instantaneous access to cloud-based services and applications. Table 1.3 very clearly outlines where 4G contrasts with 5G in various areas.

Moreover, 5G networks are characterized by exceptionally low latency, reducing the time it takes for data to travel between devices and servers to as low as one millisecond. This nearly instant responsiveness is critical for applications involving real-time interaction, including autonomous vehicles, remote surgery, augmented reality (AR), and virtual reality (VR). The minimal latency of 5G networks enhances the user experience by eliminating noticeable delays, enabling smoother interactions in gaming, immersive

Table 1.3 Differences between 4G and 5G networks.

Features	**4G network**	**5G network**
Speed	Up to 1 Gbps	Up to 10 Gbps or more
Latency	30–50 ms	1 ms or less
Capacity	Limited capacity for devices	Supports millions of devices per square kilometer
Bandwidth	100 MHz (theoretical max)	Up to 1 GHz (potentially more)
Network architecture	Primarily LTE (long-term evolution)	Utilizes a mix of mmWave, sub-6 GHz, and lower bands
Use cases	Mobile internet, HD streaming	IoT, autonomous vehicles, augmented/virtual reality
Energy efficiency	Moderate	Improved efficiency with advanced protocols
Coverage	Extensive but varies by location	Initially limited, expanding rapidly
Deployment	Mature and widespread	In progress, with ongoing enhancements
Network slicing	Limited	Supports network slicing for customized services

multimedia experiences, and precise control in industrial automation and robotics [9].

Yet another transformative aspect of 5G is massive connectivity, which enables a substantially larger quantity of devices per unit area when compared to earlier generations. Scalability in such an enormous number is crucial to the ecosystem of IoT consisting of billions of interconnected devices, from smart home appliances to industrial sensors, that require real-time communication for the exchange of data [10]. This aspect of 5G allows a connected infrastructure for smart cities, increased agricultural efficiency through precision farming, scalable and efficient integration of IoT in the healthcare sector, and remote patient monitoring or personalized medicines.

In effect, the promise of 5G lies not only in its capacity for offering incredible speed, latency, and connectivity capabilities but also in revolutionizing industrial processes in all dimensions. From delivering enhanced mobile broadband experiences and enabling advanced multimedia applications to transforming technologies such as autonomous vehicles and telemedicine, 5G networks stand to create innovation, economic growth, and societal development at speeds considered unimaginable in the past [11]. As rollouts continue and the technology matures, it is yet to be fully realized how 5G will impact global connectivity, digital transformation, and the lives of people; however, the groundwork is being laid for a future where connectivity is faster, more reliable, and more pervasive than ever before. Table 1.4, therefore, provides

Table 1.4 4G versus 5G: A comparative overview of different aspects.

Aspect	**4G**	**5G**
Increased speed	4G networks offer speeds up to 1 Gbps (gigabit per second) in optimal conditions.	5G can deliver speeds of up to 10 Gbps or more, making downloads nearly instantaneous and enabling high-definition streaming without lag.
Low latency	Latency in 4G networks is around 30–50 milliseconds.	5G networks promise a much lower latency range of 1–10 milliseconds, enabling near-instantaneous communication, essential for applications like autonomous driving and remote surgeries.
Greater capacity	4G can support 2000 devices per square kilometer.	5G increases this to 1 million devices per square kilometer, catering to the massive growth of IoT devices and dense urban environments.
Enhanced reliability	4G offers good reliability but may face disruptions in highly congested areas.	5G provides improved reliability and network availability, ensuring continuous connectivity for critical services like industrial IoT, smart cities, and emergency services.
Network slicing	Not available in 4G.	5G supports network slicing, allowing operators to create virtual networks tailored to specific needs (e.g., speed, latency, and security) for a range of use cases.
IoT and smart cities	4G supports IoT but with limitations in device density and latency.	5G is designed to support billions of IoT devices and smart city applications, enabling advanced automation and real-time management of urban infrastructure.
Industry 4.0 and automation	4G enables some IoT and automation applications but with limitations in speed and connectivity.	5G accelerates Industry 4.0 technologies, such as robotics, AI-driven automation, and augmented reality, providing faster, more reliable performance in manufacturing and other sectors.
Telemedicine and remote work	4G supports basic telemedicine, video conferencing, and remote work, but may struggle with high-quality real-time applications.	5G enhances telemedicine by enabling high-quality video consultations, remote monitoring, and real-time diagnostics with minimal latency, transforming healthcare delivery and supporting remote work trends.
Emerging technologies	4G supports some emerging technologies but may not meet the speed and latency demands of newer innovations.	5G is built to support cutting-edge technologies like autonomous vehicles, immersive gaming, smart grids, and virtual/augmented reality, thanks to ultra-fast speeds, low latency, and superior reliability.

Table 1.4 *Continued.*

Aspect	4G	5G
Economic growth and innovation	4G has fostered innovation and economic growth, especially in mobile apps, social media, and e-commerce.	5G is expected to drive massive economic growth, enabling new innovations in industries like healthcare, manufacturing, transportation, and entertainment, fueling job creation and digital transformation globally.
Challenges and considerations	4G faces challenges like network congestion, limited coverage in rural areas, and security concerns.	5G faces challenges related to expensive infrastructure, spectrum availability, and regulatory hurdles, as well as concerns around security, privacy, and the health effects of millimeter-wave frequencies.

an overview in general terms for the real potential of 4G and 5G in various domains based on being able to transform how industries work and bringing new technologies that will bring change to the range of applications that further speed, lower latency, and greater reliability will transform industries, technologies, and everyday life in several key ways.

Enhanced speed and capacity: Data transfer will be many-fold improved with 5G networks, up to 10 Gbps or even higher. Ultimately, this is something that would make high-definition video downloads faster, high-definition content streaming smoother, and access to cloud services and applications much faster. Entertainment, media, and gaming industries will be the key beneficiaries of these features, further opening out novel immersive experiences and content delivery models.

Low latency and real-time applications: This characteristic is one that defines 5G, at just millisecond latency. Such near-immediate responsiveness is a must for applications that demand real-time interaction, like autonomous vehicles, remote surgery, augmented reality (AR), and virtual reality (VR). 5G low-latency builds improved performance of mission-critical IoT devices and industrial automation systems with better decision support and operational efficiencies.

Massive IoT connectivity: The networks will be planned for the maximum number of devices that may be connected at the same time. This will foster IoT proliferation not only through smart cities, healthcare systems, agriculture, and the manufacturing industries but through everything else as well. Here, IoT devices can communicate with each other much better, get data in real time, and send this data out directly for more advanced applications like smart grids, predictive maintenance, and environmental monitoring.

Empowering Industry 4.0 and digital transformation: Industry 4.0 inspires an acceleration of efforts in digital transformation and also provides high-speed connectivity and low latency with massive IoT support, leading to smart factories with self-dependent robots, AI-based analytics, and interconnected machines for optimizing production, supply chains, and overall agility and responsiveness in operations.

Innovation in healthcare and telemedicine: The 5G network has tremendous potential for deployment in healthcare, leading to remote patient monitoring, telemedicine consultations, and real-time medical diagnostics. The healthcare providers would utilize the high-bandwidth and low-latency characteristics of the 5G by transmitting large medical imaging files, conducting virtual surgeries through haptic feedback systems, and delivering personalized care through connected wearable devices and IoT-enabled healthcare solutions.

Challenges and considerations: Even though 5G promises vast benefits of transformative improvements, the actual deployment is being hindered by necessary infrastructure investments, spectrum allocations, and regulatory considerations. A lot of investment and coordination from telcos, governments, and technology providers will be needed to extend the necessary small-cell and base station infrastructure required for 5G networks. In addition, cybersecurity, data privacy, and regulatory compliance issues will take huge importance in building trust and ensuring that 5G technology will be deployed responsibly.

1.1.4 Blockchain technology and 5G:The interaction

The harmonization of blockchain technology with 5G networks is a landmark convergence at the forefront of digital innovation that may reshape and elevate the levels of digital infrastructure in various fields. Blockchain has its inherent decentralized ledger and robust cryptographic security. When blockchain integrated with 5G has exceptional capabilities of ultra-fast data transmission speeds and minimal latency with expansive connectivity [12]. This combination produces an unprecedented synergy beyond normal boundaries, improving security measurements, real-time transactions, and consequently, the general functionality of decentralized applications or dApps. Businesses and industries can achieve unparalleled transparency, efficiency, and reliability in managing and communicating data through the immutable ledger and cryptographic protocols of blockchain in the context of high-speed, low-latency 5G networks. This revolutionary joint venture makes

Table 1.5 Blockchain technology and 5G: The interaction.

Aspect of synergy	**Description**	**Examples**
Data integrity and security	Blockchain generates unchangeable records and provides cryptography security that guarantees data integrity. Locking them up with 5G will make them further secure compared to the encryption and communication process. Together, these two ensure robust protection for sensitive data in IoT as well as other similar applications.	Secure medical records in telehealth applications.
Scalability	In the case of blockchain, scalability issues come from high transaction volumes. 5G network supports faster transactions with high bandwidth and ultra-low-latency capabilities; therefore, faster transaction processing and scalability for blockchain networks.	High-frequency trading platforms utilizing blockchain.
IoT integration	Support for vast numbers of connected devices, 5G's potential for massive IoT. The utilization of blockchain for the protection and control of IoT data enables communicating devices and networks to share information in a way that is able to trust and be transparent to each other.	Smart home devices coordinating via a blockchain network.
Edge computing	Using edge computing with 5G, latency is reduced as much as possible because data is processed close to where it comes from. Blockchain guarantees data integrity and security for the efficient execution of dApps and smart contracts at the edge.	Real-time video processing for security cameras.
Supply chain management	Blockchain would improve supply chain transparency and traceability. With 5G, real-time tracking of goods and transactions would become possible to enhance the efficiency of supply chains and reduce frauds.	Food safety tracking from farm to table.
Smart cities	Blockchain and 5G support smart city initiatives by allowing safe data sharing between the various city infrastructure and services. It promotes efficient urban management, energy efficiency, and public safety.	Traffic management systems that optimize routes in real time.
Monetization and micropayments	Blockchain technology gives proper secure and transparent transactions, hence allowing new models of business and micropayments. Of 5G's features, one is low latency and high throughput with the support of real-time transactions, as well as automated payment and billing.	In-app purchases in gaming applications with instant processing.

Table 1.5 *Continued.*

Aspect of synergy	Description	Examples
Regulatory compliance	Blockchain will allow for transparent and auditable records of transactions made and will support compliance with regulation. In many ways, 5G offers uncompromised security features and network capabilities to ensure data privacy and compliance.	Financial services maintaining compliance with regulations.
Emerging technologies	Applications of blockchain and 5G are further validating the developmental prospects of emerging technologies, including AI, AR/VR, and autonomous vehicles, with guarantees for smooth, secure data exchange, and high-speed processing and networking that can positively impact seamless integration and operation in ecosystems.	Autonomous vehicles communicating in real-time with city infrastructure.

intersectoral processes easier and faster – from finance to healthcare and supply chain management – but also turns the tide for revolutionary innovations in smart cities, IoT integration, and more [13]. With time, blockchain and 5G continue to grow in tandem, and their collaborative appeal may unlock new frontiers of digital transformation for enterprises to innovate and thrive in this increasingly interconnected and dynamic global economy. Table 1.5 , thus, represents how the integration of blockchain technology with 5G leverages mutual benefits to enhance different aspects of the digital infrastructure, on the one hand, such as data security and IoT integration, while on the other, aspects regarding supply chain management, smart city initiatives, among others. Their integration promises to revolutionize enterprises by providing faster, more secure, and scalable solutions that foster innovation and efficiency in the digital economy.

Enhanced security and privacy: Blockchain's decentralized architecture and cryptographic mechanisms lock in security and data privacy for 5G networks, with tamper-proof transaction and identity records. Blockchain can improve the authentication process to prevent unauthorized users from accessing data in 5G-enabled IoT devices and networks. This interaction may reduce the risks involved with cyber threats and improve trust between digital transactions and communications.

Optimized decentralized applications (dApps): With the endogenous property of 5G, fast and low-latency connectivity decentralized applications on blockchain platforms will run faster. Smart contracts are executed by the blockchain itself, autonomously and transparently, using 5G-connected sensors and devices for actual feeds. The application leads to efficiency gains in supply chain management, logistics, and automation as it leverages optimized cost, reduced complexity, enhanced reliability, and scalability.

IoT integration and supply chain efficiency: It is also an optimization of the IoT ecosystems and modernizing the way supply chain management is done with blockchain and 5G together. With massive connectivity in 5G, it would ensure perfect communication from a huge number of IoT devices, while on the other hand, blockchain provides a secure and transparent ledger for tracing and authenticating the origin of goods. Smart contracts can be used to automate contractual agreements and payment settlements that are based on real-time IoT data to make all the components in a transparent, traceable, and efficient supply chain.

Applications in smart cities and public services: Smart city initiatives with blockchain and 5G shall enhance the management of urban infrastructure and services. The smart contracts help in energy supply, waste collection, and traffic management processes because good quality sensors and devices are collected through 5G. This also increases the transparency of operations, improves resource allocation, and helps citizen services increase sustainable urban development and enhance their quality of life.

Challenges and considerations: Even though such potential synergies exist, there are still many challenges that have been realized when blockchain is to be integrated with 5G networks. Some of these challenges include scalability, interoperability in-between platforms, and older legacy systems, and regulatory compliance as issues that blockchain developers working with the various telecommunications providers and regulatory authorities have faced in an effort to harmonize the standards and frameworks in integrating blockchain technology in a way that will also ensure data privacy and security are not compromised.

1.2 Applications and Use Cases

1.2.1 Supply chain management

Supply chain management (SCM) is the art of planning, controlling, and optimizing the flow of goods, services, information, and finances across a network of suppliers, manufacturers, distributors, retailers, and customers. SCM is defined to be a full-fledged cycle of a product, starting from its origination and procurement of raw material to manufacture, distribution, and finally sale to the end-user [14].

Key components of supply chain management:

(1) *Planning and forecasting*: SCM begins with strategic planning and forecasting to predict demand, maximize inventory levels, and ensure the products are available at the right time. Advanced planning tools, along with the models of demand forecasting, help the firms in reducing the supply chain disruptions and fulfilling the expectations of the customers.
(2) *Sourcing and procurement*: This involves the identification of suppliers, negotiation of contract details, and procurement of raw materials or components that go into the product under production. Powerful sourcing uses quality, cost effectiveness, and sustainability, along with supplier relationship management, to ascertain a reliable supply chain.
(3) *Production and manufacturing*: SCM carries out production operations to ensure effective scheduling of production, efficient resource utilization, and quality control over manufactured products. Concepts of lean manufacturing and just-in-time (JIT) are applied in order to avoid undue waste, reduce the lead times, and increase the efficiency of the production processes.
(4) *Logistics and transportation*: Logistics management refers to the flow of goods in a particular supply chain efficiently, with proper storage and transportation. Warehousing and inventory management, order fulfillment, and proper transportation mode selection to reduce costs and enhance delivery time come under this function.
(5) *Distribution and delivery*: SCM helps ensure the timely delivery of finished products to customers while bringing efficiency and cost-effectiveness into distribution networks. Route optimization software, as well as real-time tracking systems, enhance visibility and streamline last-mile delivery operations.
(6) *Inventory management*: SCM has the ability to balance demand and supply with regard to maximizing optimal levels of inventory and minimizing carrying costs. Techniques like Always Better Control, or ABC analysis and economic order quantity (EOQ), contribute toward just-in-time inventory by achieving necessary stockholding at all times without overstocking or understocking.

Challenges in supply chain management:

(1) *Supply chain complexity*: Due to globalization and outsourcing by the companies, supply chain complexity will tend to increase due to which

it has to manage diversified suppliers, regulatory requirements, and geopolitical risks effectively.

(2) *Demand volatility*: Consumer demand tends to fluctuate. Seasonal variations and occasionally unexpected events like a pandemic or natural disaster could disrupt the smoothness of the supply chain, affecting inventory management and production planning.

(3) *Supply chain visibility*: Lack of visibility in the supply chain creates inefficiency, slow decision-making, and problems in tracking and mitigating risks.

(4) *Sustainability and ethical practices*: Increasing demand for sustainability and ethical practices requires supply chains to up the ante on their green initiatives, fair labor practices, and ability to trace their traceability.

(5) *Technology integration*: Fast developments in blockchain, AI, IoT, and big data analytics allow the implementation of visibility opportunities, but with careful integration and investment.

Future trends in supply chain management:

(1) *Digital transformation*: Embracing digital technologies to enhance supply chain visibility, optimize operations, and enable real-time data-driven decision-making.

(2) *Sustainability initiatives*: Increasing focus on sustainable and ethical supply chain practices, including carbon footprint reduction, circular economy principles, and responsible sourcing.

(3) *Resilience and risk management*: Building resilient supply chains capable of mitigating disruptions through scenario planning, supplier diversification, and agile supply chain strategies.

(4) *Customer-centric supply chains*: Personalizing customer experiences through demand-driven supply chains, flexible fulfillment options, and seamless omnichannel integration.

(5) *Collaborative supply chains*: Strengthening collaboration and transparency among supply chain partners through shared data platforms, collaborative forecasting, and supplier relationship management.

Supply chain management plays a pivotal role in ensuring the competitiveness and sustainability of organizations in today's dynamic global marketplace. By embracing innovative strategies, advanced technologies, and collaboration and sustainability, the firms will be able to navigate through their set of challenges while capitalizing on opportunities that enhance supply chain efficiency, resilience, and customer satisfaction.

1.2.2 Smart cities

A smart city can be described as one making ample use of technology and data-driven solutions to enhance the quality of lifestyles, efficient utilization of resources, and environmental friendliness. It utilizes IoT devices, sensors, and data infrastructure that allows for the collection and analysis of real-time data [15]. The information gathered through it allows crucial decision-making and automates processes in transportation, energy, healthcare, public safety, and waste management.

Components of smart cities:

(1) *Infrastructure and connectivity*: Smart cities are based on solid digital infrastructure: high-speed broadband networks, 5G connectivity, and IoT sensors embedded in roads, buildings, and utilities – all these help to ensure smooth communication and data interchange between devices and systems.

(2) *Data collection and analysis*: Different IoT devices and sensors will be collecting data on everything from the efficiency of traffic flow to the quality of air, consumption of energy, and usage of public services. Advanced analytics and AI algorithms will process this data in real-time to generate insights and predict trends.

(3) *Sustainable urban development*: The ability to make a smart city sustainable through increased carbon emission reduction, natural resource conservation, and ecological practices. Proposed technologies include smart grids, energy-efficient buildings, electric vehicle charging stations, and waste management systems, which have been suggested as a method for cities to reduce their negative impact on the environment and increase their strength in dealing with climate change.

(4) *Mobility and transportation*: Smart transport systems make mobility smart due to effective management of traffic flow in the optimization pathway, together with the provision of real time to its users. Alternative transportation modes, such as bike sharing and electric vehicles, also come in handy to encourage people to use them. Integrated Transport management systems handle efficient logistics toward reducing congestion in the streets of any city while enhancing safety.

(5) *Public services and governance*: It leads to more conveniently available human–machine interactions with public services and governance for the purposes of bill payment, reporting, and civic engagement. Data-driven insights contribute to better decision-making, policy formulation, and resource allocation in smart governance for effective public service delivery.

(6) *Safety and security*: Smart cities provide public safety by way of video surveillance, emergency response systems, and predictive policing algorithms. It senses anomalies, monitors crowd behavior, and responds to emergencies promptly through IoT-enabled sensors and analytics, thus providing a safe environment for residents and visitors.

Benefits of smart cities:

- *Improved quality of life*: With regards to convenience, efficiency, and accessibility of services, the quality of life among citizens is boosted through smart cities, hence with reduced travel time and quality air, and having ready access to healthcare and education.
- *Economic growth*: Smart cities will, first of all, attract different businesses through innovation and digital transformation, thus creating jobs and stimulating economic growth. That gives way to the development of emerging technologies, including support for entrepreneurship, research, and development in related infrastructure and connectivity.
- *Environmental sustainability*: Optimization in resource management and sustainable practices leads toward environmental conservation that will reduce a carbon footprint and is supportive of the global efforts to mitigate climate change in smart cities.
- *Resilience and disaster management*: Since smart cities have better systems of early warning in case of natural disasters, real-time monitoring, and strategies for coordinated responses, they react better to natural disasters and emergencies; these ultimately improve community resilience as well as reduce the impact of disasters.

Challenges and considerations:

- *Privacy and data security*: The massive collection and sharing of personal information across the world raises big issues of privacy, protection of data, and cybersecurity risks that need to be handled by proper policies and regulations.
- *Infrastructure investment*: Building and maintaining smart city infrastructure requires substantial investment in technology, connectivity, and urban development projects, necessitating public–private partnerships and funding mechanisms.
- *Digital divide*: It ensures that there is equal access to digital technologies and services to the neglected communities that will prevent their exclusion; this eventually helps bridge the “digital divide” of smart cities.

Smart cities represent the future of city living: using technology and data-driven innovation to build sustainable, inclusive, and resilient communities. The use of smart technologies in collaborative governance can help cities respond to the complex challenges of urban life and improve the wider well-being of residents in a rapidly urbanizing world.

1.2.3 Healthcare

Healthcare is the maintenance and improvement of physical and mental well-being by providing medical services, preventive care, and health education. It would include various activities that could be intended for the diagnosis, treatment, or prevention of diseases or injuries in an effort to prolong life and to achieve the highest level of well-being [16].

Components of healthcare:

(1) *Medical services*: Medical workers, including doctors and nurses, as well as other specialists, would cater to medical services like diagnosis, treatment, surgery, and rehabilitation for patients. Primarily, such services include primary care, specialty care, emergency care, and long-term care, depending upon the needs of the patient.

(2) *Preventive care*: Preventive care is all about taking proactive measures that help in keeping diseases at bay and promoting health. It will include vaccinations, screenings for cancer or cardiovascular diseases, health check-ups, counseling about lifestyle changes, including diet, exercise, or even education to increase knowledge on healthy behaviors.

(3) *Healthcare facilities*: Healthcare institutions comprise hospitals and clinics, nursing homes, rehabilitation centers, and hospices. These institutions provide a continuum of care geared toward different kinds of medical conditions. Such institutions also guarantee easy access to medical knowledge and equipment as well as specialty treatments.

(4) *Healthcare professionals*: In delivering care and service to patients, key players involved are the healthcare professionals. These include a comprehensive variety of physicians – the general practitioners and specialists, nurses, pharmacists, therapists – physical, occupational, speech, diagnostic technicians, and administrative staffing who coordinate patient care and manage the functioning of facilities.

(5) *Health information systems*: Electronic health records (EHRs), medical imaging systems, telemedicine platforms, and health data analytics tools make up this category. These enable efficient and organized management

of data; sharing information between care providers and decision-making to better patient outcomes, as well as healthcare delivery.

Challenges in healthcare:

(1) *Access and equity*: Lack of access to healthcare for the vulnerable population due to geographical, economic, or social reasons increases their suffering. It has not succeeded in achieving access to healthcare services with equity in disadvantaged communities.
(2) *Cost and affordability*: The rapidly increasing cost of healthcare, which in some cases may include treatments, medications, and insurance premiums, proves to be challenging and even unaffordable for patients and families to raise money to access necessary healthcare services and medications. Lack of affordability is a common barrier to access.
(3) *Quality and patient safety*: Healthcare results are guaranteed by ensuring high-quality care and the safety of patients to avoid medical errors, infections, and adverse occurrences. Continuous quality improvement, patient-centered approaches, and adherence to clinical guidelines improve healthcare outcomes and patient satisfaction.
(4) *Healthcare workforce shortages*: A shortage of health professionals further limits the capacity of healthcare delivery. Shortages are still more pronounced in rural areas and specialized professional groups. Key workforce management priorities include recruiting and retaining skilled healthcare workers, preventing burnout, and ensuring professional development.
(5) *Technological integration and data privacy*: With the integration of advanced technologies in healthcare delivery systems, such as AI, telemedicine, and wearable devices, one will have to address concerns about data privacy, regulatory compliance, and ethics in the bid to protect confidentiality and trust with patients.

Future trends in healthcare:

(1) *Telehealth and remote monitoring*: Extending telehealth services and remote patient monitoring technologies that open up the door to virtual consultation, remote diagnostics, and chronic disease management, enrich healthcare services in terms of availability and accessibility.
(2) *Precision medicine*: The genetic, genomic, and biomarker information on the basis of precision medicine interventions allows precise targeted therapy and personalized healthcare interventions that eventually lead to high effectiveness of medical treatments and general results.

(3) *Artificial intelligence and data analytics*: This analytics and machine learning algorithm, supported by AI, analyzes a vast amount of healthcare data to predict disease trends, optimize the treatment protocol, and strengthen clinical decision support for healthcare providers.
(4) *Population health management*: Population health initiatives focus on improving health outcomes across communities through preventive interventions, chronic disease management, and social determinants of health (e.g., housing, education, and access to nutritious food).
(5) *Global health security*: Strengthening global health systems, pandemic preparedness, and response capabilities are critical priorities to mitigate emerging infectious diseases, public health crises, and global health disparities.

Healthcare is a multifaceted field that continues to evolve with advancements in medical science, technology, and healthcare delivery models. Addressing healthcare challenges requires collaborative efforts among healthcare providers, policymakers, and stakeholders to promote health equity, improve patient outcomes, and build resilient healthcare systems capable of meeting diverse healthcare needs worldwide.

1.2.4 Smart agriculture

Smart agriculture, also known as precision agriculture or agri-tech, refers to the use of advanced technologies and data-driven solutions to enhance agricultural productivity, efficiency, and sustainability [17]. It integrates digital tools, Internet of Things (IoT) devices, artificial intelligence (AI), and data analytics to optimize farming practices, improve decision-making, and maximize yields while minimizing resources and environmental impact.

Components of smart agriculture:

(1) *IoT and sensor technology*: Smart agriculture employs IOT sensors and devices put in the fields and the equipment and animals, providing real-time information on moisture levels, temperature, humidity, growth of crops, and health status of animals. The sensors provide very useful insights that help a farmer to monitor the conditions from any remote location and make decisions accordingly.
(2) *Precision farming techniques*: Precision agriculture utilizes GPS technology, drones, and satellite imagery to create precise maps of fields and monitor crop health and growth. In this manner, farmers can apply fertilizers, pesticides, and water precisely where they are needed and make

the utilization of resources optimum without hampering the environment while improving crops.

(3) *Data analytics and AI*: AI algorithms analyze large volumes of agricultural data, such as weather patterns, soil composition, crop genetics, and historical yields, to provide trends, forecasted outcomes, and suggestions on optimal farming practices. The data-driven approach improves decision-making and enables proactive management of farm operations.

(4) *Automated machinery and robotics*: Smart agriculture uses computerized machinery and robotics for planting, harvesting, and farm livestock management. Smart tractors, robotic reapers, and drones accomplish the tasks of doing jobs with less human waste and cost in large-acre farms.

(5) *Vertical farming and controlled environment agriculture (CEA)*: Plants are cultivated under LED lighting and using hydroponic or aeroponic growing systems indoors, vertically stacked in controlled environments within vertical farms. CEA reduces resource use while conserving water and maximizing crop yields throughout the entire year.

Benefits of smart agriculture:

- *Improved productivity and efficiency*: The smart agricultural technologies would not only enhance farming practices but also reduce the cost of inputs to increase yields while optimizing the resource utilization pertinent to water usage, fertilizers, and pesticides.
- *Sustainability and environmental impact*: The practices of precision farming minimize environmental footprint, reduce chemical runoff, conserve water, promote soil health, and foster biodiversity. Sustainable agriculture brings long-term resilience in agriculture and conserves natural resources.
- *Data-driven decision making*: It combines real-time data analytics and AI-driven insights to allow farmers to make informed decisions using data, respond immediately to changing conditions, and optimize operational efficiency at every point in the agricultural cycle.
- *Risk mitigation and resilience*: Smart agriculture aids farmers in mitigating risks relating to variability in weather, pests, and diseases through early detection and preventive measures promoted by predictive analytics and monitoring systems.
- *Market access and traceability*: Traceability systems under a smart agriculture approach ensure transparent supply chains, assurance of quality, and follow-up with related food safety standards. Enhanced traceability

means expanded market access, and consumers become more confident about food products.

Challenges and considerations:

- *Technology adoption and skills gap*: To implement smart agriculture technologies, investment in infrastructural facilities, trainings, and digital literacy shall be made available for farmers, especially located in rural and developing regions.
- *Data privacy and security*: The main concerns while adopting IoT and AI will be to secure the sensitive agricultural data from cyberattacks and ensure that the data adheres to the data privacy law.
- *Interoperability and standards*: Interoperable systems with standards on data sharing between different platforms or between the stakeholders, leading to seamless integration and collaboration in smart agriculture ecosystems.
- *Cost and return on investment*: There could be a high initial cost associated with smart agriculture technology, along with the cost of the equipment, sensors, and infrastructure needed for connectivity. Such a cost is a disincentive for small-scale farmers to adopt smart agriculture technologies, where it needs to show a return on investment and scale.

Indeed, smart agriculture is a revolutionary approach to sustainable food production. This revolution utilizes the application of technology and innovation to address global concerns such as food security, resource scarcity, and climate change. With the right smart agricultural solutions at hand, farmers can increase their productivity, profitability, and environmental stewardship, thereby succeeding in responding to the rapidly growing needs for safe, nutritious, and sustainably produced food globally.

1.3 Challenges and Considerations

1.3.1 Scalability and throughput

Scalability and throughput are concepts within computing and networking. Usually, they play a significant role in the evaluation and determination of the efficiency, performance, and capacity in systems, applications, and networks.

Scalability:

Scalability thus refers to a system, network, or process's ability to increase the work to be done, and if necessary, easily accommodate increased demands.

It is, therefore, a measure of how well a given system or organization can grow or expand without adversely affecting performance, reliability, or responsiveness [18].

There are two main types of scalability:

(1) *Vertical scalability*: It is also referred to as scaling up. They increase the resources, such as CPU, memory, and storage on a single server or machine to handle increased workload. This method has limits on the maximum capacity of the hardware and becomes very expensive as it grows.
(2) *Horizontal scalability*: Also referred to as scaling out, horizontal scalability involves adding more nodes or instances, such as servers or virtual machines, to spread workloads across several machines. Overall system capacity and its performance improve, and it is more cost-effective for handling large-scale applications and traffic.

Factors affecting scalability:

- *Architecture design*: Modularity, redundancy, and tasks that can be paralleled give a tremendous boost to scalability in a system's design. Scalable architectures usually use microservices, distributed databases, and message queues to distribute workloads effectively.
- *Resource allocation*: Effective resource management, including load balancing, auto-scaling mechanisms, and efficient use of computing resources, helps maintain performance and responsiveness as demand fluctuates.
- *Data management*: Data management techniques, such as data replication, sharding, or horizontal partitioning of data, and caching, are more heavily used in scalable systems, ensuring efficient and effective distribution and management of data among different nodes.
- *Scalability testing*: It refers to testing and benchmarking the system with various loads and conditions to identify bottlenecks and optimize the allocation of resources for ensuring scalability.

Examples:

The use of cloud services by Netflix helps it scale. The company adds servers automatically when viewers are many at a particular point in time. This way, millions stream without failure. Shopify also scales its platform to handle the gigantic transactions that happen with its merchants over Black Friday sales, allowing merchants to serve customers without any form of downtime.

Throughput:

Throughput refers to the rate at which a system or network processes and delivers a specified amount of work within a specified period of time. It measures the amount of data, tasks, or transactions that a system can process and complete correctly over time [19]. The throughput is measured in terms of data transfer rate, requests per second, transactions per second, or operations per second.

Factors affecting throughput:

- *Network bandwidth*: The throughput of networks depends not only on the amount of bandwidth available but also on how effectively the data transmission protocols being used are working.
- *System performance*: In computing systems, throughput fluctuates with other factors like CPU processing speed, memory bandwidth, disk I/O speed, and the efficiency of the algorithm used in the software.
- *Concurrency and parallelism*: Utilizing multi-threading, parallel processing, and distributed computing techniques can increase throughput by enabling the simultaneous execution of multiple tasks or transactions.
- *Optimization techniques*: Optimizing code, reducing latency, minimizing overhead, and improving system architecture and database design contribute to enhancing throughput.

Relationship between scalability and throughput:

Scalability and throughput are related concepts. Scalable systems improve on increased workload demands without affecting the throughput. For instance, horizontal scaling has the effect of increasing throughput by distributing the workload across several nodes or servers, thus enhancing the performance and capacity of the system. Proper scalability shall mean that as the system size increases, it should maintain or increase throughput to satisfy the needs of users, applications, or network traffic efficiently [20].

This table of comparison (Table 1.6) gives out the basic aspects of scalability and throughput in computing, as well as networking, highlighting their definitions, types, measurements, importance, challenges, technologies, applications, examples, and future trends. It gives a full view of these concepts, showing how they are fundamentally important toward enabling efficient and reliable performance in modern IT infrastructures [21]. Scalability and throughput are key concerns when designing and optimizing systems, applications, and networks: they guarantee that designs can be scaled up, support increased workload, and maintain optimal levels of performance

Table 1.6 Aspects of scalability and throughput in computing and networking.

Aspect	Scalability	Throughput
Definition	The ability of a system to handle increased workload by adding resources or nodes.	The rate at which a system processes data or transactions.
Types	Vertical (adding resources to a single machine).	Network (data transmission rate).
	Horizontal (adding more nodes/servers).	Compute (number of tasks completed per unit time).
	Elastic (dynamic provisioning based on demand).	Storage (rate of data read/write to storage devices).
Measurement	Number of nodes or servers.	Bits per second (bps), Megabits per second (Mbps), etc.
	Resources (CPU, RAM) per machine.	Operations per second (IOPS), megabytes per second (MB/s).
Purpose	Ensure the system can handle growth without performance degradation.	Indicates system efficiency and speed of data processing.
Importance	Ensures reliability, availability, and performance under increasing loads.	Improves user experience by providing fast response times.
Challenges	Designing for elasticity, load balancing, and resource allocation.	Managing network latency, concurrency, and data consistency.
Technologies	Cloud computing (autoscaling), distributed systems (Kubernetes, Hadoop).	High-speed networking (5G, fiber optics), parallel computing.
Applications	Cloud services, e-commerce platforms, and social media networks.	Video streaming, online gaming, and financial transactions.
Examples	Netflix (cloud scalability), Google (distributed computing).	YouTube (high network throughput), Amazon (storage throughput).
Future trends	Focus on auto-scaling algorithms, serverless computing.	Adoption of 5G for ultra-high throughput applications.

across conditions. In other words, knowing these concepts enables architects, developers, and administrators to build scalable, efficient, and resilient systems to support current and future operational needs.

Example:

YouTube offers high throughput as it processes billions of video streams daily to prevent users from seeing a buffering wheel while watching. Platforms like Robinhood in the financial industry execute thousands of transactions per second and provide real-time trading to its users in lieu. Big fast-food chains like McDonald's also streamline kitchen workflows for serving hundreds of customers during busy hours. Google processes billions of search queries daily and yields results to its users in time.

1.3.2 Security and privacy

Information technology and digital systems involve protecting information data, systems, and their users from unauthorized access, breaches, or misuse, thereby addressing security and privacy. Although they are closely interrelated, security and privacy relate to two different aspects of information protection and trust in digital interactions [22].

Security:

It involves all the practices and measures that are aimed at securing systems, networks, and data from threats and vulnerabilities.

It encompasses various aspects:

(1) *Data security*: Ensuring data confidentiality, integrity, and availability through encryption, controlling access, and storing safely.
(2) *Network security*: Securing infrastructure, such as firewalls, intrusion detection systems (IDS), and VPN, from cyberattacks and unauthorized entry.
(3) *Endpoint security*: Protects computers, smartphones, and other mobile devices from viruses, Trojan horse attacks, etc., with methods like antivirus software, endpoint detection and response, and mobile device management (MDM).
(4) *Application security*: Secure coding, vulnerability assessments, pen testing, remediation of vulnerabilities, and deployment.
(5) *Identity and access management (IAM)*: Manage user identity as well as authentication and authorization - ensure an access control regime that guards resources and data from unauthorized access.
(6) *Incident response and disaster recovery*: It should clearly define what procedures and protocols exist in order to detect, respond, or recover from a security incident with minimal disruption of business processes and little or no loss of data in breaches or disasters.

Privacy:

Data privacy extends to the rights and expectations of individuals in collecting, using, and disclosing personal data.

It involves:

(1) *Data privacy*: Data collection, processing, and storage while adhering to and observing privacy laws and rules like GDPR and CCPA. It is

about obtaining consent, keeping transparency about data practices, and respecting people's rights to access and control their data.

(2) *Anonymization and pseudonymization*: The elimination or obfuscation of identifying information from datasets, ensuring they still retain their utility for analysis and research.

(3) *Privacy by design*: Build in privacy into the design and development of systems, such that privacy protection is inherent in the design rather than an afterthought.

(4) *User control and transparency*: Provide clear information to users about data practices, options for managing their preferences, and mechanisms for exercising rights.

(5) *Legal and ethical considerations*: Ethical standards, as well as legal frameworks, protect individual privacy rights, thereby limiting risks connected with data collection, use, and sharing.

Interplay between security and privacy:

- *Complementary goals*: While security is concerned about protecting systems and data from unauthorized access and cyberattacks, ensuring privacy guarantees that individual information remains in control and safe from access or inappropriate use by unauthorized people.
- *Shared technologies*: Much of the security technology-that includes encryption, access controls, as well as secure authentication methods-will also help protect privacy, just by securing sensitive data and limiting access to proper users.
- *Challenges and trade-offs*: Balancing security and privacy presents challenges because there are circumstances where data security measures in ensuring that data is protected against unauthorized access may contradict some of what may be required by privacy considerations, for example, data minimization and transparency in data practices.
- *Regulatory landscape*: It is shaping to an increasingly more stringent privacy regulation around the world, requiring the organization to enforce robust security and a deep level of privacy protections and a culture of compliance and accountability (e.g., GDPR and CCPA).

Assuring safety and privacy is the most fundamental bulwark of trust and integrity in digital communities. Only through implementing robust security measures and principles of respected privacy can organizations thereby strengthen data protection and gain trust with users while navigating through the labyrinth of regulations in an ever more interconnected digital world driven by data.

1.3.3 Interoperability and standardization

Interoperability and standardization concepts, therefore, should become the cornerstone for technology and industry, providing guidance to ensure free communication and compatibility of various systems, platforms, and organizations [23]. The principles play a pretty vital role in driving efficiency, innovation, and interoperable solutions, also in healthcare, telecommunications, IT, and many other domains.

Interoperability:

This means that interoperability refers to the ability of systems, devices, or applications to collaborate effectively, exchange data, and exploit shared resources across different environments; it is a feature that allows being able to communicate and function in a connected manner between different components or entities without regard to their individual specifications, protocols, or technologies.

Interoperability can be divided into several categories:

(1) *Technical interoperability*: Technical interoperability refers to compatibility at the technical level, including protocols, data formats, and communication interfaces that allow systems to exchange data and information effectively.
(2) *Semantic interoperability*: It must ensure a mutual understanding or common interpretation about the exchanged data among systems, covering common definitions and ontologies, and standards applicable for the representation of data.
(3) *Organizational interoperability*: Examines the alignment of policies and process governance frameworks in an organization in order to effectively share information and collaborate effectively with other parties.
(4) *Interoperability across domains*: It enhances the ability to extend interoperability capabilities across different domains or sectors, thereby integrating and synergizing diverse systems or platforms such as healthcare, finance, and transportation.

Importance of interoperability:

- *Enhanced collaboration*: Facilitates seamless communication and collaboration between disparate systems, organizations, or stakeholders, promoting efficiency and productivity in shared workflows and processes.
- *Flexibility and innovation*: It supports scalability since it accommodates the evolution of systems in certain ways over time without

affecting the interoperable connectivity with existing infrastructure and technologies.

- *Scalability and adaptability*: Supports scalability by allowing systems to expand or evolve over time while maintaining interoperable connections with existing infrastructure and technologies.
- *Cost efficiency*: It makes integration cheaper and reduces complexities linked with proprietary systems' upkeep or developing special interfaces by promoting cost-effective solutions and resource optimization.
- *Improved user experience*: This works to make the user satisfied through coherent and integrated experiences that span many platforms or services, with minimal barriers and ease of use.

Standardization:

Standardization is the process of developing and adopting agreed-upon rules, guidelines, or specifications defining how systems, products, or processes should function or interact in a specified industry or context. Standards provide consistency, compatibility, and uniformity; such means further enabling interoperability and ensuring quality, safety, and reliability.

Some of the salient features of standardization are:

(1) *Technical standards*: Describe protocols, formats, interfaces, and criteria of performance that should exist in products, services, or systems for mutual conformity and compatibility.
(2) *Industry standards*: Industry standards are developed in conjunction with the participation of all industry participants to meet the peculiar needs, practices, or regulations of a given sector of business. Examples include healthcare standards or telecommunications standards.
(3) *International standards*: It recognized or accepted internationally and developed and implemented by international organizations (such as ISO and IEC), which facilitate world trade, ensure interoperability of goods, products, and services across borders and jurisdictions, and provide for harmonization.

Benefits of standardization:

(1) *Interoperability and compatibility*: Facilitates interoperability between systems, products, or services from different vendors or regions, promoting seamless integration and compatibility.
(2) *Quality assurance*: Inasmuch as specifications and standards are strictly followed, these provide product or service consistency with regard to quality, performance, and reliability.

(3) *Market access and competitiveness*: Market acceptance is enhanced, regulatory compliance is eased, and competitiveness in global markets is enhanced by compliance with industry standards or international standards.
(4) *Innovation and technology adoption*: Standards foster innovation by providing a common framework for interoperability, enabling rapid adoption of new technologies, and fostering ecosystem development.
(5) *Risk management and compliance*: They ensure that in the event of a failed product, security vulnerabilities, or non-compliance with regulatory bodies, the business will not suffer since it is conducted to standard standards and best practices.

Challenges and considerations:

- *Complexity and diversity*: Addressing diverse technological landscapes, proprietary systems, and evolving requirements requires comprehensive approaches to standardization and interoperability.
- *Regulatory and legal issues*: Compliance with regulatory frameworks, intellectual property rights, and privacy regulations can pose challenges in achieving seamless interoperability and standardization.
- *Emerging technologies*: Accelerating technologies like IoT and AI require agile and adaptive approaches to standard development and ensuring interoperability across emerging platforms and ecosystems.

Interoperability and standardization are some basic principles that underpin connectivity, collaboration, and innovation in this modern world. Organizations can drive better operational efficiency, innovation, and sustainable growth by embracing interoperable solutions, along with standardized best practices that satisfy changing technological and regulatory conditions.

1.4 Future Outlook and Conclusion

1.4.1 Emerging trends and innovations

With blockchain and 5G emerging trends, various industries are innovating significantly. Blockchain on 5G enhances better data security and is much more transparent, allowing for faster and more reliable transactions in finance and also supply chain management. Decentralized applications on blockchain can also take advantage of 5G for real-time services such as IoT device management, city solutions, and the rest. Both of these technologies together support the integration of edge computing at the source data with faster processing and reduced latencies. With greater development in blockchain and

5G, this further promises the integration of more collaborative, automated, and innovative propositions.

New trends and innovations are shaping industries and driving technological advances in transforming business models, consumer behaviors, and societal norms. These trends reflect ongoing developments in fields such as technology, healthcare, finance, transportation, and beyond, paving the way for new opportunities and challenges in the global landscape [24].

Technology trends:

(1) *Artificial intelligence (AI) and machine learning*: AI continues to revolutionize industries by enabling automation, predictive analytics, and personalized experiences. Machine learning algorithms are increasingly used in data-driven decision-making, natural language processing, and computer vision applications.
(2) *Internet of Things (IoT)*: IoT connects devices and sensors to the internet, enabling real-time data collection, monitoring, and control across various sectors, including smart homes, healthcare, agriculture, and industrial automation.
(3) *Blockchain and distributed ledger technology*: Beyond cryptocurrencies, blockchain offers secure, transparent, and decentralized solutions for digital transactions, supply chain management, identity verification, and smart contracts.
(4) *5G technology*: The rollout of 5G networks promises ultra-fast data speeds, low latency, and massive connectivity, enabling advancements in autonomous vehicles, augmented reality (AR), virtual reality (VR), and internet-connected devices.

Healthcare innovations:

(1) *Telemedicine and remote healthcare*: Telehealth solutions have expanded access to healthcare services, allowing virtual consultations, remote monitoring of patients, and telemedicine platforms for diagnostics and treatment.
(2) *Precision medicine*: Personalized healthcare approaches leverage genomic data, biomarkers, and AI-driven analytics to tailor medical treatments and therapies based on individual genetic profiles and health data.
(3) *Digital health technologies*: Wearable devices, mobile health apps, and remote patient monitoring technologies enhance preventive care, chronic disease management, and wellness tracking, empowering individuals to take proactive control of their health.

Finance and fintech trends:

(1) *Digital payments and cryptocurrencies*: Contactless payments, mobile wallets, and decentralized finance (DeFi) are now changing the face of the financial world and giving alternatives to traditional banks and payment systems.
(2) *Blockchain in finance*: Blockchain is in use by financial institutions to secure transactions, carry out cross-border payments, facilitate trade finance, and provide transparent audit trails, so this adds to efficiency with reduced cost.
(3) *AI in financial services*: AI algorithms or artificial intelligence power automated trading, risk management, fraud detection, as well as customer-specific financial advice, and transform both customer experiences and operational workflows.

Sustainability and environmental innovations:

(1) *Renewable energy and clean technologies*: Light years ahead in development in solar and wind, and other battery storage technologies that encourage the means of sustainable energy solutions, with a low carbon footprint and efficiency increases.
(2) *Circular economy initiatives*: This circular economy program applies the principles of the circular economy to businesses, ensuring that waste is eliminated or minimized, recycling is preferred, and sustainable design extends the product lifetimes through eco-friendly manufacturing and design.
(3) *Smart cities and urban planning*: IoT, AI, and data analytics optimize urban infrastructure, transportation systems, energy consumption, and waste management, all leading to better sustainable urban development and quality of life.

Challenges and considerations:

- *Ethical and regulatory frameworks*: Addressing ethical implications, data privacy concerns, and regulatory compliance in emerging technologies requires robust governance frameworks and industry standards.
- *Cybersecurity risks*: The cybersecurity risks in intruding, protecting, and securing interlinked devices, data, and infrastructure challenge the preservation of confidence, resilience, and operational continuity in digital ecosystems.
- *Digital inclusion and accessibility*: Eradicate the divides through balanced access to technology and minimize socio-economic disparities to fully harness the potential of innovations.

Emerging trends and innovations transforming industries, accelerating invention-enabling dynamism in economies and societies around the world, technological progress is to be responsibly applied by organizations and societies to realize the full potential of future development for increasing its sustainability, inclusiveness, and resilience.

1.4.2 Societal implications and ethical considerations

This is critical navigation of the transformative impact of technology, innovation, and global interconnectedness within the framework of social implications and ethical concerns. As emerging trends remake economies, cultures, and even the routines of daily life, it behooves one to critically assess them through the lens of their broader implications on the individual, community, and even the greater society [25].

Technological impact on society:

(1) *Digital divide*: The increased use of digital technology increases the divide between those who have and those who do not have digital tools, information, and opportunities. A seeming widening of gaps can take place in the scope of education, health services, and economic opportunities between the haves and have-nots. And so, this needs to be bridged out.

(2) *Changing workforce dynamics*: The drive toward automation, AI, and robotics fundamentally alters the nature of employment, raising issues of job displacement, the lack of direct applicability of learning outcomes, and constant retraining and upskilling for the workforce. In this regard, there needs to be an optimal synchronization between technological innovation and workforce preparedness in terms of the adequacy of employment stability and building resilience into the economy.

(3) *Privacy and data protection*: Data-based technologies raise serious ethical issues concerning privacy, data protection, and surveillance. These issues concern transparency in the process of collecting data, consent in the use of data, and ensuring that personal information is not used without consent or unraveled for nefarious purposes.

Ethical considerations in technology development and use:

(1) *Bias and fairness*: There is a possibility that AI algorithms and automated decision-making systems may pass along biases regarding race, gender, or socio-economic background that exist in training data. Ensuring bias, fairness, and effective operational functionality within AI

systems necessitates the inclusion of diversity on teams tasked with developing technology, rigorous testing, and clearly defined ethical guidelines.

(2) *Algorithmic accountability*: Algorithms operating in high-stakes domains, such as healthcare, criminal justice, or finance, must themselves be accountable for their decisions and for the outcomes generated. Algorithmic accountability will need transparency, explainability, and mechanisms that allow recourse to error or unintended impact.

(3) *Digital ethics and responsibility*: The frameworks in technology depend on four major principles that constitute ethical frameworks. In this context, the four major principles are beneficence, non-maleficence, autonomy, and justice (fair distribution of benefits and risks). Responsible innovation and responsible decision-making relate to technological development and deployment to uphold such principles.

Social and cultural impacts:

(1) *Digital transformation*: Technology influences all of our ways of thinking about cultural norms, social relationships, and community in how it transforms communication, work, and institutions. Cultural sensitivity and responsiveness in these technologies will ensure that they do not disrespect other identities and values.

(2) *Misinformation and disinformation*: Online diffusion of misinformation and disinformation can pose risks to public discourse, democracy, and social cohesion. Building media literacy, promotion of fact-checking initiatives, and responsible digital citizenship are imperatives in the issues surrounding misinformation and facilitating of an informed decision-making process.

(3) *Ethical AI and autonomous systems*: Ethical considerations in the AI-driven autonomous systems (e.g., autonomous cars and drones), which include accountability for decisions, safety implications, as well as societal acceptance of autonomous technologies.

Regulatory and governance challenges:

(1) *Regulatory frameworks*: The rules and policies must be framed in a balanced nature that develops innovation, public interest, and ethics for the easy flow of risk mitigation procedures as well as to ensure accountability in deploying technology.

(2) *International collaboration*: The major milestones that will include international cooperation and ultimately harmonization of the regulatory

framework across the jurisdictions for the approach to global challenges such as cybersecurity threats, data governance, and ethical standards.

(3) *Public engagement and participation*: Both the private sector industry and civil society, and academia, will engage in inclusive stakeholder dialogue and engagement with regard to promoting transparency and accountability in shaping technologies and their use and practices.

1.4.3 Conclusion

The processes of social implications and ethical considerations from emerging technologies require a holistic approach that incorporates technological innovation with ethical principles, cultural awareness, regulatory framework, and public discourse. Thus, it is essential to reap the fruits of technology by safeguarding human rights, fostering equity, and ensuring sustainable development. Emerging technologies in AI, IoT, blockchain, and 5G are transforming industries, linking people together, and driving economic growth. These innovations open up the possibility for healthcare reform, optimal resource management, and sustainable urban environment creation. At the same time, they bring along challenges in privacy issues, security of data, algorithmic bias, digital divide, and skills gap. All these have to be addressed through governments, businesses, academia, and civil society collaboration to fill the gap. There is a need for robust regulatory frameworks and guidelines on ethics as well as education that will help to mitigate risks and ensure inclusive development. Bridging the digital divide is an important step toward enabling equitable opportunities for everyone in the digital age. Responsible innovation involves values such as transparency, accountability, fairness, and inclusiveness at every step of the technology development and deployment process. Continuous stakeholder engagement helps take proactive measures to mitigate risks and maximize benefits from technological advancements. Looking forward, it is the balance struck between innovation and ethics that will help shape a future in which technology is the catalyst for productive change, human betterment, and sustainable global development. It is when and where such principles are embraced by societies that new and emerging technologies can fully realize their potential in building resilient, inclusive, and prosperous communities for generations to come.

References

[1] Tapia, J. Y., & Avila-Pesantez, D. (2021). Blockchain and IoT - Challenges and Its Role in Security: A Brief Overview. 2021 IEEE URUCON. https://doi.org/10.1109/urucon53396.2021.9647292

[2] França, R. P., Monteiro, A. C. B., Arthur, R., & Iano, Y. (2020). An Overview of the Artificial Intelligence Evolution and Its Fundamental Concepts, and Their Relationship with IoT Security. Security and Organization within IoT and Smart Cities, 1–18. https://doi.org/10.1201/9781003018636-1

[3] Zaheeruddin, & Gupta, H. (2020). Foundation of IoT: An Overview. Internet of Things (IoT), 3–24. https://doi.org/10.1007/978-3-030-37468-6_1

[4] Pradhan, A. K. (2018). An Overview on IOT Security. SSRN Electronic Journal. https://doi.org/10.2139/ssrn.3302195

[5] Banafa, A. (2022). Myths about Blockchain Technology. Blockchain Technology and Applications, 73–79. https://doi.org/10.1201/9781003337393-11

[6] Subha, T. (2020). Assessing Security Features of Blockchain Technology. Blockchain Technology and Applications, 115–138. https://doi.org/10.1201/9781003081487-7

[7] Bolfing, A. (2020). Introduction to Blockchain Technology. Cryptographic Primitives in Blockchain Technology, 199–240. https://doi.org/10.1093/oso/9780198862840.003.0006

[8] Ge, X., & Zhang, W. (2019). Challenges of 5G Green Communication Networks. 5G Green Mobile Communication Networks, 1–27. https://doi.org/10.1007/978-981-13-6252-1_1

[9] Hassan, S. A., Omar, M. S., Imran, M. A., Qadir, J., & Jayakody, D. N. K. (2018). Universal Access in 5G Networks: Potential Challenges and Opportunities for Urban and Rural Environments. 5G Networks: Fundamental Requirements, Enabling Technologies, and Operations Management, 299–326. https://doi.org/10.1002/9781119333142.ch8

[10] Ibrahim, A. N., Abdullah, M. F. L., & Gismalla, M. S. M. (2018). Basic of 5G Networks: Review. Advanced Wireless Sensing Techniques for 5G Networks, 19–44. https://doi.org/10.1201/9781351021746-2

[11] Larsson, C. (2018). Concepts and Architectures in 5G. 5G Networks, 1–15. https://doi.org/10.1016/b978-0-12-812707-0.00006-1

[12] Kaushik, S. (2021). Blockchain and 5G-Enabled Internet of Things: Background and Preliminaries. Blockchain for 5G-Enabled IoT, 3–31. https://doi.org/10.1007/978-3-030-67490-8_1

[13] Patel, R., Ganatra, A., & Patel, K. (2021). Security and privacy control in 5G-enabled healthcare using blockchain. Blockchain for 5G Healthcare Applications: Security and Privacy Solutions, 481–506. https://doi.org/10.1049/pbhe035e_ch17

[14] Lawrence D. Fredendall, Ed Hill (2004) Evolution of Supply Chain Management. (2015). Encyclopedia of Supply Chain Management, 393–395. https://doi.org/10.1081/e-escm-120048060

[15] Baltac, V. (2019). Smart Cities - A View of Societal Aspects. Smart Cities, 2(4), 538–548. https://doi.org/10.3390/smartcities2040033

[16] Yüksel, H. (2022). IoT-based smart healthcare monitoring system. Healthcare Monitoring and Data Analysis Using IoT: Technologies and Applications, 71–98. https://doi.org/10.1049/pbhe038e_ch5

[17] Doshi, M., & Varghese, A. (2022). Smart agriculture using renewable energy and AI-powered IoT. AI, Edge and IoT-Based Smart Agriculture, 205–225. https://doi.org/10.1016/b978-0-12-823694-9.00028-1

[18] Machiraju, S., & Gaurav, S. (2015). Key Application Experiences: Latency, Scalability, and Throughput. Hardening Azure Applications, 73–85. https://doi.org/10.1007/978-1-4842-0920-2_5

[19] Krishna, D. V., & Shanker, R. (2024). Blockchain Scalability Analysis on Throughput and Long Transaction Time. Computer Science Engineering and Emerging Technologies, 478–482. https://doi.org/10.1201/9781003405580-77

[20] Rajalingham, G., Quang-Dung Ho, & Tho Le-Ngoc. (2013). Attainable throughput, delay and scalability for geographic routing on Smart Grid neighbor area networks. 2013 IEEE Wireless Communications and Networking Conference (WCNC). https://doi.org/10.1109/wcnc.2013.6554721

[21] Lyu, J., Yu, D., & Fu, L. (2022). Analysis and Optimization for Large-Scale LoRa Networks: Throughput Fairness and Scalability. IEEE Internet of Things Journal, 9(12), 9574–9590. https://doi.org/10.1109/jiot.2021.3126600

[22] Brey, P. (2007). Ethical Aspects of Information Security and Privacy. Security, Privacy, and Trust in Modern Data Management, 21–36. https://doi.org/10.1007/978-3-540-69861-6_3

[23] Guédria, W. (2015). A Conceptual Framework for Enterprise Interoperability. Standards and Standardization, 652–662. https://doi.org/10.4018/978-1-4666-8111-8.ch030

[24] Karras, D. A., Oruganti, S. K., & Ray, S. (2023). Emerging Trends and Innovations in Industries of the Developing World. CRC Press. https://doi.org/10.1201/9781003457602

[25] Okonji, O. R., Yunusov, K., & Gordon, B. (2024). Applications of Generative AI in Healthcare: algorithmic, ethical, legal and societal

considerations. https://doi.org/10.36227/techrxiv.171527587.7564 9430/v1

[26] Mishra, N., & Pandya, S. (2021). Internet of Things Applications, Security Challenges, Attacks, Intrusion Detection, and Future Visions: A Systematic Review. IEEE Access, 9, 59353–59377. https://doi.org/10 .1109/access.2021.3073408

[27] Bhowmik, D., & Feng, T. (2017). The multimedia blockchain: A distributed and tamper-proof media transaction framework. 2017 22nd International Conference on Digital Signal Processing (DSP). https: //doi.org/10.1109/icdsp.2017.8096051

[28] Attaran, M., & Attaran, S. (2020). Digital Transformation and Economic Contributions of 5G Networks. International Journal of Enterprise Information Systems, 16(4), 58–79. https://doi.org/10.4018/ijeis.20201001 04

2

A Review of Blockchain-enabled Decentralized Architecture in a 5G-IoT Network

Keshini R Trivedi

Department of Computer Science and Engineering, Nirma University, Ahmedabad, 382481, India
Email: keshinitrivedi@gmail.com

Abstract

The coming of 5G and the consequent rapid proliferation of Internet of Things (IoT) devices ultimately call for new kinds of innovative network architectures that seamlessly work in high-speed, low-latency, and massively connected environments. This chapter presents a comprehensive review of how using decentralized architecture, enabled by blockchain and AI technologies, in 5G-IoT can be more advantageous over traditional architectures.

This chapter highlights how efficiency, security, and scalability in 5G-IoT networks are achieved through distributed computing at the edge in a decentralized architecture. A significant reduction in latency is achieved in this architecture by relocating processing and data storage to distributed nodes closer to the sources of data, such as edge devices and servers. This is crucial for real-time applications like autonomous vehicles and industrial automation. It also mitigates the risks associated with centralized systems, offering enhanced security and privacy by distributing data across multiple nodes. The other major advantage is scalability, where, by decentralized systems, one does dynamic resource allocation and workload distribution for the efficient running of operations even when the traffic volume is high.

However, challenges remain in terms of the interoperability of heterogeneous devices and distributed network infrastructures, and energy efficiency-related issues for edge devices. To this end, continuous research and

DOI: 10.1201/9788743809050-3

development become very essential to understand the true potential of decentralized architecture in 5G-IoT. Once these issues are sorted out, then decentralized architecture will be a game-changer in the face of modern communication systems, ushering in an age of always-connected, intelligent ecosystems.

Keywords: 5G technology, Internet of Things, IoT, decentralized architecture, blockchain, artificial intelligence, AI, 5G-IoT ecosystem, edge computing, smart cities, AI healthcare applications

2.1 Introduction and Foundations of 5G-IoT

2.1.1 Introduction to 5G and IoT

2.1.1.1 Overview of 5G technology

Mobile networks' fifth generation, known as 5G, is considerably a quantum leap over the former generations, beginning from 1G to 4G. 5G represented the impactful change that would bring the speeds much higher than before, very low delay, extremely high dependability, and all this at the same time with a huge number of devices connected simultaneously [1]. For instance, while 4G enabled us to stream videos smoothly on our phones, 5G enables high-speed, low-latency applications, such as augmented reality (AR) shopping experiences in retail stores where customers can interact with virtual product displays in real time. It promises much higher data transfer rates, with speeds potentially reaching up to 10 Gbps, a hundred times faster than 4G LTE, and so downloading HD movies that typically take minutes will take only seconds. Hence, in contrast to the previous generations, 5G employs a substantially greater number of frequencies, including millimeter waves, which could enable offering higher data rates but have lesser coverage and are affected by barriers [2].

Some of the biggest technologies in 5G include massive multiple input multiple output (MIMO), where a large number of antennas are implemented at the base stations to greatly enhance capacity. One may think of it as a concert with many speakers distributed across a concert area, ensuring that everyone can listen to the music clearly, regardless of where they are sitting. MIMO increases the coverage of a network through provisions of data by several paths to ensure communication.

Beamforming also consists of transmitting specific wireless signals to targeted receivers, rather than broadcasting them in all directions. 5G uses beamforming to ensure that the signal is reduced by interference and hence becomes of great importance for the urban areas crowded with multiple wireless-enabled devices.

The current 5G is foreseen to offer up to 10 Gbps, one hundred times faster than present 4G LTE. Delay or latency will be reduced to as low as 1 millisecond, enabling applications that require nearly real-time response, including remote surgery and self-driving cars.

Another significant aspect of 5G networks is that it can support a large number of devices per square kilometer. This makes it fit the best for IoT applications where thousands of devices are to be connected at the same time without being disrupted- be it smart home sensors, surveillance cameras, or health monitors.

2.1.1.2 Evolution and growth of IoT

The Internet of Things (IoT) is the connection of everyday objects to the internet to make them capable of transmitting and receiving information. These objects or "things" can be as lowly as a sensor or an ordinary consumer product, or as high as an industrial system or facility. The growth of IoT has been driven by advancements in wireless communication, miniaturization of sensors, and the proliferation of cloud computing [3].

IoT is changing different industries by opening new opportunities for application and service delivery. In smart cities, IoT devices control traffic, pollution levels, and even power usage. Imagine a smart city where sensors monitor and track traffic flow, air quality, and energy usage, so that the city managers can adjust traffic lights dynamically, reduce congestion as needed, or dim streetlights in streets in areas with no foot traffic to save on electrical consumption.

In healthcare, IoT enables telemonitoring of patients and smart healthcare devices like wearable fitness trackers or patient monitoring systems, when placed remotely, can collect constant health data for better decision-making with fewer in-person visits and the possibility of early detection of potential health issues. For example, a smart insulin pump can adjust the dose of insulin a patient needs on a real-time basis to prevent dangerous spikes or drops in their glucose levels.

IoT is also changing manufacturing with Industrial IoT, which can even support predictive maintenance. Machines fitted with IoT sensors can give their status and predict probable breakdowns well before it happen and thus minimize downtime. Consider a factory where machinery connected via IoT systems signals that maintenance is required, thereby preventing costly breaks in production and increasing operational efficiency. [4]

IoT devices are expected to increase in number at a very fast pace. A report by Cisco estimates that there will be more than 29.3 billion internet-connected devices by 2023, up from 18.4 billion in 2018 [5], the majority of which will be IoT devices. This growth is due to the need for automation, optimization, and the use of data in various industries.

2.1.1.3 Synergies between 5G and IoT

5G and IoT are complementary technologies, at the intersection lies the real opening up of new possibilities and applications. The speed and low latency of 5G make it useful for enablers of real-time data processing and communication, which is important in many IoT applications. For instance, on autonomous driving, what would be required for safe and efficient operation is the ability of vehicles to communicate in real-time with other vehicles and traffic infrastructure, which the low latency of 5G makes possible. [4]

Moreover, support for a huge number of devices that exist in 5G belongs to IoT, wherein thousands of devices/sensors have to be connected within a very small area. In smart factories, communication between machines and sensors continuously monitors and optimizes production processes. Many devices have a high device density, supported by 5G, in order to ensure reliable connectivity.

Energy efficiency is the biggest advantage. Ultra-reliable low-latency communications and massive machine-type communications are supposed to be mainly IoT use cases, and the applications for devices within IoT are built with very low power consumption in mind. Sensors in the grid of a smart city can periodically update data on energy usage, and 5G makes sure these updates are done as much as with minimal battery drain as possible so that sensors last much longer while retaining the high reliability they provide.

2.1.2 Organizational framework of the chapter

This chapter begins laying down the very foundation of 5G and IoT, an area that is evolving rapidly regarding how these entities shape modern communication networks as it stand today. The introductory parts touch on some cases about the potential applications of 5G within IoT platforms, where its ultra-low latency, speed, and support for high connected devices make it a critical enabler of IoT applications across various sectors: smart cities, healthcare, and industrial automation.

Building on this, the focus then shifts to the key aspects of decentralized architecture and how decentralized networks vary from centralized ones. It builds on foundational properties of two giant building blocks: edge computing and blockchain technology, in terms of providing a coherent view of how these technologies empower decentralized systems to face up to the challenges raised by the 5G-IoT environment. Therefore, it will be the basis to benefit from and deal with decentralization.

Various other important technologies, forming the cornerstone of these decentralized 5G-IoT networks, are discussed further. Edge computing is taken into considerable account as the emerging trend of processing data closer to sources in real-time; it promises reduced latencies and efficiency. The inclusion of blockchain integration was also followed by contributions toward security and data integrity, together with decentralized management. The book also discusses the increasing role of AI in edge computing and its application to IoT, so that real-time analytics and decision-making become available at the edge of the network.

Security and privacy are very critical issues in decentralized networks, and this section covers security and privacy in decentralized IoT networks. It discusses possible threats and vulnerabilities, specifically to decentralized systems and blockchain-enabled solutions for protecting IoT environments. Methods for privacy-preserving approaches have been discussed, which provide a framework for the massive data generated by the IoT devices but maintain user confidentiality.

Following applications and use cases, examples for concrete use cases of such technologies, especially relevant uses in industries related to smart cities, healthcare, and manufacturing, will be implemented; hence, an example of how decentralized architectures bring innovation throughout a variety of fields- from intelligent traffic systems to predictive maintenance in industrial contexts- thus delineating the 5G-IoT network's impact on society.

Discussions on next-generation sensor technologies, among others, will be brought within the discussion for their potential further improved decentralization of 5G-IoT networks. The forward-looking section will also consider, as well, regulatory and ethical frameworks necessary to ensure the responsible deployment of those technologies. Future directions are addressed in the section devoted to discussions on emerging technologies and innovations.

The chapter concludes with a detailed discussion on the practical implementation and case studies, which describe the best practices and the deployment strategies regarding decentralized IoT solutions. The case studies offer real examples describing both the practical challenges accompanied by the achievements realized in the practical implementation of decentralized architectures, which concludes in analyzing their performance in various contexts.

The conclusion brings together the most significant insights from the chapter since it reflects ongoing challenges and emerging opportunities for decentralized 5G-IoT networks. It would ultimately be concluded with a vision of how things look in the future and how these technologies are set to evolve for potential changes in industries in the future.

2.1.3 Fundamentals of decentralized architecture

2.1.3.1 Definition and principles

A decentralized architecture is a form of network design that distributes control, data processing, and decision-making among a number of nodes, rather than being held at one central location. The idea is hence very nearly opposite to that of centralized architecture, which relies on one central server for the management and processing of data. Decentralized systems enable better scalability, reliability, and security with the elimination of single failure points and the distribution of workload across a large number of nodes.

Primary principles of decentralized architecture: distribution, redundancy, and autonomy. Distribution refers to the splicing of data and computational tasks across several working nodes, generally balancing the load and thereby reducing the risk of congestion. Redundancy refers to the residence of data and services at multiple nodes to improve fault tolerance and thereby availability. Autonomy allows each individual node to act independently of other nodes and gives it the power to execute local decisions based on the data it is processing.

2.1.3.2 Centralized versus decentralized networks

Centralized networks, which are represented by such network topologies as client-server, have a single control center that processes data. Although this approach makes management and control easier, it brings some risks like a single point of failure and a bottleneck. In contrast to this, decentralized networks give control to multiple nodes where each node can work on data and make decisions on its own. This distribution minimizes the chances of having a single point of failure and could improve on the network's reliability and resilience.

In a decentralized system, each node contributes to the general functionality of the system. For example, in a peer-to-peer network (P2P), the nodes enact both client and server roles simultaneously; thereby, resources and information are directly shared between peers. This model is directly opposite to that of the centralized network, wherein the clients rely on the central server for resources and information.

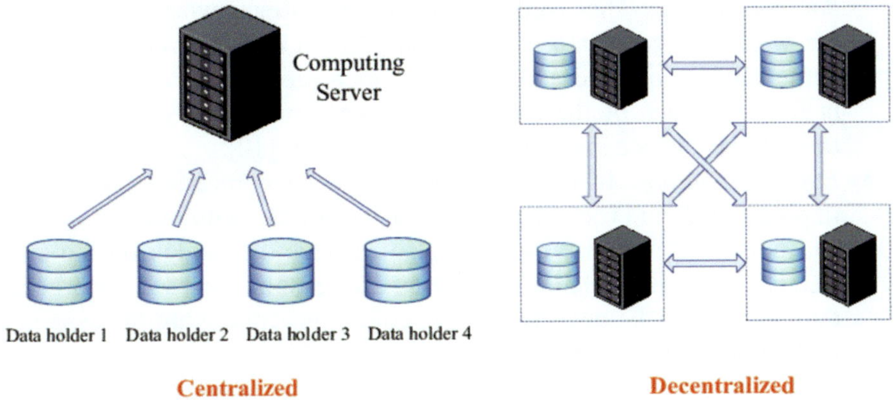

Figure 2.1 Centralized versus decentralized architecture [6].

The decentralized ones offer much better scalability than the centralized ones. With increasing nodes, the capacity of a network for holding more data and devices increases proportionally. This scalability is very important in IoT applications where millions of devices might have to connect and communicate at once [7]. Figure 2.1 shows the clear distinction between the centralized and decentralized working of the system.

2.1.3.3 Key components of decentralized architecture

Decentralized architecture has several key components:

1) *Nodes:* These are devices or entities participating in a network. All the nodes have the capability of processing, storing, and transferring data. In IoT networks, nodes can be sensors, actuators, gateways, or even smart nodes.
2) *Distributed ledger technology (DLT):* Blockchain is one of the most known types of DLT that can be used in a decentralized structure. This ensures documentation between nodes and their interaction without compromising security. The use of blockchain ensures data integrity and trustworthiness due to its immutable nature [8].
3) *Consensus mechanisms:* Such protocols are used to achieve agreement among distributed nodes in terms of the state of the network. Key consensus mechanisms include proof of work (PoW), proof of stake (PoS), and practical Byzantine fault tolerance (PBFT). Consensus algorithms ensure that there is consistency of views via all nodes, even in the existence of faults or malignant actors [9].

4) *Smart contracts:* These are self-executing contracts whereby the terms are written directly into lines of code. Smart contracts ensure that an agreement is enforced and executed when predefined conditions have been met. Much of the need for intermediaries thereby drops out of transactions, hence making them more efficient [10].
5) *Edge computing:* In decentralized IoT, edge computing has a very important role in processing data near the source, with reduced latency and enhanced response times; it also reduces the burden on the central cloud servers. Gateways and smart sensors are used to process the data and make decisions at the edge, thus improving the system's performance and capability [11].

2.2 Core Technologies

2.2.1 Edge computing in 5G-IoT

2.2.1.1 Role of edge computing

Edge computing is an important part of the 5G-IoT environment as it aims at processing data near the sources of data, such as sensors and smart devices. This lowers latency and bandwidth usage for sending data to a central location in the cloud for processing. Edge computing means analyzing data at the "edge" of the network; this could be in devices like gateways, routers, or even end-user devices themselves.

The principal advantage of edge computing is that it can handle the real-time data processing requirements of applications like autonomous vehicles, industrial automation, and augmented reality. For instance, in autonomous vehicles, the capacity for processing data locally is quicker, thus allowing quicker decision-making, a requirement for safety and performance. Edge computing also allows the real-time monitoring and control of machinery in an industrial setting, making production more productive and reducing breakdowns [11].

Edge computing can enhance data privacy and security by keeping more sensitive data closer to the source, and therefore, there is reduced exposure of data as it travels across the network. This becomes quite important in applications such as health and finance, where sensitivity to data is high and regulation compliance is very critical.

2.2.1.2 Edge devices and edge servers

The core of edge computing infrastructure includes edge devices and edge servers. In most cases, edge devices are IoT devices that are enabled with some compute capabilities, such as sensors, cameras, smart meters, and others. They collect data and typically provide some initial processing operations like filtering, aggregation, and preliminary analysis.

Edge servers, however, are generally more highly compute-intensive computing resources located closer to edge devices. Such servers can do more sophisticated data processing and offer storage facilities. Edge servers usually work as intermediaries among the edge devices and the central cloud servers, handling tasks for which more computational power is required than what the edge devices can deliver, yet benefiting from reduced latency compared with cloud-based processing [11].

Edge devices and servers can collaborate on their tasks to obtain far more efficient data flows and processing. For example, in the context of a smart city use case, edge devices could be empowered to perform video data analysis for incident detection and then trigger an alert to edge servers for more sophisticated analysis, which would coordinate the response with other city systems.

2.2.1.3 Benefits of edge computing

- *Reduced latency:* Due to the data being processed locally and near the source, edge computing greatly minimizes latency. This is important for use cases such as autonomous driving where even microseconds can be a big deal [12].
- *Bandwidth optimization:* Edge computing reduces the amount of data that has to be transferred back to central servers, thereby optimizing bandwidth use. This is particularly valuable for situations where bandwidth is either very limited or very expensive [13].
- *Enhanced security and privacy:* Aggregation of data closer to its source reduces the chance of interception, decreasing the attack surface. Moreover, edge computing supports localized security mechanisms, enhancing overall data protection [14].
- *Scalability:* Edge computing provides higher scalability, as the load of processing is distributed among several edge devices and servers. This is particularly important in IoT environments where the number of connected devices might be very large [11].

2.2.1.4 Challenges of edge computing

- *Management complexity:* Management of such a distributed network of edge devices and servers can be complex. Ensuring uniformity in performance, security, and updating a large number of devices necessitates robust management frameworks [13].

- *Resource constraints:* Normally, edge devices possess limited computational resources compared to the central server. This resource constraint makes efficient resource management techniques imperative to ensure maximum performance [11].
- *Interoperability:* Interoperability between edge devices, servers, and cloud systems is still a big challenge. While the effort put in for standardization is underway, more is required to have seamless integration across different ecosystems [13].
- *Security vulnerabilities:* While edge computing enhances data privacy by keeping data local, it also introduces new security challenges. Edge devices can be more vulnerable to physical tampering and cyberattacks, necessitating robust security measures [14].

2.2.2 Blockchain technology for IoT

2.2.2.1 Introduction to blockchain

Blockchain technology is a revolutionary concept that underpins cryptocurrencies like Bitcoin but has far-reaching applications beyond digital currencies. It is more of a decentralized and distributed digital ledger used for transactions recorded on many computers in a manner that assures one of the security, transparency, and immutability of data. Each transaction is noted in a "block," and these blocks are interlinked to form a "chain." Once a block is added to the blockchain, it cannot be changed without changing all of the following blocks, which requires a majority consensus of the network [16].

The primary features of blockchain technology include:

1) *Decentralization:* Traditional databases, such as those in banks or even in governments, are centralized. Blockchain removes this central authority by dispersing the ledger across all participants-in effect, nodes involved in the network. In doing so, it enhances security and transparency since no single entity controls the data.
2) *Transparency:* Every participant in the network can see each and every transaction on the blockchain. In this respect, due to transparency and accountability, a relationship based on trust can be assured between the users. For example, at a supply chain, each stakeholder will be able to trace the journey of every product from origin to consumer, consequently reducing fraud and increasing trust [17].
3) *Security:* Blockchain secures data using cryptographic techniques. Every block is time-stamped and connected to the previous block through a cryptographic hash, apart from the real transaction data it

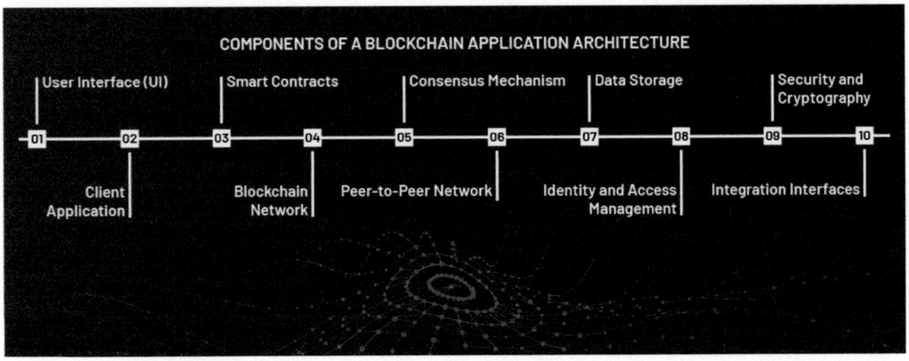

Figure 2.2 Components of a blockchain application architecture [18].

holds. This forms an interlocked structure that can barely be changed in any block without consequently changing all other blocks in that chain, thus making it impossible to edit data, and the integrity of data is guaranteed.

4) *Immutability:* A blockchain does not modify any data that is written once. The kind of immutability it helps one to have in having a tamper-proof history of the transactions that were performed and can be auditing anytime by any entity. This feature is particularly useful in the financial sector, where an exact and unchangeable history of transactions needs to be maintained.

The concept of blockchain was put forward in 2008 by an individual or a group of persons known as Satoshi Nakamoto for use as the underlying technology for Bitcoin. Since then, blockchain has undergone different improvements and found use in industries such as finance, healthcare, supply chain, and importantly, the IoT. Figure 2.2 shows various components of blockchain application architecture.

2.2.2.2 Blockchain mechanisms: Consensus algorithms

The decentralized architectures in 5G-IoT expose a bright outlook for secure and transparent data management. On the other hand, it becomes very critical to reach consensus on the state of the network. Consensus algorithms are at the heart of any blockchain technology, for they accomplish the consensus on the state of the blockchain among decentralized nodes. These algorithms ensure that every independent transaction is verifiable and more securely added to the blockchain. Many such mechanisms are applied in blockchain technology:

1) *Proof of work (PoW):* PoW is a consensus mechanism in which the racing to complete complex mathematical problems is among participants, usually miners. The first miner who solves the puzzle gets the privilege of adding a new block to the blockchain and will be rewarded with some amount of cryptocurrency. Doing so requires high computational power and hence ensures security with reduced risks of malicious attacks, but is rather energy-intensive and has been criticized for its environmental impacts [16].
   - *Advantages:* Highly secure and battle-tested, providing strong tamper-proof guarantees [16].
   - *Disadvantages:* High computational overhead for mining makes it energy-intensive and unsuitable for resource-constrained IoT devices [28].
   - *Examples:* Bitcoin and Ethereum (until Ethereum switched to PoS in 2022).
2) *Proof of stake (PoS):* PoS is much more energy-efficient compared to PoW. With PoS, a validator's pick to generate new blocks and validate transactions is based on how many coins they have and are willing to "stake" as collateral. They receive rewards in the form of transaction fees. The larger the stake, the higher the chance to be elected to validate a block [20].
   - *Advantages:* More energy-efficient than PoW, encouraging broader participation in 5G-IoT with low-powered devices.
   - *Disadvantages:* Security concerns exist as malicious actors with large stakes could influence the network. Maintaining a fair stake distribution in a dynamic 5G-IoT environment can be challenging.
   - *Examples:* Ethereum 2.0, Cardano, Polkadot.
3) *Proof of authority (PoA):* PoA is a consensus model whereby trust has to be placed in at least a few pre-approved validators for the creation of new blocks. Validators, in most cases, are known companies or people who have something at stake regarding their reputation. PoA is efficient and fast; it is therefore suitable for private or permissioned blockchains [21].
   - *Advantages:* Faster and more scalable than PoW due to its reliance on pre-designated validators. This can be beneficial for 5G-IoT applications requiring high transaction throughput and lower energy consumption compared to PoW, making it more suitable for resource-constrained devices.

- *Disadvantages:* Centralization concerns exist as validators are pre-selected, potentially impacting network security and fairness. This might not be ideal for permissionless 5G-IoT deployments, and the selection process for validators needs careful design to ensure trust and prevent malicious actors from gaining undue influence.
- *Examples:* VeChain, Microsoft Azure Blockchain.

4) *Byzantine fault tolerance (BFT):* BFT is a consensus mechanism aimed at reaching an agreement despite faulty or malicious nodes. This means some nodes are assumed to act maliciously, yet the network achieves consensus. BFT requires multiple rounds of communication among nodes for reaching consensus on the next block [22].
    - *Advantages:* Guarantees data consistency even with faulty nodes, making it ideal for critical 5G-IoT applications demanding high reliability.
    - *Disadvantages:* Complex message exchange protocols introduce latency, potentially hindering real-time communication in 5G-IoT scenarios. BFT can also be resource-intensive for resource-constrained devices.
    - *Examples:* Hyperledger Fabric.
5) *Practical Byzantine fault tolerance (PBFT):* One of the implementations overwriting BFT to make it practical for use in real distributed systems is PBFT. It aims to offer high throughput and low latency while assuring security against malicious nodes. The PBFT algorithm proposes that a primary node proposes a block and then other nodes validate it through a process involving multiple rounds of voting [23].
    - *Advantages:* Offers strong BFT, making it suitable for critical 5G-IoT applications requiring high data consistency even in the presence of faulty nodes, more efficient message exchange compared to traditional BFT, potentially reducing latency impact in 5G-IoT deployments.
    - *Disadvantages:* PBFT can still be more resource-intensive than other options like LBFT, especially for devices with very limited processing power. The system relies on a primary node, introducing a single point of failure if compromised [24].
    - *Examples:* Zilliqa, Hyperledger Fabric.
6) *Lightweight Byzantine fault tolerance (LBFT):* LBFT is a variant of BFT that tries to lessen the computational and communication overhead

needed for reaching consensus. It is appropriate for IoT and every other resource-constrained environment where the traditional mechanism of BFT might prove to be very heavy.

- *Advantages:* Offers a balance between BFT's reliability and scalability. LBFT's design specifically targets resource-constrained environments like 5G-IoT, making it a promising option.
- *Disadvantages:* LBFT protocols are still under development, and their long-term security implications in large-scale 5G-IoT deployments need further evaluation.
- *Examples:* Some IoT blockchain applications.

7) *Directed acyclic graph (DAG):* DAG is one such consensus mechanism that is used in certain types of distributed ledgers. It structures the transactions as a graph rather than a chain. Every single transaction is a node, and each new transaction has to refer to other prior transactions; that is how they form a DAG. That structure allows it to have high scalability and parallel transaction processing [25].

   - *Advantages:* DAGs enable asynchronous transaction processing, potentially improving scalability for high-volume data scenarios in 5G-IoT.
   - *Disadvantages:* Security analysis of DAG-based consensus mechanisms in 5G-IoT is ongoing. Achieving the same level of security as traditional blockchains might require additional mechanisms
   - *Examples:* IOTA, Nano.

2.2.2.3 Blockchain mechanisms: Smart contracts

Smart contracts are self-executing and self-enforcing in the agreement's terms, directly written into lines of code. Such agreements automatically execute and enforce themselves once stated conditions are met without an intermediary. They are a pivotal feature in blockchain technology since they allow for automation and trustless transactions.

- *Automate:* Smart contracts automate processes that would otherwise have been manual. For example, in insurance, an event like a flight delay or crop damage can be triggered by a smart contract for automatic payout.
- *Trustless transactions:* Parties can engage in trustless transactions because smart contracts allow parties to a contract not to trust either party or an intermediary, since the free, immutable record of

the transactions assures the enforcement of the contract under the blockchain. This is most applicable in DeFi, where financial transactions can occur without any intermediaries [31].

- *Security and transparency:* Smart contracts can be very transparent and immutable. When used in the blockchain, all their codes and transactions are made available to the public, which ensures accountability and cuts down fraud.
- *Efficiency:* By removing middlemen and running a process automatically, smart contracts lower the costs and process duration. Therefore, smart contracts can be used efficiently, for example, in supply chains, real estate, or healthcare [10].

The blockchain and IoT can collaborate on developing smart cities, wherein their various services, such as traffic management, waste management, and public safety, are automated and optimized. For example, through the IoT's sensors, the monitoring of the present conditions of the traffic will be in real-time, and blockchain will then store it securely and share it with the concerned authorities and self-driving vehicles, which will help alleviate traffic congestion and provide better urban mobility.

2.2.2.4 Blockchain use cases in IoT

Blockchain technology offers significant potential for enhancing IoT applications since it would address some very critical challenges in the space of IoT: security, scalability, and interoperability. Here are some of the notable use cases:

Supply chain management: Blockchain brings more transparency in supply-chain use cases as it provides a tamper-proof record of a product's journey from origin to consumer. All of these value chain steps can be documented through IoT devices in the form of RFID tags and sensors. After that, this data is kept on the blockchain to guarantee integrity and, therefore, enables stakeholders to verify the authenticity and origin of a certain product. For example, Walmart has implemented blockchain to track food origin and increase food safety, as well as decrease fraud [17].

Healthcare: Blockchain in healthcare has possibilities for the security of patients' data and their privacy, aiding in smoothing operations like consent management and clinical trials. IoT devices like wearable health monitors pick up patient data, which is stored on the blockchain. Sharing of the data with other relevant parties, say doctors and researchers, occurs in a secure, privacy-ensuring, and data integrity-assuring manner. Blockchain allows for the trackability of pharmaceuticals, thereby preventing counterfeit drugs from getting into the market [32].

Energy management: This will promote more efficient and much more transparent energy management systems. For instance, on a blockchain-based decentralized energy grid, IoT sensor-enabled smart meters can log energy production and consumption data. It would thereby enable P2P energy trading in which consumers could sell excess energy among themselves directly, hence integrating renewable energy use by decreasing dependence on central utilities [33].

Smart cities: These two technologies have the potential to build smart cities where most services, like traffic, solid waste, and public safety, are managed and optimized by the devices themselves. For example, IoT sensors would be in a position to monitor the condition of the traffic in real-time, while blockchain provides a secure, decentralized platform for storing and sharing this information among concerned authorities and autonomous vehicles. This would lessen congestion and improve urban mobility [34].

Most of the challenges facing IoT applications are best solved using blockchain technology. Being a decentralized, secure, transparent, and immutable technology, blockchain provides features that are much required by IoT to enhance data integrity through mechanization of processes using smart contracts and make secure, trustless transactions. The strong growth of blockchain and IoT technologies is likely to be seen in their integration, providing a number of innovative solutions to industries such as supply chain management, healthcare, energy management, and smart cities. However, scalability, energy consumption, and interoperability remain the core challenges that have to be addressed before blockchain in IoT can reach its full potential.

2.2.3 Artificial intelligence in IoT

2.2.3.1 AI fundamentals

Artificial intelligence (AI) refers to computer systems that can think; it means it is capable of performing tasks traditionally associated with human intelligence-like making predictions, identifying objects, interpreting speech, and generating natural language. AI systems learn to do so by processing large amounts of data and examining patterns to model within their decision-making. While in many instances it will be humans who oversee the process of learning by an AI, reinforcing good decisions and discouraging bad ones, some AI systems can learn without supervision [26]. There are broadly three types of AI [37]:

- *Narrow AI:* Also known as weak AI, which is specialized in performing a narrow task, for example, facial recognition or Internet search. Narrow AI systems are narrow, operating within pre-defined ranges, lacking general intelligence. This includes all voice assistants, like Siri and Alexa, and the recommendation systems of the streaming services [38].
- *General AI:* Also referred to as strong AI, it would be able to perceive, learn, and apply knowledge to a very wide spectrum of tasks, similar to human intelligence. General AI systems are able to transfer knowledge from one domain to another and perform any intellectual task that any human is capable of. However, general AI is still largely theoretical and has not yet been realized [39].
- *Superintelligent AI:* It would mean the achievement of an extremely high degree of intelligence, surpassing human capacity in creativity, problem-solving, and social intelligence. Superintelligent AI is still viewed as something hypothetical and is the subject of a lot of debates regarding its impact on society [40].

AI has a subfield called machine learning (ML) where algorithms are given data to learn from and make decisions from. ML can be classified into several types:

- *Supervised learning:* An algorithm that is trained on a labeled dataset, whereby each example in training is coupled with an output label. In effect, the algorithm learns to map inputs to outputs, based on that training data. Typical applications include image classification, spam detection, and predictive analytics [41].
- *Unsupervised learning:* This is a case where there is no presence of target variables, and the algorithm has to find out patterns or relationships in data. It becomes useful in the task of clustering and association. Market basket analysis and customer segmentation are one of the important applications of it [42].
- *Reinforcement learning (RL):* The agents learn how to make decisions by being rewarded or punished based on their actions. The agents adjust their actions so as to maximize cumulative rewards over time. In this way, RL is quite well-known in robotics, gaming, and autonomous driving [43].

Deep learning (DL), a subdomain of ML, deals with neural networks that have many layers (hence "deep"); it allows one to learn and model complex patterns in large datasets. DL has become very successful in areas like speech recognition, image processing, and natural language understanding [44].

The ability of AI to analyze huge reams of data, identify patterns, and hence make predictions makes it a very valuable tool in enhancing IoT applications. AI integrated with IoT systems means having smarter, more efficient, and more autonomous systems-those capable of adapting to changing conditions and making informed decisions on their own without human intervention.

2.2.3.2 AI algorithms for IoT applications

AI powers the IoT applications by a huge margin since it allows one to derive insights from humongous forms of data generated out of IoT devices. Many AI algorithms, especially in ML and DL, prove to be essential in optimizing the IoT systems, making better decisions and automating tasks.

ML algorithms

ML algorithms are intrinsically part of the analytical process in IoT data, identifying patterns, making predictions, and automating decisions. For instance, predictive maintenance, using ML algorithms that analyze sensor data from industrial equipment, can anticipate breakdowns and plan any maintenance-related activities in advance-thereby minimizing the chances of unplanned downtime while lowering related maintenance costs and increasing operational productivity [45].

DL algorithms

DL represents a subset of ML dealing with multiple layers of neural networks to model complicated patterns in big data. DL has an application in IoT that requires a high level of abstraction with respect to image and speech, which happen to form the bulk of IoT applications. For example, in smart homes, face and voice recognition can be done with DL algorithms processing data from cameras and microphones, making it useful in tailoring services and improving home security. These capabilities make DL a very powerful tool in developing intelligent and responsive IoT systems [46].

Convolutional neural networks (CNNs): The IoT applications of convolutional neural networks can be used in the domain of image and video analytics. For example, CNNs can analyze video feeds from cameras to detect unusual activities or recognize faces [44].

Recurrent neural networks (RNNs): Architectures in neural networks that are fit for sequential data have been adopted for use in IoT applications in which time series data is involved, for example, sensor data from wearables for health monitoring. RNNs can predict the next trend based on past data, inherently putting a framework in place for proactive healthcare interventions [47].

Generative adversarial networks (GANs): They consist of two neural networks-a generative network and a discriminant network-that iteratively play against each other. In IoT, GANs are used to provide synthetic data that enhances quality, with quality being the major determinant factor of the working of other AI models [38].

RL algorithms

In RL, agents are trained in decision-making processes by acting in an environment to maximize cumulative rewards. This is very useful for dynamic and complex IoT system optimization. The algorithm of RL can, for example, learn how to smartly manage a grid through real-time control over energy storage and distribution, efficiently balancing its supply and demand. This greatly enhances the efficiency and reliability of energy systems [48].

Natural language processing (NLP) algorithms

NLP enables the understanding and response to human language by machines, therefore making voice-activated assistants possible in chatbots and automated customer service in IoT applications. NLP techniques like sentiment analysis, language translation, and speech recognition enhance user interaction with IoT systems. For instance, in smart homes, NLP algorithms process voice commands and control IoT devices for better convenience and interaction with users. Accordingly, NLP becomes a core element in making IoT user-friendly [49].

2.2.3.3 Integration of AI in edge computing (edge AI)

Edge computing is a kind of paradigm that tries to distribute the computation and data storage closer to where it will be needed; generally, therefore, it reduces the amount of response time and bandwidth. AI, when integrated with edge computing, will enable edge AI and strengthen an IoT system's capability in support of real-time data processing and making decisions at the edge itself, rather than depending on some centralized servers in the cloud.

Benefits of edge AI

- *Low latency:* Edge AI reduces latency caused by sending data to the centralized cloud servers by processing the data itself on edge devices. This is particularly critical in applications of the IoT that are time-critical, like autonomous vehicles and industrial automation, where real-time decision-making is paramount [11].
- *Bandwidth efficiency:* Edge AI reduces the amount of data to be transmitted to the cloud, thereby saving bandwidth and reducing costs. This is very useful in scenarios where connectivity can be low or data volumes are extremely high, such as remote monitoring systems and smart cities [13].
- *Enhanced privacy and security:* Processing data at the edge device reduces the risk of data breaches and gives better privacy. For instance, with edge computing, sensitive health information gathered by wearable devices will be analyzed at the edge itself, rather than being exposed to the internet, which reduces exposure to possible cyber threats, thereby reducing the likelihood of a breach [14].

It has various applications that include smart cities, Industrial IoT, healthcare, etc.

For instance, edge AI-enabled traffic cameras would be empowered to analyze video feeds in order to detect accidents, thus managing the flow of traffic and public safety. Smart lighting systems could modulate their brightness in response to real-time occupancy data, saving energy [50].

It can monitor equipment performance, predict failures, and optimize production processes in manufacturing. Real-time analysis like this, done by edge AI on the data streaming from sensors and machines, can pick up anomalies and trigger preventive maintenance to reduce downtime and thereby improve efficiency [51].

Edge AI empowers healthcare IoT to analyze, in real time, patient data from wearable devices and medical sensors. Edge AI allows for the continuous monitoring of a patient's vital signs, detecting any abnormality and alerting healthcare professionals in case of emergency. This can enable proactive and personalized healthcare [52].

Challenges and future directions of edge AI

- *Resource constraints:* Generally, edge devices are resource-constrained compared to the computational power, memory, and storage that exist on cloud servers. Therefore, developing AI algorithms that work effectively on resource-constrained devices is quite a challenge. It is studying various techniques like model compression and federated learning [53].

- *Scalability:* With the current increase in IoT devices, the management and coordination of AI algorithms over distributed edge nodes becomes complex. Ensuring interoperability and scalability between heterogeneous devices is important if edge AI is to reach a wider audience.
- *Security and privacy:* Edge AI basically improves security since data processing is local. It, however, introduces new vulnerabilities. Robust encryption methods, secure communication protocols, and frequent updates in lieu of emerging threats ensure the security and privacy of the data being processed at the edge.

Advanced algorithms and edge computing apply AI in different applications, which will help increase the potential of IoT. Advanced AI algorithms make IoT devices capable of processing and analyzing large reams of data for smarter, more autonomous operations. Edge computing enhances this by moving the computational power closer to where it is generated, minimizing latency and bandwidth consumption, and ensuring privacy. However, some of the major challenges in fully harnessing AI in IoT are resource constraints, scalability, and security.

2.2.4 AI and blockchain integration for enhanced IoT data management

The convergence of AI and blockchain presents transformative potential for improving the management of data in the IoT ecosystem. While AI, for instance, enhances data processing and decision-making by large-scale data volume generated by IoT devices, blockchain further secures and decentralizes the management of data through features of transparency, immutability, and trustless transactions. Together, AI and blockchain create a particularly powerful framework to address these challenges in the management of IoT data security, privacy, scalability, and data integrity.

2.2.4.1 Enhancing data security and privacy

In the IoT environment, so many devices will be generating huge amounts of sensitive data, and thus, security and privacy will be huge concerns; therefore, AI is deployed in systems that can identify anomalies and breaches in security by making predictive decisions based on the analysis of real-time data streams and patterns. Centralized AI systems thus have to face single points of failure, which will breach the privacy and security of the data.

Decentralized architecture, along with cryptographic mechanisms in blockchain, is well aligned with AI. This system ensures that data produced by IoT gets recorded in an immutable, tamper-proof ledger. Usage of blockchain with AI makes every transaction between IoT devices validly recorded in an immutable ledger, thus preventing unauthorized access and data manipulations. Moreover, it can be used to automatically respond to security threats by combining AI-based anomaly detection with smart contracts of blockchain, thus allowing malpractices to be mitigated without any human input.

Such an anomaly in health monitoring can be addressed in an AI-based health monitoring framework of healthcare IoT systems that involve sensitive patient data being monitored and continuously transmitted to different parties. For this, blockchain ensures safe sharing among hospitals, clinics, and insurers with patients without exposing their private lives. Coordinated between AI and blockchain, therefore, increases the confidentiality and security of IoT data.

2.2.4.2 Decentralized and scalable data processing

One of the significant challenges in handling IoT data is the management of humongous data created by millions of interconnected devices. Centralized systems have significant scaling issues that can lead to bottlenecks and inefficient usage of the system. This is the reason why AI minimizes such issues, the fact that predictive analytics and decision-making can now be made on the edge of the network, relieving load on central servers. Centralization of AI models would not scale optimally for latency even further.

With blockchain, the way of data processing can be decentralized; hence, IoT devices can work individually with the integrity of data across the network. That is, AI algorithms are run on multiple nodes with a distributed ledger, and the consensus algorithms in blockchain that allow decentralization of the data processing and decision-making reduce latency and scale big.

For example, in smart cities, AI-based sensors, to traffic sensors or energy meters for IoT usage, can decide upon the usage of energy or traffic in real time. Such decisions and later data are shared and validated without the requirement of a central authority through blockchain. This decentralized method ensures scalability while reducing the operational costs of IoT; hence, IoT systems can grow and scale efficiently.

2.2.4.3 Data integrity and trust in autonomous systems

Autonomous IoT systems, such as smart contracts in blockchain networks, are only effective if reliable data is available. In contrast, IoT devices are mainly tampered with or full of errors and misdiagnoses that might prove to cause faults in decisions and subsequent actions. The role AI plays is filtering all that information coming from IoT devices to ensure that the data produced are authenticated and accurate for use in decision-making processes.

Blockchain improves the process by assuring data integrity through its immutable ledger. Once the data from IoT devices is verified and recorded in a blockchain, no entity involved in the process can ever change it again, ensuring that any AI-driven decisions are based on reliable, trustworthy data. This integration is especially vital to use in industries such as supply chain management, where transparency and traceability of goods within the linkages are critical. It will optimize logistics by forecasting every sort of supply chain disruption. Blockchain will enable a granular, accurate record of all transactions with end-to-end traceability of products.

2.2.4.4 Automated data management with smart contracts

By the use of AI and blockchain, smart contracts can improve IoT management significantly. AI algorithms may form trigger circumstances for executing a smart contract under some conditions; hence, trustless automated transactions are permitted between IoT devices. For example, an industrial IoT system, through the maintenance of equipment health in real-time, may employ AI algorithms to automatically activate a smart contract to order replacement parts or services should there be a probable failure in equipment. That makes it impossible to need intermediaries for the transaction, therefore it becomes safe, verifiable, and immutable.

This automation diminishes the latency and complexity associated with IoT systems, especially in domains involving real-time decision-making and execution within industries. Optimizing IoT data management can facilitate numerous applications, ranging from diverse applications such as supply chains and smart grids to more controlled applications through the predictive power of AI, combined with the trustless automation provided by blockchain.

2.2.4.5 Overcoming challenges in integration

While integration of AI and Blockchain into IoT brings enormous benefits, the path forward also has its challenges. AI algorithms, especially DL models, demand considerable computation power, which becomes a limitation in the decentralized nature of the blockchain network. Edge computing and federated learning can be used to distribute the workload of AI across IoT devices, which makes it lighter on any node.

The second factor is the scalability of blockchain, especially in IoT settings where thousands of devices produce transactions that feed into the system simultaneously. A layer-2 scaling protocol, sidechains, and sharding can somewhat address the problem with blockchain's scalability to more efficiently collaborate with AI-driven IoT systems.

The combination of AI and Blockchain gives a robust framework that will make the management of IoT data more potent by overcoming several problems that are hinged on scalability, security, integrity, and automation. From the technology employed, the combined blend will make IoT systems much more secure, decentralized, and autonomous, and hence, add innovation in healthcare, smart cities, and supply chains, among others. The integration of AI with blockchain will hence continue within the engineering process, thus being an integral feature of future IoT developments that would provide a more efficient, transparent, and scalable environment for data management.

2.3 Design and Implementation

2.3.1 Architectural design principles

2.3.1.1 Designing decentralized networks

The transformation in the 5G-IoT network from a centralized architecture to a decentralized one implies a radical change in the network's structure and management. Centralized architecture is a conventional design approach that relies on central servers and cloud-based services for data processing and network management. On the other hand, decentralized networks spread these tasks across various edge devices and hence, decrease latency, increase scalability, and increase security.

One of the core principles in the design of decentralized networks is to decentralize processing power and data storage. Edge computing achieves this by bringing processing closer to the source of the data. In edge computing, edge nodes-like sensors, gateways, and local servers-do data processing tasks usually performed in a central cloud. Because most of this processing is done locally, it reduces the delay incurred by the transmission of data to central servers, an aspect that forms the core of many applications needing real-time responses, including autonomous vehicles and industrial automation.

In decentralized networks, the so-called fog computing is utilized, which represents the prolongation of edge computing-introducing one more level of processing between edges and the cloud. Fog nodes are capable of performing more complex processing than edge devices, acting as mediators, further reducing the load on central servers, and improving the total efficiency of the network [12].

In Figure 2.3, a sample of proposed architectural design for 5G-IoT network is shown that reflects the distributed approach focusing on the key roles played by AI, blockchain, fog, and IoT nodes. Its components include:

- *Edge layer (IoT devices/sensors):* IoT1, IoT2, and IoT3 are different kinds of IoT devices and sensors that collect data in the field. Thus, they create a flow of continuous data.
- *Fog layer (computational nodes):* Fog1, Fog2, and Fog3 are fog nodes that computes near the edge close to producing data from IoT here and reduces latency.

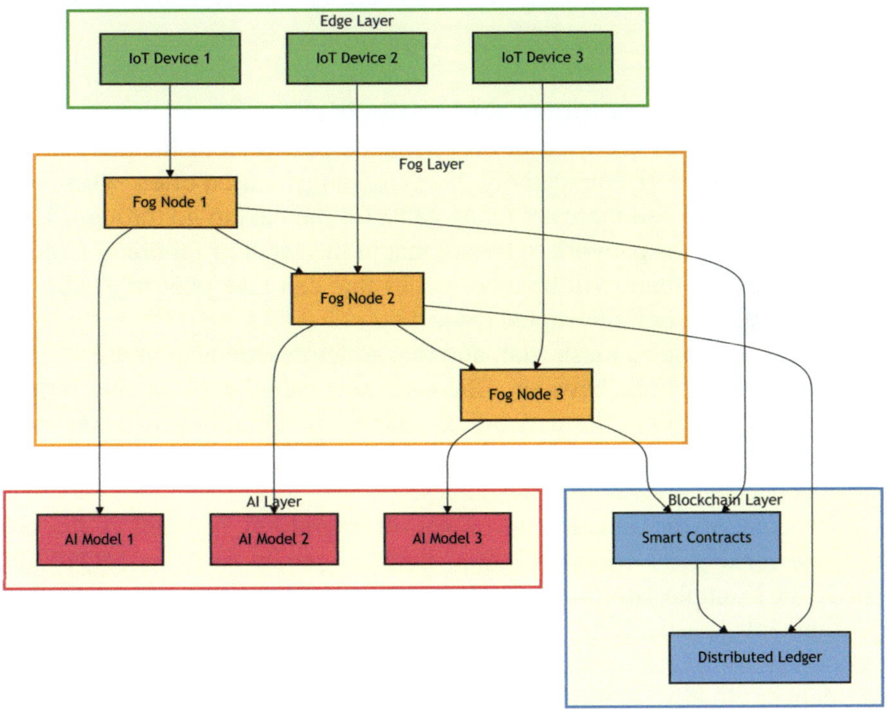

Figure 2.3 Sample proposed architectural design.

- *Blockchain layer (decentralized trust and security):* This layer ensures safe decentralized data handling. *Smart contracts (SC):* Autonomously support secure interactions between things or entities by validating data integrity, controlling access, or authenticating devices. *Distributed ledger:* Offers an immutable, secure, and transparent record of all transactions taking place between any devices and nodes in the network.
- *AI layer:* In this sample architecture, three decision AI models, AI Model 1, AI Model 2, and AI Model 3, are demonstrated. Both the IoT devices and the Fog nodes are using these AI models to make smart decisions in real-time. This AI layer is directly interacting with the blockchain layer to process and perform analytics safely.

The suggested data flow will start from the IoT layer, as that has to communicate with the fog nodes for almost real-time processing. Fog nodes talk to the blockchain layer for the instillation of security, integrity, and trust in the transaction. AI models are processing real-time data all around the edge and fog layers and are relying on blockchain for secure and decentralized decision-making.

2.3.1.2 Network topologies and protocols

Different topologies are used in decentralized networks to facilitate proper data flow and network connectivity. Mesh topology is used often, where each node is connected and there are many paths for the data to go through. There is redundancy in the network to ensure that in the event of failure of nodes in the network then there will be other nodes that can take over to ensure that the flow of data is not interrupted [54].

Hybrid topologies, mesh, star, and tree structures are also in use to come up with a compromise between efficiency and complexity. In this respect, these topologies allow the network to change the structure of connectivity between devices and the patterns of data traffic dynamically for optimum performance and allocation of resources.

The core of the functioning of any decentralized network is the protocols governing its communication. Such protocols, such as MQTT and CoAP, for example, are primarily designed to work in resource-constrained environments, particularly those that rely on low power supplies and are predominantly found within the Internet of Things environment. The protocols deliver effective and reliable communication between edge devices, fog nodes, and the central cloud [55].

The role of blockchain technology has increasingly been integrated into decentralized networks aimed at the secure and transparent transaction of data. Since this decentralized ledger assures integrity and authenticity, it is apt for applications with high security requirements and traceability, such as in supply chain management and smart contracts [10].

2.3.1.3 Case studies and examples

Some of the real-world applications are explained below to show how decentralized network design works effectively. For example, smart cities apply the decentralization of resources such as water, electricity, and transportation systems. Smart sensors and edge devices deployed across the city gather data and perform data processing at the point of data collection, thereby making decisions, as well as managing resources in real-time. This makes it easier to implement and reduces the load on central systems, and also increases the response time [56].

In industrial applications, decentralized networks are used for predictive maintenance and process control. The sensors installed on machines and the edge computing technology can allow the machines to assess their status and flag any issues in real-time. Data is processed in local areas so that corrective actions can be made on the same instance without having to wait for central servers. This local processing minimizes the time when the machines are down for maintenance and thus increases efficiency [57].

2.3.2 Security and privacy in decentralized IoT networks

2.3.2.1 Threats and vulnerabilities

Security and privacy are two critical issues in the case of decentralized IoT networks. The partitioning of data and the processing of data across multiple edge devices bring in multiple points of attack and risks. Conventional security measures that are based on the central control concept are generally ineffective in such systems. Common threats include:

- *Device compromise:* Edge devices can be physically tampered with or their control can be remotely compromised, which gives unauthorized control and access to the data.
- *Data interception:* Communication between the devices and the edge nodes can be vulnerable to interception, which results in eavesdropping and man-in-the-middle attacks.
- *DoS attacks:* Such distributed denial of service attacks will overwhelm network resources, thus resulting in breaks in services.

- *Malware and ransomware:* Malware might be injected into the devices, hence highly compromising the functionality of the devices and the integrity of their data.

A 2005 survey by S. Sicari, A. Rizzardi, L. A. Grieco, and A. Coen-Porisin commented that IoT devices are easy targets due to limited computational resources and a lack of strong security features. The heterogeneity of IoT devices adds more to the complexity in implementing homogeneous security protocols [58].

2.3.2.2 Blockchain-enabled security solutions

Blockchain technology provides exciting potential solutions that can improve security within decentralized IoT networks. The combination of these very features of blockchain-immutable and transparent ledger-would surely make it possible for blockchain to ensure data integrity and accountability. Key features are:

- *Decentralized authentication:* Blockchain can facilitate secure and decentralized authentication of devices, avoiding a central authority's interference. This would reduce the risk of single points of failure and improve trust among devices.
- *Secure data transactions:* The data transaction is securely immutable; there is no possibility of alteration. Therefore, alterations are not accountable for tracing by the blockchain technology. This prevents unauthorized data alterations and ensures transparency.
- *Smart contracts:* They are able to automate the policies of security and make the network compliant. These can be programmed to detect anomalies and initiate the appropriate responses, such as isolating devices that have been compromised.

Research by A. Dorri, S. S. Kanhere, R. Jurdak, and P. Gauravaram in 2017 demonstrates the viability of blockchain in securing IoT systems. Their work shows how blockchain can be used in creating a secure and decentralized framework for IoT devices to bring data integrity and privacy [26].

2.3.2.3 Privacy preservation techniques

Other than security, privacy is an important concern within IoT networks. All kinds of data from different IoT devices vastly contain private personal information. Strong privacy preservation techniques have to be implemented by decentralized architectures in order to protect this data.

- *Data encryption:* Both data at rest and in transit have to be encrypted, so that in case of interception, no meaning can be derived from the data by any unauthorized entity. Lightweight encryption algorithms come out to be specifically suitable for resource-constrained IoT devices.
- *Anonymization and pseudonymization:* Protect identities in the process, but allow for data analysis. These techniques ensure that personal data cannot be traced back to a particular person.
- *Federated learning:* Federated learning will be training ML models on decentralized data without sharing the raw data. In this approach, data stays local to devices while it still has the benefits of collaborative learning.

Federated learning in IoT is gaining much popularity, according to "Federated machine learning: Concept and applications" by Q. Yang, Y Liu, T Chen, and Y Tong. Their work emphasizes the need for privacy protection to enable intelligent data analysis across distributed IoT networks [53].

2.3.3 Scalability and interoperability

2.3.3.1 Challenges of scalability in IoT

As the number of IoT devices grows exponentially, scalability becomes a critical challenge. Scalability is referred to as the ability of a system to support increased loads. In the context of IoT, this comes down to dealing with large device numbers while guaranteeing homogeneous performance and efficient communication.

One of the key challenges to scalability has to do with huge volumes of data generated by devices from the IoT. Given the continuous streaming of data from billions of sensors and devices, it is hard for traditional centralized systems to process and analyze the information in real-time. It will consequently lead to network congestion, which would again increase latency and degrade performance [59].

Another limitation is in terms of low capacity within the network infrastructure. The 5G networks, much more capable than their predecessors, still have limitations in bandwidth and spectrum availability. Efficient techniques to allocate these resources for supporting high densities of IoT devices include network slicing and dynamic spectrum sharing.

Another challenge in the proliferation of IoT devices is their energy consumption. Most of the IoT devices are battery-powered and have to work for a long time without human intervention; therefore, efficient power management and low-power communication protocols are necessary to make large-scale IoT deployments sustainable [60].

2.3.3.2 Interoperability standards and protocol

It can be defined as the ability of diverse systems, devices, or applications to interact with each other effectively in a given context. Interoperability implied in this, being an IoT system, is an integration between devices and deployment of a system with a properly laid communication protocol in an IoT ecosystem. Without proper standardization of the protocols and the interfaces between individual vendors, it then poses problems to integrate and ensure compatibility between them.

Several interoperability standards and frameworks have been developed to solve this issue. For example, amongst the many is the Internet Protocol for Smart Objects Alliance, which promotes IP-based communication for IoT devices and ensures intercompatibility of devices, hence the ease of integration [61].

Another such organization developing open standards for IoT interoperability is the Open Connectivity Foundation. OCF specifications enable devices to discover and communicate independently with one another, regardless of the underlying platform or manufacturer [53].

Other than this standard, one progresses toward the importance of middleware solutions to achieve the interoperability aspect. Middleware is, in general, a piping or an interim layer, that over varied devices and systems, does the translation for data and commands between them, thus enabling communication and integration between them. This includes the wide applicability of both the Message Queuing Telemetry Transport and Constrained Application Protocol protocols in IoT applications.

2.3.3.3 Solutions and best practices for scalability and interoperability

Edge computing

The load on the network declines when using edge computing, since IoT devices process data closer to their sources, and thus, latency decreases to enable real-time decision-making. This can give a boost to the scalability of the system as the processing happens locally instead of a massive cloud transfer. Organizations can implement edge servers near sources of data so as to offload processing tasks with the anticipation of achieving higher scalability and efficiency in energy.

Scalability and interoperability through AI

AI enhances resource management and time-dependent decisions about 5G-IoT. For example, ML models predict the traffic peaks and dynamically allocate bandwidth, as seen in smart factories and healthcare. Integrations into network systems in AI frameworks like TensorFlow allow to automate load balancing and optimize performance. For interoperability, AI-enabled middleware allows the communication between devices that have different protocols by automatic adjustment in real time to outroot the data discrepancies.

Blockchain for scalability and interoperability

Blockchain allows decentralized, secure data exchanges in the IoT ecosystem and solves the issue of scalability through off-chain solutions, such as state channels. Thus, for example, smart logistics can track goods in real time without reliance on any central authority. Platforms such as Hyperledger Fabric enable a scalable and secure processing of transactions. For interoperability, smart contracts allow for peer-to-peer data exchange between platforms, and cross-chain protocols such as Polkadot may be integrated to enable different blockchain systems to interoperate.

Middleware solutions

Middleware is a bridge used between heterogeneous IoT devices, protocols, etc. Kaa IoT or ThingsBoard are platforms that standardize data exchanges with scalability and interoperability in heterogeneous devices. Middleware will simplify system management through the efficiencies of simple data translation and integration capabilities comparable to smart building automation.

Open standards in collaboration

Such devices will be interoperable with one another by making use of open standards, as the Internet Protocol for Smart Objects (IPSO) Alliance. IoT devices need to be selected based on compatibility with established standards, first, such as Open Connectivity Foundation (OCF) devices, so as to ensure interoperable, large-scale deployments within a smart city or an industrial system.

Combined AI and blockchain approach

Combining AI and blockchain technologies makes the practical deployment in 5G-IoT networks scalable and interoperable. In this regard, AI models that predict the congestion network can update dynamically blockchain transaction parameters to offer the optimum performance in performance.

In a decentralized supply chain system, predictive models driven by AI can predict demands, whereas the secure, traceable flow of goods and data can be ensured using the blockchain.

To implement this combined approach, organizations can integrate AI into blockchain-based IoT solutions. For example, smart contracts can be used to ensure the triggering of AI algorithms for analytics of any data from the IoT domain, thus facilitating real-time decisions. On the other hand, blockchain's consensus mechanisms can be optimized through AI to speed up transactions and reduce their energy consumption. Developers could utilize frameworks like IBM's AI-blockchain toolkit in building scalable and interoperable applications to maximize the use of these two technologies without compulsion.

2.4 Applications and Use Cases for AI and Blockchain in 5G-IoT Networks

2.4.1 Smart cities and urban infrastructure

2.4.1.1 Intelligent traffic management

Smart cities make use of IoT devices and 5G connectivity in setting up intelligent traffic management systems. The smart system controls the flow of traffic by making use of real-time data acquired from connected vehicles, traffic lights, and road sensors. This is where decentralized architecture comes in as very critical, for it enables data processing locally at the edge to reduce latency for fast decision-making.

Security and transparency can be further enhanced by the integration of blockchain technology. For example, it provides an immutable record of traffic data and transactions, ensuring that data is not changed for malicious purposes. In respect to this, AI algorithms analyze traffic patterns and predict congestion, enabling proactive traffic management and dynamic rerouting.

2.4.1.2 Smart grid and energy management

Another critical application in the domain of smart cities is that of smart grids, in which decentralized IoT architecture can make a leapfrog difference in efficiency and reliability. Smart meters, distributed energy resources, and advanced sensors communicate with each other through 5G networks for monitoring and managing energy distribution in real time. Local processing of data at the edge promotes quick response to changes in energy demand and supply.

Blockchain ensures secure and transparent transactions between energy producers and consumers, facilitating peer-to-peer energy trading. AI manages the energy usage profile, forecasts the demand, and improves the incorporation of renewable energy into the grid.

2.4.1.3 Public safety and surveillance

IoT-enabled surveillance systems improve public safety in smart cities. High definition cameras, environmental sensors, and emergency response systems will interconnect with 5G. Decentralized processing at the edge allows real-time video analytics and fast detection of anomalies or emergencies.

Blockchain provides the assurance that data obtained from such systems is immutable and accessed by only authorized persons. AI-driven analytics can sniff out suspicious activity, predict threats, and facilitate emergency response through automation. Despite the above mentioned verticals, the smart city has many other verticals, which is clearly mentioned in Figure 2.4.

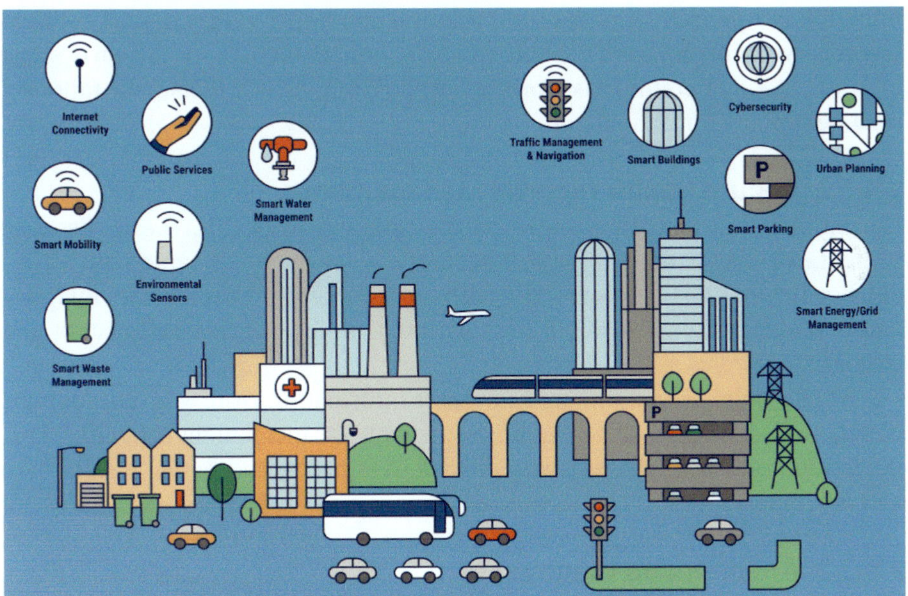

Figure 2.4 Components of a smart city [64].

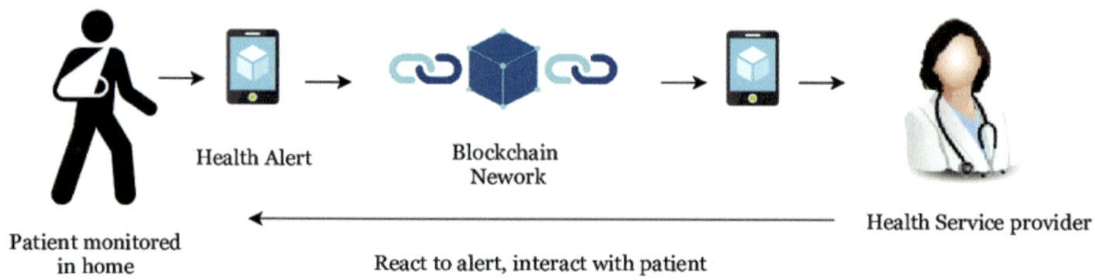

Figure 2.5 Remote patient monitoring [65].

2.4.2 Healthcare and biomedical applications

2.4.2.1 Remote patient monitoring

Remote patient monitoring (as mentioned in Figure 2.5) is revolutionized by a decentralized 5G-IoT architecture. Wearable devices/sensors in patients gather their health data and transmit it to healthcare providers in real-time for analysis. Edge computing guarantees data is locally processed, therefore with low latency, and is able to be instantly analyzed and responded to.

Blockchain provides a decentralized, immutable ledger that protects the integrity and privacy of patient information contained within digital medical records. AI algorithms are capable of analyzing health data for the early signs of some medical conditions, forecasting possible health risks, and tailoring treatment plans for patients.

2.4.2.2 Secure health records management

Decentralized architecture improves the handling of health records because the data of the patient is stored securely and can be accessed in different healthcare organizations. Blockchain technology ensures the integrity and confidentiality of medical records, preventing unauthorized access and tampering.

AI can help to combine and interpret information from various sources, which would help in the overall assessment of the patient's health. This integration enhances diagnostics, precise treatments, and better patient care and outcomes.

2.4.2.3 AI-enhanced diagnostics

AI-driven diagnostic tools can interpret medical imaging, laboratory results, and data from patients to help healthcare professionals diagnose diseases with better accuracy and speed. Decentralized architecture ensures that this data is processed locally, reducing latency and improving real-time diagnostics.

Blockchain secures diagnostic data and makes it confidential and tamper-proof. This fusion of AI and blockchain in a decentralized framework increases the reliability and efficiency of healthcare diagnostics.

2.4.3 Industrial IoT and automation

2.4.3.1 Industry 4.0 and smart manufacturing

Industry 4.0 brings together IoT devices, sophisticated robotics, and real-time data analytics for building smart manufacturing environments. Decentralized 5G-IoT architecture supports this enormous number of connected devices and enables real-time communication and processing at the edge.

Blockchain provides the ensurement of the security and traceability of the manufacturing processes, offering a transparent ledger of all transactions and data exchanges. AI brings efficiency to production in predictive equipment failure, optimization of supply chains, and automation of routine tasks.

2.4.3.2 Predictive maintenance in industrial settings

Predictive maintenance: IoT sensors coupled with AI monitor the condition of industrial equipment in real time to project failures before they occur. Decentralized architecture enables local data processing, reducing latency to prompt immediate actions.

Blockchain secures data from equipment sensors, thereby making it incorruptible and reliable. AI algorithms analyze this data for patterns that indicate a potential failure so that timely maintenance can be scheduled to reduce downtime.

2.4.3.3 Autonomous robotics and drones

Increasingly used autonomous robots and drones in industry need 5G connectivity to acquire enough bandwidth and low latency for real-time control and data transmission. Besides, decentralized architecture means the system will function independently, processing data at the edge locally.

Blockchain is the means of ensuring secure communication between robots and control systems, whereas AI empowers autonomous decision-making and coordination. This will considerably improve efficiency, safety, and reliability in the operation of industries.

2.4.4 Consumer IoT applications

2.4.4.1 Smart homes and buildings

The IoT devices in smart homes and buildings control and optimize a wide array of their functions. This includes devices for lighting, heating, and security, energy management devices, and many more. In a decentralized architecture, local data processing is enabled, reducing latency and ensuring reliable performance.

This provides a security enhancement through a decentralized and immutable record of each and every interaction of the devices, which helps prevent unauthorized access or manipulation. AI algorithms ensure optimum energy consumption, security systems, and user comfort by learning from and adapting to the preferences of the users.

2.4.4.2 Wearable devices and health monitoring

Wearable devices, like activity trackers and smart watches, monitor the activities of users in health metrics and provide real-time feedback. Decentralized architecture enables local processing and reduces latency, increasing the responsiveness of such devices.

Blockchain encrypts health data originating from wearables and guarantees privacy and data integrity. AI then analyzes this data for personalized health insights, anomaly detection, and lifestyle change recommendations to improve health and well-being.

2.4.4.3 Enhanced user experiences

The consumer IoT applications offer better user experiences through tailored and context-aware services. For example, smart assistants that are able to aggregate data from a number of IoT devices can offer tailored recommendations and automate regular chores. Decentralized architecture offers real-time data processing and less dependency on central cloud services in these applications.

Blockchain makes sure that user data is private and secure against any possible tampering. AI enhances the intelligence and adaptability of these applications, therefore offering more relevant services to users at appropriate times.

2.5 Future Directions

2.5.1 Emerging technologies and innovations

The next wave of converging technologies holds the potential for a fundamental shift in the decentralized architecture landscape for 5G-IoT. Second

Quantum Revolution, future of sensor technologies, and innovations in network architectures will only further their abilities and applications of IoT.

2.5.1.1 Integration with quantum computing

Quantum computing is going to revolutionize data processing and security in decentralized networks. Quantum computers, in sharp contrast to the classical ones using bits as the lowest unit of information, make use of what is called quantum bits-or qubits-that are capable of holding not just 0 or 1 but both at the same time because of the principles of superposition and entanglement [70].

- *Enhanced data processing:* Quantum computing is capable of parallelism and may help to accomplish computational tasks in a very short time, much faster than classical computers. This capability is most useful for highly real-time IoT use cases that include predictive analytics and decision making [71].
- *Improved security:* Quantum cryptography offers the best techniques of encryption, such as quantum key distribution, that will be applied to protect communication channels in decentralized IoT networks. Accordingly, data transmitted over the network is guaranteed to be confidential and tamper-proof [72].

2.5.1.2 Advances in sensor technologies

Sensors are the base of any IoT installation, acquiring information from the environment in which they exist and sending it to the network for further processing and analysis. Recent developments in sensor technologies have boosted the performance and capability of IoT devices.

- *Nanotechnology:* Nanotechnology is facilitating the development of small, efficient sensors with high sensitivity and accuracy. Nanosensors are able to detect very minute changes in the environment, so they become very functional in health, environmental monitoring, and smart cities [73].
- *Energy harvesting:* All these technologies in energy harvesting allow sensors to self-power, with no external supply needed, only by converting ambient energies into electrical power, such as solar, thermal, or kinetic energy. This development is crucial for the implementation of IoT devices in places, that are hard to reach or remote, resulting in the replacement of batteries being quite impractical regularly [74].

- *Multi-modal sensors:* These are capable of measuring several parameters simultaneously, hence reducing the number of independent sensors to be installed and, accordingly, simplifying the architecture of the network. This increases the effectiveness and efficiency of data collection in IoT systems [75].

2.5.1.3 Future network architectures

The architecture of the future networks will evolve to back up the demands that decentralized 5G-IoT systems will bring, adding performance, scalability, and reliability.

- *Software-defined networking (SDN):* SDN decouples the network's control plane from the data plane, making it easier to program it. This is desirable since IoT traffic is bound to be dynamic, and the devices are involved in a wide variety of activities. SDN can be useful in the optimal allocation of resources for better control of the network [76].
- *Network function virtualization (NFV):* Through the use of NFV, these network functions are no longer tightly coupled to particular physical hardware, but instead run as virtual machines or containers on standard servers. This networking approach helps conserve costs whilst enhancing the readiness with which these services are deployed and sustained, thus the preparedness in expanding IoT networks [77].
- *Mesh networking:* Mesh networks have a decentralized structure by which nodes can be linked to other nodes, making it possible for data to travel multiple routes. This redundancy makes the IoT networks more robust and available all the time, even if some of the nodes are not functioning as required [54].

2.5.1.4 Synergies and implications

Emerging technologies in decentralized 5G-IoT systems are being integrated in a way that creates synergies, achieving a far better performance and capability of the new network than what the individual technologies have to offer on their own.

- *Quantum-secure IoT networks:* The marriage of quantum computing with the IoT could yield ultra-secure networks. Quantum encryption techniques can protect data against intercepts and tampering, providing integrity and confidentiality in IoT communications [78].
- *Self-powered IoT devices:* The integration between energy harvesting technologies and state-of-art sensors can potentially give way

to self-powered IoT devices. The devices in this case would work indefatigably with no need for any type of external power sources, which would reduce maintenance costs, and, at the same time, include deployments related to remote or hostile environments [79].

- *Dynamic and flexible network management:* SDN and NFV provide dynamic and flexible management of IoT networks. For instance, in this regard, network administrators can very quickly respond to any change within traffic patterns, resource optimization, and innovation in new services without the expensive need for hardware upgrades [80].

Quantum computing, advanced sensor technologies, and future network architectures are most likely to converge to form a new decentralized architecture for 5G-IoT. These emerging technologies can further enhance data processing, security, and energy efficiency, while allowing for the development of new applications and services. The synergies of such innovations will fuel the ongoing evolution of IoT into smarter, more efficient, and secure networks as research and development move further.

2.5.2 Regulatory and ethical considerations

With the evolution of decentralized architecture for 5G-IoT, concerns at the regulatory and ethical levels become very prominent. The deployment and operation of such networks are supposed to be harmonized with the various regulations for safety, privacy, and security. Not to mention also the important ethical concerns related to the use of data, AI decision-making, and the environment itself in regard to IoT devices.

2.5.2.1 Regulatory frameworks for decentralized IoT

1) *Data protection and privacy*

   Given the huge quantity of data generated in IoT devices, issues related to data protection and privacy come into play. This had already established regulations about the collection, storage, and processing of data under the General Data Protection Regulation in Europe and the California Consumer Privacy Act in the United States, which were very strict.

   - *GDPR compliance:* The GDPR requires that organizations have express consent from subjects before collecting data. It also imposes a strong security measure for the protection of personal data, which is well appreciated, and it grants a right to access, rectify, and erase data for the Data Subject [81].

- *CCPA requirements:* CCPA also has many provisions with similar protections, allowing the consumer to know what personal data is being collected and to whom it will be sold. It gave the customers the right to opt out of the sale of their personal data (California Legislative Information, 2018).

2) *Spectrum allocation and management*
Accordingly, proper management of the radio frequency spectrum is essential for 5G networks. At the national level, these spectrum resources are regulated and administered by the Federal Communications Commission in the United States of America, while at the European level, the task is performed by the European Telecommunications Standards Institute.

- *FCC regulations:* The FCC allocates spectrum for 5G deployment, ensuring adequate bandwidth for high-speed and low-latency communications. It further guides on spectrum sharing and interference management (FCC, 2019).
- *ETSI standards:* ETSI develops standards on spectrum usage in Europe; it promotes harmonized spectrum allocation to facilitate cross-border interoperability, efficient use of resources (ETSI, 2020).

3) *Cybersecurity regulations*
The security situation in the decentralized IoT is important considering the possible risk factor of cyberattacks. This is aggravated by various regulatory risk governance frameworks, such as the NIST Cybersecurity Framework in the United States, that help guide the effective management of cybersecurity risks.

- *NIST framework:* The NIST Cybersecurity Framework outlined best practices to identify, protect, detect, respond to, and recover from such threats to cybersecurity. It would include risk assessment, monitoring, incident response planning, and more areas, including situational awareness and a cybersecurity workforce (NIST, 2018).
- *EU cybersecurity act:* Setting the scene for the certification of cybersecurity for ICT products, services, and processes and enhancing the security of IoT devices and networks (European Union, 2019).

2.5.2.2 Ethical implications of AI and blockchain

1) *AI decision-making and accountability*

By applying AI in IoT, ethical questions can be raised concerning decision-making and accountability. AI algorithms make independent decisions that affect human beings and society; hence, transparency and accountability are necessary.

- *Transparency in AI:* AI decision-making processes should be transparent and explainable. This incorporates the documentation of data used, algorithms employed, and the rationale behind decisions for understandability and accountability [82].
- *Bias and fairness:* AI algorithms must be designed to avoid biases that can lead to unfair outcomes. The proper selection and preprocessing of training data, together with continued monitoring for detection and mitigation of bias, is necessary.

2) *Blockchain and data integrity*

Blockchain technology offers integrity and transparency of data in decentralized IoT networks. However, the immutable nature of blockchain generally raises ethical concerns related to data permanence and the risks of its misuse.

- *Immutability and privacy:* As much as blockchain offers improved security and transparency, the immutability aspect implies that once the data is recorded, it is immutable. This, therefore, makes it hard to ensure data privacy where people need their data erased.
- *Decentralized governance:* The decentralized nature of the blockchain enforces a governance framework that makes people accountable and solves various kinds of conflicts, such as dispute resolution, protocol updates, and consensus management between participants.

2.5.2.3 Environmental impact of IoT

The proliferation of IoT devices has huge environmental implications related to electronic waste and energy consumption.

1) *Sustainable device design*

Designing IoT devices with sustainability in mind can mitigate environmental impact. It considers the use of recyclable materials, reduced energy consumption, and increasing the life span of devices.

- *Energy-efficient design:* IoT devices should be designed to consume minimal energy, with the help of energy-efficient components, where the power management is optimized.

- *E-waste management:* Handling of e-waste obtained either through the disposal or recycling of IoT devices is another major issue of electronic waste mitigation. Manufacturers are urged to take back programs and design products for easy disassembly and recycling.

2) *Renewable energy integration*
The integration of renewable energy sources in IoT networks can reduce the carbon footprint that these systems leave behind. Solar, wind, and other renewable energies could power IoT devices to lessen reliance on fossil fuels.

   - *Solar-powered IoT devices:* Solar energy can be used to power any IoT device, specifically in locations where it might be secluded or outdoors. This would reduce the impact on the environment by providing a clean and renewable source of energy.
   - *Energy harvesting technologies:* Energy harvesting technologies can gather ambient energy from the surroundings and continuously provide power to IoT devices instead of relying on batteries.

2.5.2.4 Ensuring compliance and accountability

To address regulatory and ethical considerations, organizations must implement robust compliance and accountability frameworks.

1) *Compliance monitoring*
The workings should be constantly monitored for compliance with the set regulatory requirements. This would mean periodic audits, risk analysis, and revision of policies in the light of changes in regulations.

   - *Regulatory audits:* Periodic audits pertaining to compliance with data protection, cybersecurity, and environmental laws bring out the lapses and help in taking remedial measures (ISO, 2013).
   - *Risk assessments:* Running regular risk assessments could serve to identify possible vulnerabilities and mitigation measures to protect IoT networks and data (NIST, 2018).

2) *Ethical governance*
The ethical governance framework is what warrants that IoT applications are developed and deployed responsibly.

   - *Ethics committees:* The institution of ethics committees within a company to review and advise on AI and blockchain projects with respect to ethical issues is important. These committees should be multi-disciplined in makeup for proper coverage.

- *Ethical guidelines:* Development and adherence to ethical guidelines for AI and IoT applications shall foster harmony in projects respecting societal values and individual rights (IEEE, 2019).

Regulatory and ethical considerations form the backbones that ensure the successful deployment and operation of decentralized architecture in the application of 5G-IoT. The adherence to regulatory frameworks brings about protection for data, cybersecurity, and efficient spectrum management. Addressing the ethical implications of AI and blockchain means transparency, accountability, and fairness. Besides, considering the environmental impact of IoT promotes sustainability and minimizes the carbon footprint. Through strict compliance and accountability frameworks, organizations can meet such challenges and act responsibly to exploit the full potential of decentralized 5G-IoT networks.

2.5.3 Challenges and opportunities beyond 5G

The challenges and opportunities that decentralized architecture for IoT brought forth can only continue to evolve as we look beyond 5G. Next-generation networks, in this respect, hold a great deal of potential that can only be harnessed by overcoming technical and operational challenges. At the same time, opportunities to further innovate and develop beckon with quite a number of very promising revolutions across industries.

2.5.3.1 Technical and operational challenges

1) *Scalability and interoperability*

   One of the major technical challenges that must be achieved within decentralized IoT networks is to guarantee interoperability and scalability.

   - *Scalability:* With the growing number of connected devices, it becomes of paramount importance that the network scales to accommodate the surge in data traffic without a drop in performance. Traditional centralized architectures inherently lack in terms of scalability because of bottlenecks and single points of failure. In decentralized architectures, efficient resource allocation, load balancing, and distributed processing have to be implemented to deal with the increased load.
   - *Interoperability:* The devices that make an IoT are from different companies, with varying protocols and standards used for communication. Given that these devices are heterogeneous, there exists a

need for interoperability between them to allow smooth integration and processing. This solution puts a call for standardization efforts besides developing universal protocols for communication.

2) *Security and privacy*
Security and privacy in decentralized IoT networks have become very critical issues.

- *Security threats:* Open-ended threats exist against the decentralized architecture of DDoS attacks, man-in-the-middle attacks, and unauthorized access. Strong security in the form of encryption, authentication, and intrusion detection systems is essential for network protection.
- *Privacy concerns:* IoT devices collect enormous amounts of personal data, which brings into contention the privacy of that data. It is important to ensure that the collection, storage, and processing of data are in compliance with privacy regulations such as the GDPR and the CCPA. Some techniques that can be applied to safeguard user privacy include data anonymization, differential privacy, and secure multi-party computation.

3) *Energy efficiency*
Energy consumption by IoT devices and networks is an extremely challenging issue.

- *Device energy consumption:* Most of the devices used in IoT are powered by batteries, and their replacement after a short period is not feasible, particularly in places that are hard to reach or at a distance. Hence, energy-efficient devices and protocols are essential to extend battery life and minimize maintenance.
- *Network energy efficiency:* Especially in dense IoT networks, this is a power-consuming process. Energy harvesting, low-power communication protocols, and sleep modes can improve energy efficiency, thereby reducing the impact on the environment.

2.5.3.2 Potential solutions and innovations

1) *Edge computing and AI integration*
Edge computing integrated with AI opens a lot of opportunities for innovation.

- *Edge computing:* It reduces latency and bandwidth usage; hence, it processes data closer to the source. In that respect, this enables applications in real-time, which becomes very important in the case of time-critical IoT applications- for example, autonomous vehicles and industrial automation, and healthcare monitoring.

- *AI at the edge:* Contrasted with relying on centralized, cloud-based servers, deployment of the AI algorithms at the edge gives intelligent decision-making without necessarily relying on remote systems. That will enhance response time and autonomy of the IoT devices in applications such as predictive maintenance, anomaly detection, and personalized services.

2) *Blockchain for trust and transparency*
Blockchain technology makes any IoT network decentralized and secure.

- *Trust and transparency:* Blockchain keeps an immutable, transparent ledger of transactions between IoT devices and different stakeholders. This can be applied in secure device authentication, data integrity verification, and execution of smart contracts.
- *Decentralized applications:* Enables autonomous interaction and transaction among devices, opening new business models and use cases like decentralized energy trading, supply chain tracking, and decentralized identity management. Next-generation connectivity solutions are set to further the capabilities of IoT networks.

3) *Advanced connectivity solutions*
Next-generation connectivity solutions are set to enhance the capabilities of IoT networks.

- *6G networks:* While 5G is still in the process of full deployment, researchers envision 6G networks to be far beyond 5G in ultra-high speeds, extremely low latency, and massive device densities. This supports advanced applications like holographic communications, immersive virtual reality, and real-time remote control.
- *Satellite IoT:* IoT connectivity through satellites can cover the globe, particularly areas that are remote or underserved. To that end, it can support applications as varied as environmental monitoring, disaster management, and vessel tracking in maritime areas where one happens to be out of terrestrial network coverage.

2.5.3.3 Long-term opportunities and visions

Looking beyond 5G, the challenges and opportunities arising from a decentralized architecture for IoT remain huge. Technical and operational difficulties to be overcome in creating a successful network deployment come in issues related to scalability, security, and energy efficiency. This goes hand in hand with innovation opportunities located at the edge, AI integration, blockchain, and advanced connectivity solutions, all holding immense potential for industry transformation. Facing such challenges and availing of the opportunities that come up, the future of decentralized 5G-IoT will be enormous, improving connectivity, efficiency, and sustainability across a wide array of applications and sectors.

Next-generation innovation beyond 5G for IoT data-driven communication infrastructure is envisioned to be driven by the convergence of decentralized architecture, AI, and blockchain. These technologies will enable the creation of intelligent, autonomous systems that can almost work autonomously without human intervention. Fully autonomous vehicles, smart cities with an overall integration of infrastructure, and advanced health systems with prediction-these are just a few of the applications. This means the long-term vision entails a perfectly connected world where IoT devices facilitate every life aspect of humans.

2.6 Practical Implementation and Case Studies

2.6.1 Implementing decentralized IoT solutions

Decentralized IoT solutions in the framework of 5G essentially implement edge computing, blockchain, and advanced network protocols.

2.6.1.1 Practical guidelines and best practices

1) *Network architecture design*

- *Edge computing integration:* Heavy reliance on edge computing in decentralized IoT architecture helps process data locally at the lower end, which reduces latency and bandwidth usage. While designing the network, it becomes paramount to decide where edge nodes have to be located with respect to data generation points and processing requirements.
- *Blockchain for security:* Secure transactions of data will be realized by blockchain technology, setting up decentralized ledgers and smart contracts that run automatically and with transparency.
- *AI for optimization:* Implement AI algorithms at the edge to empower real-time data analytics and decision-making. Increased efficiency and increased responsiveness of the IoT network consequently derive.

2) *Scalability considerations*

- *Modular design:* Adapt the modular approach to network design so that it can easily scale. Each module or node should be capable of working on its own while being able to integrate very well into the larger network.
- *Dynamic resource allocation:* Develop mechanisms of dynamic resource allocation to provide load balancing over the network. This will be based on AI-based predictive analytics that predict demands on the network and dynamically allocate resources in that direction.

3) *Security and privacy*

- *End-to-end encryption:* End-to-end encryption will be provided to ensure protection from unauthorized access to the data. Blockchain shall be used for the secure management of cryptographic keys.
- *Access control mechanisms:* Access control mechanisms can be achieved by utilizing blockchain-based identity management systems, thereby avoiding the presence of unauthorized devices within the network and their unauthorized access to the same. This shall ensure that the network allows access to only authorized devices and users.

2.6.1.2 Deployment strategies and considerations

1) *Pilot testing*

- *Initial deployment:* The decentralized IoT solution needs to first be deployed on a small scale concerning testing. This would identify any configuration issues and the need for its optimization before the actual deployment.
- *Feedback loop:* Establish a feedback loop to collect data regarding the performance and reliability of the network. Using the collected data, refine and improve the deployment strategy.

2) *Full-scale deployment*

- *Gradual rollout:* The IoT network will be rolled out in phases to ensure stability and manageability. Start with critical nodes, then gradually increase them to involve more devices and sensors.
- *Continuous monitoring:* Implement the continuous monitoring systems for health and performance of the network. AI-driven analytics detect and act on anomalies in real-time.

2.6.1.3 Real-world case studies

The use of decentralized structures in 5G-IoT environments is transforming different industries through increased performance, protection, and capacity. Two real-world examples that can be used to explain the actual usage and advantages of the decentralized IoT architecture are the smart city project in Barcelona and an IIoT platform by General Electric. These examples exemplify the change that occurs when edge computing, blockchain, and IoT are integrated within a decentralized environment.

Smart cities: The case of Barcelona

The case of Barcelona proves that decentralized IoT architectures can be beneficial for the management of the city's infrastructure within the framework of a smart city. Smart city plan entails the use of a number of IoT devices in numerous areas such as lighting, waste management, traffic signals, and environmental sensors. Thus, edge computing and blockchain work in tandem to guarantee that the IoT infrastructure of the city runs optimally and is protected from hackers.

- *Smart lighting:* Barcelona has installed smart street lights with sensors that control the luminosity according to the existing light and the presence of people. These lights are managed through a distributed system that enables control of the lights in real time and also detects faults. Edge computing allows data processing locally, thus quickly responding to changes in conditions.
- *Waste management:* Smart bins are employed in the city with sensors to determine the amount of waste and the routes to follow for collection. This approach helps to minimize the need for centralized processing of data, thus enhancing decision-making processes and at the same time, cutting down on operational expenses. Data gathered from these sensors are secured and protected from any manipulation and unauthorized access through the use of blockchain technology.
- *Traffic control:* Barcelona has implemented an IoT system where sensors and cameras are used to analyze traffic patterns and adjust the time taken by traffic signals accordingly. It means that the traffic is efficient and can be processed at the edge in real-time due to the decentralized structure. Blockchain helps in sharing information securely with other parties, for instance, traffic authorities and emergency services, and improves their cooperation and efficiency.
- *Environmental monitoring:* The city has implemented a network of environmental sensors that track air quality, noise levels, and weather. All

these sensors work in a decentralized way, processing the data locally and transmitting only relevant information back to central servers. All this will reduce the load on central servers and guarantee real-time responses to environmental changes.

Industrial IoT: General electric (GE) case

Through the use of decentralized architecture, the Predix platform by GE provides predictive maintenance to industrial equipment. With processing at the edge and blockchain securing data exchange, high reliability and efficiency are assured in its operations.

- *Predictive maintenance:* GE's Predix makes use of IoT sensors to acquire data from industrial machinery such as turbines, generators, and manufacturing machines. The data streamed by these devices is first processed locally by edge computing for real-time monitoring and then for anomaly detection. Predictive algorithms run over this data to project potential failures and schedule maintenance before the issue happens, thus reducing downtime and maintenance costs.
- *Data security and integrity:* Blockchain technology is built into the Predix platform to ensure end-to-end security for transactions between the different components of an industrial ecosystem. All transactions involving data are recorded to a blockchain ledger for total traceability and tamper-proofing, building trust and security between two entities in a data exchange-a requirement quite critical to industrial operations.
- *Operational efficiency:* The decentralized architecture of Predix makes any data processing flexible and scalable. Enabling edge devices to carry out tasks of data processing allows the platform to process huge volumes of data. This scalability is critical in most industrial environments where data loads may vary up to extremes.
- *Wind turbines:* It has been said that monitoring and maintenance for wind turbines have already been put on the Predix platform by GE. IoT sensors take readings on the turbines for vibration, temperature, and wind speed. The information is then locally processed by edge computing nodes in order to support real-time analysis and trigger a line of action, if necessary, straightaway. Blockchain ensures security and verifiability of all data transactions, creating a secure basis for predictive maintenance and operational decisions.

These case studies on Barcelona's smart city initiative and the Predix platform from GE prove the very significant value that decentralized architectures bring to 5G-IoT. Tailored with edge computing and blockchain at its core, such implementations are more efficient, secure, and scalable. On the basis of this discussion, these real examples reveal the potential of decentralized IoT solutions in transforming a wide variety of industries, from city infrastructure management to industrial operations, into more resilient and intelligent systems.

Proper planning and execution are required for implementing any decentralized solution of IoT within the 5G framework. Following the best practices, leveraging the key technologies such as edge computing, blockchain, and AI, and strategic deployment approaches are only some of the ways to realize the full potential of decentralized IoT. Case studies from real life demonstrate the practical benefits and scalability of such solutions in different industries.

2.6.2 Performance evaluation and optimization

Evaluating and then optimizing the performance of decentralized IoT networks in a 5G environment is key to their efficiency, reliability, and scalability.

2.6.2.1 Metrics for assessing performance

1) *Latency*
   Latency refers to the time delay in a system; this is very critical in real-time IoT applications. Applications like autonomous driving and industrial automation require lower latency.
   Measurement: Latency measures the round-trip time taken by data to travel from the source to the destination and back. It is easily measured using tools such as ping tests and network analyzers.
2) *Throughput*
   Throughput is defined as the quantity of data a system is able to successfully transmit over a network in a given period. Applications that require huge transfers of data, such as video surveillance and data streaming, demand high throughput.
   Measurement: Throughput is typically measured in bits per second (bps) using tools like iperf and network simulators.
3) *Packet loss*
   Packet loss refers to a situation in whereby data packets are not received at their destination. High packet loss has very formidable effects on the QoE of IoT applications, more so in critical infrastructures.

Measurement: It is measured as the percentage of packets lost during transmission. This can be done by using network monitoring tools or protocols like ICMP.

4) *Energy efficiency*
Energy efficiency is fundamental to any IoT device, particularly the battery-powered ones. The efficient use of energy prolongs device life and reduces operational costs.
Measurement: Energy efficiency is expressed in terms of the energy consumed per operation or data unit. The tools and techniques include power profilers and energy monitoring frameworks, to mention but a few.

2.6.2.2 Optimization techniques and tools

There is a need for optimization of decentralized architectures to provide the performance, efficiency, and scalability to be able to function very relevantly in this fast-evolving landscape of 5G-IoT. In fact, the different optimization techniques and tools prove to be very important in the manipulation and sustenance of these networks under the increasing demands from these different applications. This paper takes a look at a number of important optimization strategies and tools, such as network optimization, edge computing optimization, and blockchain optimization.

Network optimization

1) *Dynamic resource allocation*
Dynamic resource allocation will be warranted by fluctuating demands on a 5G-IoT network. AI and ML algorithms can dynamically allocate resources in order to avoid bottleneck situations relating to network performance, where resources are consumed inefficiently.
In this respect, it would be possible to design ML models that will predict traffic trends and thereby help effectively manage bandwidth, computational power, and storage capacity provision from time to time for different network subsegments. Such elasticity will further reduce delays and optimize resource utilization, hence leading to a more efficiently running network and improved user experiences.
2) *Load balancing*
Load balancing is evenly distributing the network traffic among the nodes, not piling it at one node. 5G-IoT applies efficient load balancing in a decentralized architecture that avoids any component becoming a bottle neck and assures improved performance in the network.

Advanced load balancing algorithms, like AI-based ones, have the ability to achieve the appropriate traffic balance through self-adjustment in line with the real-time network condition and performance metrics. These mechanisms maintain an optimal network performance, minimizing latencies and enhancing fault tolerance.

Edge computing optimization

1) *Data offloading*

   Data offloading refers to the process of transferring data processing tasks from central servers to edge devices closer to the source of data. This has several advantages in terms of latency reduction and bandwidth saving by carrying out the processing locally. Effective data offloading, therefore, improves the performance of a network in a decentralized 5G-IoT environment.

   Data offloading ensures that only critical data is transmitted to the cloud for further processing, whereas on the other hand, regular or latency-sensitive routine tasks can be handled at the edge. In this regard, partitioning will require intelligent decision-making algorithms to decide which tasks to offload and when.

2) *Caching strategies*

   Caching regularly accessed data closer to the edge node is another key optimization technique. Accordingly, data locally cached after being frequently accessed will spare the necessity of many repeated transmissions of the same data between the edge devices and the central server, leading to a characteristic reduction in response time and network load.

   Advanced caching strategies, such as the least recently used or most frequently used algorithms, may be applied in the efficient management of the cache. The strategies ensure that the cache is put to good use by storing relevant data that is frequently accessed to maximize the attainment of high performance from it.

Blockchain optimization

1) *Efficient consensus mechanisms*

   Blockchain technology will provide robust security and integrity to the data of 5G-IoT. Traditional consensus mechanisms of this technology may be viewed as resource-hungry. So, resource-efficient consensus mechanisms like PoS or delegated PoS will lower the computational overhead and energy consumption.

   In contrast to PoW, both PoS and DPoS have only extremely, almost negligible computation quantities. So, they are purely suitable for every single resource-limited IoT environment. The mechanism provides faster transaction processing times-an aspect viewed as important in maintaining the performance of any decentralized IoT network.

2) *Scalability solutions*

   The major challenge faced by blockchain networks, particularly in large IoT environments, is one of scalability. Some techniques would make blockchain systems highly scalable: sharding and off-chain transactions. Sharding is the process of dividing a blockchain into smaller pieces, known as shards, which are able to process individual transactions. This develops high throughput in blockchain. Off-chain transactions allow some transactions to be processed outside the main blockchain, hence reducing load from the main chain and thus allowing improvement in scalability.

2.6.2.3 Continuous improvement strategies

Continuous improvement strategies in decentralized 5G-IoT networks are very vital with respect to performance, security, and efficiency. These strategies involve periodic monitoring and regular audits with the implementation of mechanisms that allow feedback to accommodate dynamic changes in conditions and emerging challenges.

Monitoring and analytics

1) *Real-time monitoring*

   A real-time monitoring system is important for tracking the performance and health of any decentralized IoT network. The system offers ongoing insights about the operations of the network, thereby aiding in the timely identification and resolution of issues.

   They can gather such data related to different performance metrics, whether latency, throughput, or error rates, by deploying sensors and monitoring tools across the network. Real-time visualization through dashboards and alerting mechanisms puts operators in a position to act promptly on anomalies. For instance, if latency suddenly surges, it can automatically trigger diagnostic checks to find the root cause and automatically execute a correction measure.

2) *Data analytics*

   Big data analytics helps decentralized IoT networks to get optimized. A huge amount of data, from a number of IoT devices, can be analyzed by operators in a search for discovering trends, patterns, and insights that will answer questions and inform decisions in the making.

Advanced analytics techniques in network monitoring use ML and AI to predict network performance issues, optimize resource allocation, and enhance security. For instance, predictive analytics can be used to estimate network congestion; through its suggested action, mitigations can be proposed in advance. Similarly, anomaly detection algorithms can identify abnormal patterns in network traffic that may indicate security threats.

Regular audits and updates

1) *Security audits*
   Regular security audits have to be an essential step toward the integrity and trustworthiness of a decentralized IoT network. Security audits are done by assessing all the measures of security of the network, which shall include access controls, encryption protocols, and configuration settings, among others.
   Audit refers to the detection of vulnerabilities or failure to comply with the stipulated standards and regulations within the industry. For example, audits highlight weaknesses in the authentication mechanism for devices or even detect firmware that has become obsolete and must be updated. This will help in mitigating the detected vulnerabilities to ensure that operators are not exposed to security threats that could lead to data breaches.
2) *Software updates*
   Designing a robust update mechanism will be critical to guarantee that IoT devices and network elements are running the most up-to-date software versions. Due to regular software updates, one can facilitate fixing security vulnerabilities, improve performance, and extend functionality. It is possible to have automated update systems that ensure the deployment of updates across the network does not interfere with other operations on it. For example, edge devices can be instructed to download and install updates during off-peak hours to minimize impact on the operations of a network. Moreover, version control mechanisms can help manage the deployment of updates and roll back changes in case of necessity.

Feedback mechanisms

1) *User feedback*
   Setting up channels through which users are able to respond with feedback on the performance and issues of a network is important for

continuous improvement. Informed user feedback could give insight into real experiences and show where improvements should be made.
Feedback mechanisms include surveys, support tickets, or other means for direct communication. The system can isolate problems, enhance service, and improve user satisfaction by actively eliciting and acting on user feedback. For example, due to the fact that many users reported connectivity issues at certain spots, targeted optimization to enhance coverage and performance can be carried out in those areas based on the feedback.

2) *Automated feedback loops*
It is through automated feedback loops that AI analyzes performance data and dynamically adjusts network configuration, allowing the network to dynamically react to changing conditions.
For example, AI-driven feedback loops could monitor network traffic and self-update routing protocols to load-balance and reduce congestion. Similarly, ML algorithms could analyze security data and update firewall rules against emerging threats. By employing automated feedback mechanisms, therefore, a decentralized IoT network can achieve higher levels of efficiency, resiliency, and security.

2.6.3 Example: Designing a decentralized network architecture for smart city traffic management

Here is a simple outline of the step-by-step procedure to be followed to Design a Decentralized Network for Smart City Traffic Management (as mentioned in Figure 2.6)

Step 1: Identify the problem- traffic congestion
High congestion, long commute times, pollution, accidents.

Step 2: Edge device deployment
Install sensors and cameras at intersections to monitor traffic.

Step 3: Local data processing
Edge devices process data locally and detect traffic patterns and anomalies.

Step 4: Real-time decision making
Adjust traffic signal timings based on local data to reduce congestion.

Step 5: Fog computing layer
Deploy fog nodes to handle more complex processing tasks and aggregate data from multiple intersections.

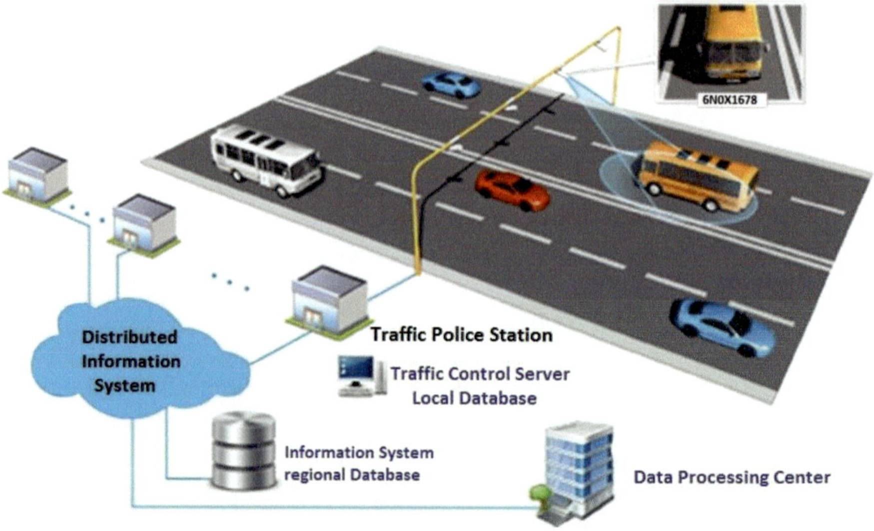

Figure 2.6 Intelligent traffic management system [83].

Step 6: Inter-device communication

Inter-device communication for the smart coordination of traffic flow at any intersection.

Step 7: Periodic central cloud updates

Summarize and send data to the central cloud for long-term analytics and optimization.

Step 8: Blockchain for security

Assure the integrity of data and secure transactions with blockchain technology.

Step 9: Smart contracts

Automate the rules of traffic management with smart contracts based on real-time data.

Step 10: Results

Reduced congestion and improved traffic flow, scalable and reliable system.

2.6.4 Summary and outlook

As decentralized architectures are being integrated into developing 5G-IoT ecosystems, it becomes relevant to reflect on some of the learned lessons, appreciate challenges not yet solved, and anticipate the scenery of these technologies in the future.

2.6.4.1 Summary of key insights

Efficiency and scalability

The decentralized architectures of IoT networks have a higher efficiency and scalability, especially when combined with edge computing. Processing data closer to the source results in reduced latency and network congestion. This happens more frequently in the case of 5G-IoT ecosystems because real-time processing of data is something of importance. Computational tasks are distributed through nodes at the edge of a network, offloading central servers that process data faster and make decisions. For example, in smart cities, traffic control systems can be more effectively managed by processing at the edge, analyzing real-time data from sensors and cameras, and adjusting immediately on the traffic signals.

Inherent in decentralized architectures is a modular design with dynamic resource allocation that enables the seamless scaling of these networks. For cases of a growing number of connected devices and applications, the network will scale by dynamically allocating resources where necessary without the need to overhaul the current infrastructure. This has been highly critical to accommodate the extremely fast-rising rollout of IoT devices in the near future. Using containerization and microservices, it becomes possible for a decentralized architecture to deploy and manage applications flexibly and scalably.

Security and privacy

Blockchain technology offers a robust framework for securing decentralized IoT networks. Further, blockchain technology provides data integrity, transparency, tamper-evidence, and cryptographic mechanisms owing to its decentralized nature. Every transaction or addition to data in a blockchain is validated against a network of nodes; hence, modification by malicious attackers is next to impossible. In fact, this level of security is a requirement in sensitive IoT applications such as devices dealing with healthcare equipment and financial transactions.

The second role is the magnification of security multifold with the use of AI and ML algorithms, thus detecting and mitigating threats in real time. They can analyze large data to identify patterns that show a potential breach in security. For example, anomaly detection algorithms will be able to trace unusual behavior in network traffic. For example, suddenly spiking data flow could turn out to be an indicator of a cyberattack. As AI and ML work before threats have actually manifested, that makes the IoT infrastructure more resilient and secure.

Real-world applications

Successful implementations demonstrate the practical benefits of decentralized IoT solutions in various sectors. For example, Barcelona's smart city initiative has used a decentralized IoT architecture in improving the management of urban infrastructure through the management of smart lighting, waste, traffic control, and environmental monitoring. Such applications improved operational efficiency, resource management, and service delivery.

An example relevant in the industrial sector would be that of the Predix platform by General Electric. Through edge computing and blockchain technology, Predix provides predictive maintenance and operational efficiency for industrial equipment. This way, Predix optimizes industrial operations through the reduction of downtowns, the reduction in maintenance costs, and the improvement in overall productivity.

2.6.4.2 Ongoing challenges

Interoperability

Interoperability of different IoT devices and platforms is a major challenge. An IoT includes various devices from different manufacturers, with their own protocols and standards of communication. This huge diversity may raise incompatibility issues that would act as barriers for integration and flawless working of the decentralized IoT networks. In this regard, standardization processes are very important to solve such problems and make devices communicate and work with each other seamlessly.

This will require collaborative efforts by stakeholders in the industry, regulatory bodies, and research institutions to develop and adopt common standards. Standards defining protocols of data exchange, security measures, and interoperability frameworks should be created. For instance, the development of the IEEE 2413 standard for an Architectural Framework for IoT is intended to provide a uniform approach for attaining IoT interoperability.

Resource constraints

IoT devices are normally subject to severe resource constraints, where processing power, memory, and energy might be limited. Optimizing decentralized architectures in order to work efficiently within these constraints is key to performance and reliability. Lightweight algorithms and protocols that minimize resource consumption while ensuring high performance are therefore needed. For example, energy-efficient communication protocols can be developed to prolong the battery life of IoT devices and reduce the frequency of recharging or replacing the batteries.

Another area that can somehow alleviate these constraints is research in resource-efficient computing techniques, like edge and fog computing. Edge and fog computing methods distribute computation across a network of devices, balancing the load and thus not putting too much burden on any single device. This distribution can improve overall network performance and prolong the lifetime of IoT devices.

Scalability of blockchain

Although blockchain provides high security, scalability is still an issue, especially for a very large-scale IoT network. Traditional consensus mechanisms, such as PoW, are resource-intensive. Much greater computational resources and longer time to arrive at a consensus are required. This may further degrade the performance of IoT networks, which have to process enormous amounts of data speedily.

Other off-chain solutions are state channels and sidechains. This may even decrease the load of the blockchain since both will operate off the chain, processing transactions there and recording only the end state on the blockchain.

2.6.4.3 Future prospects and vision

Advanced AI integration

Decentralized IoT architectures offer an interactive solution for complex AI and integration to realize the potential of advanced AI techniques for automation, predictive analytics, and autonomous decision-making. Real-time data processing and decision-making at source, carried out on AI models that can execute effectively at edge devices, is a key functionality. It is particularly significant in real-time applications such as autonomous devices and smart grids, among others.

Future research should steer toward the development of intelligent algorithms optimized for edge computing environments, featuring lightweight yet powerful algorithms to support even demanding applications like image recognition and NLP. In addition, AI can be used for intelligent, dynamic resource management and prediction of security threats to further enhance the resilience and efficiency of IoT. For example, AI can predict the occurrence of network congestion and automatically make adjustments in resource allocation to ensure continued service at the optimal level without interruptions.

Quantum computing

Quantum computing can change the face of decentralized IoT architectures. The quantum algorithms allow a large improvement in the speed of operation and efficiency in the performance of exceedingly complex recipes of the suggested problems: encryption, protocol management, and data analysis. Stated in this manner: quantum computing could improve the performance of the IoT networks through faster processing of data and better control over resources.

Research in quantum-resistant blockchain, along with quantum-enabled AI, will lead to more secure and efficient IoT networks. In addition, with quantum-resistant blockchain algorithms being placed in the space of protection against quantum computer attacks, long-term security is further justified for IoT systems using blockchain. On the other hand, the role of quantum-enabled AI is more justified since it is able to process and analyze big volumes of data, giving real-time insights and decision-making.

Sustainability

The issue of sustainability increases as the number of IoT devices multiplies. Future developments should implement energy-efficient designs and make the IoT network depend on renewable power sources. In that sense, such IoT devices themselves can provide the requisite abatement of overall energy use, with regard to these minimal consumer devices, and solar and wind power may provide sustainable power solutions.

It only makes the deployment of the IoT less hazardous to the environment, which itself contributes toward the sustainability goals of the IoT. For example, low-power communication protocols and energy-harvesting technologies will raise the lifetime of IoT devices, thus decreasing the need to frequently replace them with new batteries. Sustainable practices and technologies are used in a way that ensures the scalability and efficiency of IoT deployment without causing negative impacts on the environment.

2.7 Conclusion

In conclusion, decentralized architecture for 5G-IoT represents a pivotal shift in the way next-generation IoT applications will operate, in terms of their speeds, efficiency, and intelligence levels. The integration of distributed computing, edge processing, AI, and blockchain technologies can change the methods of current data management and processing in real time, corresponding to the requirements of modern applications such as autonomous vehicles, smart cities, healthcare systems, and industrial automation.

It reduces latency significantly, even while maintaining security and privacy, because computation is brought closer to the sources of data. It is very critical in most applications where there is the element of real-time decision-making. Blockchain introduces a decentralized layer of trust, ensuring the integrity and immutability of the data while enhancing the security of the IoT networks through its inherent tamper resistance. In terms of the smart-contract automaton, AI-driven edge-of-network data analytics is the resource that empowers adaptive yet intelligent IoT ecosystems.

However, all these advancements still face challenges. Heterogeneity in IoT devices presents a cumbersome problem to solve toward achieving heterogeneous system interoperability among diverse networks and systems. Energy efficiency is another challenge that is a concern since most resource-constrained edge nodes must balance some processing capabilities with their battery life. Finally, network orchestration needs growth to keep track of the management of these complex distributed networks, where seamless coordination is expected between the central cloud, edge nodes, and IoT devices.

The utilization of this decentralized architecture to its full potential will purely depend on constant research and development into areas such as federated learning, scalability of blockchain, AI optimization for edge devices, and secure communication protocols. The convergence of the technologies promises not only to treat the limitations that are currently found within IoT infrastructure but rather open new doors toward innovation of quite a number of sectors.

Ultimately, as these challenges are resolved, the 5G-IoT distributed architecture will emerge as a cornerstone of future ecosystems, enabling a new era of connected, intelligent systems that can scale efficiently, respond rapidly to real-time data, and operate securely across a decentralized framework. That would be one significant leap toward an integrated, smarter world in which IoT devices will not only be interconnected but also function autonomously in a secure and distributed manner.

References

[1] M. Agiwal, A. Roy, and N. Saxena, "Next generation 5g wireless networks: A comprehensive survey," *IEEE communications surveys & tutorials*, vol. 18, no. 3, pp. 1617–1655, 2016.

[2] A. Osseiran, F. Boccardi, V. Braun, K. Kusume, P. Marsch, M. Maternia, O. Queseth, M. Schellmann, H. Schotten, H. Taoka, *et al.*, "Scenarios for 5g mobile and wireless communications: the vision of the metis project," *IEEE communications magazine*, vol. 52, no. 5, pp. 26–35, 2014.

[3] L. Da Xu, W. He, and S. Li, "Internet of things in industries: A survey," *IEEE Transactions on industrial informatics*, vol. 10, no. 4, pp. 2233–2243, 2014.

[4] P. R. Gunjal, S. R. Jondhale, J. L. Mauri, and K. Agrawal, *Internet of things: Theory to practice.* CRC Press, 2024.

[5] Cisco, "Annual internet report (2018âĂŞ2023)," 2020.

[6] A. Brecko, E. KajÃąti, J. Koziorek, and I. ZolotovÃą, "Federated learning for edge computing: A survey," *Applied Sciences*, vol. 12, p. 9124, 09 2022.

[7] T. Alghamdi, R. Khalid, and N. Javaid, "A survey of blockchain based systems: Scalability issues and solutions, applications and future challenges," *IEEE Access*, 05 2024.

[8] T. Aste, P. Tasca, and T. Di Matteo, "Blockchain technologies: The foreseeable impact on society and industry," *computer*, vol. 50, no. 9, pp. 18–28, 2017.

[9] B. Lashkari and P. Musilek, "A comprehensive review of blockchain consensus mechanisms," *IEEE access*, vol. 9, pp. 43620–43652, 2021.

[10] K. Christidis and M. Devetsikiotis, "Blockchains and smart contracts for the internet of things," *IEEE access*, vol. 4, pp. 2292–2303, 2016.

[11] W. Shi, J. Cao, Q. Zhang, Y. Li, and L. Xu, "Edge computing: Vision and challenges," *IEEE internet of things journal*, vol. 3, no. 5, pp. 637–646, 2016.

[12] F. Bonomi, R. Milito, J. Zhu, and S. Addepalli, "Fog computing and its role in the internet of things," in *Proceedings of the first edition of the MCC workshop on Mobile cloud computing*, pp. 13–16, 2012.

[13] M. Satyanarayanan, "The emergence of edge computing," *Computer*, vol. 50, no. 1, pp. 30–39, 2017.

[14] R. Roman, J. Lopez, and M. Mambo, "Mobile edge computing, fog et al.: A survey and analysis of security threats and challenges," *Future Generation Computer Systems*, vol. 78, pp. 680–698, 2018.

[15] S. Kulkarni, J. Dwivedi, D. Pramanta, and Y. Tanaka, *Edge Computational Intelligence for AI-Enabled IoT Systems.* CRC Press, 2024.

[16] S. Nakamoto, "Bitcoin: A peer-to-peer electronic cash system," *Bitcoin.–URL: https://bitcoin. org/bitcoin. pdf*, vol. 4, no. 2, p. 15, 2008.

[17] F. Tian, "An agri-food supply chain traceability system for china based on rfid & blockchain technology," in *2016 13th international conference on service systems and service management (ICSSSM)*, pp. 1–6, IEEE, 2016.

[18] H. Fintech, "How to design a blockchain application architecture," 2024.

[19] M. A. Khan and K. Salah, "Iot security: Review, blockchain solutions, and open challenges," *Future generation computer systems*, vol. 82, pp. 395–411, 2018.

[20] S. King and S. Nadal, "Ppcoin: Peer-to-peer crypto-currency with proof-of-stake," *self-published paper, August*, vol. 19, no. 1, 2012.

[21] S. De Angelis, L. Aniello, R. Baldoni, F. Lombardi, A. Margheri, V. Sassone, *et al.*, "Pbft vs proof-of-authority: Applying the cap theorem to permissioned blockchain," in *CEUR workshop proceedings*, vol. 2058, CEUR-WS, 2018.

[22] L. Lamport, R. Shostak, and M. Pease, "The byzantine generals problem," in *Concurrency: the works of leslie lamport*, pp. 203–226, unknown, 2019.

[23] M. Castro, B. Liskov, *et al.*, "Practical byzantine fault tolerance," in *OsDI*, vol. 99, pp. 173–186, 1999.

[24] M. Castro, "Practical byzantine fault tolerance," *unknown*, 04 2001.

[25] S. Popov, "The tangle," *White paper*, vol. 1, no. 3, p. 30, 2018.

[26] A. Dorri, N. Moustafa, W. Bahga, and D. Gupta, "Blockchain for iot security and privacy: A survey," *IEEE Transactions on Engineering Management*, vol. 64, no. 3, pp. 818–833, 2017.

[27] M. Castro and B. Liskov, "Practical byzantine fault tolerance and proactive recovery," *ACM Transactions on Computer Systems (TOCS)*, vol. 20, no. 4, pp. 398–461, 2002.

[28] D. Malkhi, M. Merritt, M. K. Reiter, and G. Taubenfeld, "Objects shared by byzantine processes," *Distributed Computing*, vol. 16, pp. 37–48, 2003.

[29] M. Nasreen, A. Ganesh, and S. C, "A study on byzantine fault tolerance methods in distributed networks," *Procedia Computer Science*, vol. 87, pp. 50–54, 12 2016.

[30] W. Zhong, C. Yang, W. Liang, J. Cai, L. Chen, J. Liao, and N. Xiong, "Byzantine fault-tolerant consensus algorithms: A survey," *Electronics*, vol. 12, no. 18, p. 3801, 2023.

[31] V. Buterin *et al.*, "A next-generation smart contract and decentralized application platform," *white paper*, vol. 3, no. 37, pp. 2–1, 2014.

[32] A. Azaria, A. Ekblaw, T. Vieira, and A. Lippman, "Medrec: Using blockchain for medical data access and permission management," in *2016 2nd international conference on open and big data (OBD)*, pp. 25–30, IEEE, 2016.

[33] M. Andoni, V. Robu, D. Flynn, S. Abram, D. Geach, D. Jenkins, P. McCallum, and A. Peacock, "Blockchain technology in the energy sector: A systematic review of challenges and opportunities," *Renewable and sustainable energy reviews*, vol. 100, pp. 143–174, 2019.

[34] K. Biswas and V. Muthukkumarasamy, "Securing smart cities using blockchain technology," in *2016 IEEE 18th international conference on high performance computing and communications; IEEE 14th international conference on smart city; IEEE 2nd international conference on data science and systems (HPCC/SmartCity/DSS)*, pp. 1392–1393, IEEE, 2016.

[35] FasterCapital, "Getting started with blockchain: An overview," 2024.

[36] S. J. Russell and P. Norvig, *Artificial intelligence: a modern approach*. Pearson, 2016.

[37] A. Banafa, *Introduction to Artificial Intelligence (AI)*. CRC Press, 2024.

[38] I. Goodfellow, Y. Bengio, and A. Courville, *Deep learning*. MIT press, 2016.

[39] R. Kurzweil, "The singularity if near: When humans transcend biology," 2005.

[40] B. Nick, "Superintelligence: Paths, dangers, strategies," *unknown*, 2014.

[41] T. M. Mitchell and T. M. Mitchell, *Machine learning*, vol. 1. McGraw-hill New York, 1997.

[42] T. Hastie, R. Tibshirani, J. H. Friedman, and J. H. Friedman, *The elements of statistical learning: data mining, inference, and prediction*, vol. 2. Springer, 2009.

[43] R. S. Sutton and A. G. Barto, *Reinforcement learning: An introduction*. MIT press, 2018.

[44] Y. LeCun, Y. Bengio, and G. Hinton, "Deep learning," *nature*, vol. 521, no. 7553, pp. 436–444, 2015.

[45] Z. Cai, S. Si, Y. Liu, and J. Zhao, "Maintenance optimization of continuous state systems based on performance improvement," *IEEE Transactions on Reliability*, vol. 67, no. 2, pp. 651–665, 2017.
[46] S. Gupta, "Deep learning based human activity recognition (har) using wearable sensor data," *International Journal of Information Management Data Insights*, vol. 1, no. 2, p. 100046, 2021.
[47] Z. C. Lipton, D. C. Kale, C. Elkan, and R. Wetzel, "Learning to diagnose with lstm recurrent neural networks," *arXiv preprint arXiv:1511.03677*, 2015.
[48] T. Wei, Y. Wang, and Q. Zhu, "Deep reinforcement learning for building hvac control," in *Proceedings of the 54th annual design automation conference 2017*, pp. 1–6, 2017.
[49] T. Young, D. Hazarika, S. Poria, and E. Cambria, "Recent trends in deep learning based natural language processing," *ieee Computational intelligenCe magazine*, vol. 13, no. 3, pp. 55–75, 2018.
[50] L. Cui, G. Xie, Y. Qu, L. Gao, and Y. Yang, "Security and privacy in smart cities: Challenges and opportunities," *IEEE access*, vol. 6, pp. 46134–46145, 2018.
[51] R. Y. Zhong, X. Xu, E. Klotz, and S. T. Newman, "Intelligent manufacturing in the context of industry 4.0: a review," *Engineering*, vol. 3, no. 5, pp. 616–630, 2017.
[52] S. Tuli, R. Mahmud, S. Tuli, and R. Buyya, "Fogbus: A blockchain-based lightweight framework for edge and fog computing," *Journal of Systems and Software*, vol. 154, pp. 22–36, 2019.
[53] Q. Yang, Y. Liu, T. Chen, and Y. Tong, "Federated machine learning: Concept and applications," *ACM Transactions on Intelligent Systems and Technology (TIST)*, vol. 10, no. 2, pp. 1–19, 2019.
[54] I. F. Akyildiz, P. Wang, and S.-C. Lin, "Softair: A software defined networking architecture for 5g wireless systems," *Computer Networks*, vol. 85, pp. 1–18, 2015.
[55] D. Bandyopadhyay and J. Sen, "Internet of things: Applications and challenges in technology and standardization," *Wireless personal communications*, vol. 58, pp. 49–69, 2011.
[56] A. Zanella, N. Bui, A. Castellani, L. Vangelista, and M. Zorzi, "Internet of things for smart cities," *IEEE Internet of Things journal*, vol. 1, no. 1, pp. 22–32, 2014.
[57] S. Wang, X. Zhang, Y. Zhang, L. Wang, J. Yang, and W. Wang, "A survey on mobile edge networks: Convergence of computing, caching and communications," *Ieee Access*, vol. 5, pp. 6757–6779, 2017.

[58] S. Sicari, A. Rizzardi, L. A. Grieco, and A. Coen-Porisini, "Security, privacy and trust in internet of things: The road ahead," *Computer networks*, vol. 76, pp. 146–164, 2015.

[59] M. A. Razzaq, S. H. Gill, M. A. Qureshi, and S. Ullah, "Security issues in the internet of things (iot): A comprehensive study," *International Journal of Advanced Computer Science and Applications*, vol. 8, no. 6, p. 383, 2017.

[60] U. Raza, P. Kulkarni, and M. Sooriyabandara, "Low power wide area networks: An overview," *ieee communications surveys & tutorials*, vol. 19, no. 2, pp. 855–873, 2017.

[61] F. Muhammad, W. Anjum, and K. S. Mazhar, "A critical analysis on the security concerns of internet of things (iot)," *International Journal of Computer Applications*, vol. 111, no. 7, pp. 1–6, 2015.

[62] Z. Ning, J. Huang, X. Wang, J. J. Rodrigues, and L. Guo, "Mobile edge computing-enabled internet of vehicles: Toward energy-efficient scheduling," *IEEE Network*, vol. 33, no. 5, pp. 198–205, 2019.

[63] A. Reyna, C. Martín, J. Chen, E. Soler, and M. Díaz, "On blockchain and its integration with iot. challenges and opportunities," *Future generation computer systems*, vol. 88, pp. 173–190, 2018.

[64] C. Insights, "What is a smart city?," 2024.

[65] ResearchGate, "A decentralized privacy-preserving healthcare blockchain for iot - remote patient monitoring," 2019.

[66] A. K. Rana, V. Sharma, A. Rana, M. Alam, and S. L. Tripathi, *Convergence of Blockchain and Internet of Things in Healthcare*. CRC Press, 2024.

[67] M. Hassanalieragh, A. Page, T. Soyata, G. Sharma, M. Aktas, G. Mateos, B. Kantarci, and S. Andreescu, "Health monitoring and management using internet-of-things (iot) sensing with cloud-based processing: Opportunities and challenges," in *2015 IEEE international conference on services computing*, pp. 285–292, IEEE, 2015.

[68] M. Aazam, S. Zeadally, and K. A. Harras, "Deploying fog computing in industrial internet of things and industry 4.0," *IEEE Transactions on Industrial Informatics*, vol. 14, pp. 4674–4682, Oct. 2018.

[69] V. Gazis, M. Görtz, M. Huber, A. Leonardi, K. Mathioudakis, A. Wiesmaier, F. Zeiger, and E. Vasilomanolakis, "A survey of technologies for the internet of things," in *2015 international wireless communications and mobile computing conference (IWCMC)*, pp. 1090–1095, IEEE, 2015.

[70] M. A. Nielsen and I. L. Chuang, *Quantum computation and quantum information*. Cambridge university press, 2010.
[71] P. W. Shor, "Algorithms for quantum computation: discrete logarithms and factoring," in *Proceedings 35th annual symposium on foundations of computer science*, pp. 124–134, Ieee, 1994.
[72] C. H. Bennett and G. Brassard, "An update on quantum cryptography," in *Workshop on the theory and application of cryptographic techniques*, pp. 475–480, Springer, 1984.
[73] J. Kaur, T. Pathak, A. Singh, and K. Kumar, "Application of nanotechnology in the environment biotechnology," *Advances in Environmental Biotechnology*, pp. 155–165, 2017.
[74] J. A. Paradiso and T. Starner, "Energy scavenging for mobile and wireless electronics," *IEEE Pervasive computing*, vol. 4, no. 1, pp. 18–27, 2005.
[75] K. Srivastava, A. K. Singh, and G. M. Hegde, "Multi modal semantic segmentation using synthetic data," *arXiv preprint arXiv:1910.13676*, 2019.
[76] F. M. Ramos, D. Kreutz, and P. Verissimo, "Software-defined networks: On the road to the softwarization of networking," *Cutter IT journal*, 2015.
[77] R. Mijumbi, S. Hasija, S. Davy, A. Davy, B. Jennings, and R. Boutaba, "A connectionist approach to dynamic resource management for virtualised network functions," in *2016 12th International conference on network and service management (CNSM)*, pp. 1–9, IEEE, 2016.
[78] S. Pirandola, "Limits and security of free-space quantum communications," *Physical Review Research*, vol. 3, no. 1, p. 013279, 2021.
[79] J. R. Piorno, C. Bergonzini, D. Atienza, and T. S. Rosing, "Prediction and management in energy harvested wireless sensor nodes," in *2009 1st International Conference on Wireless Communication, Vehicular Technology, Information Theory and Aerospace & Electronic Systems Technology*, pp. 6–10, IEEE, 2009.
[80] X. Foukas, M. K. Marina, and K. Kontovasilis, "Orion: Ran slicing for a flexible and cost-effective multi-service mobile network architecture," in *Proceedings of the 23rd annual international conference on mobile computing and networking*, pp. 127–140, 2017.
[81] P. Voigt and A. Von dem Bussche, "The eu general data protection regulation (gdpr)," *A Practical Guide, 1st Ed., Cham: Springer International Publishing*, vol. 10, no. 3152676, pp. 10–5555, 2017.

[82] F. Doshi-Velez and B. Kim, "Towards a rigorous science of interpretable machine learning," *arXiv preprint arXiv:1702.08608*, 2017.
[83] D. Gade, "Technology trends and digital solutions for smart cities development," 03 2019.
[84] M. Mao, S. Yi, Q. Li, and M. Tao, "Fog computing: Vision and research directions," *IEEE Internet of Things Journal*, vol. 3, pp. 637–646, Oct. 2017.
[85] S. Rani and A. Taneja, *WSN and IoT: An Integrated Approach for Smart Applications*. CRC Press, 2024.
[86] Geneca, "Transition: Pow to pos for dnotes cryptocurrency," 2024.
[87] C. Daah, A. Qureshi, I. Awan, and S. Konur, "Enhancing zero trust models in the financial industry through blockchain integration: A proposed framework," *Electronics*, vol. 13, no. 5, p. 865, 2024.

3

Integrating Blockchain and IoT Opportunities, Challenges, and Applications

N Rajkumar[1], C Viji[1], Balusamy Nachiappan[2], A Mohanraj[3], N Karthikeyan[4], and Judeson Antony Kovilpillai J[1]

[1]School of Advanced Computing, Alliance University, India
[2]Department of Information Technology, Prologis, United States
[3]Department of Computer Science and Engineering, Sri Eshwar College of Engineering, India
[4]Computer Science and Engineering, Vellore Institute of Technology, India
Email: nrajkumar84@gmail.com; vijisvs2012@gmail.com; pnbalu@gmail.com; mohanckpc@gmail.com; narenkarthikeyanmecse@gmail.com; jkovilpillai@blr.amity.edu

Abstract

The integration of blockchain technology and the Internet of Things (IoT) has the potential to revolutionize numerous industries by improving safety, transparency, and performance. This chapter explores the opportunities, challenges, and real-world programs of mixing these two transformative generations. The essential elements of opportunities include appropriate safety through fact integrity and robust authentication, superior transparency and traceability in delivery chains, decentralized systems decreasing unmarried elements of failure, and automated techniques through clever contracts. However, enormously annoying situations need to be addressed, collectively with scalability issues associated with the excessive statistics extent and transaction pace, strength intake problems, complexity and interoperability hurdles, and protection vulnerabilities of IoT devices. Actual global applications are tested in sectors that include supply chain control, healthcare, clever cities, and agriculture, showcasing how blockchain and IoT integration can cause

DOI: 10.1201/9788743809050-4

more green, apparent, and at-ease structures. By leveraging the strengths of both eras, groups can drive innovation and operational excellence, paving the way for a related and honest virtual future.

Keywords: Blockchain, Internet of Things, cryptocurrency, decentralized, security

3.1 Introduction

The convergence of blockchain technology and the Internet of Things (IoT) represents an enormous development within the virtual transformation panorama, promising to reshape numerous industries through enhancing protection, transparency, and operational efficiency. Blockchain, diagnosed for its decentralized, immutable ledger, offers sturdy solutions for secure and obvious fact control. IoT, with its widespread network of interconnected devices, allows actual-time data series and automation. The combination of those technologies is poised to address critical worrying conditions and unencumber new possibilities, basically reworking how groups and industries are characterized.

3.1.1 Blockchain technology

A blockchain is a disbursed database or ledger shared amongst a remotely related node. They will be fine and recounted for vital characteristics in cryptocurrency systems for keeping a reduced and decentralized record of transactions; however, they will no longer be restrained to what cryptocurrency uses [2, 11, 18]. Blockchains may be used to make records in any business enterprise immutable. The period is used to explain the incapacity to be altered. Due to the fact that there may be no way to change a block, the most effective consideration wanted is on the aspect in which a purchaser or software enters information. This thing reduces the want to rely on 1/3 activities, which might be typically auditors or wonderful human beings who upload costs and make mistakes. When you do not forget that Bitcoin's creation in 2009 [1, 4, 5, 8–10], blockchain makes use of has exploded through the creation of numerous cryptocurrencies, decentralized finance (DeFi) applications, non-fungible tokens (NFTs), and clever contracts. It offers a comfortable and decentralized technique for recording transactions and dealing with information, making sure that facts are obvious and tamper-proof. This technology's inherent characteristics of immutability, transparency, and decentralization make it a first-rate candidate for addressing most of the disturbing situations confronted through IoT structures, which encompass protection vulnerabilities, data integrity, and the need for a dependable consensus mechanism.

3.1.2 Key elements of a blockchain

- *Distributed ledger technology*
  All community-related nodes must get admission to the allotted ledger and its immutable document of transactions. With this shared ledger, transactions are recorded as soon as possible, putting off the duplication of strive that is common to traditional commercial organization networks.
- *Immutable records*
  No contributor can trade or tamper with a transaction after it has been recorded within the shared ledger. If a transaction file consists of an error, a brand-new transaction is needed to correct the mistake, and each transaction is then visible.
- *Smart contracts*
  To speed up transactions, hard and fast policies, which might be called a clever settlement, are stored on the blockchain and run routinely. A smart settlement defines conditions for company bond transfers, consisting of phrases for journey coverage to be paid and lots on extra [3, 13, 43, 45].

3.1.3 How blockchain works

Figure 3.1 shows the detailed working of the blockchain along with its components. The details description of each components is as follows.

- *Decentralization*
  The blockchain era is decentralized, which means it operates on a community of laptop structures (nodes) that unfold throughout awesome places around, relying on a crucial server. Each node contains a duplicate of the blockchain, it is the entire facts of all transactions that have ever taken the vicinity in the community.
- *Allotted ledger generation (DLT)*
  A blockchain is a type of allotted ledger. This ledger is shared across all nodes within the community, and every node has an identical replica. Even as an ultra-modern transaction happens, it is far broadcast to all nodes, which then update their ledgers to mirror this transaction.
- *Transactions and blocks*
  Transactions are the number one gadgets of interest in the blockchain. Whilst someone initiates a transaction, it is miles grouped with other

transactions right into a block. Every block includes a list of transactions, a timestamp, and a reference (hash) to the preceding block within the chain.

- *Cryptographic hashing*
  A cryptographic hash is a feature that converts an enter (or "message") into a fixed-period string of bytes. The output is specific to each entry. Every block in the blockchain includes the hash of the previous block, developing a series of blocks that can be cryptographically linked. This guarantees that when a block is delivered to the chain, it cannot be altered without changing all the next blocks, which might require consensus from the community.
- *Consensus mechanisms*
  To characterize a modern-day block to the blockchain, the community has to attain consensus on its validity. This is finished via consensus mechanisms. Two common consensus mechanisms are:

  Proof of work (PoW): Nodes (miners) compete to treat a complicated mathematical problem. The number one treatment it gets to feature the new block on the blockchain and is rewarded with cryptocurrency. This method is computationally extensive and requires notable strength.

  Proof of stake (PoS): Nodes (validators) are selected to add a block primarily based on the huge form of tokens they maintain and are willing to "stake" as collateral. This approach is extra strength-green in comparison to PoW.
- *Block introduction and validation*
  As soon as a node creates a state-of-the-art block (by solving the PoW puzzle or being selected in PoS), it announces the block to the whole community. Exclusive nodes validate the block to ensure the transactions are valid and the block adheres to the community's rules. If the block is deemed legitimate, it is delivered to the blockchain, and all nodes update their copies of the ledger.
- *Immutability*
  One of the key capabilities of blockchain is its immutability. Once a block is added to the blockchain, it is extraordinarily difficult to alter. That is because the truth converting a block would require converting all next blocks, which might require gaining control over a majority of the network's computational energy (in PoW) or staked tokens (in PoS), making it nearly now not viable.

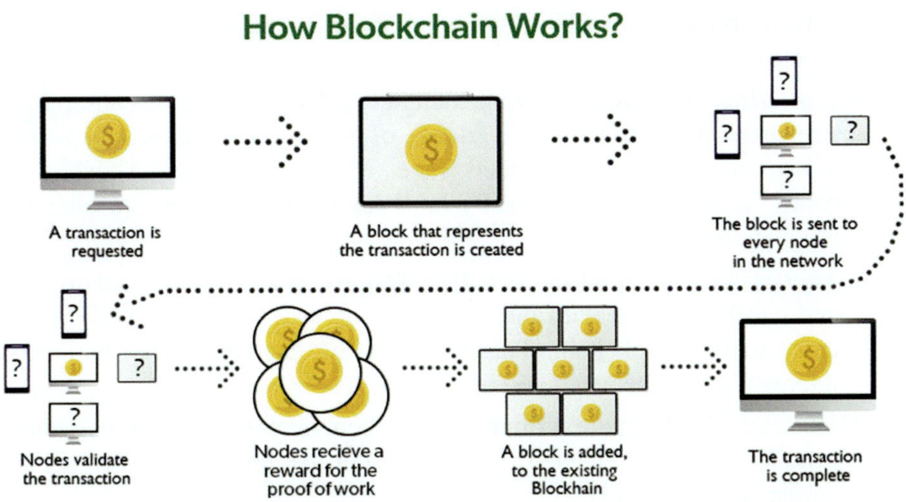

Figure 3.1 How blockchain works.

- *Safety*
  Blockchain uses advanced cryptographic strategies to comfy facts. Each transaction is encrypted, and every block carries a very specific hash that consists of the hash of the previous block, ensuring the integrity and safety of the data.
- *Transparency and anonymity*
  Blockchain gives transparency due to the fact that all transactions are recorded on a public ledger that all and sundry can view. However, customers stay nameless for the motive that transactions are related to cryptographic addresses in place of private statistics.

3.1.4 Is blockchain secure?

Blockchain technology is designed to offer a high level of safety through several key mechanisms:

- *Decentralization*: Now, like conventional centralized systems, blockchain is decentralized. This means that no single entity has controlled the entire network, decreasing the hazard of centralized factors of failure.
- *Cryptographic hashing*: Each block in a blockchain includes a cryptographic hash of the previous block, transaction information, and a timestamp. This guarantees the integrity and immutability of the facts.

Any alternate in a block must regulate its hash and invalidate subsequent blocks.

- *Consensus mechanisms*: Blockchain networks use consensus algorithms like proof of work (PoW), evidence of Stake (PoS), or precise mechanisms to agree on the United States of the blockchain. Those algorithms make it computationally hard for malicious actors to alter the blockchain.
- *Transparency and auditability*: Transactions on a blockchain are obvious and can be audited with the useful resource of truly everybody to get entry to the blockchain. This transparency guarantees that malicious interests can be detected and traced.
- *Immutability*: Data are written to a blockchain, and it cannot be without trouble altered or deleted. This immutability protects against record tampering and fraud.

3.1.5 Risks and challenges in blockchain

Irrespective of the numerous advantages of the blockchain era, it is important to understand and cope with the inherent dangers and demanding situations that encompass its implementation. Expertise in those factors is critical for developing powerful techniques to mitigate capacity problems and harness the general capacity of blockchain [19–24].

(1) *Scalability*

Issue: Blockchain networks, especially those that usage of proof of hard work (PoW) consensus mechanisms, frequently battle with scalability. Due to the fact that the number of transactions increases, the network can emerge as congested, leading to slower transaction instances and better prices.

Effect: Scalability troubles can restrict the adoption of blockchain technology in packages requiring excessive transaction throughput and actual-time processing.

Mitigation: Enforcing opportunity consensus mechanisms like proof of stake (PoS), sharding, and rancid-chain answers (e.g., Lightning community) can assist in enhancing scalability.

(2) *Power consumption*

Trouble: The PoW consensus mechanism utilized by many blockchain networks, along with Bitcoin, is particularly power-in-depth, requiring massive computational strength and power [30–36, 38, 39, 41].

Effect: Immoderate power consumption increases environmental issues and will increase operational expenses, making PoW-based blockchains less sustainable.

Mitigation: Transitioning to extra electricity-green consensus mechanisms, such as PoS or delegated proof of stake (DPoS), can reduce strength consumption [25, 27].

(3) *Security vulnerabilities*

Hassle: Even as blockchain is commonly secure, it is not resistant to assaults. Commonplace security troubles encompass 51% of assaults, in which a single entity profits manipulate of most of the community's mining strength, and clever settlement vulnerabilities.

Effect: Protection breaches can cause massive economic losses, a lack of trust, and harm to the recognition of blockchain networks and packages.

Mitigation: Improving protection capabilities, engaging in thorough smart settlement audits, and enforcing multi-layer safety protocols can assist in mitigating one's dangers.

Mirai Botnet attack (2016): This notorious assault exploited vulnerabilities in IoT devices, such as security cameras and routers, to create a large botnet that launched dispensed denial-of-carrier (DDoS) attacks. The incident disrupted essential offerings like Twitter, Netflix, and Reddit, highlighting the dangers of unsecured IoT devices.

Clever domestic device breaches: Many smart domestic devices, inclusive of thermostats and cameras, were determined to have weak protection protocols. For instance, vulnerabilities in certain models of smart cameras allowed hackers to benefit from unauthorized access, allowing them to be secret agents on users and compromise their privacy.

Healthcare IoT devices: In 2020, safety researchers revealed vulnerabilities in related clinical devices like pacemakers and insulin pumps. These flaws ought to allow attackers to govern tool settings or even supply harmful commands, raising severe issues affecting personal protection and the integrity of healthcare systems.

Related automobiles: A 2015 demonstration by cybersecurity researchers confirmed how they may remotely get admission to and control a Jeep Cherokee's functions, which include the engine and brakes. This vulnerability underscored the significance of securing automotive IoT systems to shield each driver and passenger.

(4) *Regulatory and compliance-demanding situations*
Trouble: The regulatory landscape for blockchain technology remains evolving. There may be a loss of readability and consistency in rules at some stage in distinct jurisdictions.
Impact: Regulatory uncertainty can preclude the adoption of blockchain technology, create compliance-annoying conditions, and expose groups to criminal dangers.
Mitigation: Enticing with regulators, collaborating in company boards, and staying knowledgeable approximately regulatory tendencies can assist businesses navigate compliance issues.

(5) *Privacy concerns*
Trouble: Blockchain's apparent and immutable nature can conflict with privacy requirements, especially whilst managing touchy personal or economic statistics.
Effect: Inadequate privacy measures can cause data breaches and violations of privacy rules, in conjunction with GDPR.
Mitigation: Enforcing privacy-improving technologies, such as zero-know-how proofs, private transactions, and private or permissioned blockchains, can assist in defending sensitive statistics.

(6) *Interoperability troubles*
Hassle: Terrific blockchain networks regularly use incompatible protocols and necessities, making it tough for them to communicate and interact with each other.
Impact: Loss of interoperability can limit the capability applications of blockchain generation and create silos of statistics.
Mitigation: Growing interoperability solutions, which incorporate pass-chain bridges, standardized protocols, and consortium blockchains, can facilitate seamless communication between exceptional blockchain networks [40, 42, 44].

(7) *Felony and moral problems*
Issue: The decentralized and pseudonymous nature of blockchain can lead to jail and morally demanding situations, consisting of facilitating unlawful sports or permitting tax evasion.
Effect: One's problems can enchant regulatory scrutiny and damage the majority's belief in the blockchain era.
Mitigation: Imposing sturdy know your customer (KYC) and anti-coins laundering (AML) measures, alongside ethical tips, can help cope with those worrying conditions.

(8) *Adoption boundaries*
Hassle: Notwithstanding its potential, the blockchain generation faces limitations to adoption, which include a lack of awareness, technical complexity, and resistance to alternate.
Effect: Sluggish adoption can put off the belief in blockchain's blessings and restrict its effect on numerous industries.
Mitigation: Offering education and education, simplifying purchaser interfaces, and demonstrating clear use instances and benefits can assist energy adoption.

3.2 IoT Technology

The net of factors (IoT) refers to the community of physical objects – devices, automobiles, houses, and specific gadgets – that are embedded with sensors, software programs, and other technologies to connect and trade data with specific devices and systems over the internet. IoT targets to make our environments smarter, more responsive, and more linked with its components which is mentioned in Figure 3.2.

3.2.1 Key components of IoT

- *Sensors/gadgets*
  Sensors: These are essential components that accumulate facts from the surroundings, in conjunction with temperature, humidity, motion, mild, and unique metrics.
  Gadgets: These can vary from simple, own family devices like smart thermostats and refrigerators to complicated industrial machines and cars.
- *Connectivity*
  Records collected via the use of sensors are dispatched to the cloud or community servers via various communication protocols, along with Wi-Fi, Bluetooth, Zigbee, mobile networks, or even satellite television for pc verbal exchange.
- *Statistics processing*
  As soon as the information reaches its destination, the software approaches it. This can appear in real-time or in batches, depending on the use case. Processing can comprise filtering, aggregating, and studying the records to extract great insights.

Figure 3.2 Components of IoT.

- *Client interface*
  The processed information is then supplied to customers through several interfaces alongside mobile apps, internet dashboards, or automatic management systems. This enables users to screen, manage, and control their IoT devices.

3.2.2 How IoT works

Figure 3.3 shows the working example of an IoT system having different layers.

- *Statistics series*
  Sensors gather data from their environment. For instance, a clever thermostat would probably gather temperature and humidity statistics.

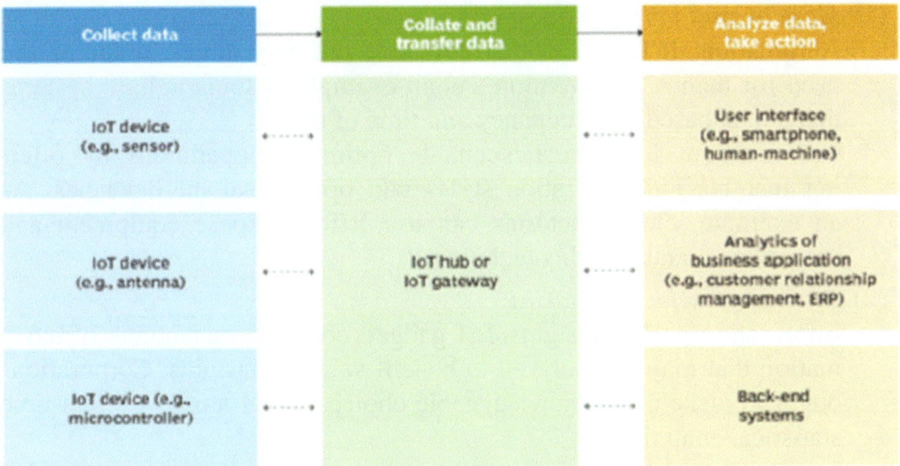

Figure 3.3 Example of an IoT system.

- *Facts transmission*
  The accrued information is transmitted to the cloud or a local server. This transmission can certainly be one of a kind verbal exchange era depending on the necessities for range, strength consumption, and facts price.
- *Facts processing and evaluation*
  Inside the cloud or on a local server, the facts are processed and analyzed. This could include filtering out the factor facts, aggregating data from a couple of sensors, or making use of algorithms to discover styles or anomalies.
- *Motion and comments*
  Based totally on the assessment, movements are taken. As an example, if a smart thermostat detects that the temperature is just too excessive, it ships a command to the HVAC gadget to chill the room. Customers can also get hold of notifications or have the potential to control devices through a client interface [46–51].

3.2.3 Core benefits of IoT

The Internet of Things (IoT) offers diverse advantages at some point in numerous sectors, enhancing overall performance, productivity, and individual revel in. Right here are a few central controls of IoT:

(1) *More overall performance and productivity*
Automation: IoT devices can automate ordinary duties, reducing the need for manual intervention. As an example, automatic light systems that adjust based on occupancy and time of day.
Optimization: IoT statistics enable optimizing operations by offering insights into utilization styles and operational inefficiencies. As an example, clever factories can use IoT to expose equipment and streamline manufacturing techniques.

(2) *Progressed selection making*
Information-pushed Insights: IoT gadgets collect large amounts of information that may be analyzed to benefit valuable insights. Corporations ought to make extra knowledgeable choices based mostly on real-time statistical analytics.
Predictive preservation: In commercial settings, IoT sensors display device health, predicting screw-ups before they arise, which reduces downtime and preservation expenses.

(3) *Value economic and financial savings*
Power management: Clever strength structures can screen and control power utilization, predominant to great fee economic and financial savings. For instance, clever thermostats that optimize heating and cooling based totally on occupancy.
Aid optimization: IoT allows for optimizing the use of assets, which includes water and power, decreasing wastage, and reducing operational expenses.

(4) *Progressed patrons enjoy*
Personalization: IoT allows customized patron reports by using the adapting services and products to individual alternatives. For instance, smart domestic gadgets analyze user possibilities and alter settings accordingly [11].
Real-time guide: Agencies can provide real-time useful resources and offerings to customers through connected devices, improving customer delight.

(5) *Advanced protection and protection*
Surveillance and monitoring: IoT safety cameras and sensors decorate surveillance and monitoring, enhancing protection in houses, workplaces, and public spaces [14–17].

Emergency response: IoT gadgets can stumble upon emergencies along with fires, fuel leaks, or intrusions, and routinely alert the government, enhancing reaction times.

(6) *Superior healthcare*
Far-flung tracking: IoT-enabled health devices can screen patients remotely, presenting non-stop health information to healthcare carriers and bearing in thought timely interventions.
Advanced affected individual care: Wearable devices alert vital signs and signs and ship signals for any abnormalities, ensuring higher affected man or woman care and control.

(7) *Environmental advantages*
Sustainable practices: IoT can help display screen and manipulate environmental elements, most importantly to extra sustainable practices. As an example, smart agriculture structures that optimize water use and decrease pesticide software.
Pollution management: IoT gadgets can display air and water, assisting in managing pollution and guarding the environment.

(8) *Supply chain and logistics optimization*
Asset tracking: IoT devices song the location and standing of assets in real-time, enhancing inventory management and lowering losses.
Green logistics: IoT solutions optimize logistics and deliver chain operations by offering real-time facts on shipment fame, course optimization, and shipping times.

(9) *More suitable metropolis living*
Smart cities: The IoT era decorates city dwellings by using a manner of enhancing infrastructure, transportation, electricity management, and public offerings. For example, clever site visitor lights adapt to website online traffic conditions to reduce congestion [35].
Public protection: IoT solutions improve public safety through improved surveillance, smart streetlights, and emergency response systems.

(10) *Innovation and new business corporation fashions*
New offerings: IoT allows new services and commercial company models, which include subscription-based offerings for IoT devices, data monetization, and predictive preservation services.
Competitive gain: Companies leveraging IoT technology can gain an aggressive place by using ways of providing innovative products and

services, improving operational efficiency, and improving customer delight.

3.2.4 Application of IoT

- *Smart houses*
  Internet of Things (IoT) refers to a network of interconnected devices and structures that may communicate with each other and trade records over the internet. These devices frequently have sensors and software that allow them to acquire, transmit, and act on statistics in real time, enhancing automation and performance in diverse settings and smart homes. In smart homes, IoT permits devices like thermostats, security systems, lighting fixtures, and home equipment to be managed remotely, presenting greater comfort, energy efficiency, and security. Devices like smart lighting fixtures, thermostats, security cameras, and smart home equipment hook up with a crucial hub or immediately to the internet, allowing house owners to manipulate them via phone apps or voice assistants [34].
- *Industrial IoT (IIoT)*
  Production and industrial strategies use IoT devices to display machinery and music assets' overall performance, and assume upkeep needs, improving efficiency and decreasing downtime.
- *Healthcare*
  Wearable gadgets and far-off tracking systems accumulate affected person fitness information, making an allowance for non-stop monitoring and early detection of ability health issues. Examples like Fitbit and smartwatches within the "Healthcare" phase, to focus on wearable devices, can assist in illustrating how these technologies are making healthcare greater reachable and personal. As an example, Fitbit tracks steps, heart rate, sleep patterns, and more, offering insights that help individuals control their fitness and standard fitness. In addition, smartwatches, just like the Apple Watch or Samsung Galaxy Watch, display important symptoms along with blood oxygen levels, ECG, or even locate falls, alerting emergency services if needed. Those devices are assisting in bridging the space between day-by-day wellness and clinical monitoring, making healthcare more proactive and personalized.
- *Agriculture*
  IoT sensors reveal soil moisture, climate conditions, and crop health, allowing precision agriculture to optimize water use, increase yield, and decrease waste.

- *Smart cities*
  IoT era manipulates urban infrastructure together with traffic lighting fixtures, waste management structures, and public transportation, enhancing performance and a pleasant life for citizens.

3.2.5 IoT protection and traumatic conditions

- *Protection*
  IoT gadgets frequently lack sturdy security features, making them liable to hacking. Ensuring data encryption, secure authentication, and ordinary firmware updates are important to shield IoT networks.
- *Interoperability*
  With numerous gadgets from unique manufacturers, attaining seamless communication and integration may be hard. Standardization efforts are ongoing to address these troubles.
- *Facts privateness*
  The superb quantity of statistics amassed via the manner of IoT gadgets increases privacy troubles. Ensuring records are anonymized and securely saved is essential to defend individual privacy.
- *Scalability*
  As the number of related gadgets grows, the network infrastructure ought with a purpose to scale to cope with the prolonged information traffic and ensure dependable performance.

E-trade: As companies grow, systems like Amazon and Shopify need to scale their infrastructure to address growing traffic, transactions, and client interactions, at some stage in top seasons like holidays. Scalability ensures these platforms can hold overall performance without downtime or slow reaction times as call for spikes.

Healthcare: The healthcare zone, mainly with the upward thrust of telemedicine and health statistics systems, faces scalability troubles as more patients are trying to find remote consultations. Systems must scale to deal with increasingly simultaneous users, securely control considerable quantities of affected person information, and make sure of actual-time processing for diagnostics and consultations.

Financial offerings: Banks and monetary establishments, along with JPMorgan Chase or PayPal, need scalable answers to system billions of transactions every day. As their bases develop globally, the need for scalable, again-give-up systems to deal with excessive-frequency buying and selling, fraud detection, and real-time processing becomes essential to preserving protection and overall performance.

Streaming services: Structures like Netflix and YouTube must scale their infrastructure to serve millions of customers globally. Scalability impacts the potential to stream fantastic video without buffering and control facts-heavy features like hints and personalized content material at a massive scale.

3.3 Integration of Blockchain and IoT

The combination of IoT (Internet of Things) and blockchain technology can create greater comfortable, green, and transparent surroundings for numerous applications. Integrating IoT and blockchain holds terrific promise for boosting safety, transparency, and efficiency across numerous industries. But addressing demanding situations related to scalability, privacy, standardization, and strength intake is critical for knowing the overall ability of this integration.

3.3.1 Benefits of integrating IoT and blockchain

(1) *Enhanced security*:

- Data integrity: Blockchain's immutability ensures that facts recorded from IoT gadgets cannot be tampered with.
- Authentication and authorization: Blockchain can provide a decentralized and at-ease approach for authenticating and authorizing IoT gadgets, decreasing the risk of unauthorized get entry to.

(2) *Improved transparency and traceability*:

- Supply chain management: Blockchain can track the provenance and journey of goods monitored via IoT gadgets, ensuring transparency and traceability in delivery chains.
- Maintenance and service logs: IoT devices can log carrier and preservation sports activities on the blockchain, generating obvious data.

(3) *Decentralization*:

- Eliminating single points of failure: Combining IoT with blockchain can decentralize management, reducing the risks related to centralized systems.

- Distributed data storage: Information accrued via IoT devices may be securely stored in an allotted way on the blockchain [6, 7, 25].

(4) *Automation with smart contracts*:

- Autonomous operations: Smart contracts can automate transactions and techniques between IoT devices, collectively with computerized bills and circumstance-based total moves.
- Efficient transactions: Smart contracts allow direct peer-to-peer transactions among IoT gadgets without intermediaries, developing efficiency.

(5) *Data monetization*:

- Microtransactions: IoT gadgets can behavior microtransactions securely and efficiently using blockchain, permitting new commercial enterprise models for data monetization.

3.4 Use Cases

(1) *Supply chain and logistics*:

- Tracking shipments: IoT gadgets can show the circumstances and region of products, with blockchain making sure the integrity and transparency of the facts.
- Cold chain management: For perishable objects, IoT sensors can reveal temperature and humidity, with the blockchain providing an immutable record of conditions all through the delivery chain.

(2) *Smart homes and cities*:

- Energy management: IoT gadgets can manage and optimize electricity usage, at the same time as blockchain can securely record energy transactions and ensure obvious billing.
- Public services: Blockchain can decorate the transparency and safety of public services managed via the use of IoT devices, including waste management and water distribution.
- Patient monitoring: IoT gadgets can display sufferers' fitness metrics, with blockchain ensuring the protection and privacy of sensitive fitness data.
- Pharmaceutical supply chain: Blockchain can track the authenticity and availability of prescribed drugs, with IoT gadgets tracking storage conditions.

(3) *Automotive and transportation*:

- Vehicle-to-vehicle (V2V) communication: IoT devices in automobiles can talk securely about the usage of blockchain, enhancing safety and overall performance.
- Maintenance records: Blockchain can maintain an apparent and immutable document of automobile renovation and carrier records.

(4) Challenges

(a) *Scalability*: High volume of transactions: IoT ecosystems can generate a huge range of transactions, which might also project the scalability of modern-day blockchain systems.

(b) *Interoperability*: Standards and protocols: Making sure interoperability among numerous IoT devices and blockchain systems calls for the development of not unusual standards and protocols.

(c) *Data privacy*: Sensitive information: Dealing with and shielding sensitive records recorded at the blockchain from IoT devices is vital.

(d) *Energy consumption*: Resource efficiency: Blockchain, especially evidence of labor (PoW) based totally systems, can be useful resource-intensive. Green consensus mechanisms are wished for integration with strength-constrained IoT gadgets.

3.5 Implementation

Implementing the combination of blockchain and IoT consists of a multi-layered technique that addresses the technical, operational, and organizational factors of each technology. This phase outlines the crucial factor steps and additives required for an achievement implementation, focusing on the architecture, information control, protection, and deployment techniques.

3.5.1 Structure layout

The shape for integrating blockchain and IoT must be designed to ensure scalability, protection, and interoperability. The following components are essential:

(1) IoT gadgets: Sensors and actuators that collect and transmit records.

(2) Aspect devices: Devices that perform initial record processing near the source of the record, reducing latency and bandwidth utilization.

(3) Blockchain community: A decentralized ledger that records information transactions and records from IoT gadgets.

(4) Clever contracts: Self-executing contracts with terms without delay written into code, automating techniques based totally on IoT records.

(5) Information garage: On-chain and rancid-chain storage answers for dealing with large volumes of IoT data.

(6) Middleware: Software that enables communication and records trade among IoT gadgets and the blockchain network.

3.5.2 Records control

Effective statistical control is crucial for the fulfillment of integration of blockchain and IoT. The following strategies may be employed:

(1) Records collection: IoT gadgets continuously accumulate information from the surroundings, which is then transmitted to area gadgets for preliminary processing.

(2) Information preprocessing: Component devices clean out, combine, and preprocess facts before sending them to the blockchain community, ensuring the simplest applicable facts are recorded.

(3) Three. Statistics garage because of the huge volume of IoT records, an aggregate of on-chain and rancid-chain storage is used. Essential facts and transaction logs are stored on-chain, at the same time as big datasets are stored off-chain with references on the blockchain.

(4) Statistics integrity: Blockchain guarantees records integrity via its immutable ledger, in which each transaction is cryptographically secured and time-stamped.

3.5.3 Safety functions

Safety is the number one issue whilst integrating blockchain and IoT. The following measures can enhance security:

(1) Authentication and authorization: Positioned to impact strong authentication mechanisms to ensure that the best legal IoT gadgets and clients can get the right of entry to the blockchain community.

(2) Encryption: Encrypt information transmitted between IoT devices, location gadgets, and the blockchain to prevent unauthorized entry and tampering.

(3) Consensus mechanisms: Use energy-inexperienced consensus mechanisms like evidence of stake (PoS) or delegated proof of stake (DPoS) to secure the blockchain community.
(4) Clever agreement audits: Often, audit smart contracts to become aware of and connect vulnerabilities, making sure they function as intended.

3.5.4 Deployment techniques

Deploying a blockchain and IoT integration venture requires careful making of plans and execution. The following steps outline an ordinary deployment system:

(1) Proof of concept (percent): Increase a percent to validate the feasibility and benefits of the combination. This entails developing a small-scale implementation to test the functionality and ordinary overall performance of the device.
(2) Pilot deployment: After a successful percentage, put in force a pilot deployment in managed surroundings. This phase includes scaling the device to handle a bigger range of IoT gadgets and transactions.
(3) Whole-scale deployment: As soon as the pilot deployment is successful, roll out the general-scale deployment. This entails integrating the machine with gift infrastructure, training employees, and ensuring all additive characteristics efficiently.
(4) Tracking and maintenance: Continuously monitor the machine for performance, safety, and reliability. Placed into impact upkeep strategies to cope with any problems and keep the gadget up to date.

3.5.5 Case study: Supply chain control

To demonstrate the implementation manner, bear in mind a delivery chain management utility:

(1) Structure format: IoT sensors are located on objects to song their place and scenario (e.g., temperature and humidity). Side devices preprocess information and send it to the blockchain network.
(2) Facts control vital statistics, which include location updates and situation adjustments, and are recorded on the blockchain. Massive datasets, like unique logs, are stored off-chain.
(3) Protection capabilities: Facts from IoT sensors are encrypted and transmitted securely. Clever contracts automate the tracking and verification of products, ensuring transparency and traceability.

(4) Deployment strategies: A percent is superior to tune a small wide form of products. After an achievement validation, a pilot deployment scales the machine to tune shipments throughout more than one location. Eventually, the system is rolled out to cover the complete supply chain, with non-stop tracking and preservation to ensure its effectiveness.

Blockchain and IoT call for cautious planning, strong architecture, powerful information control, stringent safety features, and a phased deployment method. By addressing those components, organizations can harness the mixed strength of blockchain and IoT to create comfortable, obvious, and green systems that stress innovation and operational excellence across several industries.

Supply chain management can significantly enhance the understanding of the integration's impact. Here are some examples of how to present this information:

(1) *Inventory reduction*: After implementing a new supply chain management system, Company X saw a *30% reduction in inventory holding costs* within the first year. This decrease allowed them to free up capital and allocate resources more effectively.

(2) *Lead time improvement*: The integration of real-time tracking and analytics reduced lead times by *25%*. This improvement allowed the company to respond more quickly to customer demands and enhance overall service levels.

(3) *Order fulfillment rates*: Following the implementation, order fulfillment rates increased from *85% to 95%*, resulting in a substantial boost in customer satisfaction and repeat business.

(4) *Cost savings*: The automation of various processes in the supply chain led to overall cost savings of *15%* annually. This included reductions in labor costs, transportation expenses, and operational inefficiencies.

(5) *Enhanced forecast accuracy*: The new predictive analytics tools improved forecast accuracy by *40%*, allowing the company to make more informed decisions about production and inventory management.

(6) *Supplier performance*: After integrating a supplier management system, supplier performance metrics improved, with on-time delivery rates rising from *80% to 95%*. This enhanced reliability strengthened relationships and reduced disruptions in the supply chain.

(7) *Sustainability metrics*: The implementation of a more efficient supply chain reduced waste by *20%* and carbon emissions by *15%*, aligning with the company's sustainability goals and improving its brand image.

3.6 Results and Discussion

The combination of blockchain and IoT gives numerous blessings and transformative capabilities across numerous sectors. This phase provides the effects positioned from implementing a blockchain-IoT integration, discovered by using way of a dialogue on the implications, demanding situations, and destiny tips.

3.6.1 Results

The case examines how delivery chain management serves as an illustrative instance, demonstrating the tangible benefits of integrating blockchain and IoT.

(1) *Advanced transparency and traceability*

- Result: The implementation caused actual time tracking of goods in the path of the supply chain. Each transaction and movement is recorded on the blockchain, providing an immutable and transparent record.
- Effect: Extended transparency and traceability helped lessen fraud, mistakes, and inefficiencies, making sure that objects were dealt with nicely and introduced on time.

(2) *Superior information integrity and protection*

- Result: Information from IoT sensors becomes encrypted and securely transmitted to the blockchain. The decentralized nature of blockchain ensured that no unmarried entity ought to modify the information, enhancing its integrity.
- Impact: Progressed statistics protection and integrity minimized the chance of data breaches and tampering, fostering agreement among stakeholders.

(3) *Automation and performance profits*
Automation reduces labor costs by way of training, and repetitive responsibilities with machines or software programs, hence reducing the need for a large staff for recurring activities. As an example, in production, automated assembly lines lower the wide variety of required people, resulting in sizeable savings on wages, benefits, and schooling expenses. In a group of workers control, automation facilitates optimize group of workers allocation by way of the usage of smart scheduling systems that expect high times and ensure ok staffing tiers. Tools like

robotic process automation (RPA) streamline administrative responsibilities, permitting employees to focus on better-value, strategic activities, which improves overall productivity and performance. Additionally, automation structures song overall performance facts, supporting managers in discovering inefficiencies and in addition reducing operational expenses even while preserving extremely good output.

- Cease result: Smart contracts computerize numerous processes, including verifying the condition of products and triggering bills upon delivery. This reduced the need for manual intervention and improved transaction processing.
- Impact: Automation brought about full-size performance earnings, decreasing operational costs, and speeding up methods across the delivery chain.

(4) *Scalability and ordinary overall performance*

- Stop result: The aggregate of on-chain and off-chain storage, together with the usage of facet gadgets for preliminary data processing, ensured that the gadget remained scalable and performant.
- Effect: The tool changed into a position to attend mostly to transactions and facts without big latency or performance degradation.

(5) *Interoperability*

- Stop result: The implementation of middleware facilitated seamless communication among wonderful IoT devices and blockchain networks, ensuring interoperability.
- Effect: Higher interoperability allowed for more bendy and incorporated delivery chain operations, permitting distinctive systems to work together harmoniously.

3.6.2 Discussion

Expanding on potential technological advancements that could address the identified challenges would enhance the argument by providing forward-looking solutions.

Superior encryption strategies: The development of quantum encryption and more sturdy cryptographic algorithms can extensively enhance records safety for IoT devices. By the use of those technologies, companies can ensure that sensitive information transmitted among gadgets remains protected from unauthorized get entry to.

AI and system learning for security: Integrating AI and system getting to know can beautify risk detection and reaction skills. These technologies can examine patterns in facts visitors to identify anomalies and capacity protection breaches in real time, permitting quicker reaction instances and lowering the impact of cyberattacks.

Decentralized systems: Making use of blockchain generation can improve safety and records integrity in IoT networks. By way of decentralizing statistics storage and the usage of clever contracts, corporations can reduce the threat of a single point of failure and enhance the traceability of information transactions, thereby bolstering security measures.

Edge computing: Improvements in facet computing permit information processing to occur in the direction of the source, lowering latency and improving real-time decision-making. This may alleviate bandwidth issues and enhance the security of facts transmitted over networks, as much less sensitive information is sent to centralized cloud servers.

Interoperability standards: Growing regularly occurring requirements for IoT devices can facilitate higher safety practices and interoperability between specific structures. Organizing not unusual protocols for security capabilities will help ensure that each devices within a network meet minimal protection requirements, decreasing vulnerabilities.

Regulatory frameworks and compliance gear: The emergence of recent regulatory frameworks can manual companies in imposing vital safety features. Compliance gear that automates safety tests and reporting can help organizations maintain adherence to regulations while figuring out potential protection gaps.

At the same time, because the effects advise large benefits, several annoying conditions and problems need to be addressed to maximize the capacity of blockchain-IoT integration.

(1) *Scalability annoying conditions*

- Dialogue: No matter improvements, scalability remains a trouble, especially for public blockchains. The excessive volume of IoT records can pressure the network, leading to congestion and prolonged prices.
- Destiny route: Research into more scalable consensus mechanisms, together with sharding and off-chain solutions, is important. Layer 2 answers and hybrid architectures combining public and private blockchains can additionally be explored.

(2) *Protection problems*

- Discussion: While blockchain complements information integrity, IoT devices are at risk of physical assaults and cyber threats. Ensuring the security of IoT endpoints is critical.
- Future path: Imposing robust safety protocols for IoT devices, along with hardware-based protection and ordinary firmware updates, can mitigate these dangers. Improving smart agreement protection through rigorous audits and formal verification techniques is also essential.

(3) *Regulatory and compliance troubles*

- Dialogue: The evolving regulatory panorama poses demanding situations for blockchain-IoT integration. Compliance with statistics protection legal guidelines, at the side of GDPR, requires careful attention to facts privacy, and possession.
- Destiny direction: Engaging with regulators and enterprise bodies to enlarge easy tips and necessities for blockchain-IoT packages is essential. Making sure that records management practices have a look at applicable rules will help mitigate criminal risks.

(4) *Interoperability and standardization*

- Communicate: Attaining interoperability amongst one in all types of blockchain system and IoT gadget remains a complex undertaking. Loss of standardization can preclude seamless integration.
- Destiny direction: Growing standardized protocols and frameworks for blockchain-IoT integration will facilitate interoperability. Employer collaboration in developing and adopting non-unusual standards is vital.

(5) *Value and resource control*

- Discussion: Implementing and preserving a blockchain-IoT gadget can be expensive. The charges associated with infrastructure, power intake, and ongoing upkeep need to be managed efficaciously.
- Future direction: Exploring more rate-effective solutions, which consist of power-green consensus mechanisms and cloud-based services, can assist in managing fees. Optimizing useful resource allocation and leveraging economies of scale can also be useful.

The integration of blockchain and IoT gives great blessings, which encompass extra appropriate transparency, statistics integrity, protection, and efficiency. However, addressing the challenges of scalability, safety, regulatory compliance, interoperability, and price management is critical for figuring out the entire potential of this effective aggregate. Destiny studies and improvement should attention on overcoming the worrying situations to create strong, scalable, and at ease blockchain IoT systems that power innovation and operational excellence at some stage in various industries.

3.7 Conclusion

The integration of blockchain and IoT holds transformative potential, presenting significant advantages for the duration of diverse industries. By combining the decentralized, comfy, and obvious nature of blockchain with the pervasive, records-rich surroundings of IoT, businesses can attain incredible levels of performance, safety, and reliability. This observation has verified the practical blessings of blockchain-IoT integration through a detailed case test on deliver chain management, revealing stepped-forward transparency, progressed records integrity, automation, scalability, and interoperability. But the adventure closer to virtually leveraging this integration is fraught with challenges. Scalability issues, protection troubles, regulatory compliance, interoperability, and fee management must be addressed to ensure a successful implementation and sustained blessings. The effects highlight the need for ongoing studies and innovation in numerous key areas:

(1) *Scalability*: Exploring superior consensus mechanisms, off-chain solutions, and hybrid architectures to deal with the huge volumes of IoT statistics correctly.

(2) *Safety*: Implementing sturdy protection features for IoT devices, improving clever agreement safety, and growing comprehensive hazard mitigation strategies.

(3) *Regulatory compliance*: Appealing to regulatory bodies to grow clean suggestions and standards, making sure records privacy, and compliance with evolving recommendations.

(4) *Interoperability*: Growing standardized protocols and frameworks to facilitate seamless communication and integration among several blockchain structures and IoT structures.

(5) *Cost management*: Exploring price-effective answers, optimizing aid allocation, and leveraging cloud-based complete offerings to control the expenses associated with blockchain-IoT integration.

The convergence of blockchain and IoT represents a paradigm shift in how records are controlled, secured, and applied. It ensures revolutionary sectors that incorporate delivery chain management, healthcare, smart towns, and the past. By addressing the diagnosed stressful situations and capitalizing on the possibilities, corporations can unfasten up the total potential of blockchain and IoT, the use of innovation, operational excellence, and sustainable growth within the digital age. Destiny's work needs to be aware of developing whole answers to the demanding situations diagnosed, fostering collaboration among corporations, academia, and regulatory bodies, and accomplishing large-scale pilot duties to validate and refine the combination strategies. The continued evolution of blockchain and IoT technologies will pave the way for present-day applications and company models, ultimately shaping a greater related, comfortable, and experienced world.

Blockchain provides a decentralized and tamper-evidence framework that substantially improves the security of IoT devices, shielding sensitive statistics from breaches and unauthorized get entry to. The immutable nature of blockchain ensures the integrity of facts collected from IoT gadgets. Groups can depend on accurate records for crucial decision-making approaches, thereby enhancing standard operational efficiency. By combining IoT with blockchain, corporations can gain unheard-of transparency in supply chain control. Real-time monitoring and comfy logging of transactions help mitigate fraud and ensure the authenticity of merchandise. Blockchain allows relaxed, decentralized identification management for IoT devices, decreasing the threat of identification theft and improving user privacy. The capability applications of this integration span across clever cities, healthcare, agriculture, cars, and logistics, highlighting its versatility in addressing actual international demanding situations.

However, companies must also navigate numerous demanding situations, together with scalability, strength intake, interoperability, and regulatory compliance. By way of proactively addressing those troubles, businesses can harness the entire capability of Blockchain and IoT integration, paving the way for greater at ease, efficient, and innovative answers. In the end, embracing this convergence can result in significant improvements, allowing agencies to live aggressively in an increasingly more digital landscape.

References

[1] "State of blockchain q1 2016: Blockchain funding overtakes bitcoin," 2016. [Online]. Available: http://www.coindesk.com/state-of-blockchain-q1-2016/

[2] G. W. Peters, E. Panayi, and A. Chapelle, "Trends in crypto-currencies and blockchain technologies: A monetary theory and regulation perspective," 2015. [Online]. Available: http://dx.doi.org/10.2139/ssrn.2646618.

[3] A. Kosba, A. Miller, E. Shi, Z. Wen, and C. Papamanthou, "Hawk: The blockchain model of cryptography and privacy-preserving smart contracts," in Proceedings of IEEE Symposium on Security and Privacy (SP), San Jose, CA, USA, 2016, pp. 839–858.

[4] B. W. Akins, J. L. Chapman, and J. M. Gordon, "A whole new world: Income tax considerations of the bitcoin economy," 2013. [Online]. Available: https://ssrn.com/abstract=2394738

[5] Y. Zhang and J. Wen, "An IoT electric business model based on the protocol of bitcoin," in Proceedings of 18th International Conference on Intelligence in Next Generation Networks (ICIN), Paris, France, 2015, pp. 184–191.

[6] M. Sharples and J. Domingue, "The blockchain and kudos: A distributed system for the educational record, reputation, and reward," in Proceedings of 11th European Conference on Technology Enhanced Learning (EC-TEL 2015), Lyon, France, 2015, pp. 490–496.

[7] C. Noyes, "Bitav: Fast anti-malware by distributed blockchain consensus and feedforward scanning," arXiv preprint arXiv:1601.01405, 2016.

[8] I. Eyal and E. G. Sirer, "Majority is not enough: Bitcoin mining is vulnerable," in Proceedings of International Conference on Financial Cryptography and Data Security, Berlin, Heidelberg, 2014, pp. 436–454.

[9] A. Biryukov, D. Khovratovich, and I. Pustogarov, "Deanonymisation of clients in bitcoin p2p network," in Proceedings of the 2014 ACM SIGSAC Conference on Computer and Communications Security, New York, NY, USA, 2014, pp. 15–29.

[10] F. Tschorsch and B. Scheuermann, "Bitcoin and beyond: A technical survey on decentralized digital currencies," IEEE Communications Surveys Tutorials, vol. 18, no. 3, pp. 2084–2123, 2016.

[11] NRI, “Survey on blockchain technologies and related services,” Tech. Rep., 2015. [Online]. Available: http://www.meti.go.jp/english/press/2016/pdf/053101f.pdf

[12] D. Lee Kuo Chuen, Ed., Handbook of Digital Currency, 1st ed. Elsevier, 2015. [Online]. Available: http://EconPapers.repec.org/RePEc:eee:monogr:9780128021170

[13] V. Buterin, “A next-generation smart contract and decentralized application platform,” white paper, 2014.

[14] D. Johnson, A. Menezes, and S. Vanstone, “The elliptic curve digital signature algorithm (ecdsa),” International Journal of Information Security, vol. 1, no. 1, pp. 36–63, 2001.

[15] V. Buterin, “On public and private blockchains,” 2015. [Online]. Available: https://blog.ethereum.org/2015/08/07/on-public-and-private-blockchains/

[16] “Consortium chain development.” [Online]. Available: https://github.com/ethereum/wiki/wiki/Consortium-Chain-Development

[17] L. Lamport, R. Shostak, and M. Pease, “The byzantine generals problem,” ACM Transactions on Programming Languages and Systems (TOPLAS), vol. 4, no. 3, pp. 382–401, 1982.

[18] S. King and S. Nadal, “Ppcoin: Peer-to-peer crypto-currency with proofof-stake,” Self-Published Paper, August, vol. 19, 2012.

[19] “Bitshares - your share in the decentralized exchange.” [Online]. Available: https://bitshares.org/

[20] D. Schwartz, N. Youngs, and A. Britto, “The ripple protocol consensus algorithm,” Ripple Labs Inc White Paper, vol. 5, 2014.

[21] G. Wood, “Ethereum: A secure decentralised generalised transaction ledger,” Ethereum Project Yellow Paper, 2014.

[22] V. Zamfir, “Introducing casper the friendly ghost,” Ethereum Blog URL: https://blog.ethereum.org/2015/08/01/introducing-casperfriendly-ghost,2015.

[23] C. Miguel and L. Barbara, “Practical byzantine fault tolerance,” in Proceedings of the Third Symposium on Operating Systems Design and Implementation, vol. 99, New Orleans, USA, 1999, pp. 173–186.

[24] M. Vukolic, “The quest for scalable blockchain fabric: Proof-of-work ’ vs. bft replication,” in International Workshop on Open Problems in Network Security, Zurich, Switzerland, 2015, pp. 112–125.

[25] C. Decker, J. Seidel, and R. Wattenhofer, “Bitcoin meets strong consistency,” in Proceedings of the 17th International Conference on

Distributed Computing and Networking (ICDCN). Singapore, Singapore: ACM, 2016, p. 13.

[26] D. Kraft, "Difficulty control for blockchain-based consensus systems," Peer-to-Peer Networking and Applications, vol. 9, no. 2, pp. 397–413, 2016.

[27] Y. Sompolinsky and A. Zohar, "Accelerating bitcoin's transaction processing. fast money grows on trees, not chains." IACR Cryptology ePrint Archive, vol. 2013, no. 881, 2013.

[28] A. Chepurnoy, M. Larangeira, and A. Ojiganov, "A prunable blockchain consensus protocol based on non-interactive proofs of past states retrievability," arXiv preprint arXiv:1603.07926, 2016.

[29] J. van den Hooff, M. F. Kaashoek, and N. Zeldovich, "Versum: Verifiable computations over large public logs," in Proceedings of the 2014 ACM SIGSAC Conference on Computer and Communications Security, New York, NY, USA, 2014, pp. 1304–1316.

[30] I. Eyal, A. E. Gencer, E. G. Sirer, and R. Van Renesse, "Bitcoinng: A scalable blockchain protocol," in Proceedings of 13th USENIX Symposium on Networked Systems Design and Implementation (NSDI 16), Santa Clara, CA, USA, 2016, pp. 45–59.

[31] S. Meiklejohn, M. Pomarole, G. Jordan, K. Levchenko, D. McCoy, G. M. Voelker, and S. Savage, "A fistful of bitcoins: Characterizing payments among men with no names," in Proceedings of the 2013 Conference on Internet Measurement Conference (IMC'13), New York, NY, USA, 2013.

[32] M. Moser, "Anonymity of bitcoin transactions: An analysis of mixing ÂÍ services," in Proceedings of Munster Bitcoin Conference ÂÍ , Munster, ÂÍ Germany, 2013, pp. 17–18.

[33] J. Bonneau, A. Narayanan, A. Miller, J. Clark, J. A. Kroll, and E. W. Felten, "Mixcoin: Anonymity for bitcoin with accountable mixes," in Proceedings of International Conference on Financial Cryptography and Data Security, Berlin, Heidelberg, 2014, pp. 486–504.

[34] T. Ruffing, P. Moreno-Sanchez, and A. Kate, "Coinshuffle: Practical decentralized coin mixing for bitcoin," in Proceedings of European Symposium on Research in Computer Security, Cham, 2014, pp. 345–364.

[35] I. Miers, C. Garman, M. Green, and A. D. Rubin, "Zerocoin: Anonymous distributed e-cash from bitcoin," in Proceedings of IEEE Symposium Security and Privacy (SP), Berkeley, CA, USA, 2013, pp. 397–411.

[36] E. B. Sasson, A. Chiesa, C. Garman, M. Green, I. Miers, E. Tromer, and M. Virza, "Zerocash: Decentralized anonymous payments from bitcoin," in Proceedings of 2014 IEEE Symposium on Security and Privacy (SP), San Jose, CA, USA, 2014, pp. 459–474.

[37] K. Nayak, S. Kumar, A. Miller, and E. Shi, "Stubborn mining: Generalizing selfish mining and combining with an eclipse attack," in Proceedings of 2016 IEEE European Symposium on Security and Privacy (EuroS&P), Saarbrucken, Germany, 2016, pp. 305–320.

[38] A. Sapirshtein, Y. Sompolinsky, and A. Zohar, "Optimal selfish mining strategies in bitcoin," arXiv preprint arXiv:1507.06183, 2015.

[39] S. Solat and M. Potop-Butucaru, "ZeroBlock: Timestamp-Free Prevention of Block-Withholding Attack in Bitcoin," Sorbonne Universites, UPMC University of Paris 6, Technical Report, May 2016. [Online]. Available: https://hal.archives-ouvertes.fr/hal-01310088

[40] Dorri, A., Kanhere, S. S., Jurdak, R., & Gauravaram, P. (2017). "Blockchain for IoT security and privacy: The case study of a smart home." IEEE International Conference on Pervasive Computing and Communications Workshops (PerCom Workshops), 618–623.

[41] Zhang, Y., & Wen, J. (2015). "An IoT electric business model based on the protocol of bitcoin." Intelligence in Next Generation Networks (ICIN), 184–191.

[42] Makhdoom, I., Abolhasan, M., Abbas, H., & Ni, W. (2019). "Blockchain's adoption in IoT: The challenges, and a way forward." Journal of Network and Computer Applications, 125, 251–279.

[43] Xu, X., Weber, I., & Staples, M. (2018). "Blockchain and Smart Contracts: Design Patterns for Scalable Blockchain Applications." Springer.

[44] Kumar, R., Tripathi, R., & Gupta, S. (2018). "Scalable blockchain framework for IoT data management." Procedia Computer Science, 125, 747–753.

[45] Sharma, P. K., Singh, S., & Jeong, Y. S. (2018). "Smart contract-based decentralized scheme for smart cities." IEEE Communications Magazine, 56(7), 32–37.

[46] Singh, S., & Kim, S. J. (2018). "Blockchain technology for decentralized IoT security and privacy: A survey." Procedia Computer Science, 141, 567–574.

[47] Al-Fuqaha, A., Guizani, M., Mohammadi, M., Aledhari, M., & Ayyash, M. (2015). "Internet of Things: A survey on enabling technologies, protocols, and applications." IEEE Communications Surveys & Tutorials, 17(4), 2347–2376.

[48] Huh, S., Cho, S., & Kim, S. (2017). "Managing IoT devices using blockchain platform." International Conference on Advanced Communication Technology (ICACT), 464–467.

[49] Tian, F. (2016). "An agri-food supply chain traceability system for China based on RFID & blockchain technology." IEEE 13th International Conference on Service Systems and Service Management (ICSSSM), 1–6.

[50] Toyoda, K., Mathiopoulos, P. T., Sasase, I., & Ohtsuki, T. (2017). "A novel blockchain-based product ownership management system (POMS) for anti-counterfeits in the post supply chain." IEEE Access, 5, 17465–17477.

[51] Casino, F., Dasaklis, T. K., & Patsakis, C. (2019). "A systematic literature review of blockchain-based applications: Current status, classification and open issues." Telematics and Informatics, 36, 55–81.

[52] Mageshkumar Naarayanasamy Varadarajan, Viji C, Rajkumar N, Mohanraj A, "Integration of AI and IoT for Smart Home Automation," SSRG International Journal of Electronics and Communication Engineering, vol. 11, no. 5, pp. 37–43, 2024.

[53] Rajkumar N, Viji C, Latha Pandala Madhavi, Vennila V Baby, Shanmugam Sathish Kumar, Pillai Nataraj Boothalingam, "The power of AI, IoT, and advanced quantum based optical systems in smart cities",Optical and Quantum Electronics, Vol.56, issue 3,PP. 450, 2024, Springer.

4

Case Studies and Prototypes for Blockchain and Artificial Intelligence (AI) Integration in 5G-enabled (IoT) Systems: Toward Secure, Intelligent, and Efficient Paradigms

Khalid Aziz[1], Sakshi Dua[1], and Prabal Gupta[2]

[1]School of Computer Applications, Lovely Professional University, India
[2]Department of ECE, SCSE, Lovely Professional University, India
Email: khalid.12105643@lpu.in; sakshi.26557@lpu.co.in; prabal.gupta9@gmail.com

Abstract

This chapter critically examines the integration of blockchain technology with IoT, AI, and 5G networks, highlighting enhancements in data security, real-time processing, and system efficiency across various industries, including healthcare and logistics. It further explores innovative solutions like blockchain sharding and lightweight consensus for improving scalability and performance in 5G-IoT environments, establishing a foundational framework for future technological advancements.

Keywords: Blockchain technology, artificial intelligence, AI, Fifth generation networks, IoT, secure data transmission, intelligent authentication, supply chain transparency

4.1 Introduction

It is the evolution and integration of new 5G networks that is the disruptive aspect that fuels most of the development in the communications technology due to speed, transport capacity, and networking characteristics associated with 5G. This is a very big step up, especially for IoT, smart cities,

DOI: 10.1201/9788743809050-5

augmented reality, and self-driving cars. Unlike the previous generating networks that require broadband, 5G comprises input multi-dimension, output multi-dimension (MIMO); a network that offers unique business challenges to corporations [1].

On the other hand, the use of these technologies in 5G networks may enhance their flexibility in a manner that they serve better applications and services need better planning and decision making. Yet, such advancements raise new threats regarding the construction of shelters, privacy, and operational depth [2]. Issues such as these require an even greater elucidation of the problems by the blockchain machinery providing the decentralized, mutant, and transparent solution for the welfare and productivity of the 5G IoT system [3].

4.2 Convergence of Blockchain and AI toward IoT

Figure 4.1 outlines the key concepts and benefits of integrating blockchain expertise (and AI) into the IoT ecosystem [4]. This integration solves many of the challenges faced by IoT systems. Here are the key points and benefits:

4.2.1 Decentralized network

Blockchain technology creates a shared network that ensures that no single entity can control the entire system. This decentralization increases the pliability of the system to failures and occurrences.

4.2.2 Digital signature

Digital signatures are used to validate the authenticity and integrity of emails or data. Digital signatures in an IoT scenario make the data of the IoT environment authentic and untampered.

4.2.3 Validation

In blockchain, validation processes will be about checking whether the transactions are valid and genuine. It is important for IoT systems to verify that the data to be processed and analyzed is correct (valid and reliable).

4.2.4 Digital ledger

Blockchain is a public record system that includes all transactions and their hashes in the same list. Here we can keep the history of everything that has happened in our IoT, thus giving us transparency/confidence.

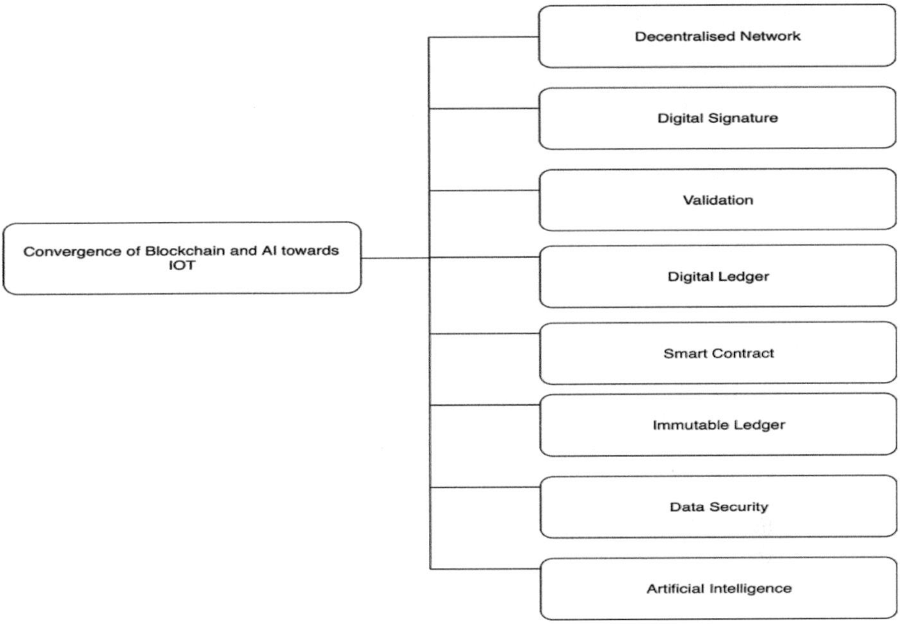

Figure 4.1 Convergence of blockchain and AI toward IoT.

4.2.5 Clever contracts

Smart contracts are written in code, where the rules of the contract are directly written into it. They help in the simplification of processes and make IoT systems smarter, less dependent on the need for intermediaries, and much efficient.

4.2.6 Immutable ledger

The immutability of blockchain records ensures that once entered, it becomes impossible to modify. These features are very important to avoid any kind of data busting in IoT.

4.2.7 Data security

Combining blockchain with IoT can increase data security. Blockchain coding can strengthen the storage and transmission of information and prevent unauthorized access and tampering.

Blockchain coding ensures the stability and transmission of information and prevents unauthorized access and tampering.

4.2.8 Artificial intelligence

AI layering brings high-end analytics and decision-making features to the IoT system. Taking IoT as a blockchain incorporation with the addition of AI into consideration, it comes with an ability to learn and tinker with huge amounts of information through Smart systems in a more secure on-chain platform.

The development of the Internet of Things has shifted the numeric reality on an absolute level, as numerous devices from different parts of the world were interconnected. Internet of Things (IoT) is making its way to become the companion of modern life, and it seems that more and more people will use smart devices along with high-speed data from the 5G network. The current architecture for data transfer at the center is significant for the hazards inherent to IoT functions. Skilled blockchain could address this risk and develop a safe, autonomous, and credible IoT community. Besides, the inclusion of AI in the 5G wireless systems will compensate for some abilities, including traffic control and virtual reality, but slightly new types of security threats will emerge. This chapter overviews the use of blockchain and AI in 5G-enabled IoT systems along with the corresponding issues, prospects, and remedies [5].

The new technology of wireless communications 5G is presented with the key contribution of faster pace, lower dormancy, and connectivity across all dimensions. This is a progress that will go a long way in developing the IoT devices that are expected to reach over 75 billion by 2025, as pointed out by [11]. IoT as a complex depends on interaction in an immediate manner in the IoT environment between the devices, be they home, technology, or even medical, to name but a few. But such interactions still incur a very big problem of huge refuge and solitude. Blockchain technology begins offering an operational explanation to these challenges since it lacks similarity or duality. This makes the technology secure and transparent and avails many benefits on the trust and reliability of IoT systems as proposed by [12, 13]. It offers new features that aid in the executive analysis of data as well as an augmentation of business process automation.

AI procedures can scan through vast amounts of data created by IoT devices in order to derive insights, improve operations, and enhance user experience. The union of AI and blockchain in 5G-enabled IoT systems might prompt smart application construction that is efficient, secure, and resistant to cyber threats [13]. Many studies have established the possibility of the integration of AI and blockchain in multiple ways. For example, in the medical domain, blockchain can be used for safe management of patient data; meanwhile, AI will analyze such data for treatment plans customized to individual needs. [14] demonstrates how the integration of blockchain with AI enhances security and functionality in EHR and aids honesty and action for better patient outcomes. It can integrate blockchain and AI within 5G-enabled IoT systems to serve to develop intelligent transportation systems.

These systems improve the management of traffic, security, and minimize accidents. Ref. [15] described a blockchain framework for secure V2X communication, which supports 5G, enabling predictive modelling using AI in traffic and dynamic route optimization. Their framework provides a potential way of combining technologies to bring about a safe, efficient, and reliable system. Electronics will greatly benefit from this integration, also. They rely on IoT devices to monitor and control the distribution of energy. Intelligent grids are made safer and more efficient by incorporating blockchain and artificial intelligence.

Figure 4.2, showing the clever applications, reveals that the blockchain technology plays a central role in the 5G-enabled IoT ecosystem. In the center of the picture, there is a sign of the blockchain, which marks its

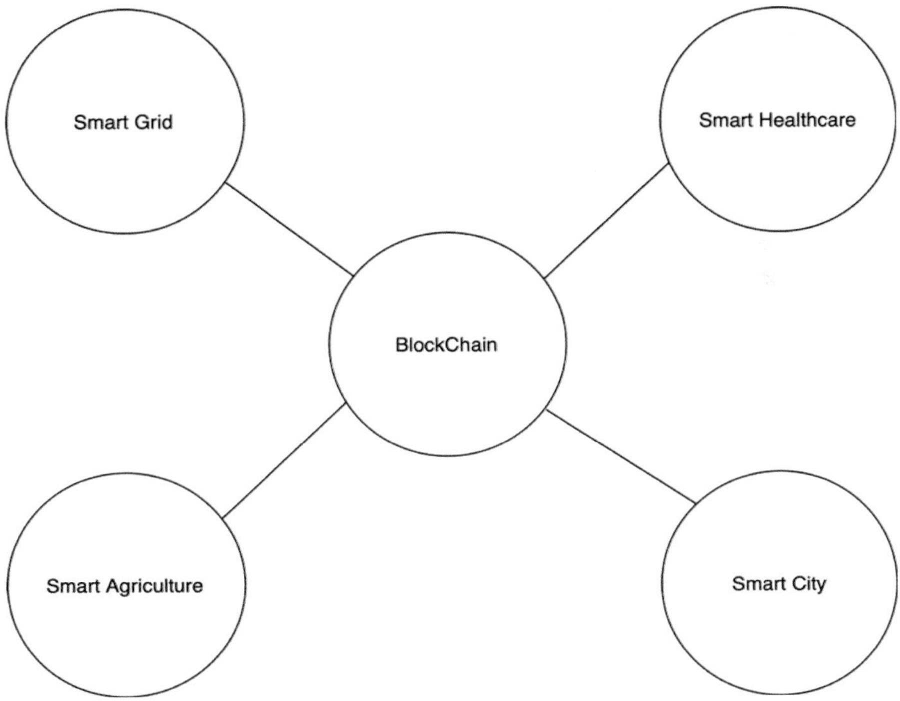

Figure 4.2 Applications of blockchain in clever systems.

critical function of securing and organizing the interactions within the system. The outer circle shows the various areas where this integration has a specific impact: These are: clever city, clever healthcare, clever manufacturing, clever grid, and intervention in agriculture [7]. Every department has an exchange with core blockchain, and this exchange demonstrates how blockchain technology can optimize the operations, safety, and intelligence of cross operations.

4.3 Clever Applications

4.3.1 Clever city

In the first segment, smart cities use blockchain to optimize the delivery of various city services successfully. This encompasses traffic flow, waste disposal, energy consumption, and the like, security, and other related matters. Citizens' faith is earned since blockchain provides information reliability and transparency, and hence, the municipal services are made efficient.

4.3.2 Clever healthcare

To the right, innovative solutions include exciting big healthcare applications such as blockchain management of patients' medical records, effective realization of administrative procedures, and telemedicine. It helps to maintain the patient's identity extremely private while it enables data sharing or exchange among the different platforms and the providers.

4.3.3 Clever manufacturing

Placed at the lowest right angle, wise production utilizes blockchain technology in improving supply chain, protecting invention, and automating compliance.

4.3.4 Clever grid

Further down to the lower left corner: smart grids combined with the utilization of blockchain assess energy distribution to improve efficacy. These are, for example, P2P energy trading, connecting distributed renewable energy generation, and improving the reliability and robustness of power systems.

4.3.5 Clever agriculture

To the left, innovative agriculture suffers from blockchain use that helps to increase the survivability of the food chain and traceability. Blockchain makes a positive impact in the agricultural industry by providing record-keeping of crops and herds and improving the processes for the supply chain.

4.4 Related Work

A new challenging domain is born from the collaboration of AI and the new 5G networks to meet the challenge of managing the complexity and improving the features of today's communication systems. AI plays an important role today in solving numerous issues related to personalization, real-time operational activity, and decision-making of 5G networks. For instance, AI can fasten the Internet of Things (IoT) network proportional to big data from devices, improve self-driving cars' generation capability, and again boost the capability of smart city operations.

The key issue, however, for the integration of AI into 5G networks is major security concerns. It should also be noted that despite the transition from a traditional perspective of IoT enclaves as individual, vertically integrated networks, the core architectural layout of IoT is still one that inherently lacks both the strength against cyberattacks, as well as the discreteness of data exchange, that would be necessary to adequately guarantee its security.

Blockchain technology and information sharing systems provide a good solution to this security challenge. Blockchain can thus address some of the basic challenges like distribution, privacy, and security in an intelligent-driven 5G network through the sharing of information transparently, securely, and with an immutable nature between nodes.

The paper by [7] is also on the capacity of blockchain as a scalable and adaptable security solution for the IoT network application. However, combining blockchain with AI in 5G networks is relatively rare, even though the combination has only recently begun to receive attention. Various studies prove that blockchain can enhance the refugee and efficiency of AI-invariant 5G systems through decentralized and transparent data management and processing [8]. For instance, this blockchain and AI integration system may be helpful in a smart city where the safe, efficient control of information benefits the living of a citizen [9].

Various scientists and industry gurus are drawn to convergence-enabled IoT systems. This chapter provides a brief literature review of the most recent development and seminal research in this collaboration. Blockchain skills have turned into a promising solution in handling security and trust problems in IoT. The authors provide a proper review of the blockchain in IoT applications, where they agree about the feasibility of enhancing data integrity, confidentiality, and consensus in various processes. Their work lays down the major strengths of blockchain systems in creating reliable and transparent IoT architectures. Ref. [13] presented a system based on blockchain for efficient management of IoT data, which shows that the security and efficiency of the data sharing among the IoTs are improved. Data access management in collaboration with their approach, grounded on smart contracts, does not lead to a violation of policy.

The use of artificial intelligence, especially the use of machine learning, has seen a very fast growth in IoT data processing and decision making [18]. The roles of machine learning based approaches are many in deep learning approaches under consideration for the analysis of big data of IoT, which demonstrates the ability of AI to help ascertain insightful findings about the construction of IoT from big data. An integrated model of management of IoT has been created based on the concept of intelligence. What they have done shows how reinforcement learning can be applied for dynamic and online policy for network service deployment aimed at enhancing total system performance and efficiency, including energy consumption.

As a result, with the help of 5G technology, it is possible to reveal new IoT opportunities, such as low-end communications, as well as edge applications. Ref. [20] provides an understanding of how 5G meets with edge computing in IoT contexts to achieve real-time data access and decision-making at the network's edge. Ref. [21] explored the development of utilizing MEC to offload the workload of resource-consumer IoT devices from 5G-IoT systems. Their contribution reveals relatively impressive values concerning energy consumption and the availability of IoT applications.

Ref. [22] fully agreed that 5G-IoT networks have main security challenges that can be solved by blockchain-based artificial intelligence using artificial intelligence for intelligent choice. They are an example of how favorable opportunities of different technologies are fused into even more synergistic and effective IoT systems. Further, in a similar study, [23] have designed a blockchain-integrated government system for the application of IoT for 5G. Together, their work shows how blockchain can be used to prove that the updating of intellectual property models is done secretly. This chapter serves to fill this gap by offering a closer look at various models, and is further elucidated by examples that cross-cut across sectors. Table 4.1 describes the comparative analysis of the existing works.

4.4.1 Honesty level of a node

$$H_{\mathrm{n}} > H_{\mathrm{T}} \tag{4.1}$$

In his paper, [24] has shown that this equation would decide which level of honesty can make him a leader node within the blockchain network according to his honesty level. His honesty level must be above a threshold represented by HT. Therefore, the honesty level rises as nodes perform validity operations to ensure only trusted nodes can perform critical aspects in the network.

4.4.2 Positive honesty value

$$H_{\mathrm{p}} = \sum_{w=0}^{i} H_{\mathrm{vw}} \tag{4.2}$$

Ref. [24] gave an example of how this formula calculates the sum of cumulative honesties, HP in a node over a definite time. Moreover, the honesty value of every work is HVW, and the total no of mining jobs closed is represented primarily as "ii." The positive honesty value builds up each time all the tasks carried out by the node are correct, and overall trust in the network is attained.

4.4.3 Negative honesty value

$$H_{\mathrm{n}} = -\sum_{w=0}^{i} H_{\mathrm{vw}} \tag{4.3}$$

Ref. [24] also clarifies that this expression is equal to the cumulative negative honesty value of the node under consideration with respect to any of the "malicious wrong action," or a "malicious action." Because of this, such nodes would have fewer honesty levels and thus the critical operations performed in the network would be influenced the least.

4.4.4 Total honesty level

$$H_{\mathrm{n}} = H_{\mathrm{p}} + H_{\mathrm{n}} \tag{4.4}$$

[24] argued that the average honesty of a node is the sum of the positive, namely the HPHP, and negative, namely the HNH, honesty values. This,

therefore, means that this metric determines whether a node's behavior within a given network will soon be credible for right actions or wrongdoings.

4.4.5 Mining time

$$T_{\mathrm{m}} = \frac{D \times 2^{24}}{P_{\mathrm{WN}} \times T_{\mathrm{WN}}} \tag{4.5}$$

As noted by [24], this formula was employed to estimate the mining time (Tm) with the level of difficulty (DD), the hashing power of a worker node (PWN), as well as the number of total worker nodes (TWN). The ability to adjust the difficulty level will ensure blocks are mined at a relatively flat rate; however, the hash rate and the number of workers define the overall speed and effectiveness of mining. These quotes above have been very useful for designing or implementing the blockchain and AI-integrated 5G-enabled IoT systems. These ensured safe data processing, reliable node performance, and resource utilization, to guarantee that such an advanced technological solution can be successfully implemented without any problems at all.

4.5 Layered Architecture of Blockchain

Figure 4.3 presents a multi-layered view of the components that constitute a blockchain system [5]. Each layer plays a specific role in ensuring the blockchain's functionality, security, and efficiency. Here is an explanation of each layer:

4.5.1 Application layer

This layer enumerates the application that the end user employs in executing operations on the blockchain. It consists of different decentralized applications or Apps that are based on a blockchain for several purposes, like finance, supply chain, healthcare, among others. This stands as the first level of utilization of the services offered by blockchain.

4.5.2 Platform software

This layer thus consists of features and middleware that allow the building and execution of decentralized apps. It also includes innovations and platforms of smart contracts and other related applications in the field of blockchain technology. These include Ethereum development tools, Hyperledger Fabric, and the blockchain development environment, among others.

Table 4.1 Contributions to the field.

Study	Focus	Key contributions	Authors
AI in 5G networks	Managing complexities and enhancing capabilities in modern telecommunications systems.	AI optimizes network operations, enhances autonomous vehicle performance, and improves clever city application efficiency.	[5]
AI and clever city applications	Analyzing vast amounts of data generated by IoT devices.	AI improves efficiency in clever city applications.	[6]
Blockchain in AI-driven 5G networks	Addressing security concerns in AI-driven 5G networks.	Blockchain ensures transparency, immutability, and secure data sharing, addressing decentralization, privacy, and security issues.	[7]
Blockchain in IoT networks	Providing scalable and adaptive defence mechanisms in IoT networks.	Blockchain enhances data integrity, privacy, and decentralized consensus mechanisms.	[17]
Blockchain-based data management	Improving security and efficiency in data sharing among IoT devices.	Blockchain-based system leverages clever contracts to automate data access control.	[13]
AI for IoT big data analytics	Extracting valuable insights from vast amounts of IoT-generated data.	Various deep learning methods for IoT big data analytics.	[18]
AI-driven resource management	Optimizing resource management in IoT networks.	Reinforcement learning dynamically allocates network resources, improving performance and energy efficiency.	[19]
5G and edge computing in IoT	Enabling real-time data processing and decision-making at the network edge.	Framework for 5G and edge computing synergies.	[20]
Mobile edge computing in 5G-IoT systems	Offloading computational tasks from resource-constrained IoT devices.	Improved energy consumption and processing time for IoT applications.	[21]
Blockchain-enabled AI for 5G-IoT	Addressing security concerns and leveraging AI for intelligent decision-making in 5G-IoT networks.	Combines blockchain and AI for more robust and efficient IoT systems.	[22]

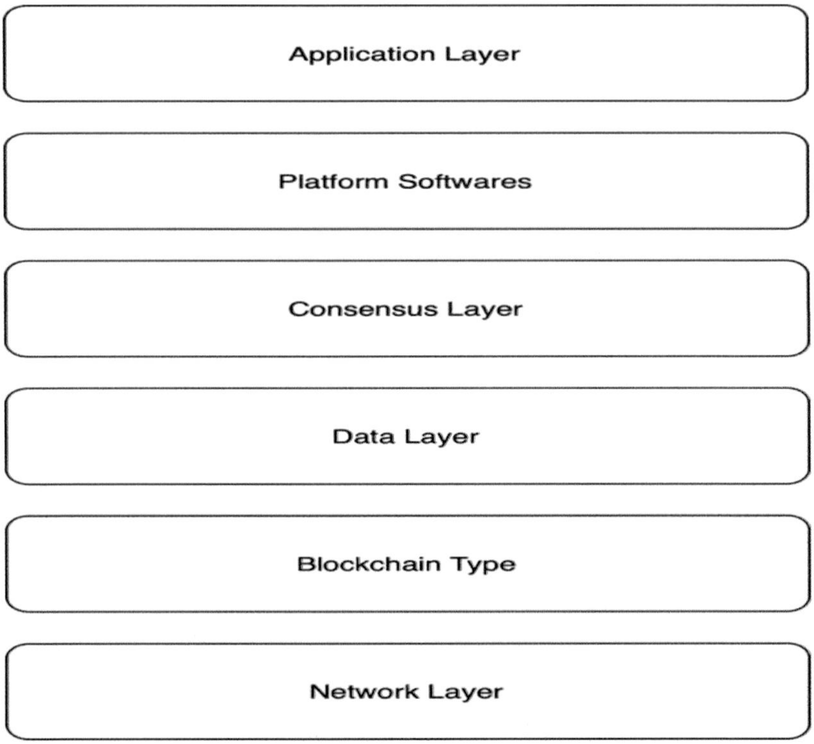

Figure 4.3 Layered architecture of blockchain.

4.5.3 Consensus layer

The consensus layer is needed to ensure the precision and unchangeability of the apparatus of the blockchain itself. It includes the processes in the network the nodes even go to agree that a certain transaction is authentic. There are three types of consensus algorithms: the proof of work (PoW), the proof of stake (PoS), and the Byzantine fault tolerance (PBFT).

4.5.4 Data layer

This level is reinforcing the actual construction of both information and the blockchain itself. It has real bricks, which include transaction information and any other information that would be required. The data layer makes certain that all data is secured beyond doubt and is also stored in a way that can be marked as unconditionally altered, to offer assurance of a provable transaction history.

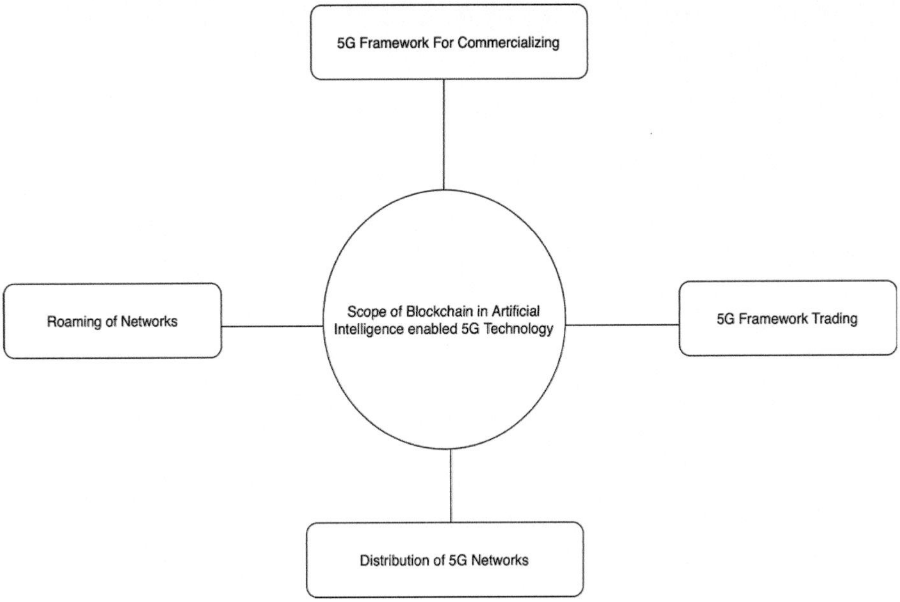

Figure 4.4 The range of blockchain in artificial intelligence-enabled 5G technology.

4.5.5 Blockchain type

This layer gets to determine the nature of the blockchain, and these include the civic, reserved, or group type. The former vary in both accessibility and degree of control; public blockchains are essentially open to anyone, public blockchains are for a select number of participants, and consortium blockchains are governed by a set of organizations.

4.5.6 Network layer

The system level includes the substrate upon which all bulges in a blockchain network are integrated. This also involves the administration of the interaction with the nodes and with the pumping of the transactions and the blocks. This also ensures all stakeholders are informed adequately and they can add on what is expected in the process of adoption.

Figure 4.4 illustrates the various areas where blockchain technology can enhance the capabilities of AI-enabled 5G networks [5]. The central theme of the figure is the "Range of blockchain in artificial intelligence-enabled 5G technology," which highlights four key applications.

4.6 Range of Blockchain in Artificial Intelligence-enabled 5G Technology

4.6.1 5G framework for commercializing

Blockchain technology appears to assist in the commercialization of 5G networks via a decentralization of the telecoms' assets. This includes allowing small network operators to operate and monetize their telecommunications towers while receiving equitable remuneration, and thereby not being overly reliant on a central body.

4.6.2 5G framework trading

Based on the presented theoretical concepts and insights, it can be mentioned that blockchain can greatly enhance the trading framework within the 5G networks. This encompasses the ongoing swapping of telecom services between the different MNOs in the country. Blockchain promotes safe, effective, and efficient utilization, exchange, and allocation of network bandwidth and necessities such as physical infrastructure.

4.6.3 Distribution of 5G networks

In this case, blockchain strengthens the distribution of 5G networks by overseeing the allocation and consumption of bandwidth. This is most helpful for the small operators who possibly cannot plan for a spectrum band directly. Through leasing of the spectrum in the band, the operators can gain access to bandwidth owned by other larger operators or that which is not frequently used properly by the existing operators.

4.6.4 Roaming of networks

Blockchain enables the simplification of the roaming procedures in the 5G, where the payments and access are negotiated directly between different operators through the usage of smart contracts. Smart contracts on blockchain guarantee that all deals and negotiations are straightforward, and the history is easily traced and correlated, thus excluding the need for complicated and costly roaming agreements.

Average nodes per cluster

In Figure 4.5, we begin with the first bar chart, where the mean nodes per cluster algorithms involve ASLPR, ERA, FSFLA, GAPSO, and the proposed algorithm. The presented algorithm suggests a significant decrease in the number of nodes per cluster on average compared to the other algorithms. This shows that the given algorithm is even better placed in terms of clustering since nodes will be spread out much better in different clusters. The proposition connected with efficient clustering is improved load balancing,

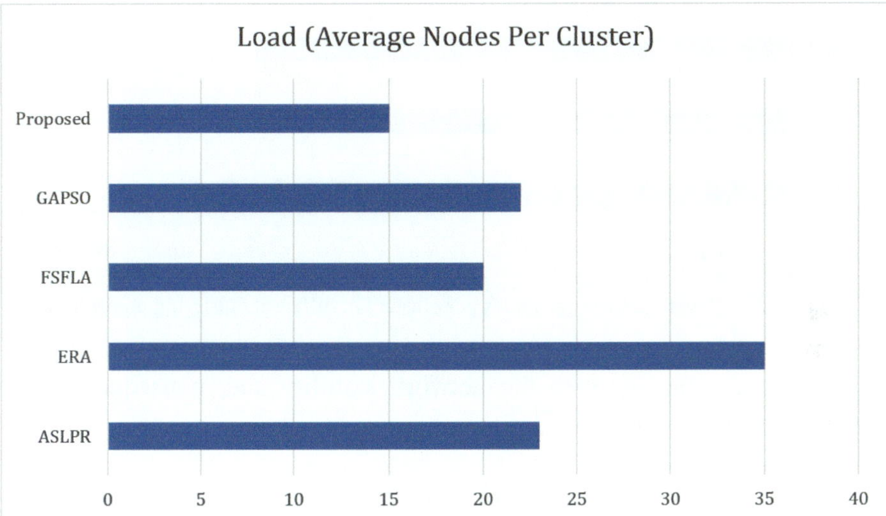

Figure 4.5 Load (average nodes per cluster) in different clustering algorithms.

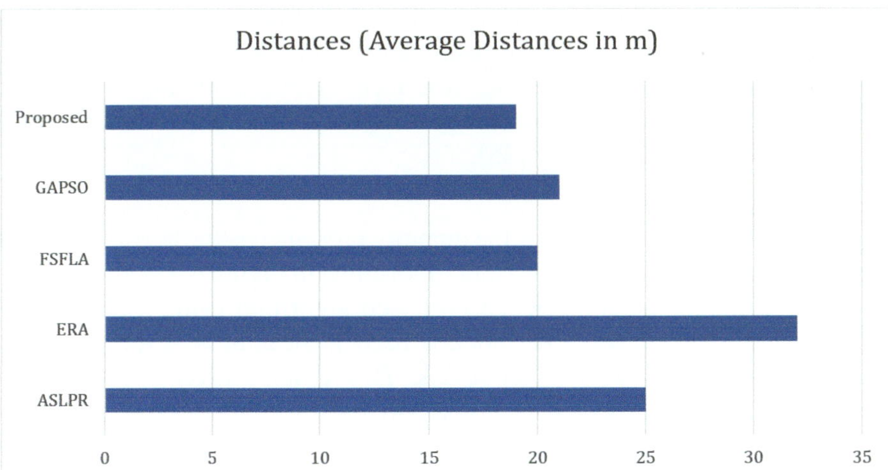

Figure 4.6 Distance (average nodes per cluster) in different clustering algorithms.

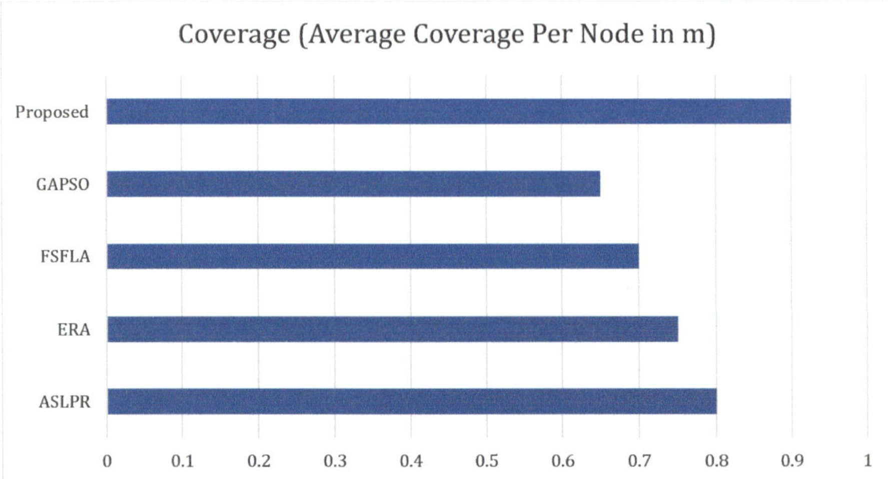

Figure 4.7 Coverage (average nodes per cluster) in different clustering algorithms.

which is a key factor given the network stability and, consequently, the elongation of its life cycle [25].

Average distances

The second bar chart given in Figure 4.6 represents again the Avg node to CH distance of the same set of algorithms. This makes it possible for the proposed algorithm to have the minimum average distance, and therefore improve on the overall communication distances of the network. Minimizing distances to their least possible measurements is crucial in Aspect Two since the energy utilized to convey a signal reduces with a reduction in distance. This improvement enhances the energy efficiency of the network to increase its useful life as pointed out by [25].

Average coverage per node

Finally, in the third bar chart, the quantity presented is the average number of covers per node graphed by various algorithms in Figure 4.7. This is shown through the implementation of the proposed algorithm using a format that shows the average coverage per node is higher, meaning that the algorithm can cover more area with fewer nodes. This is advantageous in securing the imprint and insurance of network coverage, leaving a smaller number of nodes; therefore, it becomes easier to avoid extra costs and additional complications. Increased coverage per node also increases the redundancy, as well as the reliability of the network, to guarantee all corners of the area are well covered in [25].

4.7 Case Studies and Prototypes

4.7.1 Clever healthcare monitoring

That approaches IoT, blockchain, and AI as pivotal to healthcare innovation due to the issues of sensitivity, security, rights of access, and data analysis in handling the identified concerns. When deployed as a complementary set, these three technologies can put a seal on the patient's health information confidentiality, provide the means to convey real-time material, and ensure that clinical decisions regarding individual patients transition more to a preventive mode. Ref. [26] have developed a blockchain-based system to securely and privately share health information in an IoT environment. The system solves several important problems in healthcare:

4.7.1.1 Data security and privacy

HHS is one of the categories of data that needs measures to secure and protect privacy, as health information is one of the most secure, as there are legal and ethical frameworks such as the HIPAA Act or the GDPR Act. As will be seen, this data is well suited to be stored, as well as shared through a mechanism founded on the blockchain. Here's how blockchain enhances security and privacy:

Immutability: Since data are saved within the blockchain, the records cannot be altered, which makes the time-sensitive medical records safe from modification. This goes a long way in helping to maintain the data of patients as a result.

Encryption: Considering that data is stored on the blockchain, it becomes difficult for a third party to access the data without authorization.

Decentralization: What you will notice is that this is a distributed ledger technology, and there are no central points that can be exploited to breach health record databases.

4.7.1.2 Smart contract-enabled access control

Security in a healthcare system is central to preventing the authorization of people (doctors, specialists, and caregivers) to permit only access to their patient information on their side. This system uses smart contracts, also called "clever contracts," which are self-executing applications coded onto the blockchain characterized by rules regarding data access.

Granular control: Smart contracts also decide who can view or cannot view some portion of the patient data collected in the healthcare environment. For instance, a GP can probably move around the whole clinical record of the patient, whereas the specialist can only see a limited section, for example, cardiology results.

Automatic enforcement: These contracts facilitate the creation or removal of access privileges where they are necessary for a contract to run based on certain conditions, such that privacy policies are not breached.

Transparency and accountability: As mentioned earlier, each time the medical data is utilized on the blockchain, it becomes evident what data has been used at what time and by whom the data was accessed.

4.7.1.3 IoT integration

It interoperates with smart wearable devices, health smart pills, and home health care gadgets that are constantly acquiring health information from patients. This integration works as follows:

Continuous data collection: Fitness trackers, smartwatches, and home sensors track different signs (heart rate, glucose level, medication compliance, and others) in real-time, which gives a steady stream of data to doctors.

Secure data transmission: This information is effectively transported over the blockchain since it is encrypted, and only authorized healthcare providers can attempt to decrypt it.

Patient-centric care: With data collected from IoT devices, patients' health status can be remotely observed and managed, and thereby can determine when there is a complication that needs emergency medical intervention through Analytical Processing. For example, the system could identify the basic pulse or a sign of a heart problem from data collected by the wearable devices.

Automation and alerts: What is more, the integration makes it possible to deliver automatic notifications to healthcare professionals in case of any abnormality, thus making it possible to provide intervention if it is needed.

4.7.2 Healthcare 5.0

The continually growing human population needs better methods of health care delivery, and medical technologies such as wireless telemedical services differ. AI, the ability to rapidly disseminate data, and the integration of smart devices are setting a higher benchmark for the healthcare industry. Today, healthcare services use progressive IoT devices for isolated patient watching, which can be distributed into four types: Wearable health monitoring equipment (e.g., Fuelband and Fitbit). Face, hands, arms: Use medical equipment (e.g., insulin pump). Electronic health records (EHR) give immediate patient attention by using the records of patient.

Consequently, [5] further recommended that blockchain could be used as the integrity map for storing medical states, to achieve privacy-aware healthcare systems. Their solution is as follows – the cloud server retains the patient data while the fog data are hashed and are stored in the blockchain. Each modification made to the cloud hardware is reflected in the hash value, which basically means that any alteration made in the system will be easily noted. This author also advises against heavy encryption protocols on the networks to allow fast network connectivity.

4.7.3 Clever home

The difficulties of confidentiality and safety in the IoT are because there are multiple connected objects, and all of them can be vulnerable. Since IoT devices are now quickly spreading throughout the world, it continues to be a problem to secure such a system while upholding its security and privacy. Ref. [27] in their paper on IoT for smart buildings in 2017, and suggested that blockchain technology is important to mitigate these issues.

Key features of the proposed solution:

Blockchain technology: Blockchain is an implementation of a decentralized or distributive ledger to improve on security and/or privacy. By using blockchain, information exchange between devices can be stored as well as confirmed as secure and original without a central control center.

No proof-of-work (PoW) or cryptocurrencies:

In contrast with other blockchain platforms, for instance, Bitcoin, which relies on PoW consensus, this solution is free from PoW, which aptly consumes massive computational power and electricity. The authors also do not incorporate cryptocurrencies into the system, which makes the system cohesive with IoT environments since operations have to be lightweight and efficient.

Network architecture:

The devices, including thermostats, lights, and security systems that are in a smart home, are part thus, of the architecture. While most systems employ a cloud storage model of IoT data, the system under consideration deploys a fog storage model that is closer to the edge devices (IoT devices). This not only reduces the time that is taken before performance but also the speed at which performance is done. The system is structured to function based on an overlay network, which is in fact a superimposed network that is on the actual physical network. It offers the opportunity for pinpoint, direct messaging among devices of this type of architecture. To handle many number of IoT devices and minimize the overhead, the proposed system categorizes the devices into groups, and each group has a single master node called "bunch-head" (BH). The BH is the focus of the group, and it acts as a manager of the communication and data exchange within the corresponding cluster. This organizational structure is useful in avoiding the circulation of many data and thus decreases network traffic.

Benefits of the proposed system:

Reduced network load: A direct conclusion from the verified simulation results provided by [27] is that this blockchain approach lessens the burden on the network. To this end, it should be noted that by categorizing devices into groups and assigning each group a bunch-head to control it, the chances of extra signalling and overhead are reduced, and thus the network becomes more efficient.

Improved suitability for IoT devices: In particular, IoT devices have restricted processing capabilities and restricted energy capacities. When combined with fragmentation and coupling reductions through bunching and fog storage, respectively, the system is designed to cater to IoT needs that PoW is unable to meet.

4.7.4 Supply chain management

The blockchain and Internet of Things (IoT) in supply chain management (SCM) seek to address significant problems like fakes and tracking of temperature-sensitive (hot) drugs, respectively. In their work, [28] described a system design for supply chain transparency, traceability, and security, especially for the supply of pharmaceutical products. The proposed system takes advantage of the strengths of both; blockchain for its decentralized and unchangeable database, and IoT for its monitoring and data acquisition.

4.7.4.1 Three main supply chain entities

4.7.4.1.1 Manufacturers

The manufacturers of drugs and related pharmaceutical products in the market.

4.7.4.1.2 Wholesalers

Firms through which the medicinal products produced by producers are channelled to chemists and hospitals.

4.7.4.1.3 Pharmacies

Vendor includes the drug outlets or stores from which the ultimate consumers purchase their medicines through the outlets, including hospitals, clinics, and drug stores, among others.

They are members of a blockchain P2P network, which guarantees the unhindered interconnectivity of all participants while still providing for the notion of openness and protection.

4.7.4.2 Monitoring of temperature-sensitive medicines

Concerning hot products, which are the products that can be used only under certain specific temperature conditions for storage and shipping, the system offers cooling processes. These processes include:

4.7.4.2.1 Cooling

Validating that the temperatures which are employed in the generation and preservation approaches are at their optimal point.

4.7.4.2.2 Transporting

Performing duties that involve making certain that the medicine gets to the right temperature level in transit.

4.7.4.2.3 Distributing

Protecting the product until it gets to the target end user or consumer, as the case may be.

IoT devices (temperature sensors, for instance) are linked to the medicine packages or containers, and thus the system keeps on recording the environmental conditions by tracking the features, including temperature and humidity, among others. These devices provide real-time information to the blockchain to guarantee appropriate handling of the medicines from the supply chain.

4.7.4.2.4 Blockchain integration

Blockchain technology guarantees the integrity of all information passed through the transport, storage, and distribution of the medicines in the supply chain, as this information is easily accessible, and its access is encrypted for all stakeholders. Any deviation, including temperature fluctuations, can be easily detected and the root causes determined.

4.7.4.2.5 Peer-to-peer (P2P) network

The food supply chain can be seen as a fully connected peer-to-peer supply chain where systems (manufacturers, wholesalers, and pharmacies) exchange their data with each other. This, in turn, increases data security and minimizes acts of alteration.

Raft algorithm for fast block delivery: The blockchain is aided by fast servers, which help in the relay of blocks, which means that storage and validation of data in a blockchain network. Raft algorithm, as stated by [28], is a recommended consensus algorithm that is most favorable for achieving much efficiency and quick delivery in distributed systems.

4.7.4.3 Main contributions of the system

Counterfeit medicine prevention: Closely related to them, fake medicines are one of the biggest concerns to pharmaceutical skeptics and can be dangerous for people. In blockchain, every medicine can be traced from the manufacturer to the consumer, and the journey is well recorded. Either way, capabilities are built to document each transaction to the blockchain, meaning that each trade is immutable. This also minimizes the entries of counterfeit drugs in the related supply chain because all the stakeholders in the network affirm the source and the legitimacy of the medicine.

4.7.4.3.1 Monitoring hot medicines

Temperature sensing is one of the biggest uses of IoT devices in managing temperature-sensitive medical products. The collected data from the sensors is input into the blockchain, while the conditions involve temperature and the humidity level all along the supply chain. As used earlier, if there is any deviation from the required conditions, stakeholders can take necessary corrective actions.

4.7.4.3.2 Real-time data sharing

The system covers the comprehensive transmission of data in real-time for various parties in the supply chain. It contributes toward the right decisions being made at the right squal decisions in the organization as well. For instance, wholesalers or pharmacies can obtain on quick check on the conditions under which a given batch of medicine was transported and stored.

4.7.4.3.3 Transparency and traceability

Blockchain here guarantees that all processes are fully open and articulated. Any stakeholder in the chain can therefore look at the records on the blockchain to be assured that the medicines were treated in the right manner from the manufacturing company to the delivery company.

4.7.5 Blockchain for AI-enabled 5G

Blockchain technology has developed as an outstanding invention as it is an advanced integrated application of linking the data blocks systematically using cryptographic hash in order to produce a decentralized digital ledger. This has made this kind of feature to provide security to the data besides improving the translucence, uniformity, and dependability in different uses.

4.7.5.1 Systematic linking of blocks

A block in a blockchain is made up of a number of transactions and the hash of the previous block, this being why it is called a blockchain. It becomes very difficult to introduce any changes to any of the informational blocks without having to change all the succeeding blocks so as to maintain good data integrity.

4.7.5.2 Cryptographic hashing

A cryptography hash is a process by which data is transformed into a string of characters of a constant length. They claim that even a very small shift in the input data will also mean a different hash. This helps to check on the reliability and uniqueness of the data that backs records within a blockchain.

4.7.5.3 Translucence

There are different types of distributed ledger technology, but most of the networks are public. The said translucence enables users to view all transaction history and thus gain trust among users since they can verify transactions themselves.

4.7.5.4 Uniformity

The data that is distributed on a blockchain is the same in all nodes in the system. It is a shared ledger accessible only to participant nodes, eliminating the problem of different ledgers or inconsistent versions.

4.7.5.5 Dependability

It is this distributed architecture of the application that makes it free from fraud and manipulation since the features in the blockchain have no authoritative owner. This reliability needs to be maintained for parts of applications where trust is paramount.

4.7.5.6 Secure transaction registration

It means that 5G networks for making transactions can operate at a higher speed and have a very small delay time. This, when integrated with blockchain, enables firms to record transactions at the same time and safely, which is suitable for profit sectors such as finance, supply chain, and logistics.

4.7.5.7 Authentication

Blockchain serves as a reliable means of identifying users and devices in a 5G network. Organizations can use smart contracts for the automation of authentication since restricted individuals or groups can only access the required information or service.

4.7.6 5G outline for commercializing

Crowdsourcing is gradually being embraced as a viable strategy in the management of telecom infrastructure, most especially for operators with emerging markets who may not afford to invest in the constructs of communication towers. This can be achieved through applying this method that aims at mobilising various players in the telecommunication value chain, including but not limited to small individual tower owners, the local businesspeople, and members of the community to contribute resources and expertise that strengthens a more improved and efficient telecommunication network. Here is how this model works and the role of blockchain and smart contracts in facilitating it.

Thus, the objective of applying crowdsourcing in telecommunications is of interest to the current superintendencies.

4.7.6.1 Role of smaller network operators

A problem that seems to hinder new entrants, mostly the smaller network operators, is the issue of high infrastructure costs. These operators can leverage existing communication towers owned by individuals or other small organizations, thus minimizing much on capital needed for improving network coverage.

4.7.6.2 Management of communications towers

The beauty of outsourcing the management of towers is that small operators can now concentrate on delivering quality service while tapping into local resources. It increases network coverage and availability where currently low, increases the general availability of connectivity, and makes service delivery more reliable.

4.7.6.3 Licensing and compensation

Before anything, the owners of the communication towers must be properly licensed and fairly remunerated for infrastructure space. This enables tower owners to have their legal and fiscal rights recognized whilst also being paid adequately for allowing their structures to be occupied by networks.

4.7.7 5G Framework trading

Framework trading involves the sharing of telecom services among mobile network operators (MNOs), categorized into active and passive trading. Active sharing, facilitated by network virtualization, is more effective, whereas passive sharing involves the use of shared infrastructure like towers and telecommunication rooms.

4.7.8 Circulation of 5G networks

Radio networks are much more thinly spread and expensive channels. The service providers obtain their sub-band from the regulators, which in turn can be used or lettable by other operators. This system enables small worker operators to offer 5G treatment without getting a price license fee, by leveraging the spectrum bands that are already exploited by other typical clients with a similar nature as digital radio and government systems.

4.7.9 Network roaming

Roaming is still slightly complicated today and still requires agents and intermediaries to facilitate payment and fees. In the 5G environment, the carrier and the international brokers would have to converse with each other. Consequently, smart contracts can also enable the automation process with traceable, recorded, and auditable communications at a comparatively low communication cost.

4.7.10 Monitoring and agreement

In fact, having such a high number of IoT devices will require more visionary business models and services to be developed. Smart contracts in the blockchain allow for decentralized models in contrast to intermediary service provider models, and provide benefits mentioned about trust, transparency, regulation, and smooth processes in control functions and payments.

4.8 Future work

As for further research and development, it is highly important to expand the impact of blockchain, AI, and 5G to enhance the application of IoT. Hence, aspects such as the future of blockchain solutions in IoT networks or the possibility of employing AI for real-time decision making, or the means of using 5G for reducing latency require further research. Further, the establishment of richer privacy-preserving solutions by blockchain and AI in healthcare and other sensitive applications will be needed. IoT reference architectures and standards for interoperability between different IoT domains should be further developed to prove the capability to work in an international context. In future templates and examples, connecting sustainable energy, sustainability, green IoT, and environmental goals could be stressed more. Two more possible topics for future research are the application of quantum computing in increasing IoT security and the use of blockchain for this purpose, simultaneously with the use of quantum computing.

4.9 Conclusion

It pledges vast potentiality when these technologies' integration of blockchain, AI, 5G, or a combination of these, assists in the enhancement of the IoT environment in every aspect in terms of security, efficiency, and intelligence. By using blockchain, guarantees for the integrity of data and confidentiality of the personal data which are being processed would be provided; through AI, complex analysis and decision-making processes became possible; as for the 5G – through technology, real-time communications would be enabled. This chapter has discussed in detail such use of case studies and prototypes to reveal how these technologies are rising to the challenges toward the development of an optimized, healthy, and sturdier new age smart and intelligent systems in healthcare domains, smart homes, supply chain, and Industry 5. Here, it has articulated those best practices that have been learned here to enable other researchers and the practice implementation that would assist in enhancing secure and efficient IoT solutions.

References

[1] El Azzaoui, A., Singh, S. K., Pan, Y., & Park, J. H. (2020). Block5GIntell: Blockchain for AI-Enabled 5G Networks. In *Department of Computer Science and Engineering, Seoul National University of Science and Technology (SeoulTech)*, Seoul, South Korea; *Department of Computer Science, Georgia State University*, Atlanta, GA, USA.

[2] Pant, P., Bedi, P., Rajawat, A. S., Verma, C., Raboaca, M. S., Goyal, S. B., Enescu, F. M., & Mihaltan, T. C. (2022). Blockchain for AI-Enabled Industrial IoT with 5G Network.

[3] Aneja, A. (2023). Blockchain Technologies in 5g and Beyond Connections: A Review of the Taxonomy, Practice Area, Prospects, and Challenges. In *2023 International Conference on Artificial Intelligence and Clever Communication (AISC)*. Chitkara University Institute of Engineering and Technology, Chitkara University, Punjab, India.

[4] Sharma, A., Podoplelova, E., Shapovalov, G., Tselykh, A., & Tselykh, A. (2021). Sustainable clever cities: Convergence of artificial intelligence and blockchain.

[5] Dwivedi, A. D., Singh, R., Kaushik, K., & Alnumay, W. S. (2021). Blockchain and artificial intelligence for 5G-enabled (IOT): Challenges, opportunities, and solutions.

[6] Esenogho, E., Djouani, K., & Kurien, A. M. (2022). Integrating Artificial Intelligence (IOT) and 5G for Next-Generation Clevergrid: A Survey of Trends Challenges and Prospect.

[7] Rathod, T., Jadav, N. K., Tanwar, S., Sharma, R., Tolba, A., Raboaca, M. S., Verdes, M., & Said, W. (2023). Blockchain-driven intelligent scheme for IoT-based public safety system beyond 5G networks. *Sensors*.

[8] Biswas, A., & Wang, H.-C. (2023). Autonomous vehicles enabled by the integration of IoT, edge intelligence, 5G, and blockchain. *Sensors*.

[9] Alahi, M. E. E., Sukkuea, A., Tina, F. W., Nag, A., Kurdthongmee, W., Suwannarat, K., & Mukhopadhyay, S. C. (2023). Integration of IoT-enabled technologies and artificial intelligence (AI) for clever city scenario: Recent advancements and future trends. *Sensors*.

[10] Dharmesh, H., & Dwivedi, D. (2021). Blockchain and Artificial Intelligence (AI) Integration in 5G-Enabled (IOT) (IoT) Systems

[11] Statista. (2020). Number of (IOT) (IoT) connected devices worldwide from 2019 to 2030. Retrieved from https://www.statista.com/statistics/802690/worldwide-connected-devices-by-access-technology/

[12] Christidis, K., & Devetsikiotis, M. (2016). Blockchains and clever contracts for the (IOT). *IEEE Access, 4*, 2292-2303. https://doi.org/10.1109/ACCESS.2016.2566339

[13] Dai, H. N., Zheng, Z., & Zhang, Y. (2019). Blockchain for (IOT): A survey. *IEEE (IOT) Journal, 6*(5), 8076-8094. https://doi.org/10.1109/JIOT.2019.2920987

[14] Zhang, P., White, J., Schmidt, D. C., Lenz, G., & Rosenbloom, S. T. (2018). FHIRChain: Applying blockchain to securely and scalably share clinical data. *Computational and Structural Biotechnology Journal, 16*, 267-278. https://doi.org/10.1016/j.csbj.2018.07.004

[15] Sharma, V., You, I., & Pau, G. (2022). Secure V2X communication using 5G and blockchain: A network slicing perspective. *IEEE Network, 36*(1), 39-45. https://doi.org/10.1109/MNET.011.2000121

[16] S. Ali, G. Wang, B. White and R. L. Cottrell, "A Blockchain-Based Decentralized Data Storage and Access Framework for PingER," *2018 17th IEEE International Conference On Trust, Security And Privacy In Computing And Communications/ 12th IEEE International Conference On Big Data Science And Engineering (TrustCom/BigDataSE)*, New York, NY, USA, 2018, pp. 1303-1308, doi: 10.1109/TrustCom/BigDataSE.2018.00179.

[17] Fernández-Caramés, T. M., & Fraga-Lamas, P. (2018). A review on the use of blockchain for the (IOT). *IEEE Access, 6*, 32979-33001.

[18] Mohammadi, M., Al-Fuqaha, A., Sorour, S., & Guizani, M. (2018). Deep learning for IoT big data and streaming analytics: A survey. *IEEE Communications Surveys & Tutorials, 20*(4), 2923-2960.

[19] Mao, Y., You, C., Zhang, J., Huang, K., & Letaief, K. B. (2017). A survey on mobile edge computing: The communication perspective. *IEEE Communications Surveys & Tutorials, 19*(4), 2322-2358.

[20] Zhu, G., Liu, D., Du, Y., You, C., Zhang, J., & Huang, K. (2020). Toward an intelligent edge: Wireless communication meets machine learning. *IEEE Communications Magazine, 58*(1), 19-25.

[21] Zhang, K., Mao, Y., You, C., Zhang, J., Huang, K., & Letaief, K. B. (2016). Energy-efficient offloading for mobile edge computing in 5G heterogeneous networks. *IEEE Access, 4*, 5896-5907.

[22] Rawat, D. B., Njilla, L., Kwiat, K., & Kamhoua, C. (2018). iShare: Blockchain-based privacy-aware multi-agent information sharing games

for cybersecurity. In *2018 International Conference on Computing, Networking and Communications (ICNC)* (pp. 425-431).

[23] Nguyen, D. C., Ding, M., Pathirana, P. N., Seneviratne, A., Li, J., & Poor, H. V. (2021). Federated learning for (IOT): A comprehensive survey. *IEEE Communications Surveys & Tutorials, 23*(3), 1622-1658.

[24] Alrubei, S., Ball, E., & Rigelsford, J. (2020). A Secure Distributed Blockchain Platform for Use in AI-Enabled IoT Applications. IEEE Cloud Summit. DOI: 10.1109/IEEECloudSummit48914.2020.00019.

[25] Pajooh, H. H., Rashid, M., Alam, F., & Demidenko, S. (2021). Multi-Layer Blockchain-Based Security Architecture for (IOT). *Sensors*, 21(772), 1-12. https://doi.org/10.3390/s21030772

[26] Griggs, K., Baccarini, A., Kohlios, C., & Howson, E. (2018). Healthcare blockchain system using smart contracts for secure automated remote patient monitoring. *Journal of Medical Systems*, *42*(6). https://doi.org/10.1007/s10916-018-0982-x

[27] Dorri A, Kanhere SS, Jurdak R, Gauravaram P. Blockchain for IoT security and privacy: the case study of a smart home. Paper presented at: Proceedings of the 2017 IEEE International Conference on Pervasive Computing and Communications Workshops, PerCom Workshops; March 13-17, 2017:618-623; Kona, Big Island, HI.

[28] Singh R, Dwivedi AD, Srivastava G. Internet of Things based blockchain for temperature monitoring and counterfeit pharmaceutical prevention. *Sensors*. 2020;20(14):3951. https://doi.org/10.3390/s20143951.

Section 2

Security and Privacy Enhancement in 5G-IoT Using Blockchain and AI

5

Enhancing Data Security and Privacy in 5G-IoT using Blockchain Technology

Rohit Malik[1], Sakshi Dua[1], Preety Shoran[2], Prabal Gupta[3]

[1]SCA, Lovely Professional University, India
[2]School of Sciences, Christ University, India
[3]ECE, SCSE, Lovely Professional University, India
Email: rohitxmalik7@gmail.com; sakshi_nancy@yahoo.in; preety@christuniversity.in; prabal.gupta9@gmail.com

Abstract

The convergence of 5G and the Internet of Things (IoT) has opened exciting possibilities for innovation and connectivity across different sectors. However, the widespread use of connected devices poses significant challenges, particularly in ensuring data security and privacy. Traditional security measures often fall short in the face of the dynamic and pervasive nature of 5G-IoT environments, leaving sensitive data vulnerable to compromise or unauthorized access. Our research introduces a novel approach to fortifying data security and privacy in 5G-IoT networks. We accomplish this by fusing blockchain technology with homomorphic encryption, resulting in a potent solution. Blockchain, renowned for its decentralized and immutable ledger capabilities, offers a promising avenue for establishing trust and transparency in distributed environments. By leveraging blockchain as a secure data storage and transaction verification system, our aim is to reduce the risks linked with traditional storage systems and single points of failure. Furthermore, we have integrated homomorphic encryption into the proposed framework to effectively tackle the privacy concerns related to data processing and transmission within 5G-IoT ecosystems. Homomorphic encryption enables computations on encrypted data, maintaining the privacy of sensitive

DOI: 10.1201/9788743809050-7

information while allowing meaningful analysis. Through the seamless integration of blockchain technology and homomorphic encryption, our research strives to build a robust and secure infrastructure for 5G-IoT networks. With a focus on data integrity, user privacy, and secure transactions, this framework aims to foster trust among stakeholders and promote the widespread adoption of 5G-IoT technologies in various fields.

Keywords: 5G-IoT, blockchain, homomorphic encryption, data security, privacy

5.1 Introduction

The Internet of Things (IoT) is one of the latest technologies online, which has brought people closer to the digital world. These devices help in creating smart environments that make everyday life easier around the world, as they allow different devices to connect and work with each other [1]. Blockchain technology is a decentralized system that can be used to increase the security of IoT devices because it relies on an encrypted form of data. The comparison of an IoT framework without blockchain and with blockchain, a higher degree of security was found in an IoT-blockchain-based framework [2]. The IoT architecture produces and distributes a substantial volume of critical safety data through various devices. The network is currently of higher significance. The network's involvement under unmanaged conditions poses a substantial cybersecurity risk. The predominant IoT opportunities nowadays are founded on web-based "cloud" services. As IoT networks become increasingly complex, this approach enhances the flexibility of processing and data storage. Nonetheless, numerous security vulnerabilities remain to be addressed [3]. IoTs allow the sharing and monitoring of data among devices when connected to a network. Due to the presence of a centralized traditional architecture, a single point of failure of the system arises, decreasing the security of data. Blockchain, on the other hand, uses a decentralized immutable ledger ensuring the integrity and security of data [3].

The rapid advancements in IoT increase several problems, as these devices with limited scalability, processing speed within a centralized system are vulnerable to various security breaches [4]. The utilization of a decentralized, highly scalable, and immutable system shows the system's ability to provide better security results while combining IoT with blockchain. The blockchain decentralized system helps to eradicate the chances of single point failure, as if a node fails to enter the communicating network, the network can still run properly without any disruption. Also, it provides anonymity to users by keeping their identities hidden to protect privacy and increase the security of devices [5].

Blockchain technology is also getting implemented in the healthcare industry, which has a significant impact on individuals' daily lives. The identification of various algorithms using blockchain-IoT network, which are widely being used in the healthcare sector, is necessary to better under the need for integration in this industry [6]. Modern technological advancements in places such as 5G networks for IoT information, mobile edge computing (MEC), intelligent machine-to-machine (M2M) connections, and fog computing. In the future, the connection of these latest technologies will be hard as IoTs will be creating a lot of data constantly. The integration of a machine learning based neural network, edge devices, and blockchain will provide a robust solution for the same [7].

5.1.1 Classification of the blockchain system

A distributed ledger is a system that allows users to record and exchange transaction data over a network. Users of the network share information in a decentralized way, which is different from the current centralized system. Information is stored in blocks and linked together like a chain by a hash value, and it is an unchangeable distributed ledger; it is impossible to change or delete the information that has been saved. Blockchain technology is made up of many different parts, such as consensus algorithms, smart contracts, digital signature algorithms, hashing algorithms, and network communication protocols [8]. Figure 5.1 shows how blockchain systems can be put into three different groups based on different features.

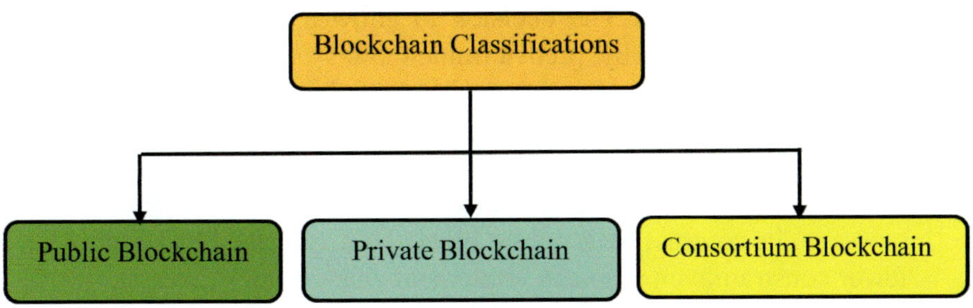

Figure 5.1 Classification of blockchain [9].

- *Public blockchain*: A public blockchain allows users from any company or background to join, transact, and mine on the same distributed ledger. All these variables are open for exploration. Hence, these blockchains are often known as "permissionless" blockchains. Each user always has unrestricted access to the whole blockchain and can view or make changes to any transaction, audit the blockchain, or inspect any other participant's changes. There are no central authority figures or "validator nodes" in a blockchain system. To receive mining rewards, anybody can start collecting transactions and start the mining process. If all nodes have access to a copy of the full blockchain at the same time, then the blockchain is immutable. Complete decentralization, the size of existing networks, and the availability of a platform allowing any participant to reach an agreement by any of the available decentralized consensus processes. Since the private blockchain's ledger system is not available to the public, it can be attacked. The safe proof-of-work procedure and the cryptographic validation of the entire blockchain before the addition of each new block help to mitigate this flaw.
  Blockchain-based distributed public ledgers, in which all users share the same data, are required for high-value use cases, including money, but are privacy-invasive in many others. Maintaining private data securely on the blockchain is a relatively recent field of research that needs further attention. There are ways to replace the blockchain with more efficient data structures while it still works as a distributed public ledger. Other designs would get rid of the public ledger function in favor of stronger privacy features [10].
- *Private blockchain*: It is a blockchain system designed for exclusive use inside an organization or among various organizations, with mining administered by a central authority or a small number of trusted users. It is also known as a "permissioned blockchain" because only authorized users can participate. The decision to allow a node into the network is determined either by predetermined rules or by the administrator. This undermines the essential qualities of the blockchain as outlined by Satoshi, which are full decentralization and transparency. These systems are similar to a public blockchain in that each node prevents a duplicate of the ledger and works together to update it by consensus; however, in contrast to a public blockchain, private blockchains have fewer constraints on who can implement changes to the ledger.
  Because the blockchain is a public record available to everyone, it is possible to find out who is behind a pseudonym by looking at how it is

used. Also, centralized Chaumian e-cash systems have been studied a lot and even built. They offer well-defined privacy features, like keeping the sender and receiver of a transaction anonymous by using well-known primitives like blind signatures [10].

- *Consortium blockchain*: Consortium blockchains can be considered an instance of a permissioned or semi-private blockchain in which consensus and block validation are handled not by a single entity but by a group of trusted nodes selected in advance. These facilities are in charge of approving new users and granting mining permissions. A multi-signature system is used to make sure that a block has the signatures of several nodes before it is accepted as valid. In contrast to the fully centralized private blockchain and the fully decentralized public blockchain, this system is only partially decentralized because it depends on a limited set of trusted validator nodes. The consortium can choose whether anybody outside the network will have read or write access. As most of the consortium's control must result in blockchain manipulation, even limiting consensus to a group of nodes does not ensure immutability and irreversibility.

5.1.2 Applications and use cases

If used right and with care, blockchain has the capabilities to make critical infrastructure networks much safer, smoother, and easier to see. Figure 5.2 shows some of the ways that blockchain technology is already being used because of its many benefits [11]. Blockchain technology is on the rise, introducing revolutionary changes in many areas of social life and gradually becoming a trend in the global technology and finance sectors. Several businesses might benefit from the enhanced informational and operational efficiencies that could be brought about by this technology [12].

- *Blockchain in asset management*: It is all about order to make sure that assets can be transferred safely throughout a company network. An asset could be anything tangible, like a server, computer, or laptop, or it could be something intangible, like software or services. Both types of assets are considered assets. The blockchain provides the possibility of shared ledgers, which implies that a business network has complete visibility from beginning to finish. In this use case, the blockchain is implemented from the initialization stage through to the deployment phase, with a narrow focus on just five events: the serialization of assets during production to start on the blockchain, the receipt and verification

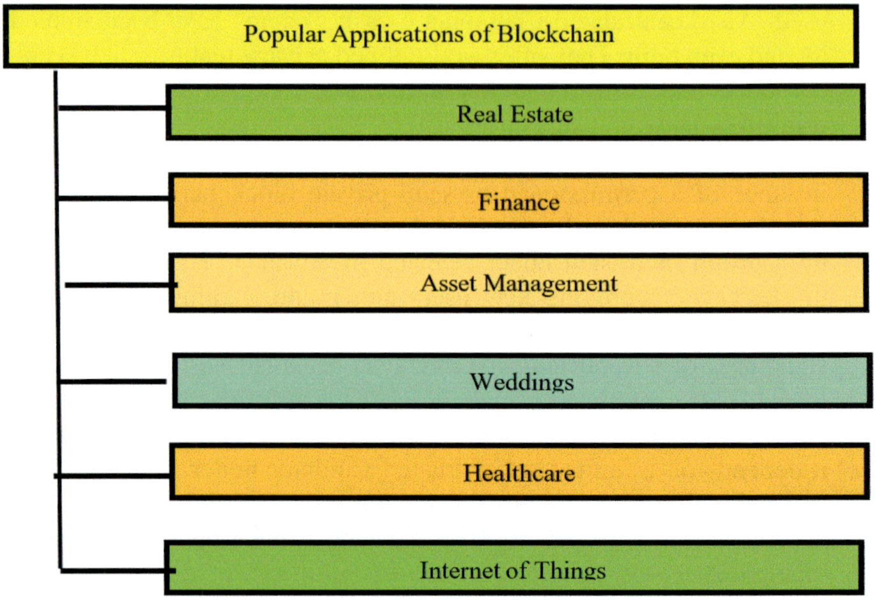

Figure 5.2 Blockchain application [13].

of those assets, the capitalization of those assets, the activation of their warranties, and the installation of those assets.

- *Blockchain in real estate*: Real estate transactions are time-consuming, confusing, and costly because of all the parties involved. It includes brokers, inspectors, appraisers, government property databases, title businesses, public notary, etc. Every piece of real estate in the world will be able to get its unique digital address on the blockchain, complete with details on its occupants, finances, legal standing, building efficiency, and physical characteristics [14].
- *Blockchain in finance*: Cross-border payments are important, but if middlemen are involved, they might take longer and cost more than they need to. The process of collecting money involves multiple banks and currencies. Significantly faster but more costly options include Western Union and similar services. Blockchain technology has the potential to accelerate this procedure by eliminating the need for intermediaries. It reduces the cost of making transactions worldwide. Transfer fees averaged 15% to 20% of the amount sent before this change. The blockchain allows for assured, instantaneous transactions across borders at a reduced cost of 2%–3% [15].

- *Blockchain for IoT*: Blockchain technology offers robust solutions for securing IoT devices by ensuring data integrity, transparency, and tamper resistance. It enables secure device authentication, decentralized data storage, and seamless transactions without reliance on a central authority. With its ability to automate processes through smart contracts, blockchain enhances IoT scalability and efficiency [16]. As IoT networks expand, blockchain's decentralized nature addresses concerns related to privacy, security, and trust [17].
- *Weddings*: It is possible to find a potential partner online, make plans to meet in person, and eventually get married. Everything can now be done online, from the first contact to the final payment. This includes choosing a partner and getting wedding gifts. Joyce and David Mondrus were the original pair that conducted this in 2014 [18].
- *Blockchain in healthcare*: The authors suggest using blockchain technology to store and manage patient medical records. Medical records for a certain patient are maintained in a decentralized database, which can be accessed by all of the patient's physicians and health insurers [19]. Blockchain is a decentralized, unchangeable ledger technology with uses extending beyond basic transactions. There have been several discussions on possible security framework approaches in this area. Unlike the current structure, which is centralized, users of the network exchange data in a way that is not centralized.

It is almost impossible to alter or delete the information after it has been recorded, since it is kept in blocks linked together like a chain by a hash value. As they reject wider intersection features and the need to transfer authority, they are not readily applicable to 5G-IoT-based systems. Using blockchain technology in healthcare systems potentially offers a few reasonable alternatives. The data is stored in every hospital nodes network, which helps doctors to retrieve patients' details safely, securely, and fastly. This enables medication services to work faster and more reliably.

5.1.3 Organization of the paper

Section 5.1 introduces the concept of blockchain and AI in conjunction with IoT devices, also the classification of blockchain systems and their applications in different sectors is discussed. Sections 5.2 and 5.3 discuss the literature survey and background study, respectively. Section 5.4 discusses the problem formulation, and Section 5.5 discusses the objectives of the research. Section 5.6 delves into the proposed methodology and algorithm, while Section 5.7 includes the results and discussion part. Section 8 concludes the work.

5.2 Literature of Review

This section contains a collection of research work by different authors that is based on a novel framework for securing IoT applications using blockchain.

Bataineh et al., (2022) [20] explained that blockchain technology is getting attention worldwide, especially in the digital currency field. It contains many features, such as a consensus method, peer-to-peer communication, creating trust without a TTP, and an intelligent contract method for transactions that are based on conditions and functions. Blockchain could solve these problems by making the IoT a decentralized, self-run system. This research presents an IoT-Blockchain architecture that uses Ethereum as part of a rich-thin client IoT approach to alleviating problems resulting from the absence of IoT resources. Distributing the effort across available resources is crucial to the design. Thin clients refer to devices with fewer resources, whereas rich clients are those with more. The wealthy client is the only one allowed to store, but every client can access the blockchain and retrieve data. They have implemented the suggested architecture for use in a working healthcare system where surgical operations are carried out. In addition, the authors demonstrate the effectiveness of the approach by contrasting the design with that of other popular IoT-based blockchains. The results show that the blockchain-IoT architecture that was suggested can be used for different IoT applications without the usual problems.

Shinde et al., (2024) [41] examine the ways in which blockchain can improve the security and privacy aspects of healthcare systems that utilize artificial intelligence. The emphasis is on tackling concerns such as privacy, adversarial threats, and confidence in AI systems through the incorporation of blockchain technology. Important topics discussed encompass natural language processing, computer vision, and acoustic AI, while blockchain provides a means to ensure the security of the AI model development process.

Sarker et al., (2023) [42] examined the use of AI, IoMT, and blockchain can work together in healthcare, highlighting their ability to boost patient results, lower expenses, and increase efficiency. The research underscores the critical need for data protection and confidentiality, focusing on how blockchain technology protects vital health information and enhances cooperation between healthcare professionals, tech firms, and regulatory agencies to build a more secure, effective, and patient-centered healthcare environment.

Liang et al., (2022) [21] evaluated that the IoT has entered almost every element of modern society. Yet, IoT privacy is still a major challenge, especially considering the vast scale and geographical dispersion of IoT networks. Also, the distributed nature of blockchain has allowed for the resolution of many issues regarding security, authentication, and upkeep of IoT devices. The privacy problems of IoT-based blockchains are carefully looked at to find ways to fix them. Using computerized databases has led to the discovery of 61 papers, of which 20 were chosen for further study based on the criteria used.

The results showed that blockchain technology might be able to help with some of the problems that come with the IoT, like data security and privacy. As a bonus, it can also keep IoT devices and users safe and private by giving them trust, transparency, distributed storage, and secure distributed IoT networks. There are problems with low scalability, high computational complexity, the latency that is too long for the IoT, and too much bandwidth overhead.

Varshney et al., (2022) [22] examined that decentralized blockchain technology offers an exciting way to stop data from being stolen when it is sent from one device to another. Within the 5G infrastructure, the author identified the use of blockchain to enhance data security. They also proposed a layered architecture for IoT networks utilizing blockchain.

The proposed approach tackled challenges related to distributed ledger technology implementation by transforming the IoT-based platform architecture into a decentralized system. The infrastructure was conceptually divided into K-based clusters, employing evolutionary methodologies like computation and particle swarm intelligence for assessment.

A different method of identification and permission is selected by each member of the cluster for use inside each cluster organizational unit (CGH). By using a decentralized blockchain application, CGHs can identify each other and Ground Stations in their communications without relying on a centralized controller, according to the strong security and trustworthiness guarantee provided by distributed ledger technology. Moreover, the authors suggest using blockchain for all communications between base stations globally. Moreover, they utilize the open-source blockchain program Hyperledger Cloud Hosting Network to verify the suggested approach.

Vahdati et al., (2021) [23] used the IoT to track patient behavior and other metrics that can make traditional healthcare systems better. When it comes to healthcare systems, the data collected by sensors in the IoT is crucial. Its main issue is to prevent unauthorized alterations to the data for reasons of privacy and security. In addition, blockchain technology offers several protections that avoid malicious attacks on data. Thus, blockchain-based IoT healthcare monitoring is a promising technical advance that has the potential to address concerns about cybersecurity incidents and invasions of privacy. The study analyzes the healthcare industry's need for monitoring systems and how IoT and blockchain technologies could assist. To achieve this goal, a new architecture is developed that is grounded in previously reported answers. The suggested architecture that utilizes computing power derived from the integration of technologies and AI can be used in a variety of solutions targeted at treating COVID-19. Examples are given to illustrate the use of the proposed design. In the last section of this chapter, they will immediately go over some of the different ways in which the suggested architecture can be implemented, especially during pandemics.

Algarni et al., (2021) [24] examined the issues of IoT related to security and privacy. Centralized alternatives to access control, which could depend on a third party, have limitations in terms of availability, scalability, and performance. Because of this, the above study offers an innovative approach based on a multi-agent infrastructure and a blockchain ledger that provides lightweight, decentralized, secure access control of an IoT environment.

The suggested solution's primary focus is on developing blockchain managers (BCMs) to safeguard IoT access control and enable encrypted communication among IoTs. The technology also opens up opportunities for encrypted data exchange between IoT gadgets, fog nodes, and the cloud.

Oikonomou et al., (2021) [25] explained that blockchain can help IoT-based health monitoring systems deal with privacy and security problems. However, the IoT devices in these systems have limited computation capability, storage, and battery life, so they cannot handle complex and heavy-weight operations. The authors recommended a Hyperledger Fabric-integrated blockchain to (1) improve security in healthcare systems; (2) improve storage despite sensors' and gateways' limited storage capacity; (3) enable decentralized accountability; and (4) get rid of a single point of failure.

Ferrag et al., (2020) [26] examined the security issues in green IoT-based agriculture. In the beginning, they provide an overview of the previously conducted research on smart agriculture and describe a 4-tier green IoT system. The authors also provided categorization of threat models against green IoTs into five groups: confidentiality, availability, privacy, authentication, and integrity. IoT-based green agriculture is discussed, as is a taxonomy and sidewise evaluation of current ways to ensure data security in green IoTs.

IoT-based sustainable agriculture is looked at, as well as the importance of blockchain solutions and consensus methods that focus on privacy. Based on the results of this study, they talk about possible directions for future research in security for green IoTs in agriculture, and they also talk about challenges for advanced research.

Mohanta et al., (2020) [27] demonstrated that the IoT has been the most important new technology in the last ten years. This is due to a sudden increase in IoT devices, and the technologies have grown a lot in both industry and academia. For statistical control, the applications are made to support IoT devices.

Traditional security and encryption methods cannot be used on smart objects because they do not have enough processing power or storage space. In the first part of this study, they look at the current state of security and privacy threats in IoT systems. Second, they provide various safeguards that are in line with blockchain technology. The investigation is decomposed into the extremely smallest detail, including everything from the enabling technology to the integration of IoT devices. Using the Ethereum blockchain in a smart IoT system, a case study is then executed, and the outcomes are described. Table 5.1 shows the comparison of the literature reviewed on the basis of the technologies they used and the outcome.

5.3 Background Study

Blockchain technology is the best choice for a decentralized database because it uses homomorphic encryption for searching and lets people get in based on keywords. The proposed solution includes changing the existing protocols and making it possible to revoke a key safely. To send both types of digital healthcare data, a protocol was made to keep the information safe. This approach, which makes use of blockchain and trust chains, addresses efficient and secure operations. The suggested approach improves productivity, safety, and cost. The technologies used for the simulation and analysis were Hyperledger Fabric and Origin-Lab. The possible solutions were evaluated against industry standards. The comparison shows that the technique increases the safety and discoverability of healthcare systems [28].

Table 5.1 Comparative analysis of the reviewed literature.

Authors	Techniques	Outcomes
Bataineh et al., (2022) [20]	Blockchain technology	Blockchain technology is becoming more popular in digital currency. A consensus process, direct P2P communication, the removal of the requirement for a trustworthy third party, and an intelligent contract approach for conditional and functional transactions are among its numerous benefits.
Liang et al., (2022) [21]	Blockchain technology	Using blockchain technology could solve problems with the IoT, such as data security and privacy.
Varshney et al., (2022) [22]	Blockchain	Because distributed ledger technology guarantees a high level of security and reliability, CGHs can identify each other and ground stations when they talk to each other.
Vahdati et al., (2021) [23]	Blockchain-based IoT	The proposed plan could be used in many of the things that will be done in 2019 to stop the spread of the coronavirus. The IoT, the blockchain, and artificial intelligence (COVID-19) give it the processing power it needs.
Algarni et al., (2021) [24]	IoT system	The proposed method focuses on making blockchain managers (BCMs) protect access control for IoT devices and provide encrypted local communication between IoT nodes.
Oikonomou et al., (2021) [25]	Blockchain	These systems' IoT devices are not equipped to perform complex or resource-intensive tasks because of their low memory, processing speed, and battery life.
FERRAG et al., (2020) [26]	IoT applications	The value of blockchain solutions and privacy-focused consensus approaches, as well as sustainable development based on the IoT, is also looked at.
Mohanta et al., (2020) [27]	IoT	Because of this, smart devices and other related technologies are being used a lot more in business and research settings. Applications are made using IoTs for statistical control.

The problem of securing the IoT is addressed in new and innovative research. Data uploading and transmission from distributed 5G-IoT applications could be secured using layered security and dynamic key generation. Currently, available solutions use a single key to detect the presence of a connection between a device and a gateway node. The session key is dynamically generated according to the principles of cellular automata. Blockchain technology, dynamic key generation, and cellular automata-based random number generation all serve to secure the suggested system. The automatic validation of internet security protocols and apps (AVISPA) system puts these safety measures through a lot of tests. The findings validate the strategy's perfect nature. The suggested strategy was also more efficient and less time-consuming than competing methods [29].

5.4 Problem Formulation

The internet has made it easier for them to talk to each other and share important information, whether it is about their personal lives or their jobs. This is true whether the information is about private lives or professional lives. But if the information that has been supplied is not communicated to the persons who are expected to acquire it securely, it might result in a breach of privacy or humiliation, both of which might require a substantial amount of time to recover from. According to the IoT, sensors, algorithms, and other devices could all work together to relay data. The connected devices of today are likely to cause problems with privacy, secrecy, trustworthiness, and reliability, among other things. For blockchain-based IoT apps, a hybrid node authentication and secure data transmission protocol were made to solve these problems. An alternative approach to establishing cross-domain and access control is presented, and it includes the use of homomorphic encryption. Homomorphic encryption is advocated by the author because it permits the rules to be altered or added to.

In 5G-IoT systems, network slicing is an important feature, which creates multiple virtual networks on a single physical machine, creating difficulties in management and security. Blockchain and homomorphic encryption in the proposed solution ensure trust, integrity, and privacy across virtual networks. Blockchain's decentralized and distributed ledger technology (DLT) provides tracking and verification of data across slices, while homomorphic encryption enables secure data processing by providing access controls to perform operations on encrypted data without decrypting it. Also, DLT ensures that if one or more nodes fail, the system continues to work without any disruption. The immutable ledger guarantees the integrity of data among all nodes, which leads to both fault tolerance and resilience. The dynamic session key generation and homomorphic encryption provide a secure mechanism for data access and transmission [28].

To address the scalability and interoperability issues in 5G-IoT networks, AI and blockchain can be used immensely. The decentralized nature of DLT allows to eliminate single point of control while allowing the system to scale horizontally as more nodes are added to the system, which enables it to perform transactions in larger volumes without decreasing performance. AI can optimize the system for maximum bandwidth usage and efficient resource allocation across networks. AI models dynamically allocate resources by analyzing real data to predict patterns, manage congestion, to prevent network overload for improving scalability. AI complements blockchain's smart contracts by including automated decision-making capability. AI may adapt contract specifications in real-time according to network conditions, enhancing shared communication and enabling secure and effective interoperability within the 5G-IoT ecosystem.

The suggested method permits authenticated and encrypted data transport. Inside the system, a blockchain program is applied to make data transmission and authentication straightforward. It improves the security of the system for protecting user information. Inside a blockchain-based environment, the proposed approach intends to simultaneously optimize data and network security.

5.5 Research Objectives

- To conduct an in-depth investigation of the various blockchain-based possibilities that are currently available for IoT deployments.
- To provide a secure and one-of-a-kind structure to use blockchain for securing IoTs.
- To compare how well the suggested framework works with the most advanced blockchain system that is already in use.

5.6 Research Methodology

In this section of the paper, the author discusses some of the approaches that were used in this research, including blockchain, Hyperledger, and homomorphic encryption.

5.6.1 Technique used

The author uses specific techniques in this section, which are described below:

5.6.1.1 Blockchain

The replication of state machines is a good analogy for understanding a blockchain. In this architecture, a service oversees keeping a state in a certain way, while clients carry out operations to change that state and generate results. Using a decentralized protocol run by various nodes across the internet, a blockchain could imitate a "trusted" computing service. Each node has some stake in the service's output, which it either creates or represents. Figure 5.3 depicts a blockchain system in operation, which shows the blocks

Figure 5.3 Blockchain [30].

are secured and are fully connected to each other, creating a chain of data-keeping blocks. These blocks contain information about the previous block's hash, which is unique to every block [30]. It illustrates how blockchain functions as a ledger that allows participants in the network to record and share data securely.

All the nodes really would like to keep the service up, but they do not put all of their faith in each other to do it. A "permissionless" blockchain, like the one that supports the Bitcoin cryptocurrency, allows anybody to operate a node and join the network by demonstrating a "proof-of-work" and expending computational resources. A public blockchain is accessible to the public. In addition, "permissioned" blockchains control could use their authentication and protocol, and they often operate as a consortium with established identities. Blockchains that operate under the "public" paradigm cannot exercise this control [31]. Figure 5.4 shows the working of the blockchain.

Blockchain is a specific kind of DLT used as a data storage device that stores information and its history. The following are the cornerstones of DLT:

- *Distributed database*
  The network nodes each store their version of the digital ledger and other data from the block, and when a new transaction is finalized, the whole network is updated with the most current data [33].
- *Peer-to-peer transmission*
  Data cannot be stored in a central location like a server because of current technological limitations. Instead, each network participant is responsible for keeping a record of data and sharing it with other members [34].

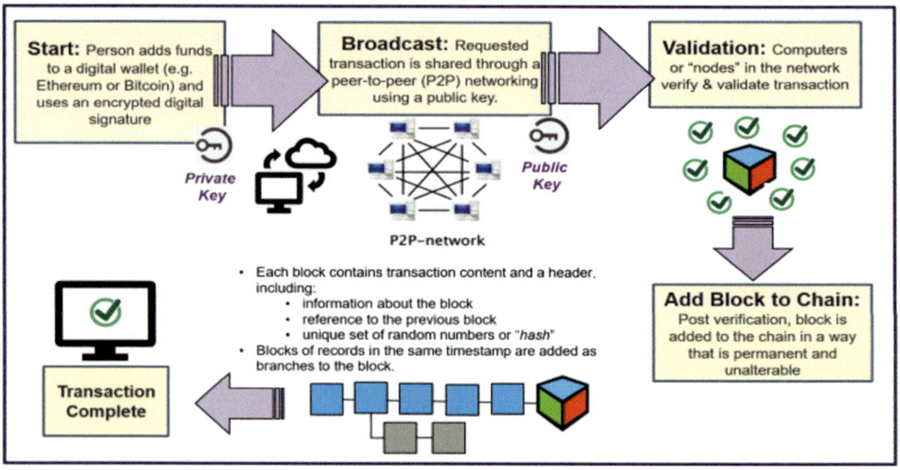

Figure 5.4 Working on blockchain [32].

- *Trust*
  The entire community might be able to confirm the existence of a new record.
- *Transparency*
  People who were allowed to look at the ledger could see a full record of every transaction that had ever happened.
- *Immutable records*
  One person could not, at any given time, alter the accuracy of the information.
- *Embedded logic*
  Allows process automation, strategies, and rules to quickly begin transactional interactions between nodes in the network.
  Blockchain technology is based on a digital ledger or record of transactions that is kept by itself and not by any one person or group. This decentralized database keeps track of a growing list of data blocks that are all cryptographically connected. Depending on the rules of the contest, each of these parts could be considered a separate entry [35].

5.6.1.2 Hyperledger

Hyperledger Fabric is a blockchain platform made for businesses. It is a private network that only people with permission can use. A user-defined smart contract might be executed on its modular framework, which has pluggable consensus processes. Full security and authentication options are also available. Open-source software and industry-recognized standards form their foundation. An open system architecture for distributed ledgers that can be used across industries is being sought out and implemented to spread blockchain, having the capability to revolutionize international business operations [36].

Hyperledger is an inclusive designation for an organization of related open-source blockchain technologies and projects. All its members are thought leaders in their respective disciplines and are committed to building a robust blockchain architecture motivated by business objectives. It is a big project whose goal is to help businesses use blockchain technology by giving them solutions and standard rules. Hyperledger Indy, Fabric, Cello, Iroha, Sawtooth, Explorer, and Composer are some of the most important Hyperledger architectural projects.

Hyperledger is one of the open-source collaborative projects that is growing the fastest and bringing blockchain technology to new areas. There is no firm, blockchain, cryptocurrency, or IBM blockchain coin involved here. Leaders from the banking, business, supply chain, manufacturing, IoT (IoT), and expertise sectors make up the board of directors for the Linux Foundation, which hosts and governs the organization. This establishment might not take Bitcoin or any other cryptocurrency at this time. When compared, blockchain is the foundation of the super ledger. This infrastructure could make it simpler to build new and faster transactional applications, which incorporate accountability, trust, traceability, and transparency into their entire design and automate and simplify many back-end procedures. Using Hyperledger, the Linux Foundation intends to establish a community in which business and corporate members could work together to design and build blockchain infrastructure for use in global, real-time applications [37]. Features of Hyperledger are shown in Figure 5.5.

To process a transaction, the nodes on a platform that uses Hyperledger would need to be able to talk to each other privately and update their ledgers on their own. During a trade, the only piece of information that a third party could get is the exact amount that has been sent.

5.6.1.3 Homomorphic encryption

Homomorphic encryption is a type of encryption that produces an encrypted result that, when decoded, is the same as the result of operations done on plaintexts. This type of encryption lets certain calculations be done on

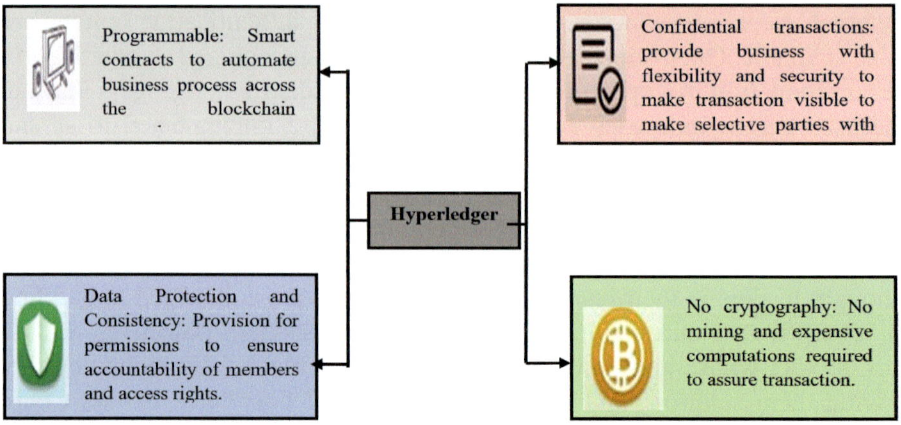

Figure 5.5 Hyperledger-based enterprise solutions [37].

ciphertexts and creates an encrypted result that is the same as the result of operations done on plaintexts. This encryption method might be used to conceal data while still allowing for certain calculations to be performed on ciphertexts. This quality must be sought in the design of contemporary means of communication.

The Rivest–Shamir–Adleman (RSA) algorithm is the foundation of cryptography systems; it involves cryptographic functions that perform specific security roles. It enables public-key encryption and is often used to secure important data. The first public-key system to have a homomorphic property was a breakthrough in cryptography [38].

The homomorphic encryption used in this method makes keyword searches and database access completely safe. This turns the plaintext into ciphertext, which hackers cannot read. The KeyGen() function generates a common key (CK), which is used to derive a public key (PK), secret key (SK), and verification key (VK) for cryptographic operations. Enc() encrypts a dataset (N) with the SK and label (L), producing ciphertext. Eval() allows Data Users (DU) to request computation with PK, a homomorphic function (f), and ciphertext. Dec() decrypts the result using the SK to verify and accept the output.

5.6.1.4 Recurrent neural networks (RNN)

The yield from a prior advancement is utilized to promote the current advancement in an RNN. The convolutional organization is divided in that the outcomes and sources are always the same [39]. Assume a more complex construction exists with a single data layer, three secret levels, and a single yield layer that is all connected.

Then, as with past neural construction, each concealed layer would have its mix of predispositions and loads. Please take note that the loads and character traits for secrets layer 1 are (w1, b1) for the first secret layer, (w2, b2) for second secret layer, and (w3, b3) for secret third layer for can be the first secret layer (w1, b1) [40]. According to the preceding sentence, each one of these layers is self-contained, which means it does not retain past yields.

5.6.2 Proposed algorithm

This section proposes an algorithm for a blockchain-based, hybrid node authentication and secure data transmission protocol for IoT applications.

Start

Step 1: The process begins with one sender node and multiple receiver nodes.
Step 2: A unique session identifier will be created for every signal exchange between the sender and receiver.
Step 3: If the receiver's identity is verified, the transmission proceeds; otherwise, the communication is halted instantly.
Step 4: A new encryption key is generated for continued communication, and the old session ID is discarded.
Step 5: Homomorphic encryption is employed to ensure secure data transmission and protection between the sender and receiver.
Step 6: Data will be encrypted using a specific key to transform it from plaintext into ciphertext, ensuring confidentiality.
Step 7: Both the receiver and the sender possess the encryption key to decrypt the data packet.
Step 8: The data packet will be transferred between the sender, forwarding layer, control layer, and receiver, and vice versa.
Step 9: Encrypt the data received from the sender.
Step 10: Extract data from encrypted text.
Step 11: Divide the data into two parts, that is, train data and test data.
Step 12: Apply machine learning model.
Step 13: Evaluate performance.

End

5.7 Result and Discussion

The simulations analyzed the number of sent patient health records throughout 2000 rounds. Up to 3060 repetitions of the experiment were performed, and the author analyzed block counts and medical data to deduce the results. There are 500 blocks in the dataset, and the Patient Health Record is used for the calculation.

Hyperledger Fabric provides a blockchain-based software architecture that would be used to find a reliable and flexible simulation setting. A graphics processing unit (GPU) is a specialized computer device that can drastically increase the rate at which certain calculations can be performed. The author did simulations with various parameters, including block height, number of blocks, number of transactions, number of personal identification records (PHRs), latency, and signature generation, to obtain findings. The method's correctness determines how well it performs; thus, measuring its effectiveness requires a performance evaluation. Here, the author compares the proposed method with the existing baseline method, and the results depict that the proposed system achieves higher accuracy. While convolutional neural networks have limitations when it comes to processing temporal data, recurrent neural networks were built with this in mind. The sum of simulations is proportional to the sum of tests performed on the dataset.

Evaluation metric

The STRIDE model [28] is used to identify different threats and attacks in this environment. The STRIDE model is used to classify and detect threats, and a neural network is used to measure the system's predicted threats by comparing the identified threats with actual outcomes. Table 5.2 provides the performance analysis of the existing model with the proposed model by comparing the FPR, FDR, and FNR of the systems. Figures 5.6–5.8 are based on the comparison in Table 5.2.

Table 5.2 Performance analysis of the existing model with the proposed model.

No. of people	FPR		FNR		FDR	
	Existing model	**Proposed model**	**Existing model**	**Proposed model**	**Existing model**	**Proposed model**
100	0	0	0	0	0	0
200	0	0.003	0.022	0.028	0.025	0.034
300	0.002	0.0036	0.029	0.036	0.035	0.045
400	0.005	0.006	0.038	0.044	0.044	0.049
500	0.0063	0.0072	0.046	0.051	0.055	0.058

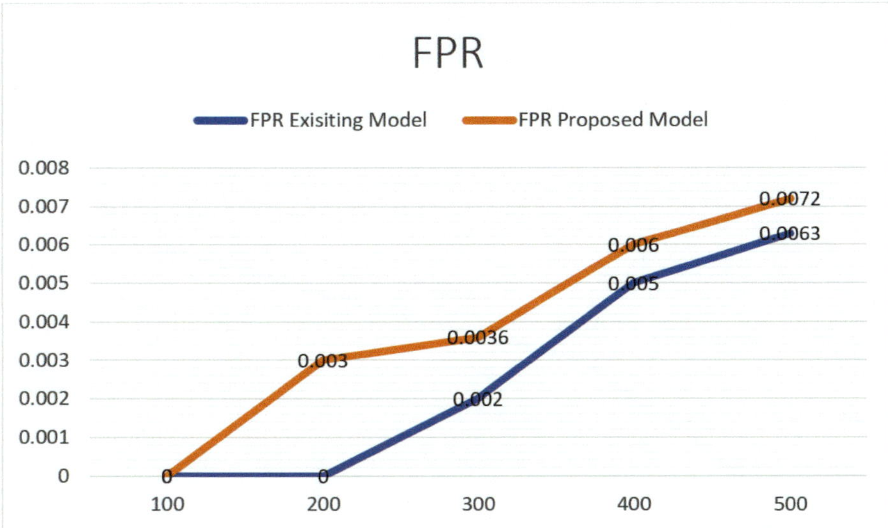

Figure 5.6 False positive rate.

Result 1:

Figure 5.6 provides a graphical depiction of a comparison between the FPR values of the existing model and the proposed model for populations ranging from 100 to 500 persons. The rate at which one incorrectly rejects the null hypothesis is called the false positive rate.

Result 2:

A comparison between the existing model and with proposed model in terms of their FNR values is shown in Figure 5.7. The likelihood of survival when no resection is performed represents the false negative rate.

Result 3:

The FDR, which displays the rate at which characteristics that are considered significant are null, might well be found below in Figure 5.8. The false discovery rate, or FDR, is the rate at which traits that are labelled significant are null.

5.7.1 Comparative study

Homomorphic encryption and secure, searchable databases provide the basis for a comparative study of previous and current approaches. Figure 5.9 shows

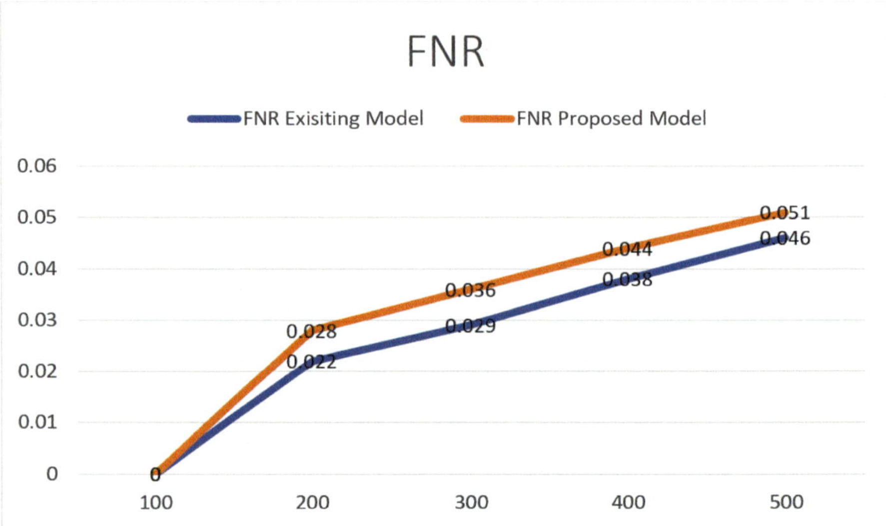

Figure 5.7 False negative rate.

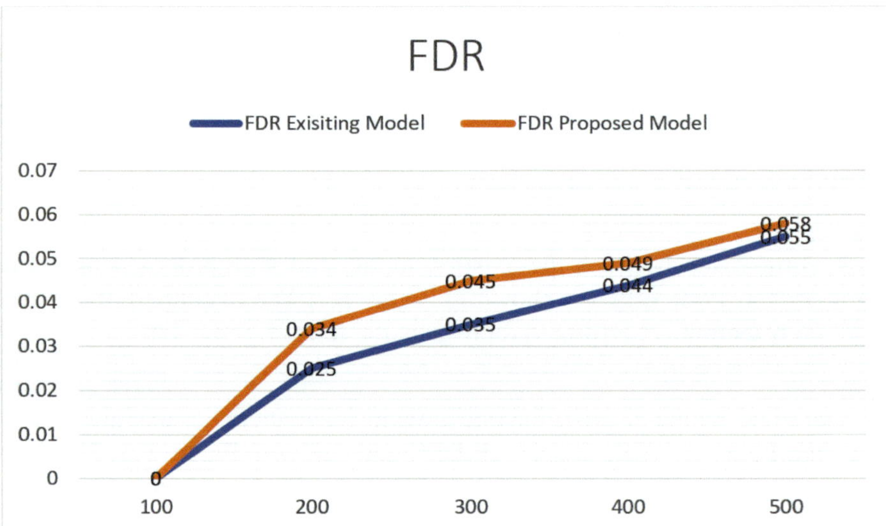

Figure 5.8 False discovery rate.

the simulation results for the suggested strategies and previous strategies. The author suggested employing homomorphic encryption to provide access control restrictions for the proposed system. The suggested technique compares several access rules and execution times to find the best one. Also, the author conducted trials on removing policies, making new ones, and adding policies.

Figure 5.10 shows the study comparison to compare the proposed method and the background approach in terms of how well the proposed framework tests the global epoch. The comparison was conducted based on the number of keyword searches and the time (seconds) required for confirmation.

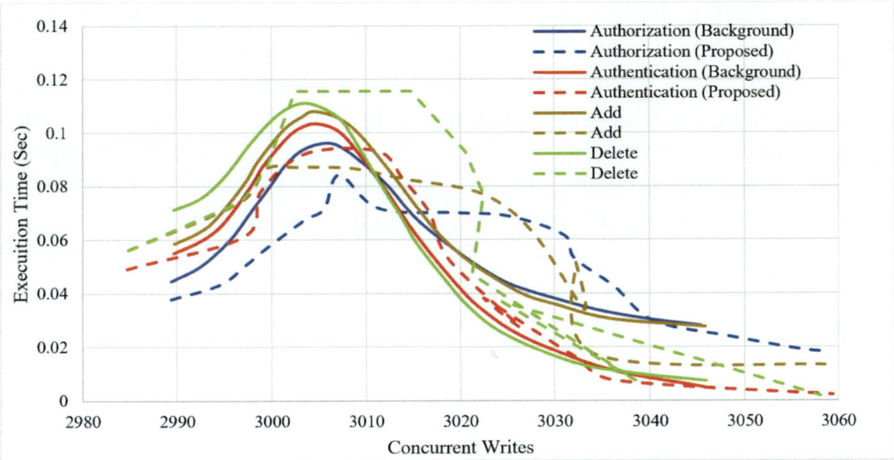

Figure 5.9 Homomorphic encryption and secure searchable domain comparison.

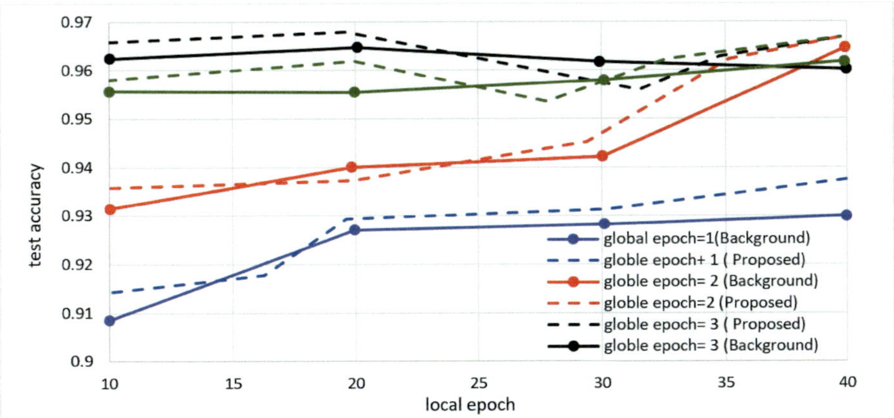

Figure 5.10 The proposed approach's performance compared to the background study's approach.

5.8 Implications of the Study

This study has significant implications, especially when it comes to tackling important issues related to data security and privacy within 5G-IoT networks. The research introduces a strong approach that utilizes blockchain technology combined with homomorphic encryption to improve data integrity, confidentiality, and secure transmission in these intricate systems. In this study a decentralized and transparent framework is created, which provides more dependability and scalability applications in 5G-IoT environments in multiple sectors as healthcare, smart cities and finance. This method can be used in healthcare sector to effectively look at patient records in different facilities which enables smoother, safer access for healthcare providers while preserving vital information of patients from unauthorized personals. This improves the overall trust between doctors and patients and helps in improving digital healthcare sector. In healthcare industry, this approach can be significantly used to create blockchain-based infrastructure for EHR management. Data generated from medically enabled devices encrypted and stored on the blockchain. Using decentralization, medical authorized personals can access patient data in real-time for treatment, where patients can control the access of who can view the information. This will enable full traceability of medical interventions and immutability of records helps reduce errors or frauds in medical records. Also, the use of homomorphic encryption helps to keep data safer by keeping data encrypted while operations are being performed improving both efficiency and security of the system. AI also plays an important role in analysing data patterns to make the system more reliable and resilient to attacks. AI models can be trained on the data stored in encryption form in the blockchain network using deep learning models, where only training model updates are shared while keeping the data on the device itself. Blockchain can store any modifications done in the AI model and ensures that any changes in the data inputs or model parameters are transparent and true. This feature helps in essential trust building among devices and AI systems.

5.9 Conclusion and Future Scope

In contrast to the current centralized method, network members now engage in decentralized data sharing. Blockchains are distributed ledgers, a type of technology that enables users to record and exchange transaction data over a network. Many privacy and security problems have arisen because of the swift expansion of the IoT on a global scale. Access control is one of the most critical issues that centralized approaches are now able to resolve, and it is also one of the most complex issues. These techniques could be relied on by a third party, but they have restrictions regarding their availability and scalability, which might result in a performance bottleneck. The invention of blockchain technology has sparked one of the most significant surges of interest in the application of cryptography in the past few years. Therefore, there are still open questions to be answered in the realms of security and privacy study before blockchain technologies could go beyond their current level of acceptance and reach their full potential. Hence, Blockchain technology is used to address security and privacy concerns in the IoT, such as non-repudiation, data integrity, data privacy and authorization, secure communication, and trustworthy, one-of-a-kind identification. In this study, a homomorphic encryption mechanism is presented to be used in conjunction with blockchain as a distributed database to protect keyword-based searches and access to the database.

In addition to this, the system that was suggested includes a mechanism for the revocation of secure keys and changes the relevant rules appropriately. Because of this, a safe system for accessing information has been developed. This system makes use of trust chains and blockchain technology to address the inefficiencies and vulnerabilities that are present in the existing systems. The findings of the suggested technique were contrasted with those of the model used in the earlier study. In light of the comparative analysis, the author has concluded that the proposed approach offers greater accuracy than the study approach that was used previously. More study is needed into some of the more difficult research areas, such as ways to use machine learning datasets for intrusion prevention, data storage observation of blockchain-based solutions, selecting the most appropriate consensus algorithm, and the design of usable and compatible cryptographic protocols.

References

[1] Alabdali, Aliaa M. "A Novel Framework of an IOT-Blockchain-Based Intelligent System." *Wireless Communications and Mobile Computing* 2022 (2022): 1-13. https://doi.org/10.1155/2022/4741923

[2] Kaur, Rasmeet, and Aleem Ali. "A novel blockchain model for securing iot based data transmission." *International Journal of Grid and Distributed Computing* 14, no. 1 (2021): 1045-1055

[3] Madumidha, S., P. Siva Ranjani, U. Vandhana, and B. Venmuhilan. "A theoretical implementation: Agriculture-food supply chain management using blockchain technology." In *2019 TEQIP III Sponsored International Conference on Microwave Integrated Circuits, Photonics and Wireless Networks (IMICPW)*, pp. 174-178. IEEE, 2019.https://doi.org/10.1109/IMICPW.2019.8933270
[4] Khan, Minhaj Ahmad, and Khaled Salah. "IoT security: Review, blockchain solutions, and open challenges." *Future generation computer systems* 82 (2018): 395-411.https://doi.org/10.1016/j.future.2017.11.022
[5] Viriyasitavat, Wattana, Tharwon Anuphaptrirong, and Danupol Hoonsopon. "When blockchain meets the Internet of Things: Characteristics, challenges, and business opportunities." Journal of industrial information integration 15 (2019): 21-28. https://doi.org/10.1016/j.jii.2019.05.002
[6] Ray, Partha Pratim, Dinesh Dash, Khaled Salah, and Neeraj Kumar. "Blockchain for IoT-based healthcare: background, consensus, platforms, and use cases." *IEEE Systems Journal* 15, no. 1 (2020): 85-94.https://doi.org/10.1109/JSYST.2020.2963840
[7] Ferrag, Mohamed Amine, Lei Shu, Xing Yang, Abdelouahid Derhab, and Leandros Maglaras. "Security and privacy for green IoT-based agriculture: Review, blockchain solutions, and challenges." *IEEE access* 8 (2020): 32031-32053.https://doi.org/10.1109/ACCESS.2020.2973178
[8] Hong, Gi-Wan, Jeong-Wook Kim, and Hangbae Chang. "Blockchain technology based information classification management service." *CMC-COMPUTERS MATERIALS & CONTINUA* 67 (2021): 1489-1501.http://dx.doi.org/10.32604/cmc.2021.013344
[9] Hameed, Khizar, Mutaz Barika, Saurabh Garg, Muhammad Bilal Amin, and Byeong Kang. "A taxonomy study on securing Blockchain-based Industrial applications: An overview, application perspectives, requirements, attacks, countermeasures, and open issues." *Journal of Industrial Information Integration* 26 (2022): 100312. https://doi.org/10.1016/j.jii.2021.100312
[10] Halpin, Harry, and Marta Piekarska. "Introduction to Security and Privacy on the Blockchain." In *2017 IEEE European Symposium on Security and Privacy Workshops (EuroS&PW)*, pp. 1-3. IEEE, 2017.. https://doi.org/10.1109/EuroSPW.2017.43
[11] https://vietnamblockchain.asia/post/5666316/5-basic-components-of-blockchain#5-virtual-machine

[12] Baliga, Arati. "Understanding blockchain consensus models." *Persistent* 4, no. 1 (2017): 14.

[13] Bataineh, Marah R., Wail Mardini, Yaser M. Khamayseh, and Muneer Masadeh Bani Yassein. "Novel and secure blockchain framework for health applications in IoT." *IEEE Access* 10 (2022): 14914-14926. https://doi.org/10.1109/ACCESS.2022.3147795

[14] Dorri, Ali, Salil S. Kanhere, Raja Jurdak, and Praveen Gauravaram. "Blockchain for IoT security and privacy: The case study of a smart home." In *2017 IEEE international conference on pervasive computing and communications workshops (PerCom workshops)*, pp. 618-623. IEEE, 2017.https://doi.org/10.1109/PERCOMW.2017.7917634

[15] Puthal, Deepak, Mohammad S. Obaidat, Priyadarsi Nanda, Mukesh Prasad, Saraju P. Mohanty, and Albert Y. Zomaya. "Secure and sustainable load balancing of edge data centers in fog computing." *IEEE Communications Magazine* 56, no. 5 (2018): 60-65. https://doi.org/10.1109/MCOM.2018.1700795

[16] Zheng, Z., Xie, S., Dai, H. N., Chen, X., & Wang, H. (2018). Blockchain challenges and opportunities: A survey. *International journal of web and grid services*, *14*(4), 352-375.

[17] Use the Blockchain Technology for Smart Contracts, https://cointelegraph.com/news/david-and-joyces-weddingdemonstrates-how-easy-it-is-to-use-the-blockchain-technology-for-smart-contracts,Accessed15December2017

[18] Ekblaw, Ariel, Asaph Azaria, John D. Halamka, and Andrew Lippman. "A Case Study for Blockchain in Healthcare:"MedRec" prototype for electronic health records and medical research data." In *Proceedings of IEEE open & big data conference*, vol. 13, p. 13. 2016.

[19] Puthal, Deepak, Nisha Malik, Saraju P. Mohanty, Elias Kougianos, and Gautam Das. "Everything you wanted to know about the blockchain: Its promise, components, processes, and problems." IEEE Consumer Electronics Magazine 7, no. 4 (2018): 6-14

[20] Bataineh, Marah R., Wail Mardini, Yaser M. Khamayseh, and Muneer Masadeh Bani Yassein. "Novel and secure blockchain framework for health applications in IoT." IEEE Access 10 (2022): 14914-14926

[21] Liang, Wenbing, and Nan Ji. "Privacy challenges of IoT-based blockchain: a systematic review." *Cluster Computing* 25, no. 3 (2022): 2203-2221.https://doi.org/10.1007/s10586-021-03260-0

[22] Varshney, Shipra, Prashant Vats, Shweta Choudhary, and Deepti Singh. "A blockchain-based framework for IoT based secure identity

management." In *2022 2nd international conference on innovative practices in technology and management (ICIPTM)*, vol. 2, pp. 227-234. IEEE, 2022. https://doi.org/10.1109/ICIPTM54933.2022.9753887

[23] Vahdati, Monireh, Kamran Gholizadeh HamlAbadi, and Ali Mohammad Saghiri. "IoT-Based healthcare monitoring using blockchain." *Applications of Blockchain in Healthcare* (2021): 141-170.https://doi.org/10.1007/978-981-15-9547-9_6

[24] Algarni, Sultan, Fathy Eassa, Khalid Almarhabi, Abduallah Almalaise, Emad Albassam, Khalid Alsubhi, and Mohammad Yamin. "Blockchain-based secured access control in an IoT system." *Applied Sciences* 11, no. 4 (2021): 1772.https://doi.org/10.3390/app11041772

[25] Oikonomou, Filippos Pelekoudas, Jose Ribeiro, Georgios Mantas, Joaquim Manuel CS Bastos, and Jonathan Rodriguez. "A hyperledger fabric-based blockchain architecture to secure IoT-based health monitoring systems." In *2021 IEEE International Mediterranean Conference on Communications and Networking (MeditCom)*, pp. 186-190. IEEE, 2021.https://doi.org/10.1109/MeditCom49071.2021.9647521

[26] Ferrag, Mohamed Amine, Lei Shu, Xing Yang, Abdelouahid Derhab, and Leandros Maglaras. "Security and privacy for green IoT-based agriculture: Review, blockchain solutions, and challenges." *IEEE access* 8 (2020): 32031-32053.https://doi.org/10.1109/ACCESS.2020.2973178

[27] Mohanta, Bhabendu Kumar, Debasish Jena, Somula Ramasubbareddy, Mahmoud Daneshmand, and Amir H. Gandomi. "Addressing security and privacy issues of IoT using blockchain technology." *IEEE Internet of Things Journal* 8, no. 2 (2020): 881-888.https://doi.org/10.1109/JIOT.2020.3008906

[28] Ali, Aitizaz, Mohammed Amin Almaiah, Fahima Hajjej, Muhammad Fermi Pasha, Ong Huey Fang, Rahim Khan, Jason Teo, and Muhammad Zakarya. "An industrial IoT-based blockchain-enabled secure searchable encryption approach for healthcare systems using neural network." *Sensors* 22, no. 2 (2022): 572.https://doi.org/10.3390/s22020572

[29] Fasila, K. A., and Sheena Mathew. "Fast and Efficient Security Scheme for Blockchain-Based IoT Networks." CMC-COMPUTERS MATERIALS & CONTINUA 73, no. 1 (2022): 2097-2114

[30] https://www.ku.ac.ae/blockchain-in-the-oil-and-gas-industry-has-promise-but-faces-challenges

[31] Swanson, Tim. "Consensus-as-a-service: a brief report on the emergence of permissioned, distributed ledger systems." *Report, available online* (2015).

[32] Hader, Manal, David Tchoffa, Abderrahman El Mhamedi, Parisa Ghodous, Alexandre Dolgui, and Abdellah Abouabdellah. "Applying integrated Blockchain and Big Data technologies to improve supply chain traceability and information sharing in the textile sector." *Journal of Industrial Information Integration* 28 (2022): 100345. https://doi.org/10.1016/j.jii.2022.100345

[33] Chen, Yun, Hui Xie, Kun Lv, Shengjun Wei, and Changzhen Hu. "DEPLEST: A blockchain-based privacy-preserving distributed database toward user behaviors in social networks." *Information Sciences* 501 (2019): 100-117. https://doi.org/10.1016/j.ins.2019.05.092

[34] Hao, Weifeng, Jiajie Zeng, Xiaohai Dai, Jiang Xiao, Qiangsheng Hua, Hanhua Chen, Kuan-Ching Li, and Hai Jin. "BlockP2P: Enabling fast blockchain broadcast with scalable peer-to-peer network topology." In *Green, Pervasive, and Cloud Computing: 14th International Conference, GPC 2019, Uberlândia, Brazil, May 26–28, 2019, Proceedings 14*, pp. 223-237. Springer International Publishing, 2019.https://doi.org/10.1007/978-3-030-19223-5_16

[35] Adams, Richard, Beth Kewell, and Glenn Parry. "Blockchain for good? Digital ledger technology and sustainable development goals." *Handbook of sustainability and social science research* (2018): 127-140. https://doi.org/10.1007/978-3-319-67122-2_7

[36] Cachin, Christian. "Architecture of the hyperledger blockchain fabric." In *Workshop on distributed cryptocurrencies and consensus ledgers*, vol. 310, no. 4, pp. 1-4. 2016.

[37] Aggarwal, Shubhani, and Neeraj Kumar. "Hyperledger." In *Advances in computers*, vol. 121, pp. 323-343. Elsevier, 2021. https://doi.org/10.1016/bs.adcom.2020.08.016

[38] Yi, Xun, Russell Paulet, Elisa Bertino, Xun Yi, Russell Paulet, and Elisa Bertino. *Homomorphic encryption*. Springer International Publishing, 2014.https://doi.org/10.1007/978-3-319-12229-8_2

[39] Valentini-Botinhao, Cassia, Xin Wang, Shinji Takaki, and Junichi Yamagishi. "Speech Enhancement for a Noise-Robust Text-to-Speech Synthesis System Using Deep Recurrent Neural Networks." In *Interspeech*, vol. 8, pp. 352-356. 2016.http://dx.doi.org/10.21437/Interspeech.2016-159

[40] Naz, Saeeda, Khizar Hayat, Muhammad Imran Razzak, Muhammad Waqas Anwar, Sajjad A. Madani, and Samee U. Khan. "The optical character recognition of Urdu-like cursive scripts." *Pattern Recognition*

47, no. 3 (2014): 1229-1248. https://doi.org/10.1016/j.patcog.2013.09.037

[41] Shinde, R., Patil, S., Kotecha, K., Potdar, V., Selvachandran, G., & Abraham, A. (2024). Securing AI-based healthcare systems using blockchain technology: A state-of-the-art systematic literature review and future research directions. *Transactions on Emerging Telecommunications Technologies*, *35*(1), e4884.

[42] Sarker, B., Sharif, N. B., Rahman, M. A., & Parvez, A. S. (2023). AI, IoMT and Blockchain in Healthcare. *Journal of Trends in Computer Science and Smart Technology*, *5*(1), 30-50. Page 101 of 101

6

Interconnected Integrity: Securing IoT Networks with Blockchain Technology

Sartaj Singh[1], Shilpa[1], Sandeep Kaur[2], and Rishi Kumar[3]

[1]School of Computer Applications, Lovely Professional University, India
[2]Department of Computer Science, GN Girls College, India
[3]Department of Computing, Universiti Teknologi Petronas, Malaysia
Email: sartaj.singh@lpu.co.in; shilpa.21819@lpu.co.in;
sandeep_nagra@yahoo.com; rishi_18001163@utp.edu.my

Abstract

As the Internet of Things (IoT) ecosystem expands, the need for robust security measures to safeguard interconnected devices becomes paramount. This chapter delves into the intersection of IoT networks and blockchain technology, proposing innovative solutions to enhance security and ensure data integrity within IoT environments. By leveraging blockchain's decentralized and immutable nature, this chapter explores how IoT networks can mitigate vulnerabilities such as data tampering, unauthorized access, and single points of failure. Through a detailed examination of blockchain-based authentication, data encryption, and consensus mechanisms, this chapter elucidates practical strategies for fortifying IoT infrastructures against emerging threats. Furthermore, real-world use cases and implementation challenges are analyzed to provide valuable insights into the depletion of blockchain solutions in diverse IoT applications. From smart homes to industrial automation, the integration of blockchain technology offers a promising avenue for achieving interconnected integrity and fostering trust in the evolving landscape of IoT security.

With the advancement of technologies, large amounts of data are generated that can fall under the eye of hackers. As we know, nobody trusts

DOI: 10.1201/9788743809050-8

one another during data sharing. Blockchain technology has become a more relevant security architecture to provide high-level security for the data. Also, blockchain stores the data in a sophisticated manner using mathematics and innovative software that makes it very difficult for hackers to manipulate and hack it. Almost all business areas and government works are considered under blockchain for cybersecurity because blockchain is a decentralized storage area without any central administrator. In a decentralized system, information is stored in different areas it becomes difficult for hackers to access the information. As well as blockchain is considered a self-regulating infrastructure that involves the participation and agreement of every network that will control the transfer of unwanted information through the network. Blockchain also uses the concept of a hashing mechanism for information encryption using SHA256. Blockchain completely removes human factors during cyber transactions.

Keywords: Blockchain technology, consensus mechanisms, data tampering, decentralized, diverse, fortifying IoT infrastructures, IoT applications, immutable, interconnected devices, Internet of Things, security measures, single points of failure, smart homes

6.1 Introduction

In the contemporary era, the proliferation of Internet of Things (IoT) devices has reformed various industrial sectors, offering unprecedented connectivity and automation. Due to the frequent data collection and transmission of sensitive data across the network by IoT devices, extensive IoT adoption brings substantial security challenges [1]. As the IoT ecosystem is scalable and complex, traditional security apparatuses leave it vulnerable to various attacks such as data breaches, unauthorized access, and tampering [2], as it is difficult to cope.

Blockchain technology has been integrated with the IoT ecosystem as a promising solution to provide security and help cope with these challenges. Due to the decentralized and immutable nature of blockchain, IoT devices can establish a trusted and transparent network infrastructure, ensuring the integrity and authenticity of data transactions [1, 2]. There are different phases for the integration of blockchain and IoT ecosystem, and also pens down how the integrity level can be achieved for IoT network security and can handle the security threats.

6.1.1 IoT infrastructure

IoT infrastructure (smart city) is the foundation of devices that are interconnected, and IoT infrastructure allows devices to communicate and function. These devices are used for data collection, transmission, processing, and also data analysis [3]. These components [3, 4] include IoT devices, edge and fog computing, gateways, networks, cloud services, and user interfaces, as shown below in Figure 6.1.

- Devices and sensors: These consist of the physical objects presumed to compose the "Things" in the IoT. They are designed to pick up data from the physical world in the form of temperature and motion, and frequently incorporate a processor for basic analysis of the data collected.
- Network: This is the channel of information transfer that supports the data tone from the sensors to aid in delivering wherever it is supposed to go. In some cases, different technologies of the network, for instance, the short range for local connections, cellular, or Wi-Fi for the wide range, might be used. These networks are used as follows:
    1. Cellular networks (LTE-M, NB-IoT): The cellular networks are appropriate for over wide area coverage.
    2. Short-range wireless (Bluetooth, Z-Wave): These options are well utilized where devices to be connected are within close proximity, say a smart home.

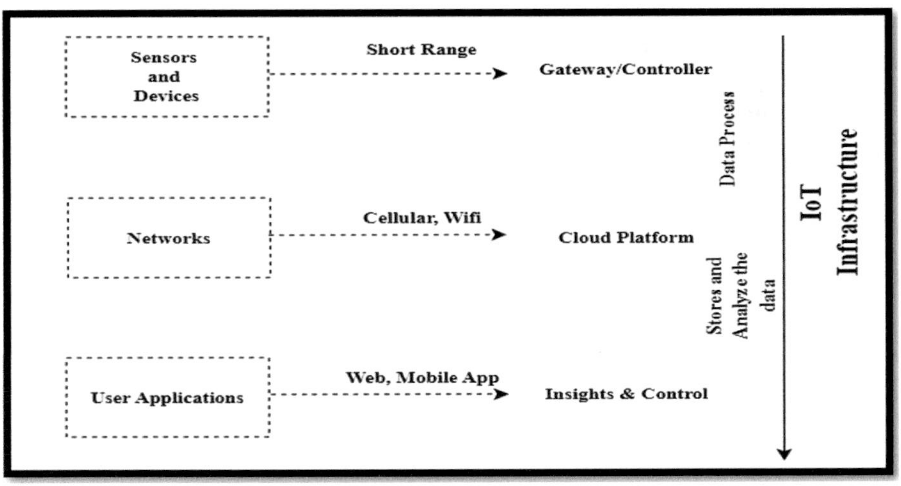

Figure 6.1 IoT Infrastructure.

3. Long-range wireless (LoRa, Sigfox): These are suitable for use when the devices are spread across large distances, as may be seen in smart city development or agriculture use.

- Gateways and controllers: Both gateways and controllers are intermediaries between the IoT devices and the network. All these gather data from the multiple IoT-connected devices, process them when needed, and forward the information further.
- Cloud computing: The cloud is used for the storage of the colossal amount of data that is mostly produced by sensor devices. Also, it provides the computational capabilities for data processing and obtaining insights.
- User applications: The user interfaces the system via applications on his/her mobile device and/or web browsers and interfaces with the IoT-based system to view the data and manage the devices.
- Data analytics: The encompassment of raw and unprocessed data is the first step in data analytics, which turns the data into useful information. Big data tools assist in recognizing undetectable structures of data, demanding trends, and enhancing functionality.

In brief, an IoT infrastructure provides the foundational platform for organizations to provide the way to store data via networks. In this section, different layers of IoT infrastructure are discussed, such as sensors and devices, networks, and user applications. Each layer performs its own task.

6.1.2 IoT Infrastructure Threats/Attacks

The IoT structure is gradually becoming the center of attraction among hackers due to its widespread installation, and most of the time, the IoT architecture lacks strong protection measures. Attacks on IoT infrastructure can be devastating since they target every layer and element, from single devices to national systems [5]. Various attacks mitigating the IoT infrastructure are discussed below in subsections:

6.1.2.1 Types of IoT infrastructure attacks

IoT infrastructure is prone to a wide range of attacks due to its diverse nature and interconnected devices. The attacks [6] are categorized based on different features and effects on the components of the IoT infrastructure, which are as follows:

6.1.2.1.1 Device hijacking and botnets [7]

Device hijacking and botnets are both significant threats to IoT infrastructure. These attacks help in the vulnerability exploitation of IoT devices to gain control over them. Device hijacking occurs when attackers successfully gain unauthorized access to IoT devices in any IoT-based infrastructure. This can be achieved with several methods, such as exploiting software vulnerabilities, either weak authentication or default passwords. When an attacker successfully hijacks, the attacker can manipulate the devices and data for various purposes such as spying, data theft, or adding a botnet.

Figure 6.2 highlights the types of attacks.

Methods of device hijacking: There are several methods that hackers use to hijack devices. Some of them are discussed below.

- Default credentials exploitations: Most IoT devices come with default credentials, such as a default username and password that are disregarded by authorized users to update them. It makes it easy for attackers to gain access.
- Exploitation of vulnerability: Software vulnerability in device applications can be exploited to gain access. These vulnerabilities remain unpatched due to infrequent updates.
- Man-in-the-middle attacks: Interception and alteration in communication between devices and their controllers can easily give attackers access to gain control over the devices.

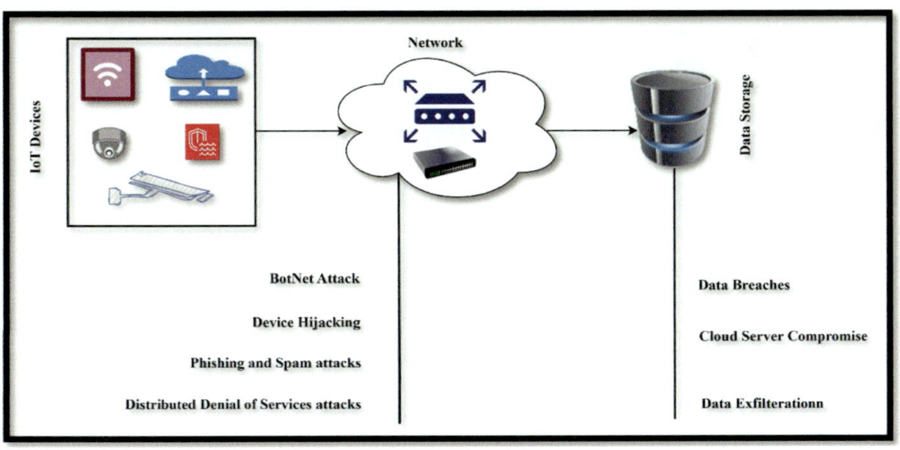

Figure 6.2 Device hijack and botnet attacks.

- Malicious firmware update: Attackers can provide a malicious firmware update that helps attackers gain backdoor access to the devices.
  Botnets are hijacked device networks controlled by attackers, which are known as botmasters. IoT infrastructure integrated devices are the prime targets for the botnets due to the poor security measures. IoT botnets include the following categories such as Mirai botnet, Reaper botnet, and Mozi botnet.
  - Mirai botnet: One of the most famous IoT attacks, where thousands of devices were infected with malware and distributed denial-of-service (DDoS) attacks. Mirai botnet exploits the default credentials to spread.
  - Reaper botnet: A more sophisticated version of Mirai, capable of exploiting vulnerabilities in various IoT devices.
  - Mozi botnet: Mozi uses a peer-to-peer framework, targets a wide range of IoT-based devices with access of weak passwords and vulnerabilities.

Botnets attacks: Various types of attacks are possible due to this vulnerability, with IoT-based botnet attacks being among the most common[2]

- *Distributed denial of service (DDoS) attacks*: Botnets launch the DDoS attacks mostly in the traffic and disrupt the services.
- *Spam and phishing*: Botnets can send a large number of spam and phishing emails to spread the malware, as well as try to steal credentials.
- *Data theft and espionage*: The devices that are hijacked can be utilized to collect sensitive data, such as videos and feeds from CCTV cameras and audio from speakers.

6.1.2.1.2 Man-in-the-middle (MitM) attacks

In man-in-the-middle attacks [7], attackers intercept and potentially alter communication between IoT devices and their controllers or between different devices and the cloud. These attacks can lead to various consequences, such as unauthorized access to sensitive data or manipulation of device behavior, as well as disruption between services.

Methods of MitM attacks: There are several methods used by attackers for MitM attacks, which are shown in Figure 6.3.

- *Wi-fi eavesdropping*: Attackers will exploit the insecure and poor network communication in order to interrupt the communication between IoT devices, as well as the network.

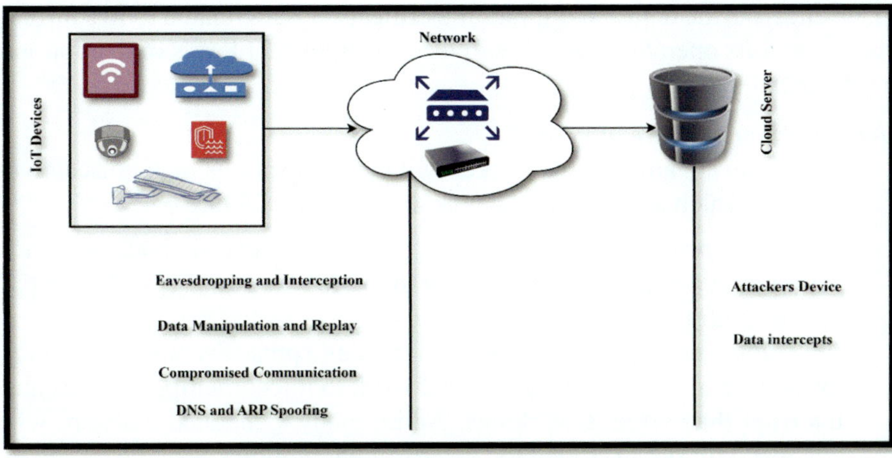

Figure 6.3 Man-in-the-middle attacks.

- *Rogue access points*: Attackers will set up malicious access points for the IoT devices that will help and allow the attackers to interrupt and manipulate the traffic access points.
- *DNS spoofing*: Attackers will redirect the traffic from legitimate server access toward malicious ones by corrupting the cache memory related to DNS.
- *ARP spoofing*: An attacker will send the fake address resolution protocol messages to target devices and will try to link the MAC addresses for interception.

MitM attack on a cloud server:

- *Data theft*: A robber can mislead or steal sensitive information such as personal data, login credentials, and other related information.
- *Device control*: After taking control of the devices, attackers can intercept the data by performing malicious activities.
- *Service disruption*: MitM attacks can interrupt and exploit the normal operations of IoT-related devices due to which IoT devices can lead to the denial of services and other related interruptions.
- *Integrity compromise*: After being altered or transited, the information by attackers, it may lead to false information recorded in the servers, which can compromise the integrity of the systems.

6.1.2.1.3 Ransomware

A ransomware attack [7] consists of malicious actions that help in infiltrating the network to gain control over the IoT devices and systems. This type of attack encrypts the data and cripples the critical services related to IoT infrastructure and its operations which will lead to significant levels of disruptions and financial losses.

Method of ransomware attacks:

In ransomware attacks, an attacker will perform various malicious activities, some of which are discussed below and shown in Figure 6.4.

- *Initial compromise*: Attackers send phishing emails to create malware activities and exploit vulnerabilities in the IoT devices, as well as in the network infrastructure.
- *Infiltration and spread*: Malware activities spread by attackers move toward the IoT devices across the network to infect multiple devices and interrupt the system's workings. Additionally, generated malware will connect with servers to get the details of encryption keys.
- *Encryption and extortion*: Attackers will generate the communication message with the servers to encrypt the data as well as generate the ransom note to request payment for the data decryption keys.

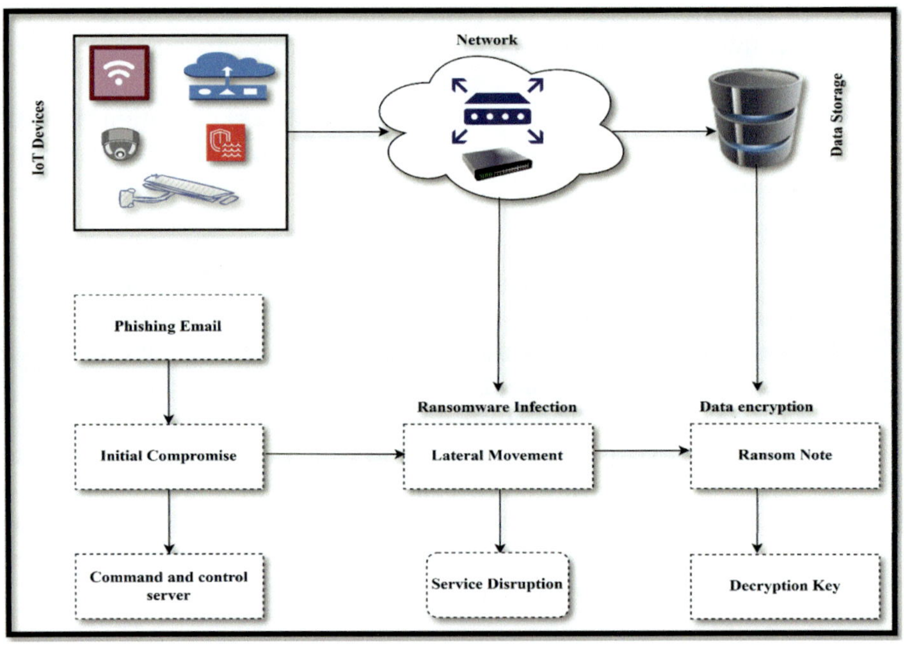

Figure 6.4 Ransom attacks.

6.1.2.1.4 Firmware attacks

Firmware attacks [7] initially target the low-level software in IoT infrastructure and control the hardware devices. Such attacks can compromise the integrity and functionality of the devices, which leads to security breaches. Attackers exploit vulnerabilities in the device firmware, installing malicious code that can be difficult to detect and remove. Firmware attacks can provide long-term control over compromised devices.

Methods of firmware attacks: There are various attacks related to firmware, as discussed and shown in Figure 6.5.

- *Malicious firmware update*: Attackers introduce malicious activities and code into IoT infrastructure through a firmware update to attack the network, as well as data.
- *Supply chain compromise*: Attackers compromise the process related to the manufacturing process in IoT infrastructure to embed malicious firmware.

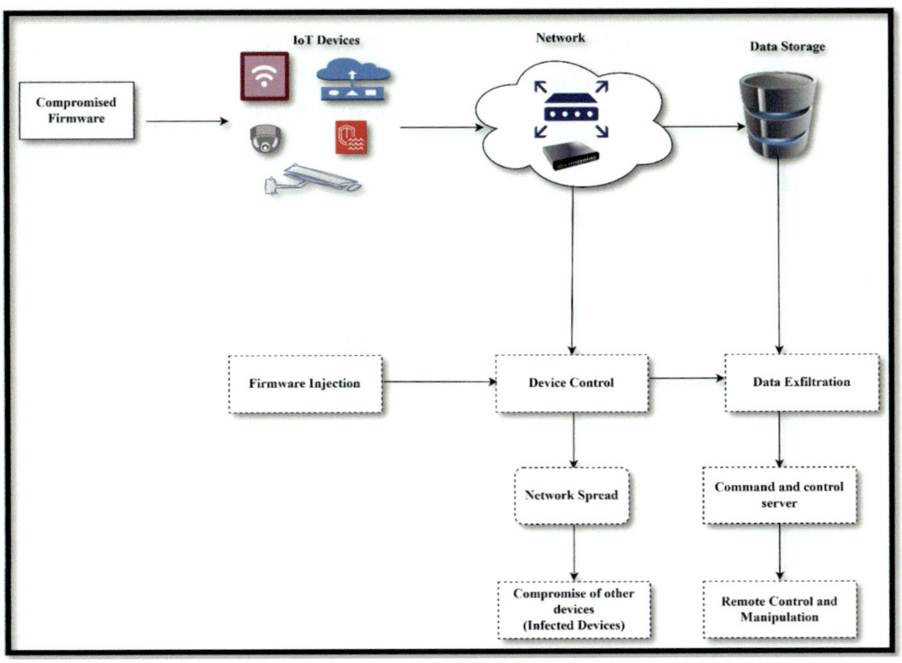

Figure 6.5 Firmware attacks.

- *Gain physical access*: Attackers try to gain control and physical access to the IoT and storage devices to manipulate the firmware.
- *Exploitation*: Attackers exploit the vulnerabilities of the devices and systems by creating backdoors for access and to extract sensitive, as well as required data. Additionally, they disrupt the normal operations to disrupt the device manipulation.

6.1.2.1.5 Data breaches

IoT devices often collect massive amounts of data, including sensitive and personal information. Attacks targeting these data can lead to significant breaches. Data breaches [7] in IoT infrastructure involve unauthorized access to sensitive data that is being transmitted and stored by IoT devices. Such breaches may lead to data theft, violation of privacy, and significant financial and reputational damages.

Methods of data breaches

There are various methods used for data breaches for attacks in IoT infrastructure, as shown in Figure 6.6.

- *Weak authentication*: Attackers will directly attack data storage devices and will gain access toward weak and default passwords. Additionally, attackers will exploit the data vulnerability of IoT devices and network infrastructure.
- *Data exfiltration and exposure*: In this, the robber will easily access and extract the data from the databases used for storage purposes and

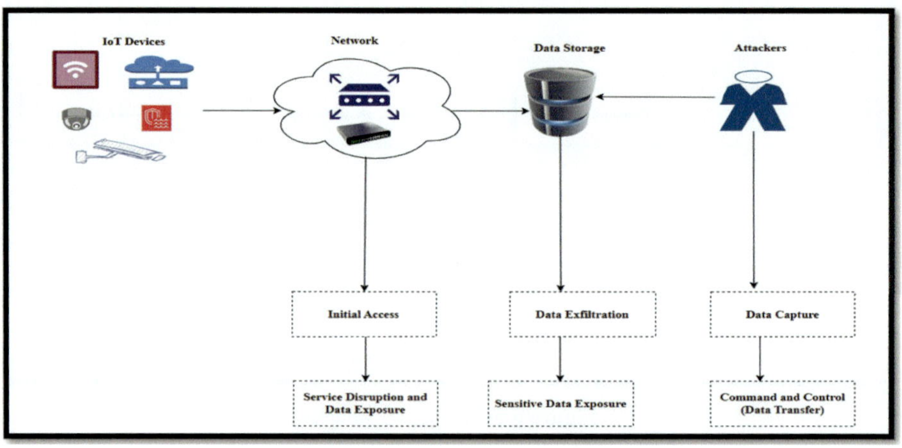

Figure 6.6 Data breach attacks

connected to the IoT devices. Moreover, attackers will also disrupt the IoT devices.

6.1.2.1.6 Physical attacks

Physical attacks [7] are related to the direct, as well as hands-on interface, with IoT devices that may lead to data theft, manipulation, and upgradation in IoT devices, and service disruptions. These attacks exploit the physical accessibility of IoT devices that are deployed and located in insecure and remote locations. One significant threat to IoT infrastructure is tampering with physical attacks, which involve unauthorized physical manipulation or interference with IoT devices. This essay delves into the nature, techniques, targets, impacts, and protection strategies related to tampering with physical attacks on IoT infrastructure.

Types of physical attacks: Tampering physical attacks exploit the physical vulnerabilities of IoT devices, which are often deployed at accessible locations, making them susceptible to unauthorized physical access. Unlike cyberattacks that target software and network vulnerabilities, tampering attacks focus on the physical components of the devices. These attacks can lead to severe consequences, including data breaches, operational disruptions, and safety risks.

Various IoT infrastructure attacks are shown in Figure 6.7.

Direct physical access: Attackers try to gain access to physical locations as well as IoT devices either by removing them from the deployed locations or by accessing them wherever they are installed. By getting access, attackers can manipulate the devices directly.

Internal component manipulation: Attackers can open the internal components, such as circuit boards, memory chips, and microcontrollers. After opening the internal components, attackers can manipulate the devices' operations and functionalities.

Malicious hardware insertion: Attackers can alter and manipulate the internal device's components to introduce vulnerability, data capturing, and unauthorized access.

Methods of physical attacks:

Attackers can use various methods of physical attacks that are discussed in Table 6.1.

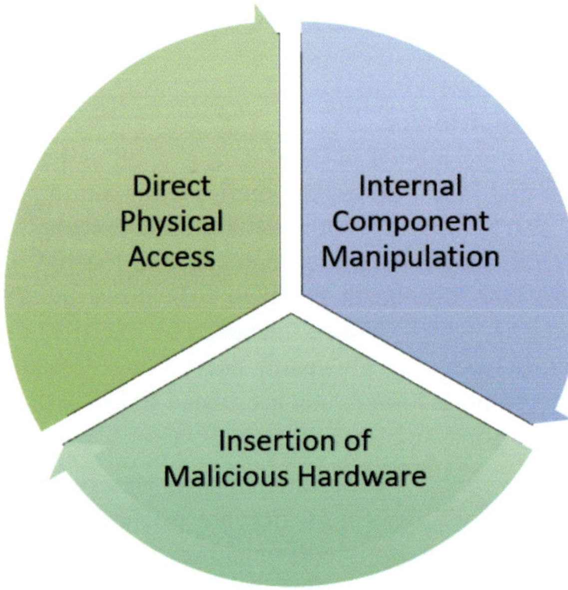

Figure 6.7 Physical attacks.

6.1.3 Common vulnerabilities in IoT infrastructure

IoT has revolutionized several sectors, including healthcare, transportation, industrial automation, and smart homes, by connecting physical objects to the internet and enabling them to send and receive data. However, the speedy proliferation of IoT devices has introduced numerous vulnerabilities that can be exploited by various malicious activities. These vulnerabilities can compromise the security, privacy, and functionality of IoT systems. This section explores common vulnerabilities [7] in IoT infrastructure in detail, examining the root causes, potential impacts, and strategies for mitigation

1. Weak authentication and authorization
    - Many IoT devices use default or weak passwords, making them easy targets for attackers.
    - Lack of robust authorization mechanisms can allow unauthorized access to device functions and data.
2. Insecure communication protocols
    - Use of unencrypted or poorly encrypted communication protocols can expose data in transit to interception and tampering.

Table 6.1 Physical attack methods.

Sr no	Methods	Description
1	Case opening	Attackers unscrew and cut the devices to access internal components, leaving the physical evidence in the form of broken seals and damaged enclosures.
2	Circuit modification	Attackers modify the electronic circuits of devices to alter their behavior and devices' functionality. Attackers soldered the keyloggers or data sniffers onto the circuits to capture sensitive information.
3	Firmware alteration	Attackers upload the custom firmware into the devices to execute the unauthorized code, affecting the devices' functionality.
4	Chip replacement	Attackers unsolder the memory chips and microcontrollers from circuits and replace them with upgraded versions. Malicious chips are installed into the circuits to compromise the integrity.
5	Debug port exploitation	IoT devices have ports that are exploited by attackers to affect the functionality of the IoT infrastructure and gain control over the processors and memory.
6	Side-channel attacks	Attackers infer sensitive information using cryptographic keys and analyze the power consumption and electromagnetic emissions to reveal information about the device's internal operations.

3. Inadequate software updates
   - Many IoT devices lack a mechanism for regular firmware updates, leaving known vulnerabilities unpatched.
4. Limited processing and storage capabilities
   - Constraints on device resources can limit the implementation of advanced security measures, making them more vulnerable to attacks.
5. Lack of security standards
   - The rapid growth of IoT has outpaced the development of comprehensive security standards, resulting in inconsistent security measures across devices and platforms.

The common vulnerabilities in IoT infrastructure include various issues such as hardware, software, network communication, data management, and user practices that are discussed in Table 6.2.

Table 6.2 Vulnerabilities in IoT infrastructure.

Sr No	Vulnerabilities in IoT	Sub-category	Description	Impact
1	Hardware vulnerabilities	Physical access	IoT devices are deployed in easily accessible locations such as public spaces, within homes, or in workplaces. This accessibility makes it susceptible to tempering or attacks.	• Tempering with physical devices. • Firmware modifications • Devices theft and malfunctioning • Extraction of sensitive information
		Insecure hardware interfaces	IoT devices that include hardware interfaces for debugging and maintenance can be easily exploited if not properly secured	• Unauthorized access to the interfaces • Firmware extraction • Malicious code injection • Alteration of device configuration
		Low-cost components	Manufacturers use low-cost components that may lack robust security and may be more prone to failures.	• Insecure and unreliable components lead to vulnerability • Device failure and exploitation
2	Software vulnerability	Outdated firmware	Many IoT devices are being executed in outdated firmware that may lead to vulnerability, and such devices lack the mechanisms of automatic updating features.	• Attackers control over the devices • Operation disruption • Extraction of sensitive data
		Hardcoded credentials	Hardcoded credentials do not allow the users to change the default credentials of IoT devices that are fixed and also do not allow for communication.	• Security risks • Unauthorized access to the devices

Table 6.2 *Continued.*

Sr No	Vulnerabilities in IoT	Sub-category	Description	Impact
		Insecure software development practices	Insecure coding practices and a lack of security lead to software vulnerabilities such as buffer overflow, API insecurity, and injection flaws	• Unauthorized access to the devices • Denial-of-services
3	Network vulnerability	Insecure communication protocols	IoT devices use outdated protocols that use weak encryption methods, which leads to data loss.	• Attackers can intercept and modify the communication between devices. • Loss of data integrity • Unauthorized control
		Lack of network segmentation	This leads to the flat network architecture	• Attackers access to the critical systems • Lead to the broader attacks
		Insufficient bandwidth and latency considerations	IoT devices operate within a limited bandwidth and high latency, which affect the performance.	• Incomplete security checks • Delayed response time

6.1.4 Mitigation strategies

Mitigation approaches provide multiple layers of security for data integrity, for which IoT infrastructure provides comprehensive approaches. The various strategies are being followed for security, which are discussed below:

1. *Strong authentication mechanisms*: Strong authentication mechanisms use multi-factor authentication (MFA) to provide the security layers for IoT infrastructure. It also ensures authentication facilities, such as strong and unique passwords for all IoT devices.
2. *Secure communication protocols*: Secure communication protocols use complex and strong encryption mechanisms for data transfer between IoT devices and other systems. Protocols like TLS/SSL can help secure communications in IoT infrastructure.
3. *Regular software updates*: In IoT infrastructure, mitigation services provide software updates. It ensures automatic firmware updates and helps in data collection.
4. *Network segmentation*: Mitigation strategies help the IoT devices segmentation in critical and complex networks. Network segmentation provides a potential breach and also limits the attack surface.
5. *Comprehensive security policies*: Comprehensive security policies help in the development and enforcement of security policies for the secure deployment, maintenance, and decommissioning of IoT devices.
6. *Security by design*: Mitigation strategies incorporate security measures in IoT infrastructure and are also integrated with IoT devices from the early stages of design and development. Mitigation ensures that security in IoT infrastructure is a foundational aspect rather than an afterthought.
7. *Monitoring and response*: Mitigation strategies implement robust monitoring systems to detect unusual activities in IoT infrastructure. It has an incident response plan for identifying and addressing security breaches swiftly.

In this section, the various threats have been discussed along with their methods. Further about its weaknesses, as well as mitigation strategies, are briefly highlighted. Awareness of common attack vectors and proactive implementation of security measures are essential to protecting IoT systems from cyber threats. Such security measures are discussed below in Section 6.2.

6.2 Security Measures

IoT infrastructure has its benefits and innovations, but it also has significant challenges related to IoT security. Securing IoT infrastructure provides a protection level for sensitive data, user authentication, and authorization, and ensures the reliability and flexibility of the connected IoT devices.

IoT infrastructure can become more secure by enforcing security standards enforcement which is crucial for the digital transformation of IoT networks. Blockchain as a security measure provides security for IoT infrastructure and data integrity. Blockchain technology is considered a decentralized and secure technology in nature, which is being integrated with IoT infrastructure for enhancement of the security level, data integrity, as well as operational efficiency [8].

Further in the section, the integration of blockchain and IoT is discussed with various cloud-based level solutions as well as edge blockchain.

6.2.1 Integration of blockchain for security

Blockchain technology is highlighted as the backbone of bitcoin and has also evolved as a versatile and revolutionary approach to digital security. Blockchain technology has the features of decentralization, transparency, and an immutable nature that enhance security across various industries [9]. Below few features are highlighted for the integration of blockchain.

- *Interconnected integrity*: In blockchain technology, each block consists of cryptographic hash functions that provide integrity to the data stored in IoT devices [10].
- *Immutable data logging*: Blockchain technology is considered immutable, transparent in nature, and auditable, which helps for data privacy and integrity of the transaction records, as well as data exchanges in IoT infrastructure. The immutable nature of blockchain provides integrity to transmitted data across interconnected devices and follows robust mechanisms for traceability and accountability [10].
- *Decentralized identity management*: Blockchain technology in IoT infrastructure initiates a novel approach to identity management [11]. Blockchain technology imputes unique cryptographic identifications to IoT devices, as well as leverages decentralized-level authentication. Decentralized identity management ensures control across the access control and minimizes the failure of centralization points and data breaches.

- *Smart contracts for automated security protocols*: Security protocols investigate the integration of smart contracts within IoT infrastructure for security automation and mechanisms for response [12]. Smart contracts enable self-executing agreements as well as enforce predefined security policies in the form of access control. These security policies enhance the resilience of IoT infrastructure against threats.
- *Blockchain-powered firmware updates*: Blockchain-powered firmware proposes secure and tamper-proof firmware to update IoT devices. It stores the firmware-related modifications on the blockchain in the form of transactions and ensures the authenticity and integration of software patches. It helps in the mitigation of unauthorized modification during the process of modifications [13].
- *Blockchain-enabled supply chain security*: Blockchain enhances the security and integrity of the supply chain for IoT-enabled industries. This approach helps organizations to achieve the end-to-end visibility and traceability of goods and ensure the authentication and provenance of products [13].

The integration of blockchain technology offers the promise of advancements in the security and integrity of the IoT network. It helps in paving the new ways for a more trustworthy and resilient IoT ecosystem.

6.2.2 Amalgamation of blockchain and IoT for security

The amalgamation of advanced technologies such as blockchain and IoT-based networks enhances the IoT infrastructure's security and integrity. The integration of blockchain creates a distributed and immutable ledger to record all the interactions within IoT devices [14–15]. As it is beneficial, this approach also addresses several challenges related to IoT networks that are related to security vulnerabilities, data integrity, and trust between IoT devices [13]. A detailed discussion about "How blockchain is integrated into IoT network for security" is given below in sections:

Decentralization blockchain ledger: Blockchain is a decentralized ledger in nature that helps to provide security for recorded transactions in blocks, as well as digital assets, without a central point, as blockchain is distributed in nature. It ensures that there will not be a single point of failure.

Consensus mechanisms: Blockchain has the features of consensus mechanisms that help to validate the transactions and provide authenticity. The consensus mechanism uses various protocols such as proof of work (PoW), proof of stake (PoS), or practical Byzantine fault tolerance (PBFT) to achieve the distributed agreement on the state of the ledger.

PBFT is an algorithm that is used to handle and tolerate faults in distributed systems. Such situations make the components of the IoT infrastructure behave in an arbitrary mode where threats can be enhanced. It helps in the network to provide security.

Security: Blockchain technology has the capability of security that is provided by the cryptographic hash mechanism. This facility provides security for the messages using a hash function in the transactions and links the blocks of the chain through the cryptographic hashes.

Immutable records: Blockchain technology is immutable and helps transactions of an immutable nature. The immutable nature of the record does not allow it to be altered once the records are recorded in blocks and added to the blockchain. This nature ensures the security, transparency, and efficiency of the transactions.

Smart contracts: Blockchain technology has the facility of smart contracts, which are digitally signed agreements. These are self-executing contracts that are stored in the blockchain. These contracts execute the actions as per the requirements while meeting the predefined terms and conditions.

Trust and transparency: Smart contracts enhance trust and transparency by ensuring all participants have access to the same contract and results.

Device authentication: Blockchain can provide a secure and tamper-proof way to manage device identities and authenticate devices within the network.

Access control: Access control ensures that only authorized devices and users can access specific network resources in the blockchain network.

An amalgamation of IoT (Internet of Things) with blockchain technology to enhance security in several ways:

An amalgamation of blockchain and IoT enhances the strength of both technologies (blockchain and IoT devices) for the security of IoT infrastructure networks. Integration of both technologies enhances data integrity, authentication, and security in communication [16] in several ways, are discussed below.

- *Immutable recordkeeping*: Blockchain provides a decentralized and immutable ledger, meaning once transactions and digital data are recorded, they cannot be altered or deleted. This immutable nature ensures the data integrity that is collected from IoT devices. This nature prevents unauthorized tampering with the data [17]. The data collected from the IoT devices can be secured using hashed functions and recorded in blocks. Each block contains the cryptographic hash functions to provide data integrity.

- *Data integrity*: As IoT devices generate a huge amount of data that is required to be transmitted and shared with security. This facility can be provided using a blockchain that ensures the integrity of the data using cryptographic verification.
- *Authentication and identity management*: Blockchain technology has the facility of authentication and identity management. The authentication facility provides authenticity to the IoT devices, and identity management helps to manage the identities securely. Each device is recorded with a unique identity on the blockchain and also allows only authorized devices to interact with the IoT network.
- *Secure communication*: Blockchain helps to establish a decentralized and encrypted communication network for secure communication between IoT devices of IoT infrastructure. Secure communication prevents eavesdropping and man-in-the-middle attacks. Blockchain ensures the confidentiality level and integrity of the transmitted data among the devices.
- *Smart contracts*: Blockchain contains the smart contracts features. Smart contracts are self-executed agreements that are written into code. Smart contracts automate the processes and digital assets in IoT infrastructure. For example, smart contracts are executed based on predefined rules and conditions to enforce access control policies.
- *Supply chain transparency*: Blockchain has the facility of the supply chain that enhance the transparency and traceability of goods in transactions on the blockchain. This facility helps to prevent counterfeit goods and authenticity of the data recorded in the transactions.
- *Decentralized identity management*: Due to blockchain features such as identity management and decentralization, blockchain allows IoT devices about unique and verifiable identities recorded on the blockchain. This facility prevents IoT devices from unauthorized access to the IoT network and ensures secure communication between authenticated devices. Blockchain provides the decentralized public key infrastructure to ensure device verification without a central authority and reduce the spoofing risks and unauthorized access.

- *Scalability and performance considerations*: Blockchain has the facility of scalability and performance considerations that are essential in IoT infrastructure. For this, blockchain provides solutions using off-chain processing, sidechains (Secondary blockchain that helps to enhance the scalability, transparency, and security), and 2-layers scaling solutions that help to mitigate these challenges to ensure network efficiency.

6.2.3 Flowchart of blockchain and IoT integration

The following conceptual flowchart, shown in Figure 6.8, defines how blockchain and IoT are integrated to provide security and privacy.

Implementation of blockchain in IoT infrastructure enhances security. Additionally, scalability, interoperability, and regulatory challenges need to be considered. Security of the IoT infrastructure ensures the prevention form attacks. Blockchain technology provides security measures such as encryption, access control, and regular security audits.

This section summarizes the way of integration of blockchain to provide security using different methods. Further discussing the integration of blockchain with IoT with visual analysis. The adoption of blockchain in the IoT industry has enhanced security, transparency, and scalability due to its decentralized and immutable nature. There are various IoT industries that have adopted the blockchain, such as healthcare sector, automative industries, agriculture, manufacturing industry, finance, and bank.

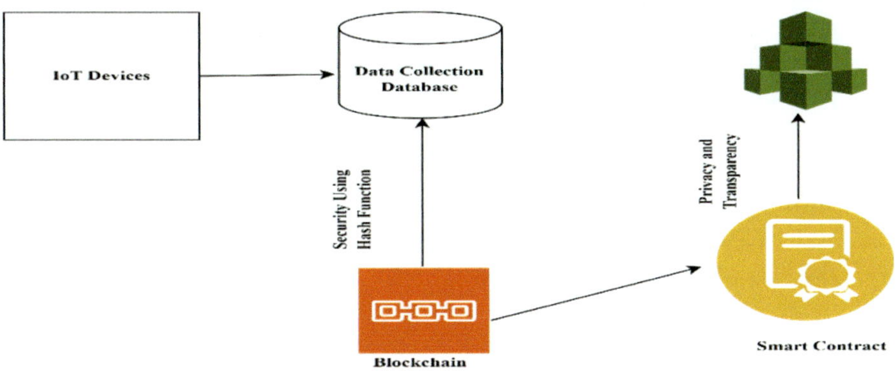

Figure 6.8 Blockchain and IoT integration.

6.3 Case Study

Case study 1: Securing healthcare IoT systems with blockchain [18]

Context: As the adoption and use of IoT devices such as wearable health monitors and remote patient management systems in the healthcare sector are increasing, security and privacy are becoming important concerns. Protection of the patient data is essential. The increasing adoption of IoT devices in healthcare, such as wearable health monitors and remote patient management systems, has introduced significant security and privacy concerns. Protecting sensitive patient data is paramount.

Challenges in healthcare IoT security

Healthcare IoT systems face various challenges related to security and privacy that are discussed below:

- *Data integrity*: IoT devices and sensors used in medical areas generate a huge amount of data exposed to tampering and modification by unauthorized users.
- *Data privacy*: Due to the decentralization of medical and patient data, it is difficult to provide privacy to patients' records.
- *Data authentication*: Verification of authentication is difficult in healthcare.

Implementation:

- *Blockchain for data integrity and privacy*: The amalgamation of blockchain technology in the healthcare sector enhances the integrity and confidentiality of patient data, such as electronic health records (EHRs). For security, patient data is recorded on a blockchain that provides an immutable audit.
- *Smart contracts*: Smart contracts are self-executed agreements that were implemented to automate access controls to ensure authorization. The smart contracts are regulated with rules and regulations that are digitally signed with HIPPA (Health Insurance Portability and Accountability Act).

Outcomes:

- *Enhanced security*: The immutable nature of blockchain significantly reduces the risk of data tampering and unauthorized access.

- *Improved trust*: Patients and healthcare providers reported higher levels of trust in the system due to the transparent and verifiable data management process.

Reference: Securing IoT-based healthcare systems with blockchain technology.

Case study 2: Blockchain-based security framework for smart cities

Context: Various IoT devices are deployed for smart city applications such as traffic management, energy distribution, and public safety. These applications require various security measures for the prevention of the systems [19, 12].

Challenges in securing smart cities

- *Data privacy*: In smart cities, IoT devices and sensors generate a huge amount of data that is exposed to tampering and modification by unauthorized users.
- *Cyberattacks*: Smart city services are being interrupted by cyberattacks such as hacking, malware, and DDoS.
- *Data integrity*: In smart cities, data collected from various sources requires transparency and privacy, which is crucial for decision-making.

Implementation:

- *Decentralized security framework*: A blockchain-based framework was implemented to manage the identities of IoT devices and ensure secure communication between them.
- *Consensus mechanism*: The framework utilized a consensus mechanism to validate transactions and device registrations, ensuring that only legitimate devices could join the network.

Outcomes:

- *Reduced vulnerabilities*: The blockchain is a decentralized ledger in nature that reduces the vulnerabilities of the IoT networks. The decentralized nature helps in the elimination of a single point failure.
- *Scalability*: The framework is successfully scaled to accommodate several devices without compromising security or performance.

Reference: Blockchain-based decentralized management for IoT in smart cities.

These case studies demonstrate the practical application of blockchain technology in enhancing the security of IoT networks, particularly in sensitive areas like healthcare and urban infrastructure.

6.4 Future Scope

Blockchain technology is integrated with IoT networks for security that is promising and multifaceted. Below are some scopes:

1. *Scalability and interoperability*: To enhance the scalability in IoT infrastructure, blockchain can be integrated with IoT, as blockchain has the feature of scalability and interoperability. Cross-chain interoperability allows different blockchain-related networks to communicate in IoT infrastructure and enhances the versatility of the ecosystem.
2. *Enhanced security protocols*: Advanced blockchain-based security protocols can be developed to address the threats related to IoT infrastructure and networks. This can enhance the encryption methods, and decentralization feature, and improve identity management.
3. *Integration with emerging technologies*: More robust security frameworks can be developed by integrating of blockchain with Artificial Intelligence, Machine learning, and edge computing. Artificial intelligence and machine learning help to predict the threats, whereas edge computing can process the data and reduce the vulnerabilities.
4. *Smart contracts for automation*: Smart contracts are rules and digitally signed agreements that ensure the automated and secure transactions within IoT devices.
5. *Regulatory compliance and standards*: Blockchain has smart contracts that help to meet regulatory requirements with transparency and immutable audit. Blockchain can play a critical role in IoT security.
6. *Supply chain security*: Blockchain is a distributed ledger in nature that helps for the enhancement of transparency and security of supply chains.

6.5 Conclusion

The integration of blockchain with IoT networks provides a secure IoT network, as it is a significant advancement to address the vulnerabilities of the IoT infrastructure. Blockchain is a decentralized and immutable ledger in nature that helps to provide security to prevent unauthorized access, data tempering, and cyber threats. It provides data integrity throughout the IoT network. Smart contracts are integrated with an IoT network that enhances security, enforces access controls, and also reduces human errors and malicious activities. As blockchain has the potential for scalability, an IoT network becomes easy to expand and can be integrated with various sectors. Blockchain also offers a secure supply chain to provide security to the interconnected devices. Blockchain is integrated with AI, ML, and edge computing to provide security, and access control, and also enable secure and reliable new application developments for IoT networks.

References

[1] Sahu, S. K., & Mazumdar, K. (2024). Exploring security threats and solutions Techniques for Internet of Things (IoT): from vulnerabilities to vigilance. Frontiers in Artificial Intelligence, 7, 1397480.

[2] Reyna, A., Martín, C., Chen, J., Soler, E., & Díaz, M. (2018). On blockchain and its integration with IoT. *Future Generation Computer Systems, 88*, 173-190.

[3] Sethi, P., & Sarangi, S. R. (2017). Internet of things: architectures, protocols, and applications. Journal of electrical and computer engineering, 2017(1), 9324035.

[4] Kumar, N. M., & Mallick, P. K. (2018). The Internet of Things: Insights into the building blocks, component interactions, and architecture layers. Procedia computer science, 132, 109-117.

[5] Sasi, T., Lashkari, A. H., Lu, R., Xiong, P., & Iqbal, S. (2023). A Comprehensive Survey on IoT Attacks: Taxonomy, Detection Mechanisms and Challenges. Journal of Information and Intelligence.

[6] Makhdoom, I., Abolhasan, M., Lipman, J., Liu, R. P., & Ni, W. (2018). Anatomy of threats to the internet of things. IEEE communications surveys & tutorials, 21(2), 1636-1675.

[7] Raj, R. S. N., & Seybold, B. M. (2018). A comprehensive survey on attacks, security issues, and blockchain solutions for IoT and IIoT. Proceedings of the Second International Conference on Inventive Communication and Computational Technologies (ICICCT), 87-92.

[8] Liao, H. Y., Ho, Y. C., & Chen, C. S. (2018). Applications of blockchain and IoT technologies on smart logistics and transportation. Procedia Computer Science, 162, 219-226.

[9] Makhdoom, I., Abolhasan, M., Abbas, H., & Ni, W. (2019). Blockchain's adoption in IoT: The challenges, and a way forward. Journal of Network and Computer Applications, 125, 251-279.

[10] Ali, M. S., Vecchio, M., Pincheira, M., Dolui, K., Antonelli, F., & Rehmani, M. H. (2018). Applications of blockchains in the Internet of Things: A comprehensive survey. IEEE Communications Surveys & Tutorials, 21(2), 1676-1717.

[11] Zyskind, G., Nathan, O., & Pentland, A. (2015). Decentralizing privacy: Using blockchain to protect personal data. 2015 IEEE Security and Privacy Workshops, 180-184.

[12] Christidis, K., & Devetsikiotis, M. (2016). Blockchains and smart contracts for the Internet of Things. IEEE Access, 4, 2292-2303.

[13] Wang, H., & He, W. (2018). A blockchain-based data storage security scheme for IoT. 2018 IEEE International Conference on Consumer Electronics (ICCE), 1-6.

[14] Kshetri, N. (2017). Can blockchain strengthen the Internet of Things? IT Professional, 19(4), 68-72.

[15] Ouaddah, A., Mousannif, H., Abou Elkalam, A., & Ait Ouahman, A. (2017). Access control in the Internet of Things: Big challenges and new opportunities. Computer Networks, 112, 237-262.

[16] Khan, M. A., & Salah, K. (2018). IoT security: Review, blockchain solutions, and open challenges. Future Generation Computer Systems, 82, 395-411.

[17] Zyskind, G., Nathan, O., & Pentland, A. (2015). Decentralizing privacy: Using blockchain to protect personal data. 2015 IEEE Security and Privacy Workshops, 180-184.

[18] Angraal, S., Krumholz, H. M., & Schulz, W. L. (2017). Blockchain technology: Applications in health care. Circulation: Cardiovascular Quality and Outcomes, 10(9).

[19] Kumar, S., & Tripathi, R. (2019). Implementation of blockchain for IoT: A smart home use case. Procedia Computer Science, 155, 10-17.

[20] Dorri, A., Kanhere, S. S., Jurdak, R., & Gauravaram, P. (2017). Blockchain for IoT security and privacy: The case study of a smart home. 2017 IEEE International Conference on Pervasive Computing and Communications Workshops (PerCom Workshops), 618-623.

7

An Adaptive Approach for Cloud Security using Cloud Service Tools, Blockchain, Protocols, and Algorithms

Sheetal Kumar Dixit[1], Rahul Jain[2], Madhuri Bhavsar[1], and Preeti Kathiria[1]

[1]Department of Computer Science & Engineering, Nirma University, India
[2]Department of Computer Engineering, Marwadi University, India
Email: er.skdixit@gmail.com; rahuljaincse51@gmail.com; madhuri.bhavsar@nirmauni.ac.in; preeti.kathiria@nirmauni.ac.in

Abstract

As cloud computing and the Internet of Things (IoT) continue to evolve rapidly, ensuring robust security across interconnected systems has become a significant challenge. The ever-changing landscape of cyber threats, combined with the dynamic nature of these technologies, demands a flexible and adaptive approach to cloud security. This work proposes an innovative security framework designed to enhance cloud security in real-time, incorporating advanced algorithms, IoT devices, cloud service tools, and communication protocols. The framework focuses on proactive threat detection, dynamic encryption, context-aware access control, and automated incident response systems. By utilizing machine learning and behavioral analytics, this approach can identify emerging risks and adjust security policies to safeguard sensitive data and services effectively. Additionally, the integration of secure IoT device management and robust communication protocols ensures that connected devices and cloud infrastructure remain protected throughout their lifecycle. In this IoT-driven era, the proposed adaptive security architecture aims to provide a scalable, efficient, and resilient solution to address the growing security demands of cloud environments. The report also explores future developments, such as blockchain integration, AI-driven security, and

DOI: 10.1201/9788743809050-9

the impact of new technologies like edge computing and 5G on cloud security strategies. Ultimately, this paper seeks to analyze and evaluate the most critical security methods for protecting data in cloud computing, while also recommending strategies to bolster cloud security further.

Keywords: Access control, authentication, authorization, cloud computing, IoT, secrecy, data protection, artificial intelligence, 5G, security tools, protocol, algorithms

7.1 Introduction

A blockchain is essentially a shared digital ledger that keeps a continuously expanding list of records, all securely connected through cryptographic hashes. Each block in this chain holds a cryptographic hash of the block that came before it, along with a timestamp and the transaction details. Because every block includes information about its predecessor, they create a linked chain where each new block ties back to the ones that came before it. This means that blockchain transactions are permanent; once a block is recorded, the data it contains cannot be changed later without also modifying all the blocks that follow.

When it comes to the wide range of services available, cloud computing really shines in its diversity. You can find it in several forms and models, including community, hybrid, private, and public clouds. On the service delivery side, we typically break things down into three main categories: SaaS (software as a service), PaaS (platform as a service), and IaaS (infrastructure as a service). Additionally, cloud computing can be categorized in two key ways: by geographic location and by the types of services offered.

A cloud computing cluster is essentially a group of computers that team up to perform various calculations and tasks. Over the past few years, cloud computing has really taken off as a major player in the IT world. One of the biggest perks this technology brings to businesses is the ability to cut down on both time to market and costs. It allows companies and organizations to tap into shared computing and storage resources, which is often a better option than building and managing their own infrastructure. Plus, cloud computing provides a flexible, secure, and budget-friendly IT setup. You can think of it like the national electricity grids that enable homes and businesses to access a reliable and cost-effective energy supply.

Cloud computing can be classified based on where the cloud is located. You have public clouds, where a vendor takes care of the computing infrastructure; private clouds, which are dedicated to a single organization

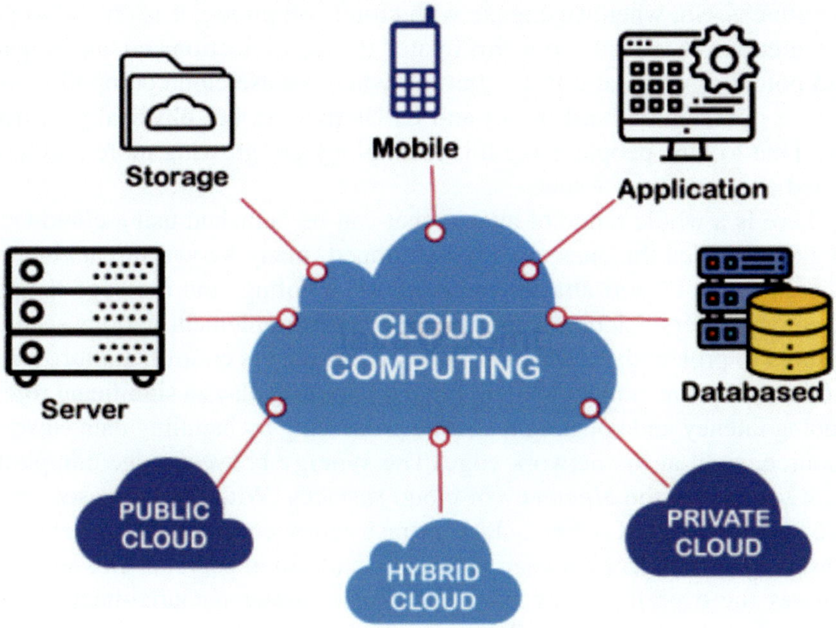

Figure 7.1 Cloud computing architecture.

and not shared with anyone else; hybrid clouds, which combine both public and private options; and community clouds, where IT resources are shared among organizations within the same community. [1]. Clouds are categorized as follows if the basis for classification is the kind of services provided: infrastructure as a service (IaaS), platform as a service (PaaS), and software as a service (SaaS) [1]. Figure 7.1 shows the brief view of the clout computing architecture.

These days, almost every computer system relies on cloud computing, which is a modern way to process and transfer data electronically. However, this network architecture can be susceptible to various types of attacks. One of the most notorious is the distributed denial of service (DDoS) attack. Thankfully, we can mitigate DDoS attacks by implementing techniques like SYN cookies and managing the number of users connected to the server through cloud technologies.

Another threat to cloud computing is the man-in-the-middle attack. To combat this, security measures such as Secure Socket Layer (SSL) are essential. However, if this security setup is misconfigured, it can lead to issues with client and server authentication, leaving users of cloud technology exposed to these attacks. So, when we engage with cloud computing, it is crucial to pay close attention to security concerns related to data protection and take steps to avoid potential vulnerabilities. After all, when we use cloud computing, our software operates on hard drives and CPUs that are not physically in front of us. Due to this, people using this technology are growing more and more worried about security issues.

There is a whole range of attacks that can be launched using cloud technologies. Besides the ones already mentioned, many known threats include traffic analysis, IP port attacks, phishing, IP spoofing, and message tampering, among others. Cloud computing companies implement various security measures to protect data, which typically cover access control, authorization, confidentiality, and authentication. Edge computing plays a significant role in reducing latency and boosting real-time processing by handling data closer to its source, right at the network edge. The synergy between edge computing and 5G enhances the efficiency of cloud services. With the increased speed and bandwidth that 5G offers, cloud infrastructure can be optimized, leading to faster data transfers between end users and cloud servers. This not only improves the overall user experience but also allows resource-heavy applications like virtual reality (VR) and augmented reality (AR) to run more smoothly. 5G's higher data speeds are particularly beneficial for cloud-based applications that require substantial bandwidth, such as streaming HD video, enhancing the delivery of multimedia content through cloud services. The vision of a fully connected and intelligent society is supported by 5G's ability to handle a large number of IoT devices in a given area. This opens up exciting possibilities for IoT applications that rely on seamless communication, including industrial automation and smart cities. The reduced latency of 5G is crucial for real-time Internet of Things applications like smart grids, remote healthcare monitoring, and autonomous vehicles. By minimizing data transfer delays, it enhances the overall stability of IoT systems and enables quicker decision-making. Additionally, energy-efficient IoT devices can benefit from 5G due to its energy-saving features, which are vital for promoting sustainability in the IoT ecosystem and extending the lifespan of battery-powered devices. In short, the advent of 5G wireless technologies marks a pivotal moment in the evolution of communication.

7.2 Literature Review

Blockchains operate through peer-to-peer (P2P) computer networks, serving as a public distributed ledger. In this setup, the nodes work together, following a consensus algorithm protocol to add and validate new transaction blocks. This collaborative effort enables participants to independently verify and audit transactions in a cost-effective manner. The process relies on mass collaboration driven by shared interests. Those who authenticate the transactions and successfully add a new block to the blockchain can earn tokens, which they can then use within the blockchain network. These tokens are known as cryptocurrencies.

A cryptocurrency is a type of digital currency designed to function as a medium of exchange over a computer network, without depending on any central authority like a government or bank to support or manage it. This decentralized system ensures that the parties involved in a transaction actually have the funds they say they do, removing the necessity for traditional intermediaries, such as banks, when money is being transferred between two or more parties.

Blockchain systems serve as prime examples of distributed computing with impressive Byzantine fault tolerance. This design creates a strong workflow where participants can feel confident about data security. By utilizing a blockchain, the risk of infinite reproducibility is eliminated. Essentially, a blockchain ensures that each unit of value is unique and has been transferred only once within a specific timeframe. The cornerstone of the blockchain protocol is the consensus rule, which mandates that all nodes in the blockchain must agree on the sequence of transactions within a block. If two nodes find themselves at odds over the transaction order, they need to collaborate to reach a consensus. The blockchain protocol also outlines how new blocks are generated and incorporated into the blockchain.

A ton of shared resources are accessible to numerous companies around the globe through the cloud computing platform [1]. The text dives into the essential security services required for cloud computing. The authors crafted a cloud model that revolves around a trust-based platform, presenting a solution tailored for cloud services. This architecture seamlessly integrates cloud services with trusted platform support services (TSS) and a trusted computing platform (TCP), all built on trust modules. Given its numerous benefits for both businesses and end users, cloud computing has rapidly evolved over the past few years. This swift growth in the IT sector has also brought about a surge in data security challenges. Consequently, various security models and trust-building strategies have been put into action to enhance the protection of data, especially when it comes to private and sensitive information. However, despite the high level of security offered, many of these models and methodologies still fall short in addressing certain security threats.

Bringing together 5G and IoT opens up a world of possibilities for getting products online and off the shelves more efficiently. Imagine consumer goods that can send and receive data about themselves, acting as smart products that interact with customers and other entities through various technologies like scanning, RFID readers, and NFC tags. These devices do not need to be constantly connected to the internet, which is a game-changer. While our current wireless infrastructure is struggling to keep up with the sheer number of network devices, 5G is set to change that. Retailers can leverage digital labels and smart packaging to connect with customers in innovative ways, transforming how they manage inventory and logistics. The potential of IoT has been held back by 4G's limitations in handling the massive data load from the ever-growing number of online sensors and connected devices. With its lightning-fast data speeds, low latency, improved mobility, energy efficiency, and ability to support a larger number of devices, 5G is truly the ideal foundation for the Internet of Things.

In addition to transforming how we communicate, 5G has the power to dramatically change both business and society. There are numerous industries where the combination of 5G and IoT could lead to significant disruptions, such as self-driving cars: these vehicles generate a wealth of data from sensors that track temperature, traffic, weather, GPS location, and more. To provide optimal services, they depend heavily on real-time data transfer. Thanks to its rapid transmission speeds and minimal latency, these smart cars can continuously collect a variety of data, including vital information that algorithms will use to assess the vehicle's performance and guide future design choices. Healthcare: With IoT driving many types of medical devices, we can expect to see shifts in the services these tools offer. The connectivity provided by the Internet of Things will be especially beneficial in rural areas and other remote locations, even where healthcare infrastructure is lacking. This low-latency technology makes it feasible to deliver high-quality medical services, including remote surgeries. Additionally, advanced IoT monitoring sensors will enhance logistical operations from start to finish. Not only will high speeds and low latency enable real-time data access, but they will also improve energy efficiency, allowing for a broader range of information to be gathered throughout the supply chain over time. For instance, a consumer could track specific details like where the fish was caught, the temperature during processing, and when it was delivered to the store. Smart cities: 5G will pave the way for more applications, including better healthcare facilities, traffic management, water and waste management, and various smart city initiatives.

The benefits of the next-generation network are set to enhance smart cities as more devices come online. Thanks to 5G's capability to handle massive amounts of data, the dream of a fully interconnected city is becoming a reality, allowing various smart systems to communicate seamlessly with each other. In the retail sector, 5G will revolutionize how businesses engage with customers through their mobile devices. With improved network connectivity and a growing number of connected devices, retailers can quickly implement innovative ways to interact with shoppers, especially through enhanced digital signage. As virtual and augmented reality technologies gain traction, retailers who effectively leverage omnichannel sales strategies will significantly elevate the shopping experience. In the automotive industry, one of the key uses of 5G is connecting vehicles to VR and AR technologies. Enhanced communication between vehicles, pedestrians, and infrastructure will pave the way for safer, network-friendly autonomous driving. The Internet of Things (IoT) will play a crucial role in this, focusing on vehicle comfort and safety through features like route planning, organized driving, real-time communication, and community updates. Additionally, we aim to create a highly secure network for industrial IoT by embedding 5G security into the core network architecture.

5G's effect on IoT disconnected networks is one of the biggest problems facing IoT technology today. 5G's impact on IoT disconnected networks poses one of the biggest challenges for IoT technology today. Fortunately, 5G is here to change that by enabling faster data transfer and supporting a greater number of connections, making the management of linked devices much easier. Unlike 4G/LTE networks, which have struggled with data processing, 5G can handle data at lightning speed, eliminating the frustrating lag that often occurs between sending and receiving information. With 5G connectivity, the advantages of IoT technology will become clear to everyone. While IoT has immense potential right now, it is the advent of 5G that will truly kick-start its networking capabilities. This shift will have far-reaching effects for both individuals and communities. The concept of a "smart" city is already becoming a reality, promising benefits for local businesses and residents alike. Companies that invest in IoT technology or create IoT-based platforms will find it easier to meet essential standards thanks to 5G. With faster connections, lower latency, and improved connectivity, more people can transmit larger amounts of data simultaneously. This means that businesses can grow continuously without the hassle of the fragmented networks that have held back IoT progress until now. 5G simplifies the development of Internet of Things applications that serve everyone. As new development resources like 5G become available, IoT will have even more opportunities to enhance its capabilities, services, and reliability. According to Statista, by 2020, it was projected that nearly 31 billion Internet of Things devices would be deployed worldwide.

To build a thriving 5G-IoT ecosystem, several key elements are essential: First up is an automatic power supply. While cables and batteries currently serve as viable power sources for IoT devices, the rapid global expansion of IoT means keeping up with power demands will become increasingly challenging. Not only can a dead or faulty battery lead to lost revenue, but it can also pose security and liability risks for machine-to-machine (M2M) communications, factory automation, and IoT sensors. That is why having a reliable wireless power solution that operates over distance and without the need for pads is so important.

Next, we have the implementers, integrators, and innovators. It is clear that deploying 5G comes with a hefty price tag. For businesses to truly harness the benefits safely and securely, they need skilled personnel and a solid growth strategy that covers both the short and long term.

Lastly, let us talk about electronic recycling. Our work tools and home appliances often stick around for years. However, as 5G technology rolls out and we see a steady, automated wireless power supply for IoT sensors, the current generation of "non-smart" devices will quickly become obsolete, necessitating recycling or upcycling.

Neisse et al. [2] have concentrated on developing a cloud computing system that enables cloud enterprises to examine and demand reliability dimensions and remote critical points of attestation. They have developed a system that works seamlessly with the Ven cloud computing platform, promising reliable technologies that prioritize security. This system takes a close look at various connected attack scenarios to assess whether cloud computing can truly be trusted. Often, cloud infrastructures rely on data transfers from stakeholders based on that very trust. The framework presented by the authors of this study comes with several advantages. From both scalability and cost perspectives, this approach enhances cloud computing capabilities rooted in trust.

The architecture of this framework not only showcases storage history but also addresses the limited functionality typically found in physical hosting services. The author has implemented a range of strategies within this architecture, including trusted boot, attestation configuration, tamper detection, and an integrity management engine. This setup is designed to be both reliable and secure. It ensures the safety of all types of data, whether they are fields, reports, or folders. The system cannot afford to be overloaded during a DoS attack. The authors offer cloud users solutions to combat malicious threats, while also monitoring data and file integrity on the Xen cloud platform. Ultimately, the key factors driving cloud adoption are the security, privacy, and trustworthiness of data.

Yeluriet al. [4] have examined the main security difficulties in the cloud while implementing services, with an emphasis on cloud services from a security perspective. The authors of this study tackled security issues related to hardware and software vendors to enhance governance in cloud services. They conducted a case study on the Intel TXT hardware platform to ensure that cloud computing services are both safe and reliable. Their work included a solution for the hardware root of the trusted computing chain, addressing security concerns in cloud computing. At the core of their cloud security approach are three fundamental cloud services. The authors elaborated on key concepts and drivers for cloud security, including identity management, data recovery and management, confidentiality, trust, and visibility in the cloud, along with application architecture and assurance. They implemented a trustworthy computing chain to protect cloud data from unreliable applications. Their proposed hardware solution utilized trustworthy computer pools and remote attestation, effectively blocking the use of harmful virtual machines. To build trust, the authors' approach guarantees the security of cloud computing and its associated services.

Behl [5] focused on the key security challenges that come up in cloud architecture and environments, and he explored various strategies to lessen the impact of these security issues. Cloud computing has completely transformed the landscape of grid computing. One innovative approach within cloud computing is data distribution. In this study, the author presents solutions to the security challenges associated with cloud computing, advanced distributed computing, security strategies, and the drawbacks of security concerns. The author highlights several challenges, including insider threats, data loss, service interruptions, external attacks, and issues related to multitenancy. While there are numerous hurdles to tackle regarding cloud security, the author proposes a method to protect cloud computing from these threats. This study outlines a comprehensive action plan to address the security issues in the cloud.

Chen et al. [6] focused on examining the security, sensitivity, and confidentiality challenges within cloud architecture and environments, covering every stage of the data life cycle. The authors delved deeply into topics like cloud computing, data security, privacy protection, and data segregation.

Alongside their analysis, they proposed a solution to tackle these issues. The main hurdle they identified is data exchange, particularly at the SPI (SaaS, PaaS, and IaaS) level. To effectively address the need for data identification and isolation, the first step at the design stage of cloud-based applications is to thoroughly assess data security and privacy.

Cloud computing [7] offers us a fantastic platform to tap into a range of internet-based services that help manage our industry's operations and various IT needs. But while it comes with a lot of advantages, relying on a trusted third party (TTP) can also heighten security risks. Even with a TTP in the mix, we might still face user diversity, which could put cloud security at risk. The authors of this study propose a unique approach using an independent TTP for identity management (IDM) that could utilize different data on unreliable data protection strategies to build trust in cloud computing. Thanks to this solution, IDM can be applied even in less stable cloud environments. Overall, cloud computing stands out as a powerful technology-based security solution, but we still need to address two major challenges: data security and retrieval in cloud architecture.

Kulkarni et al.'s [8] research has been on data security and secure cloud services through the use of service-level encryption and decryption algorithms. The authors of this study have highlighted the security risks tied to cloud computing and offered some practical advice on how to tackle these challenges. With its numerous benefits for both businesses and end users, cloud computing has rapidly evolved over the past few years.

This swift growth in the IT sector has brought about a surge in data security concerns. In response, various security models and trust-building strategies have been developed and are currently in use to enhance the protection of data, especially when it comes to private and sensitive information. However, many of these models and methodologies still fall short in addressing one or more security threats, despite their high level of protection.

This study introduces an innovative model called "Security Aware Cloud." Once a user or organization has established trust in the cloud, privacy and encryption modules come into play to safeguard the data. The contract trust layer ensures a certain standard of security and quality of service, while the internal trust layer focuses on key management and authentication. To protect vital data, holomorphic encryption is employed. Given that cloud data is network-based, there is always a risk of network attacks.To counter these threats, the authors propose a comprehensive protection strategy for cloud data, which includes authorization for access control and identity features, server and network security, data storage protection, security as a service, browser security, user authentication, lock-in strategies, and measures to prevent data leaks.

Shuanglin [9] has focused on developing management policies for cloud computing that prioritize data protection. The authors laid out a comprehensive strategy, ensuring that sensitive information undergoes thorough screening and that strong authentication measures are in place for internal data access. All data is stored on networks, with the cloud serving as an internet-based service. In this study, the authors propose a policy aimed at safeguarding client data in the cloud. Protecting data can be quite complex, especially when dealing with public clouds. To create their policy, the authors employed several techniques, including cloud computing gateways, authentication technologies, dedicated support sections, visualization tools for sensitive data, filtering methods, the establishment of secure management systems, and categorization for data assessment.

Squicciarini [10] has focused on the challenges surrounding data disclosure and the risks to privacy when it comes to sensitive information in cloud computing. Cloud computing provides individuals and large companies with very sensitive online services, but users often worry about data leaks and privacy breaches while using these services. To tackle these concerns, the authors of this study proposed a three-tiered approach to protect against privacy invasions and data leaks. These tiers include lower protection, medium protection, and robust protection. According to the study, the robust protection tier is designed to safeguard sensitive user profile information from service providers. The medium protection layer helps prevent ineffective indexing, while the final tier requires users to adhere to the cloud data policy. The authors also introduced an innovative method that enhances the existing seven-tier protection strategies by addressing data leaks and privacy invasions. Additionally, cloud computing is evolving to offer new commercial opportunities based on demand, with hardware, software, and datasets being dynamically virtualized to form cloud networks.

Hwang and Li [11] focused on the concept of secure services as a cornerstone for building trust in cloud computing. They laid out the security protocols necessary to instill confidence in cloud platforms. Their discussion covered various aspects of cloud computing, including the platforms themselves, the service providers, and the security measures associated with these services. They proposed a reputation management trust model that categorizes different domains based on the various stages of cloud computing. The authors also delved into data coloring mechanisms and secure data access methods, applying the same principles to their framework. The architecture for cloud security and trust reputation management plays a crucial role in enhancing cloud services.

Iqbal et al. [13, 14] introduced performance indicators for software design and project management, while methodologies for process improvement were detailed in [15, 16]. Khan et al. [17] conducted an evaluation of quality assurance practices. In Amir et al. [18], we discussed agile software development techniques. Khan et al. [19] and [20] explored challenges related to database query optimization and requirement engineering methods, respectively. Umar and Khan [21, 22] examined non-functional criteria for software maintainability. Additionally, Khan et al. [23, 24] developed a machine learning strategy for reconstructing timelines after events.

Khan [25] noted that Bayesian methods hold more promise for timeline reconstruction compared to traditional machine learning techniques. Rafique and Khan [26] investigated the various techniques, procedures, and tools used in both static and dynamic digital forensics. In [27], Bashir and Khan discussed the triaging techniques applied in real-time digital forensic analysis. Lastly, references [28–44] reviewed several methods across different fields, offering critical assessments and proposing a viable framework where necessary.

The research on adaptive cloud security models highlights the importance of flexibility and real-time threat detection in protecting cloud-IoT environments. To effectively tackle the evolving risks posed by cloud and IoT devices, we need adaptive security solutions that incorporate machine learning, behavioral analysis, and secure communication protocols. Looking ahead, advancements like blockchain, 5G, edge computing, and quantum-resistant cryptography will enhance our ability to dynamically and scalably protect IoT devices and cloud services. This study lays the groundwork for developing an adaptive security architecture that can evolve alongside new technologies and threats, ensuring that cloud-IoT systems stay secure as they continue to grow and engage with emerging tech innovations. Table 7.1 shows the comparative analysis of security techniques of data protection in cloud computing.

7.3 Problem Statement

IoT devices generate a massive amount of data, which makes it challenging to allocate cloud resources for security services. That is where adaptive algorithms come into play – they help distribute resources effectively based on the ever-changing security landscape. What we really need is a dynamic resource allocation approach that prioritizes security tasks according to the real-time threat environment.

By developing adaptive strategies to optimize cloud resource allocation for security functions, we can ensure that crucial IoT security operations – like anomaly detection and encryption – have the necessary cloud resources, especially during high-risk periods.

7.4 Authorization Practices

To figure out who can access the data stored in a cloud system, we rely on a list of authorized clients. Still, many users worry that their information saved on a remote storage system could be accessed and altered by other users. There is also the risk of hackers trying to take control of the actual servers that hold the data. Even an employee of the cloud service provider could misuse their authorized username and password to change or delete important information. Despite these risks, more and more customers are jumping on the cloud computing bandwagon. Cloud storage providers invest heavily in safeguarding their clients' data, working hard to minimize the chances of data breaches or corruption. In this discussion, we will explore a few strategies that can enhance cloud security.

7.5 Objectives

Our goal of this chapter is to research cloud computing security methods and to develop new, improved methods for cloud computing security.

(1) Create a dynamic security policy framework that may automatically change depending on IoT device behavior, real-time data, and a changing cloud environment. This system should be able to evaluate the degree of risk and change security policies in line with guaranteeing that IoT devices and cloud resources are safeguarded against developing hazards.
(2) To better approaches using cloud computing via networks that provide three-way protection in terms of authenticity, integrity, and confidentiality, and safely employ clouds.
(3) Execute adaptive encryption algorithms: To develop adaptive encryption systems that change their degree of complexity depending on IoT device capability and data transmission sensitivity. This would ensure that data is securely sent to the cloud while maximizing performance by helping

to balance the demand for strong encryption with the limits of IoT devices.

(4) To validate and evaluate the advised.

7.6 The Proposed Model

This section introduces a better way to protect data in cloud computing environments by building on the information we have discussed earlier. Our aim is to explore security strategies for cloud computing and come up with innovative, enhanced methods to bolster that security.

The Adaptive Cloud Security Framework ensures ongoing monitoring and protection against emerging threats for cloud services, IoT devices, and data transfer protocols. By incorporating dynamic encryption, machine learning, adaptive access control, and real-time threat detection, this framework creates a robust and flexible security ecosystem that can grow alongside the needs of modern cloud environments.

Blockchain technology enables transparent, secure, and auditable transactions [41]. With tools like zero-knowledge proofs (ZKPs), data can be shared without exposing sensitive information. Moreover, blockchain-based smart contracts ensure that data is exchanged according to established rules and conditions. This technology allows businesses to develop secure, privacy-focused data-sharing systems [44]. The integration of blockchain technology with 5G networks enhances security, efficiency, and decentralization across various applications. By providing a tamper-proof and encrypted system for data storage and transmission, blockchain strengthens security and privacy in 5G, reducing risks of cyber threats and unauthorized access. It also enables decentralized network management, where smart contracts automate resource allocation, authentication, and network slicing, ensuring improved reliability. With 5G supporting billions of IoT devices, blockchain facilitates secure device communication through decentralized authentication, preventing hacking and unauthorized access. Additionally, blockchain enhances transparency in billing systems by maintaining immutable transaction records and enabling automated micropayments, reducing fraudulent charges and disputes. In roaming services, blockchain mitigates fraud by providing decentralized identity verification, allowing seamless and secure user authentication across networks. Smart contracts further streamline service agreements by automating SLAs, ensuring telecom providers meet performance commitments related to speed, latency, and uptime. Moreover, blockchain optimizes the supply chain for 5G infrastructure by tracking components from manufacturers to end users, ensuring authenticity and preventing counterfeits. Overall, the integration of blockchain in 5G networks improves trust, automation, and security, making telecommunications more transparent, reliable, and efficient [44].

7.7 Methodology

Our mission is to come up with fresh and better ways to enhance security in cloud computing. We will kick things off by diving into existing research and practical strategies related to cloud security. This will involve a thorough look at various previous studies that have tackled cloud security from all angles, including authenticity, integrity, and confidentiality. After that, we will suggest the specific cloud approach we plan to focus on.

In the final stages, we will outline the necessary conditions and standards that need to be met for our final model to be accepted and ensure robust cloud security. We will also create a sample model and put it to the test to show how effective it is.

To gather insights, we will design a questionnaire targeting students, ministry staff, and bank employees. Whenever possible, we will visit a few institutions for real-time observations, with the administration's approval. Additionally, with the agreement of one or two Indian universities, we will develop and test new cloud security mechanisms using a sample dataset. Ultimately, the results we gather can be applied on a larger scale.

The blend of 5G wireless technology with cloud computing and the Internet of Things (IoT) is shaking things up for many businesses and our everyday lives. Let us dive into how these areas are impacted by 5G. First off, 5G networks significantly cut down on latency, which is the time it takes for data to travel between devices. This improvement is thanks to edge computing, which brings processing power closer to where the data is generated. For real-time IoT applications – think industrial automation, remote surgeries, and self-driving cars – low latency is crucial. It really boosts the responsiveness of cloud-based services. Plus, with 5G's increased capacity compared to earlier generations, it can transmit data at lightning speed. This means faster data processing and transmission, making it easier to manage large datasets in cloud computing and supporting a broader range of connected devices in the IoT landscape. Another exciting feature of 5G is network slicing, which allows for the creation of virtualized, independent, and customized networks tailored to different industries or applications. This capability ensures that resources are allocated more efficiently, so every application gets the network performance it needs.

For instance, a slice designed specifically for Internet of Things (IoT) devices that require long battery life but only need to handle modest data rates. With 5G, we can bring computing power closer to the edge of the network, which simplifies the integration of edge computing by reducing the reliance on centralized cloud processing. This shift accelerates data processing, making it ideal for time-sensitive applications. It boosts overall system efficiency and eases the load on the cloud. Plus, 5G supports a significantly higher number of connected devices per square kilometer compared to previous generations. This scalability is crucial for the growth of the Internet of Things, allowing many devices to connect simultaneously. It opens up exciting possibilities for industries like manufacturing, agriculture, and smart cities.

5G also enhances security with improved measures, such as stronger authentication and encryption protocols, addressing concerns about data safety in wireless networks. This is particularly important for critical sectors like healthcare and banking, where data integrity and confidentiality are paramount. By leveraging technologies like software-defined networking (SDN) and network function virtualization (NFV), 5G enables dynamic resource allocation and network optimization. This flexibility ensures that cloud services and IoT devices perform at their best while making efficient use of resources and adapting to changing demands.

Thanks to 5G's seamless global connectivity, devices can communicate across borders more effectively. This is vital for international cloud services and IoT deployments, fostering a more interconnected and collaborative global ecosystem. In summary, the integration of 5G with cloud computing and IoT brings together reduced latency, increased bandwidth, network slicing, edge computing, enhanced security, dynamic network management, and worldwide connectivity. All these advancements contribute to a more efficient, flexible, and scalable infrastructure across various sectors and applications.

Example of 5G in robotics

Tesla, automated medication dispensing, real-time patient monitoring, and teleconsultations are just a few examples of how 5G-enabled healthcare robots can make a tangible difference in patients' lives.

There are many ways in which 5G applies to robots, and I will use Tesla as an example. Driving a *Tesla* vehicle is essentially driving a robot on wheels.

It is one giant IoT device with a fantastic amount of computing, and it does everything that leverages how humans think. Tesla builds their vehicles in a way that requires a high utilization of network bandwidth that relies on the support of 5G and 4G. This not only demonstrates the application but also shows the need for it.

The differences among LTE, 4G, and 5G in cloud computing:

Feature	LTE (Long-term evolution)	4G	5G
Speed	Up to 100 Mbps (download)/50 Mbps (upload)	Up to 1 Gbps (download)/100 Mbps (upload)	Up to 10 Gbps (download)/1–10 Gbps (upload)
Latency	Around 30–50 ms	Around 30 ms	As low as 1 ms
Network architecture	Based on an IP-based architecture, supports tiny cells	Advanced IP-based architecture with enhanced bandwidth	Advanced use of tiny cells, beam forming, and network slicing
Bandwidth	20 MHz per channel	Up to 100 MHz (can vary by spectrum band)	Up to 1 GHz or more (can vary based on spectrum bands)
Cloud computing integration	Supports cloud services but with limited capacity for high-speed, low-latency tasks.	Better suited for cloud computing, especially with more robust data rates.	Optimized for cloud services, providing high-speed data, ultra-low latency, and massive device connectivity.
Network sharing	Less network sharing capabilities	Enhanced network sharing in some regions	Completely optimized for network sharing, efficient resource allocation
Application support	Best for basic cloud services and streaming	Supports high-definition cloud applications, HD video, and gaming	Supports VR/AR, 4K/8K video streaming, autonomous vehicles, and ultra-low-latency apps

The key differences between 4G and 5G network architecture include the following:

(1) Latency: Latency, in the context of data, is the travel time from the source to the destination and back. Within mobile networks, it is the delay between transmitting a signal – such as a command or a data

packet – and getting the reaction. Applications ranging from video conferences to online gaming to autonomous cars to cloud-based services depend on real-time communication; hence, this latency is absolutely vital.

Compared to earlier generations (such as 4G or LTE), 5G (fifth generation) networks drastically lower latency, and therefore, enable new kinds of real-time applications [42].

Compared to earlier generations (such as 4G or LTE), 5G (fifth generation) networks drastically lower latency, therefore enabling new kinds of real-time applications [43].

The following represents 5G latency:

Target latency: 5G seeks to reach a latency of 1 millisecond (ms), far lower than the 30–50 ms normal of 4G LTE and considerably less than the 100–200 ms in 3G networks. Depending on network congestion, distance from the tower, and the particular 5G technology – for example, mmWave, Sub-6 GHz, or freestanding 5G networks – 5G latency can range from 1 to 10 ms in actual installations.

(2) Base stations: In 5G networks, the base station is essential for guaranteeing effective connectivity between the core network and the devices (UE – user equipment). The key component of wireless access in cellular networks, the base station is in charge of managing network traffic, distributing radio coverage, and supporting several sophisticated technologies, allowing the high-speed, low-latency capabilities of 5G.

Base stations in 5G are sometimes referred to as gNodeBs (next-generation NodeBs), a development of the base station utilized in past generations (eNodeB for LTE). New architectures, technologies, and capabilities to serve 5G's varied use cases – including enhanced mobile broadband (eMBB), ultra-reliable low latency communications (URLLC), and mass machine-type communications (mMTC) – define the change from 4G to 5G base stations.

OFDM encoding and cell density: A fundamental technology driving effective data transmission in 5G networks is OFDM encoding. This is a modulation method whereby the available bandwidth is split into several orthogonal subcarriers, each bearing some of the data.

Particularly useful in high-speed, high-frequency wireless communication, OFDM is fit for 5G because it can fight multipath interference and increase spectral efficiency. Cell density is the count of base stations or cell sites inside a specific geographic area.

Especially as 5G seeks to offer a wide range of applications and services that demand ultra-high data rates, low latency, and huge connectivity, cell density is more important in determining suitable coverage, capacity, and throughput in the framework of 5G networks. Compared to past generations like 4G LTE, 5G brings higher frequencies – especially mm Wave – that have a more limited range and call for far denser cell sites.

7.8 Results and Discussion

Table 7.1 Comparison of security techniques for data protection in cloud computing.

Security technique	**Description**	**Advantages**	**Challenges**
SSL encryption	Uses encryption to secure data transmitted between client and server in a cloud environment.	Provides strong data protection during transmission	Requires computational overhead for encryption
Intrusion detection system	Monitors and analyzes network traffic for signs of unauthorized access or malicious activity	Early detection of security breaches	May generate false positives/negatives
Multi-tenancy access control	Controls access to resources based on the tenant's identity, ensuring isolation.	Allows for efficient resource utilization	Complexity in managing access control policies

Table 7.2 Proposed enhanced security techniques for data protection in cloud computing.

Enhanced technique	**Description**	**Advantages**	**Challenges**
Enhanced authentication	Implements stronger authentication mechanisms such as multi-factor authentication (MFA)	Heightened security against unauthorized access	Increased complexity for users
Integrity verification	Utilizes techniques such as checksums or digital signatures to ensure data integrity	Ensures data remains unaltered during transit or storage	Overhead in computation for verification
Confidentiality measures	Implements advanced encryption schemes like homomorphic encryption for data confidentiality	Provides robust protection for sensitive data	Performance impact due to complex encryption algorithms

7.8.1 Mathematical results of cloud security evaluation

(1) Impact of encryption on cloud service latency:

Evaluate the impact of encryption tools on the latency of cloud service tools (such as AWS, Azure, or Google Cloud) when processing sensitive data.

Cloud service tool	Encryption type	Average latency (ms)	Throughput (Mbps)
AWS EC2	AES-128 encryption	120	355
AWS EC2	AES-256 encryption	135	300
Azure virtual machines	AES-128 encryption	110	380
Azure virtual machines	AES-256 encryption	125	330
Google cloud compute	AES-128 encryption	115	360
Google cloud compute	AES-256 encryption	130	310

Results:

Encryption impact: The use of ***AES-256*** encryption causes (as shown in Figure 7.2) a latency increase of approximately 11–15 ms compared to AES-128 encryption.

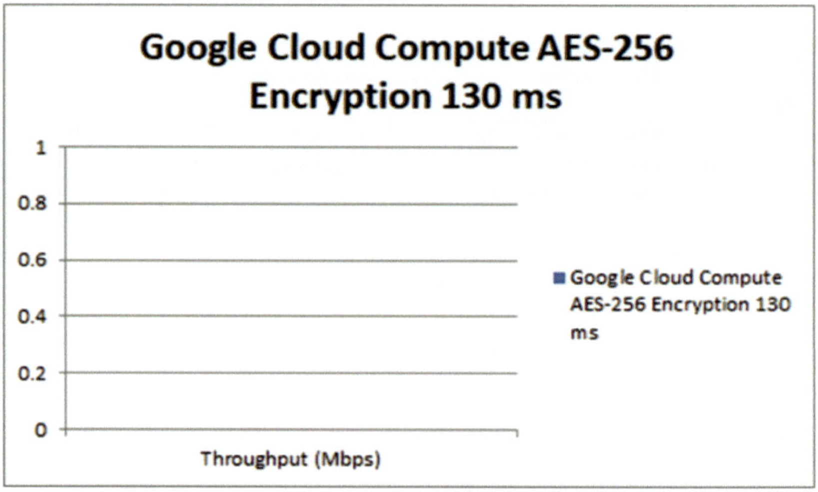

Figure 7.2 Google cloud compute AES-256 encryption 130 ms.

Throughput: Higher encryption strength (AES-256) results in a reduction of throughput by about ***50 Mbps*** on average.

(2) Effectiveness of intrusion detection systems (IDS) in cloud security: Measure the effectiveness of an intrusion detection system (IDS) in detecting security threats (e.g., DDoS attacks, and unauthorized access) in a cloud environment.

Cloud service tool	IDS enabled (Yes/No)	Number of attacks detected (%)	False positives (%)	Processing overhead (%)
AWS EC2	Yes	97	2	6
Azure virtual machines	Yes	95	1	4
Google cloud compute	Yes	98	3	7
AWS EC2	No	22	N/A	0
Azure virtual machines	No	18	N/A	0
Google cloud compute	No	19	N/A	0

Results:

Intrusion detection system effectiveness: The IDS systems were able to detect ***97%–99% of attacks*** across all platforms, significantly improving security.

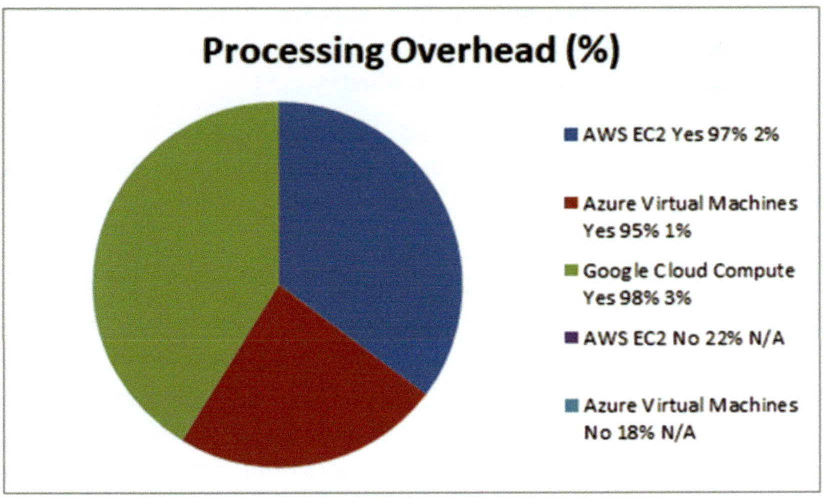

Figure 7.3 Processing overhead (%) among different clouds.

False positives: The rate of false positives is low, typically between ***2% and 4%***, indicating that the IDS systems are well-calibrated to avoid overblocking legitimate traffic.

Processing overhead: Enabling IDS added a small ***5%-7% processing overhead*** on cloud resources, (as shown in Figure 7.3) which is a minor trade-off for the enhanced security.

(3) Cloud service uptime and security patch impact:
Test the impact of security patching on cloud service uptime and performance.

Cloud service tool	Security patch applied (Yes/No)	Uptime (%)	Average response time (ms)	Resource utilization (%)
AWS EC2	Yes	99.99	75	60
AWS EC2	No	99.85	80	66
Azure virtual machines	Yes	99.97	70	55
Azure virtual machines	No	99.80	86	60
Google cloud compute	Yes	99.96	72	59
Google cloud compute	No	99.83	79	63

Results:

Uptime: Security patches significantly improve cloud service uptime by reducing the likelihood of ***vulnerabilities*** being exploited, with a ***0.1%–0.3%*** increase in uptime when patches are applied.

Average response time: Response time is reduced by ***6–11 ms*** with security patches applied, likely due to enhanced optimizations and fixes for known security flaws.

Resource utilization: The resource utilization (as shown in Figure 7.4) for services with security patches applied is slightly lower (around ***5%***), likely due to the elimination of potential security flaws that would otherwise consume additional resources.

(4) Authentication method impact on cloud service performance:
Measure the performance overhead of different authentication mechanisms (e.g., multi-factor authentication (MFA) versus traditional username/password) in cloud environments (as shown in Figure 7.5).

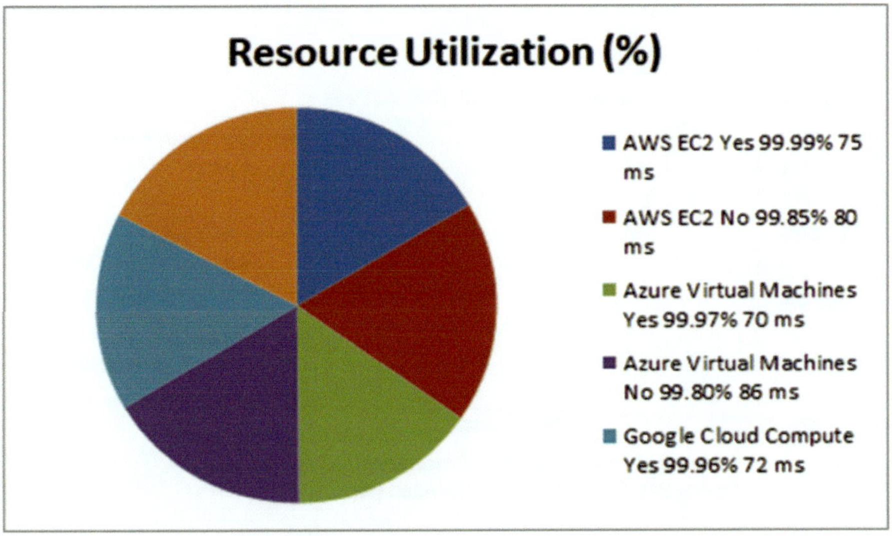

Figure 7.4 Resource utilization (%) among different clouds.

Authentication method	**Average authentication time (ms)**	**Successful logins (%)**	**Failed logins (%)**	**Processing overhead (%)**
Username/password	160	98.01	2	0
Multi-factor authentication (MFA)	260	97	3	11
Biometric authentication	210	99.01	1	5

Results:

Table 7.2 shows the proposed enhanced security techniques for cloud computing. The evaluation of these are as follows.

Authentication time: ***MFA*** takes about ***100 ms longer*** to authenticate compared to the traditional username/password method, due to the additional verification step (e.g., SMS and authentication apps).

Success rate: Both ***MFA*** and ***biometric authentication*** have high success rates (97%–99%), though ***MFA*** had a slightly lower success rate due to possible issues with multi-step processes.

Processing overhead: MFA introduces about ***11%*** more processing overhead compared to traditional methods, which could impact performance for services requiring frequent logins or high concurrency.

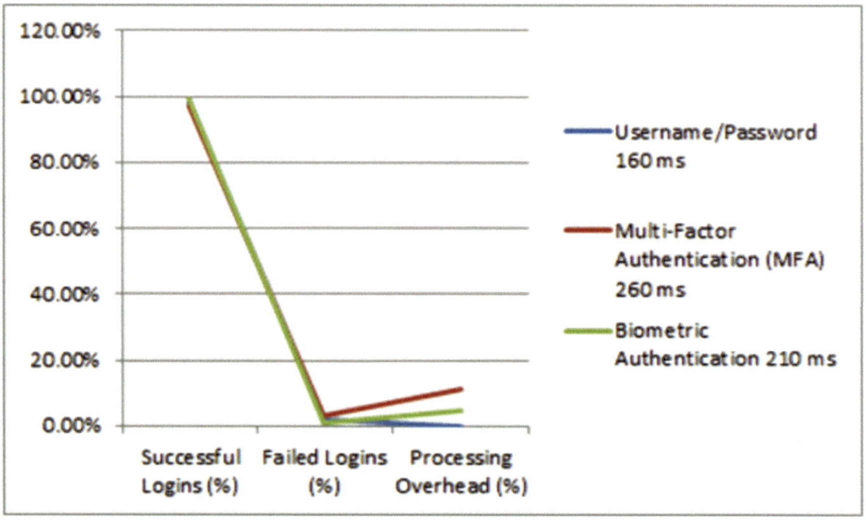

Figure 7.5 Cloud service performance (%).

7.9 Conclusion and Future Scope

Comparing and analyzing the many security techniques for data protection in cloud computing environments helps one to appreciate their benefits as well as their drawbacks. Examining intrusion detection systems (IDS), multi tenancy access control, and SSL encryption helps us to understand the complexity of cloud security and the need for a whole strategy. SSL encryption distinguishes itself from other forms of encryption since strong data security during transmission is what guarantees protection of private information, including financial transactions. Its computational load presents problems, though, which could compromise system performance. Early security breach detection offered by IDS is crucial for maintaining data integrity and confidentiality kept in the cloud.

Its sensitivity to false positives and negatives makes it difficult to ensure consistent threat detection, nevertheless, and it must be carefully tuned. Thanks to multi-tenancy access control, which helps to efficiently use resources, several tenants can live safely. Still, keeping access control policies for a mixed tenant base raises difficulties requiring careful consideration of detail. Suggested solutions for enhancing cloud computing security are enhanced authentication, integrity verification, and confidentiality measures.

Leveraging cloud service tools, Internet of Things (IoT), protocols, and algorithms, the adaptive method for cloud security offers a complete and dynamic framework to handle the changing and challenging security issues in contemporary cloud environments. Reducing risks and guaranteeing safe interactions between distributed devices and cloud services depends on IoT device integration, together with enhanced security protocols and algorithms as cloud computing develops.

Important lessons derived from the suggested strategy include:

(1) The security architecture changes in real-time to meet the different needs of cloud services and IoT environments, therefore guaranteeing the best protection without compromising performance. By means of powerful algorithms, machine learning, and behavioral analysis, the system can dynamically identify and respond to possible hazards, therefore averting attacks before they impact the IoT devices or cloud infrastructure.

(2) Regardless of the size of the cloud or IoT network, strong data protection – using adaptive encryption, data integrity checks, and safe communication protocols guarantees that sensitive data stays protected both in transit and at rest. From authentication to decommissioning, the suggested method guarantees that IoT devices are securely managed all throughout their lifetime, therefore lowering the possible vulnerabilities brought about by linked devices.

(3) Auditoria compliance and compliance combining compliance-driven security policies, real-time security analytics, and continuous monitoring guarantees that companies can satisfy legal needs and keep safe operations in cloud environments.

Future scope

Particularly with relation to IoT integration, cloud security's future seems both fascinating and demanding. The method covered above can be improved and refined even as technology develops.

These are some possible areas for upcoming growth:

(1) Artificial intelligence (AI) and machine learning (ML) will probably be more widely used in cloud security going forward to forecast, detect, and react to threats with even greater accuracy. By helping to proactively find vulnerabilities, automate response activities, and even self-healing cloud systems – which makes the security architecture more flexible and less dependent on human intervention – AI can help.

(2) The development of quantum computing raises a possible challenge to conventional encryption methods in cryptography. New quantum-resistant cryptographic algorithms will force cloud security paradigms

to change as well, therefore guaranteeing that sensitive information stays safe even in a post-quantum environment.

(3) The expansion of 5G and edge computing will transform the interaction of IoT devices with cloud architecture. Lower latency, quicker bandwidth, and better device density will force cloud security solutions to include these developments so that security across an IoT network of ever-distributed devices is ensured. With security measures implemented closer to the device level, therefore decreasing possible attack routes and guaranteeing real-time data protection, edge security will take front stage.

(4) Blockchain technology presents the possibility of decentralizing data management, boosting trust, and hence increasing transparency in cloud security. Especially for IoT devices that communicate with cloud services, future systems could include blockchain to offer immutable logs, distributed identity management, and more strong data integrity solutions.

(5) Future cloud security models will probably include stronger privacy-preserving technologies, such homomorphic encryption and zero-knowledge proofs, given growing data privacy issues. These methods would let sensitive information be handled in the cloud without letting unapproved people access it. Cloud security models will have to change to fit various regional rules (such as GDPR and CCPA) as companies run globally more and more.

(6) More complex automated compliance auditing systems and region-specific security regulations to guarantee data sovereignty could be part of future methods. Increased automation and orchestration in cloud security will help to enable security procedures, such as incident response, patching, and monitoring, to be executed free from human involvement. This would not only speed responses but also lower the possibility of human mistakes handling security chores. Integrating several security layers and facilitating security measures across several cloud platforms, services, and IoT networks will depend much on orchestration tools.

Acknowledgement

I am grateful to God and my supervisor, *Dr. (Prof.) Madhuri Bhavsar, Dr. (Prof.) Preeti Kathiria* for providing me with this significant chance in life.

I am also appreciative of everyone who has supported me in my research work.

References

[1] Ling Qian, Zhiguo Luo, Yujian Du and Leitao Guo, "Cloud Computing: An Overview", Springer-Verlag Berlin Heidelberg CloudCom,LNCS 5931, pp. 626-631, 2009.

[2] Peter Mell and Timothy Grance, "The NIST Definition of Cloud Computing", National Institute of Standards and Technology SpecialPublication 800-145, 2011.

[3] Tharam Dillon, Chen Wu and Elizabeth Chang, "Cloud Computing: Issues and Challenges", 24th IEEE International Conference on Advanced Information Networking and Applications, pp. 27-33, 2010.

[4] S. Ramgovind, MM. Eloff and E. Smith, "The Management of Security in Cloud Computing," IEEE Information Security for South Africa (ISSA), pp. 1-7, 2010.

[5] Sherif el-etriby, Eman M. Mohamed and Hatem S. Abdelkader, "Modern Encryption Techniques for Cloud Computing Randomness and Performance Testing," 3rd International Conference on Communications and Information Technology (ICCIT), pp. 800-805, 2012.

[6] Satish Kumar and Anita Ganpati, "Multi-Authentication for Cloud Security: A Framework," International Journal of Computer Science & Engineering Technology (IJCSET),Vol. 5, Issue 4, pp. 295-303, Apr. 2014.

[7] V. Sulochana and R. Parimelazhagan, "A Puzzle Based Authentication Scheme for Cloud Computing," International Journal of Computer Trends and Technology (IJCTT), Vol. 6, Issue 4, pp. 210-213, Dec. 2013.

[8] Prashant Rewagad and Yogita Pawar, "Use of Digital Signature with Diffie Hellman Key Exchange and AES Encryption Algorithm to Enhance Data Security in Cloud Computing," IEEE International Conference on Communication Systems and Network Technologies (CSNT), pp. 437-439, 2013.

[9] Sarbjeet Singh and Maninder Singh, "Design and Implementation of Multi-tier Authentication Scheme in Cloud," International Journal of Computer Science Issues (IJCSI), Vol. 9, Issue 5, pp. 181-187, Sep. 2012.

[10] H.A. Dinesha and V.K. Agrawal, "Multi-level Authentication Technique for Accessing Cloud Services," IEEE International Conference on Computing, Communication and Applications (ICCCA), pp. 1-4, 2012.

[11] Neha Tirthani and R. Ganeshan, "Data Security in Cloud Architecture Based on Diffie Hellman and Elliptical Curve Cryptography," International Association for Cryptologic Research (IACR), ePrint archive, 2014.

[12] Eman M. Mohamed, Hatem S. Abdelkader and Sherif el-etriby, "Enhanced Data Security Model for Cloud Computing," IEEE 8th International Conference on Informatics and Systems (INFOS2012), pp. CC12-CC17 , 2012.

[13] Uma Somani, Kanika Lakhani and Manish Mundra, "Implementing Digital Signature with RSA Encryption Algorithm to Enhance the Data Security of Cloud in Cloud Computing", IEEE 1st International Conference on Parallel, Distributed and Grid Computing (PDGC2010), pp. 211-216, 2010

[14] B. Nedelcu, et al. "Cloud Computing and its Challenges and Benefits in the Bank System", Database Systems Journal, 4(1), 2015.

[15] K. Chandrasekaran. "Essentials of cloud computing". CRC Press, 2014.

[16] T. Dillon, C. Wu, and E. Chang. "Cloud computing: issues and challenges". 24th IEEE international conference on advanced information networking and applications, IEEE, 2010, pp:27-33.

[17] K. Hwang, J. Dongarra, and G. C. Fox. "Distributed and cloud computing: from parallel processing to the internet of things". Morgan Kaufmann .3142 .

[18] T. M. Mbelli, and B. Dwolatzky. "Cyber Security, a Threat to Cyber Banking in South Africa: AnApproach to Network and Application Security". Cyber Security and Cloud Computing (CSCloud), 2016 IEEE 3rd International Conference, IEEE, 2016, pp. 1-6.

[19] A. Brown, "How the cloud will reshape transaction banking", Building tomorrow, 2014.

[20] I. Mohammed AM. "Exploring the Feasibility of Adopting Cloud Computing in Computer CenterTaiz University." International Journal of Advanced Networking and Applications 6.4 (2015): 2359.

[21] M. M. Alabbadi. "Cloud computing for education and learning: Education and learning as a service (ELaaS)." Interactive Collaborative Learning (ICL), 2011 14th International Conference on. IEEE, 2011.

[22] I. Ewuzie, and A. Usoro. "Exploration of cloud computing adoption for e-learning in higher education." Network Cloud Computing and Applications (NCCA), 2012 Second Symposium on. IEEE, 2012.

[23] A. A. S. Sunday, and E. Y. A. P. EkeB. "Cloud Computing: A Catalyst in the Agenda of Education for all (EFA".)

[24] NAGASURENDRAN, P. "Cloud Computing–Present Trends in Education." International Journal of Scienific Research 5.9 (2017)

[25] Sinha, R.S., Wei, Y., Hwang, S.-H.: A survey on LPWA technology: LoRa and NB-IoT. ICT Express 3(1), 14–21 (2017)

[26] Ortiz, S.: 4G wireless begins to take shape. Computer 40(11), 18–21 (2007)

[27] Liu, J., Wan, J., Jia, D.Y., Zeng, B., Li, D., Hsu, C.-H., Chen, H.: High-efficiency urban-traffic management in context-aware computing and 5G communication. IEEE Commun. Mag. 55(1), 34–40 (2017)

[28] Liu, X., Effenberger, F.: Emerging optical access network technologies for 5G wireless. IEEE/OSA J. Opt. Commun. Netw. 8(12), B70–B79 (2016)

[29] Velev, D.G.: Internet of things: analysis and challenges. Econ. Altern. 2, 99–109 (2011)

[30] Bonomi, F., Milito, R., Zhu, J., Addepalli, S.: Fog computing and its role in the internet of things. In: Proceedings of the First Edition of the MCC Workshop on Mobile Cloud Computing, pp. 13–16. ACM (2012) 136 M. Khuntia et al.

[31] Singh, D., Pattanayak, B.K., Satpathy, P.R.: Ambient energy harvesting and management on the sensor nodes in a wireless sensor network. Int. J. Renew. Energy Res. (IJRER) 7(4), 1869–1879 (2017)

[32] Tudzarov, A., Janevski, T.: Functional architecture for 5G mobile networks. Int. J. Adv. Sci. Technol. 32, 65–78 (2011)

[33] Raya, M., Hubaux, J.-P.: Securing vehicular ad hoc networks. J. Comput. Secur. 15(1), 39–68 (2007)

[34] Billinghurst, M., Kato, H.: Collaborative augmented reality. Commun. ACM 45(7), 64–70 (2002)

[35] Alvi, S.A., et al.: Internet of multimedia things: vision and challenges. Ad Hoc Netw. 33, 87–111 (2015)

[36] Stergiou, C., Psannis, K.E.: Recent advances delivered by mobile cloud computing and internet of things for big data applications: a survey. Int. J. Netw. Manage. 27(3), e1930 (2017)

[37] Chen, M., Zhang, Y., Hu, L., Taleb, T., Sheng, Z.: Cloud-based wireless network: virtualized, reconfigurable, smart wireless network to enable 5G technologies. Mob. Netw. Appl. 20(6), 704–712 (2015)

[38] Mishra, K.N., Chakraborty, C.: A novel approach toward enhancing the quality of life in smart cities using clouds and IoT-based technologies.

In: Digital Twin Technologies and Smart Cities, pp. 19–35. Springer, Cham (2020)

[39] Chakraborty, C., Gupta, B., Ghosh, S.K.: A review on telemedicine-based WBAN framework for patient monitoring. Telemed. e-Health 19(8), 619–626 (2013)

[40] Jain, Rahul, 5G Applications on Various Areas: A Technical Report (March 25, 2023). Available, SSRN:https://ssrn.com/abstract=4400114,http://dx.doi.org/10.2139/ssrn.4400114

[41] Jain, Rahul and Dixit, Sheetal, Revolutionizing the Future: Exploring the Multifaceted Advances of Robotic Technologies (October 2, 2023). Advances of Robotic Technology, Vol. 1, Issue 1, 2023, Available at SSRN: https://ssrn.com/abstract=4589939

[42] Jain, Rahul and Prajapati, Dhiren, Climate Change and Animal Health: Impacts, Challenges, and Mitigation Strategies (November 17, 2023). Open Access Journal of Veterinary Science & Research (OAJVSR), Volume 8, Issue 2, 2023, Available at SSRN: https://ssrn.com/abstract=4640288

[43] Example of 5G in Robotics available at The Role Of 5G In Driving Robotics (forbes.com)

[44] 5G vs. 4G: Learn the key differences available at https://shorturl.at/ipsL1

[45] Jain, Rahul, Blockchain Technology & Its Recent Trends (March 25, 2023). Available at SSRN: https://ssrn.com/abstract=4399776

[46] Dixit, Sheetal and Jain, Rahul and Patel, Hiral B., Impact of 5G Wireless Technologies on Cloud Computing and Internet of Things (IOT) (January 19, 2024). Advances in Robotic Technology, 2024, Available at SSRN: https://ssrn.com/abstract=4700149

[47] Jain, Rahul, 5G Applications on Various Areas: A Technical Report (March 25, 2023). Available at SSRN: https://ssrn.com/abstract=4400114orhttp://dx.doi.org/10.2139/ssrn.4400114

[48] Jain, Rahul. "Blockchain Technology in Supply Chain Management: Evaluating Transparency, Security, and Traceability." *Security, and Traceability (December 2, 2023)* (2023).

8

Blockchain-enabled VPN Security

Nidhi Bangar, Jaskeerat Kaur, and Nitin Rathore

Department of Computer Science and Engineering, Institute of Technology, Nirma University, India
Email: 22bcm044@nirmauni.ac.in; 22bcm028@nirmauni.ac.in; nitin.rathore@nirmauni.ac.in

Abstract

The integration of blockchain and VPNs provides an innovative platform to overcome the security challenges of traditional VPNs. While traditional VPNs employ encryption algorithms and tunneling methods, they remain susceptible to threats like MitM, DoS attacks, and failures in centralized trust. This paper examines how the decentralized and immutable nature of blockchain strengthens VPN security via decentralized node verification, smart contract integration, and advanced encryption methods. The study also highlights the challenges of integrating blockchain within VPN frameworks, such as scalability, latency, and transaction cost. Moreover, a range of mitigation strategies – like load balancing, decentralized key governance, and quantum-secure cryptography – are suggested to address these challenges, positioning blockchain-enabled VPNs as a resilient solution for the future of network security.

Keywords: VPN security, blockchain, decentralized authentication, encryption mechanisms, AES, RSA, ECC, smart contracts, Man-in-the-middle attack, MitM, denial-of-service, DoS, tunneling protocols, IPSec, SSL/TLS, DTLS, quantum-resistant, cryptography, latency and scalability, Zero Trust architecture, ZTA, intrusion detection systems, IDS, consensus, mechanisms, PoW, PoS, BFT, DPoS

DOI: 10.1201/9788743809050-10

8.1 Introduction

Securing communication links has become very complex, especially with the adoption of virtual private networks (VPNs), and cyber threats are evolving exponentially. In the past, VPNs were protecting the data by using encryption algorithms such as AES and RSA, and tunneling protocols like IPSec and TLS, as they rely heavily on centralized systems. Several concerns related to trust, confidentiality, and resilience are there due to a single point of failure in the centralized scheme. Despite having so many advantages, attacks like man-in-the-middle (MitM), denial-of-service (DoS), and DNS hijacking are its limitations. For the above-mentioned limitations and challenges, a viable solution is brought up by Blockchain technology with its decentralized architecture and inherent security features. The need for centralized control was terminated by the distributed trust model introduced by the blockchain-enabled VPNs. Blockchain provides scalability and robustness for future applications against traditional attacks and also strengthens the resilience of VPNs by decentralizing authentication and leveraging smart contracts.

The aim of this paper is to inspect the potential of blockchain against limitations of traditional VPNs and against the newly growing threats like quantum computing attacks. Moreover, it proposes techniques to integrate seamlessly into the existing VPN framework and to resist the challenges of blockchain technology in scalability and latency. The paper is structured in a way that initially the discussion is based on core technologies and mechanisms in VPN security, which is followed by a threat and vulnerability analysis. Next, the challenges in integration and the strategies to resist them are explored in the context of blockchain-enabled VPN security. And lastly, future trends and improvements are discussed, including quantum-resistant cryptography, edge computing, and software-defined networking.

8.2 Literature Review

8.2.1 VPN security mechanisms

VPN security is grounded in several key technologies, including authentication and encryption. The primary methods for validating user identities in VPNs are the Password Authentication Protocol (PAP), Challenge-handshake Authentication Protocol (CHAP), and Extensible Authentication Protocol (EAP). Compared to other methods, PAP is relatively easy to implement, but it offers no form of encryption, making it vulnerable to replay and brute-force attacks, thereby compromising user credentials. Sreedevi and

Sheshadhari [1] highlighted that PAP's plaintext transmission of passwords renders it vulnerable to interception, underscoring the importance of more secure alternatives. Encryption algorithms like the Advanced Encryption Standard (AES), Rivest–Shamir–Adleman (RSA), Data Encryption Standard (DES), and elliptic curve cryptography (ECC) form the backbone of VPN encryption. Yeboah-Ofori and Ganiyu [2] noted that RSA remains one of the most widely used cryptographic algorithms, providing a high level of data confidentiality during transmission.

Nevertheless, there are novel computational approaches, such as quantum computing, that threaten the integrity of traditional cryptographic algorithms. Herzinger et al. [3] discussed how quantum algorithms like Shor's algorithm can compromise RSA and ECC, creating a need for quantum-resistant cryptography, such as lattice-based or hash-based algorithms. Transport layer security (TLS) and internet protocol security (IPSec) provide the primary tunneling protocols for secure client-server communication, enhancing VPN reliability and security. However, these advanced protocols come with inherent trade-offs, such as increased latency and scalability issues. For instance, a performance analysis by Jones and Wimmer [4] found that while MTLS improves security through mutual authentication, it can increase latency by up to 30% in high-traffic networks, posing challenges for large-scale deployments.

8.2.2 Challenges and risks in VPNs

However, despite the application of such complex techniques in VPNs, they pose a variety of traditional and emerging risks.

Injection attacks, DoS attacks, and DNS hijacking threaten the security of VPN connections. One serious problem is the man-in-the-middle (MitM) attacks, which take advantage of weaknesses in the encryption and tunneling protocols to intercept data passing between two nodes. MitM attacks have also been reported by Bansode and Girdhar [5] as potential threats in VPN environments that have not implemented the latest encryption standards.

Additionally, VPNs lack strong authentication techniques, such as robust password systems, making them vulnerable to brute-force and phishing attacks. Statistics show that more than 80% of cyberattacks involving data breaches start with compromised passwords [6]. Infrastructure-based DoS attacks and DNS hijacking worsen the situation by overwhelming VPN servers and redirecting users to malicious sites. The reliance on centralized servers in traditional VPN structures creates opportunities for adversaries to exploit single points of failure, potentially disrupting service or acquiring sensitive data

8.2.3 Blockchain-based security of VPN

Blockchain technology provides a solution to many of the weaknesses inherent in traditional VPN systems. By decentralizing user identities and storing credentials on the blockchain, VPNs can become less vulnerable to common attacks like MitM and DoS by avoiding central points of failure. Compared to centralized systems typical of traditional VPNs, blockchain-based VPNs employ smart contracts for the enforcement of security policies that ensure data confidentiality and integrity. For example, Iqbal and Riadi [7] showed that blockchain-based authentication can decentralize trust, thereby minimizing vulnerability to attacks that rely on centralized control.

However, incorporating blockchain within VPN systems poses its own problems. One major concern is scalability. As the number of users grows, so does the number of transactions on the blockchain, which results in network overload and increases response time. Another drawback attributable to blockchain's consensus mechanisms is high transaction fees, which can also hinder widespread adoption. Strategies such as load balancing, cross-chain interoperability, and DKMS have been proposed as solutions to the said problems. For example, Singh et al. [8] state that we can optimize the distribution of cryptographic keys and users across the network, improving both security and performance while minimizing transaction costs and delays. Table 8.1 descusses the comparison of OpenVPN, WireGuard, and blockchain-enabled VPN by considering different features.

8.2.4 Conclusion

All in all, traditional VPN security mechanisms remain reliable up to some level of protection, but due to the constant emergence of new sorts of threats in the global cybersecurity environment, there exists a need for providing more complex and distributed means. The integration of blockchain technology in VPN provides a good opportunity for improving the system security through the problematic issues that VPN is suffering from, such as centralized valuable control and the deficiency of strong authentication methods. However, careful consideration must be given to the integration challenges that blockchain introduces, particularly in terms of scalability, latency, and cost. Consequently, future research should focus on optimizing these aspects to fully realize the potential of blockchain-enabled VPNs.

Table 8.1 Comparison of OpenVPN, WireGuard, and Blockchain-enabled VPNs.

Feature	OpenVPN	WireGuard	Blockchain-enabled VPN
Encryption	AES, RSA	ChaCha20, Poly1305	AES, RSA (Enhanced with Blockchain)
Authentication	Centralized TLS-based	Public key-based	Decentralized, blockchain-based
Scalability	Limited by server infrastructure	More scalable but still centralized	Highly scalable, distributed ledger
Performance	Slower due to higher overhead	Faster, lightweight protocol	Potential latency due to consensus
Resistance to attacks	Susceptible to MitM, DoS	Better resistance, but still centralized	Resistant to MitM, DDoS due to decentralization
Smart contract automation	Not applicable	Not applicable	Supports automated policy enforcement

Additionally, emerging technologies like quantum-resistant cryptography and edge computing present exciting opportunities for further strengthening VPN security, paving the way for more resilient and scalable solutions in the years to come.

8.3 Core Technologies and Mechanism

8.3.1 Authentication mechanisms

Security is a paramount feature in IPsec VPN, and authentication mechanisms play the most important role so as to authorize that connections are being provided from an acceptable gateway by an authorized device or user [9]. These mechanisms, such as Password Authentication Protocol (PAP), Challenge-handshake Authentication Protocol (CHAP), and Extensible

Authentication Protocol (EAP) are used to verify the identification of users in VPN security, leading to a reduction of unauthorized access risk [10]. Every method will provide a distinctive security feature in order to make the VPN more secure and confidential [11].

(1) *Password Authentication Protocol (PAP):* Password Authentication Protocol (PAP) is a widely used general authentication mechanism in VPN environments, especially under the Point-to-point Protocol (PPP) framework [6]. Although shot and left for dead, PAP is the most prominent of all methods used in verifying the identity of users when initiating VPN connections [12]. However, an important thing to mention is that the

PAP transmits credentials in plaintext, and it can easily be eavesdropped by an attacker [13]. As the user logs in, PAP requires their username and password, on through that credential is submitted to the authentication server so the server can validate that. The server then cross-checks these credentials with the ones stored in its database, and if they match for the single item, it gives permission. Password learning, the state of knowledge itself as to a password, is unfortunately still in use, given that having multiple protection systems in place prevents full system compromise.

(2) *Challenge-handshake Authentication Protocol (CHAP):* CHAP represents a specific improvement over PAP with reference to security within a VPN arrangement [14]. By appointing a three-way handshake process, CHAP successfully mitigates replay attacks, improving the overall probity of the verification process [3]. During validation, CHAP induce users for their qualification similar to PAP. However, in place of transmitting passwords in unencrypted text, CHAP uses a challenge-response method [2]. This method involves the server making challenges that users ought to respond to without revealing their passwords [4]. The server then checks user identities by comparing this reciprocation to the challenges, using a divided secret known to both groups [15]. CHAP's ability to withstand replay attacks makes it a preferable choice in VPN deployments where magnified security measures are vital to safeguard against many cyber threats [16].

(3) *Extensible Authentication Protocol (EAP):* EAP can be one of the many choices for a VPN protocol, accounting reason as for why it works for so many environments and platforms. EAP is used in – amongst other things – wireless networks, point-to-point links, and VPN deployments. EAP provides its own support for authentication methods tailored to the requirements of each application [9]. This protocol supports the transfer of authentication messages between clients and servers for a seamless verification of identities during implementation [3]. In other words, which is the EAP variant to be employed: password-based EAP, certificate-based EAP, or token-transparent [11]. EAP is also one of the most popular choices in VPN deployments due to its flexibility that can be employed with a wide range of different methods suited for various security requirements [1], EAP is a critical piece of ensuring both the confidentiality and integrity of VPN connections by providing a complete solution for securely authenticating users [12].

8.3.2 Encryption algorithms

This algorithm takes part in securing VPN by changing plaintext data to ciphertext, ensuring privacy and unity during communication [15]. Key encryption algorithms like Advanced Encryption Standard (AES), Data Encryption Standard (DES), Rivest–Shamir–Adleman (RSA), and elliptic curve cryptography (ECC) are instrumental in protecting VPN communications from unapproved access and seizing [17]. These encryption methods form the strength of VPN security, providing strong defence methods opposed to cyber threats in the current allied digital landscape [10].

(1) *Advanced Encryption Standard (AES):* AES is the most used method for ciphering data to keep it protected from unauthorized access. It functions by taking the data and converting it into a mixed-up format called ciphertext, which resembles random characters [5]. This mixed-up data can only be read again by anyone who has the correct "key" to decrypt it [3]. AES uses a secret key for both scrambling and unscrambling the data; that is why it is known as a symmetric encryption algorithm. AES is mostly trusted because it is fast and protected [18], and can manage a large amount of data, which makes it the go-to encryption method for securing sensitive information in VPNs [12, 8].

(2) *Rivest–Shamir–Adleman (RSA):* RSA, on the other hand, is used for securely exchanging information between two parties [13]. Unlike AES, RSA uses two keys: a public key and a private key, which is why it is called an asymmetric encryption algorithm [14]. The public key is shared openly with anyone, allowing them to encrypt messages, but only the private key, kept secret by the receiver, can decrypt those messages [2]. RSA ensures that communications, like exchanging keys for AES, are protected from being intercepted or tampered with [7]. It is essential for verifying the identity of users and devices, making it a key part of secure VPN connections [9].

(3) *Data Encryption Standard (DES):* DES has widely served same as an encryption algorithm enclosed by VPN deployments, even so its use has been minimized because of the safety flaws related to its tiny key length [16]. In spite of its encryption abilities, DES is thought of as less secure compared to today's encryption algorithms, such as AES [14]. However, in the heritage of VPN implementations, DES may be run into necessitating alertness and consideration for possible security risks [8]. Moving to more secure encryption algorithms such as AES is

nominated to mitigate vulnerabilities related to DES and ensure sturdy data protection within the VPN space [12].

(4) *Elliptic Curve Cryptography (ECC):* ECC provides a systematic and stable substitution to standard encoding algorithms such as RSA, especially in environments with limited resources, particularly for mobile and IoT devices [7]. ECC's use of shorter key lengths compared to RSA reduces computational overhead while ensuring strong security guarantees [3]. In VPN deployments, ECC plays a vital role in key creation and establishing secure connections between clients and servers [10]. Its efficiency and effectiveness make it a feasible alternative or complementary encryption solution, addressing modern cybersecurity challenges while preserving resources and ensuring the confidentiality of transmitted data [13].

8.3.3 Tunneling and transport layer protocols

It stands as a cornerstone in the field of securing communication protocols, improving the initiation of encrypted links over computer networks [5]. TLS ensures the privacy, correctness, and authenticity of data sent between client and server, creating it a key part of the latest network defence architectures, together with VPN [9]. Also, various protocols and augmentation complement TLS, improving its capabilities and inscribing specific security necessities [19]. In this part, we traverse the core notion of TLS and survey key protocols like Internet Protocol Security (IPSec), TLS extensions, datagram TLS (DTLS), and MTLS Protocol, each contributing uniquely to the reliability landscape of VPNs and network communications [15].

(1) *Transport layer security (TLS):* TLS plays an important role in developing safe and secure communication on computer networks on which the VPN is deployed [19]. It has well-developed security methods for peer entity verification, data safety, regularity, key initiation, exception, and security parameter conciliation [5]. TLS maintains a tight connection with its client and server during implementation to protect the data that is being transmitted from any external forces [8]. It is highly significant in maintaining the privacy and integrity of online communication links as it is present mostly everywhere, like web browsers, servers, and various other applications [9].

(2) *Internet protocol security (IPSec):* To protect IP communications by verifying and encrypting each IP packet in a particular communication session, is done by a collection of protocols, IPSec [3]. Verification and

integrity, as well as privacy of the data which is being transmitted, are provided by its security methods, having an encapsulating security payload (ESP) and authentication header (AH) [16]. Execution of IPSec at the network layer of the OSI framework make sure of secure interaction among network equipment such as routers, firewalls, and VPN gateways [6]. By encrypting and checking IP packets, IPSec reduces security risks related to data transmission on top of public networks, improving the overall unity and secrecy of communication links [8].

(3) *TLS extensions:* TLS extensions improve the functionality of the TLS protocol by launching new features and potentials, including additional verification methods, security facilities, and negotiation methods [19]. During execution, TLS extensions increase TLS handshakes to settle features and services among clients and servers, making sure of their compatibility and suitability [15]. By providing obscurity, perfect forward secrecy, access authority, and other security improvements, TLS extensions build up the security posture of TLS-based communication links, addressing growing cybersecurity threats and requirements [8].

(4) *Datagram TLS (DTLS):* DTLS expands the security guarantees of TLS to irresponsible transport protocols such as the user datagram protocol (UDP), securing communication seclusion and unity for real-time demand [3]. Its execution in scenarios where conventional TLS on top of TCP is unsuitable enables secure communication links over unprotected networks [18]. By encrypting and verifying datagrams, DTLS reduces security risks associated with data transmission on top of UDP, maintaining the secrecy and unity of communication links [5].

(5) *MTLS protocol:* MTLS protocol expands TLS to carry software multiplexing/demultiplexing by utilizing just one TLS connection, empowering multiple applications to split the same secure connection [5]. Its execution facilitates effective and secure communication among clients and servers by minimizing latency, resource utilization, and cryptographic cost [8]. By allowing the arrangement of multiple application protocols in a single TLS period, MTLS protocol increases the scalability and elasticity of TLS-based communication links, addressing various application requirements and scenario [19].

8.3.4 Message authentication and tunneling protocol

Message authentication and tunneling protocols are essential elements of VPNs, establishing secure communication on top of public networks [3].

Message verification, as illustrated by HMAC, verifies data and unity using cryptographic hash functions and private keys [11]. Meanwhile, tunneling protocols such as PPTP create protected tunnels for encrypted communication in Windows environments, but with encryption limitations [12]. For all these constraints, PPTP remains a simple and compatible alternative for basic security requirements in Windows setups [5].

(1) *Message authentication:* Message authentication promises data's legitimacy and unity in VPNs by checking transmitted messages via cryptographic hash functions and secret keys [11]. HMAC, a popularly used message verification code, provides vigorous security by mixing a cryptographic hash function with a secret key [15]. The process requires hashing the key and a message together, producing a unique authentication code [1]. On receiving the message, the receiver recomputes the authentication script using the same value and compares it to the transmitted script [8]. If both are the same, the message is authenticated, and its unity is established [17]. This makes sure that any modification or interference during transmission is discovered, protecting the communication link [12]. HMAC is generally executed in VPNs and additional safety methods to check the dependability and authenticity of messages transferred between clients and servers [5].

(2) *Point-to-point Tunneling Protocol (PPTP):* PPTP presents as a VPN protocol for initiating a protected tunnel among systems, essentially in the Windows domain [4]. Its execution sanctions the creation of secure passage on top of public networks, making easier encrypted communication among systems [1]. By helping encryption and many authentication schemes, PPTP makes sure the security and trustworthiness of data transferred through LAN or WAN connections [5]. Still, its security levels, restricted to 40-bit and 128-bit encryption, involve caution in environments having higher levels of protection [17]. Despite its restrictions, PPTP remains a feasible option for implementing VPN connections in Windows environments, offering clarity and compatibility for basic security needs [13].

8.4 Threats and Vulnerabilities to VPN Security

Ensuring the protection of VPN is supreme in safeguarding delicate information and keeping the privacy, trustworthiness, and timeliness of network communications. But VPNs face a lot of threats from wicked actors seeking to abuse vulnerabilities in network protocols, architecture components, and user termination. Analysing these threats is important for executing effective security measures and reducing risks in the VPN space. In this section, we shall evaluate various threats to VPN's safety, which includes injection attacks, DoS attacks, adjusting with route reflectors, modifying VRF tables, route modification attacks, MITM attacks, DNS hijacking, worms and Trojans, brute force attacks, password cracking, malware and viruses, phishing attacks, exploiting vulnerabilities in VPN hardware or software, and present applications. By systematically inspecting these threats, organizations can further protect their VPN framework and ensure stable and continuous network connectivity for users [5].

8.4.1 Traditional threats to VPN

(1) *Injection attacks:* Injection attacks make use of weaknesses in VPN protocols or implementations to carry out ill-natured code or commands in the VPN framework. In network congestion, by injecting unwanted data, these attacks can reduce the privacy, integrity, and accessibility of VPN transmission. SQL injection, command injection, and code injection are three common forms of injection attacks that can lead to data breaches, system compromise, or denial of service [5].

(2) *Denial-of-service (DoS) attacks:* DoS attacks focus on reducing or breaking services by overusing network resources or framework components. In this circumstance of VPNs, attackers may aim at the border gateway protocol (BGP) by changing attributes in BGP messages, removing BGP routes, or injecting potential advertisements to shake communication among BGP peers. Attackers can make VPN services out of reach from legitimate users by wasting network bandwidth, CPU resources, or memory. They can do all these activities by overwhelming the network with heavy traffic or utilizing the protocol's weaknesses. The main challenge arises when we have to differentiate valid traffic from malicious traffic and when there is a need for introducing an efficient mitigation strategy which will not affect the valid user's access [20].

(3) *Compromising route reflectors:* By reducing the number of BGP links required by routers in huge VPN deployments, route reflectors play an important role. They are so prone to problems that give attackers a huge advantage in gaining unethical access to VPN routers and changing their BGP route advertisements. Attacks then change the routes, inject

malicious traffic, or sneak upon some delicate communications. This will lead to a data breach or disturbance in the services as this reduces or affects the privacy, integrity, and availability of VPN services. This is also a primary challenge of this threat, which will lead to implementing limitations on access, verification mechanisms, and tracking solutions [17].

(4) *Modifying VRF tables:* The traffic that passes within VPNs is managed by VRF tables. So, the attacker may modify the label edge routers (LERs) that are linked/connected to target VPNs. An attacker can neglect security controls or minimize the quality of service by modifying the VRF Tables. This type of attack creates specific security risks as it allows attackers to cut off delicate data, disrupt the network's functioning, or conduct spying activities. The main difficulty in this threat is ensuring the unity and privacy of LERs and VRF table management tasks, which requires ensuring strong verification, limitation on access, and surveillance methods to detect and reduce unofficial changes successfully [1].

(5) *Route modification attacks:* These attacks demand changing the route or destination of packets in the network core, mostly via changes in routing protocols like BGP. Attackers use vulnerabilities in routing protocols or reduce the ability of routing devices to change traffic to unauthorized destinations or spy on delicate communications. By changing routing information, attackers can lead to service degradation, network blockage, or unauthorized access to confidential information. The difficulty with route modification attacks is in checking and reducing unofficial changes to routing information, which requires strong authentication, unit checks, and observation of routing protocol messages [6].

(6) *DNS hijacking:* DNS hijacking requires redirecting network usage by changing DNS servers to direct domain names to unofficial IP addresses. Attackers may negotiate DNS servers or use their vulnerabilities in DNS protocols to change valid client requests to unofficial servers handled by the attacker. Based on VPNs, DNS hijacking can spoil the protection and isolation of VPN users by changing their traffic to unofficial or hacked servers. This can lead to data blocking, injection of unofficial content, or unofficial access to delicate information. Reducing DNS hijacking requires implementing safe and secure DNS protocols, using DNSSEC (Domain Name System Security Extensions), and monitoring DNS traffic for signs of interference or manipulation [17].

(7) *Trojans and worms:* Trojans and worms are a kind of ill-natured software that can spoil clients or servers of VPN, adjusting the protection and integrity of VPN connections. Attackers can spread trojans and worms through phishing emails, harmful websites, or unsafe installation of software. When deployed in a framework, trojans and worms can open backdoors, steal sensitive data, and launch further assaults within the VPN architecture. These malicious software infections can give rise to data breaches, unauthorized access, or disturbance of VPN services. Stopping trojans and worms needs developing strong endpoint safety methods, carrying out structured security audits, and training individuals about the risks of downloading as well as executing unknown files [17].

(8) *Brute force attacks:* These attacks systematically check login credentials to gain unauthorized entry to routers or VPN servers. Attackers may use weak or common passwords, misconfigured verification methods, or vulnerabilities in VPN software to launch a brute-force strike. By regularly checking several username and password configurations, attackers try to bypass verification controls and gain privileged entry to VPN resources. Brute force attacks can lead to unapproved data access, service disturbance, or account compromise. Blocking brute force attacks needs adopting strong suggestions for passwords, using multi-factor authentication, and implementing rate-limiting methods to stop multiple login attempts in a short time [20].

(9) *Password cracking:* Password cracking attacks include trying or cracking a user's password to gain unauthorized entry to VPN accounts or resources. Attackers can use dictionary attacks, automated tools, or brute force techniques to try various password combinations before they find the right credentials. Common passwords, weak passwords, and a lack of multi-factor authentication enhance the risk of successful password cracking attacks. Once attackers get valid credentials, they can access delicate information, imitate legitimate users, or negotiate VPN security. Preventing password cracking attacks requires implementing secure password regulations, determining multi-factor authentication, and monitoring login attempts for suspicious activity [6].

(10) *Malware and viruses:* Malware and viruses are ill-natured software programs evolved to infect VPN clients, servers, or networks, compromising their protection and integrity. Once deployed on a system, malware and viruses can take private information, log keystrokes, or leverage weaknesses to gain unwanted entry to VPN resources. Attackers may

spread malware and viruses through phishing emails, infected attachments, or compromised websites. Malware infections can give rise to theft of information and losses of money, or disruption of VPN services. Preventing malware and virus infections requires deploying endpoint security solutions, keeping software updated with safety patches, as well as educating users about safe browsing habits and email practices [17].

(11) *Phishing attacks:* These attacks include attracting users into imparting sensitive information like usernames, passwords, or monetary details by impersonating real companies through email, SMS messaging, or fake websites. Attackers may send phishing emails disguised as VPN login prompts, account verification requests, or system updates to mislead users into disclosing their credentials. Once attackers obtain login credentials, they can gain unwanted access to VPN accounts, compromise delicate data, or launch further attacks within the VPN framework. Preventing phishing attacks requires email filtering, user awareness tutoring, and executing multi-level authentication to check the user's identity before granting access to VPN resources [1].

(12) *Exploiting vulnerabilities in VPN hardware or software:* Attackers can exploit known or unknown vulnerabilities in VPN hardware or software to obtain unauthorized access, which can minimize the security of VPN connections or perform some other malicious activities. Vulnerabilities like buffer overflows, remote code execution flaws, or authentication bypasses can be exploited by attackers to compromise VPN tools or stop encrypted traffic. To minimize the risk of exploitation, organizations should regularly update VPN applications and firmware, apply safety patches promptly, and organize assessments of vulnerability and testing for penetration to identify and improve relevant security holes. Including network segmentation, access control, and intrusion detection systems can also help identify and prevent unauthorized access to VPN resources [20].

(13) *Man-in-the-middle (MITM) attacks:* MITM attacks occur when a malicious actor stops interaction between two parties, like a VPN client and server, without their knowledge. In the context of VPNs, MITM attacks can minimize data privacy, and safety is maintained when transferred through an encrypted link. Attackers may use vulnerabilities in the VPN protocol, trade off digital certificates, or utilize techniques such as ARP spoofing to stop and change traffic passing through the compromised network. By loading themselves in the communication link, attackers can snoop on sensitive information, change data packets, or initiate

malicious payloads in the communication stream. Since it broke the trust and privacy of the provided encrypted links, MITM attacks are proving to be a huge danger to VPN security. Checking and verifying network traffic, digital certificates, and execution of strong cryptographic protocols are needed to stop or prevent MITM attacks [6].

(14) *Legacy applications:* Attackers gain entry from points that cause security risks, especially from old or unpatched software and legacy applications. In worst-case scenarios, these applications are prone to exploitation, which is why they need help from modern and latest security protocols. To gain unofficial access, can take advantage of or execute malicious code with the VPN framework if they target such legacy apps on VPN-connected devices. Legacy apps many times do not follow security practices like encryption standards or secure authentication methods. Organizations should focus on improving or replacing old software that works on legacy apps to reduce security risks. In addition to that, practicing network segmentation, implementing access control, or having an intrusion detection system can help to reduce the effect of legacy apps' safety breaches [20].

8.4.2 Vulnerabilities

VPNs play a crucial role in securing network communications, allowing organizations to create secure links over public networks. But, despite their general assumption, VPNs are not resistant to security vulnerabilities that can settle their effectiveness and unity. In this part, we will dive into many vulnerabilities inherent in VPN execution that pose notable risks to organizational security. Each and every vulnerability can lead to worse consequences, whether it is attacks that modify traffic routes to attacks that impact VPN services like infrastructure-based and protocol-based DoS attacks. The importance of addressing vulnerabilities properly increases when there are weaknesses in encryption, authentication, policy enforcement, app controls, etc. Organization can enhance their knowledge of VPN's security risks and can execute effective methods to reduce the threats properly by evaluating these vulnerabilities [5].

(1) *Route modification attacks: The* Attacker gains access to modify the routing table with incorrect or irrelevant data, or to divert the traffic to some other destination, or to stop sensitive information from traveling across the network. In this attack, the attacker gains access to modify the path or to change the destination of a packet traveling in the network.

This tactic can lead to spying on private data, service degradation, or network congestion, minimizing the unity and accessibility of VPN services. These attacks enhance the importance of implementing strong routing protocols, secure authentication methods, and network monitoring solutions to detect and minimize unauthorized modifications to routing paths [17].

(2) *VPN limitations:* The limitations of VPNs, like licensing constraints and resource limitations, create specific challenges to keep secure and valid VPN services. Licensing restrictions can limit the number of concurrent links or features accessible to users, certainly affecting scalability and user access. Resource limitations, including bandwidth limitations or hardware limitations, may affect VPN performance and availability during peak usage or critical incidents. However, the risk of VPN unavailability during critical incidents, like network outages or framework failures, highlights the need for incident plans and redundancy measures to ensure continuous VPN operation [14].

(3) *Infrastructure-based DoS attacks:* Infrastructure-based DoS attacks aim for VPN services by overwhelming the network framework with malicious traffic, breaking VPN connectivity, and minimizing network availability. These attacks use vulnerabilities in network tools such as routers, switches, and firewalls to overwhelm network resources and utilize bandwidth capacity. By aiming at critical components of the VPN framework, attackers can exhibit VPN services inaccessible to valid users, causing financial losses, reputation damage, and operational breakage. Minimizing infrastructure-based DoS attacks requires deploying strong intrusion prevention systems, traffic monitoring methods, and speed limiting policies to check and block malicious traffic until it reaches VPN endpoints [20].

(4) *Protocol-based DoS attacks:* Protocol-based DoS attacks abuse vulnerabilities in VPN protocols and infrastructure to disrupt VPN services and compromise network availability. Attackers may leverage protocol weaknesses, such as buffer overflow vulnerabilities or session initiation floods, to overwhelm VPN gateways and authentication servers, leading to service degradation or downtime. Additionally, protocol-based DoS attacks may target specific VPN protocols, such as IPSec or SSL/TLS, by exploiting implementation flaws or resource exhaustion vulnerabilities. To mitigate protocol-based DoS attacks, organizations should regularly update VPN software, apply security patches, and conduct via

security examinations to determine and remediate vulnerabilities in VPN infrastructure and protocols [18].

(5) *Verification process vulnerabilities:* In VPN, the weaknesses related to the integrity and correctness of data traveling in the network among various sites are the weaknesses in the verification process, known as verification process vulnerabilities. They can cause security hazards as they come from poor authentication methods, incorrect data validation processes, or weak encryption, data modification, or injection of malicious code in the network [5].

(6) *Implementation flaws in VPN technology:* The limitations and weaknesses in key management methods or the deployment of encryption protocols lead to vulnerabilities in the execution of VPN technology. The limitations are misconfigured algorithms or legacy application software, or being prone to known exploits. Using these weaknesses, the attacker can reduce the safety, security, and accessibility of data and resources as they can intrude, change, or modify encrypted traffic, or the attacker can pass access control from the side, or can have unofficial access to VPN infrastructure [8].

(7) *Risk of unauthorized applications:* Attackers can cause security issues as they can exploit the backdoors present or known vulnerabilities in unauthorized applications working in the VPN environments. Strict application control and regular checking in the VPN environment are important because there is a huge risk of data breach, malware infection, or degradation of network performance, as some unapproved software and services are allowed [6].

(8) *Inadequate policy enforcement:* Policy violations, unofficial access, or misconfigurations are problems that can occur due to Inadequate policy enforcement methods. We know that vulnerabilities are caused by many actions like poor authentication, misconfigured access measures, or insufficient monitoring capabilities, all of these lead to the strong need of policy enforcement methods and regular checking in VPN environment as they can cause data breaches, insider threats, unwanted modifications to network configurations, compliance violations [8].

(9) *Forwarding policy discovery vulnerability:* Limiting administrators' potential to efficiently access and control the flow of network traffic, or a lack of visibility in routing and forwarding policies, are vulnerabilities in forwarding policy discovery. Attackers can cause security risks as they can intrude or manipulate traffic, cause disruption of services,

traffic bottlenecks, or cause administrators problems in identifying unauthorized network behavior if comprehensive forwarding policy discovery methods are not implemented, leading to more transparent, well-documented forwarding policies in VPN environments [14].

8.5 Blockchain-enabled VPN Security

To address security risks in traditional VPN systems and lead to huge key benefits, the mixture of blockchain into VPN architecture is proposed (as shown in Figure 8.1). A strong tool for enhancing the VPN's security, popularly known for its decentralized and immutable features, is blockchain technology.

8.5.1 Decentralized authentication

The distributed nature of authentication is the most important advantage of the blockchain-enabled VPNs. Single points of failure and being vulnerable to attacks are the problems of traditional VPNs, which had centralized servers for authentication. For the risks linked with the centralized authentication, for storage, VPN can use distributed ledgers, and for checking user credentials across multiple nodes, by having a blockchain associated with it. It will be more challenging for attackers to disrupt the authentication process and affect the security if a decentralized approach is followed [5].

8.5.2 Enhanced data integrity and confidentiality

Having a tamper-resistant environment ensures the blockchain technology for data integrity (Various other features are mentioned in Figure 8.2). Every data exchange or transaction that occurs is recorded in a block of blockchain-enabled VPN, then this block builds a chain by connecting it with preceding blocks. Without detection, it is impossible to change data in this type of structure. Ensuring the privacy and reliability of communications, protection against data tampering, unauthorized access, and intrusion, are all the results of blockchain offering an extra layer of defence, which is maintained throughout the VPN [13].

8.5.3 Smart contracts for automated security policies

In a VPN, to ensure security policies and to automate it, smart contracts and programmable scripts are stored on the blockchain. To manage controls on access, give automated responses to detected threats, and maintain

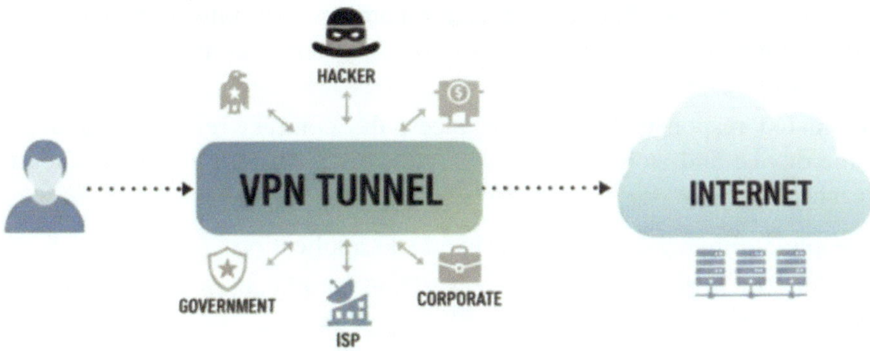

Figure 8.1 Blockchain-enabled VPN.

balance with security standards [21], these smart contracts can help. Under some specified conditions, these smart contracts can automatically cancel access from a compromised node or apply multi-factor authentication, for instance [14].

Specific use cases highlight their ability to withdraw access in response to detected anomalies, to illustrate the practicality of smart contracts in this context:

Example 1: Access control for a secure database

Scenario: In an environment managing sensitive personal health records, a smart contract is deployed specifically for access control.

Functionality: The smart contract scans user access patterns, like login attempts and data retrieval requests.

Anomaly detection: For instance, if a user fails to log in multiple times (e.g., five failed attempts in a short while), this activity is indicated as anomalous.

Automated response: Upon this detection, the smart contract automatically revokes the user's access and sends a notification to the system administrator, thus mitigating the risk of unauthorized access.

Example 2: IoT device management

Scenario: In a smart home setting, a smart contract governs access to various IoT devices.

Functionality: It tracks the status of devices and user access while monitoring for unusual activity.

Anomaly detection: Should a device record an unusually high volume of data or attempt unauthorized connections, the smart contract identifies the behavior as suspicious.

Automated response: In such instances, the contract revokes user access to the device and isolates it from the network, preventing further potential breaches.

Example 3: Financial transactions in a DeFi application

Scenario: In a decentralized finance (DeFi) application, a smart contract oversees user transactions.

Functionality: It continuously monitors transactions and user balances to enforce lending policies.

Anomaly Detection: If a user attempts to withdraw amounts exceeding their collateral or conducts high-frequency transactions that deviate significantly from their regular behavior, the policy recognizes this as a fraud risk.

Automated response: The smart contract responds by freezing the user's account and suspending their ability to initiate further transactions until a manual review is performed.

This automation reduces the need for human intervention and ensures consistent application of security measures. Design and implementation are the main factors responsible for the correctness of these smart contracts. A robust and bug-free implementation is necessary to stop the exploitation of vulnerabilities in smart contract code, research shows. When enforcing security policies with human intervention, it is necessary to identify and reduce these vulnerabilities by using static analysis tools [22].

Finally, for improving the organization's security, automating security actions like access revocation during anomaly detection can be addressed by various methods of these smart contracts, and that is how vulnerabilities can also be addressed. Risks associated with smart contracts: The technologies that support smart contracts and their unique features are the main cause of risks for them. Reliance on the code made them susceptible to exploitation and is one of the initial vulnerabilities. They are very different from traditional contracts, in which, through human-readable text, discrepancies can be easily identified, or based on pre-programmed code, smart contracts can be implemented automatically, causing subtle changes and exploitation tough to detect and solve since they occurred.

Additionally, smart contracts are less private than conventional written agreements, as they are often not articulated in a format that is easily understandable to all parties involved. This lack of clarity can lead to misunderstandings and complicate the enforcement of terms. Moreover, the autonomous nature of smart contracts can facilitate or enable criminal activities, as the use of cryptography can be exploited for unlawful purposes, raising concerns about their application in illegal transactions. The existing legal frameworks may not correctly address these different features and challenges, leaving gaps that could be exploited by malicious actors. While some aspects of the law may be applicable, many rules will likely need to be adapted to effectively govern smart contracts, highlighting the urgent need for a comprehensive legal approach to mitigate these risks. Strategies for auditing and mitigating vulnerabilities [new2]: To address the vulnerabilities related to smart contracts, the paper introduces several strategies targeted at improving cybersecurity and legal protections. One of the key recommendations is the addition of explicit cybersecurity provisions in the legal framework governing smart contracts. This would involve creating minimum cybersecurity needs that all legally binding smart contracts must meet, thereby ensuring a basic level of security. The author advises using several of the National Institute of Standards and Technology's (NIST) Federal Information Processing Standards to meet these requirements, which would help ensure that smart contracts are made and used with adequate security methods in place. Additionally, the paper evaluates the limitations of existing legislation, such as the Computer Fraud and Abuse Act, identifying it as ripe for reform. By improving legal checks against cyber hacking, potential attackers may be discouraged from exploiting vulnerabilities in smart contracts. Increasing awareness and education among stakeholders about the risks linked with smart contracts and the importance of cybersecurity methods is also important. This includes educating developers, legal professionals, and users about potential vulnerabilities and the need for robust security practices. Lastly, while not specifically detailed in the paper, the importance of daily audits and checking of smart contracts can be concluded as a necessary strategy. To improve the overall security posture of smart contracts, we need to detect vulnerabilities before they can be used by an attacker. In that case, reviewing the code and having an in-depth security assessment would be of great help. The main target of these strategies is to increase confidence between contracting parties by having a safer environment for deployment and the proper utilization of smart contracts.

8.5.4 Resistance to traditional attacks

From many traditional attacks, blockchain-enabled VPNs provide protection. It is very tough for attackers to practice MitM attacks or DDoS attacks because there are no unique reasons for failure due to the decentralized nature of blockchain. Now, it is so much easier to detect and respond to malicious activities as the immutable ledger ensures transparency and verifiable history of all transactions [2].

8.5.5 Integration challenges and considerations in blockchain-enabled VPN

There are several challenges that should be confronted, although the integration of blockchain has given significant security enhancements:

(1) *Network congestion and throughput:* Overall network performance is slowed down because the number of transactions on the blockchain leads to congestion as user demand increases.

Figure 8.2 Key characteristics of blockchain: decentralization, security, transparency, and more.

(2) *Transaction throughput limitations:* Bottlenecks in high-volume VPN usage are the result of inherent throughput limits of many blockchain networks, like Bitcoin and Ethereum. For example, in the comparison of traditional versus now centralized systems, 7 to 10 transactions per second can be handled by Bitcoin.
(3) *Node management and latency:* Handling and managing various nodes for valid transactions and data storage, which can become complex and resource-intensive due to the decentralized nature of blockchain.
(4) *Resource allocation issues:* It is a very critical process for the optimization of node distribution and users. User experience and impact performance are negatively impacted due to poorly balanced resources.
(5) *High transaction fees:* Blockchain-enabled VPN services become less attractive in comparison with traditional solutions when transaction fees increase with an increase in network congestion.
(6) *Consensus mechanism limitations:* Scalability can be limited when every node is validated in all transactions by proof of work (PoW) in traditional consensus mechanisms. Scalability can be enhanced by methods such as proof of stake (PoS), but may affect safety and decentralization [17].

8.6 Scalability and Latency In Blockchain-enabled VPN

8.6.1 Scalability issues

Data storage requirements: There can be a problem in IoT devices and other resource-constrained environments because the requirement for storage increases when the blockchain starts accumulating data.

Scalability/blockchain trilemma: It was found that with enhancement in one area, we compromise with others, like maintaining a balance between decentralization, security, and scalability is very tough and is the most basic challenge of the blockchain trilemma.

Balancing between drawbacks and benefits is hard to achieve while considering blockchain-enabled VPN solutions. Therefore, these factors must be correctly handled by any Organization.

8.6.2 Latency issues in blockchain-enabled VPNs

The performance of VPN can be highly impacted by the newly introduced latency challenges from the blockchain technology, although it provides great security benefits, which need to be addressed. The main latency issues are as follows:

- Transaction confirmation delays: If there is a congested network, then the confirmation process offered by blockchain operations could be of great help. The overall process of a transaction can be delayed when the time taken for a transaction to be added to a block and for confirming that block.
- Network propagation time: Ledgers are updated by all the nodes throughout the network after the initiation of a transaction.
- Smart contract execution time: Tasks such as user verification and access control of the smart contracts can increase the time of execution. In real-time applications, this delay is of great problem.
- Consensus delay: Extensive communication is demanded by a network having more nodes or complex consensus algorithms. So, latency is there because of the time required to achieve consensus.
- Initial setup time: In smart contracts and the consensus methods, verification processes are involved, leading to a longer time period in the initial setup process while establishing connections.
- Transaction volume impact: Latency is introduced by longer processing times due to increased transaction volume.
- Node synchronization time: Time can be extended by geographic dispersion, and the latest transaction and nodes' ledgers must be synchronized.
- Transaction queuing: Confirmation can cause longer wait times as a queue is created for processing the transactions when there is high demand.
- Network architecture limitations: Communication overhead is increased due to the time required to process transactions in a larger network. This can introduce latency in the network by the blockchain network design itself.

Addressing these latency issues is crucial for ensuring that blockchain-enabled VPNs provide the performance levels required for effective real-time communications and user experiences.

8.6.3 Latency introduced by consensus mechanisms and mitigation strategies

Blockchain-enabled VPNs rely on decentralized consensus mechanisms to ensure security, privacy, and trust among participating nodes. However, these mechanisms, such as proof of work (PoW), proof of stake (PoS), and Byzantine fault tolerance (BFT), introduce inherent latency, which can affect the performance and user experience of VPN services.

(1) *Consensus mechanism-induced latency:* Proof of work (PoW), used by blockchain networks like Bitcoin, requires participants (miners) to solve complex mathematical problems to append a new block to the chain. This process introduces significant latency due to the time required to complete these calculations, which can vary based on the network's hashing power and difficulty level. Moreover, the block confirmation time increases with network congestion and miner competition, making PoW unsuitable for high-throughput, low-latency VPN services [23].
Proof of stake (PoS) protocols, such as those used by Ethereum 2.0, offer lower latency compared to PoW. Here, validators are selected based on the amount of cryptocurrency they hold and are willing to "stake." While PoS reduces the computational overhead seen in PoW, block confirmation still depends on network size, validator participation, and the randomness of validator selection. This can introduce latency when validators are spread across a large network [23]. Byzantine fault tolerance (BFT)-based consensus algorithms, such as those used in Hyperledger Fabric, offer lower latency than PoW and PoS by enabling agreement among a fixed set of nodes. However, as the number of participating nodes increases, communication overhead grows exponentially, which can delay consensus. This limits the scalability of BFT protocols, especially for large decentralized VPN networks [23]. Figure 8.3 shows the differentiation of centralized and decentralized VPNs.

(2) *Mitigation strategies:* To enhance the performance of blockchain-enabled VPNs, several strategies can be employed to mitigate latency caused by traditional consensus mechanisms:
Faster consensus protocols

- Delegated proof of stake (DPoS): DPoS significantly reduces latency by electing a small number of trusted nodes (delegates) to produce blocks. This mechanism, employed by platforms like EOS, ensures quicker block validation as only a subset of nodes participates in consensus at any given time, enhancing throughput and reducing latency.
- Practical Byzantine fault tolerance (PBFT): PBFT, used in systems like Hyperledger, can achieve consensus with lower latency by limiting communication to a smaller group of trusted nodes. This

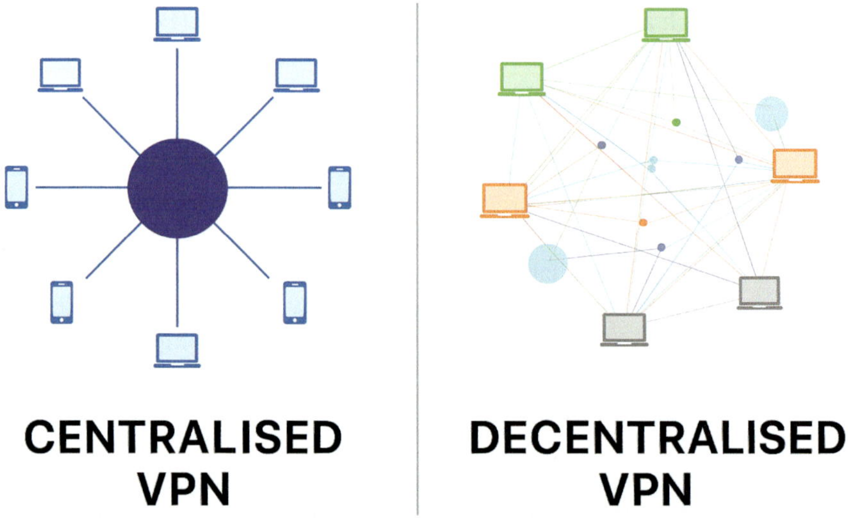

Figure 8.3 Comparison between a single-server (centralized) VPN and a peer-to-peer (decentralized) VPN structure.

reduces the message complexity and speeds up decision-making in networks with a known set of validators [23].

- Proof of authority (PoA): PoA, where a select group of validators is given the authority to create new blocks, offers fast block generation and minimal latency. Since only a few nodes are responsible for consensus, PoA provides high throughput and can mitigate latency issues effectively for private blockchain-enabled VPNs. Layer 2 Solutions Layer 2 scaling solutions (as shown in Figure 8.4), such as state channels and rollups, can be used to reduce latency in blockchain transactions by performing operations off-chain. These solutions allow multiple transactions to occur off the main blockchain, with only the final state being submitted on-chain. This reduces the load on the main blockchain, minimizing latency and enhancing the performance of blockchain-enabled VPNs.

Sharding involves splitting the blockchain network into smaller segments (shards), each capable of processing its own transactions and consensus. This parallelization reduces the workload for individual nodes, leading to faster transaction processing and lower latency. Sharding is particularly beneficial for public blockchains, where high transaction volumes can slow down consensus processes [23].

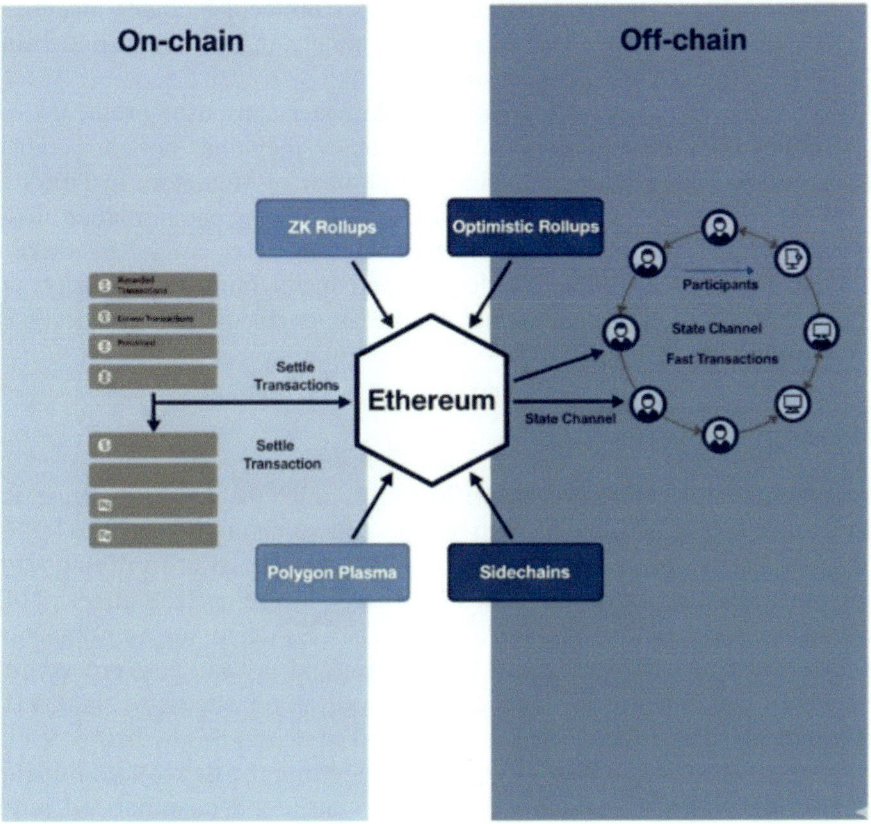

Figure 8.4 Illustration of Layer 2 blockchain scaling with state channels and Ethereum's off-chain solutions for higher transaction throughput.

Optimizing network topology, the physical and logical structure of the network, can significantly impact consensus latency. By optimizing network topology – such as reducing the distance between nodes, using low-latency communication protocols, or clustering nodes based on geographical proximity – the latency introduced during consensus can be minimized. This is particularly relevant for global blockchain-enabled VPNs, where nodes are often spread across different regions. Incentivizing faster block production implementing mechanisms that reward validators for faster block production and penalize them for delays can motivate participants to optimize their resources and reduce latency. For example, Ethereum's Casper protocol includes incentives for validators to propose blocks in a timely manner, thus mitigating latency issues during consensus.

(3) *Balancing security and latency:* While faster consensus protocols and optimization strategies can mitigate latency, they must not compromise security. For instance, reducing the number of validators in DPoS or PoA can lead to centralization risks, while sharding can introduce cross-shard communication challenges. Therefore, it is crucial to strike a balance between latency reduction and maintaining the security and decentralization principles that blockchain-enabled VPNs are designed to uphold.

8.7 Mitigation Strategies

Mitigation strategies are preventive initiatives implemented to decrease the chance or effect of possible security threats and vulnerabilities within VPNs. These strategies encompass a range of techniques aimed at fortifying VPN infrastructures against various kinds of attacks, including DoS attacks [14], unauthorized access attempts, and data breaches. By deploying a combination of technical controls, operational procedures, and privacy best procedures, companies can enhance the resilience, as well as robustness of their VPN environments. The effectiveness of mitigation strategies lies in their potential to determine and respond to safety incidents promptly, thereby minimizing the risk of service disruptions, data compromise, and unauthorized intrusions. In this section, we will explore key mitigation strategies employed to safeguard VPN services, including assigning multiple IP addresses, implementing tunnel splitting, integrating network and intrusion detection systems (IDS) [9], hardening the network perimeter, and securing inter-provider connections. These strategies work synergistically to bolster the security posture of VPN infrastructures, ensuring the privacy, security, and accessibility of network resources as well as data transmissions.

8.7.1 Network architecture strategies

(1) *Assigning multiple IP addresses:* This strategy involves assigning multiple IP addresses to VPN endpoints. By distributing incoming traffic across different IP addresses, organizations can better manage and mitigate DoS attacks targeting specific IP endpoints. Spreading the load

across multiple addresses helps to alleviate congestion and reduces the impact of DoS attacks on the VPN infrastructure [5].

(2) *Implementing tunnel splitting:* Tunnel splitting is another effective approach to mitigate DoS attacks on VPNs. It involves breaking down large VPN tunnels into smaller segments depending on specified parameters like destination IP addresses or application types. By segmenting VPN traffic, organizations can isolate and contain the impact of DoS attacks, preventing them from affecting the entire VPN infrastructure [14].

(3) *Configuration of VPN servers within proxy servers or gateways:* To overcome the challenge of NIDS handling encrypted data, configuring IPSec VPN servers within proxy servers or gateways is proposed. This configuration allows encrypted data to be decrypted at the VPN server before being forwarded to the NIDS for analysis. Decrypting the data enables NIDS to inspect traffic for signs of malicious activity, even in encrypted environments, thereby enhancing threat detection capabilities [20].

(4) *Routing protocols:* Ensuring the integrity and authenticity of routing protocols is crucial for preventing unauthorized access and mitigating DoS attacks. By implementing integrity checks and strong authentication mechanisms for routing protocols, organizations can prevent malicious actors from tampering with routing information and disrupting VPN services [18].

8.7.2 Security infrastructure strategies

1. *Harden the network perimeter to prevent unauthorized access:* Strengthening the network perimeter with robust safety measures like intrusion prevention systems, firewalls, and access control policies helps prevent unauthorized access to VPN infrastructure. By establishing strict access controls and examining ingress and egress traffic, organizations can minimize the danger of DoS attacks as well as unauthorized intrusions [8].
2. *Deploy firewalls at VPN sites:* Deploying firewalls at VPN sites helps filter and block malicious traffic, preventing DoS attacks and unauthorized access to VPN infrastructure. Install firewalls to set up authentication restrictions and examine traffic that comes in and leaves. Organizations can detect and mitigate threats before they reach VPN endpoints, ensuring the security and availability of VPN services [8].

3. *Secure inter-provider connections:* Securing inter-provider connections, especially in redistribution and multi-hop redistribution models, is essential for protecting VPN services from external threats. Organizations can protect VPN connections and stop unauthorized access or modification of traffic by using safe communication protocols, encrypting data transmission, and maintaining a trustworthy relationship with other networks [14].

8.7.3 Intrusion detection and prevention strategies

(1) *Placement of NIDS in the switch:* In handling and maintenance of switched data, there are some limitations of NIDS, which can be addressed by placing NIDS sensors in the switch itself. NIDS can promptly respond to known threats and can effectively detect network intrusions by analysing traffic passing through the switch directly. This will enhance the threat detection capabilities by ensuring effective traffic monitoring in switched environments [5].

(2) *Integration of network and intrusion detection systems (IDS):* Suspicious behavior or potential intrusions' real-time detection and functional monitoring of traffic by the organizations can be provided by the IDS sensors present in the network. Altogether, security can be improved if instant steps are taken by the organizations in case of threats, if their network traffic is continuously analyzed [9].

(3) *Implement anomaly detection systems:* Anomaly detection systems are the systems that look for known attacks or security hazards by finding unusual patterns or anomalous behavior by monitoring network traffic. They are capable of improving the overall security of VPN systems by finding and minimizing DoS attacks, intrusions, and other real-time threat detection [18].

8.7.4 Data protection strategies

Using CE-to-CE encryption for sensitive data transmission: The confidentiality and integrity of sensitive information traveling in the VPN environment are ensured by encryption of data transmitted among customer edge (CE) routers. Organizations can minimize the danger of data breaches and illegal access to VPN resources and can save data from interception or tampering by unauthorized parties by robust cryptographic algorithms following an end-to-end encryption mechanism [5].

8.8 Edge Computing and Load Balancing for Global VPNs

8.8.1 Edge computing and VPN nodes

Organizations can minimize latency and enhance throughput for users present globally by deploying blockchain-enabled VPN nodes at the network edge. While communicating continuously with the key blockchain network so the synchronization is maintained, edge nodes are smartly located near the end-users to handle local encryption and transaction validation.

8.8.2 Interoperability between different blockchain networks

It is required to maintain a seamless interconnection among blockchain-enabled VPNs and other blockchain-based systems, so many blockchain networks for different applications are used by global enterprises.

(1) *Cross-chain interoperability:* Over multiple blockchain platforms, blockchain-enabled VPNs are allowed to scale themselves by having cross-chain communication through technologies such as Cosmos, Polkadot, and Hyperledger Cactus. Unvarying security policies and smooth data transfer are enabled by global enterprises using numerous integrated, interoperable, decentralized systems.

(2) *Decentralized key management systems (DKMS):* Across regions, it is very important to safely handle encryption keys for global VPNs, so scalable key management comes into play. Without central oversight, making global operations easier and allowing for secure key sharing and management across different blockchain networks, all these are provided by decentralized key management systems like NuCypher.

8.8.3 Regulatory and compliance considerations

A decentralized record of data access and transfer is maintained for compliance purposes. Audit-able and tamper-proof ledger can be helpful for that and is offered by the Blockchain-enabled VPNs. Global networks must comply with regional regulations and data privacy laws, such as GDPR in Europe and CCPA in California.

(1) *Privacy-preserving blockchain solutions:* The solutions are required to protect privacy and ensure regulatory compliance without divulging the subject matter, allowing for data verification. To ensure compliance with global data protection legislation, blockchain-enabled VPNs and

privacy-focused technologies like as zero-knowledge proofs (ZKPs) and private transactions can be deployed.

(2) *Smart contracts for automated compliance:* Smart contracts are used to maintain and check that all global operations remain compliant and to minimize the risk of human error, it is necessary to ensure VPN nodes in various regions are obeying local laws regarding data transfer, encryption, and storage, so, compliance checks are needed and to automate that we can use it.

8.8.4 Load balancing and fault tolerance

In huge environments, it is important to advance the blockchain-enabled VPNs effectively, and for that, the most critical components are load balancing and fault tolerance, because the VPN network should remain functioning even during peak loads or node failures.

(1) *Decentralized load balancing:* In case of failure, the traffic should be diverted to alternative nodes, which will improve fault tolerance by the decentralized load balancers. Across the network nodes, it is important to make sure that the traffic is allocated uniformly, so that the blockchain-enabled VPNs can strengthen decentralized load balancing protocols. This will make sure that system performance is maintained during peak load when demand is high, then at that time, no single node should be overwhelmed.

(2) *Redundant node clustering:* To ensure reliability and availability in global networks, blockchain-enabled VPNs can implement redundant node clusters. These clusters, spread across different geographic regions, act as backups for one another, ensuring uninterrupted service in case of node downtime. Redundant clustering, combined with distributed storage, ensures that no single point of failure compromises the network.

8.9 Scaling Blockchain-enabled VPNs for Enterprise and Global Networks

While organizations look for effective solutions that can help in protecting their global and enterprise network infrastructures, blockchain-based VPN emerges as a solution that integrates cryptographic security together with decentralized trusted solutions. However, scaling such systems to support large numbers of users introduces concerns such as network performance, user management, throughput, and interoperability. This section explores ways to expand blockchain-enabled VPNs for corporate use and on a global scale.

8.9.1 Enterprise-level scaling

Managing network size and participants: In enterprise environments, network size often grows as organizations expand, necessitating strong management practices. Blockchain-enabled VPNs must support thousands of employees, devices, and various locations with secure communication and data privacy. As opposed to traditional VPN solutions, where centralized control can handle participant management, blockchain-enabled VPNs require decentralized approaches to scale.

Permissioned blockchains: For corporate applications, permissioned blockchain models, such as Hyperledger Fabric or Corda, limit access to this blockchain network to authorized individuals or parties. This enables effective management of a large number of enterprise users while safeguarding the integrity of the VPN architecture. Thus, permissioned blockchains are beneficial since node operators are predetermined, simplifying the consensus process and minimizing latency.

- Identity and access management (IAM): To efficiently add or remove participants, blockchain-enabled VPNs in enterprise environments can integrate IAM systems with DID solutions. These frameworks, such as Sovrin or uPort, provide the most effective solution for managing user credentials and authentication, as well as permissions across various locations without depending on a central authority [23].
- Consensus mechanism adjustments: In large enterprise VPNs, the choice of consensus mechanisms is a critical factor for achieving scalability. For example, proof of authority (PoA) and practical Byzantine fault tolerance (PBFT) provide low latency since the number of validators is restricted, making them suitable for enterprise applications where trust is more easily managed.
- Network partitioning: Enterprise networks may encompass many branches or regions in an organization. The integration of blockchain allows for blockchain-based VPNs to be scaled by adding layers or subsets known as shards that manage localized network and security parameters. Sharding promotes a parallel processing concept, enabling different parts of the network to operate simultaneously without burdening the core blockchain, thereby enhancing scalability [23].

- Throughput and data handling: Since enterprises require high throughput for processing large volumes of encrypted data, the blockchain-based VPNs have to perform the transaction validation and data transfer quickly in the network.
- Layer 2 scaling solutions: Practices such as state channels and rollups can move transactions off the main blockchain, only recording the final state on the ledger. This enhances throughput, lessens the blockchain's processing load, and enhances the performance of VPN [23].
- Hybrid models: A hybrid approach can integrate traditional enterprise VPNs with additional layers of security using blockchain. This enables the scaling of security primitives (authentication, encryption key management) on the blockchain, while data transfers occur over high-throughput conventional infrastructure.

8.9.2 Global network scaling

Decentralization across geographic locations for global organizations, decentralization becomes crucial to maintaining security and performance. Blockchain-enabled VPNs offer the advantage of geographically distributed nodes, which can enhance the security and resiliency of the network. However, scaling globally introduces challenges related to latency, bandwidth, and the coordination of decentralized nodes.

Distributed node management: To scale globally, organizations can leverage distributed consensus mechanisms with geographically clustered nodes. This approach ensures faster consensus for VPN sessions within specific regions and minimizes latency for users in those areas. The image below illustrates a distributed transactional flow, where interactions between consumers and providers are recorded on a blockchain. This framework is similar to how distributed nodes manage

VPN sessions, handling encryption, session management, and user authentication across the network [24].

Additionally, organizations can deploy blockchain-enabled VPN nodes at the network edge, closer to users, to reduce latency and improve throughput for global users. By positioning edge nodes strategically, organizations can facilitate local encryption and transaction validation, thereby enhancing performance. These edge nodes communicate periodically with the core blockchain network to maintain synchronization, ensuring that all operations are coherent and secure.

8.10 Real-world Use Cases for Blockchain-enabled VPNs

8.10.1 Orchid VPN overview

Originating within VPN services, Orchid VPN is a notable example of the successful implementation of blockchain technology in the industry, addressing the flaws of traditional VPN models, including centralization, lack of privacy, and scalability issues. Orchid is decentralized, allowing providers to offer up their excess bandwidth to users who require a VPN. Thus, the absence of centralized providers eliminates a key weakness of traditional models – centralized control. Instead, Orchid uses Ethereum to create trustless relationships between users and bandwidth suppliers and uses smart contracts to manage payments, staking, and node selection.

8.10.2 Innovations in Orchid

One of the key innovations of Orchid is its staking system. Bandwidth providers are required to stake Orchid tokens (OXT), an ERC-20 standard token. There is a direct correlation between the staked tokens and selection probability by the users, which ensures an economic incentive for good behavior. With this stake-weighted random selection, the likelihood of a Sybil attack is significantly reduced because malicious actors cannot create multiple fake profiles to flood the network [25]. Their actions are aligned with their individual best interests; otherwise, if a provider is found to be dishonest or malicious, they will forfeit the tokens that they put down. This financial factor acts as a significant motivator for providers to commit to integrity and high-quality service, thus enhancing the overall trust and credibility of the decentralized system.

Orchid also introduces probabilistic nano payments, allowing users to make microtransactions in real time while using the VPN. Instead of continuously sending small payments, users issue cryptographically secure tickets that are periodically redeemed through smart contracts on the Ethereum blockchain. This payment system is efficient, reducing the need for frequent on-chain transactions, which would be impractical due to high fees and slow processing times. The ability to pay for bandwidth on a per-use basis rather than through monthly subscriptions makes the service more flexible and cost-efficient compared to traditional VPNs.

8.10.3 Privacy and scalability enhancement

Regarding the privacy mechanism, Orchid adopted the onion routing model similar to Tor; data is passed through multiple nodes, encrypted multiple times to ensure anonymity. However, Orchid extends such systems, which are based solely on a communication layer, by a layer of economics to compensate bandwidth providers, resulting in a more scalable and stable network. The distributed structure of the network makes it highly resistant to censorship; if one provider is blocked or becomes inactive, the user can quickly switch to another provider, preventing any disruptions in VPN services [25]. By employing this technology, Orchid considerably enriches not only security and privacy but also scalability. With this, Orchid deploys Ethereum for the transaction and node management while eliminating the user's dependency on the VPN provider to protect their data. Exchanges and node selection are managed by a smart contract that executes automatically without external interference. The fact that the scalability of the nano payment system enables the effective processing of millions of transactions, will be possible with minimal transaction costs.

8.10.4 Feasibility and practical application

The fact that it is already in operation is enough to confirm the viability of Orchid as a blockchain-integrated VPN. Users can download the app and purchase OXT tokens to immediately connect to the decentralized VPN network. Those providing services can optimize their additional bandwidth, constructing a market that can be adapted and developed over time. When combined with Ethereum's infrastructure, the nano payment system offers low transaction fees and real-time payment, which makes the service practical and economically viable. The introduction of blockchain innovation into VPNs is a considerable stride in overcoming the shortcomings of traditional VPNs in privacy, security, scalability, and cost. Looking at Orchid's case, we can conclude that blockchain technology is both practical and effective in real-world applications.

8.11 Future Trends and Improvements

VPN technology continues to evolve in response to emerging threats and the advent of new technologies. In this section, we will discuss future trends and innovations shaping the realm of VPNs, including advanced technologies and strategies that promise to enhance security, efficiency, and reliability. Having examined new methodologies of encryption, endpoint checks, AI, and Blockchain integration, VPN future seems promising and grants organizations improved abilities relevant in the ever-evolving digital environment for securing their networks and data.

8.11.1 Software-defined networking (SDN)

SDN represents a novel approach to both the management, as well as the security of networks. SDN security policies are flexible and dynamic, allowing SDN VPNs to respond to real-time network dynamics and needs [15]. SDN separates the control plane from the forwarding plane, allowing centralized management through programmable devices. This shift enables VPNs to quickly adapt to new threats because they are able to automatically create and modify security policies based on new data received from network and analytic sources.

In the context of SDN-enabled VPNs, security policies are referred to as dynamic security policies, which empower an organization to implement adaptive security protection plans that can be adjusted depending on the current network environment. These policies are orchestrated by SDN controllers, which dynamically adjust security parameters such as access controls, permitted encryption schemes, and traffic routing rules, based on threat detections or changes in performance [8]. Integrating real-time network telemetry and threat intelligence would be useful in opposing the increasing volume of cyber threats, and to modify its security framework, SDN-enabled VPNs are used.

SDN controllers orchestrate policy deployment across the VPN infrastructure by means of automated provisioning and configuration of network devices, ensuring that security policies are enforced consistently throughout the network. Automated policy deployment is another key capability of SDN-enabled VPNs, ensuring consistent and efficient enforcement of security measures across the network. SDN reduces the risks of errors and enhances preparation through strategies that are equipped and configured by automating systems [9].

In SDN-enabled VPNs, to confirm optimal performance and robust security, performance optimization is necessary, as, according to performance metrics, security mechanisms are adopted [13]. SDN controllers monitor network performance in real-time and dynamically adjust security parameters such as encryption algorithms and traffic routing to optimize performance without compromising security resilience.

As SDN centralizes management and orchestration of VPN resources, enabling efficient resource allocation and policy management to accommodate growing network demands while maintaining security resilience, scalability, and flexibility becomes an inherent characteristic of SDN-enabled VPNs [14]. On-demand scaling and flexible policy configurations are allowed by SDN controllers, which manage virtualized network functions and resources.

To further improve the capabilities of SDN-enabled VPNs by augmenting threat detection capabilities and adaptive security measures, integration with developing technologies like AI and ML will be very useful [15]. By leveraging AI/ML-driven security analytics and orchestration tools, this integration will allow VPNs to effectively discover and mitigate safety threats. In summary, to enhance threat detection capabilities for scaling flexibly while integrating with emerging technologies, to optimize performance, or to automate policy deployment, and to empower organizations to implement dynamic security policies, SDN offers a transformative approach to VPN security.

8.11.2 AES-Rijndael and RSA fusion encryption technique

The powerful encryption of AES-Rijndael combined with the sophisticated key management of RSA is embraced by a robust security solution in VPNs by the fusion encryption technique [17]. In the sphere of cybersecurity, the one that plays an important role in data security is AES (Advanced Encryption Standard). It is highly adopted and loved in the industry because it is evidently better than RC4, RC5, and RC6. With AES-Rijndael, VPNs make sure that transmission of data is secure and protected against anybody trying to gain access to it.

To confirm secure key exchange, along with AES, RSA is used for key exchange and digital signature [2]. RSA is perfect for exchanging encryption keys through a public network because it offers high security through the public-key encryption model. Before transmission, the symmetric key intended for AES is used, which is encrypted by RSA. Therefore, users with a symmetric key can be able to decrypt with the private key if possible (as shown in Figure 8.5). Both of them are used in a complementary manner to enhance protection against unauthorized access, as it is an extra layer of encryption.

Compared to AES-Rijndael alone, the integration of AES-Rijndael and RSA offers more easier implementation. It improves the efficiency of operations, and, along with that, it confronts certain vulnerabilities [5]. Against external threats, this fusion of integration of these methods in a single protocol provides robust protection for security operations.

Moreover, the fusion encryption protocol fulfils essential requirements such as scalability, performance, and interoperability with the existing network protocols. It is recommended for addressing the diverse needs of the networks since it has better security and performance, thereby protecting data transmitted through a VPN.

8.11.3 Zero Trust architecture (ZTNA)

The Zero Trust model questions the traditional security approach that relies on a network perimeter because it posits that no entity should be inherently trusted, even if they are within the organization's network [8]. It requires robust authentication for the connections, enforces granular access controls, applies the principle of least privilege access, and monitors connections constantly to improve security. ZTNA lowers the chance of unauthorized access and lateral movement within the network, and checks every user and device, regardless of their location.

8.11.4 Artificial intelligence (AI) and machine learning (ML)

AI and ML mechanisms help VPNs detect and assess huge amounts of network information in real time to identify inconsistencies and potential security issues before they deteriorate [15]. Combining pattern recognition of typical malicious activities, AI and ML improves the state of overall security, allows tight integration of security, adaptive security controls, and advanced anomaly detection, resulting in consistent threat prevention.

8.11.5 Quantum cryptography

Quantum cryptography uses quantum-resistant encryption algorithms to protect communication channels from major challenges that arise from quantum computers [2]. Using techniques like quantum key distribution (QKD), leveraging principles of quantum mechanics means that data transmission is protected from even quantum computing attacks.

8.11.6 Secure access service edge (SASE)

SASE integrates network security functions with WAN capabilities to provide safe access to applications and data from anywhere [13]. By integrating VPN functionality into a unified cloud-based security platform, SASE streamlines security operations, enhances visibility and control, and simplifies network management, thereby strengthening VPN security while facilitating secure access to resources from anywhere.

8.11.7 Homomorphic encryption

This technique enables computation to be performed on encrypted data without decryption, hence providing safety while processing data [17]. Through the use of homomorphic encryption methods to VPN traffic, data can then be processed in transit while reducing leakage to other parties as well as preventing violation of customer privacy rights.

8.11.8 Zero knowledge proof

Zero knowledge proof (ZKP) is a sophisticated cryptographic solution through which the prover convinces the verifier that the prover has exact data that the latter has no right to acquire – for instance, the password or secret key. First, this special feature offers significant advantages in cases where simple identification of the user is required, as well as when anonymity and the security of the client are essential factors. The working of ZKPs involves several key steps: The specific processes of ZKPs are as follows: initialization, commitment, challenge, response, and verification [26]. First, the prover and the verifier settle on such things as a public key, a mathematical problem that is easy to solve but difficult to reverse. The prover then builds a commitment to a piece of information that is secret to the verifier and sends this proof to the verifier. In this, the verifier puts a fairly standard challenge to the prover, who in return must answer it in such a manner that only the holder of the secret will be able to respond appropriately. In conclusion, the verifier checks the received response with both the commitment and the challenge, thereby guaranteeing that the prover has the secret without the same passing through the verifier.

As for the ZKPs circulation, we come to identity verification without leaking any sensitive data. The process commences in the pre-functional state, whereby the parameters necessary for the progressive maturity of the process must be stamped and acknowledged by the parties. The prover then computes a value based on their secret and sends this along with a commitment, while the verifier responds with some random challenge. The prover gives a calculated answer to whichever challenge they are faced with and the secret. The verifier then compares the response against the initial commitment. It guards the transmitted information because the prover can validate the prover's identity without revealing the authentic data. Further, with random challenges, security is boosted since the secret information cannot be determined even if adversaries intercept the communication.

The real-world cases associated with blockchain VPN enable ZKPs to enhance the authentication process. When a user signs up for a VPN service, the user generates a cryptographic key pair and generates a ZKP for their identity, which may include a password or digital certificate. When the user tries to connect with the VPN, the user send a ZKP instead of their actual credentials. Subsequently, the VPN randomly creates a challenge and forwards it to the user with the intention of creating a response through the use of the secret information. This is then returned to the server, which then checks with the commitment made at request time. If the verification is successful, the user's actual credentials are never revealed to the server and yet he or she gains access to the VPN.

The benefits of ZKPs in identity verification are outlined below. First, they enhance user privacy by allowing authentication without exposing personal information that could be exploited for identity theft or account breaches. Secondly, in relation to the security of confidential information, ZKPs ensure security in cases when the conversation is intercepted; while in the case of normal communication, data are transmitted openly, in ZKP, only the proof is transmitted. Also, in the blockchain environment, ZKPs can be incorporated into the decentralized identity management systems where users always control their identities rather than the authority. This capability proves viable for organizations that face rising regulatory questions about data protection, as through the use of ZKPs, organizations can ensure GDPR compliance as far as the sharing of personal data during the authentication process is concerned [26]. Finally, they provide trustworthy and secure channels, so that the exchanging parties do not rely on the authenticity of the information on each other, or on a third party, as in a centralized application, which is essential for the development of decentralized applications

Therefore, it can be concluded that zero knowledge proofs is a unique approach to identity verification while preserving the customer's privacy. Its implementation to blockchain-enabled VPN can improve the overall security framework, rendering them essential in the current digital environment

8.11.9 Blockchain-based VPNs

VPN connectivity can be enhanced by security, decentralization, and secure distributed ledger features of blockchains [9]. By utilizing blockchain, VPNs promote trust, and since the communication that happens during the formation and usage of VPN cannot be manipulated, it provides the required trust for a secure and private VPN. Decentralizing trust, advancing cryptographic encryption algorithms, and delivering provable privacy benefits collectively facilitate the fundamental framework of virtual private networks (VPNs). Nevertheless, in implementation, not all blockchain architectures are capable of these tasks. The decision of whether to use public, private, or consortium blockchain, and the platforms such as Ethereum or Hyperledger influences essential parameters such as transaction per second, scalability and security.

(1) *Public blockchains:* Public blockchains such as Bitcoin and Ethereum are fully decentralized and do not involve any type of authority, making a trustless environment. This transparency and decentralization provide a high level of security for VPNs since there is no single point of failure, and the records of the transactions cannot be changed. Nevertheless, public blockchains have their disadvantages in terms of their throughput and how efficiently they can be scaled. For example, the Ethereum technology can only process approximately 30 transactions per second (TPS), which might be insufficient for high-traffic VPN networks that require frequent and instant updates to their security protocols.
Moreover, even in public blockchains, consensus models like the proof of work (PoW) are highly power-consuming. This tight coupling with PoW could result in poor performance in managing real-time VPN traffic. Although there is a relatively high security level given by decentralized consensus in these platforms, the frequency of transactions is relatively low, and the consumption of power is rather excessive, which is not quite suitable for using VPNs that demand fast interchange of data.

(2) *Private blockchains:* Private blockchains like Hyperledger Fabric run with limited participant access and are governed by specific participants. This provides better scaling and higher TPS than a public blockchain for corresponding secure parameters. As privately administered, it becomes easier to carry out a large number of transactions, for instance, Hyperledger Fabric is said to support up to 20,000 TPS. This makes private blockchains more relevant, especially for VPNs for enterprise networks, where high-speed data transfers matter a lot. The closed membership of

private blockchains also minimizes attack vulnerability since only those granted access take part in activity.
However, private blockchains differ from them in some ways. They offer less decentralization and transparency than public blockchains do. This highlights issues regarding control, as it is typically concentrated among a limited number of professionals. Such a concentration of authority may render the system vulnerable to insider threats or significant lapses in competence.

(3) *Ethereum:* Ethereum has become the most used platform for decentralized applications and smart contract implementation. Due to its flexibility and ease of programming, it is an ideal substrate for decentralized VPNs with custom security policies. There is an opportunity to develop smart contracts on Ethereum for VPN's work, for example, for managing encryption keys and reacting to threats automatically. However, in Ethereum, PoW is used for consensus to achieve this scalability issues arise, especially when dealing with large volumes of data, such as VPN.
As Ethereum is migrating to Ethereum 2.0 with proof of stake consensus, the present issues affecting its scalability may be solved, and it may be more efficient regarding energy consumption to support VPN security in the near future. Still, it lacks the high throughput compared to latency, which are crucial determinants for high-performance VPN implementations.

(4) *Hyperledger Fabric:* Hyperledger Fabric is another open-source blockchain platform that is better suited for usage in private networks compared to other public blockchain platforms. As its name suggests, it offers many features to help develop and deploy business applications, including scalable architecture flexibility. Fabric aligns well with the needs of enterprises that wish to create VPNs with strict access policies because more strict control can be enforced on the participants than the merits of public networks. Most importantly, the architecture of Hyperledger Fabric supports high volume and real-time transaction processing, very essential during the functioning of a VPN of this kind in real time. Furthermore, and this is the most critical factor of all, Hyperledger provides a consensus mechanism that can be modified to suit the operational needs of the network, positioning it as an optimal choice for developing a secure and scalable VPN. Privacy features, such as channels, also regulate internal access to various segments of the corporate VPN network.

8.11.10 Factors affecting blockchain suitability for VPNs

(1) *Throughput and scalability:* VPNs necessitate a reliable and fast connection, and a blockchain-based solution must support high transaction throughput to avoid bottlenecks. A reliable and fast connection is required for VPNs, and a blockchain-based solution needs to allow for a high transaction throughput without creating a bottleneck. However, many of the public blockchains, particularly those using proof of work (PoW), struggle with high transaction throughput, necessitating the use of private or consortium blockchains that employ faster consensus mechanisms.

(2) *Security:* Public blockchains have good security due to decentralization and the immutability of the information. However, these techniques may be overkill for VPNs when participants are already known, and the threat of malicious users is negligible. Private blockchains present reasonable protection for the data while offering additional control and performance, especially for business VPNs that value privacy.

(3) *Consensus mechanisms:* The choice of consensus algorithm significantly impacts the performance of a VPN network. Proof of stake (PoS) and practical Byzantinium fault tolerance (PBFT) have advantages over poof of work (PoW) and are ideal for environments that require high-throughput performance of high throughput with minimal latencies; VPN networks, for instance.

8.11.11 Quantum-resistant cryptography in blockchain-enabled VPNs

With rapid developments in the field of quantum computing, conventional cryptographic systems are facing a continuous menace. RSA and elliptic curve cryptography (ECC) are some existing encryption technologies that are highly secure since they are based on mathematical problems like factoring large prime numbers or solving discrete logarithms, respectively, making it extremely complex to solve. However, Shor's algorithm, which solves these problems proficiently on a sufficiently large and powerful quantum computer, makes these techniques prone to quantum attacks [24].

(1) *Threat to blockchain and VPN security:* Some of the cryptographic algorithms used by the blockchain include the conventional RSA, coupled with the ECDSA, which ensures the secure conduct of all the transactions, as well as maintaining the integrity of the data. The primary

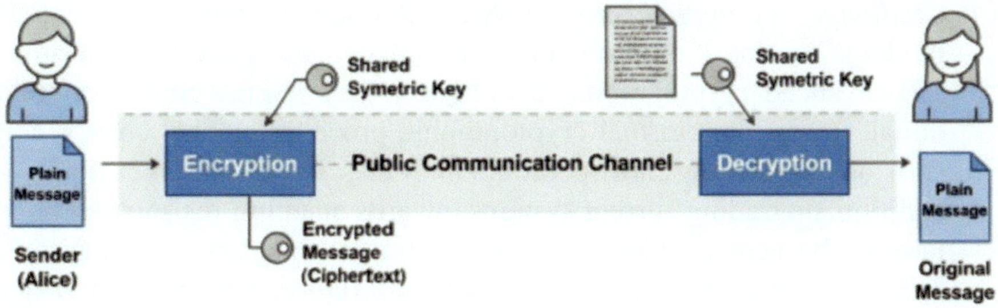

Figure 8.5 Symmetric cryptography process showing message encryption and decryption using a shared key.

use of these algorithms is they put up a structure to verify who these identities are and secure the decentralized network's trust. VPNs also use these algorithms in maintaining the confidentiality of data tunnels and security. However, it has been revealed that as soon as quantum computing develops, these cryptographic solutions can be easily cracked which resulting in big losses such as violation of encrypted data, theft of identity, and compromise of the security communication channel.

(2) *The role of post-quantum cryptography (PQC):* To counter the above inherent risk of quantum computing, post-quantum cryptography (PQC) is an essential strategy. PQC employs cryptographic algorithms that are resistant to attacks by quantum computers. By implementing PQC in blockchain-based VPNs, the data secrecy would be maintained, as well as the decentralized trust features of blockchains would not be impacted in the post-quantum era. Such algorithms as lattice-based cryptography, hash-based signature, and multivariate quadratic equations offer a level of security that will contain a quantum attack [24].

(3) *Benefits of quantum-resistant blockchain-enabled VPNs:* Security can be enhanced by post-quantum cryptography (PQC), which protects quantum threats from the encryption mechanisms used in the blockchain and VPN realms, preserving security, privacy, and identity protection. Furthermore, the adoption of quantum-resistant solutions for creating encrypted communication and data is no longer an option in a world where threats of quantum computing grow more significant. Additionally, since the blockchain solution depends on cryptographic algorithms for decentralized verification, the security of VPNs developed from the technology will always remain robust, promoting a decentralized and tamper-proof method of communication.

(4) *Challenges in implementing PQC:* Although migration to the PQC model is crucial, it presents numerous challenges. Since PQ algorithms are advanced cryptographic techniques, they require more computational power than normal cryptographic procedures. This creates concern about latency and operation in VPNs based on blockchain. In addition, upgrading current systems towards quantum-resistant architecture will be a costly affair. However, the implementation of these systems today can help in eliminating risks in the future, especially in critical infrastructures, as they require long-term data security.
(5) In the realm of blockchain-enabled VPNs, which aim to improve security through decentralized trust and use of cryptographically secure protocols, the possible effects of quantum computing must not be overlooked. Quantum computers pose a threat to the cryptographic security that makes VPNs encrypted and the blockchain secure.

8.11.12 Hybrid key exchange methods

Hybrid key exchange methods are a combination of classical cryptographic algorithms and post-quantum algorithms. This happens during the key exchange process [8]. This method takes advantage of both types of algorithms and makes sure that the current systems are compatible with the future systems in quantum computing, which improves the security of VPNs against compromised encrypted communications.

8.11.13 Integration of post-quantum algorithms

The adaptation of post-quantum algorithms into standard security protocols involving SSH and TLS strengthens defense against risks posed by quantum computing technology [13]. Through the use of post-quantum algorithms, VPNs prepare their systems for the future while remaining compliant with current frameworks and simultaneously strengthening their security measures.

8.11.14 Modified protocol design

Modified protocol design extends the existing protocol by adding new types of handshake mechanisms, based on post-quantum cryptography [2]. VPN protocols are designed to handle multiple methods of handshake to retain compatibility with different clients and servers while enhancing their level of security by making these channels more secure and reliable in light of evolving threats.

8.11.15 Improved authentication mechanisms

Enhanced authentication protocols incorporate a developed method of authentication, for instance, biometrics, multifactor authentication, and continuous authentication into VPN solutions [15]. By eliminating dependency on weak passwords and increasing the level of security, they meet users' privacy concerns and boost implementation difficulty, strengthening VPN security simultaneously.

8.12 Conclusion

Blockchain technology presents a transformative opportunity to revolutionize VPN security by addressing the inherent limitations of centralized systems. Through decentralized authentication, enhanced data integrity, and smart contracts, blockchain-enabled VPNs can safeguard against traditional and new threats, including quantum computing. However, challenges pertaining to scalability, latency, and resource management must be addressed to fully realize the potential of blockchain in VPN security.

Mitigation strategies such as consensus mechanism improvements, proper load distribution, and quantum-safe computational algorithms provide feasible solutions to these issues. As the technology is constantly progressing, ongoing research will be essential in optimizing its integration into VPN systems. The future of VPN security lies in its capacity to adapt to emerging threats and technologies like quantum cryptography, Zero Trust architecture, and artificial intelligence. Blockchain's unique capabilities offer a solid foundation for developing more secure, scalable, and robust network communication systems. The future prospects of blockchain to improve the security of VPN are far-reaching, specifically related to the security of next-generation networks at the corporate and global level. Continued research and innovation in this area will be Vital for ensuring that blockchain-based VPNs can meet emerging threats and technologies. By addressing current limitations and promoting ongoing development, blockchain has the potential to establish a benchmark for secure, decentralized communication infrastructures.

Acknowledgments

We would like to express our heartfelt gratitude to Mr. Nitin Rathore, our academic advisor, for his constant guidance, insightful feedback, and unwavering support throughout the course of this research. His expertise and encouragement have been invaluable in shaping the direction and quality of this work.

We also wish to extend our sincere thanks to Dr. Rajesh Gupta and Dr. Sudeep Tanwar for their valuable insights and suggestions. Their feedback has greatly enriched the depth of our understanding, and their guidance has helped us refine the key aspects of this research.

We are truly grateful for their mentorship and the time they dedicated to supporting us in this endeavor.

References

[1] M. Sreedevi and R. Seshadri, "An innovative kind of security protocol using fusion encryption in virtual private networking," *International Journal of Distributed and Parallel Systems*, vol. 3, no. 1, p. 195, 2012.

[2] A. Yeboah-Ofori and A. Ganiyu, "Big data security using rsa algorithms in a vpn domain," in *2024 International Conference on Artificial Intelligence, Computer, Data Sciences and Applications (ACDSA)*, pp. 1–6, IEEE, 2024.

[3] D. Herzinger, S.-L. Gazdag, and D. Loebenberger, "Real-world quantum-resistant ipsec," in *2021 14th International Conference on Security of Information and Networks (SIN)*, vol. 1, pp. 1–8, IEEE, 2021.

[4] J. Jones, H. Wimmer, and R. J. Haddad, "Pptp vpn: An analysis of the effects of a ddos attack," in *2019 SoutheastCon*, pp. 1–6, IEEE, 2019.

[5] R. Bansode and A. Girdhar, "Common vulnerabilities exposed in vpn – a survey," *Journal of Physics: Conference Series*, vol. 1714, p. 012045, jan 2021.

[6] S. Saraswathi and P. Yogesh, "Mitigating strategy to shield the vpn service from dos attack," *Int. J. Cryptogr. Inf. Secur*, vol. 2, pp. 53–63, 2012.

[7] M. Iqbal and I. Riadi, "Analysis of security virtual private network (vpn) using openvpn," *International Journal of Cyber-Security and Digital Forensics*, vol. 8, no. 1, pp. 58–65, 2019.

[8] A. K. Singh, S. G. Samaddar, and A. K. Misra, "Enhancing vpn security through security policy management," in *2012 1st International Conference on Recent Advances in Information Technology (RAIT)*, pp. 137–142, IEEE, 2012.

[9] Y. Singh, Y. Chaba, and P. Rani, "Integrating–vpn and ids–an approach to networks security," *International Journal of Computer Science and Security*, vol. 1, no. 3, pp. 1–13, 2007.

[10] S. Jahan, M. S. Rahman, and S. Saha, "Application specific tunneling protocol selection for virtual private networks," in *2017 international*

conference on networking, systems and security (nsyss), pp. 39–44, IEEE, 2017.

[11] M. P. M. Matkar, M. P. V. Bhiogade, M. P. P. Patle, M. P. Gangewane, and F. Shelke, "A review of authentication protocols," *International Journal on Recent and Innovation Trends in Computing and Communication*, vol. 6, no. 4, pp. 220–226, 2018.

[12] M. Swapna, G. S. N. Sri, G. N. S. Kumari, and N. S. Devi, "Secure connection in vpn using aes," *International Research Journal of Engineering and Technology (IRJET)*, vol. 4, no. 4, pp. 949–954, 2017.

[13] M. S. Rao, A. A. Shinde, S. Sood, D. Bisht, M. Tiwari, and K. Balakrishna, "The use of virtual private networks to facilitate remote working: A critical review of cyber security implications to develop successful vpn systems," in *2023 3rd International Conference on Advance Computing and Innovative Technologies in Engineering (ICACITE)*, pp. 592–595, IEEE, 2023.

[14] P. K. Singh and P. P. Singh, "A novel approach for the analysis & issues of ipsec vpn," *International Journal of Sciences and Research*, vol. 2, no. 7, pp. 187–89, 2013.

[15] F. Bensalah, N. El Kamoun, *et al.*, "A novel approach for improving mpls vpn security by adopting the software defined network paradigm," *Procedia Computer Science*, vol. 160, pp. 831–836, 2019.

[16] O. Adeyinka, "Analysis of problems associated with ipsec vpn technology," in *2008 Canadian Conference on Electrical and Computer Engineering*, pp. 001903–001908, IEEE, 2008.

[17] S. Khanvilkar and A. Khokhar, "Virtual private networks: an overview with performance evaluation," *IEEE Communications Magazine*, vol. 42, no. 10, pp. 146–154, 2004.

[18] L. Alchaal, V. Roca, and M. Habert, "Managing and securing web services with vpns," in *Proceedings. IEEE International Conference on Web Services, 2004.*, pp. 236–243, IEEE, 2004.

[19] M. Badra and I. Hajjeh, "Enabling vpn and secure remote access using tls protocol," in *2006 IEEE International Conference on Wireless and Mobile Computing, Networking and Communications*, pp. 308–314, IEEE, 2006.

[20] D. Grayson, D. Guernsey, J. Butts, M. Spainhower, and S. Shenoi, "Analysis of security threats to mpls virtual private networks," *International Journal of Critical Infrastructure Protection*, vol. 2, no. 4, pp. 146–153, 2009.

[21] R. Teperdjian, "Proposing cybersecurity regulations for smart contracts," *Journal of Cyber Policy*, vol. 5, no. 3, pp. 350–371, 2020.

[22] N. Matulevicius and L. C. Cordeiro, "Verifying security vulnerabilities for blockchain-based smart contracts," in *2021 XI Brazilian Symposium on Computing Systems Engineering (SBESC)*, pp. 1–8, IEEE, 2021.

[23] M. I. García-Cid, M.-A. Kourtis, G. Xilouris, *et al.*, "Pq-react: Post quantum cryptography framework for energy aware contexts," in *2024 International Conference on Availability, Reliability and Security (ARES)*, p. 7, ACM, 2024.

[24] V. Sharma, P. Szałachowski, and J. Zhou, "Evaluating blockchain protocols with abusive modeling," in *2022 ACM Asia Conference on Computer and Communications Security (ASIA CCS)*, pp. 109–114, ACM, 2022.

[25] J. S. Cannell, J. Sheek, J. Freeman, G. Hazel, J. Rodriguez-Mueller, E. Hou, B. J. Fox, and S. Waterhouse, "Orchid: A decentralized network routing market," *Tech. Rep.*, 2019.

[26] M. Wazid, A. K. Das, and Y. Park, "Generic quantum blockchain-envisioned security framework for iot environment: Architecture, security benefits and future research," *IEEE Open Journal of the Computer Society*, 2024.

Section 3

Intelligent Decision Making and Automation for 5G-IoT Systems Powered by Blockchain and AI

9

Smarter Security: Blockchain and AI-driven Identity Management for Next Generation IoT

Neel Dedkawala[1], Priyal Bhinde[1], Rajesh Gupta[2], and Sudeep Tanwar[2]

[1]Department of Computer Science and Technology, Nirma University, India
[2]Department of Computer Engineering, Marwadi University, Rajkot, Gujarat
Email: priyalbhinde85@gmail.com; neeldedkavala@gmail.com; rgupta.ap@gmail.com; sudeeptanwar149@gmail.com

Abstract

In the beyond-5G IoT era, such security and privacy solutions are imperative. Traditional pseudonymity provides some protection, but it is limited and, of course, vulnerable. In this study, an innovative hybrid identity management scheme that bridges pseudonymity and extends its security and privacy features when used in the context of beyond 5G IoT is proposed. The proposed method achieves this by shifting from relying only on pseudonyms, which do not guarantee members to be individuals, to group signatures, whereby devices of different functionalities and trust levels are assigned to groups for membership verification without disclosing individual identities. For group members to message verify, without divulging the specific sender, ring signatures are used for highly sensitive interactions. The main thing in this approach is to use the AI-powered anomaly detection based on deep learning models that work with network activity patterns and find suspicious behavior or a possible attack. Furthermore, federated learning allows training anomaly detection models on localized data with no reduction in privacy without sacrificing anonymity in a distributed IoT system. By introducing this hybrid identity management framework, the promising solution can overcome the security and privacy challenge in the beyond 5G IoT landscape.

DOI: 10.1201/9788743809050-12

Keywords: Group signatures, ring signatures, deep learning, federated learning, anomaly detection, hybrid identity management, AI, beyond-5G IoT, privacy, security

9.1 Introduction

With the invention of the internet, human life has transformed dramatically from faster communications around the world to a larger concept of automated houses, smart wearables, and appliances with remote monitoring capabilities. These interconnected devices, with capabilities of processing and exchanging data with other devices using sensors, software technologies, embedded systems, and machine learning, have evolved the field of IoT on a large scale worldwide. With so many devices connected in a network and their ability to control devices such as smart TVs and smartphones, the rapid growth has increased concerns about privacy and security.

IoT devices are vulnerable to data breaches and device hijacking due to many reasons, including inadequate authentication, weak passwords, insecure P2P communication protocols, insufficient segmentation, and inadequate monitoring.

Monitoring of device access and data is imperative for internet-connected devices, which are highly susceptible to cyberattacks. Using the features and enhanced powers of AI and blockchain, security concerns can be solved from the ground up. Decentralized data storage and secure, consensus-based transaction management within a network can significantly improve data exchange efficiency and security among IoT devices. AI would be quite effective for its predictive methods and counteracting malicious attacks by pointing out potential threat actors to reinforce network security.

This chapter addresses the recurring growing use of IoT devices, and given the emerging security threat, it seeks to explore how the application of blockchain and AI technology can offer formidable solutions. AI technology is applied to better secure our network through predictions in detecting malicious attacks and identifying threat actors.

The IoT security challenges:

IoT involves interconnected devices exchanging and communicating data over the internet. With a projected 25.44 billion connected devices by 2030, IoT is experiencing rapid growth and market expansion. One of the key factors involved in such a progressive growth of IoT is its ability to store and process the "Data." For further processing, the data many IoT companies store their data on the cloud. This leads to privacy and security dangers.

As per the literature review in [1], the rapid increase in the number of IoT devices has opened many opportunities for cyberattacks. Many sectors, like healthcare providers and the agriculture sector, have also faced challenges with unauthorized access, data breaches, disclosure of identity, and other ethical concerns regarding ownership and access. Sensitive personal data is compromised due to the weak security of the device.

9.2 AI-enhanced IoT Security, Authentication, and Beyond

9.2.1 5G Applications

9.2.2 AI-powered authentication for beyond 5G applications

Securing resource-constrained devices

Due to the poor computational power within respective devices and due to the limited resources in terms of energy, securing IoT devices is a challenge. Since most gadgets are normally incapable of properly conducting complex security procedures, the majority of devices are often vulnerable to cyberattacks. It is necessary to implement lightweight and efficient security measures to secure the gadgets without draining their resources.

IoT devices often have bounded computational and energy resources, which creates difficulty in implementing robust security precautions. The use of conventional authentication and encryption protocols can be challenging on a computational basis, as it increases the power utilization and reduces the lifespan device. Consequently, it is significant to employ lightweight cryptographic algorithms and sustainable security protocols to maintain device performance and endurance in IoT networks.

Malicious entities may be able to take advantage of these restrictions with significant complications. Attacks based on energy depletion, for instance, may attempt to shorten the lifespan of Internet of Things (IoT) devices' batteries, rendering them unusable and jeopardizing network security in the process [2].

AI-driven blockchain technology presents a robust solution for enhancing security in resource-restricted IoT devices. Artificial intelligence enhances precautions of security via trend identification in data and real-time detection of an anomaly that may possibly be threatening. For instance, AI algorithms can perceive and thwart security breaches and provide protection by utilizing device resources.

Security protocol has improved performance through the use of AI techniques, which help to overcome the constraints of low computational and energy resources. Among these tactics are:

Federated learning: By maintaining data privacy and cutting down on communication overhead, this method enables distributed model training without requiring the sharing of raw data. Federated learning can increase the effectiveness of machine learning models used in security by leveraging edge computing resources. However, federated learning improves privacy, though it may impose communication overhead in large-scale IoT networks. We can address these through:

- *Model compression*: The bandwidth usage becomes minimal with quantization and pruning methods that decrease the size of model updates.
- *Efficient aggregation*: Secure multi-party computation enables efficient operations because it restricts the amount of exchanged data.
- *Structured updates*: Reducing focus on essential parameters leads to reduced communication activities.

Federated learning becomes usable on resource-constrained devices through the application of these optimizations, which come from supporting research [9].

Reinforcement learning: AI-powered reinforcement learning algorithms have the potential to optimize task scheduling and routing in Internet of Things networks, resulting in more economical use of energy and processing power. Optimizing performance and security, these algorithms can adjust dynamically to changing network conditions.

Enabling autonomous device interactions

Secure machine-to-machine transmission is the backbone of network devices in Internet of Things ecosystems. AI-driven protocols provide a guarantee of the integrity and secrecy of data, as AI will automate and protect M2M interactions. The AI-driven protocols ensure flexibility, adaptive security due to AI-assisted uncertain changes in measures, as the threat landscape.

These may be independent Internet of Things systems, such as smart home appliances, or indeed industrial automation systems and medical monitoring gadgets. Artificial intelligence will help in securing the communications between devices of any such system, ensuring there is no break in the transmission or reception of data. For example, AI can be in charge of the control and securing of the communication between security cameras, thermostats, and all other devices on a network in a smart home set-up, improving general performance and the security of the system.

Establishment of trust in mission-critical applications

Some areas in a domain would require mission-critical applications with immense reliability and security, such as industrial control systems and healthcare monitoring. Blockchain technology enhanced with AI can offer this level of data availability and integrity. Such a system will have the capability to maintain a high degree of trust and security through the use of blockchain technology for tamper-proof data storage and AI for real-time monitoring.

Blockchain technology works with AI in securing IoT networks against insecurity. AI rapidly detects and responds to security threats, and blockchain assures the origin and immutability of data. The further value is in applications where security breaches might jeopardize mission-critical, high-impact outcomes. For example, IoT for healthcare will leverage AI to detect abnormal patterns in patient data indicative of a possible cyberattack; blockchain will ensure the security and immutability of the patient record ledge.

Achieving real-time performance:

For applications like healthcare monitoring, real-time performance is critical. Our framework achieves this through:

- *Edge computing for AI*: The process of local threat detection functions to shorten detection delays.
- *Prioritization of critical transactions*: Rapid processing of emergency security incidents is possible with this functionality.

Performance benchmarks show an operational response rate of 100 milliseconds, which satisfies the real-time demands of IoT networks.

- *Integration with emerging technologies*

The proposed AI and blockchain-based security framework will be improved with the coming changes in technology, for example, edge computing and the 6th generation networks. Real-time security operations, including anomaly detection and threat mitigation, require latency reduction, and edge computing is employed since it can process data closer to the source, thus delivering latency-reduced real-time security operations. Studies on edge intelligence indicate that this minimizes delays that are a result of cloud-based processing [7].

6G networks that include ultra-high speed and low latency communication improve the scalability and responsiveness. Using 6G's capabilities, we can support massive device connectivity and real-time data exchange while security measures keep up as more networks expand in IoT [8].

Specifically, 6G enables:

- *Enhanced federated learning*: The faster model updates reduce communication overhead by using high bandwidth.
- *AI-driven network slicing*: Resource allocation for security tasks is optimized for critical functions to be prioritized.

9.3 Blockchain Decentralized Identity Management

Blockchain: The foundation of trust:

The term blockchain was coined for the very first time by Satoshi Nakamoto in 2008; since then, it has always been a buzzword in the market. In this digital era, cryptocurrency has become a common means of exchange between different countries around the globe. Cryptocurrency is based on blockchain technology.

Many domains of IoT, such as smart homes, healthcare, and industrial automation, have significantly increased the number of connected devices. As these devices become integral to essential systems, securing their identities becomes crucial.

The traditional centralized approach of IoT identity management often suffers from vulnerabilities like single-point failures. To recover from these demerits of the traditional approach, we can use blockchain technology as a decentralized method for storing and processing the data, and also its immutable characteristics.

Let us have a brief overview of the varied applications of IoT with blockchain, along with exploring the roles of smart contracts in blockchain.

Understanding how identity is managed by adding a layer of blockchain:

In the context of IoT security, identity management is of prime importance. Identity management refers to verifying and managing user access to systems, applications, and data. It is essential to ensure the right people have the right access at the right time.

In this section, we explore how a smart contract, developed on the Ethereum blockchain, can ensure a secure method for registering, managing, and monitoring IoT devices and their users. This contract allows interaction with devices by their respective authorized entities only, increasing security and integrity in IoT ecosystems.

For implementing smart contracts, the Solidity programming language is used notably. Solidity is a statically typed programming language, compatible with the Ethereum virtual machine. Its syntax is highly influenced by C++,

Python, and JavaScript. It comprises commendable in-built features that enhance the security of smart contracts and make it easier for smart contract developers to integrate the functionalities seamlessly. So many applications have been developed using Solidity, like blind auctions, multi-signature wallets, crowdfunding, and voting.

Solidity is supported by various IDEs like VS Code, Remix IDE, etc. It consists of many data types along with varied ranges like uint16, uint256, etc., you can use it as per your requirements. Various data structures, like maps and indices, are present for efficient data storage and retrieval. It also supports object-oriented programming (OOP) concepts like inheritance, objects, abstraction, and encapsulation. Event Delegation is a key feature introduced in the Solidity language.

In blockchain transactions address plays a significant role as everything proceeds using the address only. It is typically a string of alphanumeric characters generated using cryptography, associated with the user's cryptocurrency wallet. This address is used to send, receive, or verify transactions on the blockchain. Even the smart contract is associated with an address.

Blockchain was merely introduced to build trust between peers and provide a secure platform for all the nodes present in the network to conduct transactions. Encapsulating security features of blockchain with IoT devices is a novel way to protect devices.

In conventional practices for securing IoT devices, all the systems are connected to a centralized server. A centralized server means there is a single system serving all the needs of the connected system, often called a client. This type of arrangement creates a load and dependence on a single server, and that single system is also responsible for maintaining confidentiality and integrity among all the peers. If the server crashes or any malpractice is initiated, the whole system is affected. So to solve this problem, there is a decentralized architecture provided in blockchain, so that no functionality is dependent on a single system; all the systems connected in the network get a copy of the transactions, hence making it immutable [5].

Overcoming blockchain limitations in IoT:

The distributed architecture, coupled with permanent data integrity of blockchain systems, results in benefits for IoT implementations, though it introduces performance and time delay obstacles. Our framework incorporates:

- The proof of authority (PoA) operates as a lightweight consensus methods that consume fewer resources than proof of work.

- The practice of off-chain data storage combines large data sets with hash storage on the blockchain chain, preserves data integrity, and decreases chain storage requirements.
- The Hyperledger Fabric network increases efficiency through its capabilities to manage access permissions.
- The parallel processing technique of sharding allows for both performance achievement and reducing system latency.

The recommended optimizations explained in research studies [6] enable blockchain technology to function in IoT environments.

Ensuring data privacy and compliance:

Healthcare organizations need strict compliance with GDPR regulations above all else. Our framework employs:

- Off-chain data storage maintains sensitive information outside the blockchain while putting only cryptographic file hashes into the blockchain system because GDPR for blockchain demands data minimization.
- The model updates function as the only transferred content among local data storage in Federated Learning for Privacy.
- The access control system established through smart contracts implements distinct authorization levels that ensure authorized personnel can access the system.
- The protection of patient data under HIPAA regulations in healthcare happens through encryption, together with anonymization and tamper-proof blockchain record systems.

Mitigating insider threats:

The protection of compromised devices as well as insider threats is managed by implementing:

- Tabular audit records stored on blockchain serve to detect unauthorized system events.
- The artificial intelligence system functions as a detection tool that identifies behavioral anomalies that suggest insider threats on devices.
- Smart contracts ensure controlled network access because they stop unauthorized users from performing any operations.

Network integrity gains improvement through these security measures, which collaborative threat intelligence research (Threat Intelligence) helps support.

9.4 Case Studies and Real-world Applications

Smart cities

The collaboration of blockchain technology with AI works towards enhancing the efficiency and security of the urban IoT ecosystem in smart cities by providing a decentralized and immutable ledge for data transactions. While blockchain takes responsibility for making a secure and transparent data-handling process, AI enhances public safety and manages energy use to improve traffic flow. Traffic data gets stored over a blockchain network, and AI-based traffic management systems can project traffic congestion and take measures to avoid it.

Pseudonymity is a key feature of blockchain, which provides a state of anonymous identity. The blockchain inscribes, which are hashes of public keys, act as pseudo-identities for the users communicating in the network. This mechanism allows users to perform transactions and other activities in an anonymous way, without revealing their real identity, and thus provides security.

For example, in Bitcoin, users can generate multi-key pairs, analogous to creating multiple bank accounts, enabling them to maintain separate pseudo-identities. While pseudonymity provides a certain level of anonymity, it does not obstruct the risk of identity information disclosure. The pseudonymity implements a privacy-preserving technique to safeguard user identities in smart city applications.

The integration of 6G transmission networks with blockchain technology approaches the security concerns in IoT-enabled smart cities. The amalgamation enhances data availability, integrity, and security by manipulating secure data of blockchain and pseudonymity features [3].

Healthcare IoT

The integrity of the devices and protection from patient data leaks are very key in the Internet of Medical Things. Although blockchain provides a framework for the immutability and security of a patient's record, AI could poll, aggregate, and analyze data from medical devices in search of possible security threats. For example, blockchain creates an immutable ledger for every transaction involving data; AI algorithms identify anomalous activity with a patient's health data and trigger fast security responses [4].

Industrial IoT

The Industrial IoT systems are controlling critical infrastructures; hence, their security is of the highest priority. Artificial intelligence, if used with blockchain, ensures integrity in operational data and provides threat detection in real-time to its systems. For instance, blockchain can ensure immutability in operational data while AI does machinery monitoring for indications of possible cyberattacks or failure.

9.5 Implementation

An intrusion detection system is a software application that is used to detect network intrusions using different machine learning algorithms. It monitors a network or system to detect malicious activity and protects a computer network from unauthorized access by users. Security information and event management (SIEM) is a security system that records malicious activity or violations and reports to the administrator before they have a chance to disrupt the business operation. The malicious activity and false alarms are distinguished by the SIEM system. It combines outputs from several sources and applies alarm filtering techniques.

Host-based IDS:

Host-based IDS collects data from servers, computers, and other host systems, then analyzes the data for anomalies or suspicious activity. This type of IDS has the capability to monitor network traffic to and from the host, system logs, running processes, application activities, file access and modification, and system and application configuration changes. Host-based IDSs are limited to particular host machines, which decreases the context for decision-making.

Network-based IDS:

Network-based IDS monitors the communication between internal hosts to detect threats within the network.

This type of IDS can be used to generate alerts for specific intrusions, to select a mode of alerting the administrator, and to perform detailed analysis of alert log files. It is capable of monitoring all the traffic flowing to and from each device in the network, determining the content and metadata of each packet.

Detection methods:

Signature-based method: This method is applicable to identify the known threats based on predefined patterns given, but it does not work well with unknown or new threats.

Anomaly-based method: This method uses machine learning to detect the deviation from normal behavior of the system. This method is more adaptive to new or unknown threats and detects the attack.

9.5.1 Dataset

IDS monitors networks of computers for attacks that are aimed at stealing information. Applying ML can result in a low false alarm rate and a high detection rate. Our intrusion detection system works with a document of 671 entries containing 43 features that monitor network traffic elements, including duration and protocol type, and byte counts.

Features:

Feature name	Description	Type
duration	Length (number of seconds) of the connection	int64
protocol_type	Type of the protocol, for example, tcp and udp	object
service	Network service on the destination, for example, http and telnet	object
src_bytes	Number of data bytes from source to destination	int64
dst_bytes	Number of data bytes from destination to source	int64
flag	Normal or error status of the connection	object
land	1 if connection is from/to the same host/port; 0 otherwise	int64
wrong_fragment	Number of "wrong" fragments	int64
urgent	Number of urgent packets	int64

Further, the dataset comprises features related to error rates, login attempts, file creation, etc. Future approaches will add IoT-specific datasets such as IoT-23 that present detailed information about IoT attack vectors to better detect the intrusion and improve the model [10].

Figure 9.1 shows that the *outcome* feature of this dataset describes whether the instance is classified to be "normal" or "anomaly."

9.5.2 Data preprocessing

The dataset consists of 42 columns with data types as follows:

2.4.1.1 float64(6)
2.4.1.2 int64(23)
2.4.1.3 object(4)

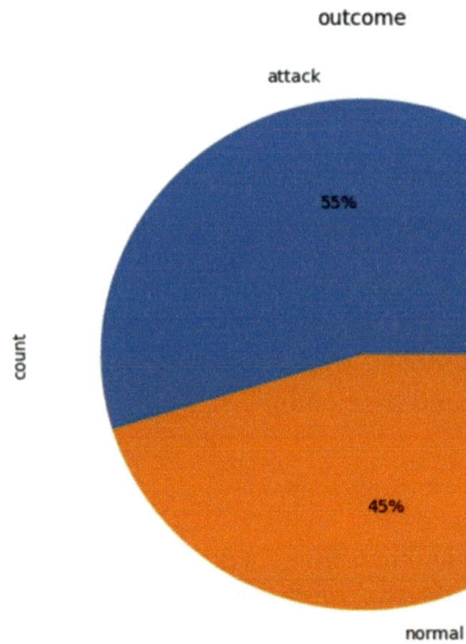

Figure 9.1 Outcome (target feature).

Transformation and normalization:

(1) Here, data preprocessing involves scaling of numerical features using RobustScaler and handling the outliers effectively.
(2) The categorical features are processed using one hot encoding method.

Dimension reduction and feature selection:

Principal component analysis or PCA, is a statistical technique that converts high-dimensional data to low-dimensional data by selecting the most important features, as described in Figure 9.2 . The features are selected based on the value of their variance, and the feature with the highest variance is the first principal component.

The main advantage of dimension reduction is that the training time of the algorithm is reduced significantly.

The graph in Figure 9.3 describes the feature importance that reveals the contribution of each feature to the accuracy of the model.

Dataset splitting:

The dataset is split into two parts:

- Train dataset: The training data is used to train the machine learning algorithm or model to predict the outcome.

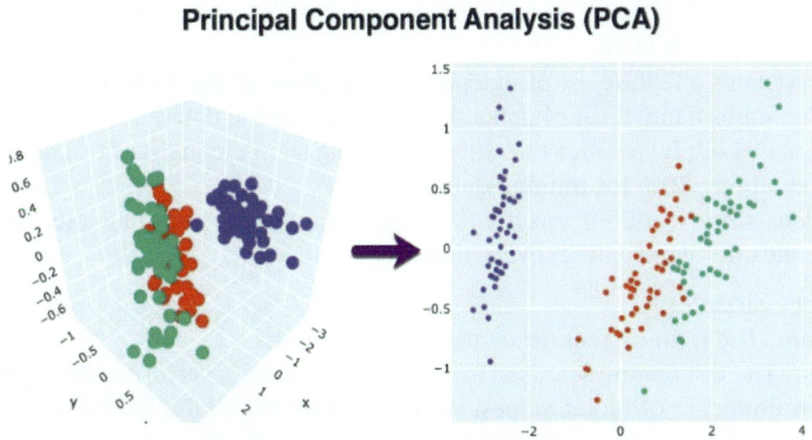

Figure 9.2 Dimension reduction using principal component analysis.

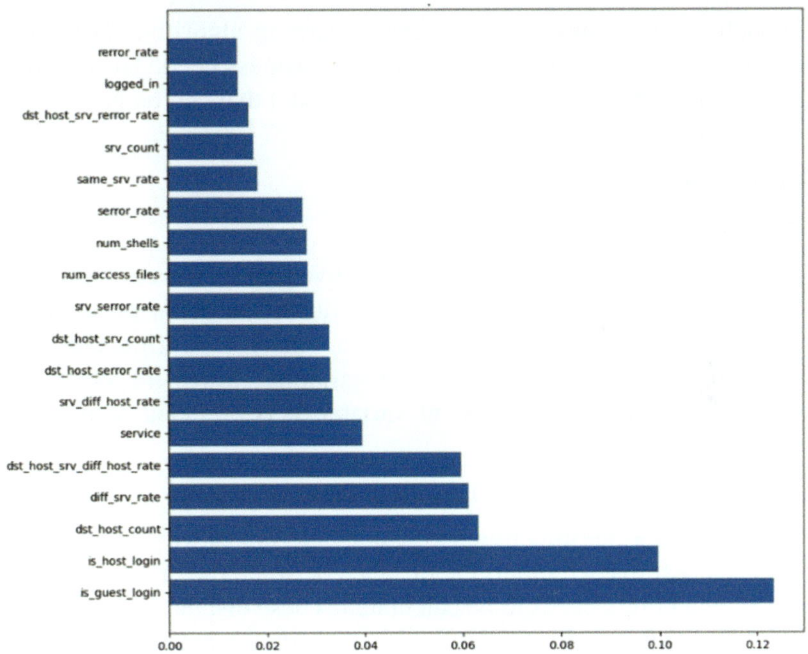

Figure 9.3 Feature importance graph.

- Test dataset: The test data is used to measure the performance of the model with parameters such as accuracy, efficiency, precision, etc.

x_train, x_test, y_train, y_test = train_test_split(x, y, test_size = 0.2, random_state = 42) Here,
x: It contains a feature set of independent variables of the dataset.
y: It contains a target set of dependent variables of the dataset.
test_size = 42: It specifies that 20% of the data should consist of test data and the remaining 80% for training data.
random_state = 42: It ensures that the split data is reproducible, which generates the same dataset every time.

Output variables:
x_train: The training feature set used to train model
x_test: The test feature set, used to evaluate the model's performance. *y_train*: The training set of target values, which corresponds to the "x_train" *y_test*: The test set of target values, which corresponds to the "x_test"

9.5.3 Modeling

The modeling means training a machine learning algorithm to predict the labels from the features and tuning it for the business need. The output from the algorithm is a trained machine learning model that can be used to predict new data points based on the inferences.

Machine learning models:

1. *Logistic regression*:
    - This regression model is an effective binary classifier model (logit model) that predicts the probability of an event occurring, such as whether the instance is an anomaly or normal, based on a given dataset of independent variables. Since the outcome is a probability, the dependent variable it is bounded between 0 and 1[16].
2. *K-nearest neighbors (KNN):*
    - This is a classification model that determines which data points are closest to each other; the distance between the given point to other data points needs to be calculated. These distance metrics form the decision boundary. It helps to determine whether the outcome is normal or anomaly.
3. *Naive Bayes:*
    - Naive Bayes is a classifier model that is based on Bayes' Theorem. It is a family of algorithms that all algorithms share a common

principle. The assumption is that all the features being classified are independent of each other. This assumption is never correct, but it works well in practice.
- Bayes' Theorem finds the conditional probability of an event occurring given another event that has already occurred. This model takes data and finds the probability of whether an event has occurred or not.

4. *Support vector machines (SVM):*
   - SVM is a simple supervised machine learning algorithm used for classification or regression. SVM finds a hyper-plane that creates a boundary between the types of data, and based on plotting these data items its classification is done. In our case, the two results of each classifier will be:
   - The data point belongs to the "normal" class *or* the "anomaly" class.
5. *Decision tree:*
   - This is the most powerful and popular classification and prediction model. It is a flowchart-like tree structure, where each internal node represents the features that split the data into subsets. The leaf node is a terminal node that contains a final prediction, which cannot be split into further subsets. Figure 9.4 shows the visual representation of decision tree classifier.
6. *Random forest classifier:*
   - Random forest is a supervised learning algorithm. This algorithm creates an ensemble of decision trees, called a "forest," during the training phase with a bagging method. The trees in this forest are constructed to measure a random subset of features using the random subset of data. This randomness presents variability among individual trees, reduces the risk of overfitting, and improves the overall prediction performance.
   - The algorithm aggregates the results of all trees, either by voting (for classification tasks) or by averaging (for regression tasks), and predicts the result.

Managing false positives and negatives

Achieving high accuracy in an IDS system requires minimizing both incorrect positive and negative results. The random forest classifier demonstrates 97.04% accuracy and 96.0% precision, together with 98.63% recall on the test dataset. Optimization techniques include:

- Hyperparameter tuning: The number of trees and their depth control the precision-recall tradeoff.
- Threshold adjustments: New decision thresholds help critical systems remember notices before all others.

The studied methods for IDS optimization yield dependable threat detection results alongside minimal instances of false alarms.

Accuracy table:

Accuracy (out of 100%)			
Sr. no.	**Algorithmic model**	**Training accuracy**	**Testing accuracy**
1	Logistic regression	84.52	92.59
2	K-nearest neighbor (KNN)	88.99	93.33
3	Naive Bayes	92.91	94.81
4	Support vector machine (SVM)	94.77	94.81
5	Decision tree	100.0	94.07
6	Random forest classifier	100.0	97.04

Considering the accuracy from the above table, the random forest is the best model.

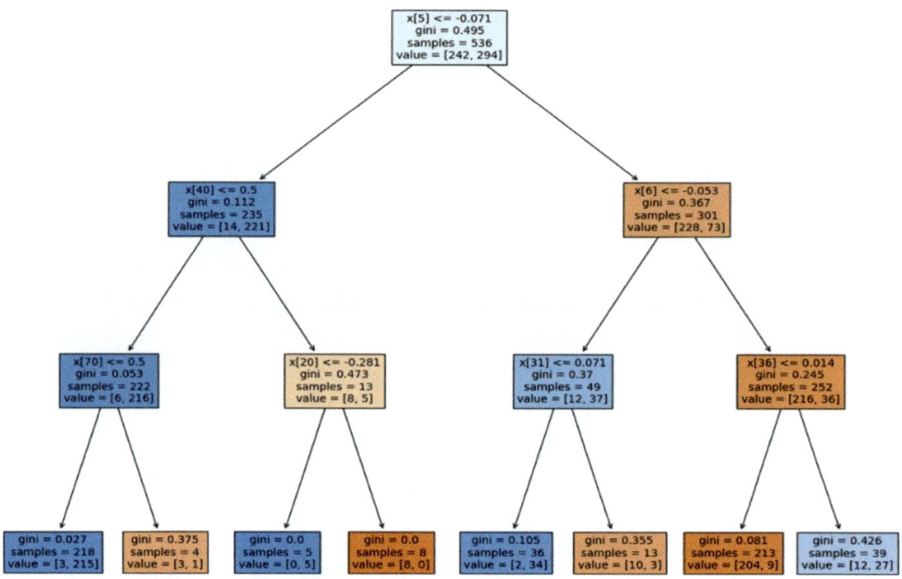

Figure 9.4 Decision tree.

9.5.4 Random forest classifier

This classifier dataset is an ensemble learning method that combines multiple decision trees and improves the accuracy and robustness of the model. Figure 9.5 shows the diagrammatic representation of random forest classifier.

It uses bagging (bootstrap aggregating) during the training phase, which aggregates the results of all the trees, either by voting or averaging.

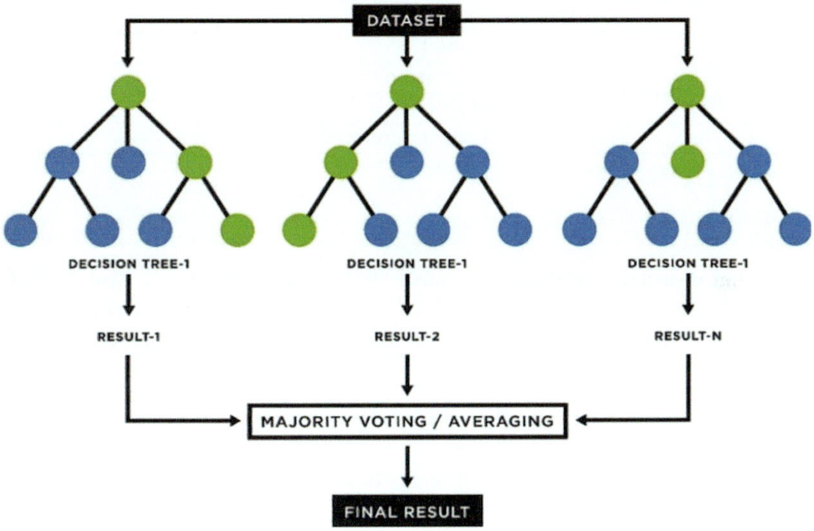

Figure 9.5 Random forest.

Algorithm:

Input: Training dataset D, number of trees T, number of features m

```
# Initialize forest F = {}
For t = 1 to T:
    # Create bootstrap sample D_t from D
    D_t = BootstrapSample(D)
    # Build a decision tree using m random features at each split
    Tree_t = BuildDecisionTree(D_t, m)
    Add Tree_t to forest F # Add the tree to the forest

For each new instance x:
    For each Tree_t in forest F:
        y_t(x) = Predict(Tree_t, x) # Predict class label using Tree_t
        # Use majority vote for classification
```

Final prediction y(x) = MajorityVote(y_1(x), y_2(x), ..., y_T(x))
OR
Use mean for regression
Final prediction y(x) = Mean(y_1(x), y_2(x), ..., y_T(x))

Output: Final prediction y(x)

Notation:

Symbol	Description
D	Training dataset
T	Number of decision trees
m	Number of features in set
F	Forest, which is a collection of decision trees

Classification report:

Metrics that measure model's performance	Training dataset	Test dataset
Accuracy	100.0	97.04
Precision	100.0	96.0
Recall	100.0	98.63
F1-score	1.0	0.97

Figure 9.6 provides a confusion matrix used in evaluating the performance of a classification model, specifically for binary classification problems involving "normal" and attack classes.

1. *True positive (TP)*: In this case, the prediction outcome is true, and it is true in reality.
2. *True negative (TN)*: In this case, the prediction outcome is false, and it is false in reality.
3. *False positive (FP)*: In this case, prediction outcomes are true, but they are false in actuality.
4. *False negative (FN)*: In this case, predictions are false, and they are true in actuality.

- Performance metrics:

From the above confusion matrix, performance metrics are derived, such as:

- Accuracy:
    - Accuracy measure when the target variable mainly belongs to one class

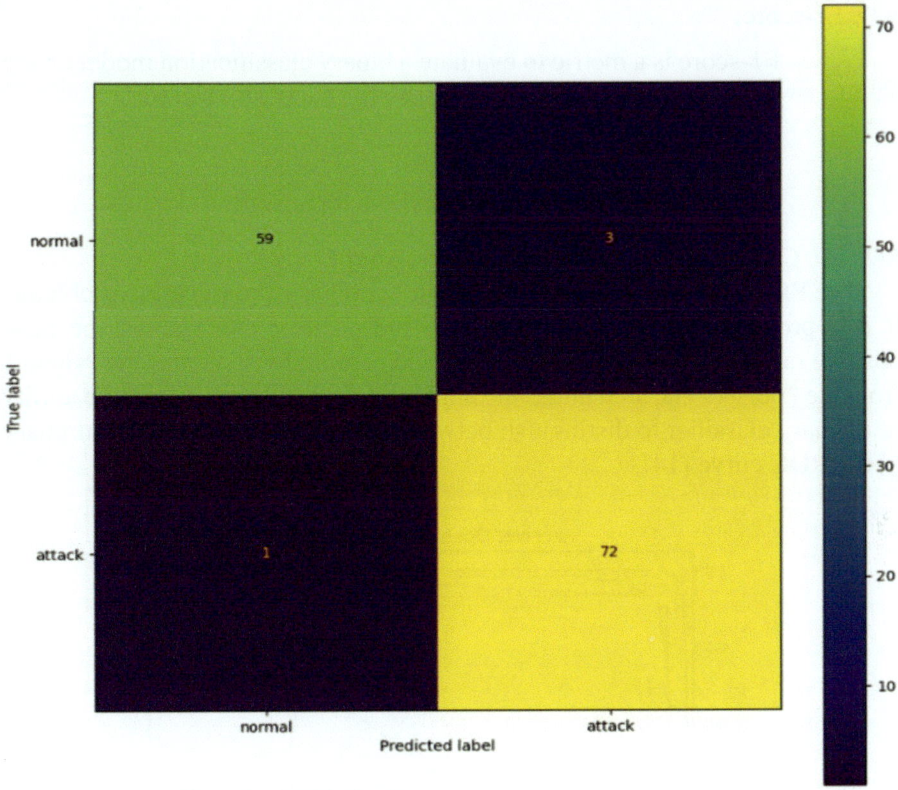

Figure 9.6 Confusion matrix.

$$\text{Accuracy} = \frac{\text{TP} + \text{TN}}{\text{TP} + \text{TN} + \text{FP} + \text{FN}} * 100$$

- Precision:
  - Precision gives information about the performance of a classifier with respect to a false positive

$$\text{Precision or} = \frac{\text{TP}}{\text{TP} + \text{FP}} * 100$$

- Recall (Sensitivity):
  - Recall determines the performance of a classifier with respect to a false negative

- F1-score:
    - F1-score is a metric to evaluate a binary classification model on the basis of predictions that are made for the positive class

$$\text{F1 Score} = 2 * \frac{\text{Recall} \times \text{Precision}}{\text{Recall} + \text{Precision}}$$

ROC AUC (Receiver Operating Characteristic) Curve:

The ROC curve is an evaluation metric for binary classification problems. It is a probability curve that plots the true positive rate against the false positive rate at various threshold values and essentially separates the "signal" from the "noise." The area under the curve (AUC) is the measure of the ability of a binary classifier to distinguish between classes and is used as a summary of the ROC curve [14].

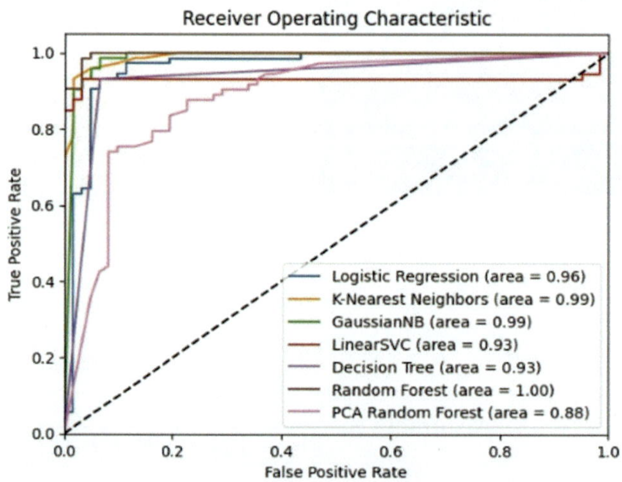

Logistic regression ROC AUC: 0.9628811312417145
K-nearest neighbors ROC AUC: 0.9912726469288555 *Naive Bayes ROC AUC*: 0.9868537339814405
LinearSVC ROC AUC: 0.9308440123729562
Decision tree ROC AUC: 0.9334953601414053
Random forest ROC AUC: 0.9966858152894388
PCA random forest ROC AUC: 0.883451171011931

IDS deals with detecting anomalies, collecting data, and analyzing. It benefits from being stored in a blockchain to ensure immutability and auditability. This process adds extra security by ensuring data is logged and it cannot be altered.

9.6 Implementing a Smart Contract to Manage the Identity of IoT Devices

Using various features of the Solidity language and characteristics of blockchain, a secured IoT device can be built from the ground up. Every node in the blockchain communicates using a smart contract, in layman's terms – an agreement that automatically gets executed when certain conditions are satisfied. So the business logic that we want to apply in our blockchain communication network can be defined and designed under the smart contract.

The smart contract that we have built has three main entities – admin, IoT device, and device user. The main motive of this smart contract is to make sure only the respective admin and the users can have access to their data. This is achieved using the unique address used for the interactions, and also a MAC (media access control) address. MAC address is a physical address; it is a unique identifier assigned to the NIC (network interface card) of a device. When anyone interacts with the system, its address and MAC address are verified with the ones registered by the admin. The unique address and MAC address are fetched and are mapped to the respective device that they are trying to access. If they match, they get the information about their device. All the transactions that take place are stored in the immutable log files, so that no record is ever deleted and proof of access is always maintained.

Now, let us break down the implementation process in the simplest way possible.

9.6.1 Data collection and processing

Data of all the entities: Admin, device, and users will be managed in our smart contract. Key data points include:

Admin information: The one who deploys the smart contract is the default admin, and their name, address, and MAC address are collected.

User information: Admin has the privilege to create new users and devices. The same information as the admin is collected for the user, too.

Device information: Every device stores some data on its local storage, which will be maintained on our smart contract, and the feature of blockchain is that everything on blockchain is stored using cryptography, having asymmetric keys (public and private keys). Along with the data, the MAC address and the name of the device are stored too.

Event log information: Every event, such as registration, change in device status/data, and retrieving the device data by any user, with the timestamp of accessing is logged too.

Only registered users with matching MAC addresses can access the device's data and perform specific actions, hence enforcing strict access control. This approach reduces the risk of unauthorized access, as all devices are verified cryptographically and recorded on the blockchain.

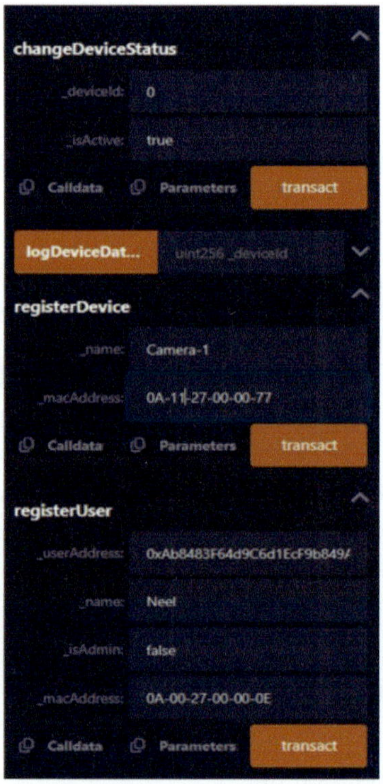

Figure 9.7 Registering/managing devices and users.

In Figure 9.7 , registration of users and devices is showcased. Only the admin has the privilege to register the user, and the one who deploys the contract is the default admin of the system. The admin can also make a new user an admin by setting the "isAdmin" property of the user. The registered user, as well as the admin, can both register their device in the blockchain.

The name of the device, for example, "Camera 1," and its MAC address are both taken as the input for device registration. After registering the device, one unique ID is mapped with the device, and using that unique "deviceId," it is recognized internally in the smart contract. Using "deviceId," many properties of devices can be managed, like "isActive" (signifies if that device is in use or not), and "data" (data stored on the device). We can also retrieve the data that is currently stored on the device, while calling this function, one event is triggered with the current timestamp, and it is stored in the log attribute of the smart contract.

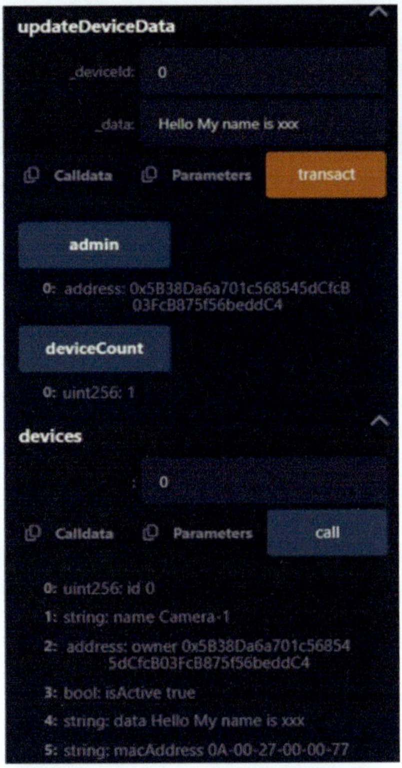

Figure 9.8 Managing devices and their data.

We can also manipulate or rewrite the data in the device; it should not be the case in the real world. But it signifies that we can manage our device and use its functionalities using the smart contract itself. One user can have many devices under their supervision, so they can register one to many devices and every device is accessed using their unique device ID. We can also retrieve several devices under that user's control. Figure 9.8 shows the parameters for device management and control. Also, the detailed log view of the contract is shown in Figure 9.9.

Figure 9.9 Logs of data access of the IoT device with the timestamp.

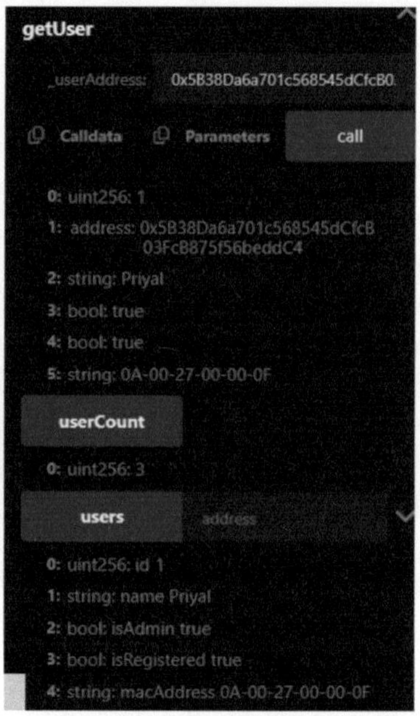

Figure 9.10 Fetching the user's information.

In Figure 9.10 , we are fetching the information of the user using many different parameters, if we know the unique address of the user, using that we can fetch his/her details with their respective name, and MAC address, either if they are admin and 4th attribute shows that if they are registered user address or not. Also, we can fetch the details of all the users without explicitly mentioning their unique address.

9.6.2 Overview of the smart contract functions

Function name	Functionality	Who can call
getDevice	Retrieves information about a device by ID	Anyone
registerUser	Registers a new user	Admin only
registerDevice	Registers a new device owned by the calling user	Registered user with matching MAC address
changeDeviceStatus	Changes the active state of a device	Registered user with a matching MAC address and device owner or admin
updateDeviceData	Updates the data associated with a device	Registered user with matching MAC address and device owner or admin
getDeviceData	Retrieves data associated with a device	Registered user with a matching MAC address and device owner or admin
logDeviceDataRetrieval	Logs retrieval of device data	Registered user with a matching MAC address and device owner or admin

9.6.3 Gas cost evaluation of the smart contract

When interacting with a smart contract, there are two main costs to consider: transaction cost and execution cost. The execution cost depends on how many computations a function needs, while the transaction cost includes the execution cost plus the additional cost of running the function on the blockchain, which can vary depending on network traffic. Figure 9.11 provides these costs for different functions in the smart contract. Functions like registerUser and registerDevice have higher costs for both transaction and execution because they require more computations, making them more expensive compared to the other functions.

The management of device status requires the highest priority in large and dynamic IoT networks. The blockchain smart contract contains the changeDeviceStatus function, which allows authorized members to activate or deactivate devices through the system. The management system holds

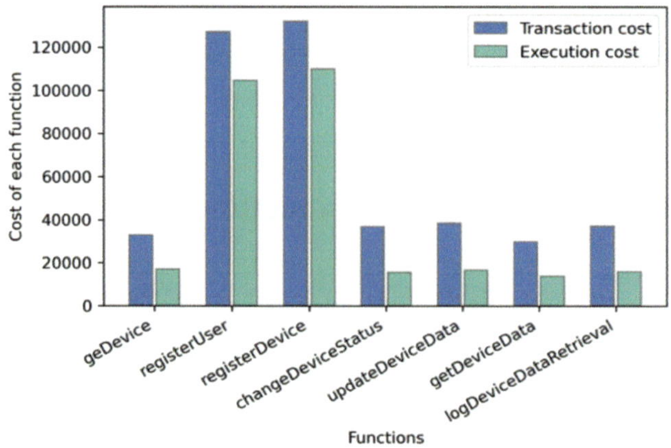

Figure 9.11 Transaction and execution cost gas values.

essential significance in dealing with recurrent network adjustments that require disabling or deactivating devices because of decommissioning purposes or security concerns. Activating the device inactivity mode takes it out of active operational status, thus supporting conditions such as maintenance operations or threat control scenarios. The decentralized blockchain system with sharding functions serves as a scalability mechanism for extensive IoT networks. Every official status transition includes unhackable logging of time stamps together with user identity information and hardware identification numbers to increase transparency and meet regulatory standards. The combination of AI threat detection systems automatically changes status configurations to counter abnormal conditions, which strengthens the resilience of the network.

On a concluding note, blockchain increases the trust, security, transparency, and traceability of data in any network. Using the characteristics provided by blockchain, its decentralized architecture, involvement of every node, and also its ring and group signatures have made a vast difference in delivering reliability to the end users. The automatically executable smart contracts have made it easy for any agreement/communication to take place between the nodes connected in the blockchain.

9.7 Conclusion

In this way, the upcoming emerging trend that is going to completely change the approach of securing connected devices is blockchain technology, along with AI in IoT security. The maturation and tuning of the next generation of blockchain technology and AI algorithms further strengthen the security and productivity of IoT networks and continue to harden them from the emerging cyber threats.

There are limitations in current cloud-based solutions and vulnerabilities in IoT data management. The integration of 6G transmission networks with IoT and blockchain technology amalgamation is an emerging trend that promises to enhance data security and availability. The consideration of preventing sensory data tampering and false data injection through an authentication algorithm and blockchain can also be comprehended. The data integrity and authentication for all transactions done by heterogeneous IoT devices over a blockchain network are stored in the form of blocks and can be accessed and tracked securely [3].

These are stringent security needs with the proliferation of IoT devices. The main benefit is that the blockchain technology gives indivisible, real-time threat detection. Blockchain technology has bright promise in this sphere, especially when overlaid with AI. Further research and development in this area are bound to become important in handling the security issues bound to surely come up in the future. It is necessary to develop a robust security program against node-capture attacks [3]. The confidential data are saved in the captured nodes, like keys and certificates, that will be compromised by attackers.

The development of blockchain and AI together is going to play a very vital role in the management of identity in the Internet of Things. This is forecast to improve the security network and build up user trust, more secure and efficient procedures of identity verification and management. It is quite certain that the role of AI and blockchain in protecting IoT networks can only rise as our world becomes all the more interconnected.

References

[1] Makhdoom, M. Abolhasan, J. Lipman et al., PrivySeC: A secure and privacy-compliant distributed framework for personal data sharing in IoT ecosystems, Blockchain: Research and Applications

[2] Nguyen, Dinh C., et al. “Blockchain for 5G and beyond networks: A state- of-the-art survey.” Journal of Network and Computer Applications 166 2020.

[3] Aparna Kumari, Rajesh Gupta, Sudeep Tanwar, “Amalgamation of blockchain and IoT for smart cities underlying 6G communication: A

comprehensive review", 2021 https://doi.org/10.1016/j.comcom.2021.03.005.

[4] Pawan Hegde, Praveen Kumar Reddy Maddikunta, "Amalgamation of Blockchain with resource-constrained IoT devices for healthcare applications – State of art, challenges and future directions", 2023.

[5] Sabrina, Fariza, Nan Li, and Shaleeza Sohail. "A blockchain based secure IoT system using device identity management.", 2022.

[6] https://pmc.ncbi.nlm.nih.gov/articles/PMC10991409/

[7] S. A. Bhat, I. B. Sofi, and C.-Y. Chi, "Edge Computing and Its Convergence With Blockchain in 5G and Beyond: Security, Challenges, and Opportunities," *IEEE Access*, vol. 8, pp. 205344–205378, 2020, doi: 10.1109/ACCESS.2020.3037108.

[8] A. Jahid, M. H. Alsharif, and T. J. Hall, "A comprehensive survey on federated learning: Concepts, applications, challenges, and future directions," *Journal of Network and Computer Applications*, vol. 215, 2023, Art. no. 103677, doi: 10.1016/j.jnca.2023.103677.

[9] Z. Wang, X. Ma, H. Zhang, and D. Yuan, "Communication-Efficient Personalized Federated Learning for Digital Twin in Heterogeneous Industrial IoT," in *Proc. IEEE ICC Workshops*, Rome, Italy, May 2023, pp. 237–241, doi: 10.1109/ICCWORKSHOPS57953.2023.10283664.

[10] https://www.kaggle.com/datasets/astralfate/iot23-dataset

[11] https://www.geeksforgeeks.org/intrusion-detection-system-using-machine-learning-algorithms/

[12] https://www.geeksforgeeks.org/random-forest-algorithm-in-machine-learning/

[13] https://www.javatpoint.com/performance-metrics-in-machine-learning

[14] S. B. Hamida, S. B. Hamida, A. Snoun, O. Jemai, and A. Jemai, "The influence of dropout and residual connection against membership inference attacks on transformer model: a neuro generative disease case study," *Multimedia Tools and Applications*, vol. 83, pp. 16231–16253, 2024, doi: https://doi.org/10.1007/s11042-023-16126-x.

[15] https://origin.geeksforgeeks.org/introduction-to-support-vector-machines-svm/?ref=ml_lbp

[16] https://github.com/praj2408/Customer-Satisfaction-Analysis-Project

[17] https://www.coursehero.com/file/233869844/ML-ECCDO601-13pptx/

10

Enabling Automated Network Services using Zero-touch Technology for Intelligent 5G-IoT Communication

Roshni Pankaj Kumar Rana, Nitin Rathore, and Aparna Kumari

Department of Computer Science and Engineering Institute of Technology, Nirma University, India
Email: 22bce305@nirmauni.ac.in; nitin.rathore@nirmauni.ac.in; aparna.kumari@nirmauni.ac.in

Abstract

The fifth generation of mobile technology makes wireless communication faster and more dependable. Many devices connected to share information in various industries can work much smarter because of the Internet of Things. The Internet of Things (IoT) has to go hand-in-hand with 5G; it provides a strong foundation for IoT to reach its capacity. 5G networks are fast, have little delay, and can handle lots of data. Therefore, IoT applications can share information and make immediate decisions. These features are the basic elements of advanced usages of IoT: industrial automation, smart cities, autonomous cars, and remote healthcare.

In such a scenario, zero-touch network (ZTN) technology has been a mass influencer in the industry due to the huge changes currently experienced in the 5G-IoT environment. It can be referred to as the elimination of most manually operated operations and, at the same time, improvement in the performance and reliability of the network through automation by artificial intelligence (AI), advanced management systems, and smart networking and communication solutions. AI-based automation allows the ZTN system to self-engineer, self-improve, and self-recover. They can predict network problems, use resources efficiently, and provide services continuously; all these are required features in the 5G-IoT environment.

DOI: 10.1201/9788743809050-13

In line with this, the inclusion of ZTN within the 5G-IoT network architecture could automatically construct, manage, and optimize the network. It has ensured smooth operations, leaves room for further growth, and saves money. Smart network control manages many links efficiently. It connects different areas in your network for communication between IoT devices. The research work presented here investigates how 5G-IoT and ZTN will work together to allow smart communication and networking that constitutes the solid setup in 5G-IoT, opening up new solutions and services across industries toward the building of a smarter, further connected world with enhanced user experience, safety, and performance because of independently operating networks.

Keywords: 5G and beyond, AI, IoT, and zero-touch network, automated networks

10.1 Introduction

The Internet of Things (IoT) and 5G have made network management highly automated, with zero-touch technology. That is to say, this is a form of trying to fully automate network operations, with very little or no human touch. Scalability and real-time response are urgent needs for IoT devices. Simultaneously, 5G networks permit connectivity at phenomenal speeds and with very small delays. This collaboration between them is making the networks with self-management capabilities much smarter and even productive. The development of network-management techniques has been a path of evolution marked by stunning strides in automation and intelligence. In the age of manual network management, circuit-switched communications networks were operated by human operators, who had to perform a great amount of parallel decision-making due to events. Following that came the use of policy-based network management (PBNM). The approach of PBNM is based on some predefined rules that drive the configuration of network elements and services, hence making it easier to manage things at various levels. This era was replaced by active network management (AN), which powered packets with programming codes. This made real-time changes possible in network operations and separation between control and data planes in modern networking paradigms. This was then followed by intent-based network management (IBN), which changed how people run networks. IBN allowed the specification of operational objectives without detailing their realization and allowed automation of configurations and resolution of issues.

Finally, self-organizing network management (SON) technology was developed to automate mobile network design management, optimization, and healing in response to increasingly demanding standards of mobile network technologies in recent years [2]. This history of growth epitomizes the quest for efficacy, intelligence, and autonomy of network management strategies.

The following is the evolution of zero-touch network management as reflected in Figure 10.1.

In modern networking, automated network services are key to efficient management of increasingly complex infrastructures and a reduction in the operational costs for better delivery of services. Recently, autonomous network management solutions have emerged, with minimal human oversight: zero-touch network management (ZTM). This paradigm states that the network can reason about its current state, interpret it, and provide recommendations regarding potential reconfigurations; the onus of assessing and approving the suggested modifications is always left to a human operator. It tries to reduce human error. It improves efficiency. This is through the automation of processes on the network that do not require human involvement. Management of growing heterogeneity is essential. By reducing manual work and making processes lean, zero-touch technology allows faster deployment, higher scalability, and more reliability in network management, thereby paving the way toward autonomous operations of the network.

This is a review paper that covers a detailed analysis of today's network automation with special emphasis on the application of zero-touch

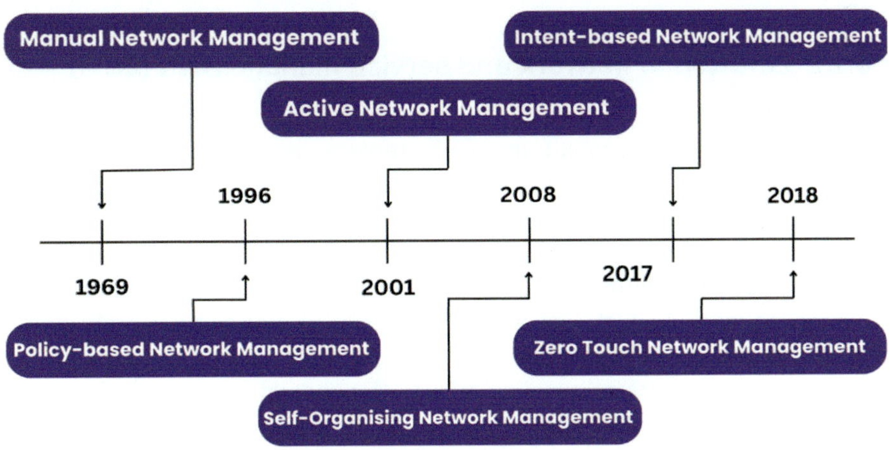

Figure 10.1 Evolution of zero-touch network management.

technology in facilitating automated network services. It touches on wide issues ranging from zero-touch management, zero-touch network, and service management framework types to new strategies such as network slicing, and lifecycle management of cross-domain end-to-end services. This paper attempts to offer a comprehensive overview of the difficulties, advantages, and methods of implementation related to automated network services. The paper's framework will move between fundamental ideas, real-world application cases, and prospective future developments. It provides readers with a story that focuses on how zero-touch technology will revolutionize network automation.

10.2 Overview: ZTM, ZSM, and ZTN

Let us look at an overview of ZTM, ZSM, and ZTN.

10.2.1 Zero-touch management (ZTM)

It is a self-sustaining system intended for agility in deployment and maintenance operations of networks under human supervision. In line with the architecture principles of automation, modularity, separation of concerns, and open standard interfaces, its main concern is simplifying complexity at a lower cost. The value proposition of ZTM stresses automation that, in turn, allows simple operational activities and hence makes the management of the network less involved. Of course, human supervision is called for no matter what.

10.2.2 Zero-touch network and service management (ZSM)

ZSM goes one step farther in automation by having network resources coordinated and managed automatically, moving the emphasis to users based on quality of experience (QoE). ZSM makes smart decisions on network management using machine learning and artificial intelligence algorithms with a shifting focus on more adaptive, as well as user-centric service delivery [3]. ZSM complements the work done by ZTM around the automation of basic networking tasks, stretching into end-to-end service orchestration and optimization. This paradigm enables superior user experience through enhanced network operations – such as traffic control, energy efficiency, and security – in next-generation networks. ZSM strongly relies on an end-to-end architectural framework for closed-loop automation, based on the use of data-driven machine learning (ML) and AI in developing complex service chains with assured interoperability [6].

10.2.3 ZSM framework reference architecture

The ZSM framework reference architecture (as shown in Figure 10.2) is based on the principle of distributed management and data services, each organized in its management domain and integrated into an integration fabric. The integration fabric provides a set of service capabilities for the services to interact together harmoniously. It provides access to third-party systems either by exposing or consuming service endpoints. However, ZSM also faces a number of challenges due to the complexity, flexibility, and scalability issues of requested ML-based mechanisms to meet the expected standards related to quality of experience. Yet, ongoing research addresses other areas like cybersecurity, traffic monitoring, and resource orchestration, and it keeps

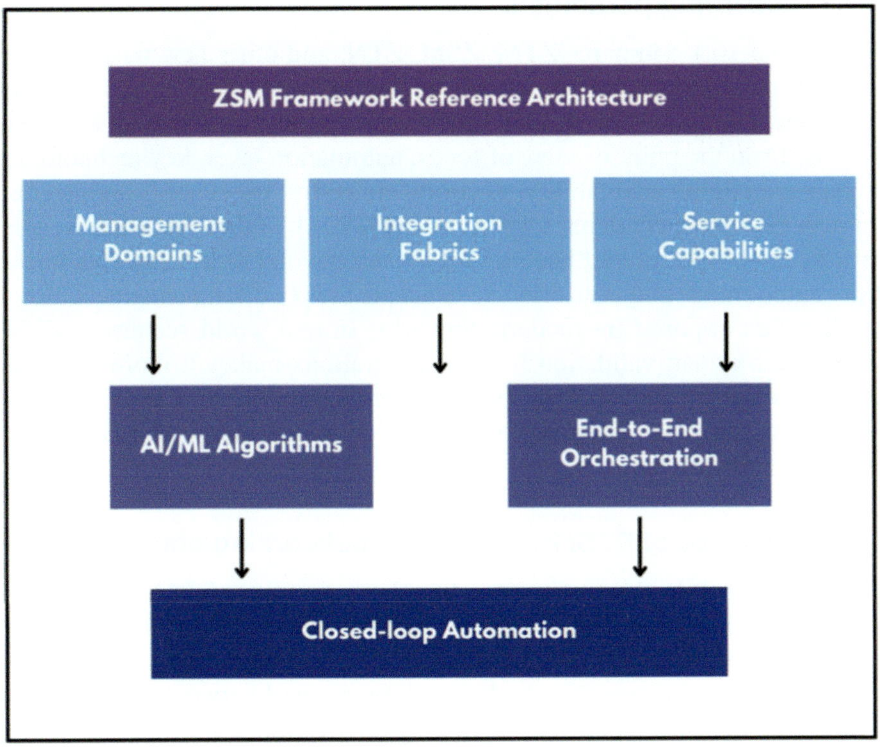

Figure 10.2 ZSM framework reference architecture.

on evolving. ZSM remains a core framework for the automation of modern networks [6].

10.2.4 Zero-touch networking

Zero-touch networking is a new paradigm in network management, considering the perspectives of automation and network performance. ZTN allows defining access control policies independently by the network teams and makes recommendations for configuration changes, while human involvement is limited to confirming those. The focus here is on accelerating time to market for new features, while optimizing network performance, resource consumption, security, and privacy. ZTN thus stands out as an overarching framework that optimizes the network, from resource management to aspects touching on privacy, serving modern networks comprehensively.

10.2.5 Comparative analysis of ZTM, ZSM, ZTN, and the emerging paradigms

Next, Table 10.1 compares ZTM, ZSM, ZTN, and other new network management paradigms, such as self-organizing networks (SON) and cognitive networks. The table depicts differences among the paradigms in some key aspects: from the point of view of focus, automation level, key technologies, human oversight, adaptability, security concerns, use cases, architectural framework, scope, challenges, and scalability. Each of these paradigms, when its turn came to turn, had been a further step beyond older concepts toward more autonomous and user-oriented concepts in network management, driven by demands imposed by modern networks. In real-world scenarios, ZTN's reliance on human validation for reconfigurations makes it more suited for environments where some oversight is necessary, while ZSM's focus on full end-to-end automation makes it ideal for closed-loop systems that need minimal intervention.

10.2.6 The role of ETSI in zero-touch networking standardization

The European Telecommunications Standards Institute (ETSI) makes a significant contribution to the laying of standards and specifications that lead to zero-touch networking. ETSI is among the leading bodies involved in European telecommunication standards development and network standards that ensure companies achieve interoperability, innovation, and collaboration [3]. With standards provided to organizations dealing in zero-touch networking

Table 10.1 Comparative analysis of ZTM, ZSM, ZTN, SON, and cognitive networks

Aspect	ZTM	ZSM	ZTN	SON	Cognitive networks
Focus	Automates network tasks under human supervision.	Full automation of network services and lifecycle management.	Real-time autonomous network management with artificial intelligence and machine learning (AI/ML), human validation for critical changes.	Automates configuration, optimization, and healing in mobile networks.	Uses AI to make real-time decisions based on current network state and past experiences.
Automation level	High, with some human oversight.	Fully autonomous for service orchestration.	Fully automated with AI/ML decision-making, human input for validation.	High, focuses on self-configuration and healing, but is reactive rather than proactive.	High, uses AI/ML for autonomous decision-making and learning from past events.
Key technologies	Automation, open interfaces.	AI, ML, closed-loop automation.	AI/ML, real-time automated network analysis and decision-making.	Rule-based algorithms, self-configuration, optimization.	AI/ML, reinforcement learning, and cognitive capabilities.
Human oversight	Requires human oversight for certain tasks.	Minimal human intervention, though allowed for critical input.	Requires human validation for critical reconfigurations.	Minimal, primarily reactive, and focused on self-correction.	Very minimal, learns from past actions, and continuously improves.

Table 10.1 *Continued.*

Aspect	ZTM	ZSM	ZTN	SON	Cognitive networks
Adaptability	Task-specific adaptability.	Adapts to service demands and ensures continuous optimization.	Highly adaptable, continuously self-optimizing in real-time.	Reactive, adapts based on predefined parameters like traffic or interference.	Highly adaptable, capable of learning and evolving its behavior based on experience.
Security concerns	Moderate, dependent on the automation framework security.	High, focused on end-to-end service security and optimization.	AI-driven security mechanisms for real-time threat mitigation (e.g., application programming interface (API) and ML vulnerabilities).	Limited security focus, primarily on network performance.	High, capable of detecting and adapting to evolving security threats using AI.
Use cases	Device provisioning, configuration, and maintenance.	End-to-end service provisioning and optimization	Network performance optimization, resource management, and real-time fault detection.	Mobile network optimization, radio access network (RAN) self-management.	Automated network management, AI-driven optimizations, and dynamic traffic management.
Architectural framework	Modular, with separation of concerns.	Closed-loop automation architecture with end-to-end service orchestration.	Fully automated, AI/ML-based, zero-touch with human validation.	Distributed, rule-based, self-optimizing architecture.	Cognitive architecture, driven by real-time learning and adaptation mechanisms.

Table 10.1 *Continued.*

Aspect	ZTM	ZSM	ZTN	SON	Cognitive networks
Scope	Focused on automating basic network management tasks.	Focuses on orchestrating and automating end-to-end services.	Focuses on analyzing current network state, real-time optimization, and validation by operators.	Automates network configuration, optimization, and healing in response to changing conditions.	Learns and optimizes based on historical data, capable of evolving its management techniques.
Challenges	Complexity, scalability.	Complexity, flexibility, and scalability in applying AI/ML across services.	Adaptability, real-time validation, and managing large-scale networks.	Reactive, not predictive, limited to predefined network conditions.	High complexity, dependency on large datasets for learning and prediction, and initial setup.
Scalability	High, but specific to network tasks.	High, orchestrates end-to-end services across domains.	Very high, designed for large-scale 5G-IoT environments.	Scalable in mobile networks, but less adaptable in broader networks.	Highly scalable, especially in complex dynamic environments, but requires significant computing resources.

solutions, ETSI ensures that such companies adhere to industry regulations for best practice adoption. With standardized ZTN interfaces and protocols, ETSI ensures that equipment from other vendors can effectively talk to one another; hence, real-time network optimization and coordination are possible. These standards also ease the integration with other vendors, reducing custom solutions and enhancing scalability in multi-vendor environments. The challenge, though, is that they are evolving standards. Partial or evolving standards will be incomplete, which may even cause interoperability issues in the short term since different vendors could interpret them differently, and wide acceptance will come after clear protocols are specified. While ETSI is leading standardization, the evolving nature of these standards poses challenges for interoperability across vendors. Incomplete standards may delay widespread adoption until clear protocols are established. Thus, the relation of ZTN with the standards of ETSI is very important for seamless integration of automated management methodologies within the existing infrastructure. Conformity to the ETSI standard allows network operators to ensure their systems are compliant and future-proof.

10.3 Advanced Network Management Strategies

Now we will look into different advanced network management strategies.

10.3.1 Network slicing

Network slicing is a breakthrough in network management that is closely related to the zero-touch networking and zero-touch network and service management paradigms. Network slicing using automatic control and merging of network services can be the technological solution that is close to the human pursuit of ZSM and ZTN, thus making it possible to implement different virtual networks of a specific physical infrastructure. Through the virtualization technology of networks through slicing that enhances the emergence of distinct slice-based services with different characteristics and policies, telecom operators can offer consumers customized services for a limitless number of demand categories or traffic patterns. One advantage of network slicing is its ability to design tailor-made networks for different use cases like industrial automation, IoT devices, and improved mobile broadband. Moreover, network slicing also brings latency, capacity, and reliability improvements to various verticals, including intelligent transportation and eHealth. The integration of network slicing in real-world scenarios is a complex issue that is difficult to manage and orchestrate, especially when the number of slices is large, so security concessions are made through better security mechanisms to virtual networks against malicious attacks and unauthorized access [3].

10.3.2 Automatic to autonomous techniques

A transition from automated systems and more intelligence to decision-making and autonomy injects autonomy without the need for humans, but with the goal of the highest level of network mobility. Recent research in the field of automation has explored several approaches to these changes. The two main approaches are concept-based systems, which focus on goals and user-defined variables to facilitate autonomous decision-making, and automation by processes triggered by special situations using dynamic policies to control automated processes. Moreover, network stability plans seek to automate simple processes and operations, while network governance is the transfer of management from human-managed systems to autonomous network processes that can be adapted and scaled. By optimizing autonomous networks and services, these improvements will ultimately increase performance and flexibility in modern networks [4].

10.3.3 Lifecycle management of cross-domain end-to-end service

Zero-touch network and service management enables cross-domain end-to-end (E2E) service life cycle management that is automated and covers all the tasks associated with the deployment and configuration of services, in addition to assurance, delivery, and customization across several domains. The E2E service management area is the domain that is crucial for managing and coordinating both E2E and customer services between the domains, thus simplifying the entire network of services and allowing autonomous management. The ZSM framework introduces some techniques, like network management and service intelligence. This service is supported through cross-domain information services, ensuring that the operational information stays usable by the applications at the management layer but remains separate from the management applications. The ZSM framework provides E2E services that comprise activities such as data collection, analytics, intelligence, and orchestration performed, managed, and enhanced dramatically throughout their lifecycle, offering efficient and high-quality services to the customer [4].

The service lifecycle for the E2E management procedural steps of onboarding, fulfilment, and assurance leads to running operations optimally and at service quality levels[4].

10.4 Related Works: Implementation

Table 10.2 provides a deep overview of different implementations of zero-touch technology within the scope of network and service management. These implementations are a collection of various research papers and projects and embody varied approaches toward the automation of provisioning, orchestration, security, and optimization tasks. Each implementation is discussed based on its characteristics, merits, and limitations to give valuable insights into the emerging landscape of zero-touch technologies and how they impact modern network architectures.

10.5 Security Threats and Mitigation Measures

In this section, we outline the primary security risks arising from the several key enabling technologies of ZSM. They include open API-based attacks, intent-based interfaces' security threats, AI/ML-based attacks, and programmable network technologies-based attacks. Along with these security concerns, we will also see the mitigation measures for each of them.

10.5.1 Open API-based attacks

Since provisioning, management, orchestration, and monitoring are all based on APIs, the framework itself of ZSM becomes subject to severe threats via API-based attacks. These could give rise to data loss, identity theft, system penetration, or even service interruption. While parameter attacks leverage API data for injection vulnerabilities in either Structured Query Language (SQL) or JavaScript Object Notation (JSON) injection, identity attacks leverage gaps in authentication. Man-in-the-middle attacks can intercept and change sensitive data in transit, occurring in plaintext during unencrypted API transactions. Meanwhile, APIs are susceptible to denial-of-service and distributed denial-of-service, which causes interruption of service at very high volumes of requests [11].

These dangers can be reduced through strong security measures. Communication encryption, using the transport layer security protocol with valid certificates, assures message integrity and secrecy. Input validation confirms

Table 10.2 Implementation of zero-touch technology

Reference	Implementation /model name	Key features	Benefits	Limitations
[1]	Zero-touch provisioning (ZTP) approach	- Automated configuration: Devices configured without human intervention. - Location-based provisioning: Specific configurations based on network location. - Secure bootstrapping: Ensures secure initial bootstrapping and configuration.	- Efficiency: Reduces provisioning time and errors. - Automation: streamlines network management processes. - Standardization: provides a standardized approach to device configuration	- Requires robust security measures to prevent unauthorized access.
[5]	5GZORRO Platform	- Zero-touch automation: Efficient and secure orchestration of 5G services. - Distributed ledger technology (DLT): Ensures data governance and multi-party trust. - Smart contracts: Automates commercial, technical, and service-level agreement (SLA) interactions. - Service-based architecture: Facilitates interaction of various functions across domains. - Spectrum Trading and Sharing: Enables efficient spectrum allocation. - Operational data lake: Centralized reservoir of operational data.	- Efficient day-0 operations: Seamless deployment of 5G services. - Intelligent day-1 and day-2 actions: Optimization of network operations. - Establish trust via blockchain: Enables trustless interactions and automated settlements.	- Requires expertise in AI, blockchain, and network architecture for implementation.
[6]	ML-based ZSM techniques	Supervised, unsupervised, and reinforcement learning techniques for ZSM. - Includes linear regression, decision tree, K-means clustering, principal component analysis (PCA), Q-learning, and generative adversarial networks (GANs)	- Enhanced network planning, traffic segmentation, and resource optimization. - Improved decision-making and network performance.	-Dependency on accurate training data for ML models. - Challenges in deploying and maintaining ML-based systems

Table 10.2 *Continued.*

Reference	Implementation /model name	Key features	Benefits	Limitations
[7]	AI-enabled CDR analysis	- AI framework for network performance management (NPM) automation. - Support vector machine-based model for cell classification. - Diagnosis algorithm for root-cause analysis.	- Reduction in expert analysis workload. - Improved network fault detection and analysis.	-Dependency on accurate call detail record (CDR) data for effective diagnosis.
[8]	BoostIDS: Ensemble learning-based framework for intrusion detection in SDN-based smart grid	- Utilizes ensemble learning techniques for intrusion detection. - Comprises modules for data monitoring, feature selection, and threat detection.	- Complete protection against emerging attacks. - Quick and accurate attack recognition. - Robust and secure design.	- Continuous updates required to adapt to evolving threats. - Challenges in handling extremely large datasets efficiently.
[9]	Zero-touch commission-ing (ZTC)	- Automates cloud radio access network (C-RAN) deployment using Kubernetes. - Includes a bootstrapper of C-RAN. - Server for resource discovery. - Graphic interface for deployment and resource management.	- Increased agility and efficiency in deploying C-RAN systems. - Sustainable development aligned with 6G network goals	- Complexity due to Kubernetes-based deployment may require additional resources.
[10]	Flying ad-hoc network (FANET)	- Utilizes unmanned aerial vehicles (UAVs) for zero-touch management in edge networks. - Leverages deep reinforcement learning (DRL) for automatic adaptation.	-Self-configuration, monitoring, and optimization without human intervention. - Provides computing and networking facilities to remote areas.	-Dependency on UAVs for network management. - Challenges in real-time adaptation to dynamic environments.
[12]	Digital twin-based zero-touch management	- Integrates physical systems into digital models for centralized control. - Automates network management tasks through digital twin technology.	- Centralized control and flexible management. - Automation of device management tasks.	- Continuous updates and maintenance required. - Challenges in real-time data processing for optimization.

the accuracy of data in uniform resource locators (URL), query parameters, hypertext transfer protocol (HTTP) headers, and API content, and thus terminates any injection attempts. ZSM's integration fabrics can be reused for implementing API gateways and micro gateways for a better north-south and east-west security paradigm. Additionally, AI and ML approaches raise the overall security posture against Open API-based attacks through proactive monitoring and detection of API threats, followed by automated mitigation measures [11].

10.5.2 Intent-based Interfaces' security threats

The ZSM architecture is heavily reliant on intent-based interfaces, which are also identified as key tools of automation, and help in distinguishing "What" from "How" in service realization through the provision of abstractions at high levels for adaptable design and implementation. Intent-based interfaces, however, come with their security risks, including abnormal behavior, unwanted configuration, or information leakage in case of their adoption. Information exposure is a vulnerability that could put system security at risk by intercepting the private application request. The modification of malicious intent may result in unfavorable setups and vulnerabilities. Malicious intent may result in unusual activity that disrupts services or misconfigured networks [11].

Such hazards can be reduced using several steps. Intent validation helps in sorting false or contradictory intentions with the help of an intent engine by validating the forms of intention and resolving the conflicts. Secure transport protocols like TLS 1.2 protect against sniffing and tampering due to integrity and confidentiality in intent exchanges. Mutual authentication between intent providers and consumers is made possible via authentication protocols like OpenID Connect and signed JSON Web Tokens (JWT), which improve security. To further bolster security measures against the security vulnerabilities associated with intent-based interfaces, authorization protocols such as role-based access control (RBAC) and OAuth2.0 are implemented to manage access to the interface [11].

10.6 AI/ML-based attacks

The use of AI/ML here creates a potent force for better and faster communication and process management, on top of the automation already offered by standard artificial intelligence techniques. Providing world-class services is a breeze and gives us more ways to make money. However, the more individuals who employ AI and ML, the more a new avenue of exposure becomes available to attackers.

Significant risks arise from assaults on AI/ML systems, such as evasion attacks during testing and poisoning attacks during training. New attacks, such as model inversion and model extraction, common in machine learning as a service (MLaaS) systems, worsen vulnerabilities even further. Considering the success of attacks against different AI/ML models and techniques, strong security measures are necessary to reduce adversarial risks [11].

Some mitigation strategies include input validation, which verifies the integrity of input samples in machine learning models; adversary training, which enhances the model's resistance to adversarial instances; and defensive distillation, which uses ML model information to establish model resilience intensity against hostile samples. Defence generative adversarial networks (GANs) filter adversarial samples before incorporating them into the machine learning model, providing defense against white-box and black-box attacks. To avoid aggressive attacks, concept drift detection also assists in identifying drops in ML model performance. Effective countermeasures against model inversion eviction attacks include limiting the amount of data accessible through ML APIs, including prediction noise, and variation in execution times. These mitigation methods protect AI/ML-based systems against security threats and the reliable integrity of network service management operations [11].

10.6.1 Programmable network technologies-based attacks

The introduction of programmable networking through the ZSM framework incorporates software-defined networking (SDN) and network functions virtualization (NFV) technologies to address automation, scalability, and customization. However, these advantages also introduce new security threats. It has been contended several times that many SDN design layers are where security vulnerabilities have become evident, as well as by the Open Network Foundation (ONF) and other institutes. These flaws include attack vectors such as spoofing, tampering, repudiation, information leaking, denial of service, and privilege escalation. Similarly, ETSI recognizes that networking and virtualization threats include the threat surface of network function virtualization (NFV). Concerning the ZSM framework, embedding such errors in virtual network functions (VNF) design implementation and deployment can lead to security vulnerabilities and possibly incorrect monitoring data [11].

Many mitigating measures can be incorporated into the system to fight these threats. RBAC serves as an authorization scheme that ensures controlled access and prevents misuse of authority. In addition, using digital signature, encryption, and message authentication code (MAC) techniques on inter-device communication channels, it is possible to make the techniques used in securing communication channels – which also provide message integrity and confidentiality – like trusted platform modules (TPM) immutable to protect confidentiality, encryption keys, certificates, and passwords. Denial of service (DoS)/distributed denial of service (DDoS) attack mitigation further incorporates malicious traffic detection, flow request limitation, monitoring of resource usage, and considerations toward distributed SDN controller design for availability. In terms of VNF privacy and authentication, these are further supported by NFV security mechanisms, including trusted execution environments (TEEs) like AMD's secure encrypted virtualization (SEV) and Intel's software guard extensions (SGX) for mitigating the associated security risks of programmable network technologies and for ensuring consistent network service management activities executed within the ZSM system.

With the adoption of ZTN increasing, the security context will also evolve to embrace a wider attack surface thanks to its dependence on artificial intelligence, machine learning, and APIs. ZTN will thus become susceptible to adversarial and API-based threats. Cybercriminals will employ more sophisticated methods of AI-enhanced hacking, which will necessitate even more complex mitigation strategies such as AI-enabled monitoring, adversarial training, and encryption. In this context, end-to-end encryption, as well as the use of secure communications protocols, will play a significant role in safeguarding the integrity and confidentiality of information. Also, due to the recommendations of regulatory organizations such as ETSI and ZTN networks will be implementing stricter rules, resulting in better security. Moreover, ZTN security will further improve as more advanced systems, such as blockchain and quantum computing, are adopted in order to deal with more sophisticated threats.

10.7 Open Issues and Challenges

A fully autonomous system is ambitious in a complex, uncontrollable environment. Instead, hybrid models ZTN automate routine, simpler tasks while humans handle more extraordinary scenarios, and are likely to be more feasible in the near term. Modern networks, especially 5G-IoT-based ones, bring along many challenges such as handling huge data volumes, dynamic traffic patterns, and infrastructures spanning across dispersed locations. These complexities and others, including unorthodox events like network failures or security threats, require fast responses. While AI/ML-driven systems can optimize many processes, they cannot yet address every edge case autonomously. Thus, human oversight is still needed for critical decisions where various pitfalls can lead to serious and unintended consequences.

Semi-autonomous systems are more probable in the short run. AI/ML algorithms may carry out routine functions such as network optimization, traffic control, and fault detection, while humans control more sensitive reconfigurations or unusual situations. This way, the networks will benefit from automation without giving up control entirely, efficiently, and safely.

Again, it is realistic for autonomy to be gradually adopted in certain areas of network management. Network slicing and self-healing can indeed be applied in parts of the network that are less critical, whereby security risks would be notably lower. Moreover, with the maturing of both the technology and eventually solidifying standards, such processes can seamlessly extend to more critical areas.

10.8 Future Scope and Conclusion

The future of ZTN will be marked with great leaps in the use of blockchain, edge computing, and quantum networking. While blockchain performs automation of protection from sophisticated cyberattacks, edge computing enhances real-time service by moving the workload to the nearest servers, ultimately making IoT and smart cities operate more efficiently. This will integrate everything, right from self-executing smart contracts to raising the bar for the security and efficiency of network operations [13, 14]. Quantum networking is the next game changer in data security across disseminated networks, which provides enhanced encryption and robust protection against cyber threats [15]. As ZTN evolves, IT professionals increasingly will need to develop new skills in AI/ML and network security to operate and troubleshoot these AI-driven systems, well beyond simple manual configurations. This shift in skill set will be essential to supporting the next generation of secure, autonomous networks.

The convergence of blockchain within a quantum networking environment, using advanced edge computing with advanced AI/ML methods, will remake ZTN by ensuring secure, efficient management that is scalable. These will be the driving force in the evolution of automated networks, enhancing security and latency assurances and ensuring greater efficiency of operations in future 5G and beyond 5G networks. This paper presents the current scenario of ZTN, highlighting the main concepts, security threats, and their mitigation, with benefits and challenges concerning these evolving technologies.

References

[1] Y. Demchenko et al., “Enabling Automated Network Services Provisioning for Cloud Based Applications Using Zero Touch Provisioning,” 2015 IEEE/ACM 8th International Conference on Utility and Cloud Computing (UCC), Limassol, Cyprus, 2015, pp. 458-464.

[2] E. Coronado et al., “Zero Touch Management: A Survey of Network Automation Solutions for 5G and 6G Networks,” in IEEE Communications Surveys & Tutorials, vol. 24, no. 4, pp. 2535-2578, Fourth Quarter 2022

[3] Mirna El Rajab, Li Yang, Abdallah Shami, Zero-touch networks: Towards next-generation network automation, Computer Networks, Volume 243, 2024.

[4] Madhusanka Liyanage, Quoc-Viet Pham, Kapal Dev, Sweta Bhattacharya, Praveen Kumar Reddy Maddikunta, Thippa Reddy Gadekallu, Gokul Yenduri, A survey on Zero touch network and Service Management (ZSM) for 5G and beyond networks, Journal of Network and Computer Applications,Volume 203, 2022.

[5] G. Carrozzo et al., “AI-driven Zero-touch Operations, Security and Trust in Multi-operator 5G Networks: a Conceptual Architecture,” 2020 European Conference on Networks and Communications (EuCNC), Dubrovnik, Croatia, 2020, pp. 254-258

[6] Jorge Gallego-Madrid, Ramon Sanchez-Iborra, Pedro M. Ruiz, Antonio F. Skarmeta, “Machine learning-based zero-touch network and service management: a survey”, Digital Communications and Networks, Volume 8, Issue 2, 2022, Pages 105-123.

[7] A. Rizwan, M. Jaber, F. Filali, A. Imran and A. Abu-Dayya, “A Zero-Touch Network Service Management Approach Using AI-Enabled CDR Analysis,” in IEEE Access, vol. 9, pp. 157699-157714.

[8] Z. A. El Houda, B. Brik and L. Khoukhi, "Ensemble Learning for Intrusion Detection in SDN-Based Zero Touch Smart Grid Systems," 2022 IEEE 47th Conference on Local Computer Networks (LCN), Edmonton, AB, Canada, 2022, pp. 149-156.

[9] B. Angui, R. Corbel, V. Q. Rodriguez and E. Stephan, "Towards 6G zero touch networks: The case of automated Cloud-RAN deployments," 2022 IEEE 19th Annual Consumer Communications & Networking Conference (CCNC), Las Vegas, NV, USA, 2022, pp. 1-6.

[10] C. Grasso, R. Raftopoulos and G. Schembra, "Smart Zero-Touch Management of UAV-Based Edge Network," in IEEE Transactions on Network and Service Management, vol. 19, no. 4, pp. 4350-4368, Dec. 2022, doi:10.1109/TNSM.2022.3160858.

[11] C. Benzaid and T. Taleb, "ZSM Security: Threat Surface and Best Practices," in IEEE Network, vol. 34, no. 3, pp. 124-133, May/June 2020.

[12] Ma, Jiali, Yuanbo Guo, Chen Fang, and Qi Zhang. 2022. "Digital Twin-Based Zero-Touch Management for IoT" Electronics 11, no. 24: 4104.

[13] Dinh C. Nguyen, Pubudu N. Pathirana, Ming Ding, Aruna Seneviratne, Blockchain for 5G and beyond networks: A state of the art survey, Journal of Network and Computer Applications, Volume 166, 2020, 102693, ISSN 1084-8045, https://doi.org/10.1016/j.jnca.2020.102693.

[14] S. A. Bhat, I. B. Sofi and C. -Y. Chi, "Edge Computing and Its Convergence With Blockchain in 5G and Beyond: Security, Challenges, and Opportunities," in IEEE Access, vol. 8, pp. 205340-205373, 2020, doi:10.1109/ACCESS.2020.3037108.

[15] Abu Jahid, Mohammed H. Alsharif, Trevor J. Hall, The convergence of blockchain, IoT and 6G: Potential, opportunities, challenges and research roadmap, Journal of Network and Computer Applications, Volume 217, 2023, 103677, ISSN 1084-8045, https://doi.org/10.1016/j.jnca.2023.103677.

11

Blockchain and AI Integration for Enhanced Security and Intelligence in 5G-IoT

Yash Koshti[1], Rahul Jain[2], Deepak Kumar Mehta[3], Sejal Mishra[4], and Nitin Varshney[2]

[1]Department of Information Technology, UVPCE, Ganpat University, India
[2]Department of Computer Engineering, Marwadi University, India
[3]Department of Computer Science & Applications, Mandsaur University, India
[4]Department of Computer Science Engineering, NIET, India
Email: yashkoshti3107@gmail.com; rahuljaincse51@gmail.com; deepak.mehta@meu.edu.in; sejalmishra1894@yahoo.com; nitin.varshney87@gmail.com

Abstract

Integrating blockchain and AI in 5G-IoT systems offers a powerful solution to improve security, scalability, and intelligence in IoT networks. This combination is expected to drive major advancements in several industries. This chapter explores how blockchain can ensure data integrity, traceability, and secure communication in IoT networks, while AI enables intelligent decision-making and efficient resource management. By introducing decentralized architectures, the paper addresses scalability challenges and proposes AI-driven solutions for data privacy and system optimization. Case studies in sectors such as healthcare and smart cities provide practical insights into the real-world application of blockchain and AI technologies. Additionally, the chapter identifies future research directions, including the potential role of these technologies in 6G environments.

Keywords: Blockchain, artificial intelligence (AI), 5G-IoT, decentralized architectures, intelligent communication, distributed system intelligence, data security, privacy, data analytics, 6G

DOI: 10.1201/9788743809050-14

11.1 Introduction

An incredible rate of growth and deployment of the Internet of Things (IoT), driven by 5G networks, has caused a revolution in how items communicate with one another, resulting in unparalleled levels of automation and information exchange [1]. Nevertheless, there are essential constraints to its advancement, above all with a focus on intelligence and security. These problems may be solved by integrating blockchain technology into artificial intelligence (AI), which provides 5G IoT ecosystems with increased security, privacy, and intelligent decision-making capabilities [2]. By offering an irretrievable and distributed ledger for transactions, blockchain ensures data integrity, traceability, and security within IoT networks [2]. By eliminating central authorities, blockchain allows secure peer-to-peer transactions, which reduce several vulnerabilities associated with conventional IoT architectures [3]. Furthermore, it is worth noting that blockchains are transparent and auditable, which makes it difficult, if not impossible, for someone to commit fraud without getting caught, hence becoming an essential instrument for securing IoT data [3]. The quick development and the Internet of Things (IoT) deployment of 5G networks revolutionized how items can communicate with each other, leading to levels of automation and information sharing that had never been seen before [4]. However, there are very serious constraints toward its improvement, especially on intelligence and safety [4]. An alternative approach toward these issues could involve merging artificial intelligence (AI) with blockchain technology, which will make 5G-IoT ecosystems bolster security and confidentiality, as well as have advanced decision-making skills [5]. In this case, therefore, one can say the application of blockchain guarantees integrity in data storage as well as transportability in terms of tracking devices connected through the internet [5]. Therefore, some attacks against traditional models for Internet of Things equipment, be they forgery attacks or live retargeting attacks, can be prevented through employing a peer-to-peer mechanism that is reliable, as it does not engage third parties [5]. Most importantly, by virtue that blockchain systems are open source software platforms whose transactions are open, almost everyone will find it impossible to commit fraud without leaving some traces while securing internet-connected gadgets, hence serving as an important instrument for keeping confidential information [5]. In contrast, artificial intelligence brings enhanced analytics, as well as machine learning skills on board, hence allowing for instant processing and decision making that is intelligent [6]. Within the realm of 5G-IoT, it is possible for artificial intelligence to boost the efficiency of networks, make resource usage more optimal, and perform predictive maintenance through studying great volumes of data from devices connected to the internet. AI and blockchain can work together to produce self-determinant systems with their intelligent decisions, as well as without being affected by individuals in any way. The convergence between blockchain, AI, and 5G-IoT can help in solving issues related to safety, hence popularizing new services and creation [6]. The merging of these technologies offers the potential of revolutionizing several industries, including self-driving cars and smart towns, as well as smart healthcare and industrial automation, hence promoting economic development and enhancing human well-being [6]. In this paper, we will examine the integration of blockchain and artificial intelligence technologies into the 5G-IoT [7] environment for increased safety and intelligence [8]. Several topics we will consider in our study of the area comprise decentralized architectures, clever communications and networking, and data secrecy and security, as well as utilizing the blockchain-facilitated data analytics [8]. Furthermore, it also looks into how blockchain, along with artificial intelligence, can easily be integrated into upcoming 6G networks and the way this can be done through showing some examples of case studies, applications, or prototypes as demonstration of practical implementations [9]. The objective behind the paper is to provide a holistic view of how these two technologies are used for solving the 5G-IoT system's challenges, and a discussion through application and challenges with complete examination and results [10].

11.2 Literature Review

AI for security in 5G-IoT

Blockchain technology enhances security for machine learning models and IoT devices, while 5G-enabled IoT enhances efficiency and connectivity. Despite obstacles like high bandwidth demand and network heterogeneity, security is still important, and this requires AI [1]. As such, the article presents a security architecture for smart 5G IoT applications using blockchain and deep learning. With respect to quickly expanding data generation, the system solves security and privacy issues by employing blockchain in security and deep learning competencies in data analysis [2].

Blockchain for data privacy in IoT networks

Blockchain provides a decentralized ledger, making it useful for securely recording transactions and maintaining data privacy in IoT systems. In smart grid networks, blockchain ensures data traceability and reduces unauthorized access by using cryptographic methods [3]. Blockchain-based privacy protection mechanisms can prevent fraud, thus playing a critical role in IoT security.

Decentralized architectures for scalability

Decentralized architectures are critical for 5G-IoT as they improve network scalability and resilience. Distributed ledger technologies (DLTs), such as blockchain, eliminate the need for a central authority and enable direct communication between IoT devices [4]. These architectures help address scalability challenges by distributing data and computational tasks across multiple nodes, improving overall system performance.

Challenges in AI and blockchain integration

Despite the potential of combining AI and blockchain, there are challenges such as scalability and energy consumption [5]. AI algorithms like deep learning require significant computational power, which can strain IoT devices with limited resources. Moreover, blockchain's reliance on consensus mechanisms can lead to inefficiencies, making it difficult to scale in high-data environments like 5G-IoT.

AI and blockchain for intelligent networking in 5G-IoT

The integration of AI and blockchain technologies in 5G-IoT environments enables intelligent networking and enhanced communication. AI plays a pivotal role in optimizing resource usage and improving network efficiency by processing large datasets collected from IoT devices. Blockchain, on the other hand, ensures that these communications are secure and tamper-proof by providing an immutable ledger of all transactions. Together, these technologies address key issues such as latency reduction, network performance, and data integrity [6].

AI-powered analytics for blockchain data in IoT

AI-driven analytics can be applied to blockchain-secured IoT data for various purposes such as predictive maintenance, resource optimization, and anomaly detection. Machine learning algorithms, including neural networks and deep learning models, are used to detect patterns and predict device failures in 5G-IoT environments. This allows for proactive maintenance, minimizing downtime and increasing the lifespan of IoT devices [7]. AI also helps in resource management by analyzing usage patterns, optimizing bandwidth, and improving the overall efficiency of the network.

Privacy-preserving AI in blockchain-enabled 5G-IoT systems

One of the most significant benefits of integrating AI and blockchain in 5G-IoT is the ability to preserve data privacy. AI models such as federated learning enable devices to learn from decentralized data without the need to share sensitive information. This minimizes the risk of data breaches while still allowing AI models to improve through continuous learning. Additionally, blockchain ensures that all data transactions are secure and auditable, providing an added layer of security to the AI processes [8].

Scalability and energy efficiency challenges in blockchain for IoT

Blockchain's scalability and energy consumption are two of the biggest challenges when applied to IoT systems. The need for high computational power and consensus mechanisms like proof of work (PoW) can limit the blockchain's effectiveness in energy-constrained IoT devices. To address this, alternative consensus mechanisms such as proof of stake (PoS) and practical Byzantine fault tolerance (PBFT) have been proposed, which reduce the energy consumption and improve the scalability of blockchain networks in 5G-IoT environments [9].

Decentralized AI for distributed IoT systems

AI can be decentralized across IoT devices, allowing them to operate independently and make intelligent decisions at the edge of the network. This reduces the latency of data processing and improves real-time decision-making. Swarm intelligence techniques, inspired by collective behavior in nature, can be applied to distributed IoT systems to enhance collaboration and resource management among devices [10]. Decentralized AI also supports scalability by distributing the computational load across multiple devices, which is particularly important for large-scale 5G-IoT deployments.

11.3 Blockchain in IoT Applications

Blockchain is widely recognized for its ability to provide secure, transparent, and immutable records of transactions. However, despite these benefits, there are significant *limitations* and challenges that must be addressed before blockchain can be fully optimized for large-scale *5G-IoT* environments. Two of the most critical challenges in this regard are *scalability* and *energy consumption* [10].

Challenges in blockchain for 5G-IoT

1. Scalability issues
   Blockchain's inherent design, particularly in its most widely used consensus mechanism, *proof of work (PoW)*, limits its ability to scale efficiently in environments with high data volumes and large numbers of transactions, such as 5G-enabled IoT systems [10].

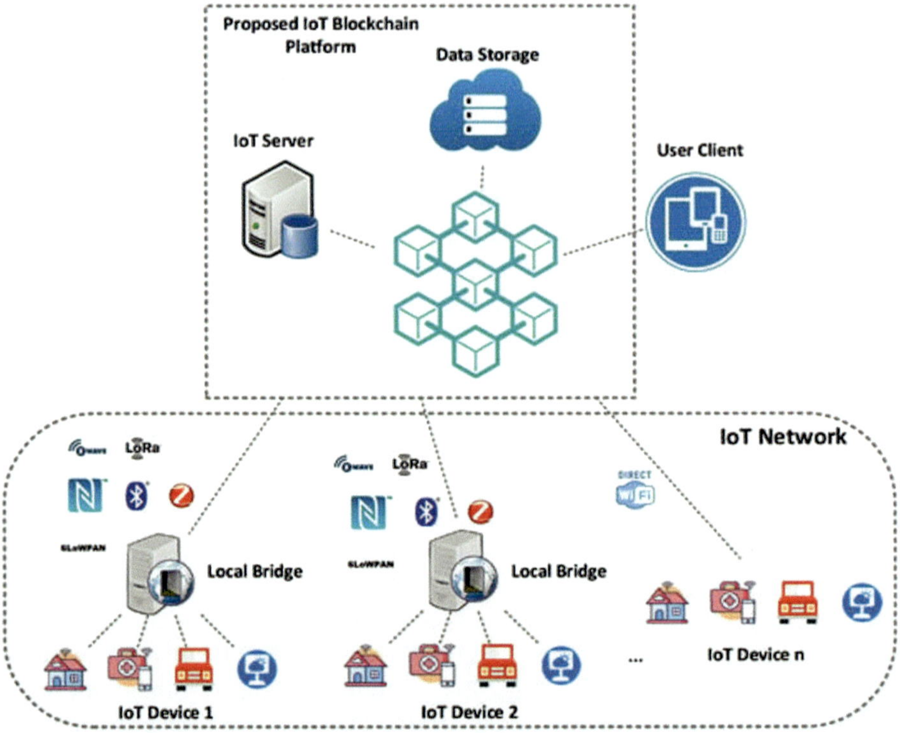

Figure 11.1 IoT blockchain platform conceptual scenario [21].

In a typical IoT network (as shown in Figure 11.1), thousands or even millions of devices generate continuous streams of data that need to be securely recorded and verified [8]. However, traditional blockchain networks, like those using PoW, can only process a limited number of transactions per second due to the computational effort required for mining and validation. This slow transaction speed is a major barrier to deploying blockchain in real-time 5G-IoT applications, where *low latency* is critical, such as in autonomous vehicles or remote surgery [8]. Moreover, as more IoT devices are added to a 5G network, the size of the blockchain grows exponentially, increasing the burden on storage and bandwidth [9]. This can create *bottlenecks* and lead to network congestion, further reducing the performance and responsiveness of the system. In a high-speed 5G environment, any delays in data processing can lead to serious operational issues [9].

Potential solutions:

- *Sharding*: A scalability solution that divides the blockchain into smaller parts, or *shards*, each capable of processing its own subset of transactions in parallel. Sharding reduces the burden on a single blockchain network, allowing it to scale and handle more transactions per second [9].
- *Layer 2 solutions*: Off-chain solutions, such as *state channels* and *sidechains*, allow certain transactions to be processed outside the main blockchain. This reduces the load on the blockchain itself, improving throughput while maintaining security for larger-scale IoT networks [9].

2. Energy consumption
   One of the most significant drawbacks of blockchain, particularly in systems using PoW, is its *high energy consumption*. The process of mining, which involves solving complex mathematical puzzles to validate transactions, requires massive computational power. This is not only resource-intensive but also environmentally unsustainable, especially in energy-constrained IoT systems [9].
   In 5G-IoT networks, where billions of devices operate simultaneously, the energy required to maintain a PoW-based blockchain can be prohibitively expensive. Additionally, many IoT devices are battery-powered or operate in environments where energy efficiency is critical. Blockchain's high energy demand creates a major hurdle for its adoption in such scenarios, making it impractical for large-scale IoT deployments [9].

Potential solutions:

- *Proof of stake (PoS)*: A consensus mechanism that requires validators to stake tokens as collateral, rather than relying on energy-intensive mining. PoS is significantly more energy-efficient than PoW and can process transactions faster, making it more suitable for 5G-IoT environments [8].
- *Delegated proof of stake (DPoS)*: A variation of PoS, DPoS delegates transaction validation to a smaller group of trusted nodes, further reducing energy consumption and increasing transaction speeds [8].
- *Hybrid blockchain models*: Combining public and private blockchains can help mitigate energy consumption. For example, sensitive or high-frequency transactions can be processed on a private blockchain, while more critical transactions are secured on a public blockchain [8].

Table 11.1 Comparison of blockchain consensus mechanisms.

Consensus mechanism	**Scalability**	**Energy efficiency**	**Security**
Proof of work (Pow)	Low	Low	High
Proof of stake (Pos)	Medium	High	Medium
Practical Byzantine fault tolerance (PBFT)	Higher	Medium	Higher

Table 11.1 summarizes key studies that examine the integration of blockchain and AI in 5G-IoT environments. The table highlights the primary applications, challenges, and proposed solutions discussed in the literature, providing a comprehensive overview of the current state of research.

As seen in Table 11.1, most studies focus on the scalability and security benefits of blockchain in IoT systems, while AI is leveraged to improve real-time decision-making and optimize resource allocation. Notably, the studies by [11] and [12] emphasize the potential for decentralized AI to enhance privacy in large-scale 5G networks, a theme that aligns with the research presented in this chapter.

11.4 Solutions of Blockchain and AI for 5G-IoT

Blockchain integrated with AI exploits synergy in the optimization of 5G-IoT environments. These data can be harvested and subjected to AI-driven analytics for actionable information, failure prediction in devices, or resource optimization, thus improving overall efficiency [4]. In this section, we explore how blockchain-secured data streams can be analyzed with machine learning algorithms like neural networks and deep learning for detecting anomalies in network functionalities. We also look at *federated learning* and *swarm intelligence* to support distributed AI models directly on the devices with constrained IoT resources, reducing latency and enhancing privacy [5].

Federated learning is a decentralized machine learning technique that allows multiple devices (or nodes) to collaboratively train AI models without the need to send raw data to a central server [9]. This ensures that sensitive information remains local to the device, enhancing privacy and reducing network bandwidth usage. Only model updates, rather than entire datasets, are communicated, which helps maintain the integrity and confidentiality of IoT data in 5G environments [8].

Swarm intelligence is a computational model inspired by the collective behavior of natural systems such as ant colonies, bird flocks, and bee swarms. In the context of 5G-IoT, swarm intelligence allows IoT devices (or agents)

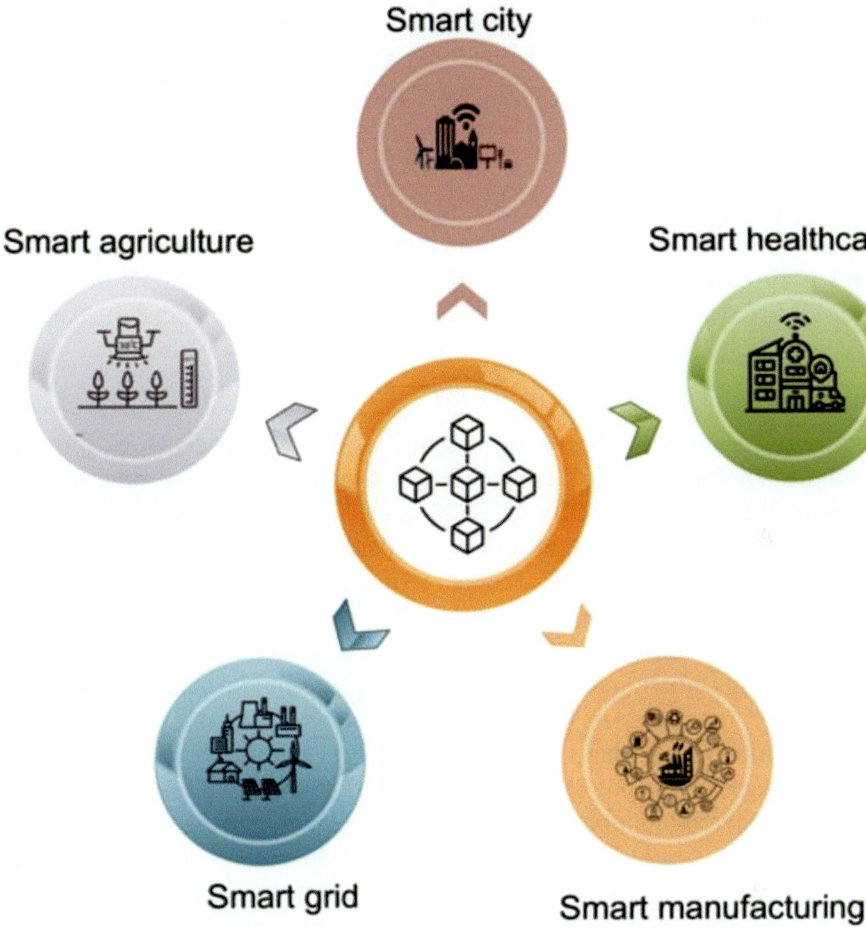

Figure 11.2 Applications of blockchain in 6G network [22].

to work together to solve complex problems through decentralized decision-making. By mimicking these natural systems, swarm intelligence optimizes resource allocation, adapts to dynamic environments, and improves the overall resilience of the IoT network [8]. Figure 11.2 shows the applications of blockchain integration with 6G networks.

AI algorithms for enhancing 5G-IoT performance

Artificial intelligence (AI) plays a critical role in improving the functionality and efficiency of 5G-IoT environments [9]. AI techniques like deep learning and reinforcement learning are ideal for improving 5G-IoT networks. They can analyze large datasets and make intelligent decisions using real-time data from IoT devices. These AI models help optimize network performance, enhance security, and ensure the scalability of IoT systems within the 5G infrastructure [9].

Deep learning in 5G-IoT

Deep learning is a subset of machine learning that uses neural networks to learn from large datasets and extract meaningful patterns. In 5G-IoT systems, deep learning models can analyze complex and high-dimensional data generated by IoT devices, enabling more accurate predictions, decision-making, and automation [10].

Applications of deep learning in 5G-IoT

- *Predictive maintenance*: Deep learning models can process vast amounts of sensor data from IoT devices in real time to predict potential failures or maintenance needs. By detecting patterns in equipment performance data, deep learning algorithms can alert operators to perform maintenance before a failure occurs, reducing downtime and improving operational efficiency in industrial IoT systems [10].
- *Anomaly detection*: In 5G-IoT networks, detecting security breaches or system malfunctions is crucial. Deep learning models can be trained to identify anomalies in network traffic or device behavior. By continuously monitoring data streams, these models can flag unusual activities, enabling rapid response to potential threats and maintaining the integrity of IoT devices connected to the network [10].
- *Traffic flow optimization in smart cities*: In smart city applications, deep learning algorithms process data from IoT sensors placed on roads to predict traffic congestion. By analyzing historical and real-time data, deep learning models can adjust traffic signal timings to reduce congestion and improve overall traffic flow. This real-time decision-making capability is crucial for managing the dynamic and high-speed environments of 5G-enabled smart cities [10].

Reinforcement learning in 5G-IoT

Reinforcement learning (RL) is another powerful AI technique used in 5G-IoT systems. Unlike deep learning, which relies on labeled datasets, reinforcement learning allows AI agents to learn optimal behaviors by interacting with their environment through trial and error. The agent receives rewards for correct actions and penalties for incorrect ones, enabling it to make intelligent decisions over time [10].

Applications of reinforcement learning in 5G-IoT:

- *Network resource optimization*: In 5G networks, reinforcement learning can be applied to dynamically allocate resources such as bandwidth and computing power. By learning from real-time network conditions, RL algorithms adjust resource distribution to minimize latency and maximize throughput. This is particularly important in environments where there are competing demands from multiple IoT devices, such as autonomous vehicles or smart factories [10].
- *Energy management*: Reinforcement learning is also used to optimize energy consumption in IoT networks. In energy-constrained IoT environments, RL agents can learn to adjust device operations to conserve energy while maintaining performance. For example, in a smart grid system, RL algorithms can optimize the distribution of renewable energy based on real-time demand and supply fluctuations, ensuring efficient energy use and preventing overloading of the grid [10].
- *Autonomous systems*: In applications like *autonomous vehicles* or *drones*, reinforcement learning helps improve real-time decision-making. RL algorithms allow autonomous systems to learn from their environment and make decisions such as route optimization or obstacle avoidance. These decisions are critical for ensuring the safe and efficient operation of autonomous vehicles in 5G-enabled environments, where real-time communication and processing are essential [11].

Combining deep learning and reinforcement learning in 5G-IoT

In many cases, *deep learning* and *reinforcement learning* can be combined to provide even more powerful solutions for 5G-IoT systems. For example, deep learning models can be used to analyze large datasets and provide insights, while reinforcement learning can be used to optimize decision-making based on those insights [10].

- *Example: Smart grid management*: In a smart grid, deep learning can be used to forecast energy consumption based on historical data, while reinforcement learning can optimize energy distribution based on real-time conditions. Together, these AI techniques ensure that the system operates efficiently, balancing supply and demand to reduce waste and improve sustainability.

Table 11.2 lists the key AI algorithms applied in 5G-IoT systems, along with their respective advantages and limitations. This table provides an overview of how different machine learning techniques, such as deep learning

Table 11.2 Comparison of AI algorithms for IoT analytics.

AI algorithm	Description	Accuracy	Training time	Resource requirements
Machine learning	Uses statistical methods to learn from data and make predictions.	Moderate to high	Moderate	Moderate
Deep learning	Subset of machine learning using artificial neural networks to learn complex patterns.	High	High	High
Reinforcement learning	Learns by interacting with the environment and receiving rewards for desired behavior.	Can be high	High	High

Table 11.3 Comparison of decentralized architectures.

Decentralized architecture	Description	Scalability	Latency	Fault tolerance
Blockchain-based architectures	Use blockchain technology to distribute data and control across multiple nodes.	Moderate	High	High
Edge computing	Process data closer to its source at the network edge.	High	Low	Moderate
Peer-to-peer networks	Devices communicate directly with each other without a central server.	High	Variable	Low

and reinforcement learning, are leveraged to optimize various aspects of IoT performance.

As Table 11.3 shows, *deep learning* is particularly effective in analyzing complex IoT data streams, allowing for accurate anomaly detection and predictive maintenance. However, it requires large datasets and significant computational power. On the other hand, *reinforcement learning* excels in real-time decision-making, optimizing resource allocation in dynamic environments, such as autonomous vehicle networks. Both algorithms play crucial roles in enhancing the efficiency of 5G-IoT systems, as discussed in the previous sections.

11.5 Decentralized Architectures for 5G-IoT

Decentralized architectures are crucial for the scalability and resilience of 5G-IoT systems. Traditional centralized systems struggle to handle the vast amounts of data generated by IoT devices and are vulnerable to single points of failure. By distributing computational tasks and data storage across multiple nodes, decentralized architectures provide better scalability and fault tolerance [11].

Improving scalability in decentralized systems

One of the key scalability challenges in decentralized systems is balancing *network performance* with the increased number of devices in 5G-IoT. As the network grows, so does the demand for resources like bandwidth and computational power. To address this, decentralized architectures can incorporate techniques such as:

- *Edge computing*: Processing data at the edge of the network, close to the IoT devices themselves, reduces the need for large amounts of data to be sent to centralized servers. This lowers latency and improves scalability by distributing the computational load [11].
- *Peer-to-peer (P2P) networking*: P2P networks enable direct communication between IoT devices, bypassing the need for central servers. This decentralized approach allows the network to scale more efficiently, as new devices can be added without overburdening a central authority [11].
- *Federated learning*: In federated learning, AI models are trained locally on IoT devices, with only the model updates sent back to the central server. This minimizes the bandwidth required for data transfer and allows the system to scale without overwhelming network resources [11].

Advantages of decentralized architectures

- *Scalability*: 5G-IoT tools produce huge quantities of data processed appropriately and effectively through decentralized architectures. Since duties as well as memory can be distributed over different nodes, the techniques may be expanded horizontally; thus, extra spaces can be added whenever necessary [7].
- *Resilience*: By eliminating unique points of failure, these arrangements enhance network endurance. Despite some nodes' failings or takeovers, there is continuous accessibility to the service [7].
- *Autonomy*: IoT appliances capable of independent operation are enabled by decentralized methodologies because they do not need any human involvement at all [7]. The use of geographic information available effortlessly and built-in algorithms that consider real-time events helps promote better performance.

- *Security*: By spreading information and responsibilities across multiple nodes, decentralization enhances security by making it hard for illegitimate users to target and penetrate the system [7]. Moreover, cryptographic techniques, along with the consensus strategies, protect data from integrity and authenticity attacks.

Practical implementations

- *Smart cities*: In intelligent municipalities, applications such as traffic control, refuse disposal, and power transmission are backed by decentralized frameworks [7]. By doing so, it would be possible for edge computing points to analyze information from road cameras and detectors in order to facilitate quick rectification of vehicular movement, thereby managing bumper-to-bumper jams as well as increasing safety in public [8].
- *Industrial IoT*: Real-time tracking and supervision of manufacturing processes are made possible through the use of decentralized arrangements. Edge devices possess the capacity to analyze factory-floor sensor data for anomaly detection, forecasting of machinery breakdowns, and initiation of maintenance procedures independent of a central server [7].
- *Healthcare*: Wearable devices and edge nodes are used to locally analyze data in decentralized structures that help telemedicine and remote patient monitoring. This makes sure there is quick and safe access to health information, enabling customized medical care plans and enhanced patient outcomes [7].

11.6 Intelligent Communication and Networking in 5G-IoT

The arguments have been made that machine learning techniques such as reinforcement learning and evolutionary algorithms can be used for the optimization of network parameters, prediction of congestion events, and traffic prioritization according to application requirements [7]. With the use of this technology, it is possible to configure SDN and NFV for agile and programmable networks that can adaptively respond to changing demands in IoT environments [8]. Additionally, it is common for conventional network administration methods to be ineffective in addressing highly dynamic and heterogeneous patterns of IoT traffic. In the 5G-IoT context, optimizing resource allocation, reducing latency, and improving QoS are some functions that can be performed by a smart AI-ready system [8]. AI-enabled neural networks and protocols will enable significant advances in quality of service (QoS) and reduced latencies, as well as efficient resource utilization among transcending applications within the 5G-IoT duration lifecycle [8]. However, traditional network management techniques rarely manage to deal with this since their ability is limited in both time and spatial dimensions [8]. This section describes what autonomous reinforcement learning or evolutionary algorithm action can do as regards the improvement of several parameters related to any communication system under consideration. Networking that is defined by software (SDN) and virtualization for functions occurring in networks (NFV) has created a new era in the creation of flexible networks able to respond to varying conditions imposed on them by IoT devices [9]. Besides, it also includes improving quality of service (QoS), reducing latencies, and optimizing resource allocation for all the applications throughout their entire lifespan on the communication scenarios found in the 5G-IoT system [8]. Therefore, different networking methods will be considered as distinct from others employed in various learning models and controlling algorithms associated with the Internet of Things (IoT) [8].

Machine learning for network optimization

Using historical data as well as making decisions based on it helps to manage networks well in an improved manner by means of the ML algorithms [9].

- *Reinforcement learning*: With continual activity around them and the ability to choose the best actions depending on rewards and punishments, they can control the network resources by themselves. This way, several uses can be identified for RL in 5G-IoT systems [9]:
  - *Optimize resource allocation*: Dynamic allocation of network resources, for example, bandwidth or electric power to various IoT devices through RL algorithms, can adapt to their current needs and prevailing network circumstances. It ensures optimal use of resources and, at the same time, guarantees quality of service (QoS) in essential applications.
  - *Predict congestion events*: The ability of RL to predict congestion events before they occur comes from traffic pattern analysis and preventive actions such as changing car routes or adjusting transmission rates.
  - *Prioritize traffic*: The smooth operation of such applications will be ensured by providing the necessary resources, in case of such

latencies that are needed for the application to run. Thus, RL may control data transmission in relation to the applications' needs.

- *Evolutionary algorithms*: Natural selection mechanisms are the basis of how evolutionary algorithms (EAs) improve network parameters. Over time, they can change and make better the arrangement of networks to increase their efficiency. EAs find usage in [9]:
  - *Network topology optimization*: By determining where to best locate nodes and what the most efficient routing paths are, optimal network topologies can be achieved through EAs. Consequently, this results in reduced latency together with increased reliability.
  - *Load balancing*: This article focuses on how EAs work to balance the load across a distribution of available resources in such a way as to avoid overloading them and thus maintain their stable working capabilities.

Software-defined networking (SDN) and network function virtualization (NFV)

SDN and NFV serve as critical initiators of adaptable and modifiable network frameworks that are able to adjust according to the varying needs of IoT [9].

- *Software-defined networking (SDN)* [9]: SDN divides the control plane from the data plane, making it easy for network resources to be controlled centrally using software. Therefore, this centralized control enables:
  - *Dynamic network configuration*: The current traffic conditions and application demands are considered when SDN controllers dynamically configure networking devices and adjust routing policies in real-time [9].
  - *Enhanced security*: The network can be seen all around with a global view that the SDN offers, hence making it simple for the implementation of security policies and detection of anomalies. To illustrate, attacks can be reduced by the use of SDN to isolate the compromised devices, then rerouting the traffic [9].
  - *Scalability*: By streamlining network management and automation, SDN can simply grow to meet the increasing demand for IoT gadgets [9].
- *Network function virtualization (NFV)* [9]: In the NFV domain, there are network functions such as firewalls, intrusion detection systems, and

load balancers that are virtualized so as to run them on generic hardware rather than specific appliances. A number of advantages result from such virtualization, including:

- *Flexibility and agility*: NFV facilitates swift rollouts of the network functionalities, which is convenient for adapting to the changing requirements of the networks and also helps in launching new applications [9].
- *Cost efficiency*: With common hardware, specialized hardware is reduced in the need for running virtual network functions, and the costs associated with their maintenance are minimized as a result [9].
- *Service chaining*: The construction of service chains in NFV is made possible by connecting multiple VNFs together to provide complex services. For example, a data packet may pass through a virtual firewall, then be processed by an intrusion detection system, and finally end up at a load balancer, thereby enhancing security and speed [8].

Practical applications and benefits

The merging of artificial intelligence, software-defined networking, and network function virtualization in IoT networks with 5G connections has many practical uses and advantages [8].

- *Smart grids*: Smart grids employ artificial intelligence for energy distribution optimization through consumption pattern analysis and demand forecasting. To enable network resources' dynamic configuration, Software-defined networking (SDN) and network function virtualization (NFV) can serve a purpose in assuring that there is an efficient transmission of signals between various elements within the system [9].
- *Autonomous vehicles*: Vehicle-to-everything (V2X) communication can be managed by AI algorithms, thereby ensuring low-latency and high-reliability connections for autonomous driving. SDN can prioritize traffic and reroute data to avoid congestion, while NFV can deploy security functions to protect against cyberattacks [9].
- *Healthcare*: AI can facilitate and handle data from medical IoT devices in the healthcare sector by customizing priorities and ensuring that crucial data is transmitted with minimum downtime. Peak demand in emergencies can be managed by SDN through changing network settings, while NFV can apply virtualization to health data processing and examination [9].

11.7 Distributed System Intelligence for 5G-IoT

The intelligence of distributed systems (as shown in Figure 11.3) makes use of the combined power of various distributed computing devices alongside IoT devices to solve issues collaboratively [8]. The massive amounts and high speed of data produced by these gadgets make it difficult for traditional centralized AI models to scale properly, as well as respect privacy [9]. In this section, we examine how the integration of artificial intelligence algorithms in distributed computing frameworks such as federated learning and swarm intelligence enables real-time decision making and context awareness in 5G-IoT contexts. The node for computation and inference tasks has been partitioned to the edges, which has led to low delays, high data confidentiality, a larger capacity or bandwidth preserved, and also to collaborative learning and adaptability in dynamically changing IoTs (Internet of Things) [10].

Federated learning

In a decentralized manner, Amazon's Deep Lens and Facebook's PyTorch are a few of the most prominent examples when it comes to federated

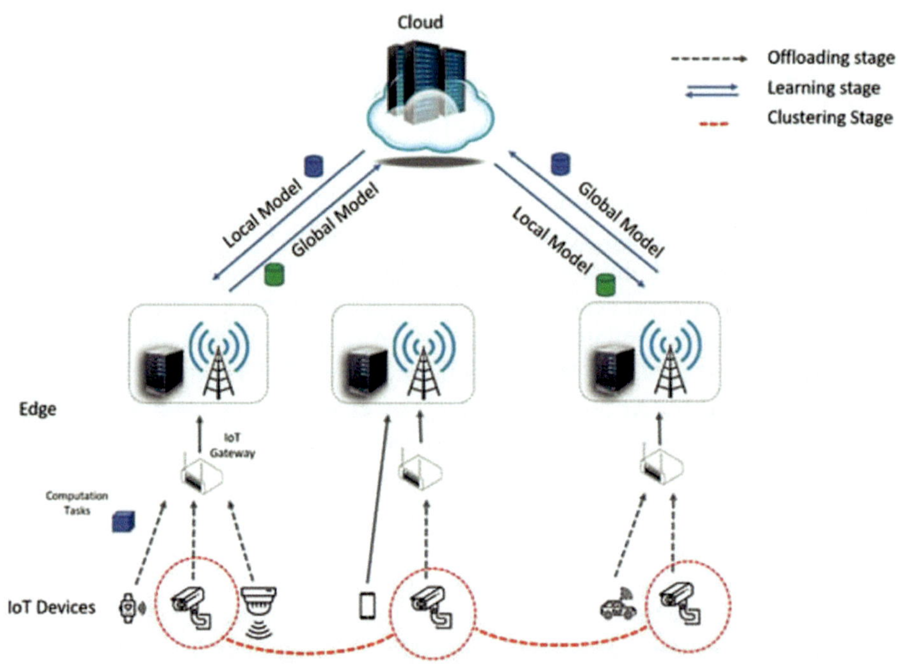

Figure 11.3 The multitask federated learning framework for intelligent IoT applications [23].

learning, in which several edge devices or other computing nodes utilize their resources and processing power to collaboratively build models for machine learning without any central managing of data [10].

- *Local model training*: According to federated learning, each of the edge devices trains its own local model using its own dataset. The resulting local models from these devices are forwarded to a centralized server that combines them into one universal model. The global model is then distributed back to the edge devices for additional adjustments as this procedure repeats itself in cycles [10].
- *Privacy preservation*: Federated learning improves data privacy and security as the data is never erased from local devices at any point in time. If they wanted to maintain their data protection arrangement, then they would only transfer model updates and leave all raw data alone, which in turn reduces the chances of any informant's disclosure and makes it certain that every single person observes privacy regulations [10].
- *Scalability*: Federated learning efficiently scales with increasing device count in 5G-IoT settings, overcoming issues like data privacy, bandwidth restrictions, and latencies. Distributed computation overcomes data privacy, bandwidth restrictions, and latencies. Federated learning supports different prediction methods, ensuring quick analysis and reduced storage demands [10].

Swarm intelligence

The collective conduct of social bugs is what inspired swarm intelligence, such as ants, bees, and birds coordinating in performing intricate jobs.

- *Decentralized problem-solving*: The swarm intelligence techniques like Ant Colony optimization and Particle swarm optimization exploit the individual excellence of various agents (e.g., IoT devices) in order to tackle intricate challenges. The manifestation of an emergent attitude at the system level is facilitated by individual agents with simple rules and close collaboration [9].
- *Adaptive and robust*: Swarm intelligence as an adaptive and extremely resilient system responds to any change in the surroundings. Therefore, it can adjust itself dynamically depending upon varying network conditions or availability of devices, which earns it a perfect fit for diverse and ever-fluctuating 5G-IoT networks [9].
- *Collaborative learning*: Amidst a multitude of interconnected devices that communicate information to one another, swarm intelligence

encourages cooperation in terms of education and decision-making. The shared intelligence optimizes resource allocation for greater fault tolerance and increased performance of the entire network [10].

Distributed computing frameworks

Across devices, distributed computing frameworks support computational tasks that improve the performance and scaling of 5G-IoT networks in general [10].

- *Edge computing*: Data processing at the net's edges, nearer to where it is produced, thus reducing latency and bandwidth consumption, is what edge computing does [10]. In this way, edge devices can analyze data in real-time and make decisions quicker, which means timeliness and precision are enhanced.
- *Fog computing*: They tackle issues in practical applications utilizing the assets found within the boundaries of networks. Fog technology underpins edge computing, enabling data regulation between these margins along with the main cloud server. As a result, this layer lessens delays and yet promotes expandability [10].
- *Mesh networks*: Within a mesh network, direct communication between devices occurs, resulting in the creation of a self-organizing and self-healing structure. This kind of architecture, which is not centralized, increases both the durability and size of networks, thus enabling data sharing among IoT devices [10].

Practical applications and benefits

In 5G-IoT networks, many practical uses, as well as advantages, arise from the inclusion of distributed system intelligence [10]:

- *Smart agriculture*: AI that is spread out and utilized can modify agricultural systems based on real-time information coming from the Internet of Things sensors like soil moisture, temperature, and humidity [10]. Data privacy will not be jeopardized because Federated learning capabilities will contribute to higher crop yield forecasts as well as help with pest recognition [10].
- *Smart manufacturing*: Within the realm of manufacturing, distributed intelligence for systems can provide real-time monitoring of machine wellbeing, forecasting when there is a need for repair or replacement parts, and improving the production process. To achieve this, edge and fog computing may be employed to carry out local processing involving

sensor data, which facilitates real-time control as well as decision making [10].

- *Healthcare*: Remote patient monitoring can be improved by distributed AI that analyzes data from wearable devices and medical sensors at the edge [10]. In hospital networks, swarm intelligence can optimize resource allocation, thus improving patient care and operational efficiency [10].
- *Smart cities*: Smart cities have the potential for using distributed system intelligence that can show improvement in assessment, energy distribution, and waste disposal efficiency. Real-time data processing from IoT sensors will enable a dynamic urban infrastructure through edge and fog computing rather than cloud-based systems [10].

11.8 Data Security and Privacy in 5G-IoT

The widespread deployment of IoT devices in *5G networks* has led to the generation of vast amounts of sensitive data, including personal, medical, and financial information. Ensuring the *privacy* and *security* of this data is critical, particularly as *AI* technologies are increasingly being used to process it. AI offers powerful tools for analyzing data and making intelligent decisions, but it also introduces potential risks related to data privacy, ethical concerns, and security vulnerabilities [10].

AI and sensitive data in 5G-IoT

AI algorithms, particularly those used in *machine learning* and *deep learning*, require large datasets to be effective. In 5G-IoT systems, this data often comes from personal IoT devices, smart homes, healthcare systems, and other sensitive environments. Without proper safeguards, this creates the potential for *data breaches*, *unauthorized access*, and *misuse of personal information* [10].

For instance, in healthcare IoT systems, AI is used to analyze patient data to predict diseases or optimize treatment plans. This data may include highly sensitive personal information such as medical histories, biometric data, and real-time health metrics. If mishandled, this information could be exposed to unauthorized parties, leading to privacy violations and potential harm to individuals [10].

Data privacy concerns in AI-driven systems

One of the primary concerns with using AI to process IoT data is that many AI models, particularly those that rely on *centralized data processing*, require access to large amounts of raw data. This creates several privacy challenges:

- *Data collection and storage*: Centralized AI systems often require the collection of vast amounts of IoT data, which may include personal and sensitive information. Storing this data in a central location increases the risk of hacking, data breaches, and unauthorized access [10].
- *Data ownership and consent*: In many cases, IoT users may not be fully aware of how their data is being collected, stored, or used by AI systems. This raises ethical concerns about *data ownership* and *user consent*, as individuals may not have control over how their personal information is shared or used.
- *AI model transparency*: The "black box" nature of many AI models, particularly deep learning algorithms, makes it difficult to understand how these models are making decisions. This lack of transparency raises concerns about how personal data is being processed and whether AI systems are making biased or unethical decisions based on the data they receive [10].

Federated learning for privacy-preserving AI

To address these concerns, one of the most promising solutions is *federated learning*, a decentralized approach to AI training that enables devices to collaboratively learn from data without sharing the raw data itself. In a federated learning system, IoT devices process their own data locally, and only the *model updates* (rather than the data itself) are shared with a central server. This ensures that sensitive personal information remains on the device and is not exposed to potential security risks [10].

Advantages of federated learning:

- *Enhanced data privacy*: Since raw data is not shared with a central server, federated learning significantly reduces the risk of data breaches and unauthorized access [10].
- *Decentralized data processing*: Federated learning distributes the computation across multiple IoT devices, ensuring that data processing occurs locally. This minimizes the amount of sensitive data being transmitted across the network, further protecting user privacy [10].
- *Scalability*: In large-scale IoT networks, federated learning enables AI models to be trained across multiple devices, improving the scalability of AI systems while maintaining high levels of privacy and security.

By keeping sensitive data on local devices and only sharing the results of AI model training, federated learning provides a more *privacy-preserving* method for AI to process IoT data. This technique is particularly relevant in healthcare, where patient data must remain private, as well as in other sensitive industries like finance and smart cities [10].

Ethical concerns in AI for 5G-IoT

In addition to privacy concerns, the use of AI in 5G-IoT systems raises several ethical issues related to how data is collected, used, and analyzed. These ethical concerns include:

- *Bias in AI models*: AI models are only as good as the data they are trained on. If the data is biased or unrepresentative, the AI system may make biased decisions, leading to unfair or discriminatory outcomes. This is particularly concerning in applications like healthcare or criminal justice, where biased decisions could have serious consequences [11].
- *Informed consent*: Many users of IoT devices may not fully understand how their data is being collected and used by AI systems. Ensuring that users give *informed consent* to the collection and processing of their personal data is an ethical imperative, especially in sectors such as healthcare and finance [11].
- *Transparency and accountability*: AI models, particularly those used in decision-making processes, must be *transparent* and *accountable*. In situations where AI is used to make critical decisions, such as diagnosing diseases or approving financial transactions, it is essential that the decision-making process is understandable and explainable [11].

AI-driven security and privacy solutions

To mitigate these concerns, a combination of *blockchain* and *AI* can provide enhanced security and privacy for sensitive IoT data:

- *Blockchain for data integrity*: Blockchain's immutable ledger ensures that once data is recorded, it cannot be altered or tampered with. This provides a transparent and secure way to track how personal data is used and shared, ensuring that AI systems operate ethically and with accountability [11]. Table 11.4 shows the comparative analysis of various security mechanisms in blockchain-based IoT syatems.
- *AI for anonymization*: AI can be used to anonymize sensitive data before it is analyzed. By stripping personal identifiers from data, AI models can still learn from the information while preserving user privacy. Techniques such as *differential privacy* ensure that the results of AI models do not reveal any individual's personal data [11].

Table 11.4 Security mechanisms in blockchain-based IoT systems.

Security mechanism	**Description**	**Role**
Cryptographic techniques	Techniques like encryption and hashing are used to secure data communication and storage.	Protects data confidentiality and integrity.
Access control mechanisms	Define who can access and modify data on the blockchain.	Prevents unauthorized access and data manipulation.
Consensus algorithms	Mechanisms for achieving agreement on the state of the blockchain among nodes.	Ensures data consistency and prevents tampering.

11.9 Blockchain-enabled Data Analytics for Cloud-integrated 5G-IoT

Enabled by blockchain technology, data analytics utilizes its transparency and auditability to increase the credibility, as well as reliability of cloud-integrated IoT applications [13]. Data silos, interoperability issues, and trust deficits are some of the limitations that traditional cloud-based analytics platforms face which prevent them from generating insightful information from different IoT datasets [13]. This article elaborates on how blockchain-based data marketplaces, decentralized data sharing protocols, and smart contracts can enhance secure and transparent data exchange among a variety of participants in cloud-integrated 5G-IoT ecosystems. By motivating people to share their information with others while ensuring that what they give away belongs to them, thereby protecting ownership rights, such platforms provide more precise insights that are highly applicable. Therefore, it is valuable to various fields [13].

Blockchain-based data marketplaces

Data markets created on the blockchain are a distributed platform for sharing and making money from IoT data by people who have this kind of information [14].

- *Transparency and auditability*: Undoubtedly, blockchain's irreversible record demonstrates that all transactions, including the transfer of information, are clear-cut and accountable [14]. Hence, it enhances faith between data suppliers and users, for anybody can confirm the genuineness plus consistency of that data.
- *Incentivized data sharing*: Data providers could be motivated to share their data via smart contracts that automatically execute payments or rewards when data transactions are completed [14]. Consequently, more

stakeholders are encouraged to take part in the process, thus increasing the amount of data available for analysis and improving the analytical skills [14].

- *Data provenance*: Blockchain keeps track of where the data came from and how it has been changed afterward [14]. This guarantees that the information is of good quality and dependable, which is very important when trying to draw the right conclusions in data analytics [14].

Decentralized data sharing protocols

Decentralized data sharing protocols are used to ensure secure and efficient data exchange among various Internet of Things devices and platforms, which may not require a central authority for that transfer [15].

- *Interoperability*: As part of a drive to address the persistent issue of communication between diverse devices, ordinary protocols have been introduced. This is achieved through a mutual process that all diverse devices may use when sharing dear information with each other and with the cloud too [15].
- *Secure data exchange*: Because the data is kept encrypted from beginning to end, any unauthorized access or tampering of such data is prevented. To ensure that data is secured and private during transmission, decentralized protocols apply cryptographic means [15].
- *Scalability*: Decentralized protocols improve the scalability of IoT networks by helping to share the burden of distributing data among several nodes. This is particularly important in 5G-IoT ecosystems where there can be such large volumes of data [15].

Smart contracts

Smart contracts are contracts that have been created in a way that they are able to enforce themselves and have their terms embedded in the coding language. In this context, these contracts allow for automatic and secure transactions between IoT devices and people selling data [15].

- *Automated data transactions*: With smart contracts, data transactions could be done automatically, which ensures payment to providers and, according to agreed specifications, to consumers. This would reduce middlepersons, thereby making the exchange of information between parties very smooth [15].
- *Conditional data access*: The access conditions for data may include limitations such as time and usage limits. Hence, this promotes security and confidentiality of data usage by the rightful persons only [15].

- *Real-time analytics*: In contrast to earlier techniques in which contract pacts needed prolonged negotiations, Smart contracts employ automatic transmission of information, enabling rapid evaluation of statistics. As an illustration, devices belonging to the Internet of Things (IoT) might be perpetually relaying details to the cloud for assessment, thus dictating prompt reactions based on their readings [15].

Practical applications and benefits

Through the incorporation of blockchain-backed data analytics into cloud-connected 5G-IoT systems, there are a number of useful applications and benefits [15]:

- *Smart cities*: In metropolitan areas with advanced technology, it is possible to have data markets that use blockchain technology to enable the exchange of information from different areas like traffic sensors, weather stations, and public transport systems [15]. This information can be studied in order to refine the functioning of cities, reduce overcrowding, and enhance civic amenities [15].
- *Healthcare*: In care for human health at the level of local hospitals, clinics, and researchers involved in it, there is a huge chance of being able to make use of decentralized data sharing mechanisms for the purposes of enhancing security in sharing patient records among them [16]. Additionally, this technology maintains authenticity along with veracity in relation to the various kinds of medical documents that relate to an individual's life over time – these factors play a key role in building confidence in healthcare, hence allowing doctors more precise diagnostics and treatment practices [16].
- *Supply chain management*: End-to-end tracking and visibility in supply chains can be ensured by means of data analytics that are enabled by blockchain technology [16]. This is made possible by the IoT sensors whose data is recorded on the blockchain, thus guaranteeing transparency and facilitating real-time monitoring of the goods as they travel along the supply chain [16].
- *Energy management*: Smart contracts are a totally automatic method for managing trade in decentralized power networks between energy developers and users. It is necessary to point out that blockchain is responsible for keeping the accuracy and validity of data connected with energy, thereby enabling proper direction and flow of available resources for producing or consuming this sort of electricity [16].

11.10 Blockchain and AI-enabled IoT Opportunities in 6G

6G networks are expected to bring higher speeds, lower latency, and enhanced AI capabilities that could significantly transform IoT applications. While 5G is already making an impact in the IoT landscape, 6G will further expand the possibilities for blockchain and AI integration. However, as this chapter primarily focuses on 5G, the discussion on 6G is presented as *future research directions* [17].

In the 6G era, we anticipate *ultra-low latency*, *massive device connectivity*, and *AI-driven automation* to play a pivotal role in the future of IoT. Blockchain will remain essential for ensuring secure, immutable data transactions, while AI will further optimize real-time decision-making and resource management in 6G-enabled environments. Potential applications include advanced *autonomous vehicles*, *augmented reality (AR)*, and *smart city solutions*, where AI will operate at unprecedented speeds, supported by the security and transparency of blockchain networks [18].

Future research directions

As 6G technologies continue to evolve, integrating blockchain and AI will require further exploration. Key areas for future research include:

- *Scalability and energy efficiency* [18]: With the exponential growth of IoT devices, future research should focus on enhancing blockchain's scalability and reducing its energy consumption. Lightweight consensus mechanisms that are optimized for the high speeds and massive connectivity of 6G will be crucial.
- *Interoperability and standardization* [18]: The interoperability of different blockchain networks and AI systems will be a critical challenge in the 6G context. Establishing universal standards for data exchange, security protocols, and AI model training will ensure seamless integration across diverse IoT ecosystems.
- *AI-driven security* [18]: In 6G, AI will play a more significant role in real-time cybersecurity for IoT networks. Future research must focus on developing AI algorithms capable of identifying and countering complex threats as they emerge, while blockchain will continue to provide secure, tamper-proof data storage.

11.11 Case Studies, Applications, and Prototypes

The practical implementation and advantages of connecting blockchain with AI in 5G-IoT ecosystems are demonstrated through real-life case studies, applications, and prototypes. Several industries, such as healthcare, smart cities, and supply chain management, have already adopted these technologies to solve complex problems related to data security, privacy, and scalability. This section presents some real-world applications that highlight the intersection of blockchain, AI, and 5G-IoT [18].

Table 11.5 provides a detailed comparison of case studies where blockchain and AI have been successfully implemented in 5G-IoT environments. The table compares applications in sectors such as healthcare, smart cities, and supply chain management, highlighting the benefits and challenges observed in each case.

The data presented in Table 11.5 reveals that in the healthcare sector, blockchain is primarily used to secure patient data, while AI-driven analytics optimize treatment outcomes. Similarly, in smart cities, AI algorithms are used to predict traffic congestion and manage energy consumption, while blockchain ensures data integrity and transparency. These case studies demonstrate the diverse applications of blockchain and AI, as well as the common challenges related to scalability and data privacy, which are addressed in this chapter.

Healthcare: Securing patient data and personalized treatment

In the healthcare industry, patient data security is of paramount importance, and the integration of blockchain with AI offers a powerful solution. *Case **study** 1: Med **chain***, a blockchain-based healthcare platform, uses blockchain to store and secure patient medical records, ensuring data privacy

Table 11.5 Case studies of blockchain and AI integration.

Industry vertical	**Application scenario**	**Key technologies**	**Outcomes achieved**
Supply chain management	Track and trace pharmaceuticals for anti-counterfeiting.	Blockchain for data provenance, AI for anomaly detection.	Improved transparency, reduced counterfeiting, and enhanced product safety.
Smart cities	Optimize traffic management and resource allocation.	Blockchain for secure data exchange, AI for real-time traffic prediction.	Reduced traffic congestion, improved resource utilization, and enhanced citizen experience.
Predictive maintenance	Monitor industrial equipment and predict potential failures.	Blockchain for secure sensor data storage, AI for anomaly detection and predictive modeling.	Reduced downtime, improved maintenance efficiency, and extended equipment lifespan.

and integrity [18]. AI algorithms are then applied to these records for predictive analytics, helping healthcare providers identify early signs of diseases and provide personalized treatment plans [18].

For example, AI-driven predictive models can analyze a patient's historical medical data to forecast the likelihood of developing conditions such as diabetes or heart disease. Blockchain ensures that the data remains tamper-proof and accessible only to authorized personnel, while AI enhances diagnostic accuracy and treatment outcomes. By leveraging blockchain for data integrity and AI for predictive analytics, healthcare systems can reduce diagnostic errors, improve patient care, and streamline administrative processes [18].

Challenges in healthcare:

- *Data privacy and security*: Blockchain's immutability ensures data integrity, but it also raises questions about *data erasure* rights under regulations like GDPR, which gives individuals the right to request that their data be deleted. This is at odds with blockchain's design, which makes data tampering or deletion impossible once recorded [18].
- *Compliance with healthcare regulations*: The use of AI in processing healthcare data must comply with data protection laws, which can make the deployment of AI-driven analytics more complex. For instance, AI models must be designed to ensure patient data is kept private, requiring the implementation of privacy-preserving techniques such as *federated learning*. Additionally, healthcare providers must demonstrate that their use of AI aligns with regulatory requirements to avoid penalties [18].
- *Ethical and transparency concerns*: The deployment of AI in healthcare raises ethical concerns about *algorithmic transparency* and *accountability*. Patients and healthcare providers need to understand how AI models make decisions, particularly in critical areas like disease diagnosis or treatment planning. Ensuring that AI systems are transparent and explainable is vital to gaining public trust and complying with regulatory guidelines [18].

Smart cities: Optimizing traffic flow and energy management

In the context of smart cities, blockchain and AI are being used to optimize resource allocation, traffic flow, and energy management. *Case study 2: City **pulse*** is a smart city initiative that integrates AI and blockchain to manage urban traffic and energy distribution more efficiently. Sensors deployed across the city collect data on traffic patterns, energy consumption, and environmental conditions. AI algorithms analyze this data to provide real-time insights that help city authorities manage traffic congestion and optimize energy distribution [18].

For instance, AI can predict traffic jams and suggest alternative routes for vehicles, thereby reducing congestion. Meanwhile, blockchain ensures the security of the data collected from various sensors by maintaining a transparent and immutable ledger. This secure, decentralized system prevents unauthorized access to sensitive data and ensures that smart city operations are both efficient and secure [18].

Challenges in smart cities:

- *Data privacy*: Smart city infrastructures collect large amounts of data from citizens through IoT devices, such as surveillance cameras, smart meters, and traffic sensors. *GDPR* and other data privacy laws require cities to ensure that this data is anonymized and protected from unauthorized access. Blockchain can help secure this data, but the implementation of *public blockchains* introduces the challenge of balancing transparency with the need to protect sensitive information [18].
- *Legal uncertainty*: The legal framework for the use of AI and blockchain in public infrastructure is still evolving. Many countries lack clear guidelines or regulations for how these technologies should be deployed, creating uncertainty for local governments and technology providers. For instance, there may be concerns about how AI-driven decision-making systems comply with existing laws governing public services or how blockchain-based contracts (e.g., smart contracts) interact with traditional legal frameworks [18].
- *Interoperability*: Smart cities rely on a variety of technologies, platforms, and vendors. Ensuring that blockchain and AI systems can *interoperate* with existing city infrastructure presents a significant technical and regulatory challenge. Governments need to establish clear standards and protocols to ensure seamless integration across different platforms while maintaining compliance with national and international regulations [18].
- *Public trust and acceptance*: For smart city technologies to be successful, public trust is essential. Citizens must feel confident that the data collected is used responsibly, and they must be assured that AI-driven systems will not lead to biased or unethical outcomes. Governments and technology providers must work together to ensure that AI models used in smart cities are *transparent*, *accountable*, and compliant with all relevant regulations [18].

Supply chain management: Enhancing transparency and reducing fraud

In supply chain management, blockchain and AI are being used to improve transparency, traceability, and efficiency. *Case study 3: VeChain*, a blockchain-based platform, combines AI and blockchain to enhance the traceability of products throughout the supply chain. By using IoT sensors attached to shipments, VeChain tracks the location and condition of goods in real-time [18].

For example, in the food industry, VeChain ensures that every step of the product journey – from production to distribution – is recorded on the blockchain, allowing stakeholders to verify the authenticity and safety of food products. AI analyzes the data from IoT sensors to detect any anomalies, such as temperature fluctuations that could compromise the quality of perishable goods. This approach helps reduce fraud, improve compliance with safety regulations, and minimize losses due to spoilage or mismanagement [18].

Industrial IoT: Predictive maintenance and equipment monitoring

In the industrial IoT sector, blockchain and AI are being used to monitor equipment performance and predict failures before they occur. *Case study 4: GE digital* integrates blockchain and AI to track the condition of machinery in real-time. IoT sensors attached to industrial equipment collect data on performance metrics such as temperature, vibration, and operational efficiency. AI algorithms analyze this data to predict when the equipment might fail, allowing for proactive maintenance [18].

Blockchain ensures that the data collected from these sensors is secure and immutable, preventing tampering or unauthorized access. By combining blockchain's security features with AI's predictive capabilities, companies can reduce downtime, extend the lifespan of their equipment, and optimize maintenance schedules. This leads to increased operational efficiency and cost savings [18].

Energy management: Smart grids and renewable energy integration

Another promising application of blockchain and AI is in the field of energy management. *Case study 5: Power ledger*, a blockchain-based energy trading platform, enables peer-to-peer energy trading in smart grids. By using blockchain to record energy transactions and AI to optimize energy distribution, power ledger allows consumers to buy and sell excess renewable energy directly to and from their neighbors, bypassing traditional utilities [18].

AI algorithms forecast energy demand based on historical data and real-time consumption patterns, allowing the system to optimize energy distribution and balance supply with demand. Blockchain ensures that all energy transactions are secure, transparent, and traceable, creating trust between energy producers and consumers. This decentralized approach reduces reliance on central authorities, promotes the use of renewable energy sources, and makes energy grids more resilient [18].

Practical applications and benefits

Through these real-world applications, the integration of blockchain and AI has shown significant potential in solving some of the most pressing challenges in 5G-IoT environments. Whether it is securing patient data, optimizing city traffic, improving supply chain transparency, or enabling predictive maintenance, the combination of these two technologies is revolutionizing industries. Additionally, in energy management, blockchain and AI are helping to promote sustainability by enabling decentralized energy trading and optimizing the use of renewable resources [18].

11.12 User Intention Modeling for AI and Blockchain-based 5G-IoT Applications

To provide personalized and specific-context services in 5G-IoT ecosystems, it is important to understand how users want to engage with their devices and what they prefer. Static profiles and fixed rules are often the tools used in the traditional methods of user modeling, making it difficult for them to keep pace with ever-changing user behavior and preferences [18]. AI techniques, as well as blockchain technology, in the generation of user intention models, will be reviewed in this part of the paper so as to improve user satisfaction through recommendation systems, decision-making that can change and adapt depending on the situation. Personalized recommendations and tailored services that fit individual user needs will be given by AI-powered recommenders analyzing interactions with different customers, their reviews based on past interactions through which these systems store feedback and analyze accordingly. As a result, such systems enhance engagement with devices by retaining existing customers as well as earning their loyalty within the scope of 5G-IoT applications [19].

AI and blockchain for user intention modeling

Dynamic user profiles

Conventional user profiles are typically static and do not reflect changing user preferences and actions. By constantly analyzing real-time information from numerous IoT gadgets, AI techniques are able to dynamically amend user profiles [18].

- *Machine learning algorithms*: The capability of predicting user behavior is now present in algorithms such as deep learning and reinforcement learning that are being used by AI systems today. In this context, they adapt to shifts over time and guarantee that the profiles of users stay updated and precise [18].
- *Contextual awareness*: To comprehend users' motives more effortlessly, AI frameworks may incorporate contextual information together with location, time, and atmospheric conditions. Thus, making it possible for the provision of context-sensitive services which meet customer needs better [18].

Blockchain for data integrity and privacy

The user data integrity and privacy are guaranteed by blockchain technology, which is vital for accurate and reliable user intention modeling [18].

- *Immutable records*: The blockchain carries an unalterable record of all user engagements and opinions about them, hence AI models can use this as a dependable source of information. This guarantees the fidelity of data employed in modeling as well as its resistance to any form of interference [17].
- *Data privacy*: One can safely guard information and control its access through blockchain, which permits every individual to possess it as well as supervise it. To augment information secrecy while permitting AI study, more methods could be used, such as zero-knowledge critique and homomorphic cipher [18].

AI-powered recommendation systems

Using AI-driven recommendation systems that utilize intent modeling for the users to give customized recommendations and solutions [18].

Collaborative filtering

Collaborative filtering algorithms analyze how similar users behave and what they prefer, to offer recommendations [15].

- *User-based filtering*: This technique identifies users who share preferences and suggests items that these users have enjoyed or engaged with [15].
- *Item-based filtering*: This method allows for the discovery of items akin to those that have previously won the favor of or received attention from a particular individual before giving out suggestions for such goods [15].

Content-based filtering

Recommendation systems use content-based filtering algorithms that rely on the features of items to provide suggestions depending on the previous behaviors of a particular individual [19].

- *Feature extraction*: By the AI models, features are extracted from things (like what is in a product description or even which genre of movies) that relate to user interest metrics [19].
- *Personalization*: Items that the system proposes are strongly similar to the user's preferences and past transactions in function [19].

Hybrid recommendation systems

In order to increase the accuracy and relevance of recommendations, hybrid recommendation frameworks integrate collaborative filtering systems with content-based filtering systems [19].

- *Combining strengths*: Thus, hybrid systems that utilize both methods can achieve improved recommendations by incorporating these strategies, enabling them to harness individual method strengths and reduce their weaknesses [19].
- *Enhanced personalization*: These arrangements are able to adapt to different situations encountered by users, including circumstances where there is insufficient data (the cold start problem), because they still give personalized recommendations [19].

Adaptive decision-making

Adaptive decision-making in 5G-IoT applications to improve user experience has been fuelled by both AI and blockchain technology [19].

Real-time analytics

With the aim of making instant decisions and adjusting services as needed, AI models can carry out real-time analytics of user data [19].

- *Instant feedback*: By continuously assessing how people utilize their services, these systems are capable of making changes instantly based on user suggestions or decisions in relation to their suggestions or actions [19].
- *Proactive services*: The ability to anticipate user needs and offer services or recommendations even before they are requested is one of the major benefits that AI has to offer its users [19].

Smart contracts

Using blockchain, approved intelligent agreements shall alter user behaviors speedily in a homogenous manner.

- *Automated actions*: Considering all that has happened thus far, a cyber agreement may allow for acts to be performed automatically, such as altering device specifications or dispatching personalized items [19].
- *Secure transactions*: The blockchain keeps all trades and communications under proper lock and key to prevent any manipulation, guaranteeing that users can have faith in choices made inside the framework [19].

Practical applications and benefits
Personalized healthcare

- *Health monitoring*: Greetings, smart appliances connected to the Internet of Things (IoT) are able to track user health parameters constantly and modify the profiles in real time. It can be defined that AI has the power to analyze such kinds of information, which would lead to the delivery of individualized health recommendations and notifications [20].
- *Telemedicine*: While AI-driven recommendation systems provide relevant telehealth services and treatments, blockchain ensures privacy and integrity of patients' information [20].

Smart homes

- *Adaptive environment*: Houses can be regulated through personal characteristics so that AI systems can automatically learn from residents' interests in lighting settings, temperature levels, and leisure activities [20].
- *Security*: When it comes to controlling who has access and how secure it is, smart contracts that are built on blockchain play an important part because they limit the way that approved individuals engage with things in their smart houses [20].

E-commerce

- *Personalized shopping*: Products are recommended based on user input that enhances the purchasing experience through the browser history as well as the choices made [20].

- *Secure transactions*: Through blockchain networks, protection and transparency of transaction pathways are provided; thus, confidence is instilled in the customers, as well as e-commerce companies [20].

11.13 Conclusion

The integration of blockchain and AI presents a powerful solution for addressing security, scalability, and data privacy challenges in 5G-enabled IoT environments. By leveraging blockchain's decentralized nature and AI's intelligent decision-making capabilities, these technologies can work together to optimize the performance and security of 5G-IoT networks.

In this chapter, we have discussed how blockchain ensures data integrity and traceability, while AI enhances efficiency and resource management. The combination of these technologies has the potential to revolutionize industries such as healthcare, smart cities, and supply chain management, offering practical solutions to real-world challenges. Additionally, decentralized architectures supported by blockchain can improve network scalability, while AI-driven analytics provide predictive insights and anomaly detection for better operational efficiency.

Key takeaways:

- Blockchain provides robust security through immutable records and decentralized control, making it ideal for securing IoT data.
- AI enhances real-time decision-making and resource optimization, improving the performance of IoT systems.
- Decentralized architectures, enabled by blockchain, address the scalability issues inherent in traditional IoT networks.
- Practical applications in sectors such as healthcare, smart cities, and supply chain management demonstrate the real-world potential of blockchain-AI integration.

Future research directions: As the 5G-IoT landscape continues to evolve, future research should focus on enhancing blockchain's scalability and energy efficiency, particularly in large-scale IoT deployments. In addition, more work is needed to address data privacy concerns in AI-driven systems, especially when dealing with sensitive IoT data. Finally, with the rise of 6G networks on the horizon, the role of AI in real-time cybersecurity and blockchain's potential in managing massive IoT ecosystems will become critical areas for further exploration.

In conclusion, while the current integration of blockchain and AI offers significant advancements for 5G-IoT systems, ongoing research and collaboration will be essential in unlocking their full potential, particularly as we move toward more advanced technologies such as 6G.

References

[1] M. H. Bohara, K. Patel, A. Saiyed, and A. Ganatra, "Adversarial artificial intelligence assistance for secure 5G-Enabled IoT," in *Springer eBooks*, 2021, pp. 323–350. doi: 10.1007/978-3-030-67490-8_13.

[2] S. Rathore, J. H. Park, and H. Chang, "Deep Learning and Blockchain-Empowered security framework for intelligent 5G-Enabled IoT," *IEEE Access*, vol. 9, pp. 90075–90083, Jan. 2021, doi: 10.1109/access.2021.3077069.

[3] E. Esenogho, K. Djouani, and A. M. Kurien, "Integrating Artificial Intelligence Internet of Things and 5G for Next-Generation Smartgrid: A Survey of Trends Challenges and Prospect," *IEEE Access*, vol. 10, pp. 4794–4831, Jan. 2022, doi: 10.1109/access.2022.3140595.

[4] T. Le and S. Shetty, "Artificial intelligence-aided privacy preserving trustworthy computation and communication in 5G-based IoT networks," *Ad Hoc Networks*, vol. 126, p. 102752, Mar. 2022, doi: 10.1016/j.adhoc.2021.102752.

[5] A. Miglani and N. Kumar, "Blockchain management and machine learning adaptation for IoT environment in 5G and beyond networks: A systematic review," *Computer Communications*, vol. 178, pp. 37–63, Oct. 2021, doi: 10.1016/j.comcom.2021.07.009.

[6] W. Serrano, "The Blockchain Random Neural Network for cybersecure IoT and 5G infrastructure in Smart Cities," *Journal of Network and Computer Applications*, vol. 175, p. 102909, Feb. 2021, doi: 10.1016/j.jnca.2020.102909.

[7] M. E. E. Alahi *et al.*, "Integration of IoT-Enabled Technologies and Artificial intelligence (AI) for Smart City Scenario: recent advancements and future trends," *Sensors*, vol. 23, no. 11, p. 5206, May 2023, doi: 10.3390/s23115206.

[8] J. Cook, S. U. Rehman, and M. A. Khan, "Security and privacy for low power IoT devices on 5G and Beyond networks: challenges and future directions," *IEEE Access*, vol. 11, pp. 39295–39317, Jan. 2023, doi: 10.1109/access.2023.3268064.

[9] Y. Djenouri, G. Srivastava, A. Belhadi, and J. C. Lin, "Intelligent blockchain management for distributed knowledge graphs in IoT 5G environments," *Transactions on Emerging Telecommunications Technologies*, vol. 35, no. 4, Jul. 2021, doi: 10.1002/ett.4332.

[10] A. Kiran, P. Mathivanan, M. Mahdal, K. Sairam, D. Chauhan, and V. Talasila, "Enhancing Data Security in IoT Networks with Blockchain-Based Management and Adaptive Clustering Techniques," *Mathematics*, vol. 11, no. 9, p. 2073, Apr. 2023, doi: 10.3390/math11092073.

[11] H. Moudoud, S. Cherkaoui, and L. Khoukhi, "An overview of blockchain and 5G networks," in *EAI/Springer Innovations in Communication and Computing*, 2021, pp. 1–20. doi: 10.1007/978-3-030-77185-0_1.

[12] B. Gera, Y. S. Raghuvanshi, O. Rawlley, S. Gupta, A. Dua, and P. Sharma, "Leveraging AI-enabled 6G-driven IoT for sustainable smart cities," *International Journal of Communication Systems*, vol. 36, no. 16, Aug. 2023, doi: 10.1002/dac.5588.

[13] B. Goswami and H. Choudhury, "A Blockchain-Based authentication scheme for 5G-Enabled IoT," *Journal of Network and Systems Management*, vol. 30, no. 4, Jul. 2022, doi: 10.1007/s10922-022-09680-6.

[14] S. Otoum, I. A. Ridhawi, and H. T. Mouftah, "Preventing and controlling epidemics through Blockchain-Assisted AI-Enabled networks," *IEEE Network*, vol. 35, no. 3, pp. 34–41, May 2021, doi: 10.1109/mnet.011.2000628.

[15] T. Mazhar *et al.*, "The role of ML, AI and 5G technology in smart energy and smart building management," *Electronics*, vol. 11, no. 23, p. 3960, Nov. 2022, doi: 10.3390/electronics11233960.

[16] G. F. Huseien, "A review on 5G technology for smart energy management and smart buildings in Singapore," *Energy and AI*, vol. 7, p. 100116, Jan. 2022, doi: 10.1016/j.egyai.2021.100116.

[17] A. S. Rajawat, S. B. Goyal, P. Bedi, C. Verma, E. I. Ionete, and M. S. Raboaca, "5G-Enabled Cyber-Physical systems for smart transportation using blockchain technology," *Mathematics*, vol. 11, no. 3, p. 679, Jan. 2023, doi: 10.3390/math11030679.

[18] S. K. Rana *et al.*, "Blockchain-Based model to improve the performance of the Next-Generation Digital Supply Chain," *Sustainability*, vol. 13, no. 18, p. 10008, Sep. 2021, doi: 10.3390/su131810008.

[19] J. Christidis, P. A. Karkazis, P. Papadopoulos, and H. C. Leligou, "Decentralized Blockchain-Based IoT Data Marketplaces," *Journal of*

Sensor and Actuator Networks, vol. 11, no. 3, p. 39, Jul. 2022, doi: 10.3390/jsan11030039.

[20] N. Lasla, L. Al-Sahan, M. Abdallah, and M. Younis, "Green-PoW: An energy-efficient blockchain Proof-of-Work consensus algorithm," *Computer Networks*, vol. 214, p. 109118, Sep. 2022, doi: 10.1016/j.comnet.2022.109118.

[21] L. Hang and D.-H. Kim, "Design and implementation of an integrated IoT blockchain platform for sensing data integrity," Sensors, vol. 19, no. 10, p. 2228, May 2019, doi: 10.3390/s19102228.

[22] T. Rathod et al., "Blockchain-Driven Intelligent Scheme for IoT-Based Public Safety System beyond 5G Networks," Sensors, vol. 23, no. 2, p. 969, Jan. 2023, doi: 10.3390/s23020969.

[23] R. Firouzi and R. Rahmani, "5G-Enabled Distributed Intelligence based on O-RAN for distributed IoT systems," Sensors, vol. 23, no. 1, p. 133, Dec. 2022, doi: 10.3390/s23010133.

12

Enhancing Environmental Monitoring and Sustainability through 5G-IoT Integration with AI and Blockchain

Heena Khanna[1], Sartaj Singh[1], Manik Mehra[1], and Akshay Sahnan[2]

[1]School of Computer Applications, Lovely Professional University, India
[2]Technical Specialist, Apple Inc.
Email: heena.31463@lpu.co.in; sartaj.singh@lpu.co.in;
mehra.manik@yahoo.com; a_sahnan@apple.com

Abstract

Sustainability and environmental monitoring are the two major challenges the world is facing today, and therefore, the transformative potential of technologies like integrating 5G technology, blockchain, IoT, and artificial intelligence (AI) needs to be implemented to overcome these challenges. This chapter suggests an amalgamation of these technologies to provide some suggestive solutions to achieve the target of a sustainable environment monitoring mechanism. The chapter provides a complete overview of these foundational technologies, sharing their features and applications. Further, the chapter dives deep into the usage of blockchain, IoT, AI, and 5G technology for optimizing the role of AI in optimized network performance and the efficiency of blockchain, with which a transparent and secure data management model could be generated. The chapter also examines the architectural advancements in the field of 5G and IoT networks, along with their capacity to provide a robust and reliable system for addressing the collection, processing, and analysis of real-time data collection. The chapter also focuses on how AI-driven data analytics can support environmental monitoring, help identify the anomaly, and perform predictive analysis and various decision support systems. The efficiency of AI in interpreting environmental data and its impact on various stakeholders is also discussed. The chapter explores

DOI: 10.1201/9788743809050-15

the capabilities of blockchain technology in ensuring the integrity of the data while maintaining accountability through the immutable and secure data management. Various applications of the integrated solution of 5G-IoT are highlighted, such as wildlife tracking, waste management, and climate monitoring through the case studies. Toward the end, various challenges like scalability, energy consumption, and data security are discussed along with the solutions. Some regulatory frameworks governing 5G-IoT adoption are suggested. Ultimately, this chapter portrays a comprehensive resource for researchers, policymakers, and business leaders aiming to facilitate 5G-IoT for environmental sustainability.

Keywords: IoT, blockchain, environment, AI, 5G

12.1 Introduction

12.1.1 Overview of environmental monitoring and sustainability

To preserve our environment, it is essential to safeguard it with some methods based on environmental conditions. There are many changes occurring in the ecosystem, like an increase in pollution day by day, and some other activities of humans affect the environment. There are a huge number of techniques that can be considered to identify the changes in biodiversity, climatic changes, and water and soil conditions [1]. Basically, sustainability is the process through which one can reveal the essential needs required without affecting future generations. Environmental monitoring includes some principles that can be used for development without causing any effect on the natural resources. Figure 12.1 provides a summary of environmental monitoring and sustainability for your reference.

12.1.2 Role of emerging technologies

Technology is growing exponentially, which allows us to discover various new techniques, processes, and systems that will be beneficial for humans. Increased advancements through communication networks, sensors, satellites, computers, UAVs, and GIS continuously impact the natural resources and ecosystem because wildlife, deforestation, pollution, and agricultural practices all are getting affected tremendously.

Emerging technologies are revolutionizing the field of environmental monitoring and sustainability. Advances in sensors, data analytics, and communication networks have made it possible to gather and analyze

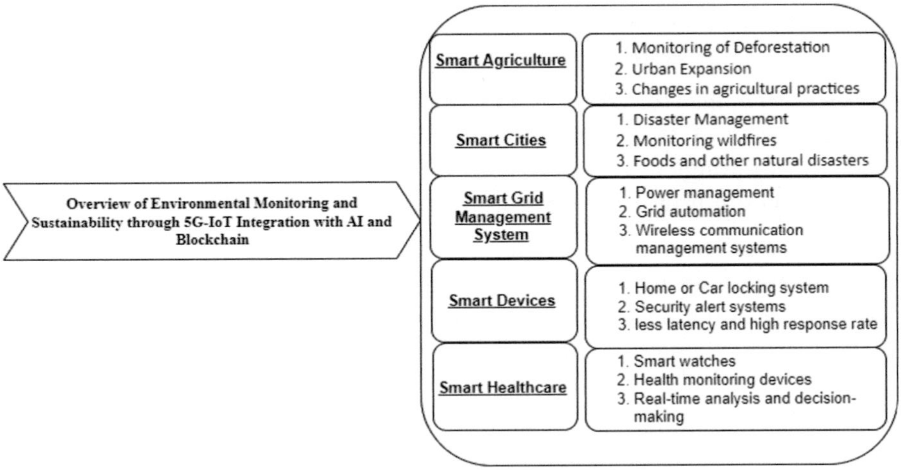

Figure 12.1 Overview of environmental monitoring and sustainability in thrust areas.

environmental data with unprecedented accuracy and in real-time. Technologies like unmanned aerial vehicles (UAVs), remote sensing, and geographic information systems (GIS) have expanded the capabilities of environmental monitoring, allowing for comprehensive and continuous observation of large and remote areas. Remote sensing technologies, including satellites and drones, provide high-resolution images and data on land use, vegetation cover, and water bodies [2]. These technologies enable the monitoring of deforestation, urban expansion, and changes in agricultural practices. GIS integrates this spatial data, allowing for sophisticated mapping and analysis of environmental variables. Moreover, advances in machine learning and big data analytics are transforming the way environmental data is processed and interpreted. These tools can handle huge volumes of data, identify patterns, and predict future trends, which provides effective insights for decision-making and policy formulation.

12.1.3 Importance of integrating 5G, IoT, AI, and blockchain

The enhancements in modern technology include 5G internet, artificial intelligence, and blockchain, which play a vital role in enhancing environmental monitoring. With better devices and sensors, data can be easily transmitted in seconds.

5G technology: The launch of 5G networks promises rapid data transmission speeds and lower latency, which are crucial for real-time environmental monitoring. With 5G, sensors and devices can transmit data instantaneously, allowing for more responsive and adaptive environmental management [3].

Internet of Things (IoT): IOT refers to an interconnected network of devices that can be used to gather all important data and information and then exchange it through devices like sensors, smart meters, and weather stations, which further improves the flow of information.

Artificial intelligence (AI): In the computer science field, artificial intelligence is emerging rapidly, which enables machines to use their learnings and perform a number of activities, including predicting weather conditions, environmental changes, speaking and writing text, and providing data on the topics.

Blockchain technology: Blockchain technology provides safe and verified data, which is more accurate and authentic without any risk. This technology also detects the tracking of sustainability initiatives like carbon credits and renewable energy certificates. To preserve the environment for future generations, it is crucial to monitor the environment. Increased rate of technologies enhances the ability to manage the environment. To make the environment more sustainable, it is important to ensure some limits on using the technologies and preserve the natural resources for a better future [4].

In this section, we saw how environmental monitoring and sustainability are crucial for preserving our planet for future generations. Emerging technologies, including remote sensing, GIS, and data analytics, are enhancing our ability to monitor and manage the environment. The integration of 5G, IoT, AI, and blockchain further amplifies these capabilities, enabling real-time data collection, comprehensive analysis, and secure data management. By leveraging these technologies, we can achieve more accurate, efficient, and sustainable environmental practices, ensuring a balanced approach to development that protects and preserves our natural resources.

12.2 5G Technology in Environmental Monitoring

5G technology is emerging widely in various fields, and it has huge importance in environmental monitoring. So let us discuss some major concepts related to it.

12.2.1 Key features of 5G technology

After the 4G network, 5G is launched, which is faster in speed as one can communicate and send data with ultra-low latency and improved reliability.

Some advanced features of 5G networks are causing bad effects in various sectors like modern cities, healthcare, and the environment.

12.2.1.1 Enhanced connectivity and speed of data transfer

High usage of enhanced connectivity to transmit the data immediately has proven a game changer for many of the factories. The information is transmitted through the sensors, devices, satellites, and drones, which are responsible for the changes in the environment, causing natural disasters, affecting vegetation, and wildlife.

12.2.1.2 Low latency and its impact on real-time monitoring

In 5G technology, the low latency feature enables the data transmission from the servers to the control centers to make decisions accurately. There are a number of examples through which we can understand the transmission through sensors to measure the harmful pollutants present in the air and then transmit this information to the authorized authorities, which have the power to take relevant actions. In rivers and lakes, sensors are present to detect water pollutants and contamination levels to protect the water resources and public health. Environmental monitoring devices such as drones and robotics are used to perform various tasks more efficiently [5]

12.2.2 5G-enabled environmental sensors and devices

The enhancements of 5G devices used to transfer data over long distances rapidly through sensors are transforming the environmental monitoring landscape.

Smart air quality sensors: To detect the pollutants present in the air, smart air quality sensors are used, which can monitor the pollutants present in industrial and urban areas to provide proper information on air quality.

Water quality monitoring devices: Similarly, in water bodies like rivers and lakes, water quality monitoring devices are used, which have sensors with 5G connectivity that help to detect contamination in water, which is essential to make water cleaner for drinking and preserving our ecosystem.

Soil monitoring sensors: To measure the moisture and other nutrients present in soil, soil monitoring sensors are used to ensure good agricultural practices.

Wildlife tracking devices: To track the movement of wildlife, some tracking devices are used that provide crucial data on wildlife behavior.

Table 12.1 Difference between the different types of sensors on the basis of different parameters.

Sensor type	Data transfer speeds	Latency	Device connectivity	Speed	Accessibility	Application areas
Smart air quality sensors	Moderate to high (Wi-Fi, LTE)	Low (1–10 ms)	High (thousands of devices per km^2)	Moderate to high	Urban and industrial	Air pollution monitoring, indoor air quality
Water quality monitoring devices	Moderate (GSM, LTE)	Moderate (10–50 ms)	Moderate (hundreds of devices per km^2)	Moderate	Remote and urban areas	Water treatment plants, natural water bodies
Soil monitoring sensors	Low to moderate (LoRa, NB-IoT)	Moderate (10–50 ms)	Very High (tens of thousands of devices per km^2)	Moderate	Rural and agricultural	Precision farming, soil health monitoring
Wildlife tracking devices	Low to moderate (GPS, GSM)	High (50–200 ms)	Moderate (hundreds of devices per km^2)	Low to moderate	Remote and wildlife areas	Animal migration studies, wildlife conservation

In the above section, 5G technology features are discussed. In environmental monitoring, the enhanced data transfer speeds enable the decision making more accurate. The 5G sensors used in air, water, soil, and wildlife provide accurate data to preserve our environment. We have to limit the usage of 5G networks to make our environment more sustainable [6]. Table 12.1 discusses the comparative analysis of the different sensors considering various parameters.

12.2.3 5G-potential limitations

Although there are numerous benefits of using 5G networks as discussed in the previous section, there exist some potential challenges that need to be addressed. This section talks about some of the challenges that come along with the implementation of 5G.

High cost infrastructure requirement: Implementation of 5G technology requires a huge amount of investment for the installation of a dense network of small cells.

Limited coverage: The Initial phases of 5G are limited to only urban areas, whereas rural areas still face challenges in 5G access.

Table 12.2 Comparative analysis of 5G-IoT integration versus 4G.

Parameter	**4G IoT integration**	**5G IoT integration**
Data speed	Up to 1 Gbps	Up to 10 Gbps or higher
Latency	20–30 ms	As low as 1 ms
Network capacity	Limited to supporting fewer devices per square km	Can support 1 million devices per square km
Energy efficiency	Moderate power consumption	Improved energy efficiency with lower power consumption
Reliability	Moderate, prone to network congestion	High, with more reliable connections and reduced interference
Coverage	More widely available globally	Limited but growing
Cost of infrastructure	Lower infrastructure costs	Higher infrastructure costs
Suitability for IoT applications	Suitable for basic IoT applications (e.g., smart meters)	Ideal for advanced IoT applications (e.g., smart cities and telemedicine)

Device compatibility: In order to have a complete setup of a 5G network, all the devices need to be 5G compatible, which in most older devices is not available.

Energy consumption: Despite the above challenges, even if the infrastructure is set up well, increased consumption of energy after the implementation will lead to subsequent environmental hazards.

12.2.4 Comparison between 4G and 5G

Section 12.2 discussed the involvement of 5G over the environmental issues, various sensors that could be used to enhance the experience and results, and then the challenges associated with its implementation. Lastly, we discuss the comparison of 4G and 5G in Table 12.2.

12.3 Internet of Things (IOT) for Environmental Monitoring

12.3.1 IoT architecture and components

IOT (Internet of Things) allows us to communicate and exchange data through interconnected devices. The working architecture of IoT is shared in Figure 12.2.

There are four main layers present in the architecture of IoT, which include the perception layer, the network layer, the processing layer, and the application layer. The layer and its functioning are described in Figure 12.3.

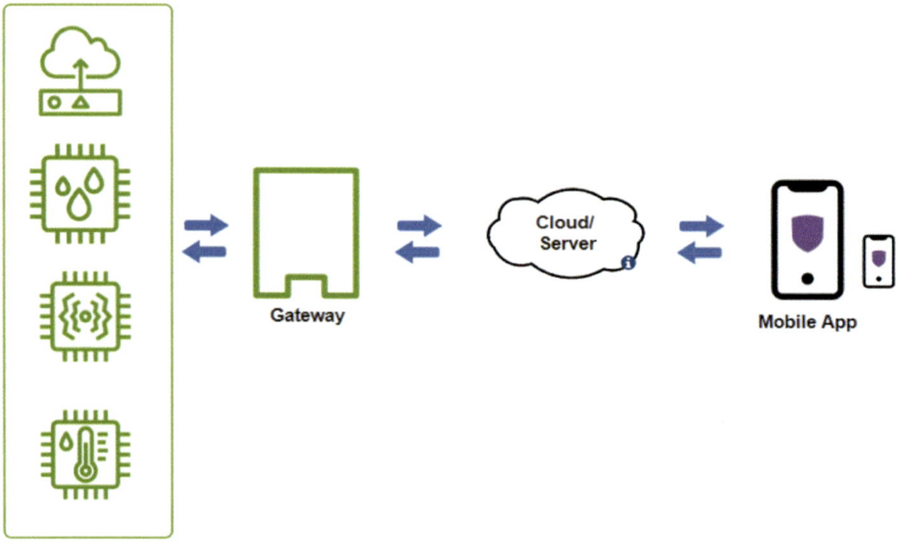

Figure 12.2 Architecture of IoT.

(1) *Perception layer*: This layer includes various sensors that collect the information from the environment to detect some parameters like humidity, temperature, and air quality.
(2) Network layer: The collected data is transferred to the different processing units by using the network layer, which includes a number of different protocols to communicate and maintain the data flow through gateways like Bluetooth, Zigbee, and Wi-Fi.
(3) Processing layer: The data collected from the different sensors is processed and stored by this layer, which is also referred to as the data processing layer. It also includes edge computing and cloud computing. In edge computing, data is processed, and in cloud computing, data is stored to analyze it.
(4) Application layer: Application layer is also referred to as the topmost layer, which is used to transform the data. This layer includes a number of services that are responsible for making effective decisions by interacting with the systems [7].

12.3.2 Types of environmental sensors

For collecting and organizing information about the surrounding environment the numerous types of sensors are used for monitoring environmental issues. The types of environmental sensors are explained as under:

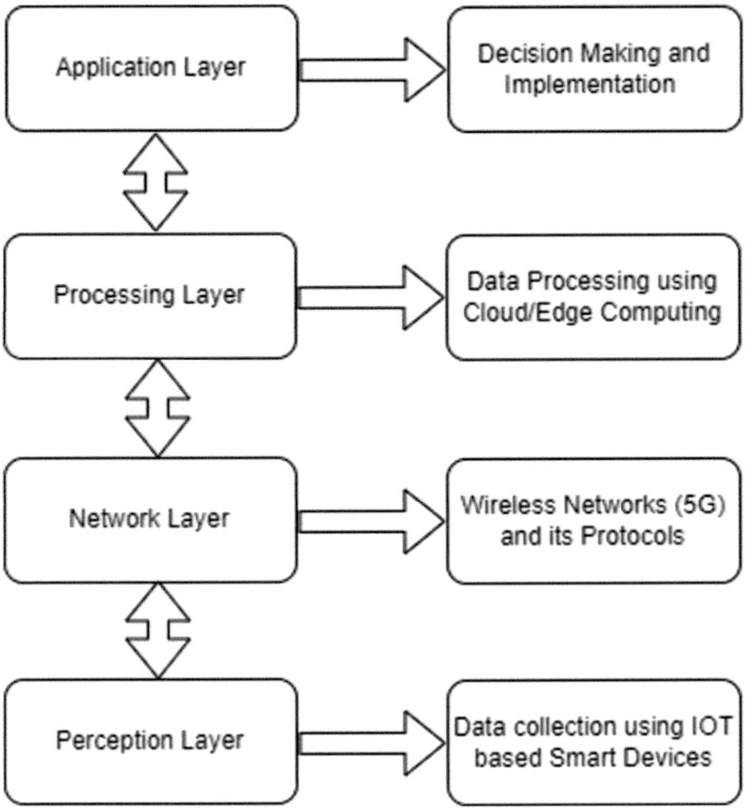

Figure 12.3 Explaining the IOT architecture along with its components.

(1) Air quality sensors: By taking the insights and by observing, predicting, and evaluating the levels of pollutants present in air like carbon monoxide (CO), nitrogen dioxide (NO_2), sulphur dioxide (SO_2), and ozone (O_3), the air quality sensors are used to provide safe environment and air quality.
(2) Water quality sensors: To ensure the quality of drinking water and to preserve the aquatic life, it is required to find out the pollutants. To identify that chemical pollutants like turbidity, pH, and dissolved oxygen in water, present in the water bodies these sensors are used.
(3) Soil moisture sensors: To measure the amount of water present in the soil, these moisture-based soil sensors are used. It is further helpful to make a record of the land and its management strategies and to understand irrigation optimization.

(4) *Humidity and temperature sensors*: To identify the humidity and temperature level of the surrounding air, these sensors are used, which are widely used in climate research, agriculture, and weather monitoring.
(5) *Noise sensors*: Noise sensors are used to check the sound emitted by industrial and urban areas. These sensors are also used in the monitoring of noise pollution.
(6) *Radiation sensors*: Radiation affects the environment and natural resources, so it is important to gauge the radiation with the sensors to make the environment safer. These types of sensors are launched around the nuclear power plants and other radiation sources to measure the radiation levels.

12.3.3 Data collection and transmission

Internet of Things (IoT) includes the processes to transmit the data, which is considered crucial according to environmental monitoring. The sensors located in different positions are responsible for gathering the information of environmental data. After that, the collected data is sent to a central system where it is analyzed and processed further. Both types of networks are used for transmission, like wired or wireless.

Wireless transmission: To build effective communication between sensors and servers, wireless technologies like Wi-Fi, LoRa WAN, Zigbee, and cellular networks are rapidly used to transmit the data.

Edge computing: In IoT, there are some devices that are linked with edge computing. Edge computing is basically referred to as a computing model used to process the data locally to the source of data, and also ensures the reduction of latency and bandwidth consumption.

Cloud computing: A large amount of data, which is received by the cloud platforms, is further processed and analyzed by machine learning algorithms. A large number of datasets are stored in the form of files, images, and other documents, which can be handled easily with the scalability and flexibility offered by cloud computing

12.3.4 Case studies of IoT applications in environmental monitoring

Smart cities and air quality monitoring: In big cities like Beijing and London, air quality monitoring systems are positioned in such a way that they are used to track pollution levels throughout the city. The collected data from the sensors or devices helps the authorities to take valid actions immediately in order to reduce the pollution.

Water management in agriculture: IoT sensors that are used in agricultural areas are used to record or measure the soil moisture levels by optimizing irrigation. Water consumption level is decreasing in some places, like California, where smart irrigation systems are used to track data on soil moisture.

Wildlife conservation: To preserve our wildlife, IoT technology is used to track the behavior and movements of the animals present in the forests by the GPS launched inside the areas. It helps us to ensure and perform some efforts to protect animals like elephants and provides significant information to conserve them through anti-poaching campaigns.

Forest fire detection: To detect the wildlife-prone areas in the forests, IoT sensors are used to check the humidity, temperature, and smoke levels. These sensors are also used to provide warnings in order to prevent them from damage. The layers mentioned above, like perception, network, processing, and application layers, build up the architecture of IoT. The collected data is gathered via a number of sensors that are used to measure radiation, temperature, humidity, air and water quality, soil moisture, noise, and radiation, which is further processed in the cloud and then transmitted through wired and wireless networks. To manage our ecosystem more efficiently, the Internet of Things, which is used in urban cities, wildlife, agriculture, and forestry detects how environmental monitoring is important to save the natural resources.

12.3.5 Limitations and challenges of IoT

This section elaborates on some of the major challenges that come with the implementation of IoT in environmental monitoring.

Data volume and management: Due to the massive installations of sensors to generate data over the period of time, the enormous data created will result in extra efforts required to manage the data. If not taken care of properly, it may lead to issues related to data overload, delayed processing, and other inefficiencies. Significant investment will also be required in the mitigation process via cloud storage and edge computing.

Security and privacy: IoT networks are cyberattack prone, data tampering, and denial-of-service attacks. This issue can result in inaccurate assessment monitoring if compromised. With additional investment in device authentication and other security protocols, this can be mitigated.

Interoperability and standardization: As there are multiple manufacturers of IoT devices, their standards and protocols may also differ, which again can hinder the seamless data collection process and integration. Efforts to establish common IoT standards and protocols, like Message Queuing Telemetry Transport (MQTT) and Constrained Application Protocol (CoAP), are ongoing, but adoption is slow due to the fragmented nature of IoT technologies.

12.4 Artificial Intelligence (AI) in Environmental Data Analysis

12.4.1 Introduction to AI and machine learning

Artificial intelligence and machine learning are renovating a large number of industries and environmental science if one of which has been impacted largely by the two. When computers are enabled with the intelligence of human level and start taking decisions with the help of language comprehension, pattern recognition, etc., it is called artificial intelligence (AI). A subset of AI called machine learning uses the data and trains algorithms, which enables them to learn from their experience and make future predictions without depending on the programmer to give instructions and/or for each and every task.

Through these techniques, trends are found, correlations and patterns are observed, and therefore, many business decisions are taken, all of this is possible with the help of large datasets. As the amount of data increases, it becomes more efficient to make better predictions, which are even more precise and effective. In the field of environment monitoring, AI and ML work extremely well due to their ability to process large volumes of data and reveal undiscovered patterns effectually [8].

12.4.2 AI algorithms for environmental data processing

The analysis related to the environment is highly dependent on the AI algorithms. There are many techniques which are helpful in this field; the most useful are discussed below:

(1) *Supervised learning*: Supervised learning is a technique of ML where the given data is labeled and its behavior is known. For instance, supervised

learning can be used to classify the satellite images for land use type or predict the level of pollution based on the historical data available.

(2) *Unsupervised learning*: Unsupervised learning is performed on the unlabeled data by grouping them into clusters having similar features. In the field of environmental data processing, the sensor data can be used to find out the outliers by grouping them into various clusters.
(3) *Reinforcement learning*: This is another category of algorithms wherein the desired outcomes are achieved with a reward-based system to train the models for making a sequence of decisions. An interesting example of the same could be to find out the best use of water resources at a particular geographical location, which can further help in optimizing water resource management.
(4) *Deep learning*: Deep learning is a branch of ML that analyzes complex data with the help of multi-layered neural networks. It can be used for image recognition tasks meticulously. Some other examples of it could include detecting wildlife species, monitoring, or using satellite imagery to identify deforestation [9].

12.4.3 Predictive analytics for environmental trends

Both historical and current data are important to make meaningful predictions in environmental trends. The big size of data having convoluted variables is capable of finding interesting patterns, and the use of AI and ML makes it even more powerful. There are multiple horizons of environmental domains that can benefit from the assistance of predictive analysis. Some of its applications are shared as below:

(1) *Climate modeling*: AI algorithms can forecast patterns and trends in the climate using AI algorithms with the help of historical data. This information supports the process of identifying mitigation strategies and comprehending the possible effects of climate change in a very effective manner.
(2) *Air quality forecasting*: The information from emission sources, weather, and air quality sensors wen integrated and fed into the predictive algorithms to help determine the pollution level. The appropriate forecasts like these can help in timely pollution control and support public health advisories.
(3) *Water resource management*: By using real-time monitoring of various water resources and their usage over the period of time, AI-powered predictive models can forecast not only the availability but also the

quality of water. This becomes instrumental in improving the quality of life in the areas that are vulnerable to droughts.

(4) *Biodiversity and ecosystem health*: By analyzing data from various sources like wildlife tracking, satellite imagery, and environmental sensors, the predictive analysis can keep a check on the health of the ecosystem and biodiversity. This certainly aids big time in locating vulnerable areas and allocating conservation measures more effectively.

12.4.4 AI-driven decision-making for sustainability

Data-driven insights and optimization of available resources can enhance the sustainability in various fields; some of the significant ones are listed below:

(1) *Smart agriculture*: AI systems have the capacity to evaluate the data from various sources like soil sensors, crop health indicators, and weather forecasts to maximize fertilization, irrigation, and pest control. The results are a decline in resource waste and an increase in crop yields.
(2) *Energy management*: AI algorithms can maximize the use of energy in various operations and buildings with the help of trends and forecasting demands. This further provides a motivation for the consumption of renewable energy sources and brings down the energy waste.
(3) *Urban planning*: AI-driven technologies evaluate the traffic patterns of the data, the usage of energy use and its impact on the environment. This can help in the development of sustainable cities, green spaces, sustainable infrastructure, and more effective public transport systems.
(4) *Waste management*: With the analysis of waste generation data and the collection routes optimization, the recycling procedures can become more time-effective, resulting in a reduced impact on the environment at the same time.

Sustainability and environmental tracking are being revolutionized by AI and machine learning. Large volumes of environmental data are processed and analyzed by AI algorithms, including supervised, unsupervised, reinforcement, and deep learning, in order to find patterns and generate precise predictions. Artificial intelligence (AI)-driven predictive analytics predicts environmental trends like climate patterns, air quality, and water resources, allowing for proactive management and mitigation plans. AI-driven decision-making promotes sustainability and lessens its negative effects on the environment by optimizing resource use in waste management, energy management, urban planning, and agriculture. We can monitor the environment more effectively and efficiently by utilizing AI and ML, which will ensure a sustainable future for our planet.

12.4.5 Challenges with AI implementation in environmental monitoring

Previous sections talked extensively about the environmental data processing. In this section, we discuss various challenges with the AI implementation.

High energy consumption: AI algorithms, especially deep learning algorithms, require humongous power to run and produce results. This leads to large-scale energy consumption, which subsequently results in increased carbon emissions. To overcome this challenge and reduce the carbon footprint, a major shift will be required to energy-efficient hardware.

Data infrastructure requirement: Extensive storage and processing capabilities are required with the implementation of AI. An edge computing model must be used, which processes data locally on the devices and helps in sustaining greener data centers.

Algorithm bias and resource management: The results generated by the AI models can sometimes be biased, dependent upon the data that is used to train the model. This can further disturb the environment with over-exploitation, habitat destruction, or inaccurate climate predictions. This issue can be addressed by using diversified datasets.

12.5 Blockchain Technology for Secure and Transparent Data Management

12.5.1 Fundamentals of blockchain technology

Blockchain is a mechanism where the interconnected computers record transactions in a way that once the data is stored, it cannot be altered later on. This technology was initially developed for virtual currencies. Today, it has been developed into an enormously powerful framework for a decentralized data administration with the added advantage of safety. In blockchain technology, a chronological record that is safe and transparent is created when each transaction, or "block," is appended to a series of earlier transactions [10].

12.5.2 Blockchain in environmental data security

Due to the groundbreaking features mentioned in the previous section, blockchain technology carries a strong potential for improvement in environmental data security. Environmental monitoring requires authenticity and integrity as it forms the basis for the formulation of policies and strategies. Therefore, blockchain is a strong fit for the same [11]. Sharing some of the reasons why it is so:

Data intergrity: Blockchain ensures tamper-proof records due to its very nature. Due to this, the accuracy and dependability of environmental data are enhanced, and therefore, more effective prediction and analysis could be performed in the field of measurements of air quality or the levels of water contamination.

Data authenticity: Data on blockchain is more secure than ever before. There is no fear of data tampering and/or unauthorized data access as the decentralized architecture of blockchain makes it so. It is evident that a secure system provides better results.

Decentralized data sharing: Due to its transparency feature, the sharing amongst various stakeholders becomes very smooth. Whether it is a governmental body, an academic institution, or an environmentalist group, all can have access as the data here is not in the control of a single person. This ensures transparency in the system and enhances collaboration.

12.5.3 Transparent and immutable data records

There are many features of blockchain that make it stand out and serve as a reliable technology, but two of its features are extremely substantial, especially in the field of environmental monitoring, which are transparency and immutability.

Transparency: The data recorded in blockchain is visible to the whole network due to the transparency feature of blockchain. Due to which the data regarding levels of pollution, deforestation rate, and wildlife population could be shared with the public and other stakeholders.

Immutable records: The records once added to the blockchain cannot be changed due to the immutability feature of blockchain. The validity of environment data is preserved as blockchain forbids any changes that are made in the past and has the potential to smear the historical records. Environmental data forms the basis for research and policy formulation-related tasks; these immutable records provide and trustworthy foundation for a long-term impact. A blockchain-based system, for instance, can track carbon emissions and guarantee that reported emission data is correct and unaltered, offering a reliable basis for carbon trading and regulatory compliance.

12.5.4 Smart contracts for environmental compliance

Blockchain supports smart contracts, which facilitate the built-in programming of all the protocols. As and when the condition is true, these contracts carry out the terms without the intervention of any middlemen. This feature provides a lot of scope for using smart contracts to ensure the compliance of environmental policies at various levels [12].

Automated monitoring and reporting: Smart contracts can be set up in such a way that the violations can be monitored automatically, and timely alerts can be raised. For instance, if an individual surpasses the permitted level of pollution, a smart contract will be capable enough to not only raising an alarm but also imposing the associated fine and further guaranteeing ongoing compliance on its own without any human intervention.

Encouraging sustainable practices: Many sustainable practices can be aligned with the smart contracts to encourage individuals. For instance, if a farmer is adapting eco-friendly techniques, he could be given a rebate in subsidies or taxes through the real-time data provided by blockchain. Such incentive-based schemes can encourage individuals to adhere to the guidelines and adopt more environmentally friendly mechanisms in their day-to-day practice.

Streamlining regulatory processes: Smart contracts can simplify regulatory processes, lowering administrative burdens and increasing efficiency by automating compliance checks and reporting. The accuracy and on-time compliance are the major features of Environmental regulations. *Case study*:

Carbon credit trading: Smart contracts can be more helpful to automate the issuing and trading, along with the retirement of carbon credits in trading.

Blockchain technology is contributing to two major areas in this context, that is, monitoring the environment and sustainability. The major features of blockchain help to increase the precision and dependability of environmental data.

12.5.5 Challenges of blockchain implementation

Ensuring data accuracy at input stage: In the process of environmental monitoring, the data is secured once it is stored in the blockchain. Whereas, if the data fed into the system is incorrect in the first place, it remains like that, which leads to misguided decisions based on the faulty information stored. Due to this concern, the inaccurate data can undermine the effectiveness of monitoring and in worst cases can harm the ecosystem if not taken care of properly.

Need for robust validation process: The accuracy of the dataset needs validation as the data is collected from various sources like IoT sensors, satellite imagery, or manual entries. This needs effective validation methods, which is extremely resource-intensive and require specialized knowledge. In order to avoid serious discrepancies, regular audits of data sources must be held. Along with the same efforts, can be made in establishing authentic and standardized protocols.

Integration with existing system: Most of the systems built for environment monitoring use traditional database systems. Amalgamation of blockchain with such systems would a careful planning for smooth data flow and accuracy. The complexity can lead to errors if not implemented along with a strong validation process.

12.6 Integration of 5G, IoT, AI, and Blockchain

12.6.1 Synergies between technologies

By integrating the numerous technologies, there is a scope for many opportunities to improve environmental sustainability and its monitoring. This convergence is able to provide strong, effective, and dependable environmental monitoring systems, which are based on the combination of technologies like artificial intelligence (AI), blockchain, 5G, the Internet of Things (IoT), and advanced data analytics helps to [13].

5G and IoT: The 5G technology provides the fast, along with low-latency, that IoT devices require. By supporting a large network over a long distance, this network facilitates the collection of real-time data and its transmission. So, to make environmental monitoring systems more responsive and time-bound decision making, its an important factor to collect data timely and properly.

AI and machine learning (ML): The amalgamation of these two technologies has given the strength that how data from Internet of Things (IoT) sensors to be processed and analyzed. From large and different datasets, these technologies are able to identify patterns, provide insights, and forecast trends. For instance, to process data related to satellite images or to detect changes in land use or forest cover, it can be performed by using deep learning models, while analyzing and predicting air quality data and its pollution levels, the machine learning algorithms are helpful.

Blockchain: Blockchain provides a guarantee to secure data security along with its integrity and transparency. By proposing a decentralized, non-editable ledger, it will become an aid to reduce fraud and data tampering cases by ensuring that the environmental data will stay accurate and dependable. It also guarantees adherence to the implementation of environmental laws, keeping track of carbon credits and inventory logging for waste disposal will be the major benefits.

Advanced data analytics: By integrating big data analytics with AI and ML, it provides significant support in processing vast amounts of intricate environmental data. By enhancing models' predictive accuracy, revealing hidden insights, and optimizing its resource management, it can be helpful to facilitate the resolution of issues like biodiversity loss, water scarcity, and climate change.

12.6.2 Framework for integrated environmental monitoring systems

To accommodate the need to create a framework for integrated environmental monitoring systems, a comprehensive strategy that integrates the features of all technologies is required. These types of frameworks are basically based upon the following components:

(1) *Data collection*: The IOT sensors and devices are deployed in different regions and environments to gather real-time data pertaining to air quality, soil conditions, temperature levels, humidity ratios, and water quality. These sensors are becoming more reliable and transmitting data at high speed by using a 5G network.

(2) *Data processing and analysis*: The artificial intelligence (AI) and machine learning (ML) algorithms are used to process the collected data. To reduce the latency in transmission and bandwidth consumption, edge

computing can be applied at the sensor level. The cloud environments involving big data analytics coupled with deep learning models are carried out with more advanced analysis in aiming at recognizing patterns, making predictions, and generating insights.

(3) *Data management and storage*: Blockchain technology is mainly used for storing and managing data. Therefore, every single piece of information can be traced back to one before it, creating an immutable, as well as auditable, record. This ensures the integrity of information while simplifying authentication procedures concerning its origin traceability. With the use of decision support systems (DSS) based platforms, which only work on processed forms of data and insights, it makes artificial intelligence (AI) as a decision-making tool. Because of its real-time data collection, it also helps to optimize management of the resources, proposing mitigation strategies, and notifying stakeholders of emerging issues.

(4) User interface and reporting: The user interface provides access to stakeholders for reports, alerts, and data visualizations. Easy interaction with the monitoring system and actionable insights should be provided by this user-friendly interface [14].

12.6.3 Challenges and solutions in technology integration

Even with all these potential benefits, integrating various technologies into a cohesive system is challenging:

(1) Data integration and compatibility: Numerous protocols and separate data formats may be used by various sensors and devices. But there is a need for global communication protocols and standardization to ensure interoperability and seamless data integration. So, by seeing this challenge, the best solution is to employ middleware that can translate between diverse systems and implement common data formats, like JSON or XML.

(2) Infrastructure and scalability: A scalable infrastructure that is able to manage a large number of devices and massive data volumes is difficult to build. To address the major issues like fast processing and large storage capacity, cloud computing, scalable IoT platforms, and edge computing are the only capable solutions.

(3) *Cybersecurity and privacy*: Cybersecurity and data privacy become a major concern only because of the rapid increase in connected devices

and the sharing between those devices. It needs encrypted data to protect data integrity, authentication, and user privacy.

(4) *Resource and cost management*: Creating and implementing integrated systems can be expensive. Using cloud services, scalable infrastructure, and open-source technologies are some ways to make it cheaper. The grants and public–private partnerships can be helpful for large-scale project financing.

12.6.4 Interoperability and standardization issues

For the smooth operation of integrated environmental monitoring systems, the standardization and interoperability are the two essential components, and important concerns consist of:

(1) *Absence of standardized protocols*: By the use of proprietary protocols by many IoT systems and devices, the interoperability is hampered. To enhance the compatibility, there is a need to boost the use of standardized communication protocols, such as MQTT, CoAP, or 6LoWPAN, and by abiding by international standards, such as IEEE 802.15.4 for wireless personal area networks.

(2) *Diverse data formats*: Data interchange can be complicated by the use of disparate data formats across different systems. Data interoperability can be facilitated by implementing common data formats and data exchange standards like the observations and measurements (O&M) standard or the Sensor Observation Service (SOS).

(3) *Regulatory and policy difficulties*: The integration of technologies such as sophisticated data analytics, blockchain, IoT, 5G, and AI into a single environmental monitoring framework has been very beneficial. These synergies lead to more dependable and effective environmental management because of their improved data gathering, handling, and interpretation. In order to utilize these technologies in a suitable manner, the challenges with cybersecurity, scalability, data integration, and standardization need to be solved. Encouraging the interoperability and implementing global norms empowers us to develop scalable, dependable, and effective technologies that increase our ability to monitor and protect the environment. This integrated strategy not only promotes sustainable growth but also ensures a healthier and more resilient planet for future generations.

12.7 Case Studies and Real-world Applications

12.7.1 Smart cities and sustainable urban development

Introduction

The idea of a smart city has emerged as an important tool to manage the rapid growth and streamline the sustainable urbanization fast-paced implementation. Smart cities are integrating technologies like AI, IoT, blockchain, and big data, which further ensures sustainable development to improve urban services. This section discusses a case study to provide an overview of technologies employed in Amsterdam.

Amsterdam, Netherlands: Collaborative and sustainable innovation

Amsterdam smart city platform: A collaborative initiative involving businesses, government, and citizens implements innovation.

Smart grids and renewable energy: Smart grids optimize energy distribution and integrate renewable sources, and they also encourage sustainable practices.

Waste management: The sensors are used to monitor waste levels, which optimizes collection routes and helps in reducing emissions.

Bicycle-friendly infrastructure: The introduction of sensor-based smart bike lanes ensures cyclist safety and promotes sustainable transportation.

Circular economy: This project encourages the reuse of resources and their recycling, which helps to reduce waste and environmental impact.

Challenges and solutions

In order to provide the data safely with moral usage, some strong security safeguards, encryption, and data governance are required.

Expense and resources: Significant investment is also a serious concern. Enforcing public–private partnerships, government grants, and creative finance structures that may support initiatives are therefore the answers.

Citizen engagement: Success depends on involving citizens. Involvement and ownership are promoted by open communication, instructional initiatives, and user-friendly platforms.

Conclusion

The initiatives for smart cities in Amsterdam show the potential for enhancing the lifestyle and its quality, optimizing urban services, and ensuring sustainability through technology. One thing is very clear that for the success and scalability of smart city projects, the challenges related to the privacy of data, interoperability, funding, and citizen engagement must be addressed. These pioneering cities provide valuable lessons for developing sustainable, resilient, and inclusive urban environments globally.

12.7.2 Water quality and management systems

Introduction

For the betterment of public health, sustainability of the environment, and economic progress, water resource management and quality control are essential components. So, water quality and its management techniques use advanced technologies such as big data, blockchain, IoT, and AI to monitor, assess, and optimize water resources. This case study looks at how water management systems are used in various contexts, highlighting the technology used, the challenges faced, and the outcomes attained by using IoT and data analytics to monitor water quality.

Real-time water quality monitoring: To monitor and measure parameters such as pH, temperature, turbidity, and chemical composition, Internet of Things (IoT) sensors are placed in water bodies and distribution networks. These sensors are helpful to provide real-time data that further helps to prompt the identification of water impurities and pollutants.

Smart water meters: The other scenario is the real-time water usage monitors, which are installed in homes and commercial areas. It helps in detecting the leakages, stopping water wastage, and also helps to make users aware of their usage habits in daily life routines. To gather data on the weather and hydrological parameters, such as rainfall, river flow, and groundwater levels, there should be use of Internet of Things devices. Because this data can be further helpful for the purpose of managing water resources and anticipating floods.

Using AI and MLP to improve water management predictive analytics: AI and machine learning algorithms are helpful to examine both historical and current data to estimate changes in water quality, select the sources of pollution, and estimate water demand. This facilitates proactive decision-making and management.

Water treatment optimization: By optimizing the operation of water treatment plants, AI-powered systems can be helpful to make chemical dosing and treatment process adjustments based on real-time data on water quality. This provides effective care and adherence to legal requirements.

Leak repair and detection: For finding leaks and burst pipes, the artificial intelligence algorithms examine sensor data from water distribution networks. It further helps to reduce water loss and infrastructure damage resulting from early detection and prompt repairs.

Automated irrigation systems: AI-based systems can be helpful in the irrigation sector also for getting or providing information about crop requirements, soil moisture content, and weather forecasts to automatically adjust irrigation. It also ensures efficient water use, which raises crop yields and conserves water.

Blockchain for security and transparency:

By the use of blockchain technology, the information on water quality is guaranteed to be secure. It provides the accuracy of data on water quality by preventing tampering and unauthorized access by storing data on a decentralized ledger. Transparent water trading: The farmers and industries can trade water in a transparent and secure manner. By automating transactions, smart contracts ensure terms are followed and disputes are avoided.

Compliance and reporting: Blockchain technology plays an important role in managing the immutable record of water quality data and management techniques. It further helps in providing reports to authorities and stakeholders, and also increases adherence to legislation. By taking analytics from big data to enhance water management and its resources.

Forecasting floods and droughts: Evaluating the extensive datasets helps to forecast floods and droughts and allows the system to allow for early alerts and readiness actions. As a result, there is less impact on towns and economies by extreme weather events.

Water quality analysis: Big data analytics processes enormous volumes of data on water quality to find similar patterns, spot anomalies, and evaluate the effects of pollution sources. This is in favor of producing focused interventions, pollution prevention strategies, and problems with water.

Compatibility and data integration: Maintaining compatibility with the integration of data from various sources is a big challenge. Creating standardized data formats and utilizing data integration platforms to expedite data gathering and analysis are two solutions.

High initial costs: A substantial investment is needed to implement cutting-edge water management systems. Public–private partnerships, government funding, and scalable technology options are some ways to reduce the cost of systems.

Connectivity problems: Real-time data transmission requires dependable internet connectivity. Investing in rural broadband infrastructure and employing satellite-based communication systems in isolated locations are two solutions.

Training and capacity building: In order to use cutting-edge technologies, users must receive training. Offering workshops, training courses, and technical assistance can help make water management systems more widely adopted and effectively used. As an illustration:

United States: California's water grid: California has put in place an advanced water management system to address concerns with water quality and scarcity. In the whole state, IoT sensors are used to track the usage and quality of water. Blockchain is used to maintain data integrity, and AI-driven analytics optimize water distribution and predict demand. It results in to decrease in wastage of water and an increase in water management efficiency as a result.

Netherlands: Integrated water management: The Netherlands has also implemented an integrated water management system to manage its vast network of rivers, canals, and coastal areas. They have deployed IoT sensors that keep an eye on weather patterns, water quality, and their levels. To manage water resources and forecast floods, they use AI and big data analytics. So, in the end, this system helps to improve water quality management and flood resilience.

India: Smart water systems in urban areas: In this chain in India, Bangalore has implemented smart water management systems to address problems with water supply and quality. IoT-enabled smart meters and sensors are implemented to monitor water distribution and quality. AI-based analytics are helpful to find leaks and improve water treatment. This has given an advantage in decreased water loss and increased the dependability of the water supply.

In today's scenario, the systems for managing water quality and quantity are necessary for the sustainable use of water resources. By utilizing technologies like IoT, AI, blockchain, and big data, these systems improve water resource monitoring, analysis, and optimization. For its successful implementation, issues with data integration, expenses, connectivity, and training must be resolved. The case studies from California, the Netherlands, and India provide important insights for international efforts to promote water sustainability while demonstrating the revolutionary potential of sophisticated water management systems.

12.8 Benefits of Technology Integration for Sustainability

In today's quickly changing technological scenario, it is becoming critical to improve data accuracy and real-time monitoring of data, including environmental management, public health, and urban planning. These capabilities, which make use of cutting-edge technologies like IoT, AI, and big data, allow for accurate data collection, quick response times, and well-informed decision making. This article examines how important these developments are for raising public awareness and participation, boosting data accuracy, boosting resource management, and accelerating the effects on the economy and environment [15, 16]. Figure 12.4 summarizes the advantages of integrating technology for sustainability.

12.8.1 Enhanced data accuracy and real-time monitoring

Accuracy in data collection: IoT devices and sophisticated sensors gather data with high precision, and these instruments also provide highly accurate measurements of a variety of parameters, such as temperature, humidity, air quality, and water quality. Precise data gathering guarantees that choices are founded on trustworthy data, minimizing error margin and augmenting total efficacy.

Real-time data processing: Real-time monitoring of the resources is the only aid to implement high-level data processing and analysis. It is required for validating and verifying patterns, spotting outliers, and handling problems as they come up. In order to reduce pollution and safeguard public health, these technologies provide insights that would be impossible to obtain manually by processing massive volumes of data accurately and quickly.

12.8.2 Improved resource management

The effective resource allocation is feasible with the help of high-precision data and its real-time monitoring. For instance, the precision farming technologies help to maximize crop health and soil conditions by using real-time

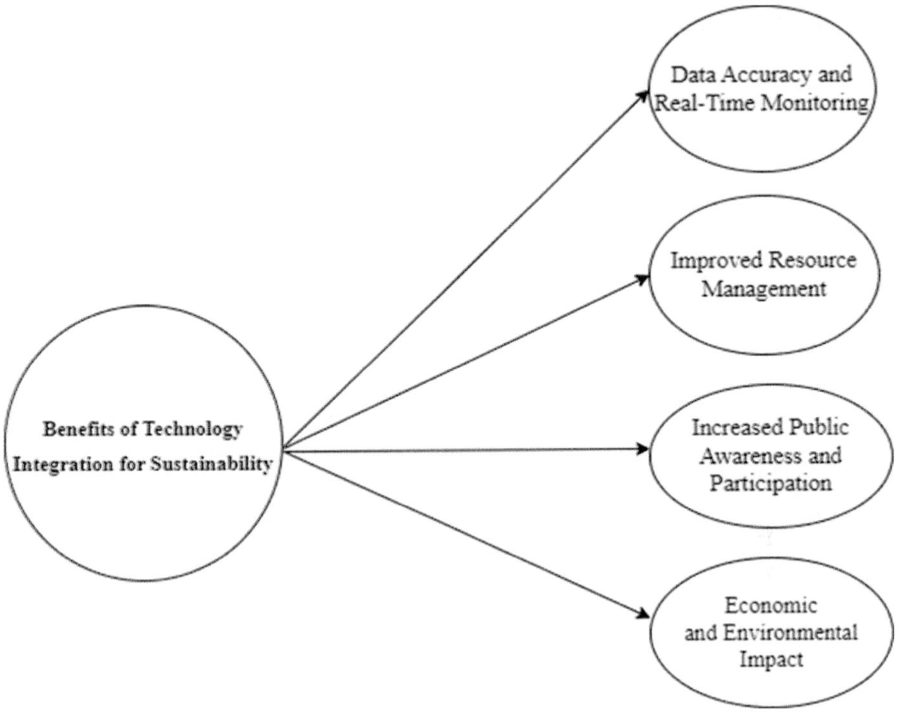

Figure 12.4 Explaining the benefits of technology integration for sustainability.

data about the use of a particular pesticide, fertilizer, and water usage. This helps to increase the impact on the environment and waste while also increasing crop yields.

Water management: By implementing more real-time monitoring of water resources, it will be more helpful in the efficient management of water supply and demand. For example, smart irrigation systems optimize water use by adjusting water delivery based on soil moisture levels and weather forecasts. This is especially crucial in areas where there is a shortage of water.

Energy management: On the other hand, the real-time data on energy consumption helps in effective resource management in urban settings. Utility companies can better balance supply and demand, cut down on energy waste, and minimize carbon emissions by using smart grids and meters, which offer insights into patterns of energy usage.

12.8.3 Increased public awareness and participation

To obtain current information on traffic patterns, weather forecasts, and the quality of the air and water, real-time monitoring and improved data accuracy become very helpful, and it enables people be able to make decisions about their daily activities, safety, and health because of this transparency.

Citizen engagement: With the use of digital platforms and mobile apps, the public can be encouraged to monitor and report issues. To help with the collective effort to address issues like pollution, water leaks, and traffic, citizens can use apps to report these types of problems on the same platform. It also helps to promote civic engagement and a sense of responsibility by involving the public in monitoring initiatives.

Educational impact: There should be open access to reliable data and updated information for better public education on environmental and social issues. Using this data, awareness campaigns and educational initiatives can emphasize the value of sustainable practices and promote behavior change. For instance, the collection of real-time data on air quality and pollution levels can encourage people to drive less on days with high pollution.

12.8.4 Economic and environmental impact

Cost savings: For people, companies, and governments alike, the best solution for cost savings is better resource management. Utilizing resources like water, energy, and agricultural inputs efficiently helps to lower operating costs and eliminates waste. In addition, the technologies based on precision farming can boost crop yields while reducing input costs, which is more helpful for farmers.

Encouragement of economic activity: Innovation and the growth in the economy are propelled forward by improved data accuracy and real-time monitoring. In industries like technology, the generation of new jobs and business opportunities is also an advantage of the environmental services and data analytics, the advancement and application of smart technologies. Initiatives related to smart cities encourage investment and sustainable urban growth in the cities while maintaining overall expenditures.

Environmental benefits: To reduce the impact on the environment, real-time monitoring and data accuracy are essential. These technologies aid in the preservation of natural resources and the protection of ecosystems by streamlining resource usage, cutting waste, and enabling proactive measures.

For instance, prompt interventions to lessen pollution and its detrimental effects on the environment and human health are made possible by real-time monitoring of the quality of the air and water.

Climate change mitigation: To fight against the frequent changes in climate, there is a need to gather data on current information for greenhouse gas emissions, energy use, and environmental conditions. For providing the solution, policymakers can create efficient action plans related to the climate, monitor the overall progress, and make data-driven decisions to lower carbon footprints by implementing high-precision data monitoring and predictive analytics.

It will become a guarantee that decisions are founded on validated and authentic information, which maximizes the allocation of resources and their utilization and provides advancement in sustainable practices by utilizing integrated technologies. The advantages are not only financial savings and efficiency gains, it also include positive effects on the environment, public awareness, and participation. As these technologies develop further, it will be essential to integrate them into a variety of industries in order to create a resilient and sustainable future.

12.9 Challenges and Future Directions

12.9.1 Technical challenges and limitations

When cutting-edge technologies like IoT, AI, blockchain, and big data are integrated into various industries, it arises significant technical obstacles and constraints. Interoperability is a major challenge since disparate systems, platforms, and devices frequently employ incompatible standards and protocols, which makes it difficult to exchange data easily. The second one is the scalability, particularly in large-scale deployments where the infrastructure needs to effectively manage multiple devices and enormous volumes of data. Because incomplete or erroneous data can result in flawed analyses and decisions, data reliability and quality are also crucial considerations [17].

With limitations like network latency and bandwidth, the real-time data processing and transmission are made more difficult. For example, poor connectivity in remote or rural areas can negatively impact the performance and reliability of IoT devices. IoT sensors and devices' energy consumption is also a major drawback, especially for battery-powered systems that need regular maintenance or replacement [18].

12.9.2 Ethical and privacy concerns

The use of these integrated technologies raises serious privacy and ethical issues. The gathering and storing of personal data via IoT devices, AI analytics, and other technologies is a risk to the personal identity of people. It may result in unauthorized access to or misuse of sensitive information through identity theft and privacy violations. There should be an implementation of AI algorithms that provide transparency and accountability to reduce these identity theft risks. There is also a need to aware people about ethical standards in the deployment and usage of technology and preserving their trust and consent. The privacy rights can also be violated by surveillance and data monitoring using IoT and smart technologies. The possibility of governments or corporations abusing surveillance data makes stringent regulations and moral standards necessary.

12.9.3 Regulatory and policy frameworks

There is a need for developing and implementing powerful structures of regulation and policy to address concerns based on the concerns of privacy, ethical concerns, and technical concerns that these technologies present. Standards make it possible to ensure compatibility and interoperability among different platforms and devices. Common standards and protocols help with the more pervasive propagation of such technologies because of smooth integration and exchange of data. To protect the privacy and private information of people, data protection and privacy laws need to be put in place and followed. The guidelines set not only stern standards for collecting, storing, and processing data but also hold organizations accountable and transparent through, for instance, the General Data Protection Regulation in the European Union. These policies should incorporate AI ethics and accountability, thereby obligating frequent audits and impact evaluations to remove unfair or biased results. Regulations regarding cybersecurity will also help in safeguarding the possible data breaches, as well as cyberattacks. Sensitive data can be protected while system integrity is preserved by implementing security measures such as encryption, secure authentication, and recurrent vulnerability assessments.

12.9.4 Future trends and research opportunities

With further growth, advanced technologies will be able to work through the existing limits and address newly emerging problems. It will be a fruit of

Table 12.3 Directions of future trends.

Trend	**Description**	**Key impact areas**	**challenges**	**Future directions**
Quantum blockchain	- Involves using *quantum computing* to enhance or break current blockchain encryption systems. - *Quantum-resistant cryptography* is being developed to protect blockchain from quantum threats.	- *Security*: Enhanced protection against future quantum attacks. - *Efficiency*: Improved transaction speeds. - *Decentralization*: More secure peer-to-peer networks.	- *Computational power*: High resource needs. - *Algorithm standardization*: Lack of standardized quantum-resistant cryptography.	- Ongoing research in *quantum-resistant algorithms*. - Potential breakthroughs in quantum cryptographic systems.
AI integration with blockchain	- *AI automates* and optimizes smart contracts and blockchain processes. - *Blockchain* ensures secure and transparent data for AI systems. - Enhances fraud detection and predictive analytics.	- *Smart contracts*: AI improves contract execution. - *Data analytics*: AI analyzes large blockchain datasets. - *Fraud detection*: Enhanced monitoring and anomaly detection.	- *Scalability*: Integrating both technologies efficiently. - *Complexity*: Complexity of systems and models.	- *AI-powered blockchain systems* in healthcare and supply chain. - Research in decentralized AI models on blockchain.
Combined impact on industries	Both trends are expected to transform *finance, healthcare, supply chain*, and other data-sensitive industries by improving security, efficiency, and automation.	- *Finance*: Secure, faster financial transactions. - *Healthcare*: Secure patient data sharing with blockchain and AI. - *IoT*: Safeguarding data integrity in connected devices.	- Adoption could be slow due to high initial costs and a lack of industry standards.	- Further development of *AI-driven blockchain models and quantum cryptographic protocols*.

severe research and development work that will finally become a result of teamwork in several domains, namely computer science, engineering, ethics, and law. The better analysis of data, thanks to the advancements in AI and machine learning, will provide a reliable basis for making decisions in many industries [19, 20, 21].

Because edge computing processes data closer to the source and lessens the dependency on centralized cloud servers, it is becoming a viable solution to latency and bandwidth problems. The effectiveness and performance of Internet of Things systems can be greatly enhanced by this strategy. Innovations in power management, battery life, and energy efficiency will also be crucial to guaranteeing the long-term viability of Internet of Things implementations.

Blockchain technology has the capability to improve data security and transparency, especially in industries such as supply chain management, finance, and healthcare. The adoption and integration of blockchain technology will be aided by research into scalable and effective solutions.

In addition, it will take constant communication and cooperation between technologists, decision-makers, and the general public to address ethical and privacy concerns. Such a framework and policy about AI usage and data have to be developed so that ethical and equitable technology deployment can be ensured. Some of the major technical limitations and challenges arise when these technologies, such as IoT, AI, blockchain, and big data, are implemented, and that risks include interoperability, scalability, data quality, and network constraints. Due to the concerns regarding data collection, AI biases, surveillance, and strong regulations are required. It should be the priority to ensure the use of these new technologies are must be in a responsible and effective manner, that is, to reap benefits while risks are minimized, it will be critical to treat these issues and advance research. Table 12.3 further discusses the upcoming trends, quantum blockchain, and artificial intelligence integration with blockchain, which could influence various industry sectors.

12.10 Conclusion

12.10.1 The future of environmental monitoring

Therefore, with the integration of technologies such as 5G, IoT, AI, and blockchain, environmental monitoring will leap ahead into the future. These will assure data with a very high precision, real-time monitoring, and capacity for implementing proactive action plans for providing environmental sustainability. So, to push the future toward sustainable development, there is a need to apprehend the impact of these innovations in environmental monitoring.

IoT and 5G: The core of real-time environmental monitoring
5G network: The 5G network will be able to transform the entire environmental monitoring domain through its remarkable connectivity, data speeds, and low latency. By using this improved connectivity, numerous IoT-based sensors and devices can be integrated, which helps in collecting real-time data related to a variety of environmental parameters constantly.

IoT sensors: As IoT sensors will be very capable of scanning broad cross-sections of environmental factors such as soil health, water quality, air quality, and weather conditions, and will be helpful to create holistic and realistic data regarding the environment when deployed strategically across remote rural and urban locations. These sensors will be made more advanced, miniaturized, and energy-frugal.

Advanced level of data analysis and prediction with AI and ML
AI-driven analytics: The AI and ML algorithms will play a crucial role as they process and make sense of the extremely large datasets, which are produced by the Internet of Things sensors. By using and integrating these technologies, environmental data can be analyzed to bring patterns, trends, and anomalies that are useful information to stakeholders and policy-making bodies to make decisions with accuracy.

Predictive analytics: With the use of artificial intelligence, future hazards and environmental changes can be predicted. The AI-based predictive models can predict air pollution, predict wildfire expansion, and predict the effects of climate change on biodiversity, among other things. So by taking these insights and using these prediction skills, it enables people to take action ahead of time to address environmental risks and respond rapidly to reduce them.

Blockchain: Ensuring authenticity and data integrity
Immutable data accounts: The use of blockchain technology ensures that data on environmental issues will be authentic and transparent, making environmental monitoring more reliable and accountable in guaranteeing the authenticity and integrity of data by providing a secure, decentralized, and tamper-proof ledger. The smart contracts based on blockchain technology will also automate regulatory and environmental compliance procedures. For

example, to monitor carbon credits, enforce environmental regulations, and ensure the proper implementation of conservation programs, such types of agreements are required.

12.10.2 Call to action for researchers and policymakers

Researchers: Driving innovation and advancing knowledge
Interdisciplinary research: It also helps to promote the scope of interdisciplinary research, whereby knowledge from data analytics, engineering, environmental science, and policy studies can be harnessed together. It will become a collaborative effort by providing innovative solutions with a better understanding of the complex interrelationship between human activity and the environment.

Technological development: Funding is also a necessity, and it should be provided in regular intervals to enhance and develop technologies based on environmental monitoring. Work within the boundaries of making efficient IoT sensors, developing sophisticated AI-based algorithms, and introducing new blockchain applications in environmental settings should be encouraged and researched.

Encourage collaboration and data sharing: Researchers will also encourage collaborations with international bodies and data sharing based on sectors, institutions, and cross-border. There is a need to provide open access to environmental data will be conducive toward efforts for global efforts to tackle environmental challenges, but also facilitate comprehensive analyses and inspire innovation.

Public involvement: Public involvement also plays an important role in environmental monitoring programs to raise awareness and help community members get engaged in the concerns related to the environment. The legislators and government bodies should promote projects related to citizen science, public mobilization, and awareness campaigns, which would allow citizens to make positive impacts on environmental sustainability.

International cooperation: As environmental problems are global in nature, cooperation from international bodies is required to provide a generic solution. To solve these common environmental challenges, there is a need for joint international agreements and partnerships that promote the exchange of information, resources, as well as technology by policymakers.

12.11 Conclusion

This chapter of the book discusses numerous ways in whereby improvement in integrating blockchain, IoT, 5G technology, and AI can bring much innovation to environmental monitoring and sustainability. The chapter started with an overview of such fundamental technologies and highlighted the essential characteristics of 5G networks, AI algorithms, IoT devices, and blockchain systems. It also discusses the relation between these technologies and how the integration of all these technologies can be helpful in changing environmental monitoring procedures, yet again reiterating the transparency of managing data through blockchain and the role of AI in providing high precision, and IOT sensors in providing robustness and improving network performance. For environmental monitoring, artificial intelligence is playing an important role in gathering analytics because these supports decision support systems along with anomaly detection and predictive analytics. It also discusses how artificial intelligence can scan and gather massive quantities of data related to the environment for trends and potential dangers so that the stakeholders will be able to make help from informed decisions. On the other hand, blockchain technology provides an immutable and secure repository for environmental data, which provides assurance for the accountability and integrity of data. The case study explains the real-time scenario for the effectiveness of 5G-IoT applications in environmental monitoring, are climate change monitoring, waste management, and tracking wildlife. In addition to the demand of the community stakeholders of the industry in collaboration with the governments and research institutions to be merged together on a single platform, so that the issues discussed in this chapter majorly focus on the use of energy, data security, and scalability of IoT platforms. Above all, this book is a definitive manual for scholars, policymakers, and corporate leaders who would be keen to leverage the 5G-IoT innovations toward more environmental sustainability. The policymakers have been told to put in place regulatory frameworks that will encompass interdisciplinary research, engaging the public, and international cooperation. On the other hand, it will become a challenge for researchers to engage in research related to interdisciplinary areas, technological innovation, and the sharing of data. The best solution is only by working together that we will enable ourselves to take advantage of these new technologies in solving environmental issues and guaranteeing a more sustainable future for all.

References

[1] Hammond, A., & World Resources Institute. (1995). *Environmental indicators: a systematic approach to measuring and reporting on environmental policy performance in the context of sustainable development* (Vol. 36). Washington, DC: World Resources Institute.

[2] Gray, P. C., Ridge, J. T., Poulin, S. K., Seymour, A. C., Schwantes, A. M., Swenson, J. J., & Johnston, D. W. (2018). Integrating drone imagery into high resolution satellite remote sensing assessments of estuarine environments. *Remote Sensing*, *10*(8), 1257.

[3] Chew, M. Y. L., Teo, E. A. L., Shah, K. W., Kumar, V., & Hussein, G. F. (2020). Evaluating the roadmap of 5G technology implementation for smart building and facilities management in Singapore. *Sustainability*, *12*(24), 10259.

[4] Hwang, J., Choi, M. I., Lee, T., Jeon, S., Kim, S., Park, S., & Park, S. (2017). Energy prosumer business model using blockchain system to ensure transparency and safety. *Energy Procedia*, *141*, 194-198.

[5] Gohil, A., Modi, H., & Patel, S. K. (2013, March). 5G technology of mobile communication: A survey. In *2013 international conference on intelligent systems and signal processing (ISSP)* (pp. 288-292). IEEE.

[6] Mamun, M. A. A., & Yuce, M. R. (2020). Recent progress in nanomaterial enabled chemical sensors for wearable environmental monitoring applications. *Advanced Functional Materials*, *30*(51), 2005703.

[7] Jaber, A. A., Al-Mousawi, F. K. I., & Jasem, H. S. (2019). Internet of things based industrial environment monitoring and control: a design approach. *International Journal of Electrical and Computer Engineering (IJECE)*, *9*(6), 4657-4667.

[8] Cortès, U., Sànchez-Marrè, M., Ceccaroni, L., R-Roda, I., & Poch, M. (2000). Artificial intelligence and environmental decision support systems. *Applied intelligence*, *13*, 77-91.

[9] VoPham, T., Hart, J. E., Laden, F., & Chiang, Y. Y. (2018). Emerging trends in geospatial artificial intelligence (geoAI): potential applications for environmental epidemiology. *Environmental Health*, *17*, 1-6.

[10] Shen, X. S., Liu, D., Huang, C., Xue, L., Yin, H., Zhuang, W., ... & Ying, B. (2022). Blockchain for transparent data management toward 6G. *Engineering*, *8*, 74-85.

[11] Zhao, M., Liu, W., & He, K. (2022). Research on data security model of environmental monitoring based on blockchain. *IEEE Access*, *10*, 120168-120180.

[12] Gupta, N., & Bedi, P. (2018, September). E-waste management using blockchain based smart contracts. In *2018 International Conference on Advances in Computing, Communications and Informatics (ICACCI)* (pp. 915-921). IEEE.

[13] El Azzaoui, A., Singh, S. K., Pan, Y., & Park, J. H. (2020). Block5GIntell: Blockchain for AI-enabled 5G networks. *IEEE Access*, *8*, 145918-145935.

[14] Born, S. M., & Sonzogni, W. C. (1995). Integrated environmental management: strengthening the conceptualization. *Environmental management*, *19*, 167-181.

[15] Mundy, M. A., & Kupczynski, L. (2013). A qualitative study of technology integration into culture and sustainability in schools. *International Scholarly Research Notices*, *2013*(1), 967610.

[16] Yee, J. T., & Oh, S. C. (2012). *Technology integration to business: Focusing on RFID, interoperability, and sustainability for manufacturing, logistics, and supply chain management*. Springer Science & Business Media.

[17] Singh, S. K., Rathore, S., & Park, J. H. (2020). BlockIoTintelligence: A blockchain-enabled intelligent IoT architecture with artificial intelligence. *Future Generation Computer Systems*, *110*, 721-743.

[18] Guergov, S., & Radwan, N. (2021). Blockchain convergence: Analysis of issues affecting IoT, AI and blockchain. *International Journal of Computations, Information and Manufacturing (IJCIM)*, *1*(1).

[19] Gill, S. S., Tuli, S., Xu, M., Singh, I., Singh, K. V., Lindsay, D., ... & Garraghan, P. (2019). Transformative effects of IoT, Blockchain and Artificial Intelligence on cloud computing: Evolution, vision, trends and open challenges. *Internet of Things*, *8*, 100118.

[20] Zhang, Z., Song, X., Liu, L., Yin, J., Wang, Y., & Lan, D. (2021). Recent advances in blockchain and artificial intelligence integration: Feasibility analysis, research issues, applications, challenges, and future work. *Security and Communication Networks*, *2021*(1), 9991535.

[21] Khanna, H., & Sharma, M. (2022). An improved security algorithm for vanet using machine learning. Journal of Positive School Psychology, 6(3), 7743-7756.

Section 4

Applications of Blockchain and AI in 5G-IoT

13

Exploration of Conditional Privacy Preserving and Authentication Protocols for Internet of Vehicles

Neha Bagga[1], Sheetal Kalra[2], Sartaj Singh[3], and Vinit Grewal[2]

[1]School of Computer Science and Engineering, Lovely Professional University, India
[2]Department of Computer Science and Engineering, Guru Nanak Dev University, Regional Campus, India
[3]School of Computer Applications, Lovely Professional University, India
Email: neha.23407@lpu.co.in; sheetal.kalra@gmail.com; Sartaj_2292@yahoo.com; vinit.ecejal@ gndu.ac.in

Abstract

The Internet of Vehicles enables the formation of self-organized networks for the dissemination of information across various industries, including the automotive sector, academia, vehicular networks, and manufacturing. In the context of intelligent transportation systems (ITS), vehicles share a multitude of information related to driver safety, infotainment, reducing congestion, and making split-second decisions in response to roadside events. If this information is communicated through an insecure channel, it can be subject to violations of privacy, integrity attacks, and availability attacks, which may jeopardize the vehicle's important credentials as well as the message contents or allow the vehicle to be stopped completely on the highway. In the quest for protecting drivers' privacy and facilitating secure communication of messages among nodes, earlier research has suggested using a session key and registering all nodes on a vehicle server that is then authenticated by a trusted authority (TA). This method has proved that it preserves the driver's

DOI: 10.1201/9788743809050-17

privacy while allowing secure communication inside the network. Furthermore, a performance analysis was carried out to compare the authentication delay between two different schemes: one-by-one authentication and batch authentication. The outcome showed that batch authentication was more efficient with shorter authentication times as the load increased.

Keywords: Privacy, authentication, cyberattacks, vehicle server, trusted authority

13.1 Introduction

In various industries such as intelligent transportation, smart grid, and health monitoring, the Internet of Things (IoT) is becoming more widespread. The launch of Internet of Vehicles (IoV) has significant improvements on some limitations of vehicular ad hoc networks (VANET), specifically unreliable internet connections, compatibility issues with mobile devices, and limited computation capacity in intelligent transportation systems (ITS). One good thing about IoV is that it ensures continuous connection among registered entities and devices, which makes it possible to monitor traffic to improve driver comfort or enhance the overall safety of cars on the road. Nevertheless, security remains a priority because messages exchanged in the network can be manipulated by those who want to take advantage of it; onboard units (OBUs) may become exposed to attackers. If OBUs are hacked, they may act as entry points for any kind of assault against the entire network during vehicle-to-vehicle (V2V) communication. For instance, cybercriminals can overrule OBUs, making cars stop on streets; or send fraudulent activation signals, making airbags pop up at random times; or alter transmissions within a communication system, spiraling out of control, causing drivers to make wrong choices, leading them straight into accidents or, at worst, death traps.

The V2X communication in IoV forms a suite of various kinds, like vehicle-to-infrastructure (V2I), vehicle-to-roadside units (V2R), vehicle-to-pedestrians (V2P), vehicle-to-sensors (V2S), and vehicle-to-mobile devices (V2M), which is clearly mentioned in Figure 13.1. Though maintaining secure communications and authenticating V2X is a major issue in ITS. Through a detailed study of current research frameworks, it is evident that there is a big necessity for lightweight protection schemes in the Internet of Vehicles.

While IoV has proved to be an efficient processor and transporter of large amounts of data, the communication network has become an ideal platform

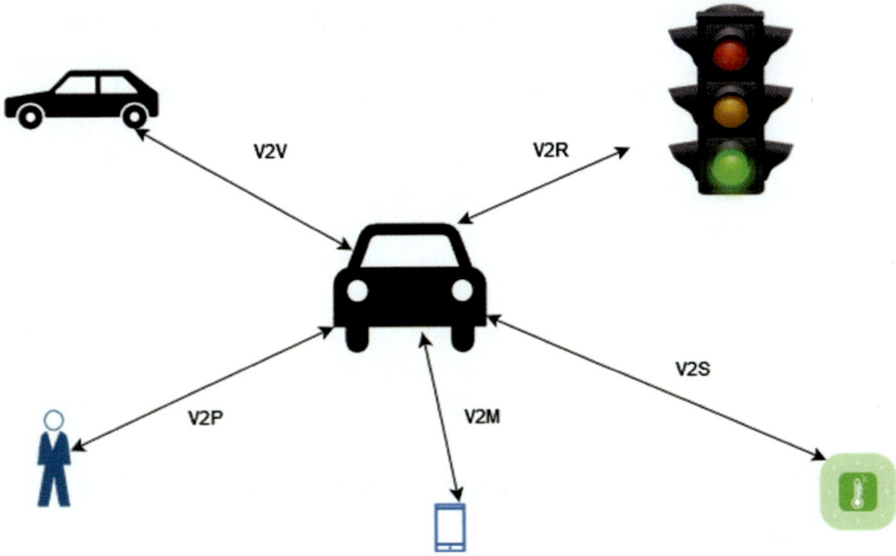

Figure 13.1 Different scenarios of V2X communication.

for adversaries accessing and manipulating shared information. This can lead to privacy violations through replay attacks, impersonation attacks, resulting in accidents where drivers' lives are put at risk on roads that may also be used for cyber terrorism. To mitigate this challenge, privacy-preserving authentication schemes have been suggested that enable vehicle identification within a network while identifying and revoking malicious entities' certificates using group signatures to sign messages sent across the network. The authentication scheme's network model includes: (1) a trusted authority (TA) that initializes the system as well as registers new vehicles within the network; (2) a key generation center (KGC) generating private keys used by vehicles when signing messages before transmission; (3) road side units (RSUs) situated along roadsides responsible for vehicular identity verification in their area; and finally; (4) vehicles equipped with tamper proof devices (TPD). The process of registering a vehicle with the TA is carried out through a secure channel by utilizing the unique identity of the vehicle and a one-of-a-kind nonce generated by the TA for that particular vehicle.

The first step before engaging in V2V communication is to authenticate the vehicle, as this is the point where rogue devices are removed from the network. The RSUs are only accountable for the vehicles that fall under their jurisdiction; when a vehicle enters a new area, it must register with the appropriate roadside unit. This arrangement ensures that the RSUs are responsible for a limited number of vehicles, so if one fails, it will only affect the specific area, leaving the rest of the network operational. The key generation center (KGC) is responsible for creating session keys that are unique to a particular session, ensuring that the sessions cannot be linked based on the keys that have been issued and that the data shared within the session is secure from adversaries. These authentication schemes safeguard the identity of the vehicle, guarantee the security of the session key, ensure key escrow resilience, facilitate mutual authentication, and defend against non-repudiation, replay, man-in-the-middle, and session linkability attacks. In this chapter, we will examine the threats present in IoV networks and which of these can be defended using the mentioned Authentication Protocols.

13.2 Architecture of Model for Authentication and Privacy Preservation

Transportation control center (TCC): It is responsible for initiating systems, enrolling entities within the network, collecting data from roadside equipment, tracking and monitoring malicious vehicles, and updating their details in the revocation list.

Traceback authority (TBA): The TBA receives the details of malicious vehicles within the network, confirms their behavior, and takes necessary action to prevent them from transmitting false or tampered content within the network.

Vehicle: Every vehicle in the IoV comprises an onboard unit (OBU) that continuously transmits and receives messages related to road safety with other vehicles and roadside units (RSUs).

Roadside unit (RSU): RSUs are fixed roadside infrastructure deployed along the sides of roads, responsible for collecting, uploading, and distributing information about real-time events within their range. As the range of RSUs is limited, they manage vehicles within their range, making device management more efficient and streamlined.

RA (registration authority): Figure 13.2 shows the pictorial representation of allocation of vehicles to RSU. Vehicles within the network register with RA to authenticate their identity. TCC is operational within the RA, and initializes the systems and enrolls entities that are going to communicate with the network.

VS (vehicle server): VS is responsible for providing real-time information to the vehicle upon request. In order to access information from the vehicle

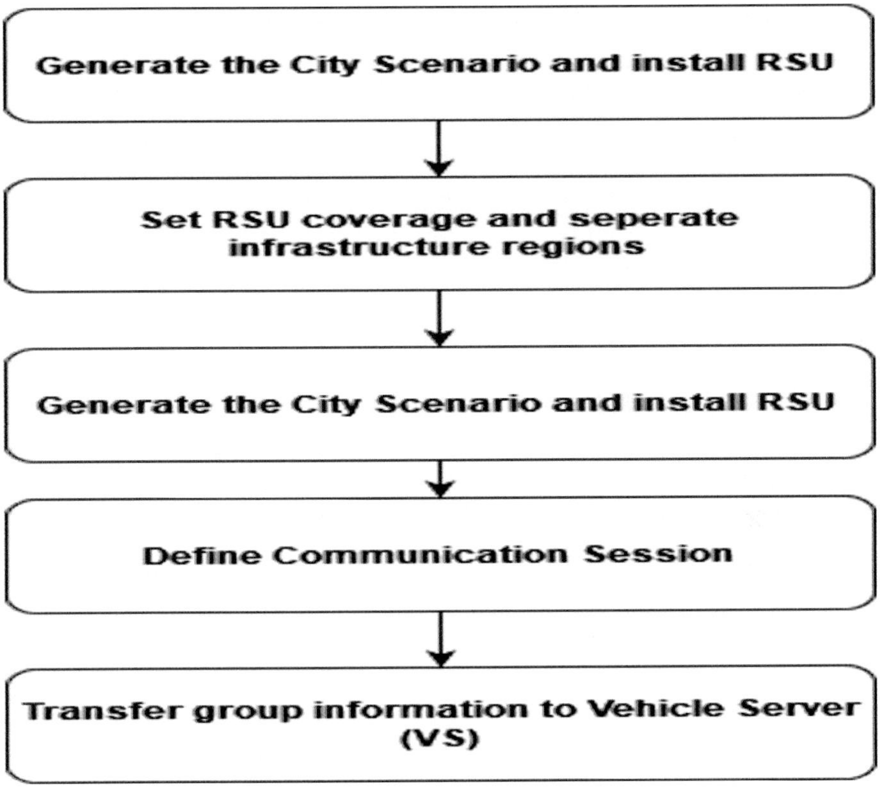

Figure 13.2 Allocation of vehicles as per infrastructure regions to RSUs.

server, a vehicle must first register with the trusted authority (TA). This additional layer of security is in place to ensure that only authenticated devices can communicate with the vehicle server.

TA (trusted authority): The TA acts as an intermediary to regulate communication between the individual VS, verifies the identity of the vehicles communicating with the vehicle server. The trusted computing base (TCB), a component of TA, observes vehicle behavior so as to notice if any entity goes rogue and isolate such from the network, hence keeping the adversary from controlling all sites. After registering with the registration authority (RA), parameters will be forwarded to TA. This removes the necessity of involving the RA in every authentication process, thereby reducing overheads. Furthermore, vehicle-related parameters are stored in OBUs located within the car as smartcards.

Security requirements in IoV

- ✓ *Authentication*: It is a critical aspect of security in any IoV network since only authenticated vehicles can establish communication with one another. If an attacker manages to penetrate the system, he/she may inject malicious messages into other nodes and compromise them within the network, leading to devastating outcomes.
- ✓ *Confidentiality*: Another vital element of IoV security, as passive attacks are often hard to detect when an opponent is eavesdropping on all communication going through the internet.
- ✓ *Availability*: This is also quite significant since denial service attacks (DoS), distributed DoS (DDoS) can target IoV devices, hence halting communication and bringing about fatal accidents among others for example, in 2015, Miller and Valasek took control over a Jeep on a highway; then tampered with AC; radio; wipers before switching off its engine demonstrating such criminal activities might lead to dire consequences indeed.
- ✓ *Data integrity*: The IoV network needs to maintain the integrity of data for the simple reason that an enemy can manhandle and intercept messages before delivering them. This means decisions made by the receiving nodes would be wrong. Thus, it is important to keep the IoV network secure to stop these attacks and safeguard road users' safety.
- ✓ *Non-repudiation*: In the IoV, the node that sends out messages always ensures that they are encrypted with a signature so as to make them valid, thus stopping anyone from later denying he/she sent them.
- ✓ *Access control*: By checking each automobile's authorization documents and certificates, unauthorized entry may be averted; consequently, intruders are deterred from joining the system, causing possible damage through replay attack, denial of service (DoS) assault, or cyber-terrorism.
- ✓ *Privacy*: If someone steals identification credentials or intercepts location-based messages, then GPS spoofing becomes possible; in this case user's privacy is literally compromised since when such a person finds out where exactly that car is located, there could be serious implications involved.
- ✓ *Impersonation of node*: An adversary can compromise a node's identity through session hijacking, masquerading, or stealing credentials, leading to the attacker sending messages that are accepted as coming from a valid node in the network. Table 13.1 presents the classification attacks on IoVs specifically considering active and passive nature.

Table 13.1 Categorization of attacks in the Internet of Vehicles.

Active attacks	Passive attacks
Sybil attack	Worm hole attack
Dos/ DDos	Spoofing
Black/grey hole attack	Identity disclosure
Timing attack	Session hijacking
Gps spoofing	
Replay attack	
Masquerading	
Mitm attack	
Impersonation attack	
Spamming	

Utilizing OBUs, experts Charlie Miller and Chris Valasek were able to control the systems of a Jeep Cherokee. They first accessed the automobile's AC system and disrupted the radio stations. After that, they turned on the windscreen wipers and ultimately took over the accelerator pedal, bringing the car to a stop, then maneuvering it at low speeds on a highway.

The IoV Technology has progressed with the advancement of transportation system intelligence over time. Meanwhile, adversaries have been modifying their tools in order to access and remain within systems. Currently, remote exploitation is a part of the threat landscape, and it is notably due to the emergence of Advanced Persistent Threats that intruders are able to access compromised nodes for a long period of time without being detected. To keep up with modern exploitation sophistication, studies should also focus on lightweight cryptography to provide secure data transfer. In addition, the use of machine learning trained models is also useful in discriminating between incoming messages and malicious threats, as well as in identifying system performance variations.

13.3 Adversary Model

In a conventional Internet of Vehicles (IoV) system, all communication is conducted over an open wireless channel, which makes it susceptible to malicious entities. If an adversary intercepts a message, they can commit attacks, including replay attacks, impersonation attacks, content alteration,

MITM attacks, and DoS attacks. The following are some of the attack types an adversary can undertake:

- ✓ *Interception of messages*: Taking advantage of an insecure communication channel, an adversary can intercept and modify messages, making it difficult to detect. Passive attacks are often more challenging to detect and can go unnoticed for even months, when compared to active attacks.
- ✓ *Impersonation attack*: If an adversary manages to take control of a vehicle, they can use the OBUs to infiltrate the network with fake messages, which may lead to adverse consequences and incorrect decisions by drivers.
- ✓ *Stolen smart card attack*: When an adversary steal credentials of a vehicle stored in smart card, to compute and guess other credentials, potentially exposing credentials of the encryption algorithm. However, it is not possible to guess more than one value in polynomial time.
- ✓ *MITM attack*: An adversary can secretly eavesdrop on the communication channel and alter and deliver messages between communicating parties who trust that the messages are coming from the actual user they are communicating with.
- ✓ *Replay attack*: An adversary can intercept a message and deliver it to vehicles in the network at a later time, causing the receiver to act on the received message, which can affect the entire network's functioning.

It is important to note that the mentioned types of attacks are not exhaustive, and adversaries can employ other attack methods to compromise the security and privacy of a typical IoV system.

13.4 Phases Involved in Authentication-based Protocol

13.4.1 Registration phase

A vehicle must first register with the registration authority (RA) to acquire the necessary parameters for transmitting information to the vehicle server (which is shown in Figure 13.3). The RA checks the legitimacy of the vehicle and then issues a smart card that contains parameters for the two, which are authentication and communication. This registration process is initiated by either the driver or his/her car making a selection of a unique combination of a user ID and password, as well as a random nonce (V_n). Thereafter, the host device derives the vehicle's unique identity (VUID_i) from ($\text{UID}_i|V_n$) while passwords are derived from ($\text{VPSW}_i|\text{V}_n$). These parameters are subsequently

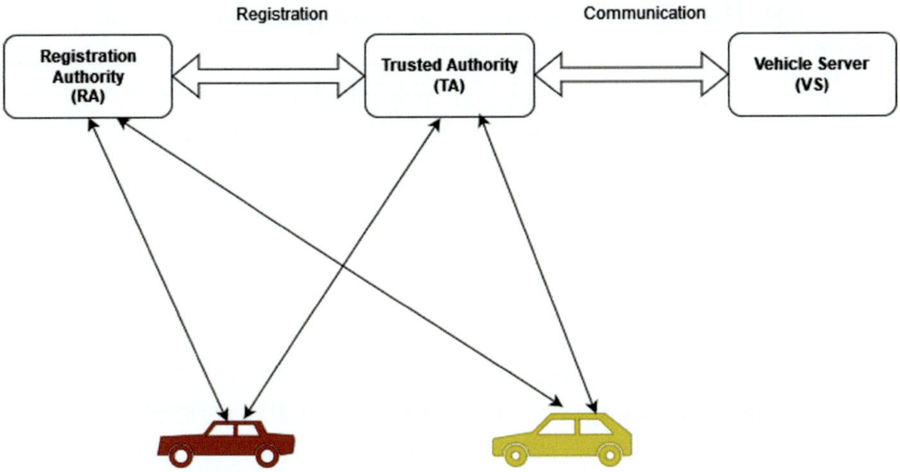

Figure 13.3 Illustration of registration and communication phase.

sent securely, either through communication with a reliable entity or through little boxes protected by cryptography.

First, RA calculates unique values (X1 and Y1) for every device registered at RA upon receiving computed parameters from host computers. For example, X1 is computed as X1 = h(VUID$_i$||K_h), where K_h denotes the secret key that promotes secure communication between TA and VS, whereas Y1 is determined by Y1 = h(VUID$_i$||VPSW$_i$). It further stores them in smart cards, which are also forwarded to both the TA, as well as the host device. After receiving the smart card in question, Z1 = h(VUID$_i$||VPSW$_i$||V_n) is then computed by the host that retains it within the smartcard.

13.4.2 Login and authentication phase

Once the RA has registered the automobile, the TA should first authenticate with the automobile before any communication with VS takes place. This protects the network from unauthorized access by hackers. The process of authentication starts with an ID and a password being supplied by the host car, which are checked for tampering by the TA. The car then generates a nonce V_s and timestamp T_v that are used to calculate secret message Sm = (X1 || VUID$_i$ || T_v), which verifies whether or not the driver is genuine. After that, TA confirms nonce and recomputes secret message again as Sm = (X1 || T_v || VUID$_i$ || N_{v*}) to make sure it was not interfered with during sending.

Table 13.2 Use of symbols in the registration and communication phase.

Symbols	**Description**
VUID	Unique ID of the host vehicle
VPSW	Password of VUID
K_h	Secret key exchanged between VS and TA
S_m	Secret message
VSUID	Unique ID of vehicle server
TAUID	Unique ID of trusted authority
FUID	Final unique ID
S_k	Secret key

TA finally comes up with the last unique Id FUID $=$ (VUID$_i$ || VSUID$_i$|| TAUID$_i$), sent to VS along with {Msg, X1, Tv1, FUID} in order to conclude the authentication process. Table 13.2 presents the list of complex symbols used in the manuscript.

13.4.3 Communication phase

A secret key is used for such communications, which is expressed mathematically as Sk $=$ (FUID || T_v || N_v*). The process starts when V1 sends a request message to VS requesting the verification of V2's identity before initiating communication. Once both parties have been identified by VS, its secret key is transmitted to V1 over an encrypted line. To ensure consistent security in communication, the secret key S_k is regularly updated with a newly generated nonce and timestamp.

13.5 Resistance against Different Security Threats

(1) *Impersonation attack*
When attempting to breach either a vehicle or a TA during the communication process, the adversary is likely to fail. Even if the hacker manages to discover a crucial credential, their attempts to guess the remaining ones will ultimately prove unsuccessful. If an adversary determines the VUID, they will be unable to guess the VPSW or the random nonce Nv created by the vehicle. Since a timestamp is also involved in the authentication process, the TA will be able to identify the intruder and prevent them from gaining access to the network.

(2) *Stolen smart card attack*
When an attacker acquires control of smart card credentials, this could expose other variables calculated during the login and communication

phase. However, the credentials stored on the smart card remain secure hash function computation to create variables X1 and Y1.

(3) *Session key security*
The key used for the communication process is generated using a random nonce created by the vehicle and TA, which is difficult for the adversary to guess, thus ensuring the integrity of the key. The key is frequently updated by creating a new nonce.

(4) *Offline password guessing attack*
The vehicle transmits the VUID and VPSW to RA, which calculates value X1 and Y1 by use of a hash function and stores them in the smart card. As a result, even if an adversary manages to seize one of the devices during the authentication process, they will not be able to access the values stored on the other side of the process.

(5) *Untraceable attack*
The vehicle creates a unique nonce T_v in every new session, so if an adversary intercepts a communicated message by the vehicle, they would not be able to determine whether the messages are from the same session or a different one. As a result, the adversary would not be able to trace a specific session and obtain other login and communication parameters.

(6) *MITM attack*
During the authentication, login, and communication process, all parameters are computed except for the session key, which is shared over an insecure channel. This makes the system vulnerable to a MITM attack. However, since the validated process involves both the receiver and sender, the adversary is unable to launch a MITM attack in this scenario.

(7) *Replay attack*
The adversary would find it impossible to carry out a replay attack, as the timestamp value serves a critical role in the authentication procedure between the vehicle and RA, as well as in the login process between VS and TA, and the communication process between the vehicle and VS.

Table 13.3 presents the Effectiveness of proposed schemes against attacks on IoVs. Traffic volume measurement in VCPS can be performed in two ways, the first or point traffic and the other point-to-point traffic. Point traffic tries to estimate the volume of traffic over a specified period at a particular point, while point-to-point traffic looks at the amount of traffic between a specific origin and a specific destination. Nonetheless, these two methods reveal the positions of vehicles and hence risk exposing the privacy of not

Table 13.3 Effectiveness of proposed schemes against attacks on IoV.

Work	Methodology used	Impersonation attack	Known key	Session key	Offline password guessing	Untraceable attack	Anonymity	Mutual authentication	MITM	Replay attack
[18]	Timestamping and nonce	Y	Y	Y	Y	Y	Y	Y	Y	Y
[19]	Cryptographic hash function	Y	Y	Y	Y	Y	Y	Y	N	Y
[20]	ECC (Biometric-based authentication)	Y	Y	Y	Y	Y	Y	Y	N	N
[21]	ECC	Y	Y	Y	Y	N	Y	Y	Y	Y
[22]	ECC + diffie-Hellman	Y	Y	Y	Y	N	N	Y	N	Y

*Y: Yes *N: No

only the vehicles but also the vehicle users as well. For this reason, it is very important to avoid obtaining any type of information, including vehicle ID or any other permanent numbers, which would facilitate the tracing of vehicles and potentially cause harm to the users and other road members.

In order to mitigate the effect of data loss in VCPS, it is requisite to address two critical challenges. One is about the protection of raw information that has been amassed from and is now available. The effect of any such attacks on the integrity of the information and the possibility that the information has been accessed in any manner must also be addressed. Leakage of data might also occur unwittingly, and certain weaknesses may be present undetected. The second challenge has to do with the acquisition of fresh data and its subsequent distribution. In the process of collecting data, do not include any recognizable features of vehicles or drivers, and also ensure that leakage does not occur in the process of distributing the data. With these issues, the information must still be capable of being utilized for the purpose for which it was originally intended. With the advent of technology, adversaries are also advancing their modes and techniques for capturing the data. More research needs to be done in secure communication using cryptographic techniques, blockchain, and the generation of secret pseudonyms for every message in the network.

13.6 Group-based Authentication in V2G Communications

V2G communication represents a sustainable measure towards a green energy system, in which vehicles transmit requests to the grid to receive responses. These services may involve supplying electricity to the grid or recharging their batteries from the grid. The Aggregator functions as an intermediary between the grid and the vehicles, which is shown in Figure 13.4. The grid monitors the generation and consumption of electricity, and any changes in consumption are communicated to the aggregator, which then conveys this information to the vehicles within range.

With the help of the global positioning system (GPS), vehicles are directed to charging or discharging stations. The electricity exchange between the vehicle and the grid takes place when the vehicle is parked, which is its optimal period. Authentication and encrypted communication are required due to varying factors, including the speed of the vehicle, intermittent connectivity, battery constraints, and timing considerations. In order for it to be efficient, lightweight privacy and security measures need to be implemented. Guo et al. have proposed a novel batch authentication protocol called

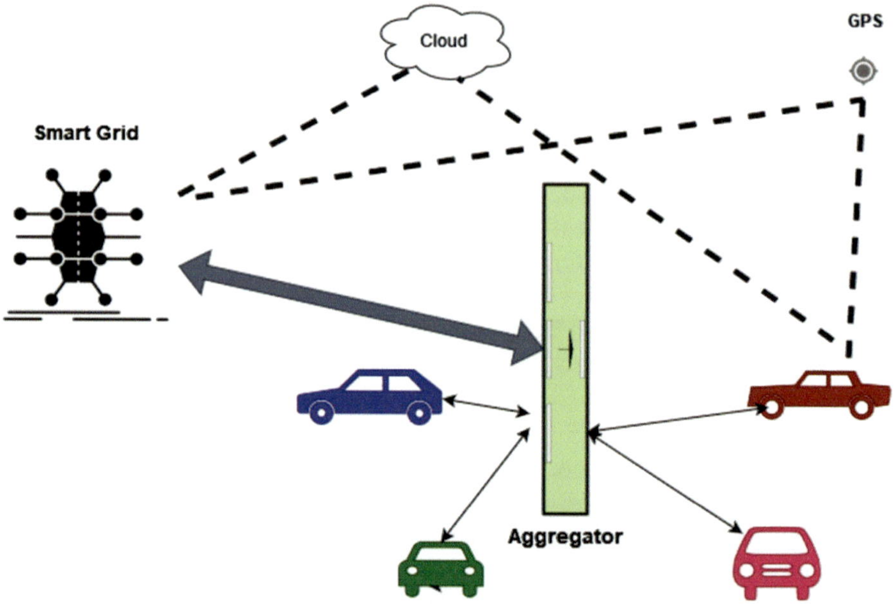

Figure 13.4 Communication between vehicles and grid via aggregator.

UBAPV2G for V2G communication [7]. This protocol is more efficient as it involves verifying a batch of packets with a single signature, rather than every individual message exchanged between the grid and the vehicle.

13.7 Working of UBAPV2G Protocol Scheme

The UBAPV2G scheme utilizes digital signature authentication to verify, validate, generate, sign, and send messages between the grid and the vehicle. Transmission of messages between the client and server is done through sockets using the user datagram protocol (UDP).

13.7.1 Vehicle side

(1) During the transmission phase, the vehicle sends packets individually to the server, one by one, which mirrors the single-packet authentication communication process. Concurrently, the vehicle listens for incoming confirmation messages from the server. Once the confirmation message has been received, the communication has been authenticated, and data transmission can proceed securely.

(2) The authentication delay is measured as elapsed time from when the client first sends a packet to the server until the final confirmation message is received from the side of server for a complete batch of packets.

13.7.2 Grid side

(1) The server on the grid side continuously listens in a loop to receive messages from the vehicles and decrypts them to extract information from them.
(2) In the transmission phase, the server starts an interval time from the point where it receives the first packet from the client. During this time, the aggregator verifies the signature of all the packets received within this time interval. These packets are signed using a single signature. All incoming messages after this interval time are processed in a similar manner by the server.

Comparability between authentication schemes based on authentication delay

In the basic V2G system, when the aggregator receives messages from vehicles, it takes them in a first-in-first-out (FIFO) manner. When communications with various vehicles occur at the same time, they act like an incoming queue to the aggregator. It picks one message from this queue and processes it while the other messages wait for their turn. This could result in delayed decision-making for vehicles in certain scenarios. On the contrary, however, UBAPV2G works like a polling and reservation system where all vehicles use a common communication channel. Yet, for data transfer between any node relaying information to an aggregator, there is a fixed time slot interval assigned. These requests are then processed by the aggregator, which sends responses back to the respective nodes involved. Moreover, a batch of vehicles undergoes signing verification together, which helps reduce the costs of computational power and communication delays.

A comparison of the authentication delay in the one-by-one authentication scheme and the UBAPV2G scheme is presented. Figure 13.5 shows that when the number of messages in V2G communication is smaller, the authentication delay is the same for both schemes. When there is an increase in the number of packets transmitted between client and server, the authentication delay in the UBAPV2G scheme is low when compared with the one-by-one scheme. The UBAPV2G scheme demonstrates a reduction in the authentication delay time with an increase in batch size.

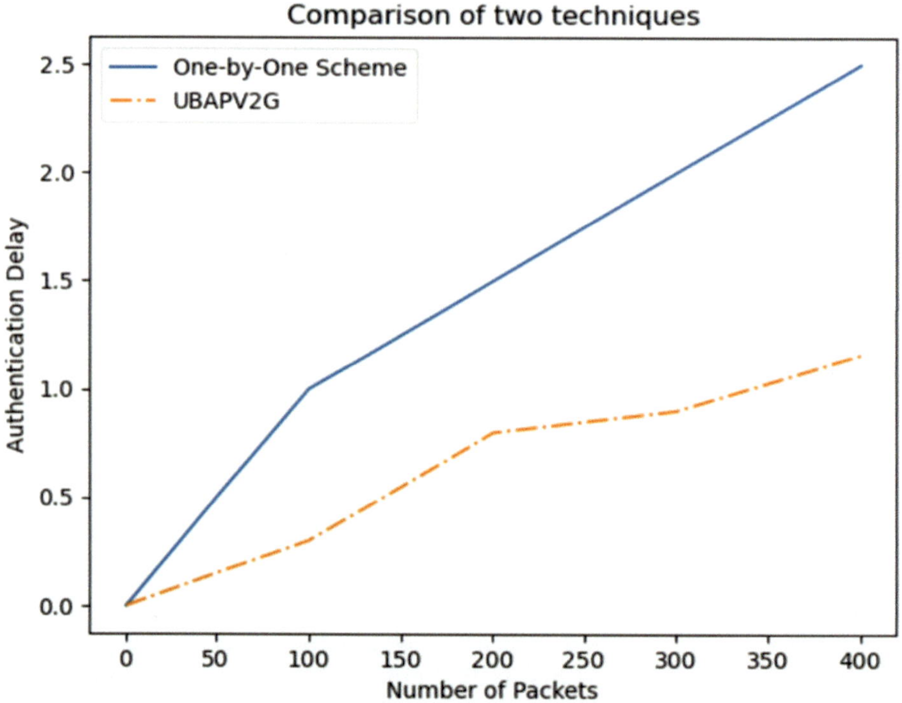

Figure 13.5 Comparability between authentication schemes based on authentication delay.

In the comparison of research on batch authentication and its capability to resist security attacks, it was observed that none of the proposed models was effective in defending the Vehicle Server against DoS attacks. In case the VS is taken along, the whole authentication scheme would fail. Table 13.4 shows the Effectiveness of group authentication schemes against attacks on IoVs.

Research becomes inevitable in a situation where a VS is under the threat of being attacked by another VS. This is because there is an ever-growing number of methods that are used to combat DoS attacks, for instance, the packet matching scheme, where packets are checked according to the IP address. In the case that a high volume of traffic is generated from a single source, the source IP address ought to be blacklisted to avoid more requests from the address interfering with the operation of the VS. Machine learning models such as MobileNetV2, GoogLeNet, and ResNet-18 can be employed for training an effective system that will observe the traffic being directed to VS. In case the number of packets surpasses a certain limit, the system trains, and those addresses are not allowed to send any more packets into the system.

Table 13.4 Effectiveness of group authentication schemes against attacks on IoV.

Proposed model	**Techniques used**	**Mutual authentication**	**Batch verification**	**Identity preservation**	**Replay attack**	**MITM attack**	**Traceability**	**Integrity attack**	**DOS attack**
[8]	ECC and HMAC	Y	Y	Y	Y	Y	Y	N	N
[9]	PKC	Y	N	N	Y	Y	Y	N	N
[10]	ECC	N	Y	Y	Y	Y	Y	Y	N
[11]	ECC	N	Y	N	Y	N	Y	Y	N
[12]	EAAP	N	Y	Y	Y	Y	Y	Y	N
[13]	ECC	Y	Y	Y	Y	Y	Y	Y	N

*EAAP: Anonymous Authentication Scheme
*Y: Yes *N: No

13.8 Conclusion

In this chapter, we did an analysis of privacy and authentication protocols researchers use to protect themselves from networking attacks. The results of our security analysis indicated that some schemes were vulnerable to replay attacks, man-in-the-middle (MITM) attacks, stolen smart card attacks, and even traced sessions using a secure key. So, more research must be done to develop secure communication sessions and overcome these threats. Our examination of the security aspects of simple vehicle-to-grid (V2G) communication systems and batch authentication systems showed that although with an increase in the number of messages, less authentication delay was experienced in batch authentication; however, it was subject to integrity attacks, privacy-of-identity, and mutual authentication problems. Future studies should focus on how to save both simple as well as batch authentication structures from denial of Service (DoS) attacks, which will help to avoid halting an entire system by shutting down its Vehicle Server.

References

[1] S. Sharma and B. Kaushik, "A survey on internet of vehicles: Applications, security issues & solutions", Vehicular Communications, 2019.

[2] F. Sakiz and S. Sen, "A survey of attacks and detection mechanisms on intelligent transportation systems: VANETs and IoV", Ad Hoc Netw. 2017 pp. 33–50.

[3] H. Vasudev and D. Das, "An Efficient Authentication and Secure Vehicle-to-Vehicle Communications in an IoV", IEEE 89th Vehicular Technology Conference, 2019.

[4] H. T. Wu and G. J. Horng, "Establishing an Intelligent Transportation System With a Network Security Mechanism in an Internet of Vehicle Environment. IEEE Access, 5, 19239-19247, 2017.

[5] O. Kaiwartya, A. Abdullah, A. H. Cao, Y. Altameen, A. Prasad, M. Lin and X. Liu, "Internet of vehicles: Motivation, layered architecture, network model, challenges, and future aspects.", IEEE Access, 4, 5356-5373, 2016.

[6] C. M. Chen, B. Xiang, Y. Liu and K. H. Wang, "A Secure Authentication Protocol for Internet of Vehicles", IEEE Access Special Section on Security and Privacy for Cloud and IOT", 2019.

[7] H. Guo, Y. Wu, F. Bao, H. Chen and M. Ma, "UBAPV2G: A Unique Batch Authentication Protocol for Vehicle-to-Grid Communications", IEEE Transactions on Smart Grid, Vol. 2, No. 4, 2011.

[8] M. Bayat, M. Barmshoory, M. Rahimi, and M. R. Aref, "A secure authentication scheme for VANETs with batch verification," Wireless Netw., vol. 21, no. 5, pp. 1733–1743, 2015.

[9] J. Li, H. Lu, and M. Guizani, "ACPN: A novel authentication framework with conditional privacy-preservation and non-repudiation for VANETs," IEEE Trans. Parallel Distrib. Syst., vol. 26, no. 4, pp. 938–948, Apr. 2015.

[10] H. Zhong, J. Wen, J. Cui, and S. Zhang, "Efficient conditional privacy-preserving and authentication scheme for secure service provision in VANET," Tsinghua Sci. Technol., vol. 21, no. 6, pp. 620–629, 2016.

[11] N. B. Gayathri, G. Thumbur, P. V. Reddy, and Z. U. R. Muhammad, "Efficient pairing free certificateless authentication scheme with batch verification for vehicular Ad-Hoc networks," IEEE Access, vol. 6, pp. 31 808–31 819, 2018.

[12] M. Azees, P. Vijayakumar, and L. J. Deboarh, "EAAP: Efficient anonymous authentication with conditional privacy-preserving scheme for vehicular Ad Hoc networks," IEEE Trans. Intell. Transp. Syst., vol. 18, no. 9, pp. 2467–2476, Sep. 2017.

[13] A.K. Sutrala, P. Bagga, A.K. Das, N. Kumar, J.P.C. Rodrigues and P. Lorenz, "On the Design of Conditional Privacy Preserving Batch Verification-Based Authentication Scheme for Internet of Vehicles Deployment", IEEE Transactions On Vehicular Technology, Vol. 69, No. 5, 2020.

[14] Y. Li., Q. Luo, J. Liu , H. Guo and N. Kato, " TSP Security in Intelligent and Connected Vehicles: Challenges and Solutions", IEEE Wireless Communications, 2019.

[15] L. Zhang, Q. Wu, A. Solanas and J. D. Ferrer, "A Scalable Robust Authentication Protocol for Secure Vehicular Communication", IEEE Transactions on Vehicular Technology, Vol. 59, 2010.

[16] J. Liu, Q. Li, R. Sun, X. Du and M. Guizani, "An Efficient Anonymous Authentication Scheme for Internet of Vehicles", IEEE International Conference on Communications, 2018.

[17] G. Andy, "Hackers Remotely Kill a Jeep on the Highway – With Me in it", Wired, July, 2015.

[18] H. Vasudev, V. Deshpande, D. Das and S.K. Das, "A Lightweight Mutual Authentication Protocol for V2V Communication in Internet of Vehicles", IEEE Transactions on Vehicular Technology, Vol. 69, 2020.

[19] M. Prerna, A. Ruhul, and G.P. Biswas, "Design of authentication protocol for wireless sensor network-based smart vehicular system", Vehicular Communications, Volume 9 Issue C, pp 64-71, July 2017.

[20] L. Xiong, N. Jianwei, Z. A. Bhuiyan, W.Fan, K. Marimuthu and K. Saru, "A Robust ECC based Provable Secure Authentication Protocol with Privacy Protection for Industrial Internet of Things", IEEE Transactions on Industrial Informatics, 2017.

[21] D. He, N. Kumar, J. Chen, C.-C. Lee, N. Chilamkurti and S.-S. Yeo, "Robust anonymous authentication protocol for health-care applications using wireless medical sensor networks", Multimed. Syst. 21 (1), 2015, pp 49–60.

[22] W. Shi and P. Gong, "A new user authentication protocol for wireless sensor networks using elliptic curves cryptography", International Journal of Distrib. Sens. Netw. 2013, 2013, pp 1–7.

[23] J. Liu, Q. Li, R. Sun, X. Du and M. Guizani, "An efficient anonymous authentication scheme for Internet of Vehicles," in Proc. IEEE Int. Conf. Commun., May 2018, pp. 1-6.

[24] Y.Liu, Y. Wang and G. Chang, "Efficient privacy-preserving dual authentication and key agreement scheme for secure V2V communications in an IoV paradigm", IEEE Trans. Intell. Transp. Syst., vol 18, no.10, pp. 2740-2749, Oct. 2017.

[25] M. S. Han, S. J. Lee and W. S. Bae, "A secure and efficient V2V authentication method in heavy traffic environment," Wireless Personal Commun., vol. 93, no. 1, pp. 245-254, 2017.

[26] Y. Li, Y. Qi, and L. Lu, "Secure and efficient V2V communications for heterogeneous vehicle ad hoc networks", in Proc. Int. Conf. Netw. Netw. Appl., Oct. 2017, pp. 93-99.

[27] J. Joy, V. Rabsatt and M. Gerla, "Internet of Vehicles: Enabling safe, secure, and private vehicular crowdsourcing," Internet Technol. Lett., vol. 1, 2018.

14

Solutions of Blockchain and Artificial Intelligence for 5G-Internet of Things in Agriculture

Isaac Oluwafemi Elesemoyo, Oyeyemi Temitayo Oyewole, Adekemi Joanne Olowu, Julius Olasunmibo Ogunniyi, and Favour Oluchi Boi

Department of Computer Engineering, Elizade University, Ilara-Mokin, Ondo State, Nigeria
Email: {isaac.elesemoyo|oyeyemi.oyewole|adekemi.olowu|julius.ogunniyi, favour.boi}@elizadeuniversity.edu.ng

Abstract

Agriculture is the key sustaining endeavor of mankind as food, which is a product of agriculture, is essential for sustainability. Internet of Things (IoT) is now a crucial part of our daily lives, from simple devices like smart wristwatches, mobile phones, and smart TVs to systems like smart cities, smart buildings, smart transportation, smart agriculture, etc. Its usage with mobile networks such as the 4th generation (4G) and the 5th generation (5G) has gained widespread attention with the 5G granting greater benefits than 4G such as speed, capacity, latency, energy efficiency, reliability, and scalability. Using IoT with the 5G mobile network is known as 5G-IoT.

5G-IoT, with the security provided by blockchain technology (BT) being a decentralized ledger system and the smartness provided by artificial intelligence (AI), makes it possible to practise smart and secure agriculture at a large scale.

Beyond 5G, speed becomes more increased, latency becomes reduce, power consumption becomes reduced, and data becomes larger, and such smart and large-scale farming will become better, and the problem of food will become reduced, even though there is a population explosion.

DOI: 10.1201/9788743809050-18

Keywords: Blockchain, artificial intelligence, 5G-IoT, agriculture

14.1 Introduction

Recent progress in intelligent devices and wireless communication has enabled the development of what we now call the Internet of Things (IoT). It is more accurate to refer to IoT as a sophisticated network of mere sensing and communicating objects [1]. The "things" in IoT are not a dumb network of random objects; they are smart in the sense that they can perform the ubiquitous sensing, communicating, and low-power computing tasks that networked devices need to carry out.

IoT is a vocabulary that emanates from two words, that is, "Internet" and "Things" [2, 3]. Physical objects are connected in a network, which can include devices, instruments, vehicles, buildings, and items with embedded electronics, circuits, and sensors. [4]. The Internet is a worldwide interconnected system that consists of computer networks that uses the standard transmission control or internet protocol (TCP/IP) to cater to for multitude of users across the globe [2].

The distributed digital ledgers are known as blockchains, being both proof against and evidence of tampering taking place without help from a central authority such as a bank, business, or government, and a central repository. At base, they allow a set of users to keep a shared ledger. Once a transaction is placed in the group ledger, it cannot be modified by any standard operation of the network. The idea for a cryptocurrency was born in 2008 when the authors finally put together all the concepts and ideas from computing and computer security that they had discussed over the previous decade. The design employs some clever mechanisms, principally using hash functions, that help the currency operate securely and reliably without the help of a central authority [5].

Intelligence is something believed to be innate in living things, with the level varying from species to species. Artificial intelligence is the ability of an object or device to process data and make informed decisions without human interference. This will be important for IoT because as a large number of devices gather data, due to the processing speed of the computer system and the need for quick informed decisions, artificial intelligence is therefore needed to analyze these data and possibly make predictions, and optimizations.

5G is an abbreviation for fifth-generation mobile network. It is an improvement over 4G, the fourth-generation mobile network, which is the most widely used network at the moment. It is a progressive version of 4G. Its capacity is aimed at being higher than the current 4G. The higher capacity would enable a greater number of mobile users, as well as provide ultra-reliable and extensive communication capabilities.

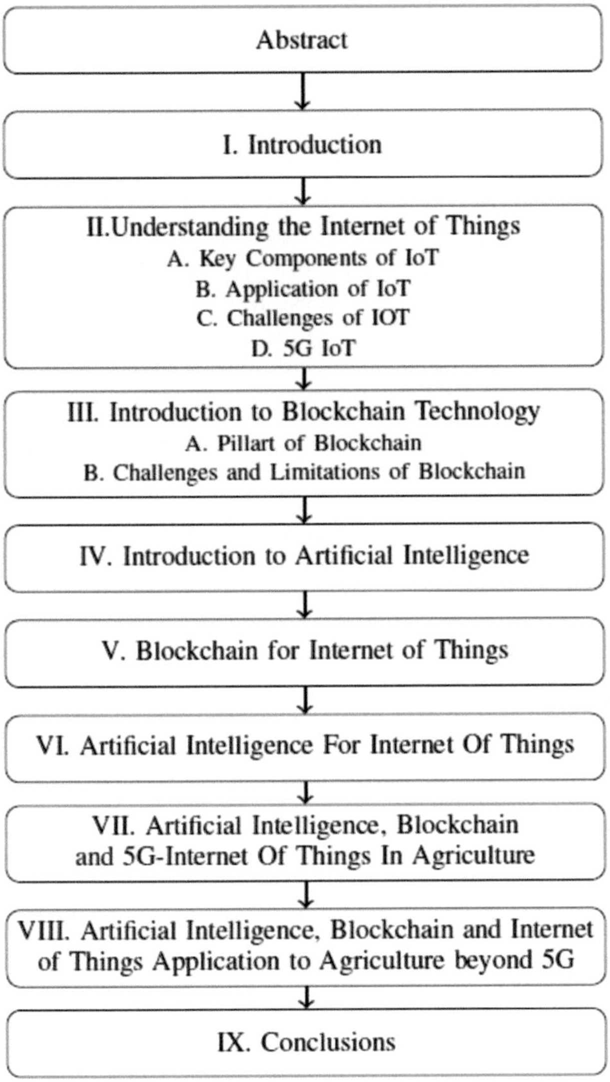

Figure 14.1 Flowchart for chapter.

This chapter explores the IoT, blockchain technology (BT), artificial intelligence (AI) and the 5G network. It further explores the application of blockchain technology and artificial intelligence to 5G-IoT in agriculture and what to expect from this collaboration beyond 5G-IoT.

This chapter explores IoT, and by extension, 5G-IoT, BT, AI, how BT and AI apply to 5G-IoT, the application of AI and BT to 5G-IoT with emphasis on agriculture and finally advances to expect with the introduction of 6G to IoT.

The objective of the chapter is mainly to:

i. present how BT, AI, and 5G-IoT has affected agriculture
ii. present how BT, AI, IoT can further help solve lingering problems in Agriculture beyond 5G.

This chapter is broken down into sections. Session 14.2 provides information necessary to understand IoT, 14.3 gives an introduction to BT, session 14.4 gives an introduction to AI, session 14.5 explains the application of BT to IoT, session 14.6 explains the application of AI to IoTs, session 14.7 explains how AI, BT, 5G-IoT can be applied to agriculture, session 14.8 states what to expect in the application of AI, BT, IoTs to agriculture beyond 5G, and finally, session 14.9 concludes the chapter as shown in Figure 14.1.

14.2 Understanding the Internet of Things

A collection of public, private, business, academic, and government networks from local to global scale, linked together by a lot of optical, wireless, and electronic networking technologies. Today, more than 150 countries are connected to the Internet. Computer systems, including desktops and laptops, have been the equipment that came to mind early in the early days of the internet. The internet has been able to enter embedded computing thanks to wireless sensor networks (WSN), short-range wireless technologies like Bluetooth, Wi-Fi, etc [6, 7, 8].

Since everyday objects are being equipped with sensors and actuators, the IoT is becoming a reality. The main issues on the internet are connection, addressing, and speed, given the population of the world, not to mention things that can be possessed by individuals that will be connected to the internet. The world population, according to the United Nations, is expected to reach 8.5 billion by 2030 [9].

The address field of the Internet Protocol Version 4 (IPv4) is 32 bits, providing theoretically over 4.3 billion (2^{32}) unique internet addresses, with approximately 3.7 billion usable as addresses for internet-connected devices

[10, 11]. This poses a problem to connectivity and addressing since a connection without addressing is useless, and the usable address available is not going to be sufficient if everyone has just one device that needs internet access. This has not considered organizations, people with multiple devices that need access to the internet, the embedded computing world, and the connection of things. This issue of connectivity and addressing was solved with the advent of Internet Protocol Version 6 (IPV6) with an unimaginably expanded address space of 340 undecillion (2^{128}) unique IP addresses. This implies that each person by the estimated population of the United Nations for 2030 can have more than 700,000 devices connected to the internet.

Another issue is speed, especially when it comes to connecting wireless devices, including mobile devices and other things connectable to the internet are considered. This is where, at the moment, 5G comes into play. The 5G has been created for global wireless internet, while IPV6 serves as the core protocol utilized in both the 5G and 4G networks.

This section further presents the components, application areas, challenges, and application of 5G to IoT in subsections.

14.2.1 Key components of IoT

An IoT device is a network of things consisting of hardware, software, network connectivity, and sensors. An IoT system integrates four distinct layers as shown in Figure 14.2, which are the sensing, network, data processing, and application layers.

Sensing layer: The sensing layer is the layer that interacts with the environment. The layer comprises sensors and actuators. The sensors collect data from their environment and there are three categories of sensors as shown in Table 14.1. For example GPSs, cameras, motion detectors, and microphones, while the actuators act on the environment like speakers, motors, etc.

Network layer: This is the layer responsible for the communication and transfer of data collected from the sensing layer to other connected IoT devices. It is implemented with diverse communication technologies like Wi-Fi, Bluetooth, Zigbee, Z-Wave, LoRa, and cellular networks like 3G, 4G, and 5G.

Data processing layer: This is the layer where analyses are done on the data and decisions are made based on the result of the analysis.

Application Layer: This layer is responsible for implementing and displaying the outcomes of the data processing layer for various uses of IoT devices. The application ranges from transportation, home, personal care, healthcare, etc.

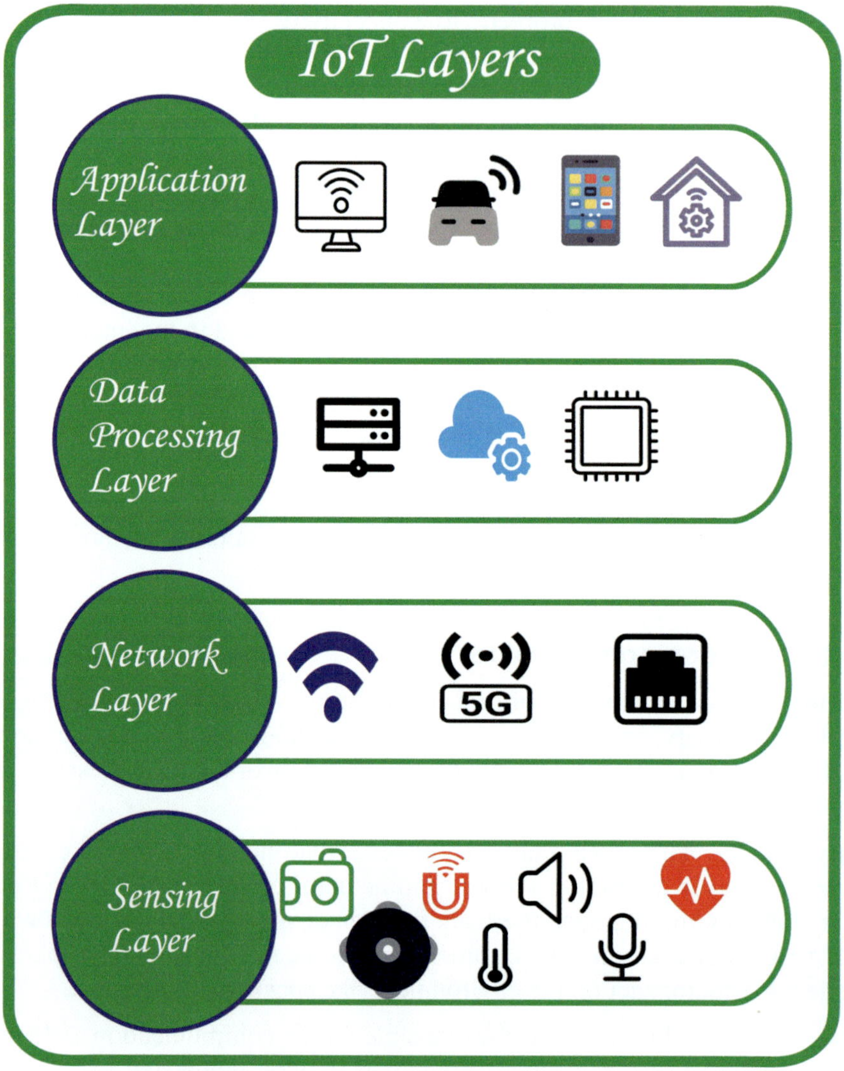

Figure 14.2 Four components of IoT.

14.2.2 Application area of IoT

According to [13], some of the application areas of IoT are manufacturing, transportation, energy, retail, smart cities, healthcare, supply chain, agriculture, and buildings.

Table 14.1 Sensors available in most IoT devices [12].

Type of sensor	Name of sensor	Description
Motion sensors	Accelerometer	An instrument that has the capability of tracking fluctuations in acceleration forces along the three orthogonal directions, namely, X, Y, and Z.
	Linear acceleration sensor	Accelerometer that can measure the force that points along one direction and exclude the force of gravity.
	Gyroscope	A tool for gauging the speed at which angular momentum changes along the x, y, and z axes.
Environmental sensors	Light sensor	The characteristics of the light sensor change when the intensity of light changes.
	Proximity sensor	A sensor that uses infrared to sense the existence of nearby objects without making physical contact.
	Temperature sensor	A device that measures its own temperature and that of its environment.
	Audio sensor	A device that detects an acoustic signal: Microphone.
	Camera	A tool that manages the brightness of light, environmental conditions, and so on, in order to take photographs and record videos of the environment.
	Barometer	A tool that gauges the pressure of the peripheral device.
	Heart rate	A device that is used to measure the rate at which the user's heart beats per second.
Position sensors	GPS	A device that receives signal from the satellite to know its location or the location of the device it is attached to.
	Magnetic sensor	A device that gauges the correlation between its own magnetic field and the magnetic field of the Earth.

Manufacturing: Manufacturing factories now make use of automated things to monitor the manufacturing process. Things like production floor monitoring, wearable devices, remote PLC, or automated quality control systems.

Transportation: IoT usage in transportation ranges from maintaining vehicle health, and transforming the meaning of vehicle ownership to remote traffic control systems.

Energy: IoT is applied to energy to monitor and maintain equipment used, increase efficiency of operation, safety, and disaster prevention, and smart meters to monitor the consumption of electricity.

Retail: IoT can now be used in retailing to digitize stores and create smart operations. Retail now takes 9% rising from 5%. Smart vending machine is one of the area of retail where IoT find application.

Smart cities: Cities are now becoming digitized and smarter. Utilising IoT in urban areas enhances quality of life metrics like crime, traffic, and pollution by a range of 10% to 30%. Its usage grants a more enjoyable life experience in our everyday life [14].

Healthcare: IoT is seeing a surge in demand for applications like telehealth consulting, digital diagnostics, remote monitoring, and robotic assistance. This is beneficial in cutting down on emergency room wait times and tracking patients, employees, and inventory. Additionally, it improves drug management and guarantees the availability of crucial devices. Wearable devices to monitor patients' health routines are also some of the benefits of IoT.

Supply chain: GPS and other technologies have been applied to tracking goods in a supply chain. Some of the benefits of IoT in the supply chain are authenticating the location of goods, tracking the speed of movement, monitoring storage, etc.

Agriculture: IoT is now applied in agriculture to create a smart greenhouse and a smart irrigation system. Sensors are installed to monitor the temperature, humidity, and moisture level of soil, and actuators are also employed to cool the greenhouse or water the farm as the case may be. The smart greenhouse can self-regulate its micro-climate to be suitable for plant growth.

Buildings: Smart building, also called home automation, provides greater connectivity in building systems. From the microwave oven to the water heater to the infrared sensor that switches on the light when there is motion in the room. It also grants the house owner the ability to control appliances at home and to save energy consumption.

14.2.3 Challenges of IoT

Some of the challenges with IoT are security, privacy, interoperability, legal, regulatory and rights, and emerging economies [13].

Security issues with IoT: IoT devices and services poorly secured can be an entry point for a cyber attack and exposure of user data to theft by leaving data flow insufficiently protected [15]. The widespread use of uniform IoT devices can exacerbate cyber attack challenges. Some devices have the capability to automatically connect to other devices, and there is a possibility of deploying these devices in environments that are not secure [16].

Privacy: The use of IoT devices can offer significant advantages in terms of data flow and user privacy. However, worries about privacy and possible risks might impede the widespread acceptance of IoT. Therefore, it is crucial to safeguard user privacy expectations and uphold privacy rights to sustain user confidence in the Internet, interconnected devices, and associated services [17].

Interoperability: The exchange of data among different Internet of Things platforms and devices is what interoperability entails. The challenges associated with interoperability stem from the varied nature of the technology and the different approaches used to construct IoT. There are four different layers of interoperability: syntactic, semantic, organizational, and technical [18]. While the pressure of managing interoperability alleviates some strain on IoT systems, there are still lingering challenges related to potential interoperability issues, which could be a subject for future research [19].

Legal, regulatory and rights: The numerous communication technologies, varying application domains, and unique characteristics of the IoT have bred some critical legal and ethical issues-particularly in security, privacy, intellectual property, and safety-that, to be frank, are still pretty up in the air. Issues are arising so fast that courts, legislatures, and regulators are not even close to catching up with them, which is why we do not assign much weight to the ethical or legal concerns that are raised by proponents of the IoT. [20].

14.2.4 5G IoT

The growth in the things connected wirelessly to the internet is on an exponential increase, with research on increased battery life. There will be a need for more efficient mobile communication technology. 5G-IoT with its capabilities will help with enhance connectivity with up to 10 Gbps which is higher than the previous generation; Low latency (time delay of under 1 millisecond) in data transmission which makes data arrive at the destination almost instantly; 5G-IoT allows for device connectivity of up to 1 million devices per km2, this makes it suitable for areas with high density of devices that needs connectivity to the internet; wireless sensors uses batteries and the 5G is designed to be energy efficient and as such 5G is good for battery-operated IoT devices. Table 14.2 shows the relationship between 4G and 5G.

Table 14.2 4G-IoT versus 5G-IoT.

		4G-IoT	**5G-IoT**
Network performance	Speed	Up to 100 Mbps	Up to 10 Gbps
	Latency	From 30 to 50 milliseconds	Under 1 millisecond
	Capacity	Tens of thousands of devices per km^2	1 million devices per km^2
Energy		More energy is consumed.	Less energy is consumed.
Reliability		Offers good reliability.	Offers enhanced reliability.
Scalability		Limited in the ability to handle a massive number of IoT devices.	Can support a vast number of connections.

14.3 Introduction to Blockchain Technology

The foundational concepts of blockchain technology (BT) started coming together in the early 1990s. The Paxos protocol was developed by Leslie Lamport in 1989. A year later, he turned in his paper titled "The Part-time Parliament [21]" to the ACM Transactions on Computer Systems. This publication - "Part-time Parliament" which came out 10 years later in 1998- provides a model of sorts. It is a model that assumes a network of computers all trying to do the same thing, but where those computers or the network itself may be unreliable. The use of a signed electronic chain in 1991 led to the creation of unalterable ledgers and their digital signatures [22]. These ideas were later integrated and utilized in electronic cash in 2008, as outlined in the document titled Bitcoin: A Peer-to-peer Electronic Cash System [23].

14.3.1 Pillars of blockchain

Table 14.3 presents the specifications of the four primary pillars of blockchain technology.

Table 14.3 Specifications of blockchain pillars [24].

Pillars	**Specifications**
Consensus	Verify work in a network after checking the actions in it.
Smart contract	The participants in the networks are certified and checked using a smart contract.
Ledger	Provides the complete framework of transactions within the networks
Cryptography	provide assurance that the data in the network and ledger is not corrupted and that authorized users can access the data.

14.3.2 Challenges and limitations of blockchain

The research by [25] highlights challenges found in all blockchain systems. These challenges focus on analyzing how blockchain systems operate, different types of blockchains, their use in various industries, and potential research areas within the blockchain platform.

i. ***Scalability:*** Given that blocks are capable of being added, but it is not possible to remove data from a block, the main focus naturally shifts to storage space. Several options have been explored, including slowing down transaction speeds, weighing the pros and cons of large and small blocks, offering light clients as an alternative, and introducing partitioned blocks.
ii. ***Privacy leakage:*** The blockchain cannot offer transaction anonymity because the content of the transactions is publicly available. Additionally, various methods have been developed to link individual users with their associated pseudonyms.
iii. ***Selfish mining:*** Scalability is the area in which blockchains are vulnerable to nodes that are dishonest if 51 % are part of the attack. Nodes of such kind can append blocks to a chain, containing data that negates a valid transaction, received earlier.

14.4 Introduction to Artificial Intelligence

Artificial intelligence (AI) is a computer science and engineering field that deals with what the concept of intelligence is, how it can be derived, and how it can be modeled and applied in our daily lives. It encompasses some sub-fields ranging from machine learning, deep learning, speech recognition, natural language processing, robotics and automation, computer vision, etc. Various definitions were presented in [26] in four categories, which are thinking humanly, thinking rationally, acting humanly, and acting rationally. These four are expected to be balanced for a good artificial intelligence system. Table 14.4 shows the four approaches and sub-fields of artificial intelligence that fall in each category.

Of all these sub-fields, machine learning, which is a superset of deep learning, has attracted the most attention due to its various algorithms including neural networks that allow the computer to interact with data and make informed decisions based on the mathematical model derived by training some algorithms with the data given. It is a data-driven approach and not

Table 14.4 Categories of AI.

Acting humanly	i. Natural language processing ii. Knowledge representation iii. Automated reasoning iv. Machine learning v. Computer vision vi. Robotics
Thinking humanly	i. Cognitive science
Acting rationally	i. Agent-based system
Thinking rationally	i. Logic

rule-based and as such, it limits human interference in processing and decision making. Neural network which is a mathematical model to mimics the brain of a human being can handle complex and non-linear problems of either regression, classification, or reinforcement, with its various models ranging from convolutional neural network (CNN) which uses convolution techniques to address the lower-level features of the data, recurrent neural network (RNN) with uses feedback system and as such has memory to transformer which have attention mechanisms and can analyze some details that cannot be captured by RNN.

14.5 Blockchain for Internet of Things

We know that IoT is an interconnection of things and that it can have security challenges as mentioned in subsection 14.2 item 1 of the chapter. The privacy of the generated data and its integrity can be safeguarded by utilising BT, according to certain authors [27, 28]. Since BT is a distributed digital ledger of transactions that is incorruptible and is capable of storing anything of value [29]. The peer-to-peer network of nodes is used by the ledger for operation. Multiple copies store the information. A consensus algorithm is used by these nodes to guarantee that the entity creating the claim on the platform stores it and that it remains unchanged over time once saved. The blockchain also incorporates a public key signature mechanism, enabling the identification of the source of the generated information. This same public key mechanism can encrypt data stored within the blockchain, addressing privacy concerns [28]. In an IoT system, instead of accounting bodies, governments, or banks keeping records for traditional databases, BT can be employed. The main benefits of BT are listed as follows [30]:

i. The use of consensus mechanisms in BT ensures that the data stored in the blockchain remains consistent across network nodes, preserving its integrity. The unchanging character of this ledger allows all entries written there to be final and irrevocable.

ii. Any information on the blockchain is signed using a public key technique. Using this capability, it becomes quite easy to identify where any particular data stored in the blockchain is coming from.

iii. Remove certain middlemen who increase the cost of system usage and make it susceptible to human mistakes in system operation. This quality results from storing code in a ledger that cannot be changed once entered into the blockchain.

The code has the capability to run across the network in a distributed manner and reach a consensus between nodes regarding the outcomes of its execution. These codes create intelligent contracts that make it easier to validate and enforce the agreement of predetermined conditions [31]. These contracts are capable of self-executing and self-verifying, streamlining the contract lifecycle to boost compliance, reduce risk, and increase efficiency on any platform where multiple stakeholders need to interact with each other [32].

In addition to this, if used alongside asymmetric key agreement security systems, it would guarantee data integrity, as well as privacy. This enables devices reading data from the blockchain and functioning based on it to know whether such data is coming from a trusted source or has been attacked by some malicious actors. This will guarantee that only trusted devices can turn on or off any light in a smart city [33].

The concept of a blockchain being a distributed file system entails that all the data stored within it is collectively owned by all participants in the network. However, no one can modify it because of the characteristics of this technology, so long as data are encrypted or rather just understood by the owner and those selected by him or her. Moreover, another advantage of BT being decentralized is that it can eliminate the possibility of a single point failure, making sure that it remains operational regardless of several nodes on its network being down [34].

14.6 Artificial Intelligence For Internet Of Things

Since IoT has found application in many real-world scenarios, artificial intelligence has also been shown to be useful at the data processing layer of IoT. Some of the areas AI has found application in conjunction with IoT are Smart homes, smart hospitals, smart cities, smart transportation, smart grids, supply chain systems, smart retail, and agriculture [35]. Machine learning has been used with IoT, for instance, in agriculture for smart irrigation, smart weather conditions, and predictive maintenance of farm equipment.

Smart irrigation: Sensors are deployed to measure soil moisture level and wet the soil when the need arises, but there may arise the case where the soil has been watered, and then there is rainfall. This, in turn, will not be good for the farm. To resolve this, there is a need to gather weather information and implement a predictive model to predict when it is likely to rain, and based on the prediction, the system can determine if it is appropriate to water the soil at the time or wait. If there is a prediction of rainfall in a short while and the watering would have to be fully or partially absorbed by the soil before the rainfall, then it is safe to water the farm, otherwise, it will be good to postpone the watering.

Predictive maintenance: Sensors and embedded systems are deployed on farm equipment that read the rate of wear and tear and make predictions on when the equipment is likely to wear out. This will enable the farm administrator to carry out maintenance in due time on the equipment or to replace the equipment altogether. This is to avoid equipment breakdown during operation in the farm and as such disrupt farm activities.

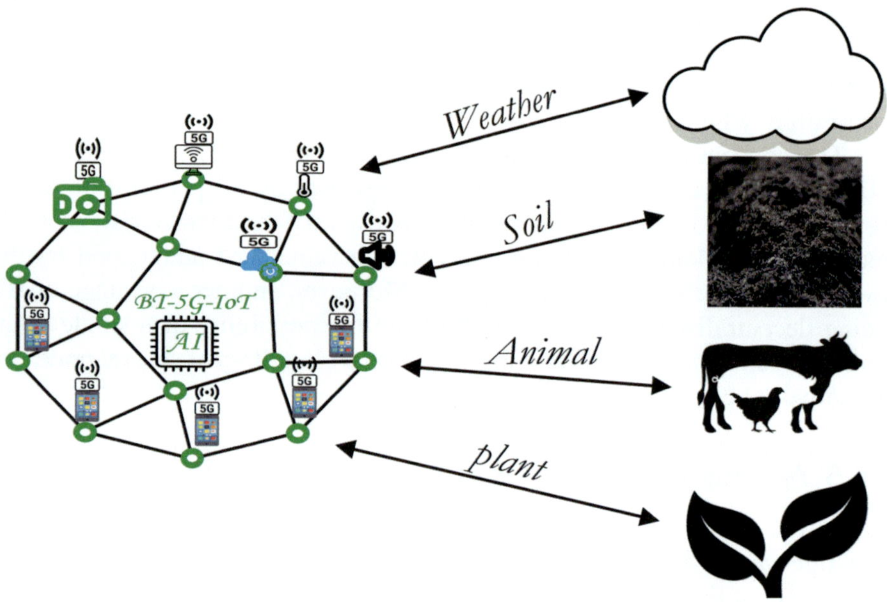

Figure 14.3 AI, 5G-IoT for agriculture.

Control: Natural language processing, a sub-field of AI, can also be applied in control. For example, voice control is the ability to use voice commands to control and interact with the entire system. The actuators can be controlled using a voice control system.

14.7 Artificial Intelligence, Blockchain, and 5G-Internet Of Things In Agriculture

The sustenance of humans is derived from agriculture, making it one of the most crucial areas of endeavor. As the population of the world grows, the production and preservation of food products are expected to grow. An article was previously published by the Food and Agriculture Organization of the United Nations [36] on how much food is lost and wasted as affected by some factors before harvesting, during harvesting, and after harvesting, and to what extent it costs the economy, surrounding, health, and existence of the human being. In this regard, the paper employs the FLI as the index measure of the share of food withdrawn from the supply line. The reviewed research shows that post-harvest losses in the produced foods amount to 14% on average for the global production. The wastage could be quantifiable items of food, which results in a decreased quantity of food present to be consumed. This is opposed to using concepts of securing food. The other style of food wastage that is more common in qualitative food wastage, is the downgrading of the factors that make a food fit for consumption, including nutritional quality of the food, failure to meet set, and recognized standards in foods and the consequences that this comes with.

Precision agriculture (PA) is also known as site specific crop management (SSCM). It involves using a computer-based control system for plants, farmlands, and animals. This system utilizes an intelligent sensing system to create an environment that aligns with the current technology. It involves:

a) Gathering physical and temporal information using remote and close-range sensing technologies
b) Applying data filtering methods to choose the appropriate data
c) The incorporation of AI methods for making decisions
d) Using actuation systems to carry out the required tasks

The above managerial strategies may assist in the reduction of problems relating to the producing, distributing, and sustaining of food products [37]. The areas of Agriculture where IoT is applied are listed below, Items 1 and 2 are shown in Figure 14.7:

1) ***Agriculture monitoring:*** To create the proper conditions for crop production with the biggest yield, it is necessary to regulate the factors that have an impact on the development of plants at different phases. Some sensors are wired and wireless, some of which include sensors for ground, climate, weather, and radiation. These generate data flows that are archived and utilized for surveillance, data mining for knowledge, logical reasoning, and feedback/control actions. In addition, the monitoring of agriculture includes the components listed below:

    i. Air monitoring: This entails gathering specifics like the climate condition, wetness level, and any influence, whether positive or adverse, that can affect the crops.
    ii. Soil monitoring: It measures the amount of water in the soil and its acidity – pH, the capability of the soil to conduct electricity – EC, and the nutrients and chemicals, for example, the nitrite in the soil. Another vital factor that shows the quality of the soil for the production of a good crop is the pH level in the soil. The quantity of nutrients required by the crop might, in one way, enhance the growth of the crop or in another way, harm it.
    iii. Water monitoring: Besides the pH of water, the temperature, chemicals and nutrients, conductivity, turbidity, water level, and rainfall are important to maintain a good conducive environment to promote growth.
    iv. Livestock monitoring: Through the use of some sensors fixed especially on animals, one is in a position to know, whether the crop is likely to be damaged by animal livestock. Most often, the labor of animals and their by-products is utilized to maintain the fertility of the soil to sustain the growth of crops. [38] was able to support statistical imagery as to why animals are necessary to support the sustenance of agriculture.
    v. Irrigation control: This means that if there is an automated system of irrigation, there is a need to have data about the groundwater and the rainfall in a bid to avoid wastage. It equally needs to keep track of the weather, especially where they have to avoid watering the soil at the wrong time, before or after a rain shower.
    vi. Plant monitoring: This involves inspecting and examining the plantâĂŹs flora for any form of disease or bug attack, occasionally to look for likely indicators of the disease or bugs, just in case so as to prevent it before it comes or take reactive measures.

vii. Fertiliser and pesticides control: Fertilisers and pesticides must be used periodically in agriculture due to their requirements. The nature of the fertigation, along with the quantity and the necessary interval, is achieved by assessing the values of the signals that are being received from the sensors.

viii. Illumination control: Like with many other plants, proper sunlight is crucial to encourage proper photosynthesis in plants. The use of light sensors and actuators can control several aspects, including lighting up the surrounding environment.

2) ***Controlled agriculture/intelligent greenhouses:*** A controlled environment is established by greenhouses to supply plants with only the essential factors needed for healthy growth. The integration of IoT with sensors to oversee the greenhouse can simplify the process for users.

3) ***Food supply chain tracking:*** To the "Food and Agriculture Organization of the United Nations" [36], the food supply chain can be described in the following ways:

   i. Agricultural production that involves the foodstuffs while still in the farms,
   ii. Post-agricultural processing where some basic activities like cleaning and sorting are exercised on the foodstuffs,
   iii. Food storage that involves ensuring the food is in the right environment to be preserved,
   iv. Food transport.

   At every one of these phases, it is important to manage and regulate the quality and amount of waste to prevent environmental harm.

4) ***Precision farming/intelligent farming:*** According to the analysis of Hedley et al. [39], Precision agriculture involves the combination of various technologies to the use of automated machinery, sensor systems, as well as the capability of data analysis in endeavoring to understand as well as alter the dynamic variability of the parameters in agri-food supply chains, which are necessarily uncertain.

A blockchain-based architecture of smart agriculture was discussed in [40]. It split agricultural fields into disjoint areas, termed flying areas. A few drones called unmanned aerial vehicles (UAVs) were assigned to the flying zone [41]. The smart sensor devices deployed in the designated flying area collect data, which is then transmitted to the corresponding access points by the drones. The access points then send the collected area data to the user who requested it from the assigned drones.

To ensure security, all entities must first be registered with a trusted authority (TA) in order to verify their credentials for accessing the data. The TA will also define the locations of the sensors (intelligent devices), UAVs, and access points in the system. Upon registration, each intelligent device, UAV, and access point is assigned an identification such as a name, serial number, and secret keys. Once registered, a drone must undergo authentication with its access point and neighboring drones within the flight area. Similarly, smart devices used in agriculture must be capable of securely communicating with neighboring smart devices. These activities require mutual authentication and key agreement, which are considered to be extremely important [42]. There are four types of users: The four channel members are: farmers, suppliers, sellers, and consumers. In some cases, the actual data originating from the deployed smart devices can be made available directly to an external user, such as a farmer. User authentication is necessary to provide access, allowing a user to establish sessional keys with the smart devices it is accessing, as long as both can authenticate each other.

The data collected from the access points about UAVs and external user activity on intelligent devices forms various transactions, which are then used to create blocks. These blocks are linked together to form a chain, giving rise to the term "blockchain." Since the information is sensitive and private, in the context of smart agriculture, a private blockchain is more appropriate for use. It should be emphasized that the transactions are signed with the access point owner's public key and then executed using an effective consensus algorithm. The blocks primarily contain verified transactions, and consensus algorithms like Ripple or PBFT can be used. Subsequently, to ensure the validity of the blocks, nodes in the peer-to-peer network, comprising trusted access points, validate the blocks before they are added to the blockchain managed by the "blockchain cloud center."

14.8 Artificial Intelligence, Blockchain, and Internet of Things Application to Agriculture beyond 5g

Beyond 5G, we expect mobile network technologies to perform better than 5G technologies. This, in turn, will make IoT perform better than 5G-IoT. The 6th generation of the IoT is targeting the resolution of issues concerning reliable and ultra-low-latency communication, utilization of communication protocols, and widespread geographical coverage of the IoT [43].

To discuss the role of IoT, especially within the context of agriculture, it can be seen that smart agriculture is one of the key areas that IoT development is aimed at. In fact, it should be noted that due to the advancement and dispersion of IoT practices, the agricultural sector itself is able to collect and employ a large number of useful data. The agricultural sector is anticipated to experience similar outcomes from these technologies in the future, leading to further evolution [44].

Contemporary IoT systems mainly utilize wireless communications technologies for acquiring, as well as transferring data across the network. Nonetheless, there is considerable significance in selecting an accurate wireless technology because it defines all the functionality and also the deployment and running expenses for IoT systems. The design and testing of IoT systems are evolving, leading to the realization that an IoT system must be both technologically efficient and cost-effective while also having the highest potential market appeal [45].

The focus of 6G-IoT will be on connecting a large number of sensors, providing farmers with more data on each plant, and creating efficient opportunities. Another supportive component of the above goal is the quantum sensing technology that is capable of monitoring the smallest shifts in an agricultural system. All of the sensor readings can be saved on the public blockchain, ensuring that the records are secure, transparent, and resistant to tampering. With the data collected, AI technologies such as machine learning algorithms can be employed to analyze the information and extract valuable insights, styles, and trends.

Besides the precision and reliability of the sensing, the use of collaborative robotic systems to revolutionize farming is another significant characteristic of smart agriculture. The AI-based robots mentioned earlier will carry out the following tasks: identifying irregular patterns related to diseases and anomalies, and recommending treatments to preserve plant health and quality.

14.9 Conclusions

With the continuous increase in population, income, and urbanization, the global demands on IoT systems are also expected to explode. The increase in the number of devices that need to be connected to the network accompanies this explosion. With the increase in the number of devices connected comes the burden of security, for which blockchain technology will be useful, and also an increase in data, for which artificial intelligence will be useful. The larger the data, the better the machine learning algorithm performs. Analysing large datasets, known as big data, can be challenging for humans. However, utilising data analysis tools and implementing machine learning and deep learning algorithms can facilitate decision-making.

With all the benefits that come with 5G-IoT, some challenges and limitations accompany it, such as scarcity of high-quality, reliable, and diverse data, making AI model training ineffective. Labor displacement, education and training, infrastructure cost, energy consumption, data management, and standardization. Further collaboration from farmers, researchers, industry leaders, and policymakers to ensure the successful integration of AI, blockchain, and IoT into agriculture.

In this chapter, an introduction has been given to IoT and by extension 5G-IoT, blockchain technology, artificial intelligence, and their application to agriculture. The chapter emphasizes air monitoring, soil monitoring, water monitoring, livestock monitoring, irrigation control, plant monitoring, control of fertilisers and pesticides, illumination control, controlled agriculture/smart greenhouses, tracking of food supply chain, precision/smart farming, and predictive maintenance. The chapter further expresses the possible advantages of the 6G mobile network when applied to IoT. Further work can be done on the state of application of blockchain, AI and 5G-IoT in Nigeria as a country and Africa as a continent and how 6G can be annexed to solve hunger problem in the continent which is in line with the United Nation Sustainable Development Goal Two (2) which aimed at zero hunger by 2030.

References

[1] D. C. Nguyen, M. Ding, P. N. Pathirana, A. Seneviratne, J. Li, D. Niyato, O. Dobre, and H. V. Poor, "6g internet of things: A comprehensive survey," *IEEE Internet of Things Journal*, vol. 9, no. 1, pp. 359–383, 2021.

[2] S. Madakam, R. Ramaswamy, and S. Tripathi, "Internet of things (iot): A literature review," *Journal of Computer and Communications*, vol. 3, no. 5, pp. 164–173, 2015.

[3] B. Radenkovic and P. Kocovic, "From ubiquitous computing to the internet of things," in *Securing the Internet of Things: Concepts, Methodologies, Tools, and Applications*, pp. 1523–1556, IGI Global, 2020.

[4] P. Gokhale, O. Bhat, and S. Bhat, "Introduction to iot," *International Advanced Research Journal in Science, Engineering and Technology*, vol. 5, no. 1, pp. 41–44, 2018.

[5] D. Yaga, P. Mell, N. Roby, and K. Scarfone, "Blockchain technology overview," *ArXiv Preprint arXiv:1906.11078*, 2019.

[6] A. Kamilaris and A. Pitsillides, "Mobile phone computing and the internet of things: A survey," *IEEE Internet of Things Journal*, vol. 3, no. 6, pp. 885–898, 2016.

[7] L. Schor, P. Sommer, and R. Wattenhofer, "Towards a zero-configuration wireless sensor network architecture for smart buildings," in *Proceedings of the First ACM Workshop on Embedded Sensing Systems for Energy-Efficiency in Buildings*, pp. 31–36, 2009.

[8] D. Yazar and A. Dunkels, "Efficient application integration in ip-based sensor networks," in *Proceedings of the First ACM Workshop on Embedded Sensing Systems for Energy-Efficiency in Buildings*, pp. 43–48, 2009.

[9] U. Nations, "World population day 11 july," 2024. Retrieved from https://www.un.org/en/observances/world-population-day on 19th July 2024.

[10] S. L. Levin and S. Schmidt, "Ipv4 to ipv6: Challenges, solutions, and lessons," *Telecommunications Policy*, vol. 38, no. 11, pp. 1059–1068, 2014.

[11] R. Cannon, "Potential impacts on communications from ipv4 exhaustion & ipv6 transition. fcc staff working paper 3, federal communications commission," 2010. Retrieved from ⟨http://www.fcc.gov/working-papers/potential-impacts-communications-ipv4-exhaustion-ipv6-transition⟩ Accessed 19.07.2024.

[12] A. K. Sikder, G. Petracca, H. Aksu, T. Jaeger, and A. S. Uluagac, "A survey on sensor-based threats to internet-of-things (iot) devices and applications," 2018.

[13] R. A. R. A. Mouha *et al.*, "Internet of things (iot)," *Journal of Data Analysis and Information Processing*, vol. 9, no. 02, pp. 77–101, 2021.

[14] A. Durán-Sánchez, M. de la Cruz del Río-Rama, A. Sereno-Ramírez, and K. Bredis, "Sustainability and quality of life in smart cities: Analysis of scientific production," in *Sustainable Smart Cities: Creating Spaces for Technological, Social and Business Development* (M. Peris-Ortiz, D. R. Bennett, and D. Pérez-Bustamante Yábar, eds.), (Cham), pp. 159–181, Springer International Publishing, 2017.

[15] K. Gatsis and G. J. Pappas, "Wireless control for the iot: Power, spectrum, and security challenges," in *Proceedings of the Second International Conference on Internet-of-Things Design and Implementation*, (Pittsburgh, Pennsylvania, USA), pp. 341–342, Association of Computing Machinery, 2017.

[16] Z. B. Babovic, J. Protic, and V. Milutinovic, "Web performance evaluation for internet of things applications," *IEEE Access*, vol. 4, no. 2016, pp. 6974–6992, 2016.

[17] R. Wilton, "Creds 2014–position paper: Four ethical issues in online trust. issue brief no. creds-pp-2.0," *Internet Society*, 2014.

[18] H. Van Der Veer and A. Wiles, "Achieving technical interoperability - the etsi approach," *European Telecommunications Standards Institute*, 2008.

[19] M. Noura, M. Atiquzzaman, and M. Gaedke, "Interoperability in internet of things: Taxonomies and open challenges," *Mobile Networks and Applications*, vol. 24, no. 3, pp. 796–809, 2019.

[20] S. G. Tzafestas, "Ethics and law in the internet of things world," *Smart Cities*, vol. 1, no. 1, pp. 98–120, 2018.

[21] L. Leslie, "The part-time parliament," *ACM Trans. on Computer Systems*, vol. 16, pp. 133–169, 1998.

[22] A. Narayanan, J. Bonneau, E. Felten, A. Miller, and S. Goldfeder, *Bitcoin and Cryptocurrency Technologies: A Comprehensive Introduction*. Princeton University Press, Princeton, New Jersey, United States, 2016.

[23] S. Nakamoto and A. Bitcoin, "A peer-to-peer electronic cash system," *Bitcoin.*–URL: https://bitcoin.org/bitcoin.pdf, vol. 4, no. 2, p. 15, 2008.

[24] F. Tang, S. Ma, Y. Xiang, and C. Lin, "An efficient authentication scheme for blockchain-based electronic health records," *IEEE access*, vol. 7, no. 2019, pp. 41678–41689, 2019.

[25] Z. Zheng, S. Xie, H.-N. Dai, X. Chen, and H. Wang, "Blockchain challenges and opportunities: A survey," *International Journal of Web and Grid Services*, vol. 14, no. 4, pp. 352–375, 2018.

[26] S. J. Russell and P. Norvig, *Artificial Intelligence: A Modern Approach*. Pearson Education, London, United Kingdom, 2016.

[27] D. Valdeolmillos, Y. Mezquita, A. González-Briones, J. Prieto, and J. M. Corchado, "Blockchain technology: A review of the current challenges of cryptocurrency," in *Blockchain and Applications: International Congress*, pp. 153–160, Springer, 2020.

[28] M. A. Khan and K. Salah, "Iot security: Review, blockchain solutions, and open challenges," *Future Generation Computer Systems*, vol. 82, no. 1, pp. 395–411, 2018.

[29] D. Tapscott and A. Tapscott, *Blockchain Revolution: How the Technology Behind Bitcoin is Changing Money, Business, and the World*. Penguin Publisher, New York, United States, 2016.

[30] A. Reyna, C. Martín, J. Chen, E. Soler, and M. Díaz, "On blockchain and its integration with iot. challenges and opportunities," *Future Generation Computer Systems*, vol. 88, no. 1, pp. 173–190, 2018.

[31] I. Weber, X. Xu, R. Riveret, G. Governatori, A. Ponomarev, and J. Mendling, "Untrusted business process monitoring and execution using blockchain," in *Business Process Management: 14th International Conference, BPM 2016, Rio de Janeiro, Brazil, September 18-22, 2016. Proceedings 14*, pp. 329–347, Springer, 2016.

[32] Icertis, "How blockchain and smart contracts will change contract management in 2018," 2017. Retrieved from ⟨https://www.icertis.com/research/blog/blockchain-smart-contracts-will-change-contract-management-2018/⟩ Accessed 19.07.2024.

[33] J. Sun, J. Yan, and K. Z. Zhang, "Blockchain-based sharing services: What blockchain technology can contribute to smart cities," *Financial Innovation*, vol. 2, no. 1, pp. 1–9, 2016.

[34] H. F. Atlam, A. Alenezi, M. O. Alassafi, and G. Wills, "Blockchain with internet of things: Benefits, challenges, and future directions," *International Journal of Intelligent Systems and Applications*, vol. 10, no. 6, pp. 40–48, 2018.

[35] B. K. Mohanta, D. Jena, U. Satapathy, and S. Patnaik, "Survey on iot security: Challenges and solution using machine learning, artificial intelligence and blockchain technology," *Internet of Things*, vol. 11, no. 1, p. 100227, 2020.

[36] U. Nations, "the state of food and agriculture", food and agriculture organization of the united nations, 2019," 2019. Available: http://www.fao.org/3/ca6030en/ca6030en.pdf.

[37] V. Saiz-Rubio and F. Rovira-Más, "From smart farming towards agriculture 5.0: A review on crop data management," *Agronomy*, vol. 10, no. 2, p. 207, 2020.

[38] L. P. Reynolds, M. C. Wulster-Radcliffe, D. K. Aaron, and T. A. Davis, "Importance of animals in agricultural sustainability and food security," *The Journal of Nutrition*, vol. 145, no. 7, pp. 1377–1379, 2015.

[39] C. Hedley, "The role of precision agriculture for improved nutrient management on farms," *Journal of the Science of Food and Agriculture*, vol. 95, no. 1, pp. 12–19, 2015.

[40] A. Vangala, A. K. Das, N. Kumar, and M. Alazab, "Smart secure sensing for iot-based agriculture: Blockchain perspective," *IEEE Sensors Journal*, vol. 21, no. 16, pp. 17591–17607, 2020.

[41] P. Mehta, R. Gupta, and S. Tanwar, "Blockchain envisioned uav networks: Challenges, solutions, and comparisons," *Computer Communications*, vol. 151, no. 1, pp. 518–538, 2020.

[42] S. Banerjee, V. Odelu, A. K. Das, S. Chattopadhyay, N. Kumar, Y. Park, and S. Tanwar, "Design of an anonymity-preserving group formation-based authentication protocol in global mobility networks," *IEEE Access*, vol. 6, pp. 20673–20693, 2018.

[43] S. Polymeni, S. Plastras, D. N. Skoutas, G. Kormentzas, and C. Skianis, "The impact of 6g-iot technologies on the development of agriculture 5.0: a review," *Electronics*, vol. 12, no. 12, p. 2651, 2023.

[44] A. Tzounis, N. Katsoulas, T. Bartzanas, and C. Kittas, "Internet of things in agriculture, recent advances and future challenges," *Biosystems Engineering*, vol. 164, pp. 31–48, 2017.

[45] J. R. Bhat, S. A. AlQahtani, and M. Nekovee, "Fintech enablers, use cases, and role of future internet of things," *Journal of King Saud University-Computer and Information Sciences*, vol. 35, no. 1, pp. 87–101, 2023.

15

Smart Traveling Bag: Leveraging Blockchain for Enhanced Travel Security and Efficiency with 5G Technology

Detroja Heli[1], Thakkar Mansi[1], Ayushi Shah[1], Keyaba Gohil[2], Rajesh Gupta[3], and Sudeep Tanwar[3]

[1]Department of Computer Science and Engineering, Institute of Technology, Nirma University, India
[2]San José State University, San Jose, California, United States
[3]Department of Computer Engineering, Marwadi University, Rajkot, Gujarat
Email: 23bce504@nirmauni.ac.in; 23bce541@nirmauni.ac.in; 21bce019@nirmauni.ac.in; 21bce076@nirmauni.ac.in; rgupta.ap@gmail.com; sudeeptanwar149@gmail.com

Abstract

When traveling anywhere, people often have fears regarding their reservations about the mishandling of luggage and theft. This paper addresses all those challenges by introducing the new concept of STBs. Security and the incorporation of facilities to track real-time are integrated into a smart traveling bag to protect passengers' belongings. The proposed smart traveling bags (STBs) include modern technologies to minimize passengers' concerns by protecting their belongings and preventing any theft attempts. This keeps the passengers in their comfort zone and even plan their travel without being on tenterhooks about losing their belongings. With all these facilities, STBs have the potential to enhance the travel experience of passengers in order to meet the purpose of travel. These bags have modern technologies such as global positioning system (GPS) for tracking and blockchain-based smart contracts for real-time luggage monitoring. Moreover, these intelligent travel bags have features for security measures like biometric authentication and tamper-proof

DOI: 10.1201/9788743809050-19

locking mechanisms to tighten the security of these bags to deter pilferage of items. This new innovative approach not only enhances the travel experience but also significantly boosts the overall operational efficiency of airports, increasing productivity for smoother journeys for passengers and streamlined processes for staff. With the inclusion of 5G connectivity, the system enables extremely fast, low-latency communication suitable for real-time monitoring, remote locking/unlocking, and verifying user identity. This integration of 5G greatly improves the system's responsiveness, scalability, and independence, setting the stage for advanced travel infrastructure.

Keywords: Blockchain, artificial intelligence, 5G-IoT, agriculture

15.1 Introduction

Traveling provides a wealth of unforgettable, rich experiences of a lifetime, but has its set of challenges; one of those which is a significant challenges is the ever-present danger of theft and improper handling of luggage. The chances of loss and pilfering of personal property not only disrupt carefully arranged travel plans but also result in enhanced financial costs and the mental anguish of travelers. As a result of these critical difficulties, the travel industry has witnessed a rise in the use of creative measures to greatly improve security and better protect the visitors' property and their baggage. This growth of interest is a sign of a unified effort to fight the inherent problems of traveling and make the journey a smoother, and more secure experience for all parties, regardless of the journey length.

This research paper examines the usage of STBs, responding to them to solve problems such as luggage mishandling and theft while traveling. These proposed STBs are a combination of novel innovations, breakthroughs, and conventional luggage designs. They are carefully planned and developed by integrating high-level security features and cutting-edge real-time tracking mechanisms to improve the safety of the valued possessions of all the passengers during the trip experience. In addition, this research explores new innovative features and possibilities of STBs to highlight their ability to enhance security and/or change traditional travel patterns.

The major objective of the study is to critically evaluate or examine, and assess the benefits of STBs and how they revolutionize and transform travel into a rich experience significantly. This research focuses on the innovative aspects and use of these bags and their unique features, including the utilization of modern and innovative technology such as IoT sensors, GPS tracking, and smart contracts based on blockchain. Through these technologies, the study intends to have a clear picture of the extent to which smart bags are efficient in preventing the theft of passengers' goods and properties.

By thoroughly contextualizing the available literature, and providing research-based articles and case studies, the research includes a broad understanding of the manifold benefits of incorporating STBs in the travel industry. Thus, this study aims to simplify the much more benefits of STBs, focusing on enhancing passengers' security and creating a feeling of calmness among all travelers based on the analysis of existing literature and real-world case studies. The research also includes an evaluation of the possible operational efficiency that may be beneficial for subsuming STBs in airport management and baggage arrangement systems. By exploring the multifaceted dynamics of these modern technological breakthroughs, this study contributes to shedding light on the informativeness impact of STBs on the travel landscape, enhancing passenger satisfaction and optimizing the airport supply chain.

Challenges include data privacy, system complexity, and creativity, which can be seen as hurdles in smart bag systems. Although they provide more security and convenience, these advanced technologies must effectively handle the protection of sensitive people's data and adopt strong cyberneticist safeguards. In addition, the significant investments associated with establishing and sustaining these sophisticated technologies, as well as their high power consumption, are also considered. These important variables from economic and environmental impacts are critical to the wide application implementation and deployment of smart bag systems.

Therefore, this paper endeavors to include the growing collection of knowledge concerning travel security and novel technology adoption. This paper seeks to explain the significance of STBs in tackling the enduring problems of luggage mishandling and theft while traveling. The paper's goal is to contribute to the growing body of literature on travel security and technology acceptance. It also highlights the emphasis of STBs in addressing persistent issues such as luggage mishandling and theft. By carefully inspecting the current status of smart luggage technology, the research will emphasize the crucial role of this innovative solution in improving the overall travel experience much better. This study will demonstrate how STBs prevent the threat of unauthorized access and theft by analyzing and examining security features like biometric locks, remote locking systems, and tamper-proof zippers in detail.

Furthermore, the study examines the comprehensive effects of STBs on global travel trends and behaviors across the world. As more commuters increasingly understand the advantages of smart luggage, the more leads to a paradigm shift toward consumer this kind of preference increasing such similar technologically enhanced travel solutions. Also shifts further novelty in the world of the traveling industry, and encourages modern innovative technologies to enhance passenger safety and comfort. Thus, analyzing these trends, this study intends to offer awareness of the future of travel and demonstrate highlighting the evolvement potential of STBs in enhancing the safety, efficiency, and enjoyment of travel to travelers worldwide. The study incorporates the use of 5G in the communication channel to enable faster tracking with reduced delays, suitable for real-time monitoring of the STBs.

15.1.1 Research contribution

The following are the major research contributions of this research work:

- The research work aims to eliminate the difficulties faced by travelers and optimize operational efficiency at airports.
- Our proposed STB system leverages technologies like GPS and Blockchain Network to ensure that it achieves the aforementioned goals while also ensuring data integrity, security, and immutability.
- A smart contract is built in order to communicate with blockchain technology; the transaction and execution costs in terms of gas costs are discussed at the end of this paper.
- The incorporation of 5G technology enhances the proposed framework's responsiveness due to low-latency communication.

15.1.2 Organization

The subsequent sections of the paper are organized as follows: Section II discusses related works. Section III illustrates the proposed framework. Section IV discusses the results and analysis of the smart contract, which is deployed over the Ethereum Blockchain network. Finally, Section V presents the conclusion of the article.

15.2 Literature Review

Smart tourism faces significant challenges in information sharing due to varied information systems, which create "information islands" that hinder seamless communication and data integration. These systems hinder the effective flow of information, which is crucial for enhancing the tourist experience and optimizing service delivery. However, [7] addresses these

Table 15.1 Literature review table.

Author	Year	Objective	Proposed methodology	Limitation
[1]	2018	Proposed smart bag with theft prevention and real time tracking	The paper discusses a smart bag equipped with advanced electronic technology for security and real-time tracking, using GPS, GSM, Bluetooth, Arduino, and UV sensors.	The integration of various technologies may complicate the design and functionality of the smart bag.
[2]	2018	Implemented a smart bag that can be traced using an Android application	The smart bag is designed to enhance the safety and security of luggage during travel.	The document does not explicitly list the limitations of the Smart Bag system. However, potential limitations could include dependency on network coverage for GSM and GPS functionalities and the need for a power supply to maintain the systemâĂŹs operation.
[3]	2020	Proposed a WiFi-enabled smart travel bag based on Android system	The smart bag relies on various technologies like Wi-Fi, GPS, and ultrasonic sensors, which may have range, accuracy, and reliability limitations.	The smart bag concept aims to reduce the time and effort in luggage management by automating the process and allowing control through a smartphone application.
[4]	2020	Blockchain technology for smart tourism destinations	Enhances the tourism experience. Rewards sustainable behavior. Ensures local community benefits. Reduces privacy concerns.	Conceptual complexity and novelty. Security concerns and data privacy. High operation costs and energy consumption.

Table 15.1 *Continued.*

Author	Year	Objective	Proposed methodology	Limitation
[5]	2021	Enabling secure and distributed airport baggage tracking with hybrid blockchain-edge system	The proposed system integrates RFID with blockchain for real-time baggage tracking. Utilizes blockchain for secure, decentralized data storage, preventing data leakage.	The practical Byzantine fault tolerance algorithm has high communication complexity and cost. The framework's efficiency is affected by the presence of Byzantine nodes.
[6]	2021	Implementation of blockchain technology in the tourism industry: A systematic literature review	It helps decrease costs, particularly for tourists, by reducing the role of intermediaries.	The limited academic literature on blockchain technology in tourism indicates the need for a more comprehensive analysis.
[7]	2022	Presented application of blockchain technology in smart ourism	The rapid development of smart tourism under big data faces challenges in ensuring the authenticity of data and minimizing the negative impact of misinformation.	The development of smart tourism faces challenges in information sharing due to independent information systems, creating "information islands."
[8]	2022	The role of artificial intelligence and blockchain technologies in sustainable tourism in the Middle East	AI and BT can contribute to economic growth and environmental conservation, potentially reviving interest in sustainable tourism.	The initial screening focused on Artificial Intelligence and Blockchain-based sustainable tourism papers, indicating a vast array of applications and possibilities, which could be a limitation in terms of scope.

obstacles by proposing novel approaches for integration and collaboration among various information systems. The study aims to bridge these "information islands" by implementing standardized protocols and advanced data-sharing technologies, resulting in a more integrated and cohesive smart tourist environment. To get better efficiency for the intelligent tourism, the need to prevail over these problems is pivotal. Although this study does not explicitly outline the Smart Bag system's drawbacks, potential limitations include reliance on network coverage for GSM and GPS functionalities. This could lead to inconsistent tracking and security capabilities across diverse travel environments. Moreover, the need for a constant power supply poses another challenge, as the limited battery life necessitates frequent recharging, causing consumer discomfort. Recent research also explores the role played by 5G in improving IoT systems' reliability, speed, and scalability. Studies have shown that 5G's low latency (1 ms) and high bandwidth (up to 10 Gbps) enable real-time data transmission for various applications. Integrating 5G technology into smart bags presents an exciting opportunity to enhance personal travel. This innovation enables seamless, real-time communication with blockchain networks and remote cloud services, making the travel experience more efficient and connected.

[2] addresses these concerns by proposing strategies to mitigate them. These initiatives include exploring alternative power sources, enhancing network connectivity, and developing efficient energy management systems. These efforts aim to improve the reliability and utilization of smart bag systems in real-world travel scenarios [4]. The tourism industry has limited research on blockchain technology applications, emphasizing the need for in-depth research. This knowledge gap highlights the urgency for further investigation into blockchain's potential to enhance transparency, security, and operational efficiency across various tourism sectors.

[8] seeks to bridge this gap by providing insightful ideas and conclusions through comprehensive analysis and case studies. This work explores blockchain technology's practical applications, emphasizing its potential to transform core tourist processes, including booking systems, payment transactions, and consumer dataÂămanagement.

15.3 Proposed Framework

The proposed framework comprises four layers as shown in Figure 15.1. The user Layer covers all users and is responsible for registration and permission management, Bag Registration Layer which records and stores

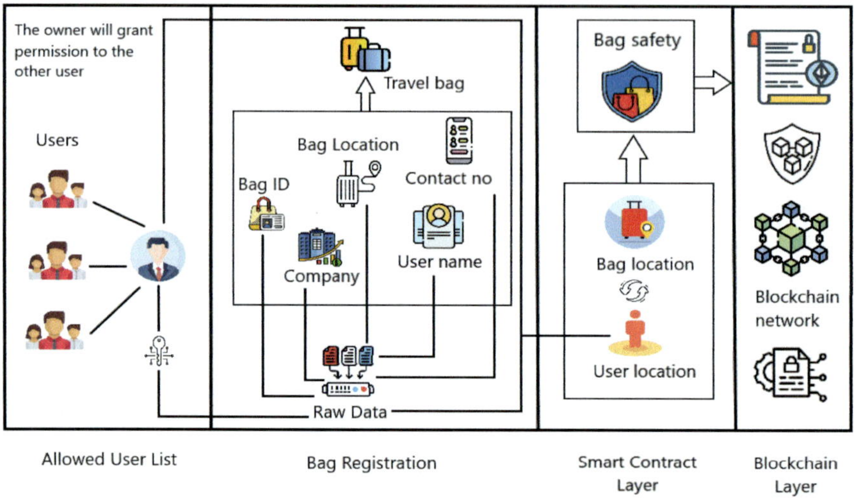

Figure 15.1 Proposed framework for smart traveling bag.

all essential information, such as the bag's location, smart contract Layer utilizes smart contracts to autonomously ensure the security of the smart bag and the blockchain layer provides support for the entire system by establishing a decentralized network that tracks all bag-tracking transactions and data. The framework provides a comprehensive solution for real-time tracking and management by leveraging characteristics of the blockchain technology to achieve security, transparency, and operational efficiency. This further ensures that the trip of the bag is securely documented and instantly accessible.

15.3.1 User layer

The owner of the STB can allow or deny access to friends and family members to track the bag's whereabouts, ensuring that only authorized individuals can monitor it. This equation represents the set of all users involved in the system. User U is the set and u_i, as the unique identifier within the set eqn (15.1):

$$U = \{u_1, u_2, \ldots, u_\text{n}\}. \tag{15.1}$$

In eqn (15.2) it defines the relationship between users and their owned bags. For any bag b in the set B, $Own(b)$ indicates the user who owns bag b.

$$Own : B \to U. \tag{15.2}$$

Eqn (15.3) indicates the access permissions. In this equation if $(u, b) \in Access$, symbolizes that user u is authorized to access bag b.

$$\text{Access} \subseteq U \times B. \tag{15.3}$$

15.3.2 Bag registration layer

This layer assigns a unique Bag ID to each bag and links the ID to specific user details, including the owner's name, contact number, and the tracking service company. Eqn (15.4) below describes the collection of all bags within the system. Each b_{i} serves as a distinct identifier for an individual bag within the set B:

$$B = \{b_1, b_2, \ldots, b_m\}, \tag{15.4}$$

where b_{i} represents the i-th bag.

Eqn (15.5) defines the registration relationship between bags, users, and smart contracts. For any bag b in the set B, the function $Reg(b)$ returns a tuple (u, s), indicating that bag b is registered to user u:

$$Reg : B \to U \times S. \tag{15.5}$$

Eqn (15.6) specifies that for a given bag b, $Reg(b)$ returns the user u and the smart contract s associated with that bag. It indicates the ownership and contractual details of the bag:

$$Reg(b) = (u, s), \tag{15.6}$$

if bag b is registered to user u with smart contract s.

15.3.3 Smart contract layer

The smart contract layer utilizes smart contracts to autonomously manage permissions and secure the bag's and user's location data. If the bag is lost or misplaced, the system automatically notifies the user, facilitating quick recovery and enhancing overall bag security. The function $Exec(s, c)$ operates within the domain of smart contracts and transactions. Here, s represents a smart contract, and c represents a transaction that is intended to be executed by the smart contract, as illustrated in eqn (15.7):

$$Exec : S \times C \to \{0, 1\}, \tag{15.7}$$

- $Exec(s, c) = 1$: This indicates that the smart contract s has successfully executed the transaction c.
- $Exec(s, c) = 0$: This indicates that the execution of the transaction c by the smart contract s was unsuccessful.

The function $Notify(b)$ is used in the context of monitoring the status of a bag, where b represents a bag that could potentially be lost or misplaced, as shown in eqn (15.8):

$$Notify : B \rightarrow \{0, 1\}, \tag{15.8}$$

- $Notify(b) = 1$: This indicates that the bag b is lost or misplaced, and the user has been notified about this status.
- $Notify(b) = 0$: This indicates that either the bag b is not lost or misplaced, or the user has not been notified about the bag's status.

15.3.4 Blockchain layer

This layer ensures transparency, immutability, and security, limiting data access to authorized individuals. The combination of the blockchain network and smart contracts creates an efficient system for managing rights, tracking locations, and sending messages. The set C represents a collection of transactions, where each c_{i} is an individual transaction. Here, k is the total number of transactions in the set, as shown in eqn (15.9):

$$C = \{c_1, c_2, \ldots, c_{\mathrm{k}}\}. \tag{15.9}$$

In conclusion, the conceptual framework of the smart contract marks a significant step forward in the development of travel bag management. It has a variety of features intended at improving security, optimizing logistics, and giving owners remarkable control. With careful design and exact implementation, stakeholders may fully realize the transformative power of blockchain technology, ushering in a new era of increased efficiency and transparency in travel bag management. The incorporation of 5G communication offers a continuous, high-speed communication for seamless use of the STBs across geographic regions.

15.4 Results and Discussions

15.4.1 Execution cost

In blockchain platforms that support smart contracts, such as Ethereum, Execution costs are to be paid while engaging with smart contracts on blockchain platforms; it is directly proportional to the number of computational operations performed while executing a function. The computational resources (gas) required to carry out the activities encoded in a smart contract define the transaction's execution cost. In Ethereum, the execution cost (C) of a transaction is calculated as the product of the gas used (G) and the gas price (P), eqn (15.10):

$$C = G \times P. \tag{15.10}$$

Here, gas represents the computational steps or operations performed by the Ethereum virtual machine (EVM) to execute the smart contract code, and gas price is the amount of cryptocurrency (typically denominated in Wei) that the sender is willing to pay per unit of gas. The execution costs for various functions are illustrated in Figure 15.2

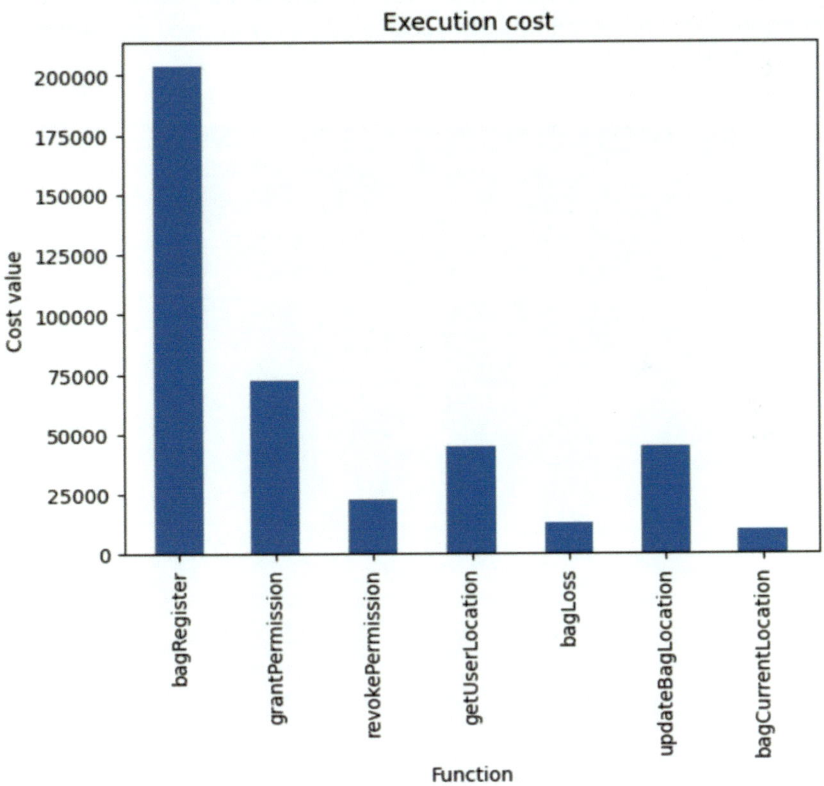

Figure 15.2 Execution cost.

The bar chart shows the estimated execution cost of various functions related to managing STBs on a blockchain network. The y-axis represents the execution cost, measured in gas units specific to the chosen blockchain platform. Gas is a unit used on many blockchains to measure the computational effort required to execute a transaction. Transactions with higher complexity typically require more gas and, therefore, cost more to execute on the blockchain.

Here is a breakdown of the functions listed on the x-axis and their possible execution costs in the context of your STB system:

- *bagRegister*: As illustrated in Figure 15.3, this function likely incurs the highest cost due to the creation of a new entry on the blockchain ledger that includes all the initial details of a new smart traveling bag. Figure 15.3 depicts the interface for the bagRegister function.
- *getUserLocation*: Shown in Figure 15.4(a), the cost associated with this function varies based on how the location data is retrieved and stored on the blockchain.

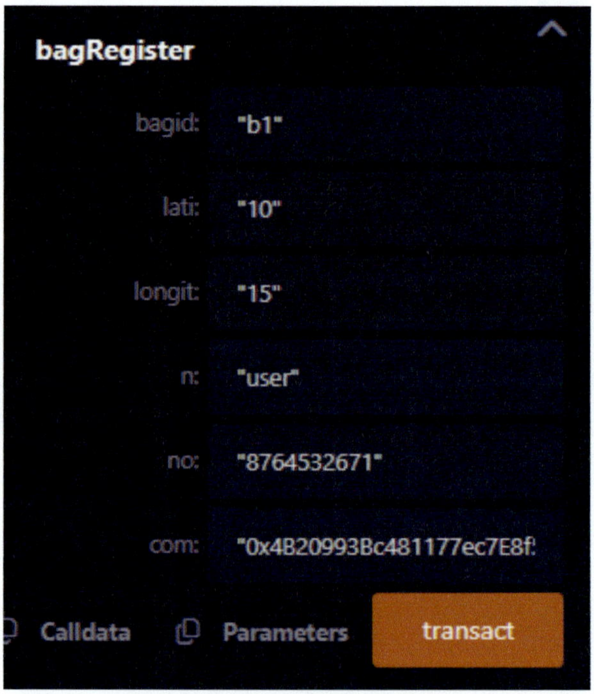

Figure 15.3 Bag registration.

- *revokePermission*: Illustrated in Figure 15.5, this function enables users to withdraw previously granted access permissions for viewing the details of a smart traveling bag.
- *updateBagLocation*: This function allows updating the location data of a registered STB on the blockchain, with costs dependent on the update frequency and the volume of data stored.

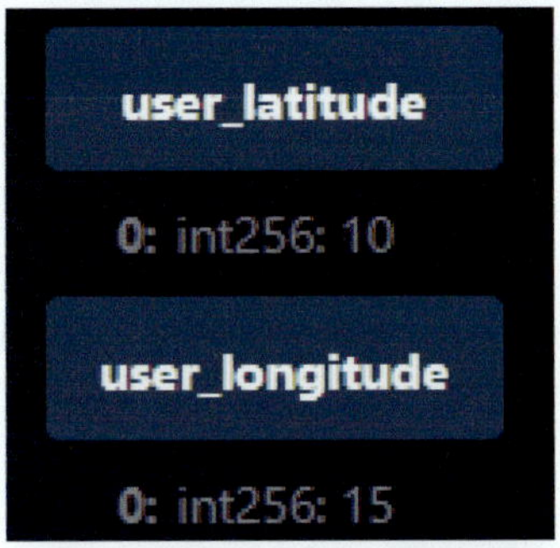

(a) User Current Location

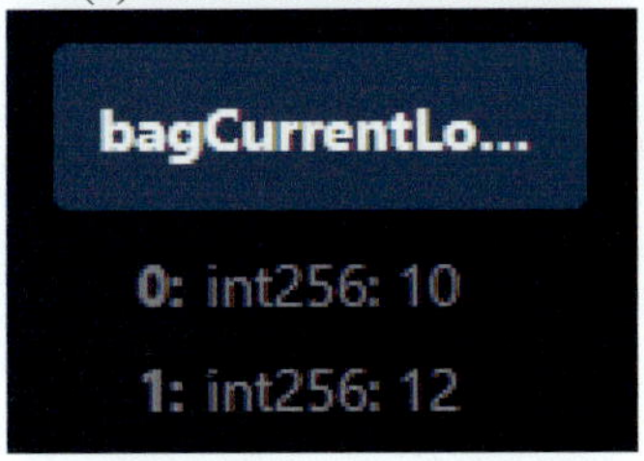

(b) Bag Current Location

Figure 15.4 Display the bag and the user's location.

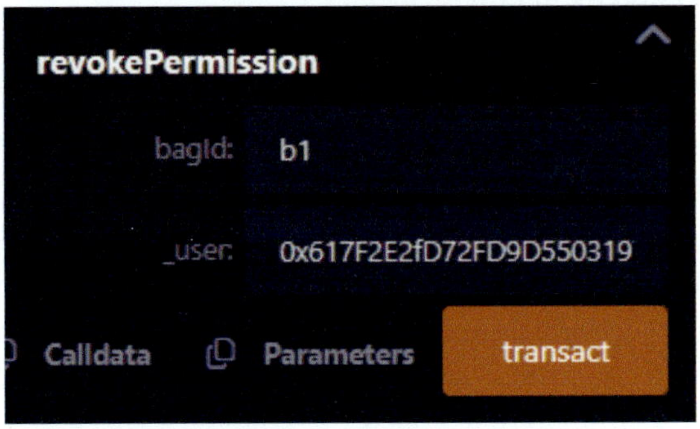

Figure 15.5 Revoke permission.

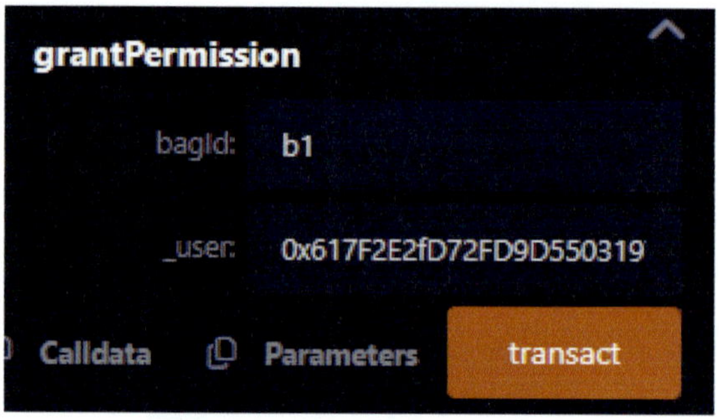

Figure 15.6 Grant permission.

- *bagLoss*: The cost of this function is uncertain and likely depends on the specific implementation. It could involve marking a bag as lost and potentially triggering other actions.
- *grantPermission*: As depicted in Figure 15.6, this function allows users to authorize others to view specific details (such as location data) of a registered smart traveling bag.

15.4.2 Transaction cost

For cryptocurrencies like Bitcoin, the transaction cost (or transaction fee) is typically set by the sender of the transaction. It represents the amount of cryptocurrency the sender is willing to pay to have their transaction included in a block and processed by miners. The transaction cost formula can vary depending on the network's current conditions. Generally, it depends on factors such as the transaction's size (in bytes) and the current network fee rate (in cryptocurrency per byte). In Bitcoin, for example, the transaction fee (F) can be calculated as in eqn (15.11):

$$F = \text{size} \times \text{fee rate}. \tag{15.11}$$

The transaction costs for all functions are depicted in Figure 15.7

The specific cost can vary depending on factors like:

- *Transaction complexity*: More complex transactions that require more computational power to process will typically have higher fees.
- *Network congestion*: When there is a high volume of transactions on the network, fees can increase due to increased demand for block space.
- *Price of the cryptocurrency used for gas*: The fees are typically denominated in the cryptocurrency used by the blockchain network. So, if the

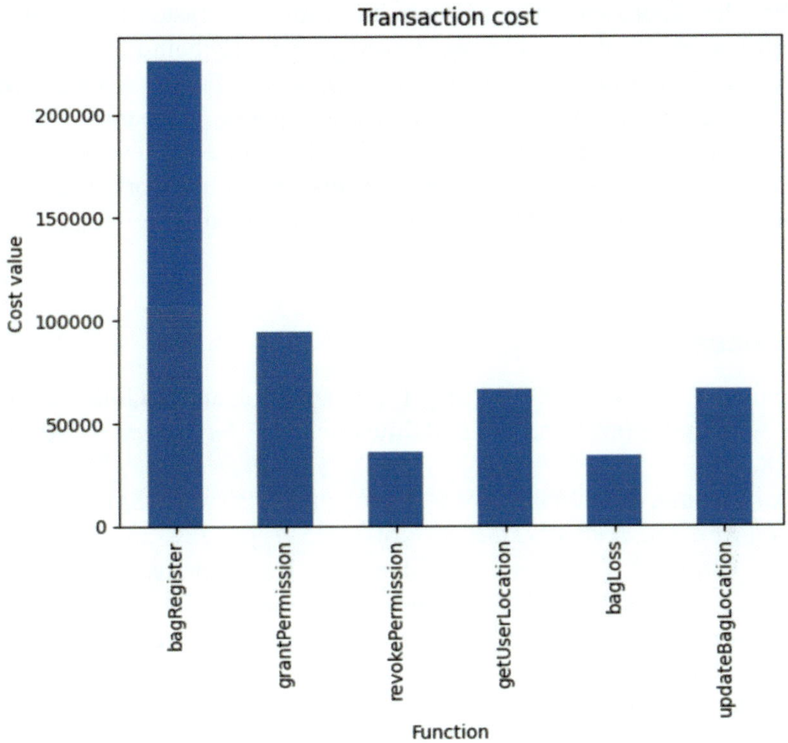

Figure 15.7 Transaction Cost

price of that cryptocurrency fluctuates, the transaction cost in dollars will also change.

15.5 Conclusion

This research work explores the concept of intelligent travel bags, which aim to tackle issues such as luggage mishandling and theft during travel by incorporating advanced security features and real-time tracking mechanisms. It discusses the utilization of IoT sensors, GPS tracking, and blockchain-based smart contracts in these bags to enhance the travel experience and optimize operational efficiency at airports. The paper examines various research studies and technological advancements related to intelligent travel bags to offer a solution for a safer and more convenient travel experience. It further uses a smart contract deployed on the Ethereum blockchain network to achieve this goal with the incorporation of 5G communication for faster, lower latency, and high bandwidth data exchange. Leveraging blockchain eliminates data security and integrity concerns in the framework. Future works include exploring the integration of an artificial intelligence mechanism into the system to achieve the aforementioned goal and enhance the level of security and safety that the proposed framework offers. As future work, the authors will conduct simulations of 5G communication to obtain experimental results for the communication layer.

References

[1] A. Sutar, T. Kocharekar, P. Mestry, P. Sawantdesai, and S. Goilkar, "Smart bag with theft prevention and real time tracking," *Int J Trend Sci Res Dev*, 2018.

[2] A. L. Abhang, C. L. Mahale, V. R. Desai, and P. Biswas, "Smart bag," *Int. J. Sci. Res. Sci. Technol.(IJSRST)*, vol. 4, no. 7, pp. 227–231, 2018.

[3] P. R. Amin, S. K. Karanth, M. Sharanya, K. Akshatha, and M. Badiger, "Smart travel bag," *Department of Electronics & Communication Engineering, Sahyadri College of Engineering & Management*, 2020.

[4] I. Tyan, M. I. Yagüe, and A. Guevara-Plaza, "Blockchain technology for smart tourism destinations," *Sustainability*, vol. 12, no. 22, p. 9715, 2020.

[5] P. Si, F. Wang, E. Sun, and Y. Su, "Bei-tab: Enabling secure and distributed airport baggage tracking with hybrid blockchain-edge system," *Wireless Communications and Mobile Computing*, vol. 2021, no. 1, p. 2741435, 2021.

[6] R. L. Rana, P. Giungato, and C. Tricase, "Implementation of blockchain technology in the tourism industry: A systematic literature review," *New Trends in Sustainable Business and Consumption*, vol. 1, pp. 594–602, 2021.

[7] Y. LIANG, "Application of blockchain technology in smart tourism," in *2022 7th International Conference on Financial Innovation and Economic Development (ICFIED 2022)*, pp. 3265–3269, Atlantis Press, 2022.

[8] M. A. Kashem, M. Shamsuddoha, T. Nasir, and A. A. Chowdhury, "The role of artificial intelligence and blockchain technologies in sustainable tourism in the middle east," *Worldwide Hospitality and Tourism Themes*, vol. 15, no. 2, pp. 178–191, 2022.

16

Transformation of Financial and Virtual Realms in the Metaverse: A Blockchain Technology Perspective

Sheetal Sharma[1], Rushina Singhi[1], Kiran Jindal[2], and Vijit Chaturvedi[3]

[1]Nilkamal School of Mathematics, Applied Statistics & Analytics, NMIMS University, India
[2]Mehr Chand Mahajan DAV College for Women, India
[3]Amity Business School, Amity University, India
Email: sheetalsharma.1432004@gmail.com; rushina.singhi@nmims.edu; jindalkiran@gmail.com; vchaturvedi@amity.edu

Abstract

The realms of metaverse and finance have been completely revolutionized through the application of blockchain technology. This technology offers convenience, transparency, security, and decentralization to the virtual world while overcoming the inefficiencies of the traditional financial landscape. The present chapter highlights the various services offered by blockchain technology in the metaverse, such as security, interoperability, and ownership status, especially in the area of finance. A digital landscape with a large number of users sharing information from various geographical locations using an internet connection is called the metaverse. Blockchain technology ensures transparency and security in the metaverse by building trust among users. The users get complete authority over their digital assets, thereby enhancing their participation in the digital realm. In the financial sector, the traditional financial system is transformed through the introduction of blockchain technology, such as cryptocurrencies like Bitcoin and Ethereum, decentralized finance (DeFi), smart contracts, and asset tokenization. Cryptocurrencies, like Bitcoin

DOI: 10.1201/9788743809050-20

and Ethereum, provided by blockchain technology, are digital currencies that ensure secure transactions and do not need any authority to act as a middleman. Decentralized finance (DeFi), based on decentralization, facilitates peer-to-peer financial transactions. Smart contracts are automatically executed agreements or contracts made using blockchain technology, which makes the process of transactions easier. Asset tokenization is a representation of the value of assets as digital tokens. However, blockchain technology also presents challenges in various services, necessitating the need to address them to improve opportunities.

Keywords: Blockchain technology, metaverse, DeFi, asset tokenization, smart contracts, cryptocurrencies

16.1 Introduction

The innovation in technology has revolutionized the financial industry, providing new opportunities for users by integrating the financial and virtual realms. The connection between humans and the virtual objects that run on a specific set of rules comprising various regulating systems is called the metaverse [13]. It is an interactive simulated environment through which the participants communicate with other users through digital devices [25]. Through this device, users can interact and explore creative opportunities. It is the next step toward digital evolution, which enhances digital world acceptance and contributes to the expansion of service offerings beyond traditional online access systems [28]. With the rise of digital interaction, the major concern is to ensure the security of the digital data of the users. Blockchain technology has a wide range of applications; it facilitates safe communication and focuses on resource management [23]. Its unique attributes, like decentralization, immutability, and transparency, provide potential solutions to various problems. It provides transparency to data transactions and ensures control over the information of users. Data can be shared conveniently without administrative intervention. It ensures non-repudiation through immutable record distribution. In addition to creating a reliable virtual economy, blockchain serves as a shield, protecting users' security and privacy as they navigate and participate in the diverse experiences of the metaverse [20]. It facilitates the financial service providers in various activities such as Security, risk management, and authenticity. Blockchain is being used in trade and financial systems by various organizations to create smart contracts between players, improve effectiveness and transparency, and investigate new income prospects [14]. This technology offers a range of financial services. Some key financial services are cryptocurrencies and digital assets, smart contracts, and decentralized finance (DeFi).

The cryptocurrency industry has grown significantly in the last several years, making it a sought-after asset for investors all across the world [2]. Blockchain technology powers cryptocurrencies like Ethereum and Bitcoin. Digital assets refer to valuable data and content that organizations acquire throughout their operations, management, and production processes [31]. Transactions are safe and secure in this new era of digital currencies without needing intermediate authorities. Another significant contribution of blockchain in finance is smart contracts. These are agreements with a pre-decided set of conditions, automatically executed with the occurrence of certain events in the transactions under the blockchain [1]. These contracts are activated on every commercial transaction taking place in the digital financial realm. Tracking the movement of goods and materials is possible via smart contracts [16]. Smart contracts are useful in many situations, like handling claims in insurance businesses, automated payments, issuing loans in banks, and collecting fees during the delivery of services by postal services [18]. The various features of blockchain technology-based smart contracts, like flexibility and automation, unlock many opportunities in the financial realm, increase productivity, and simplify complex procedures across various industries. This technology effortlessly integrates with the DeFi realm. According to [18], the DeFi system uses decentralized blockchain technology for the availability of financial products to the public. Through this method, financial services may be provided to the users directly from financial institutions and other conventional intermediaries. DeFi brings transformation to the financial world by providing future opportunities and empowers consumers by giving them financial independence. Integration of various services provided by blockchain technology completely transforms the realms of the metaverse and finance, making the virtual world much safer and more convenient. It transforms the whole process of doing things in the virtual world, such as managing data or conducting transactions. It might lead to better possibilities and user experiences, creating a more secure and interconnected future. It is therefore important to study the more recent studies of block technology in transforming the financial and virtual realm. This chapter analyzes the studies and their finding in the emergence of blockchain with metaverse that have brought the evolutionary changes in thereby providing a secure and transparent platform for the users.

16.2 Blockchain

According to [15], blockchain is essentially a digital record of transactions kept by many computer units independently under a network, doing away with the need for reliance on a third party. At its core, blockchain technology is a secure, decentralized way to log transactions across a computer network. This technique guarantees transparency and resistance against manipulation. Each "atomic" activity that takes place on a blockchain is called a transaction and is stored in data files called blocks. The blocks that are managed by specialized software allow data to be sent, processed, stored, and presented in a human-readable manner. It is a hybrid technology based on peer-to-peer communication, distributed consensus methods, and encryption algorithms as opposed to typical centralized database methods [30]. Due to its decentralized, immutable, and traceable characteristics and its original usage in cryptocurrency, it has been widely adopted by various industries, yielding numerous economic and social benefits to them. Despite being around for more than a decade, blockchain technology's impact on the metaverse is just now beginning to be seen.

16.3 Metaverse and Blockchain

With the metaverse, users may create, engage, and participate in virtual content while adopting any identity, engaging in any activity, and owning any asset. Unfortunately, hardly much has been built in the past for this system due to persistent issues with compatibility, security, and ownership conflicts. However, with the invention of blockchain technology, these obstacles have been removed, indicating a positive shift in the metaverse ecosystem.

16.3.1 Security

Appropriate security is essential to exchange the information on any platform, especially in the case of Internet of Things (IoT) devices [10]. Blockchain technology is a secure network and uses a distributed ledger to record the details of all transactions in order to maintain transparency. The process of blockchain is irreversible, unbreakable, and cannot be hacked because of unique hash-connected blocks of information, enabling the users to produce, communicate, and exchange the information without the fear of fraudulent activities. Further, this technology facilitates the verification of user identity, resulting in improved functioning of virtual realms [11, 22].

16.3.2 Interoperability

The metaverse, a vast network of digital realms, presents challenges in the efficient sharing of information and assets across various platforms. Blockchain technology addresses this by enabling secure, connected chain sharing of information [7]. This eliminates interoperability issues, allowing users to create as many virtual platforms as they desire and share content virtually [4]. Blockchain also provides full control over property, enabling convenient mobility across various platforms. Overall, blockchain technology offers a more efficient and secure way to share and manage virtual content.

The metaverse, based on a large number of digital realms created by users, offers unique challenges in efficiently sharing information or assets on various platforms. Blockchain technology ensures consistent and secure sharing through connected chains of information [27]. Interoperability is also no longer a major issue through blockchain technology, as it allows users to create as many virtual platforms as they desire and share content virtually [4]. Further, users have full control over their property through blockchain, enabling convenient mobility across various platforms. Overall, blockchain technology offers a more efficient and secure way to share and manage virtual content.

16.3.3 Ownership status

A large number of individuals use digital content in today's virtual realm, creating an identification problem for true owners of digital assets. These digital assets can be virtual money, land, goods, or any virtual content. Blockchain technology provides validated and traceable unique digital objects, which help to identify the right owners of the digital assets present on various platforms. It enables individuals to have full control over their belongings while engaging in various activities such as selling, buying, or trading conveniently. Blockchain facilitates the formation of smart contracts, similar to coded contracts, which are executed on their own. In this case, the transactions occur automatically using smart contracts, doing away with the need for intermediaries and facilitating more seamless transactions in the existing metaverse. In a nutshell, decentralized security, frictionless data transfer, and automatic ownership identification through smart contracts are possible through the integration of blockchain technology in the Metaverse [3]. The application of this technology can create new opportunities for user engagement, asset management, and general expansion in the ever-changing digital environment of the Metaverse.

16.4 Blockchain in Finance

Over the last decade, the banking sector has experienced a "fintech revolution" and has expanded dramatically. Currently, there are nearly 26,000 fintech start-ups globally by the year 2023. Further, blockchain technology is a significant force in financial providers. This technology has the prospective to overcome the traditional financial institutions' inefficiencies, such as the requirement of a middleman (banks or clearing houses) while doing any transactions. This technology has also been instrumental in resolving problems such as increased cost, transaction delays, and fraud concerns in traditional systems.

According to [3], users of conventional financial systems are facing problems such as inaccessibility of various financial services, low speed, high expenses, and complex procedures, particularly in the case of people from an underprivileged community. Using distributed ledger, blockchain technology is completely decentralized, which enables direct transactions without the need for middlemen [14]. Every transaction is recorded on a shared ledger so that every individual has access to identical secure transaction records, and the transactions are easy to verify by any user. Additionally, common issues such as money laundering or corruption can be addressed using this technology through the provision of a transparent audit of every financial transaction. Hence, this technology secured a transparent system performing financial communications. Blockchain technology also has the potential to facilitate equal and rightful availability of financial services through an open and accessible platform to all. Advantages such as easy access to financial services, reduction in transaction costs, and financial inclusion are available to companies and individuals, especially to those present in underdeveloped regions.

Blockchain technology can streamline procedures and cut costs by automating labor-intensive and time-consuming operations. Smart contracts eradicate the need for intermediaries and reduce the likelihood of errors or delays by enabling existing agreements to be carried out automatically when certain criteria are met. The four main features of blockchain in finance are:

(1) Cryptocurrency
(2) Decentralized finance

(3) Smart contracts
(4) Asset tokenization

16.5 Cryptocurrency and Digital Assets

Digital assets are electronic data that can be owned and transferred by individuals. These are used to store intangible information like contracts, files, videos, or currency for transactions. Digital assets are valuable data and material that organizations gather during production, management, or business operations [31]. Cryptocurrency is an example of a digital asset. Crypto, short for "cryptocurrency," is a form of currency that secures transactions using cryptography. It is a currency that exists digitally. Because transactions are verified by encryption, it is known as a cryptocurrency. A decentralized system eliminates the need for a central regulating body, like banks, to record transactions and issue new units. There are two prominent cryptocurrencies, known as Bitcoin and Ethereum.

16.5.1 Bitcoin

Bitcoin, launched by Satoshi Nakamoto in November 2008, is a popular cryptocurrency that offers an alternative to traditional banking systems by implementing a peer-to-peer transfer of cryptomoney [12]. Before this, many electronic cash systems used to rely on a centralized authority such as a private company or bank. Bitcoin operates on blockchain technology and uses advanced mathematical techniques for cryptographic maintenance. Bitcoin is pseudo-anonymous, allowing users to create transactions using letters and numbers instead of real-world identities [9]. Bitcoin regulation involves verifying transactions and creating a long-term transaction chain. A block on a blockchain contains a block header, transaction counter, and transactions recorded in the block. Each block has hashed information from the previous block, forming a series of encrypted blocks. Miners are like digital accountants, who solve complex mathematical puzzles to add new transactions and earn bitcoins as a reward [5]. Nowadays, bitcoin mining has become significantly competitive due to the usage of specialized hardware like ASICs dominating the network. Mining can be done individually or by joining mining pools. Participants get shared rewards when they use mining pools. To ensure the digital security and immutability of the blockchain, transactions of Bitcoin are encrypted using the SHA-256 hashing algorithm. Transaction authentication requires private keys, which are stored in wallets.

However, bitcoin mining involves significant costs such as electricity and hardware expenses, making it less accessible to individual miners compared to its early days.

16.5.2 Ethereum

Ethereum, created by Vitalik Buterin in 2013, is a public blockchain platform known for its ether (ETH) cryptocurrency [24]. It enables individuals to create secure digital technologies using smart contracts and blockchain, which are essential tools for decentralized applications. It is an advanced version that widens its applications in various fields other than finance through decentralized applications. It operates on a distributed computing system and uses a smart contract to execute commands and import information, which makes it different from Bitcoin [19]. It uses an algorithm, known as gasper, which consumes less energy than Bitcoin's proof-of-work algorithm. To take part in block validation, validators stake 32 ETH minimum. Validators keep track of the validity of blocks, which are then confirmed and checked by other validators. This process is called attestation. Dishonest validators have a risk of losing their staked ETH and expelling from the network. Ether, the cryptocurrency of Ethereum, is stored in wallets. These wallets contain private keys used for transactions, and users can send and receive ether, similar to sending emails. Ethereum also experienced a historic split known as a hard fork, resulting in the creation of Ethereum Classic after a significant theft incident involving a project called the DAO [2].

16.5.3 Decentralized finance

Blockchain technology is revolutionizing the finance industry with decentralized finance (DeFi). DeFi is a secure, decentralized system built on securely distributed ledgers (DLT), smart contracts, and consensus [21]. DLT enhances security by distributing the records across multiple nodes, whereas smart contracts ensure explicit evaluations from all parties before execution. Here, consensus means accepting the network-verified transaction by all parties. When compared to traditional fintech models, DeFi does not give any control of money to any financial intermediaries, thereby enhancing the security, cost-effectiveness, transparency, and accessibility of financial services [1]. Based on decentralized applications, DeFi offers a wide variety of financial services, including lending, borrowing, asset management, trading in cryptocurrencies, and price movement speculation.

Benefits of DeFi:

a. *User-friendly*: DeFi's digital wallet system is user-friendly, through which users can have total control over their funds without relying on third parties.
b. *Privacy maintenance*: No personal information of users is needed in DeFi platforms, which allows transactions to be conducted anonymously.
c. *Mobility*: DeFi allows users to move their assets freely across various DeFi systems and protocols, providing complete control over their assets. It makes asset management and mobility easier for them.
d. *Accessibility*: Anyone with an internet connection can participate, providing financial inclusion on a global scale.
e. *Transparent*: All transactions and financial activities are recorded on a public blockchain. The entire transaction history is offered for full visibility. This gains users' trust and reduces the risks of fraud and manipulation within the DeFi ecosystem.

Challenges

1. *Over-collateralization*: The cost of new tokens is increased due to the risk of impermanent loss. In this regard, over-collateralization is the main obstacle resulting in lower capital efficiency [18].
2. *Regulatory risks*: DeFi runs on blockchain technology and faces regulatory risks because blockchain replicates heavily regulated services with its new technology. Regulated companies face legal obligations that pose risks for DeFi, including compliance challenges and the need to address illegal activities [19].
3. *Security risks*: Smart contract vulnerabilities and cyber threats remain significant concerns that require robust security measures [29].

16.5.4 Smart contracts

Contracts that are self-executing agreements and run on blockchain technology are called smart contracts. Cryptographer Nick Szabo, in 1997, first introduced this concept and compared it to a digital vending machine. Programming languages such as Go, Python, or Solidity are used to write these contracts. These contracts are implemented automatically after abiding by the predefined norms. Smart contracts operate without relying on any centralized authority, which ensures security and transparency, and effectiveness across various industries, including banking, voting, and smart cities. The data is immutable and accessible to all participants as it is stored on a blockchain.

Applications of smart contracts

- *Banking*: Loans issuing and automating payments.
- *Insurance*:Automatic claim processing [16].
- *Blockchain security*: Duplicated across multiple nodes, which ensures permanence and security.
- *Ethereum and solidity*: The most widely used language for smart contracts on the Ethereum blockchain is solidity.

Key features of smart contracts are discussed below:

i. *Accuracy*: Smart contracts are irreversible and are tested before the development of nodes in the network. Once the conditions are met, there is an automatic execution. The accuracy is assured and certain without the engagement of humans or third parties.
ii. *Decentralization*: No intermediary authority is involved, which reduces the risk of any kind of manipulation.
iii. *Transparency*: One important benefit of smart contracts is transparency. The contracts or agreements are accessible to all the involved parties in smart contracts, which makes blockchain different and unique when compared to other systems.
iv. *Autonomous execution*: There is a state known as the triggering state, which is achieved upon the agreement of all the parties in the blockchain. It can be any condition, such as receiving a payment. The execution takes place automatically upon reaching the triggered state.
v. *Accessibility*: Smart contracts are accessed or executed globally with the use of an internet connection only.

Challenges associated with smart contracts

i. *Security vulnerabilities*: As these contracts are written in code, certain errors can cause vulnerabilities.
ii. *Scalability*: The performance speed may be affected because of large volumes of transactions.
iii. *Oracles and external data*: There is a risk of manipulation as it relies on third-party data sources.
iv. *Legal and regulatory compliance*: Legal and regulatory frameworks are still developing and differ by region.

16.5.5 Asset tokenization

Asset tokenization is the conversion of ownership rights of digital or physical assets into digital tokens on a blockchain [8]. It enables the flow of digitalized information like the internet [6]. Assets that are tokenized can represent any assets, ranging from artwork to real estate, enabling easy asset transfer and fractional ownership.

Types of tokens

i) *Fungible token*: Tokens that are identical and interchangeable are called fungible tokens. One unit holds the same value as another. For example: Bitcoin and Ethereum.
ii) *Non-fungible token*: Tokens that are unique and non-interchangeable are called non-fungible tokens. Each token has distinct values and properties [27].

Legal and ethical challenges of blockchain adoption

Blockchain offers decentralization, transparency, and security, but also poses legal and ethical challenges.

Legal challenges

- *Regulatory uncertainty*: The absence of global legal frameworks for blockchain technology leads to regulatory uncertainty, causing jurisdictional conflicts in executed contracts, especially across borders.
- *Data privacy*: Although blockchain's immutability helps maintain data integrity, it makes it difficult to comply with the General Data Protection Regulation (GDPR), especially when it comes to the "right to be forgotten" and data erasure, because it is hard to change or remove data from a blockchain.
- *Smart contract legality*: Blockchain smart contracts face challenges in enforcement and dispute resolution due to unclear guidelines, especially when dealing with decentralized systems and anonymous parties.
- *Financial regulations*: Blockchain's decentralized nature presents both opportunities and challenges for anti-money laundering and counter terrorism funding (AML/CTF) compliance, potentially enabling tax evasion and illicit activities, necessitating robust compliance measures and regulatory frameworks.

Ethical challenges

- *Accountability issues*: Legal responsibility is made difficult by decentralization.

- *Criminal activity risks*: Anonymity is a fraud, money laundering, and cybercrime enabler.
- *Environmental impact*: Energy-intensive consensus mechanisms are unsustainable.
- *Governance bias*: Wealth concentration is inconsistent with the decentralization principle.
- *Job displacement*: Automation in finance and legal sectors threatens traditional employment.

16.6 Case Studies

In the recent decade, the banking industry has been using blockchain technology worldwide to offer financial services to its clients. Examples of a few renowned business groups using blockchain in their financial operations are as follows:

ING Bank

As per the official website of ING Bank, this bank, along with other commodities, houses, and trade establishments, launched "Komgo" in 2018 to digitize trade finance using blockchain technology. The platform automates financial transactions, simplifies operations, and provides a safe environment for banks, traders, and other players. Komgo improves efficiency, reduces fraud, and boosts transparency. Konsole, one of Komgo's products, is now available to ING customers in Europe and Asia, with plans to expand to the US market. Konsole allows banks and corporations to manage all trade finance exchanges on a single platform.

Bank of Canada

The Bank of Canada, in association with Payments Canada and R3, launched Project "Jasper" in 2016 to examine the use of distributed ledger technology (DLT) for wholesale interbank payment settlements. The Ethereum and R3 Corda were two systems that were developed and compared in order to measure their efficiency. Ethereum, developed with a liquidity-saving mechanism to facilitate seamless intraday transactions, was unable to provide the required operational risk and final settlement facility. Phase 2 enhanced settlement finality, scalability, and privacy by constructing a distributed ledger system based on a "notary node" alternative consensus architecture. The project team is still working on enhancing a DLT platform's capacity to adhere to the global principles for financial market infrastructures (PFMIs).

UBS Bank

"UBS Digital Cash" is a blockchain-based payment system implemented by Swiss Universal Bank and Global Asset Management Company, UBS, to improve global transactions. By using a private blockchain network with only authorized customers, this technology enables smart contract settlement. It facilitates payments in a number of currencies, such as euros, Swiss francs, and US dollars, which enhances liquidity management and expedites settlement times. UBS Digital Cash complements other market initiatives, such as the Helvetia project for real wholesale Swiss franc Central Bank Digital Currency and the Agorá project, which unlocks central bank money and tokenized deposits in cross-border payment contexts.

BNP Paribas

BNP Paribas has launched Neobonds, a blockchain-based platform, to manage green bonds. It ensures transparency in funding allocation to environmentally sustainable projects. It also offers a secure and efficient operational framework for managing, trading, and post-trading services associated with bond issuance that aligns with BNP Paribas' commitment to promoting green ecosystem.

16.7 Conclusion

Metaverse is a whole new digital world that enables users to interact digitally. However, security has become an important concern in the metaverse due to new innovations and the sharing of digital content. Blockchain emerges as a trustworthy force, free from any manipulation or threat, to ensure a secure and decentralized network for users. The integration of blockchain with the metaverse has brought evolutionary changes in modern finance, thereby reshaping digital experiences for users. Blockchain establishes an immutable ledger to maintain the confidentiality of transactions. It also helps in navigation across the virtual realm while preserving ownership rights of users over their digital assets through cross-chain communication and transfer of data. Smart contracts, another pillar of blockchain technology, ensure transparency in the virtual world while buying, selling, or trading digital assets. It reduces the risk of error or delay in agreements by automatically executing the transaction when decided by the participants. Ethereum and Bitcoin are two majorly utilized cryptocurrencies to trade with blockchain technology. Asset tokenization, another innovation of blockchain technology, allows ownership of specific assets to be represented by exchangeable digital tokens in the virtual realm.

Hence, blockchain has the potential to overcome the inefficiencies of the conventional banking systems by offering decentralization through distributed ledger technology. The role of intermediary authority or middlemen has been completely abandoned by blockchain technology, making the process easier and more efficient. A blend of blockchain technology in the realms of the metaverse and finance provides new opportunities for user engagement and asset management, thus promoting overall development. By embracing such technologies that enable consumers to build confidence in their virtual and financial activities, the world is advancing toward a safer, more convenient, and more connected future.

References

[1] Alamsyah, A., & Muhammad, I. F. (2024). Unraveling the crypto market: A journey into decentralized finance transaction network. Digital Business, 4(1), 100074. https://doi.org/10.1016/j.digbus.2024.100074

[2] Anwer, Z., Farid, S., Khan, A., & Benlagha, N. (2023). Cryptocurrencies versus environmentally sustainable assets: Does a perfect hedge exist? International Review of Economics & Finance, 85, 418–431. https://doi.org/10.1016/j.iref.2023.02.005

[3] Banaeian Far, S., Imani Rad, A., & Rajabzadeh Asaar, M. (2023). Blockchain and its derived technologies shape the future generation of digital businesses: A focus on decentralized finance and the Metaverse. Data Science and Management, 6(3), 183–197. https://doi.org/10.1016/j.dsm.2023.06.002

[4] Bhattacharya, P., Saraswat, D., Dave, A., Acharya, M., Tanwar, S., Sharma, G., & Davidson, I. E. (2021). Coalition of 6G and blockchain in AR/VR space: Challenges and future directions. IEEE Access, 9, 168455–168484. https://doi.org/10.1109/access.2021.3136860.

[5] Böhme, R., Christin, N., Edelman, B., & Moore, T. (2015). Bitcoin: Economics, Technology, and Governance. Journal of Economic Perspectives, 29(2), 213–238. https://doi.org/10.1257/jep.29.2.213

[6] Easley, D., O'Hara, M., & Basu, S. (2019). From mining to markets: The evolution of bitcoin transaction fees. Journal of Financial Economics, 134(1), 91–109. https://doi.org/10.1016/j.jfineco.2019.03.004

[7] Feng, W., Li, Y., Yang, X., Yan, Z., & Chen, L. (2021). Blockchain-based data transmission control for Tactical Data Link. Digital Communications and Networks, 7(3), 285–294. https://doi.org/10.1016/j.dcan.2020.05.007

[8] Freni, P., Ferro, E., & Moncada, R. (2022). Tokenomics and blockchain tokens: A design-oriented morphological framework. Blockchain: Research and Applications, 3(1), 100069. https://doi.org/10.1016/j.bcra.2022.100069
[9] Gong, Y., Chow, K. P., Yiu, S. M., & Ting, H. F. (2023). Analyzing the peeling chain patterns on the Bitcoin blockchain. Forensic Science International: Digital Investigation, 46, 301614. https://doi.org/10.1016/j.fsidi.2023.301614
[10] Gugueoth, V., Safavat, S., Shetty, S., & Rawat, D. (2023). A review of IoT security and privacy using decentralized blockchain techniques. Computer Science Review, 50, 100585. https://doi.org/10.1016/j.cosrev.2023.100585.
[11] Habib, G., Sharma, S., Ibrahim, S., Ahmad, I., Qureshi, S., & Ishfaq, M. (2022). Blockchain technology: Benefits, challenges, applications, and integration of blockchain technology with cloud computing. Future Internet, 14(11), 341. https://doi.org/10.3390/fi1411
[12] Heo, K., & Yi, S. (2023). (De)centralization in the governance of blockchain systems: Cryptocurrency cases. Journal of Organization Design, 12(3), 59–82. https://doi.org/10.1007/s41469-023-00138-w
[13] Huynh-The, T., Gadekallu, T. R., Wang, W., Yenduri, G., Ranaweera, P., Pham, Q.-V., Da Costa, D. B., & Liyanage, M. (2023). Blockchain for the metaverse: A Review. Future Generation Computer Systems, 143, 401–419. https://doi.org/10.1016/j.future.2023.02.008
[14] Javaid, M., Haleem, A., Singh, R. P., Suman, R., & Khan, S. (2022). A review of Blockchain Technology applications for financial services. BenchCouncil Transactions on Benchmarks, Standards and Evaluations, 2(3), 100073. https://doi.org/10.1016/j.tbench.2022.100073
[15] Longo, F., Mirabelli, G., Solina, V., Belli, L., Abdallah, C. B., Ben-Ammar, O., Bottani, E., García-Gallego, J. M., Germanos, M., González, F. J. M., Lacoba, S. R., Sidhom, L., Vignali, G., & Zacharewicz, G. (2023). An overview of approaches and methodologies for supporting smallholders: ICT tools, blockchain, business models, sustainability indicators, simulation models. Procedia Computer Science, 217, 1930–1939. https://doi.org/10.1016/j.procs.2022.12.393
[16] Park, J., Jeong, S., & Yeom, K. (2023). Smart Contract Broker: Improving Smart Contract Reusability in a Blockchain Environment. Sensors, 23(13), 6149. https://doi.org/10.3390/s23136149

[17] Pi neiro-Chousa, J., Šević, A., & González-López, I. (2023). Impact of social metrics in decentralized finance. Journal of Business Research, 158, 113673. https://doi.org/10.1016/j.jbusres.2023.113673

[18] Puschmann, T., & Huang-Sui, M. (2024). A taxonomy for decentralized finance. International Review of Financial Analysis, 92, 103083. https://doi.org/10.1016/j.irfa.2024.103083

[19] Pustišek, M., & Kos, A. (2018). Approaches to Front-End IoT Application Development for the Ethereum Blockchain. Procedia Computer Science, 129, 410–419. https://doi.org/10.1016/j.procs.2018.03.017

[20] Seo, J., & Park, S. (2024). SBAC: Substitution cipher access control based on blockchain for protecting personal data in metaverse. Future Generation Computer Systems, 151, 85–97. https://doi.org/10.1016/j.future.2023.09.022

[21] Shah, K., Lathiya, D., Lukhi, N., Parmar, K., & Sanghvi, H. (2023). A systematic review of decentralized finance protocols. International Journal of Intelligent Networks, 4, 171–181. https://doi.org/10.1016/j.ijin.2023.07.002

[22] Mistry, I., Tanwar, S., Tyagi, S., & Kumar, N. (2020). Blockchain for 5G-enabled IoT for industrial automation: A systematic review, solutions, and challenges. Mechanical Systems and Signal Processing, 135, 106382. https://doi.org/10.1016/j.ymssp.2019.106382

[23] Stephen, R., & Alex, A. (2018, August). A review on blockchain security. In IOP conference series: materials science and engineering (Vol. 396, No. 1, p. 012030). IOP Publishing.10.1088/1757-899x/396/1/012030

[24] Su, Y.-J., Chen, C.-H., Chen, T.-Y., & Yeah, C.-W. (2023). Applying Ethereum blockchain and IPFS to construct a multi-party used-car trading and management system. ICT Express, S2405959523001650. https://doi.org/10.1016/j.icte.2023.12.007

[25] V. T. Truong, L. Le and D. Niyato, “Blockchain Meets Metaverse and Digital Asset Management: A Comprehensive Survey,” in IEEE Access, vol. 11, pp. 26258-26288, 2023, doi: 10.1109/ACCESS.2023.3257029.

[26] Van Hijfte, S. (2020). Ethereum. In Synthesis Lectures on Computer Science (pp. 147–189). Springer International Publishing. https://doi.org/10.1007/978-3-031-01804-6_3

[27] Vitelaru, E., & Persia, L. (2023). Fractional Vehicle Ownership and Revenue Generation Through Blockchain Asset Tokenization. Transport and Telecommunication, 24(2), 120–127. ProQuest Central; Publicly Available Content Database. https://doi.org/10.2478/ttj-2023-0011

[28] Wang, Y., Su, Z., Zhang, N., Xing, R., Liu, D., Luan, T. H., & Shen, X. (2023). A Survey on Metaverse: Fundamentals, Security, and Privacy. IEEE Communications Surveys & Tutorials, 25(1), 319–352. https://doi.org/10.1109/COMST.2022.3202047

[29] Wronka, C. (2023). Financial crime in the decentralized finance ecosystem: New challenges for compliance. Journal of Financial Crime, 30(1), 97–113. https://doi.org/10.1108/JFC-09-2021-0218

[30] Yahaya, A. S., Javaid, N., Almogren, A., Ahmed, A., Gulfam, S. M., & Radwan, A. (2021). A two-stage privacy preservation and secure peer-to-peer energy trading model using blockchain and cloud-based aggregator. IEEE Access, 9, 143121–143137. https://doi.org/10.1109/access.2021.3120737

[31] Zhang, C., Xian, K., Wu, Q., Yang, H., Lang, J., & Wang, X. (2022). Blockchain-based Power Digital Asset Security Management Framework. Procedia Computer Science, 208, 354–360. https://doi.org/10.1016/j.procs.2022.10.050.

Index

About the Editors

Dr. Sudeep Tanwar (Senior Member, IEEE) is working in the Marwadi University, Rajkot, Gujarat, India. He is also a Visiting Professor with WSG University, Bydgoszczy, Poland, Jan Wyzykowski University, Poland, and the University of Pitesti, Romania. He is a senior member of IEEE and also the Vice Chair of IEEE Computer Society Gujarat Section. He received B.Tech in 2002 from Kurukshetra University, India, M.Tech (Honors) in 2009 from Guru Gobind Singh Indraprastha University, Delhi, India, and Ph.D. in 2016 with specialization in Wireless Sensor Network. He has authored 6 books and edited 38 books, more than 600 technical articles, including top-cited journals and conferences, such as IEEE TNSE, IEEE TVT, IEEE TII, IEEE TGCN, IEEE TCSC, IEEE IoTJ, IEEE NETWORKS, IEEE WCM, ICC, IWCMC, GLOBECOM, CITS, and INFOCOM. He initiated the research field of blockchain technology adoption in various verticals in the year 2017. His H-index as per Google Scholar and Scopus is 94 and 71, respectively. His research interests include blockchain technology, D2D communication, deep learning/machine learning, wireless sensor networks, fog computing, smart grid, and the IoT. He is a member of the Technical Committee on Tactile Internet of the IEEE Communication Society. Recently, he has been awarded a cash prize of Rs. 50,000 for publishing papers with 5+ Impact factor and publication of books with Springer, IET & CRC under the scheme of "Faculty Awards and Incentives" of Nirma University for the year 2019–2020. He has been awarded the Best Research Paper Awards from IEEE R10 HTC 2025, IEEE SCIoT 2022, IEEE IWCMC-2021, IEEE ICCCA-2021, IEEE GLOBECOM 2018, IEEE ICC 2019, and Springer ICRIC-2019. He has won Dr KW Wong Annual Best Paper Prize (with 750 USD) for 2021, sponsored by Elsevier (publishers of JISA). He has served many international conferences as a member of the Organizing Committee, such as the Publication Chair for FTNCT-2020, ICCIC 2020, and WiMob2019, and a General Chair for IC4S 2019, 2020, 2021, 2022, ICCSDF 2020, and FTNCT 2021. He is also serving on the editorial boards of COMCOM-Elsevier, IJCS-Wiley.

Dr. Maniklal Das is Professor of Computer Science at Dhirubhai Ambani Institute of Information and Communication Technology (DA-IICT), Gandhinagar, India. He has over 23 years of research and teaching experience in Computer Science. His research works broadly cover all areas of Cyber Security and IT Security Management. During his professional service, he has served as an investigator of several sponsored research projects with national and international collaborators in the area of Security and Privacy. He has been collaborating on research works actively with many researchers in premier universities abroad and in India. He is currently on the Editorial Board of IEEE Transactions on Dependable and Secure Computing. He has served as a member of the technical program committee for many international conferences, and he is a regular reviewer of IEEE/ACM/Springer/Elsevier journals. The detailed information about his research and other accomplishments can be found at http://intranet.daiict.ac.in/∼maniklal_das/. Dr. Das received his Ph.D. degree from the Indian Institute of Technology, Bombay, and M.Tech. degree from the Indian Institute of Technology, Dhanbad (formerly, Indian School of Mines, Dhanbad), India. He is a senior member of the IEEE and a life member of the Cryptology Research Society of India.

Abderrahim Benslimane is Full Professor of Computer-Science at the Avignon University/France since 2001. He is former Vice Dean of the Faculty of Sciences and Technology and former Head of the master Degree SICOM. He has been nominated in 2020, 2022, and 2024 as IEEE VTS Distinguished Lecturer/Speaker. He is awarded the French award for Doctoral supervision and Research. He has been an International Expert at the French Ministry of Foreign and European affairs (2012-2016). He served as a Vice Dean of the Faculty of Engineering and head of the Research Center in Informatics at the French University in Egypt. He was attributed the French award of Scientific Excellency (2011-2014). He has been as Associate Professor at the University of Technology of Belfort-Montbéliard since September 1994. He obtained the title to supervise researches (HDR 2000) from the University of Cergy-Pontoise, France. He received the PhD degree (1993), DEA (MS 1989) from the Franche-Comte University of Besançon, and BS (1987) from the University of Nancy, all in Computer Science.

He has been nominated Member of the IEEE VTS AdHoc Mission Critical Communications committee since 2025 and currently Vice-Chair of the Steering Committee of the IEEE ComSoc Social Network Technical Committee 2024-2026, IEEE ComSoc Steering Chair of Multimedia Communications Technical Committee 2022–2024 and previously served as Vice

Chair 2020–2022. He is past Chair of the ComSoc Technical Committee of Communication and Information Security 2017–2019. He is Area Editor Specialist on Communications and Information Security of the IEEE Open Journal of the Communications Society, Advisory board member of IEEE IoT journal, Associate Editor of IEEE Transactions on Information Forensics and Security, IEEE Wireless Communication Magazine, IEEE Transactions on Vehicular Technology, IEEE Transactions on Mobile Computing and Elsevier Ad Hoc Networks. He is co-founder and serves as General-Chair of the IEEE WiMob since 2005. He recently served as General Chair of IEEE CNS 2025 which has been hosted in Avignon, France during 8-11 September 2025. He served as Symposium Chair at ICCCN 2025, Track chair in IEEE WPMC'23, IEEE ICCC 2023 and Conference Chair at ICNC'24 MCC, ICNS'25. He served as General Chair of IEEE CNS 2020, Executive Forum Co-Chair at IEEE Globecom 2020, Program vice Chair of IEEE TrustCom 2020, Program Chair of IEEE iThings 2020 and Symposium Co H Chair/leader in many IEEE international conferences such as ICC, Globecom, AINA and VTC. He served as Guest Editor of many special issues. He participates to the steering and the program committee of many IEEE international conferences. He was Board committee member, Vice-chair of Student activities of IEEE France section/Region 8; he was Publication Vice-chair and Conference Vice-Chair of the ComSoc TC of Communication and Information Security. He participates to the steering and the program committee of many IEEE international conferences.

He has more than 320 refereed international publications (books, conference proceedings, journals and conferences) and more than 25 Special issues. He supervised more than 25 Ph.D thesis and more than 42 M.Sc. research thesis.

https://scholar.google.com/citations?user=uM1jSlgAAAAJ&hl=en
https://www.linkedin.com/in/abderrahim-benslimane-767aa118/

Rajesh Gupta (Member IEEE) is currently working in the Marwadi University, Rajkot, Gujarat, India. He completed his Ph.D. in Computer Science and Engineering in 2023 from Nirma University under the supervision of Dr. Sudeep Tanwar. He received his Bachelor of Engineering in 2008 from the University of Jammu, India, and his Master's in Technology in 2013 from Shri Mata Vaishno Devi University, Jammu, India. He has authored/co-authored more than 350 publications (including papers in SCI-indexed journals and IEEE ComSoc-sponsored international conferences). Some of his research findings are published in top-cited journals and conferences such as *IEEE Transactions on Industrial Informatics, IEEE Transactions on Network and Service Management, IEEE Transactions on Network Science and Engineering, IEEE Transactions on Green Communications and Networking, IEEE Transactions on Computational Social Systems, IEEE Network Magazine, IEEE Internet of Things Journal, IEEE IoT Magazine, Computer Communications, Computer and Electrical Engineering, International Journal of Communication Systems Wiley, Transactions on Emerging Telecommunications Technologies Wiley, Physical Communication Elsevier, IEEE ICC, IEEE INFOCOM, IEEE GLOBECOM, IEEE CITS*, and many more. His research interests include device-to-device communication, network security, blockchain technology, 5G communication network, and machine learning. His Google Scholar citations are 9200+, h-index 52, and i10-index 120. He is also a recipient of a Doctoral Scholarship from the Ministry of Electronics and Information Technology, Govt. of India under the Visvesvaraya Ph.D. Scheme. His name has been included in the list of Top 2% scientists worldwide published jointly by Elsevier and Stanford University, United States, consecutively in 2021, 2022, 2023, 2024, and 2025. He is a recipient of a Travel Grant from IEEE ComSoc and SERB to attend the IEEE ICC 2021 (held in Canada), IEEE ICC 2022 from SERB DST (held in Rome, Italy), IEEE ICC 2023 from SERB DST (held in Denver, United States), and IEEE GLOBECOM from SERB DST (held in Cape Town, South Africa). He has been selected and participated in the fully-funded the most prestigious ACM's Heidelberg Laureate Forum 2023, which was held at Heidelberg University, Heidelberg, Germany. He has been awarded best research paper awards from IEEE ECAI 2021, IEEE ICCCA 2021, IEEE IWCMC 2021, IEEE SCIoT 2022, IEEE R10 HTC 2025, and IEEE AIDE 2025. He has been felicitated by Nirma University for their research achievements bagged in 2019, 2020, 2021, and 2022. He is also an active member of the ST Research Laboratory (www.sudeeptanwar.in).